Natural Gas Markets in the Middle East and North Africa

Natural Gas Markets in the Middle East and North Africa

Edited by
BASSAM FATTOUH and JONATHAN STERN

Contributors
SIAMAK ADIBI
RANDA ALAMI
ANDREW CLEARY
HAKIM DARBOUCHE
JUSTIN DARGIN
FEREIDUN FESHARAKI
ANDY FLOWER
FRANZ GERNER
DAVID LEDESMA
ROBERT MABRO
WANISS A. OTMAN
IAN RUTLEDGE
SILVANA TORDO
LORIAN YACOUB

Published by the Oxford University Press
for the Oxford Institute for Energy Studies
2011

OXFORD

UNIVERSITY PRESS

Great Clarendon Street, Oxford OX2 6DP

Oxford University Press is a department of the University of Oxford.
It furthers the University's objective of excellence in research, scholarship,
and education by publishing worldwide in

Oxford New York

Auckland Cape Town Dar es Salaam Hong Kong Karachi
Kuala Lumpur Madrid Melbourne Mexico City Nairobi
New Delhi Shanghai Taipei Toronto

with offices in

Argentina Austria Brazil Chile Czech Republic France Greece
Guatemala Hungary Italy Japan Poland Portugal Singapore
South Korea Switzerland Thailand Turkey Ukraine Vietnam

Oxford is a registered trade mark of Oxford University Press
in the UK and in certain other countries

Published in the United States
by Oxford University Press Inc., New York

© Oxford Institute for Energy Studies 2011

British Library Cataloguing in Publication Data
Data available

Library of Congress Cataloguing in Publication Data
Data available

Cover designed by Cox Design Limited
Typeset by Philip Armstrong, Sheffield
Printed by Information Press, Eynsham, Oxford

ISBN 978-0-19-959301-9

1 3 5 7 9 10 8 6 4 2

CONTENTS

LIST OF MAPS

LIST OF FIGURES

LIST OF TABLES

ACKNOWLEDGEMENTS

No work of this size and complexity can be brought to a successful conclusion without the efforts of many people. We would like to pay particular tribute to our co-authors not just for the effort they have put into their chapters, but also the impressive self-discipline they all displayed in meeting agreed deadlines throughout the preparation of this book. We are very fortunate to have managed to assemble the collective expertise of these authors, each of whom brings a particular insight born of personal experience of living, working and studying in these countries over a long period of time. A special word of thanks to Hakim Darbouche who played a major part in bringing together the North African section of the book.

Our grateful thanks go to everybody at the Oxford Institute for Energy Studies, but especially Laura El-Katiri. Laura's role in this book has been crucial, both in relation to coordination with authors and organisation of artwork but also her knowledge of the region and linguistic ability has made a substantive contribution to the quality of the book and the speed with which it came together. Our Director Chris Allsopp lent us his customary enthusiasm, encouragement and intellectual support, and Kate Teasdale her customary organisational support.

The maps and charts drawn by Dave Sansom contribute substantially to understanding the significance of regional geography, and the conclusions that are drawn from the research. Grateful thanks also to Judy Mabro and Phil Armstrong for their editorial and typesetting skills.

Bassam Fattouh and Jonathan Stern
Oxford, November 2010

UNITS AND ABBREVIATIONS

Gas

Billion cubic metres: Bcm
Billion cubic metres per year: Bcm/yr
Billion cubic feet: Bcf
Million cubic metres: million cm
Million British thermal units: MMBtu
Million standard cubic feet per day: mmscf/d
Thousand cubic metres: mcm
Trillion cubic feet: tcf
Trillion cubic metres: tcm

LNG

Million tons: mt
Million tons per annum: mtpa

Power

Gigawatts: GW
Kilowatt hours: kWh
Megawatt hours: MWh
Megawatts: MW

Oil

Barrels of oil equivalent per day: boed
Million barrels per day: million b/d
Million tons of oil equivalent: mtoe
Dollars per barrel: $/bbl

NOTES ON CONTRIBUTORS

Siamak Adibi is currently head of the Middle East gas team in FACTS Global Energy (FGE), a consulting company based in Singapore. Siamak specialises in the natural gas/LNG business with a focus on the Middle East, North Africa and CIS countries. He holds an MA in Energy Economics and was previously with the National Iranian Gas Export Company (NIGEC). Recently, he led a depth study with focus on gas for Middle East and North African countries in FGE. Siamak Adibi has presented at several oil and gas briefings/conferences in Asia and the Middle East. His works have been published in numerous international publications.

Randa Alami is a development economist specialising in the Middle East, and is currently a Teaching Fellow at the School of Oriental and African Studies, University of London. Previously, Randa worked as a Research Fellow at the Oxford Institute for Energy Studies and at UNCTAD, and has been a consultant to DFID, ESCWA and others.

Andrew Cleary is a partner at Integrity Research and Consultancy, specialising in fragile and natural resource-endowed environments. He has a MScEcon (Intelligence and Strategic Studies) from Aberystwyth University, and researched his dissertation on Russian natural gas. This is his first published work.

Hakim Darbouche is Research Fellow at the Oxford Institute for Energy Studies. Prior to that he was an advisor on MENA affairs to a Brussels-based international organisation. He has a PhD in International Relations from the University of Liverpool and a BA in International Relations and Development Studies from Sussex University. He has published extensively on issues of politics, energy and political economy in North Africa. In Oxford, he is a Senior Associate Member of St Antony's College and serves as a Region Head on the MENA desk at Oxford Analytica. He is also Deputy Editor of the journal *Mediterranean Politics*.

Justin Dargin is an Energy Research Fellow with Harvard University and a Fulbright Scholar of the Middle East. He is a specialist in energy law, and the Middle Eastern oil and gas market. He has many years of experience in the MENA oil and gas market. Previously, Dargin worked in the legal department of OPEC where he advised senior officials on various multilateral issues. He is the author of *Desert Dreams*, a book about the intersection of Middle Eastern geopolitics, energy and state formation. He sits on the board of directors for the International Energy Foundation.

Bassam Fattouh is a Professor in Finance and Management of the Middle East, School of Oriental and African Studies (SOAS), University of London; Senior Research Fellow and Director of the Oil Programme at the Oxford Institute for Energy Studies; and Fellow of St. Antony's College, University of Oxford.

Fereidun Fesharaki is Chairman of FACTS Global Energy, an energy consulting firm with offices in Singapore, London, Dubai, Honolulu, Beijing, Perth, and Yokohama. He received his PhD in Energy Economics at the University of Surrey and has led energy-related academic research at the East–West Center since 1985. Prior to founding FGE, Dr Fesharaki was at Harvard's Center for Middle Eastern Studies. He was the Energy Advisor to the Prime Minister of Iran and a Delegate to OPEC's Ministerial Conferences.

Andy Flower is an independent consultant specialising in LNG. He has more than 30 years experience of working in the LNG business, of which many were spent with BP. He has been involved in the development of LNG projects in Africa, Australia, the Middle East and South East Asia.

Franz Gerner is a Senior Energy Economist with 15 years experience in the gas sector focusing on gas market reform, restructuring, pricing and economic regulation. He currently works on the World Bank's gas business and dialogue in Eastern Europe and Central Asia and has previously covered Egypt and Yemen. He has published widely including a World Bank publication: *Republic of Yemen: A Natural Gas Incentive Framework*, ESMAP Report # 40099-YE/2007.

David Ledesma is an independent energy and strategy consultant specialising in LNG and gas. In his 25 years of experience in the energy and utility sector in Shell and other companies, David worked on the development of complex integrated energy projects, negotiations at government level, and in the management of joint ventures. David is a Fellow of the Oxford Institute for Energy Studies and co-author of its book *Gas in Asia* published in 2008.

Robert Mabro founded the Oxford Institute for Energy Studies in 1982 and was Director of the Institute until April 2003. He also founded the Oxford Energy Policy Club and Oxford Energy Seminar. He is an Emeritus Fellow of St Antony's College, a Fellow of St Catherine's College and a lay director on the board of ICE Futures, the oil futures exchange in London. He is also the Dean of the Oxford Energy Seminar and the honorary secretary of the Oxford Energy Policy Club. In November 2005 Robert Mabro stepped down as President of the Institute. The Board of Governors appointed him Honorary President in November 2006. He is currently the editor of the *Oxford Energy Forum*.

Waniss A. Otman is a petroleum economist who specialises in the area of risk and uncertainty analysis. He holds a PhD in risk analysis of investment in the upstream oil and gas sector, as well as related LLM, MSc, and BSc Degrees. He has written many peer-reviewed articles and authored these books: *The Libyan Petroleum Industry in the Twenty-First Century; The Libyan Economy: Economic Diversification and International Repositioning; Libya Oil and Gas Resources; Oil and Gas Fiscal Review, Iraq Energy Institute; Understanding Modern Libya; and Africa's Energy* **and** *Natural Resources in the Global Economy*.

Ian Rutledge is director of SERIS (Sheffield Energy and Resources Information Services) and Honorary Senior Research Fellow in the Management School at the University of Sheffield. His career has included three years employment as a miner with the National Coal Board. He is author of *Addicted to Oil: America's Relentless Drive for Energy Security*, published by I.B. Tauris, 2005 and 2006.

Jonathan Stern is Director of Gas Research at the Oxford Institute for Energy Studies; Honorary Professor at the Centre for Energy, Petroleum & Mineral Law & Policy, University of Dundee; and Visiting Professor at Imperial College's Centre for Environmental Policy. He is author of *The Future of Russian Gas and Gazprom* (2005), editor of *Natural Gas in Asia* (2nd Edition 2008) and many other works on natural gas.

Silvana Tordo is a Lead Energy Economist at the Oil, Gas and Mining Policy Division of the World Bank. Her area of focus includes upstream oil and gas sector policies and strategies, legal and institutional frameworks, fiscal terms and petroleum contracts, and petroleum revenue management. She is a co-author of *Republic of Yemen: A Natural Gas Incentive Framework*, ESMAP Report # 40099-YE/2007.

Lorian Yacoub is a Doctoral Researcher at the Management School, University of Sheffield. Her current research project, 'Reconstructing Oil Governance in Iraq' specifically looks at the revenues distribution between the central and regional governorates.

PREFACE

The Oxford Institute for Energy Studies has a long tradition of research on Middle East and North African energy issues. However this is the first time that we have produced an academic book on the region's natural gas markets. Natural gas in the Middle East and North Africa region is a crucial factor in the dynamics of global supply and demand for this increasingly important source of energy. The region contains nearly half the world's known reserves of conventional gas. But internal consumption of gas within the region is rising fast, and questions are being raised about the ability of countries to expand their exports.

This is partly because of population growth, but gas has also become the fuel of choice for electricity generation and water desalination, is re-injected into oil fields to enhance oil production, and is central to MENA government strategy of diversification into energy-intensive industries such as petrochemicals. Throughout the region, gas prices have been maintained far below international market levels providing a further stimulus to demand growth, diminishing incentives to use gas efficiently, and discouraging investments in the domestic gas market.

For these reasons, potential MENA gas exports may be significantly lower than projected, as many countries that were expected to become exporters are instead seeking to import gas. As well as having an impact within the region, this could have a significant impact on international gas trade particularly for Europe, which could find itself competing with MENA countries for incremental production and exports.

This book represents a timely collaboration between OIES's natural gas programme and its programme of research on oil and the Middle East. With chapters on individual countries, the focus is both on the challenges within particular countries and on the overall picture for the region as a whole.

Christopher Allsopp CBE
December 2010

INTRODUCTION

Bassam Fattouh and Jonathan Stern

Purpose of the Book

In 2009, Middle East and North African (MENA) countries accounted for more than 45 percent of global proven gas reserves. Given the potential importance of this resource base, it is extraordinary that there has been no publicly available study of the development of gas markets in this region. While there are plenty of studies of export projects in operation or in prospect, very few of these place exports in the context of a rapidly expanding domestic demand and mounting challenges of developing new gas reserves and increasing gas supplies. The primary rationale for the book is therefore to fill this considerable gap in the global gas and energy literature. However, there is a strong secondary rationale which is to critically examine the prevailing assumption in much of the gas and energy literature, that MENA countries will become an ever-larger source of internationally traded gas.

The MENA Gas Puzzle

Most accounts of MENA gas start with the data in Table 1 which demonstrate that, both in absolute terms and in relation to the number of years for which production can be maintained at current levels, the resource potential of the region is vast. Only three of the countries in Table 1 – Bahrain, Oman and Egypt – have reserve to production ratios of less than 50 years, and for most other countries the figure is closer to 100 years. These observations on reserves usually lead to conclusions about the very substantial increase in production and exports that can be expected from the region. However, in the 2000s, a new phenomenon began to appear in the MENA countries: shortages of gas leading to curtailment of exports and (in some countries) a need for imports. Iran, with the second largest reserves of gas in the world – a country which had been a significant net gas exporter in the 1970s – became a net gas importer in the late 1990s, and has continued taking more gas from Turkmenistan than it delivers to Turkey and Armenia. Abu Dhabi and Oman continued to export LNG while starting to import significant quantities of gas from Qatar via the Dolphin pipeline. Kuwait began to import LNG and Dubai prepared for similar imports. By the late 2000s, a majority of countries in the MENA region appeared to be experiencing 'gas shortages'; some observers claim that the region faces a 'gas crisis', a situation which seemed impossible a decade earlier and seems unbelievable with reference to the figures in Table 1.

Table 1: Proven Natural Gas Reserves in the Middle East and North Africa, end 2009

	Proven Reserves *(trillion cubic metres)*	*Reserves/Production Ratio* *(years)*
Middle East		
Bahrain	0.09	6.7
Iran	29.61	>100
Iraq	3.17	>100
Kuwait	1.78	>100
Oman	0.98	39.6
Qatar	25.37	>100
Saudi Arabia	7.92	>100
Syria	0.28	51.8
UAE	6.43	>100
Yemen	0.49	>100
Other Middle East	0.06	24.2
North Africa		
Algeria	4.5	55.3
Egypt	2.19	34.9
Libya	1.54	>100

Source: BP *Statistical Review of World Energy*, 2010, p.22

So, how can one begin to explain the MENA gas puzzle? An important dimension of the puzzle and perhaps the most difficult to analyse, concerns the rapid domestic demand growth in the last three decades. Middle East gas demand has roughly doubled every decade since 1980 reaching 344 Bcm in 2009. In 1980, the region consumed less than 3 percent of global demand; by 2009 the figure was nearly 12 percent. The pace of demand growth in North Africa has been similar, albeit reaching only just over 80 Bcm in 2009 (Table 2). Very substantial domestic demand developed in virtually all countries – mainly concentrated in power generation, petrochemicals and desalination – fuelled by 'cheap' gas. By the late 2000s, gas dominated the stationary energy balances of most regional countries.

The factors that have contributed to the very rapid growth in gas demand vary considerably across the region depending on a country's individual features such as the structure of its economic activity and industry, its resource endowments, and the degree of flexibility of

Table 2:   Middle East and North African Gas Demand, 1990–2009, Bcm

	2000	*2005*	*2009*	*2008* *UP percent***
Middle East	**186.0**	**279.6**	**343.9**	**79.6**
Abu Dhabi	20.6	26.7	38.2	67.8
Bahrain	8.5	10.7	12.5	83.0
Dubai	6.0	9.6	15.7	46.8
Fujairah	0	1.2	1.3*	n/a
Iran	62.9	105.0	131.3	75.5
Iraq	2.9	1.5	1.9*	53.3
Israel	0.01	1.0	1.2*	98.9
Jordan	0.29	1.6	3.0*	100.0
Kuwait	9.6	12.2	12.8*	96.5
Oman	5.7	9.4	14.72	85.8
Qatar	9.2	18.9	21.1	90.8
Ras-al-Khaimah	1.0	1.2	1.0*	66.7
Saudi Arabia	49.8	71.2	77.1	99.8
Sharjah	3.8	3.4	4.4*	99.4
Syria	5.7	6.1	6.0*	73.8
North Africa	**48.97**	**61.24**	**83.10**	**n/a**
Algeria	21.8	23.7	28.53	51.4
Egypt	18.3	26.7	44.37	94.8
Libya	5.1	5.8	5.4	75.4
Morocco	0.05	0.04	0.6*	100.0
Tunisia	3.72	5.0	4.2	93.7

*   2008 data

** UP percent = percentage of utilised production; marketed gas production = gross gas production-gas reinjection-flared gas.

Notes: the data in this Table are not necessarily consistent with that of the country chapters, which use different sources. Yemen is not included because virtually all of the gas is reinjected (and a small volume is flared) with no marketed production.

Source: Cedigaz, 2009, *Natural Gas in the World 2009*, Tables 20 and 60, pages 44 and 135; Cedigaz 2010, *2009 Natural Gas Year in Review*, pp. 25–6.

economic and energy policy. Despite the diversity of experiences, it is possible to identify some common causes for the rapid growth in domestic gas demand: a rapid economic expansion and relatively high (but volatile) GDP growth rates; an expanding population whose growth rate exceeded the world average; a concerted policy of increasing the role of gas in power generation and water desalination; an economic strategy which aims at diversification into energy-intensive industries; an energy policy that aims at increasing the productivity of the oil sector through gas injection into oil reservoirs to enhance oil recovery;

a gas pricing policy which encourages wasteful consumption; and lack of effective demand management policies.

Out of the above factors, three stand out. Demand for natural gas in the region has been strongly interlinked with that of electricity demand. In the early stages of MENA gas markets development, the industrial and residential sectors were the main drivers of gas demand growth. More recently, gas consumption in the region has been driven largely by the power generation and water desalination sectors. While the share of oil in electricity production shrank from 72 percent in 1971 to 36 percent in 2006, the share of gas increased from 15 percent to above 56 percent over the same period. By the end of the 2000s, nearly 60 percent of the MENA region's power requirements were gas-fired. This aspect of demand growth raises a series of questions: Will natural gas continue to increase its share in power generation or will gas shortages reverse the trend in some countries? How sustainable is the current policy of subsidising electricity prices? Will MENA countries be able to meet the projected increase in electricity demand in an environment of low gas and electricity prices? Or will power cuts become a common feature throughout the region?

Another factor connected with the rapid rise in gas demand is economic policy. Despite continuous efforts to reduce oil dependency, the hydrocarbon sector still accounts for the bulk of export earnings and government receipts and acts as the main engine for economic growth in most MENA countries. Leveraging on the hydrocarbon reserves has allowed major transformations in many of the region's economies and led to general improvement in the population's living standards. However, growth rates have been highly volatile mirroring volatility in oil and gas output and prices in international markets (Figure 1). Furthermore, rapid population growth during the last three decades resulted in declines or stagnation of real income per capita in many MENA economies. High population growth rates and a young population structure are putting pressure on MENA governments to generate employment opportunities for the hundreds of thousands entering the labour market each year.

Given these challenges, the diversification of the domestic economy has been a top priority, especially for resource-rich economies. The natural gas sector lies at the heart of these diversification efforts where gas has become the fuel of choice for industrialisation. A cornerstone in the development strategy of many MENA economies is the establishment of export-oriented industries such as petrochemicals and aluminium that rely on large quantities of relatively cheap gas. The central role that gas plays in the process of a country's economic

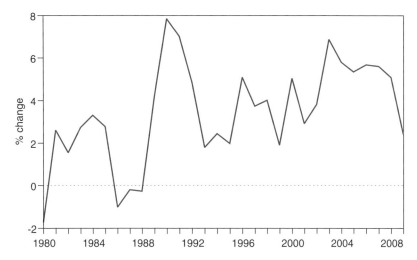

Figure 1: Annual Percentage Change in Gross Domestic Product, constant prices;
      1980–2009

Source: IMF, World Economic Outlook Database, April 2010. Composed of 20
         countries: Algeria, Bahrain, Djibouti, Egypt, Islamic Republic of Iran, Iraq,
         Jordan, Kuwait, Lebanon, Libya, Mauritania, Morocco, Oman, Qatar,
         Saudi Arabia, Sudan, Syrian Arab Republic, Tunisia, United Arab Emir-
         ates, and Republic of Yemen.

development implies that any analysis of the gas sector and the future
evolution of gas demand should be positioned within the countries'
wider economic and development strategy. This raises a series of key
questions: Does the policy of diverting gas to energy-intensive industries
optimise the use of this exhaustible and scarce resource? Will future
developments in the gas sector constrain the ability of MENA governments to achieve the ultimate goal of economic diversification? Is the
policy of promoting energy-intensive industries based on cheap gas
viable in the long term? These questions assume special importance
at times when there are concerns about gas shortages and rising costs
of developing domestic gas reserves.

Gas Pricing Issues

The region has some of the cheapest domestic gas prices in the world.
Maintaining low gas prices has been part of an overall strategy aimed at
encouraging the development of non-oil domestic industry; promoting
the interests of particular sectors; protecting the income of the citizens,
especially the vulnerable and the poor; and improving the access to
modern forms of energy such as electricity. In resource-rich economies,

it is also considered as one of the various methods for distributing the hydrocarbon rents.

The concept of subsidy is often described as 'too elusive to define'. This is reflected in the various definitions used in the literature. At the very general level, subsidy can be defined as 'any government assistance, in cash or in kind, to private sector producers or consumers for which the government receives no equivalent compensation in return, but conditions the assistance on a particular performance by the recipient'.[1] It is clear from this definition that many governments' actions can be categorised as involving subsidies. These include direct payments to consumers and producers (cash subsidies), granting loans to enterprises at low interest rates (credit subsidies), reduction in specific tax liabilities (tax subsidies), government purchase of goods and services at above market price (procurement subsidies) and provision of goods and services at below market price (in-kind subsidies). De Moor and Calamai provide a more narrow definition of subsidy as 'any measure that keeps prices for consumer below the market level or keeps prices for producers above the market level or that reduces costs for consumers and producers by giving direct or indirect support'.[2] Based on the above definition, it is clear that in order to measure a subsidy we need to compare the price actually charged to consumers and producers to some 'benchmark' or 'free market price'. The difficulty arises in identifying the benchmark or the free market price. In standard economic theory, the best benchmark to compare actual prices with is the marginal cost. Economic analysis emphasises the merits of policies that allow prices to reflect the economic cost of providing a good or service as these maximise economic efficiency. Measures of marginal costs, however, are difficult to observe in practice. Thus, economists focus instead on the concept of the opportunity cost.

To many analysts, the current policy of providing natural gas to consumers at a price below the international or regional price constitutes a classic case of a subsidy. However, this cannot be easily generalised in the MENA context. Whether a subsidy exists and how large it is depends on many factors including whether the country is a net gas importer or exporter, the nature of gas reserves (i.e. associated or non-associated) and whether the country has the necessary infrastructure to access export markets. In order to measure the size of subsidies, the price charged to domestic consumers should be compared with some measure of cost. There is more than one concept of cost to consider – the average cost, the long-term or short-term marginal cost and the opportunity cost and it is not always clear which concept one should use in the different contexts. And even when there is an agreement on the concept of cost to be used, data limitations often prevent researchers from measuring the size of the subsidy in many MENA countries.

Some observers use a different concept of subsidy based on the definition provided by the World Trade Organisation (WTO). Under the Agreement on Subsidies and Countervailing Measures, the following conditions must be satisfied for a subsidy to exist: '(i) a financial contribution (ii) by a government or any public body within the territory of a Member (iii) which confers a benefit'. Based on this definition, some argue that as long as the price charged to consumers is not below production costs, then it would be difficult to justify that a benefit had been conferred to domestic producers.[3]

Regardless of the issue of whether current prices constitute a subsidy or not, the policy of low gas prices raises a number of challenges. It intensifies the gas supply–demand gap by encouraging demand growth and limiting potential supply responses. On the demand side, low prices accelerate the growth in gas consumption. Farrell, Remes and Charles (2008) note that there are large differences in energy productivity (defined as the inverse of energy intensity of GDP) across developing countries with similar levels of economic development.[4] Their study finds that countries that subsidise energy use tend to have lower energy productivity with energy subsidies explaining around a quarter of the variation in energy productivity. The contribution of energy subsidies to explaining the variation across countries exceeds those of other factors such as a country's industrial structure and climate. On the supply side, low domestic prices reduce the incentive for exploration and development of gas reserves and investment in domestic gas infrastructure. They also create allocational distortions by biasing producers' decisions towards exports rather than supplying the domestic market. Subsidies also raise some serious distributional issues as households in high-income groups and large industries tend to capture the bulk of benefits of low energy prices.

The current gas pricing policy adopted in the region raises a series of interesting questions. Is the current policy of low gas prices sustainable or will the strains and fiscal pressures lead to price reform? Will the reform be gradual or sudden? What are some of the economic and political consequences of raising gas domestic prices? The answer to these and other similar questions are key to understanding the evolution of the gas sector in the next decade.

Production and Exports of Gas

In addressing the demand challenge, many countries in the region have been increasing their domestic gas supplies. Middle East gas production doubled during the decade 1998–2008, while North African production increased roughly by 50 percent. Furthermore, as gas became more valuable and more widely utilised, flaring of gas associated with oil production was dramatically reduced and largely eliminated in many countries. Despite these efforts, gas flaring in the region stands at about 50 billion cubic metres annually, making it the second largest flaring region in the world after Russia and the Caspian.

The 2009 *World Energy Outlook* from the International Energy Agency sees Middle East gas production more than doubling from 350 Bcm in 2008 to 800 Bcm in 2030. While it is clear that the resource base is sufficient to support such growth, political and economic factors – both domestic and international – suggest future complications and doubts. Specifically, can the region develop its gas reserves and expand gas supplies in an environment of low prices?

It is now evident that the era of low cost gas production, specifically gas associated with oil production and easily accessible non-associated gas is over. Greater depth of resource discoveries, complexity of reservoirs ('tight gas') and the presence of impurities ('sour gas') dictate an upward trend in the cost of gas production. There is also the issue of whether the region can expand its gas supplies without the support of foreign companies and foreign investment. This raises the important issue of whether the current petroleum laws and fiscal regimes provide the necessary incentive for domestic and foreign investment into the gas sector.

The rise in domestic demand and the lagged supply response in many MENA economies have serious implications on the region's export capability. As noted above, many countries in the region have already become net importers. In terms of exports, the Middle East region made a slow start. North African countries, and specifically Algeria, were pioneers of LNG to Europe and the USA starting in the 1960s, and pipeline gas to southern Europe from the 1980s. Libyan LNG exports started at a similarly early stage but were less successful, and pipeline exports started only in the mid 2000s. Substantial Egyptian LNG (and regional pipeline) exports have been operating since the mid 2000s. In the Gulf, LNG exports from Abu Dhabi date back to the 1970s, while Qatari exports started only in the 1990s but have become much larger and seem set to dominate global LNG trade. Omani LNG exports, which started in the early 2000s have grown to rival those of Abu Dhabi; in 2009 Yemen joined the ranks of LNG exporters. During the 2000s, exports from the region have increased by more than 60 Bcm and although North African exports still comfortably exceeded those of the Gulf in 2009, the latter was catching up fast primarily due to Qatari LNG exports (Table 3). In global terms, MENA countries accounted for 18 percent of total international gas exports in 2008, but more than 40 percent of LNG exports. In terms of pipeline exports, Iran was an important supplier to the southern USSR during the 1970s but following the Iranian revolution, exports ceased and only recommenced on a large scale to Turkey in the 2000s. Starting from the 1980s, North Africa became an important supplier to southern Europe – Algerian and Libyan gas to Spain and Italy. The second half of the 2000s has seen an increase in regional gas trade with both Qatar and Egypt becoming regional pipeline exporters.

Table 3: Middle East and North African Gas Exports 2000 and 2009, Bcm

	2000	*2009*	*Increase 2000–09*
North Africa			
Algeria	60.9	52.7*	-8.2
Libya	0.8	9.9	9.1
Egypt		18.3	18.3
Total	**61.7**	**80.9**	**19.2**
Gulf			
Qatar	14.0	49.4	35.4
Oman	2.8	11.5	8.7
UAE	7.0	7.0	0
Yemen	0	0.4	0.4
Total	**23.8**	**68.3**	**44.5**
Grand Total	**85.5**	**149.2**	**63.7**

* in 2009, Algerian exports were affected by the recession in Europe which substantially reduced gas demand; the 2008 figure was 58.8 Bcm.

Sources: Cedigaz 2001, *2001 Natural Gas Year in Review*, Table 4 and Cedigaz 2010, Ibid., Table 6.

Despite this impressive record in expanding supplies and playing a greater role in international gas trade, the question is whether the region can continue the export momentum of the past few years. The signs are not encouraging. Both Qatar and Egypt had imposed moratoria on new export projects. Saudi Arabia has a clear policy of not exporting natural gas. Domestic political and economic factors in North Africa are likely to constrain export growth while Iraq and Iran face serious international and domestic political challenges which may constrain their ability to develop their export capability. Despite these challenges, projections of very substantial increases in MENA exports based, at least to some extent on projects already under construction, continued to give the impression of a region with abundant exportable gas.

Regional Gas Trade

While the region is well endowed with massive gas reserves, the distribution of these reserves is highly uneven with some countries facing potential shortfalls while others have turned to gas exports to secure a major source of revenue. This raises the issue of whether any potential regional gas shortfall will be met from within the region. Over the past two decades, many schemes for gas cooperation between countries of the region have been proposed and negotiated and in some cases contracts have been signed. However, very few of the proposed projects have been implemented and consequently, inter-Arab gas trade remains very small. Regional pipeline projects face some major obstacles. Some of these are political in nature and include issues such as border disputes, regional influence, and concerns about increasing dependency on imported gas from particular countries. Others are commercial, related to expectations of cheap gas prices. For the majority of exporting countries, the answer to the economic choice between supplying rapidly growing domestic and regional markets at low prices, or an international market at much higher prices seems obvious. But there are political complexities involved in such choices.

Structure of the Book

This book tries to grapple with some of the issues and questions raised in this introductory chapter. However, it is important to stress from the outset that some of the above questions remain unanswered. This is in part due to the scope of some of the chapters and in part to data limitations and lack of public information. Many of the authors have found it extremely difficult to locate public domain data on fundamental aspects of the industry. This lack of data has been compounded by a great reluctance by companies and governments to comment openly on a range of issues that are considered commercially and politically 'sensitive'. This is not unique to the MENA region and, to some extent, is a perennial problem of all academic gas research. However, in the MENA context, these have been particularly difficult problems in the preparation of this book of which readers should be aware.

The book is structured in chapters dealing with the national gas markets of: the Gulf, North Africa and the Mashreq. The Gulf chapters are on Saudi Arabia, Iraq, Iran, Oman, UAE, Yemen, Bahrain and Kuwait. There are two chapters on Qatar: one on the evolution of the country's extensive LNG export projects and the other dealing with domestic gas development and regional exports via the Dolphin pipeline. The North African chapters focus on: Algeria, Egypt and Libya, and the transit countries of Tunisia (also a gas producer) and Morocco. An additional chapter includes an assessment of gas development in the Mashreq countries (Syria, Lebanon, Jordan), Israel and the Palestinian territories.

Notes

1   Cited in Clements, B. et al, 1995, 'Government Subsidies: Concepts, International Trends and Reform Options,' I.M.F. Working Paper.
2   De Moor, A. and Calamai, P., 1997, *Subsidizing Unsustainable Development.* Earth Council and the Institute for Research on Public Expenditure.
3   Dargin, J., 2010, 'The Gulf Natural Gas Dual Pricing Regime, Dubai Initiative Working Paper.
4   Farrel, D., Remes, J. and Charles D., 2008 'Fuelling Sustainable Development: The Energy Productivity Solution', McKinsey Global Institute, October.

CHAPTER 1

ALGERIA'S NATURAL GAS MARKET: ORIGINS AND CONSTRAINTS OF EXPORT STRATEGY

Hakim Darbouche*

Introduction

The Algerian natural gas market has experienced a chequered evolution process since its early days in the 1960s, but it has managed to emerge as one of the most mature in the Middle East and North Africa (MENA) region. Algeria is the second largest exporter of natural gas in the region,[1] and its domestic market has known sustained growth in recent years. More specifically, Sonatrach, the Algerian state energy company, has achieved remarkable results in terms of export volumes, diversity of markets and reliability of supplies despite the numerous structural and contextual constraints it has operated under since its creation in 1963. Among these inhibiting factors, direct government interference and security threats in the 1990s are the most prominent. However, while the security environment has markedly improved in recent years, the subjection of Sonatrach to strict government control seems to have been reinforced since 2006 following a botched attempt to achieve the opposite.

Geographical proximity to Europe has naturally led to the development of an interdependent relationship between Algeria and European gas consumers. Shipments of gas by subsea pipelines connecting Algeria to the southern shores of Italy and Spain have grown consistently since the early 1980s with the laying, and subsequent expansion of, the Trans-Med pipeline through Tunisia and the Maghreb–Europe line (GME) through Morocco.[2] In 2009, the volumes of gas delivered to Europe through these two systems exceeded 30 billion cubic metres (Bcm), with

*   I am deeply indebted to Ali Aïssaoui for his generous advice and guidance in the course of the research phase of this study. I am also grateful to Mostefa Ouki and Hadi Hallouche for their feedback on some aspects of this work. The comments of Jonathan Stern helped refine the final version of this text. Any mistakes, in fact or interpretation, remain my own. The first draft of this chapter was completed in September 2009. Its second and final version was submitted in March 2010

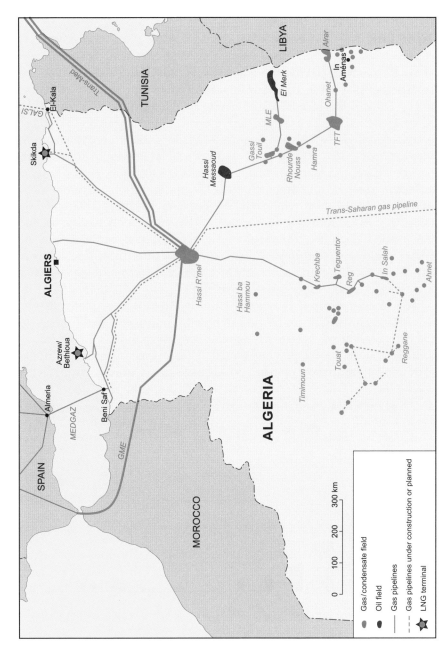

Map 1.1: Algeria: Gas Fields and Transport Infrastructure

Italy absorbing more than two-thirds of these flows.[3] Furthermore, the export flexibility enjoyed by Sonatrach as a result of its renowned LNG capability has not only meant that the Mediterranean basin absorbs about 95 percent of Algeria's gas exports, but it has also enabled the company to play an increasingly important role in the security of supply in the Atlantic basin and a minor role in Asian markets (Figure 1.1). More to the point, the exacerbation of the European Union's (EU) sense of vulnerability vis-à-vis its perceived overdependence on Russian gas supplies, owing to a saga of price disputes and related supply disruptions between Russia's Gazprom and Ukraine in 2006–2009, has spurred a collective sense of urgency within the Community to increase member states' gas intakes from more reliable suppliers like Algeria. Coinciding with Algeria's willingness to expand its gas exports to Europe in the 2000s, the EU's renewed interest in Algerian gas has translated into the construction and planning of two new submarine pipelines, Medgaz and Galsi, linking Algeria directly to Spain and Italy, respectively, with a combined initial capacity of 16 Bcm/yr.

The rapid growth of the global LNG market for most of the 2000s, driven largely by US and Asian demand, contributed for its part to the formulation of Sonatrach's ambition to expand its LNG export capacity by about 30 percent by 2013 from the current 22 million tons per annum (mtpa), leading to an increase of overall national gas

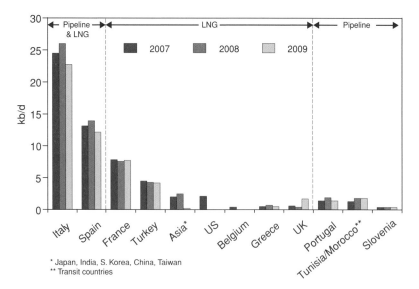

Figure 1.1: Algerian Gas Exports by Destination

Source: *BP Statistical Review of World Energy*

exports to 85 Bcm/yr by 2013 and 100 Bcm/yr by 2015. However, the devising of this export expansion strategy took place in a challenging context for Sonatrach and Algerian energy policy-makers. Despite the country's relatively important gas reserves and Sonatrach's recognised operational competence, between rising domestic consumption and stalling upstream reforms, reaching the enunciated policy targets looked set for an uphill struggle from the outset. Thus, questions regarding the outlook for Algeria's gas exports have become prevalent recently, especially amongst European consumers.

This chapter analyses the outlook for Algeria's short- to medium-term gas export strategy, with a view to assessing the impact that a number of existing and anticipated challenges along the gas value chain are likely to have on the country's export policies and objectives. To this end, the chapter will begin by setting a framework for understanding the domestic drivers of Algeria's gas export policy. It will argue that the primacy of hydrocarbons in the Algerian economy and the con-comitant strategic importance of gas exports, the role of Sonatrach as a state institution, and the dynamics of government change between 1962 and 1999 are all domestic policy factors that have traditionally defined Algeria's export strategies. The analysis will then move on to Algeria's natural gas production profile in the next decade, as well as the projected growth of domestic consumption over roughly the same time frame. In doing so, focus will be placed on the fallout of the 'nationalist' reversal of the 2005 Hydrocarbon Law in terms of foreign investment and upstream exploration, as well as the upstream dynamics of depletion and reinjection in Algeria's major gas-producing field, Hassi R'Mel. With regard to domestic consumption, the impact of current economic diversification efforts through the expansion of the petrochemical sector, and the continued upholding of domestic gas prices at artificially low levels, will be emphasised. Finally, the reasons behind the maintenance of ambitious gas export targets by the Algerian government despite the impending difficulties will be revisited in light of the above framework, and some policy recommendations for addressing the challenges ahead will be put forward.

The Domestic Determinants of Algeria's Gas Export Strategies

With the exception of the relatively brief period between independence in 1962 and the nationalisation of the oil and gas industry in 1971, overwhelming dependence on hydrocarbons has been a constant feature of the Algerian economy, with far-reaching implications for government policy-making in other issue areas. Indeed, no sooner had the state assumed control of the hydrocarbons industry than a vast industrialisation programme was launched, with express reliance on oil and gas revenues and in line with the *dirigiste* [central planning] wisdom prevailing amongst policy-makers at the time.[4] Against the parallel inertia of the agricultural and private sectors, this policy orientation soon resulted in a jump of the share of hydrocarbons in Algeria's foreign currency income to over 95 percent and in the government budget to nearly 60 percent (Figure 1.2) – a trend that has structurally remained unchanged ever since.[5] In the face of such heavy reliance on mono-sectoral performance there inevitably developed a symbiotic relationship between hydrocarbons and government domestic and external policies; not only do international market fluctuations affect the course of policy planning in Algeria, but, equally, hydrocarbon development strategies intrinsically reflect the government priorities of the day relative most notably to economic development, recovery, and international relations. And, as natural gas has represented a significant proportion of Algeria's exports from early on,[6] export strategies have been particularly reflective of the domestic imperatives underlying government policy.

Government priorities are channelled into the gas industry through the national oil company (NOC) Sonatrach. Since its inception, Sonatrach has been an integral part of the national government structure

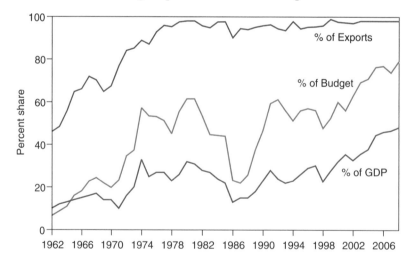

Figure 1.2: Share of Hydrocarbons in the Algerian Economy, 1962–2008

Source: Updated from Ali Aïssaoui (2001), *Algeria: The Political Economy of Oil and Gas*, Oxford University Press

in Algeria, serving as a pivotal instrument in the implementation not only of energy policy but also of wider political economy programmes.[7] Sonatrach's first mission was the preservation of the Algerian state's interests against the post-colonialist proclivities of French companies, and the philosophy underlying its creation has infused its relationship with Algerian governments ever since – notwithstanding numerous restructuring efforts aimed at decoupling the roles of both actors.[8] In view of this intimate relationship, Sonatrach's gas export policies have almost invariably been the progeny of shifting government priorities. For the most part, this government interference inhibited the full optimisation of Sonatrach's commercial interests, at times to the detriment of the broader national interest. Nonetheless, Sonatrach has achieved world-class results as a gas exporter, topping African and Arab ranks and competing with major industry players in Europe and the Atlantic basin. However, with the Algerian gas market facing challenging times ahead, questions about the status of Sonatrach and the nature of its relationship with the government become even more pertinent.

The control exerted by the government over the national oil company has been exacerbated in the case of Algeria by the intrinsically-complex dynamics of government *alternance* [change], which, in contrast to other (quasi-) monarchical energy-producing countries in the region, have rather been a source of inhibiting energy policy discontinuity, particularly in regard to natural gas exports. Being often the result of the informal power struggles that have pervaded the Algerian polity since independence, successive governments between 1979 and 1999 promulgated different gas export strategies that were at times more reflective of myopic political agendas than long-term commercial planning. The resulting dialectical approach to gas exports and depletion policy has occasionally affected Algeria's reputation with international oil companies (IOCs) and inevitably precluded Sonatrach's fulfilment of its potential as a producer and exporter of natural gas.

The role of international market factors as well as foreign governments and oil companies in influencing Algeria's gas export policies has not been negligible. However, beyond the contexts of pre-nationalisation of hydrocarbons in 1971 and the slump in global oil prices in 1986, the role of outside factors has largely been confined to a secondary effect in relation to primary domestic determinants. This can be seen in the trail of Algeria's hydrocarbon development policies and the corresponding gas export strategies.[9]

In the 1970s, Algeria's intensely socialist government embarked upon an ambitious (import-substituting) industrialisation programme that was to be largely financed by the country's unique source of revenue, hydrocarbons. For this purpose, a programme for the rapid expansion of oil and gas production and exports was put in place, in almost total diametrical opposition to the protectionist policies designed for other industrial sectors, considering its implications for foreign investment rules. Known as Valhyd (*Valorisation des Hydrocarbures*), the plan envisaged an aggressive gas depletion policy and concomitant export strategy within a thirty-year time frame. Driving this strategy was the conviction of policy-makers at the time that, in order to consolidate its political independence and Third World leadership, Algeria needed to build a viable industrial base, which, along with a 'revolutionised' agricultural sector, would set the country on a solid path of economic development. The high oil prices of the 1970s seemed to have had a limited impact on the implementation process of this incipient gas export policy.

With the unexpected change of government in 1979, an avowedly more liberal administration came into office but with immediate adverse consequences for Valhyd. As the newly-chosen president lacked domestic legitimacy, not only did he come under pressure to allow more policy-making prominence for the FLN – the state's only party-political apparatus at the time – but he also needed to accommodate the policy preferences of the party's powerful conservative factions to minimise dissent within state structures. Encouraged by a context of exceptionally high oil prices (1979–1981), the new energy decision-makers advocated a more 'nationalist' hydrocarbon development strategy, which implied moderating gas production and export targets. The resulting policy reversal and its concomitant gas pricing strategy had a far-reaching impact on Sonatrach's international commercial interests, with significant implications for LNG supply contracts with US and European buyers,[10] paving the way for a broader national economic crisis later in the 1980s.

While the downswing of the international oil market in 1986 brought about a government rethink of upstream investment terms in the form of a new hydrocarbon law, the persistent political and economic vicissitudes of subsequent years induced a reinvigoration of ambitious gas export policies, though on an explicitly less aggressive basis than Valhyd. A target of 60 Bcm/yr of gas exports by 2000 – nearly double the level of the late 1980s – became the primary objective, and re-entering the US market was considered a necessary stepping stone in this direction for Sonatrach, along with the construction of a new pipeline to Europe.[11] Despite the numerous setbacks that the new gas export strategy endured in the 1990s as a result of political instability, broader state imperatives overrode all uncertainties and gas exports reached 60 Bcm by the turn of the century.

As a new administration came into office in 1999, Algeria's gas export strategy was set on a new course. Chakib Khelil, the new energy minister, ambitiously aimed at increasing gas exports to 85 Bcm/yr by 2010 and 100 Bcm/yr by 2015.[12] The new government had inherited an economy badly damaged by a decade of civil unrest and a country totally isolated on the international scene. As a result, its overall policy agenda consisted of an important public investment plan aimed at reinvigorating vital physical infrastructure, as well as an ambitious liberalisation programme designed to attract foreign capital. More importantly, new president Abdelaziz Bouteflika needed to consolidate his political position at home after a spoilt election,[13] and redefining his country's foreign relations with major powers was part of his plan.[14] As the country's strategic export commodity, natural gas was central to the new government's strategy from both economic and geo-political perspectives. Accordingly, policy-makers went to great lengths in order to reach the new targets, including by proposing an ambitious new hydrocarbon law that aimed to introduce more liberal terms for upstream investment and redefine the role of Sonatrach as the national oil company. Although these efforts were eventually thwarted by fierce domestic opposition, the exports targets of the new strategy were stubbornly upheld.

What this ex-post analysis confirms is the defining role of the domestic factors (identified above) in the formulation of Algeria's gas export strategies since the 1970s. However, in the 2000s, a new wave of political developments precipitated the waning of political fragmentation in Algeria, presaging lesser influence of government change on future gas policies. Going forward, the emergence of new gas market dynamics is also likely to lead to reduced political interference in the process, though continuing economic dependence on hydrocarbons will remain a defining feature. Rising domestic consumption, declining reserves of 'easy gas', slowing European demand, and the growth of international LNG supply competition will gradually gain more traction in the context of Algeria's gas policy-making process. The constraints imposed by these changing conditions on policy-makers will focus efforts and resources on the rational optimisation of exports in a way that increasingly seeks to reconcile domestic imperatives and market forces. For Sonatrach, this may translate into a more consolidated commercial future at the expense of being an instrument of state policy, although this is unlikely to happen under the Khelil administration, which has already brought unwarranted instability to the company through its efforts to introduce radical, though perhaps not totally meritless, reforms.

Upstream Constraints and Production Dynamics

The investment rules governing the Algerian upstream gas business, in place since the enactment in November 1991 of the amendments to the 1986 Hydrocarbon Law, were by and large deemed fit for the purpose of Sonatrach's gas development policy in the 1990s. Indeed, the 1991 legislative 'upgrade', which offered the possibility to foreign companies to have a share in gas production and invest in the midstream,[15] paved the way for a steady increase in gas production in the 1990s (Figure 1.3), allowing Sonatrach to reach its natural gas export target of 60 Bcm/yr by 2000. However, the provisions of the existing investment framework became apparently ill suited for the new government's gas policy ambitions, and an overhaul of the Algerian hydrocarbon legislation was undertaken.

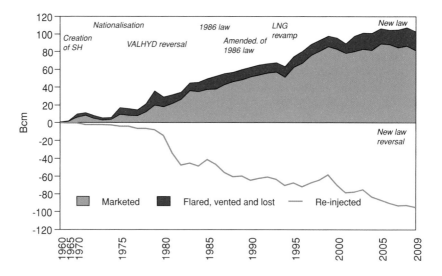

Figure 1.3: Algeria's Natural Gas Production, 1961–2009

Sources: Adapted from Aïssaoui (2001), using IEA and OPEC Annual Statistical
Bulletin (2000–2009)

'Khelil's Law': Good Intentions, Unintended Consequences

When President Abdelaziz Bouteflika came to power in 1999, the liberalisation of the energy sector was not on top of his political agenda. As one of the main protagonists of the hydrocarbon nationalisation process in the late 1960s and early 1970s,[16] his preferences with regard to this matter have remained unchanged. What the new president was most interested in upon coming into office was redressing Algeria's distressed economy and reinforcing his domestic power-base. To this end, his strategy was twofold: promote selective economic liberalisation to attract foreign investment; and rely on the hydrocarbons sector to generate the necessary revenue for economic recovery and the restoration of civil peace. Chakib Khelil was among a core team of reform-minded technocrats chosen for the implementation of the president's political programme, and appeared to have been allowed unrestrained policy-making power given his experience and personal affinities with the president.

One year into the job, Chakib Khelil set new targets for Algerian gas exports (85 Bcm by 2010 and 100 Bcm by 2015) and laid out his vision of how to achieve the new gas policy through a draft hydrocarbon law, which was made public in early 2001. As soon as it was mooted, the draft legislative framework caused a furore within Sonatrach and on the Algerian political scene more broadly. Aside from the envisaged far-reaching liberalisation of the upstream and other segments of the industry, the proposed radical changes to Sonatrach's traditional state functions and the far-fetched prospect of its (partial) privatisation aroused unprecedented protest from the company's unions and management. Stripping Sonatrach of its government prerogatives may have been desirable, but the main bone of contention was the extent to which the planned reforms would make Sonatrach compete with foreign operators in most segments of the value chain, including the marketing of gas.[17]

After a five-year intractable controversy, which saw 'Khelil's law' tweaked, shelved, dusted off, ratified and then amended significantly in 2006,[18] little of the original plan survived except the damage caused by the minister's unilateralist approach to the opposition within Sonatrach to his proposed institutional reform. The company's management was purged of all sceptical elements, leaving its reigns in the hands of a leadership eventually dissatisfied with the institutional framework within which they have had to operate since 2006. From a governance perspective, this outcome looked likely to perpetuate the dialectical dynamics of Algeria's energy policy-making – should Khelil no longer enjoy the apparent unconditional support of Bouteflika (for whichever reason) then his alienated peers will most likely seek to wrest some authority away from him and reverse the order the minister has hitherto imposed.

The corruption probe into Sonatrach's top management team that was announced in January 2010 was an indication that the Algerian national energy company was not out of the woods yet. The suspicion of wrongdoing in the award of procurement contracts will cast further doubt on the reform policies of Chakib Khelil's team, leading almost certainly to the intended curtailing of the minister's authority on the sector. Far from being the product of some (putative) factional infighting over presidential succession at the helm of the state as was widely reported,[19] the 2010 Sonatrach corruption affair points to the debilitating effect exclusionary sectoral management and failure to recognise the need for policy dialogue/change have had on important areas of the Algerian energy sector in the 2000s.

If the ratification process of the hydrocarbon law, which became 'Law 05-07' following its approval by parliament in April 2005, obeyed presidential electoral priorities,[20] its reversal before its effective entry into force a little over a year later appears to have been the result of the realisation by the re-elected president that the Algerian polity and economy had recovered enough to no longer warrant an intensive (oil and) gas depletion policy. Spurred on by a context of rising energy prices on international markets, the hydrocarbon legislative amendments decreed by Bouteflika in August 2006 went further than just reinstating Sonatrach's status as a controlling obligatory partner in all upstream concessions and introduced a windfall tax to be retrospectively levied on foreign operators when Brent prices exceed $30 per barrel.[21] However, the resulting hybrid regulatory framework revolving around Sonatrach, Alnaft (*Agence nationale pour la Valorisation des Resources en Hydrocarbures*) as licensing agency, and ARH (*Autorité de Regulation des Hydrocarbures*), as regulator of upstream and midstream activities left many onlookers uncertain as to the effect of these unexpected changes on foreign investment.

With the launch of the first E&P licensing round under the new regime – the seventh since the introduction of competitive upstream bidding by Chakib Khelil in 2000 – these concerns were soon vindicated. After a protracted enactment process of the amended Law 05-07, the details of the bidding round were unveiled in summer 2008 and attracted high initial interest from IOCs.[22] However, the results of the tender, which were announced in December, were relatively muted with only four of the sixteen blocks on offer being awarded.[23] This subdued interest could certainly be blamed on the effect of the credit crisis on the global economy and the oil markets starting in September 2008, but many foreign companies affirmed they were further discouraged from investing by the proposed contract terms.[24]

Indeed, besides the perceived unattractiveness of the provisions of the new investment regime, additional conditions were attached by

Sonatrach to the concession of interest in its most prospective gas block of all, Ahnet.[25] Preferential treatment to this effect was promised to bidders most willing to share advanced technology and swap overseas assets with the Algerian NOC. This bullish attitude on the part of Sonatrach reflected the company's new-found confidence as expressed most emphatically by Chakib Khelil in 2007 when he questioned the added value of IOCs for his country's upstream business: 'Money, I have. Reserves, I have. Markets, I have. Technology, I have access. What do you bring? Maybe you can bring me access to reserves elsewhere; that, I will give you points for. Maybe you can bring me access to markets; that, I will give you points for'[26]

The results of the 2008 licensing round will have undoubtedly constituted a setback for Algeria's enunciated gas export targets, as they meant more delays for the development of new reserves. However, considering the equally timid outcome of Egypt's parallel gas-focused international tender,[27] the Algerian bidding exercise appeared by no means isolated and part of the blame for its disappointing results shifted from the institutionalised investment terms as such to Sonatrach's emphatic display of over-confidence in 2006–2008.

By contrast, the 2009 bidding process, which saw the re-offering of the Ahnet block, was accompanied by a more inviting tone from Sonatrach. Officials from the company showed more receptiveness to feedback from IOCs and promised to 'do as much as possible within the existing law' to make it more attractive for foreign investors to participate in the 2009 licensing round. However, the results, which were announced in December 2009, displayed a similar pattern to the previous round in that only three exploration and development licences out of the ten permits offered were awarded. Nevertheless, Ahnet was awarded to a Total-led consortium, which projected first gas flows for 2015, allowing plans for the development of new reserves in the southwest to move forward.

What seems clear is that uncertainty among investors over the effect of the post-2006 hybrid regulatory regime on Algeria's energy decision-making efficiency is not a welcome development, for even if Algeria's upstream potential remains relatively attractive, added bureaucratic ponderousness through Alnaft will leave IOCs hoping for a better framework. This was certainly not the intended outcome of Khelil's original reform plan, but the political *instrumentalisation* [calculated use] of energy policy by Bouteflika left the reforming minister with no room for a 'plan B', limiting his options to the half-hearted implementation of a less-than-perfect alternative. The entire process of legislative change introduced by Chakib Khelil has so far hampered gas production, mainly as a result of the sense of uncertainty it has instilled both inside and outside Algeria; however, its future implementation need not be as inhibiting.

Natural Gas Production: Between High Potential and Quasi-stagnation

Algeria's hydrocarbon potential has invariably derived from its natural gas reserves which, as of January 2010, stood at 4500 Bcm[28] – representing two-thirds of the total national hydrocarbon reserves and the fifth largest gas reserves in the MENA region. From the early 1970s, when Sonatrach began promoting the commercial production of natural gas, the gas reserves-to-production ratio began declining at a much faster rate than the ratio for oil, stabilising at around 50–55 years in the 2000s (Figure 1.4). The stagnation of gas reserves in Algeria since the late 1990s is reflective of E&P activity trends during this period, which concentrated on the development of known reserves both southeast and southwest of Hassi R'Mel, with relatively limited prospection in the underexplored areas around the Reggane and Bechar basins.[29]

Sonatrach-operated Hassi R'Mel, Algeria's largest wet gas field, accounts for over 50 percent of proven gas reserves (2400 Bcm).[30] The rest of the reserves is scattered around the Rourde Nouss/Gassi Touil,

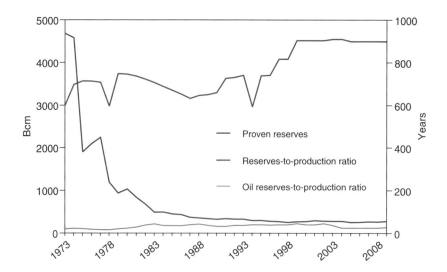

Figure 1.4: Algeria's Natural Gas Reserves, 1973–2009

Sources: BP *Statistical Review of World Energy* and OPEC *Annual Statistical Bulletin*

In Amenas/Ohanet, In Salah/Ahnet, and Reggane areas (see Map 1.1). Additional gas resources that are yet to be discovered are estimated by the US Geological Survey (USGS) at around 1000 Bcm.[31] Most of these yet-to-find resources are located in the gas-prone region southwest of Hassi R'Mel, consisting mostly of dry, tight gas with higher than average CO_2 content.[32]

Hassi R'Mel is also Algeria's largest wet producing field, accounting for an average of 64 percent of annual gross production since 2004. The development of a number of gas fields in the 2000s has gradually reduced Hassi R'Mel's share in total gas output, purposely alleviating some of the production pressure previously sustained by the field. Ohanet (2003), In Salah (2004) and In Amenas (2006), developed by Sonatrach with BHP Billiton, BP and Statoil, added a combined 23 Bcm/yr of gas to Algeria's production profile, contributing mostly to the expansion of pipeline exports through the Trans-Med and GME systems.[33] With the exception of In Salah, the gas produced from these fields is marketed by Sonatrach on its own account, while its partners normally recover their investments through natural-gas-liquids (NGLs) intakes. The marketing arrangement for In Salah gas was initially problematic because of Sonatrach's stance at the time vis-à-vis destination clauses,[34] but a temporary compromise seems to have been found until an agreement was struck with the European Commission in 2007 about the removal of territorial restrictions from existing and future gas supply contracts.[35] The only other gas development project that envisaged joint marketing was Gassi Touil, as its LNG output was earmarked for the US market, away from Sonatrach's core southern European outlets; but gas marketing remains generally Sonatrach's *chasse gardée* [exclusive domain].

Gassi Touil. The development of existing gas reserves at Gassi Touil, as well as at Hamra and Rourde Nouss, as part of an integrated upstream and liquefaction project was meant not only to bring known reserves on stream and reduce the depletion of Hassi R'Mel, but also to capitalise on the unprecedented growth of international LNG markets in the early 2000s. More importantly, Gassi Touil was considered a significant stepping stone for Sonatrach's enunciated gas export target of 85 Bcm/yr by 2010 and an important symbol of Algeria's hydrocarbon liberalisation commitment as it was the first integrated LNG project to be awarded to foreign companies. The fields assigned to the project contain around 250 Bcm of gas reserves and the concomitant new LNG train at Arzew was designed with an initial nameplate capacity of 4 mtpa.[36]

The importance of Gassi Touil for Algeria was thrown into sharper focus by the Skikda LNG accident in January 2004, as higher stakes for Sonatrach's reputation in the LNG industry added to the incipient gas exports challenge. After an aggressive and protracted bidding process, Spain's Repsol and Gas Natural were awarded the tender in November 2004, raising many eyebrows in the industry because of the consortium's particularly low bid and relative lack of track record in the execution of projects of this scale.[37] However, Sonatrach's apparent confidence about its choice soon gave way to the realisation that the winning bidders were facing serious difficulties in carrying out the project,[38] hindered by changing international business conditions in a context of high energy and commodity prices as well as increasingly bullish industry contractors.

In the face of the Spanish consortium's perceived disingenuous efforts to show commitment to its contractual engagements, Sonatrach decided to revoke the Gassi Touil contract in September 2007 and announced that it would seek compensation through international arbitration. The results of the ruling process were announced in November 2009 and the conclusion of the arbitration court advised that no compensation should be paid by either side to the dispute. Inevitably, the resulting feeling amongst IOCs is that the Gassi Touil events were symptomatic of Algeria's post-2006 renewed sense of confidence. However, the ensuing dispute should be seen as predominantly commercial. There is little doubt that strained relations at that particular juncture between the Spanish and Algerian governments on the one hand and between Sonatrach and Gas Natural on the other had contributed very little to salvaging the Gassi Touil partnership,[39] but the conspicuous failure of the Spanish consortium to fulfil its contractual obligations may have been irreparable anyway.

Besides causing potential prejudice to Sonatrach's relations with IOCs, the Gassi Touil standoff represented another setback for Algeria's gas development policy, as Sonatrach's decision to take exclusive control of the project could not reverse the resulting delays for its initial export target, which was by now being deferred to 2012/13. Indeed, in July 2008, Sonatrach awarded the engineering, procurement and construction (EPC) contracts to a number of service companies both for the liquefaction part of the project and the upstream development of one of the three main supply fields.[40] This final investment decision (FID) on the part of Sonatrach was the only one made for a gas liquefaction project in 2008,[41] challenging the extant LNG project-development rulebook.[42] The costs of the project, which had at least doubled from the initial estimates of $3 billion, were covered entirely by Sonatrach despite the explicit exclusion of IOCs from all segments of the project and the conspicuous absence of long-term supply contracts with potential buyers. In addition to being, in many ways, a watershed in Sonatrach's relations with IOCs, Gassi Touil added to Algeria's existing gas production woes, such as the challenges faced at Hassi R'Mel.

Hassi R'Mel depletion and reinjection. As can be seen in Figure 1.3, the rate of gas reinjection in Algeria's oil and gas fields represented just under 50 percent of 2009 gross production, making reinjection a 'swing variable' in the country's output profile. Used in oil reservoirs as a means of enhanced oil recovery (EOR), gas reinjection also occurs in wet gas fields to maintain reservoir pressure and optimise the recovery of NGLs. As Algeria's oldest and largest wet gas field,[43] Hassi R'Mel has for long been the single most important 'consumer' of re-injected dry gas. Today, reduced depletion pressure and the use of advanced enhanced recovery technology has relatively rationalised the rate of gas reinjection in Hassi R'Mel,[44] though the field still accounts for nearly 60 percent of total reinjection in wet gas fields with more than a third of its dry gas production being re-injected into the reservoir (Figure 1.5). The remainder of the gas re-injected as part of wet gas fields' cycling processes goes mostly into Rourde Nouss, Hamra, Alrar and Ohanet. Furthermore, the rate of gas reinjection in oil fields has grown consistently since the 1990s, driven largely by decreasing reservoir pressure in the maturing fields of Hassi Messaoud and Rourde el Baguel.[45]

The issue of reinjection in Hassi R'Mel is intrinsically linked to the field's depletion rate. It is estimated that nearly half its remaining reserves are NGLs – particularly condensate – and that these will be depleted around 2020 when the blow-down of Hassi R'Mel is likely to take place. Furthermore, according to Sonatrach's annual reports, Hassi R'Mel gas production has stabilised at an average of 95 Bcm/yr since 2003/4 (Figure 1.5). In view of the above, it is estimated that production at Hassi R'Mel will start declining in the first half of the 2010s, starting at an initial depletion rate of 2 percent per year and accelerating in the second half of the decade. The use of advanced technology can help manage super-giant Hassi R'Mel's inevitable decline, and Sonatrach has recently hired the services of the Swiss company ABB for the expansion of existing and installation of new compressors. However, the implications of the field's depletion for Algeria's gas production will be immediately palpable, especially given Hassi R'Mel's role as the linchpin of the country's gas system (see Map 1.1).

Investment. In spite of its increasing revenues since 2000, Sonatrach's

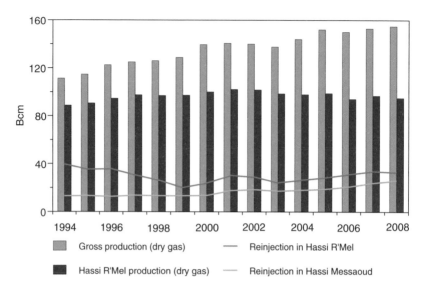

Figure 1.5: Hassi R'Mel Natural Gas Production and Reinjection Data

Source: Sonatrach and own estimates

investment in the maintenance of its ageing infrastructure seemed to have lagged behind in the Algerian NOC's programme for the best part of the last decade. Government spending priorities during this period diverted most of the foreign currency income towards a number of projects that are socially and politically more rewarding, targeting specifically the expansion of physical infrastructure and the repayment of external public debts.[46] It was not until the dramatic accident at Skikda's LNG plant delivered a stark reminder to Algerian decision-makers about the need for systematic maintenance and upgrading of the vital energy infrastructure that Sonatrach was allowed some investment 'breathing space'.[47]

Apart from the Skikda disaster, which has also been partly blamed on negligence, the result of Sonatrach's lack of investment manifests itself intermittently in domestic pipeline corrosion, which was reported to have seriously impeded its LNG output in 2008/9.[48] Some of Algeria's domestic pipelines are 40 years old and have been unable to sustain increased gas throughput. This is true of pipelines both north and south of Hassi R'Mel, all managed exclusively by Sonatrach subsidiary *Transport par Canalisation*.[49] More recently however, Sonatrach announced an ambitious five-year (2009–2013) outlay plan of $63 billion, 9 percent of which has been earmarked for the upgrading and extension of its 16200 km network of operational oil and gas pipelines.[50] Thus, if along with project delays, upstream investment uncertainty and Hassi R'Mel maturity, lack of investment has accounted for the quasi-stagnation of gas production since the late 1990s, Sonatrach's new spending commitment will be a defining component of the company's gas production and export expansion policy in the years ahead.

Production Outlook to 2020

As a result of the major delays encountered by Sonatrach in its upstream programme, Algeria's net gas production is expected to remain close to its current level of 87 Bcm until 2011/12 when the development of the 113 Bcm proven and probable reserves at the Menzel Ledjmet East (MLE) wet gas field in the Berkine basin will bring an initial 3 Bcm of gas on stream.[51] Similar field-by-field analysis, covering producing fields,[52] fields to be developed,[53] and fields under exploration,[54] indicates that production of natural gas in Algeria will increase significantly between 2014 and 2018 (Figure 1.6). The average rate of production growth during this period is estimated at 8 percent, and will be followed by a slight decline as a result of the depletion of NGLs in and the likely blow-down of mature wet gas fields Rourde Nouss and Hassi R'Mel. Subsequently, overall net production is expected to reach a plateau of 115–120 Bcm, lasting until the early 2020s before entering a probable final decline phase.

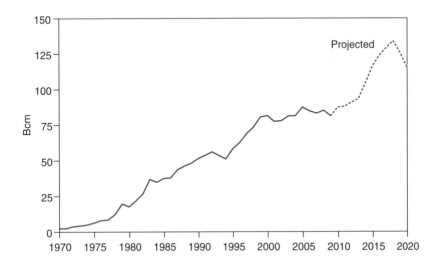

Figure 1.6: Algeria's Natural Gas Production, 1970–2020

Sources: OPEC (actual); Sonatrach and own estimates (projected).

These projections are clearly more bearish than the 2008 estimates of the IEA and the OME, and are subject to an important proviso. As most of the expected gas increments will originate in the country's vast and underexplored southwest 'frontier', the timing of their development will be crucial to the achievement of Sonatrach's objectives. Indeed, for these fields to make a timely contribution to Algeria's gas production and export requirements, development permits had to be delivered by Alnaft by early 2010, and Sonatrach will still have to complete the laying of a 700 km pipeline to Hassi R'Mel by 2013 (GR3). For in spite of the fact that gas-in-place volumes are substantial, the geology and the lack of infrastructure pose a difficult challenge. The scattered fields of Reggane Nord (Repsol-YPF), Timimoun (Total) and Touat (GDF-Suez), which are expected to produce 9 Bcm/yr of dry gas after an initial development phase by 2013, are said to be highly impermeable and contain relatively high CO_2 levels, requiring higher development costs.[55] These operational difficulties have been compounded by lengthy negotiations over marketing arrangements, but Sonatrach seems intent on overcoming these hurdles to clear the way for the development of adjacent fields, such as Ahnet, which would allow it to meet not only its export commitments but, most importantly, its growing domestic demand.[56]

Domestic Gas Consumption

The domestic use of natural gas to satisfy Algeria's primary energy requirements has been actively encouraged by government policy from the early 1970s. Gas has been relied upon as feedstock for a large industrial base, especially for fertiliser and petrochemical production, and as the 'fuel of choice' for power generation. In the particular case of the latter energy transformation industry, the rationale underlying this policy choice was to release higher-value oil products for exports by using a fuel that had hitherto been flared.[57] As a result, the power sector has become almost entirely dependent on natural gas, which represents 97 percent of its fuel input (Figure 1.7). Moreover, natural gas accounts today for around 60 percent of the country's total primary energy requirements.[58] Correspondingly, gas consumption increased sharply until the mid-1980s when deteriorating economic conditions slowed demand down to virtually stable levels until the end of the 1990s (Figure 1.8). Since then, gas consumption – including the energy sector's own use – grew at an annual rate of 4 percent, reaching 26.6 Bcm in 2008 and accelerated to 6.6 percent in 2009 to reach 28.4 Bcm.[59]

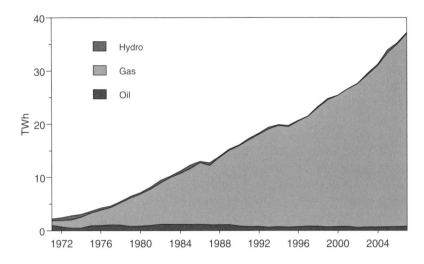

Figure 1.7: Electricity Generation by Fuel, 1971–2007

Source: IEA 'Energy Balances of Non-Energy Countries', 2009

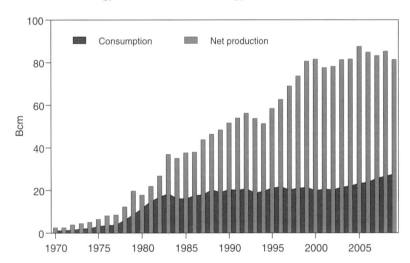

Figure 1.8: Algeria's Natural Gas Production and Consumption, 1970–2009

Sources: BP *Statistical Review of World Energy* 2010

In the 2000s, growing domestic gas demand was driven largely by the power generation and energy sectors. More broadly, sustained GDP growth since 2000, reflecting increased activity in the construction and the services industry as well as other energy-intensive sectors, translated into higher demand for gas through the power sector. What's more, the noticeably decreasing concentration of occupancy per housing unit, coupled with the increasing affordability of air conditioning systems, has put additional pressure on electricity consumption particularly through summer-load peaks. Given a global ratio of 1 ton of oil equivalent (toe) energy consumption per capita in 2008, Algeria is likely to experience a sustained increase in energy (and gas) consumption as living standards continue to improve.

However, considering Algeria's ratio of energy consumption per unit of GDP, which as a rough indicator of energy efficiency stood at 0.24 toe/$1000 in 2008 – much higher than in other countries such as Spain, Brazil and Turkey, though lower than in some MENA countries – there is clearly a lot of room for improvement in terms of the rationalisation of energy consumption. This is of course intrinsically related to the issue of domestic price management, which in Algeria constitutes a major disincentive for rational use of energy and the main stumbling block to the commercial profitability of the country's public gas and electricity utility, Sonelgaz.[60] In 2008, the pre-tax price set by ARH for the gas supplied by Sonatrach to all national users stood at Algerian Dinars 1203/1000 m³, or approximately $0.5/MMBtu. The price is readjusted annually on the basis of a formula reflecting year-on-year US Dollar exchange rate variations as well as a fixed 5 percent inflation rate. Although in recent years the government has taken a number of important steps in the way of reducing gas price subsidisation, such as bringing the price of gas feedstock sold by Sonatrach to the power generation sector to parity with that paid by industrial users,[61] the prospects for a meaningful liberalisation of pricing mechanisms remain far from realistic in the short to medium term. Current prices remain lower than the long-run marginal cost of supply, estimated by Razavi at $0.67/MMBtu,[62] and far short of the depletion premium.[63]

Domestic Demand Outlook to 2020

According to CREG estimates,[64] future growth of gas consumption in Algeria is unlikely to show any signs of abating, despite the global economic recession which does not seem to have had the same effect on the Algerian economy as in other countries. In its indicative programme for the period 2009–2018, the Algerian downstream regulator identifies three growth scenarios based on a range of socio-economic assumptions relating to population and GDP growths, to the rate of occupancy per housing unit, and to programmatic developments pertaining to various users (power generation, energy sector, domestic and commercial, industrial). Accordingly, the resulting annual growth

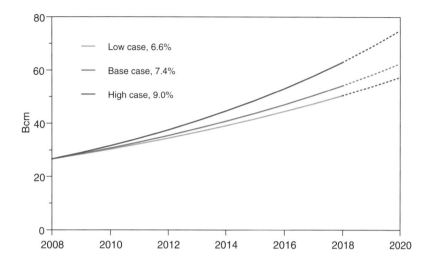

Figure 1.9: CREG 2009 Projections for Domestic Gas Consumption

Source: CREG, 'Programme indicatif d'Approvisionnement du Marché national en Gaz, 2009–2018', 2009

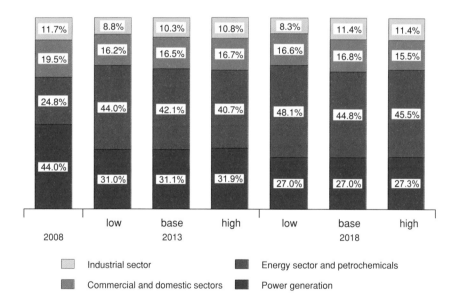

Figure 1.10: CREG 2009 Scenarios for Projected Natural Gas Consumption by Sector

Source: CREG, 'Programme indicatif d'Approvisionnement du Marché national en Gaz, 2009–2018', 2009

projections are divided between a low case at 6.6 percent, a base case at 7.4 percent, and a high case at 9 percent (Figure 1.9). The low case has been adopted in this study. This choice is informed by the belief that government forecasts tends to be bullish, knowing that they only serve as indicators, in this case of the challenge posed by domestic demand for Algeria's gas balance.

Thus, gas consumption is expected to reach 50 Bcm in 2018 and, assuming it continues to grow at about the same rate until 2020, is likely to double compared to the 2009 level. As can be seen in Figure 1.10, future growth will be strongly driven by the planned expansion of the energy and petrochemical sectors, which are expected under the low-case scenario to account for nearly half the country's gas consumption in 2018. This should come as no surprise considering the production capacity of the petrochemical projects currently under construction or in the planning stages (Table 1.2). This development programme is meant to reinforce Algeria's industrial base by capitalising on its competitive advantage in the energy sector, but it will undoubtedly have a restraining effect on gas exports. The power sector will also be a consistent driver of gas consumption growth during the same

Table 1.1: Recently-completed and Planned Power Stations in Algeria

Plant	Type	Nameplate capacity (MW)	Expected online date
Relizane	Gas turbine	3x155	May-July 2009
Arbaâ	Gas turbine	4x140	Feb-Oct 2009
Alger Port	Gas turbine	2x35.5	Apr-May 2009
Batna	Gas turbine	2x127	Apr-May 2009
M'sila	Gas turbine	2x215	June-Aug 2009
Annaba	Gas turbine	2x35.5	Mar-09
F'Kirina	Gas turbine	200	2013
Batna extension (Ain Djasser)	Gas turbine	200	2013
Messerghine	Gas turbine	400	2015
Hadjret Ennous	CCGT	3x400	2009
Terga	CCGT	3x400	2012
Koudiet Edraouch	CCGT	3x400	2012
Ras Djinet	CCGT	2x400	2014
Jijel	CCGT	2x400	2015
Hassi R'Mel	Hybrid (gas/solar)	150 (30 solar)	2010
		Total 8000	

Source: CREG, 'Programme indicatif des Besoins en Moyen de Production d'Électricité', 2008

Table 1.2: Planned Petrochemical and Other Energy-intensive Projects in Algeria

Project	Site	Nominal capacity (ton/year)	Ownership	Estimated cost	Expected completion date
Topping condensate	Skikda	5 million	Sonatrach	$380 million	2010
Sorfert ammoniac	Arzew	1.3 million ammonia 1.0 million urea	Orascom 51% Sonatrach 49%	$2.1 billion	2011
Ammoniac	Arzew	1.1 million	Fertiberia 51% Sonatrach 49%	$1 billion	2011
SBGH ammoniac	Arzew	1.3 million ammonia 1.1 million urea	SBGH 51% Sonatrach 49%	$2.5 billion	2012
Methanol plant	Arzew	1 million	Almet 51% Sonatrach49%	$786 million	2012
Aluminum plant	Béni Saf	700,000	Mubadala 51% Sonatrach 49%	$5 billion	2013
Ammoniac and derivatives	Béni Saf	660,000	Sonatrach	$1 billion	2013
Ethane steam-cracking plant	Arzew	1.4 million ethane 100,000 ethylene	Total 51% Sonatrach 49%	$3.6 billion	2013
Fuel cracking plant	Skikda	4.5 million	Sonatrach	$2.5 billion	2014
Naptha steam-cracking plant	Skikda	1.8 million	Sonatrach	$3 billion	2014
Tiaret refinery	Tiaret	15 million	Total 70% Sonatrach 30%	$6 billion	2015

Source: Algeria Ministry of Energy and Mines (2008)

Table 1.3: Recently-completed and Planned Desalination Plants in Algeria

Plant	Completion date	Capacity (cm/d)	Estimated cost
Oran (Arzew)	2006	90,000	$400 million
Algiers (Hamma)	2008	200,000	$250 million
Skikda	2008	100,000	$105 million
Ain Timouchent	2008	200,000	$204 million
Tlemcen I	2009	200,000	$238 million
Mostaganem	2009	200,000	$227 million
Boumerdes	2010	100,000	$133 million
Tipaza	2010	120,000	$180 million
Tlemcen II	2010	200,000	$251 million
Chlef	2010	200,000	$290 million
El Taref	2010	50,000	-
Tipaza	2010	100,000	$115 million
Oran (El Magtaâ)	2011	500,000	$468 million
Total		2,260,000	$2.86 billion

Source: Algeria Ministry of Energy and Mines (2008)

time frame, though it will have lost some of its current share to the petrochemical sector, according to CREG estimates. This will mainly be a reflection of the planned doubling of the electricity generation capacity, bringing 8000 MW online between 2009 and 2015, as well as the realisation of one of the world's most ambitious water desalination programmes (Tables 1.1 & 1.3).[65]

Algeria's Gas Export Policy: A New Era?

The gas export targets set by Algeria at the turn of the century were meant to be attained through a combination of upstream revival, a fuller utilisation of existing pipeline capacity, and the construction of additional LNG and pipeline infrastructure. However, even before the 5 Bcm increment from In Salah came on stream in 2004,[66] the Skikda accident had resulted in a significant loss of export capacity (about 4 Bcm). As a result, even the midway target of 65 Bcm/yr set for 2005 was nowhere to be seen, notwithstanding the successful upgrade of the capacity of the GME pipeline system to 11.5 Bcm/yr in 2005. In fact, against the challenges described above, Algerian exports have been running at less than 60 Bcm/yr for most of the period since 2005.[67] Furthermore, as the delays plaguing the Gassi Touil project became more evident, the 85 Bcm/yr target slipped by default to 2013. However, more troubling now than missing the original export target dates are questions over Algeria's ability to produce enough gas to satisfy both its growing domestic market and the array of export facilities it will have completed by 2014 (Figure 1.11).

Export Projects. Underlying Sonatrach's gas export ambition has been its instinctive commercial drive to diversify its outlets and secure market share, thus being able to reinforce its flexibility and better capture market upside. However, diversification from the Mediterranean market is only going to be possible to a relatively limited extent, as the interdependence underpinning Sonatrach's relationship with its main customers in Europe derives mainly from its comparative advantage consisting of geographical proximity, cost competitiveness and flexibility between pipeline and LNG exports. What's more, current gasline projects to southwest Europe, namely Medgaz and Galsi, as well as the expansion of the Trans-Med system's capacity to 32.5 Bcm/yr by the end of 2009 are only likely to further entrench this interdependence.[68]

In this vein, in its initial conception, the integrated LNG project of Gassi Touil was expressly targeted at the US market – Sonatrach's 'natural base'.[69] However, in light of the fundamental shifts that have occurred in the US market as a result of the development of shale gas resources this is now highly uncertain. Sonatrach will now most likely seek to place the Gassi Touil volumes in Asian or 'niche' markets in the Middle East and South America. The replacement of the damaged

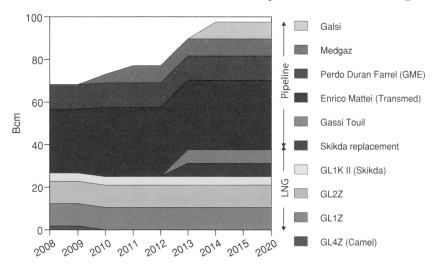

Figure 1.11: Planned Expansion of Algeria's Gas Export Capacity

Sources: Sonatrach, MEES (various issues) and own estimates

Skikda trains with an enhanced 4.5 mtpa single train will for its part consolidate Sonatrach's commercial position in the the Mediterranean and, as well as in northern Europe, when it comes on stream in 2013.[70] However, the potential of this new LNG capacity may not be fully realised until the refurbishment of existing LNG units, which is planned to take place once the new trains are operational, is completed around 2015.[71]

LNG Supply Contracts. As well as increasing its LNG export capacity, Sonatrach has been keenly investing in the downstream of its customers' markets to maximise its trading margins. This strategy has consisted of acquiring regasification capacity in major markets such as the US (3 Bcm at Cove Point), the UK (7 Bcm jointly with BP at Isle of Grain), Spain (10 percent stake in the 2.5 Bcm Renagosa plant), France (1 Bcm at Montoir de Bretagne), and possibly the Netherlands as of 2012 when new capacity at Rotterdam (LionGas LNG) comes online. Further down the value chain, Sonatrach has also deployed significant efforts to secure downstream positions in these markets – successfully in Spain, Italy and France – allowing it to sell its gas directly to end-users, though the move did generate some resistance from incumbents, particularly in Spain.

   This strategy is reflective of the structure of Sonatrach's LNG sales, which between 2004 and 2008 had become increasingly focused on spot markets.[72] Encouraged in large part by the ability of Sonatrach to capture lucrative arbitrage opportunities through its international trading offices, this changing policy gathered pace on the back of growing confidence on the part of the Algerian company to the extent that traditional long-term contracts are now said to belong in the past and shorter-term alternatives are openly advocated.[73] In this context, the non-renewal of LNG supply contracts with Gas Natural and Distrigas in 2004 and 2006 respectively may indeed have been a prelude to this enunciated policy shift. Nevertheless, departing from their quasi-doctrinal attachment to long-term contracts,[74] it is worth noting that Algerian energy policy-makers led by Chakib Khelil championed this contractual policy change at a time of booming global LNG demand and record spot prices – their apparent persistent support of a new approach seems *a posteriori* to be more in tune with the emerging realities of the Algerian gas market than the shifting international market conditions.

Outlook for Algeria's Gas Export Strategy to 2015

Compared with other North African producers, Algeria's medium-term gas export potential is less a function of reserves, conventional know-how or capital. Yet, between setting new gas export targets and meeting its enunciated plan, Algeria has failed to reach a number of benchmarks most notably in upstream development. As a result, not only did it become clear early on that the original objective of increasing exports to 85 Bcm/yr needed to be deferred to 2013, but it now seems that even this is an unlikely prospect. Indeed, it is expected that Sonatrach will only be able to reach this target around 2017/18, though this may not be sustainable, while it remains highly unlikely that it will ever accomplish its 100 Bcm/yr export ambition. This is largely attributable to the vicissitudes of the legislative reform process initiated by energy policy-makers at the start of the decade. Far from introducing an investment framework conducive to an enhanced upstream yield, the new hydrocarbon law seems to have, by default rather than by design, impeded its architects' gas export policy by undermining the prospect of a sufficient increase in production.

While there is nothing fundamentally objectionable or indeed atypical about a failure to achieve original policy targets, the trouble with Algeria's long-stated gas export plan is that the impending supply crunch will mean that the array of new export infrastructure intrinsic to this plan is likely to remain undersupplied unless important, yet potentially costly, adjustments are introduced (Figure 1.12). The first of these actions concerns the deferral of project schedules. Medgaz for instance saw its first-gas date delayed by more than a year from the original commissioning target set for the first half of 2009. Though this was partly due to falling demand on the Spanish market as a result of the economic recession, Sonatrach did not show any signs of urgency about starting to inject gas into the pipeline. The Galsi project is another likely case of deferral, in view of the fact that in 2010, despite the enthusiastic endorsement it had initially received from government and industry actors alike, its final investment decision (FID) appeared to be put on the backburner.

The second important shift that is likely to occur relates to LNG supply contracts. It seems evident that, given the current conditions pervading Algeria's gas market, Sonatrach will abandon the practice of systematic renewal of contracts on extant terms to allow itself greater flexibility. In the first instance, this would most likely apply to its current contract with Turkey's Botas upon its expected expiry in 2014. Additionally, the initially bullish announcement of policy change with regard to long-term contracts may in the less certain future serve quite a different purpose for Sonatrach. If future gas supply is clouded by uncertainty, Sonatrach will indeed only be in a position to make short-term commitments to LNG

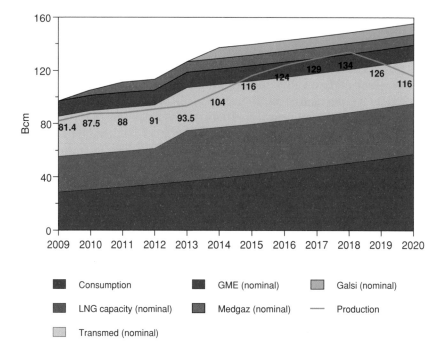

Figure 1.12: Algeria's Gas Balance to 2020

Sources: CREG (2009), Sonatrach, and own estimates

customers, especially for the new trains with no dedicated upstream reserves such as Skikda. As such, a change in the structure of supply contracts would be the result of necessity rather than policy. Though useful, such export policy adjustments will alone not be sufficient to address the looming deficit in Algeria's gas supply capacity. Further policy actions, put forward in the following section, will be needed.

Policy Recommendations

The impact of the global economic recession on European gas demand from the end of 2008 relieved Sonatrach of some of its supply pressure in 2009 and its effect is likely to continue until at least 2011/12. Indeed, IEA estimates show that Algerian 2009 gas exports to Europe were about 10 percent lower than 2008 levels, and instead of late 2009 the commissioning of Medgaz has consequently been pushed back to mid-2010. However, the issue of gas supply shortages in relation to export capacity will require more coordinated measures if impending imbalances are to be seriously addressed. The following set of policy actions should be considered as a way forward:

- *Consumption.* Given the substantial impact that the planned petro-chemical projects will have on future domestic gas requirements, relative to their actual economic added value in terms of job and value creation, the deferral of a number of them – especially those awaiting a FID[75] – should be considered. It is estimated that such a move would free up to 8–11 Bcm/yr of gas for exports. Pursuing these projects should be resumed after 2015 when predictability about the supply situation will have improved, though this should be done on a different domestic pricing-policy basis, which should make at least industry users pay near-market level prices for gas feedstock. Furthermore, the gradual shift to enhanced reinjection techniques, such as CO_2 reinjection, should be more resolutely implemented to reduce the rate of gas reinjection for oil and liquids recovery.

- *Exports.* Adopt a more rational policy on export objectives, which would imply deferring the 85 Bcm/yr target to after 2015, or indeed until such point when reaching this target becomes more feasible. Though the infrastructure capacity will be operational by then (Trans-Med expansion, Medgaz, Gassi Touil, Skikda replacement), doing so would serve the purpose of formulating a less ambiguous and more coherent policy message. In this vein, it seems logical that the Galsi pipeline should also be explicitly deferred sine die. Given the fact that Medgaz' capacity could easily be doubled and that the planned expansion of the Spain–France interconnector will justify that, Galsi would be more sensible in case the Trans-Saharan Gas Pipeline became more feasible, notwithstanding the fact that Galsi's onshore section (from Hassi R'Mel) is almost complete. This in turn is a far-fetched prospect, but keeping the project's current political momentum should be a priority for the Algerian government.

- *Production.* Taking into account the projected decline in production, mainly stemming from Hassi R'Mel, a moderate gas depletion policy should be pursued to ensure that the projected increase in domestic consumption is satisfied in the medium to long run. At the same time, alternative sources of energy should be explored, particularly nuclear and solar energy. In the current conditions, nuclear energy seems a more viable alternative, but given the strategic and logistical adjustments involved, the sooner a framework for its development is devised, including an adjustment of domestic power prices, the more timely its contribution to satisfying domestic energy requirements is likely to be. Though less obvious an alternative for now, solar energy should be developed to the extent possible, prioritising the requirements of the domestic market.

Conclusion

The evolution of Algeria's natural gas market since 2000 has taken place against a background of rapidly changing domestic and international environments, which have presented Algerian policy-makers with both opportunities and challenges. However, as the new gas development strategy was formulated in the 2000s, in manifest symbiosis with the proposed hydrocarbon legislative overhaul, it became evident that the rigid pursuit of the new law's implementation process could not but have an adverse impact on gas export policy in the event of failure. Yet, as Law 05-07 was reversed in 2006, the gas export targets of 85 Bcm/yr by 2010 and 100 Bcm/yr by 2015 were maintained against the resulting odds. Falling short of these targets, as it has by now become clearly inevitable, is not problematic in and of itself for Algeria. It is rather the implicit challenges of this shortfall as well as the longer-term supply uncertainties for Sonatrach's ability to optimise export capacity and maximise revenues that are likely to cause concern, considering the economic and geopolitical importance of gas in Algeria on the one hand, and the absence of a meaningful diversification of the national economy away from hydrocarbons on the other. Unless significant reserves are discovered in the coming years and more effective management of reservoir depletion in the main producing fields is undertaken there is little that will prevent these looming supply challenges from materialising.

A combination of subdued upstream gas development and growing domestic consumption has left the prospects of Algerian gas exports in a worse position than initially intended. A quasi production hiatus since 2006 is likely to persist until the early part of the 2010s, when a string of new fields southwest of Hassi R'Mel are expected to come on stream, boosting marketed output to 116 Bcm by 2015. Nevertheless, these and future gas upstream developments will hinge on the ability of Sonatrach to reconcile its state functions on the one hand and its increasing reliance on IOC involvement for the development of hydrocarbon reserves on the other. However, this balancing act requires less meddling with investment terms as such than significantly improving Sonatrach's decision-making efficiency.

Domestic consumption of natural gas has become a defining factor in Algeria's gas supply balance. In recent years, sustained economic growth has translated into intensified demand for power generation, which will be supplanted by the petrochemical sector as the main engine of growth in future gas consumption, which as things stand is projected to reach 42 Bcm by 2015. Moreover, socio-political imperatives have manifestly left decision-makers with little room for manoeuvre as regards price-focused demand management, and the existing constraints are unlikely to wither in the short-term. Yet, relative to other MENA countries this distortion may be more sustainable in Algeria as it will not pose an immediate and damaging threat to domestic economic development, although radical reforms will need to be urgently introduced if power generation capacity from nuclear and renewable sources is to become operational by 2020 as planned. Algeria's current financial wealth is likely to militate against such reforms, but the probable coming to power of a new political leadership after 2014 will almost certainly bring a change of approach to this and similar economic issues.

Notes

1   Before being overtaken by Qatar in 2009, it had been the biggest exporter of gas in the MENA region since 1964
2   Hayes, M.H., 'The Transmed and Maghreb Projects: Gas to Europe from North Africa' in D.G. Victor et al. (eds), *Natural Gas and Geopolitics: From 1970 to 2040* (Cambridge: Cambridge University Press, 2006). In 2000, the two pipelines were renamed Enrico Mattei Gas Pipeline and Pedro Duran Farell Gas Pipeline respectively (see Map 1.1). The traditional Trans-Med and GME appellations will be used here.
3   *BP Statistical Review of World Energy*, 2010.
4   Aïssaoui, A., *Algeria: The Political Economy of Oil and Gas* (Oxford: Oxford University Press, 2001) p.13; Dillman, B.L., *State and Private Sector in Algeria: The Politics of Rent-Seeking and Failed Development* (Oxford: Westview Press, 2000) p.4.
5   Aïssaoui, A., 'The Challenges of Diversifying Petroleum-Dependent Economies: Algeria in the Context of the Middle East and North Africa', API-CORP Research Economic Commentary, 4 (6), June 2009.
6   On average, natural gas exports since 2000 have accounted for 40–50% of overall hydrocarbon export volumes.
7   Entelis, J.P., 'Sonatrach: The Political Economy of an Algerian State Institution', *The Middle East Journal*, 53 (1) 1999, pp. 9–27.
8   For detailed analyses of these reform attempts, see: Entelis, 'Sonatrach, pp. 13–16; Aïssaoui, *Algeria*, pp. 202–220.
9   Aïssaoui, *Algeria*, pp. 88–125 provides a detailed account of these policies.

A more gas-focused account can be found in Aïssaoui, 'The Challenges of Diversifying Petroleum-Dependent Economies'.

10 Aïssaoui, A., 'Algerian Gas: Sonatrach's Policies and the Options Ahead' in R. Mabro and I. Wybrew-Bond (eds) *Gas to Europe: The Strategies of Four Major Suppliers* (Oxford: Oxford University Press, 1999), p. 17.

11 Ibid., pp. 53–55.

12 It is worth noting that Chakib Khelil was the chairman of the Valhyd implementation committee in the 1970s. It seems therefore unsurprising that he advocated a high-export policy upon his return to government in 1999.

13 Bouteflika's six opponents in the 1999 election withdrew at the last minute in protest at the candidate's explicit endorsement by the powerful military establishment, leaving him to be elected by default.

14 Darbouche, H., 'Algeria's Chequered Democracy Experiment' in M. Emerson and R. Youngs (eds), *Struggling Transitions and Proliferating Dynasties: Democratisation's Trials in the European Neighbourhood*, (Centre for European Policy Studies, Brussels, 2009).

15 Aïssaoui, 'Algerian Gas', p.48.

16 As minister of foreign affairs at the time, Bouteflika was in charge of renegotiating with the French government the provisions of the Evian Accords in relation *inter alia* to the Algerian hydrocarbons industry.

17 *Gas Matters*, February 2002.

18 Ibid., September 2006.

19 *African Energy*, 22 January 2010.

20 *Gas Matters*, January 2003.

21 The rate of the new windfall tax varies between 5–50% depending on the level of production. The measure is reported to have generated over $1 billion in 2007 and $4.3 billion in 2008 for the Algerian treasury.

22 Over seventy companies were prequalified for the bidding (*MEES*, 21 July 2008).

23 ENI, BG, Gazprom and E.On Ruhrgas won the four concessions, marking the Russian and German majors' Algerian upstream debut following their signing of a separate MoU with Sonatrach in 2006.

24 *Middle East Economic Survey [MEES]*, 29 December 2008.

25 Ahnet's proven gas reserves are estimated at 140 Bcm.

26 *Petroleum Economist*, June 2007.

27 The licensing round launched by Egypt's Gas Holding Company (EGAS) in September 2008 and concluded in March 2009, after benefiting from a one-month extension, saw only three out the seven 'prolific' offshore blocks on offer awarded (*MEES*, 9 March 2009).

28 *Oil & Gas Journal*, 2009. The estimate includes both non-associated and associated gas.

29 A number of gas discoveries were made since 2000, but these have been rather too small and scattered around to make any significant difference to Algeria's reserves (and production) profile.

30 Recent IEA (2009b) estimates put Hassi R'Mel reserves at 3100 Bcm.

31 Observatoire méditerranéen de l'Energie [OME], 2008, p.276.
32 *MEES*, 25 February 2008; *World Gas Intelligence [WGI]*, 28 November 2008.
33 Located southeast of Hassi R'Mel, Ohanet and In Amenas are wet gas fields, producing 5–6 and 9 Bcm/yr of gas respectively. Part of the 'southwest project', In Salah is Algeria's largest dry gas field. The first phase of the project, which has brought on stream three out of seven fields, produces 9 Bcm/yr and is expected to be expanded in 2013 (OME, 2008, p.282).
34 *Gas Matters*, April 2005.
35 See EC press release No. IP/07/1074, 11 July 2007. Algeria is widely believed to have softened its tone in relation to destination clauses as a result of increased pressure particularly following Gazprom's decision in 2003 to drop such territorial contractual restrictions, and also to pave the way for its European downstream plans.
36 OME, 2008, p.283.
37 *LNG Focus*, 14 October 2007. Gassi Touil initial project costs were estimated at about $2.9 billion. The Spanish consortium bid to invest around $2.1 billion, while the rest of the costs were to be covered by Sonatrach.
38 *WGI*, 7 March 2007.
39 Relations between the Algerian and Spanish governments deteriorated since the coming to power of Zapatero's PSOE in 2004, mainly as a result of diverging views over the Western Sahara dispute. And a range of commercial disputes from pipeline gas supply prices to downstream market access pervaded Sonatrach's relationship with Gas Natural in the run-up to the Gassi Touil dispute (*World Gas Intelligence*, 12 September 2007).
40 Japanese Chiyoda and Italian Saipem/Snamprogetti were awarded the construction of the new 4.7 mtpa LNG plant at Arzew after the cancellation by Sonatrach of an earlier contract award to Petrofac and IKPT, while Japan's JGC won the EPC contract for the development of the relevant Rourde Nouss field.
41 IEA, 'Natural Gas Market Review (OECD/IEA, Paris, 2009), p.107.
42 *Petroleum Economist*, September 2008.
43 Hassi R'Mel was discovered in 1956 and began commercial production in 1961. The average yield for condensate in Hassi R'Mel is about 200 grams/ m3 (*APS Review Gas Market Trends*, 10 February 2003), which means that the field is central to Algeria's valuable condensate production of which it is one of the world's leading exporters.
44 In 2000, Sonatrach signed a contract with a Japanese consortium to install three major gas-boosting compressor stations and 11 compression lines at the field in the aim of maintaining its pressure (*APS Review Gas Market Trends*, 27 November 2000).
45 Hassi Messaoud accounts for more than 60% of gas reinjection in oil fields.
46 Public investment between 1999 and 2009 is believed to have largely exceeded $200 billion, going mostly towards building new roads, schools and universities, hospitals, rail and air transport infrastructure, dams, housing and new towns. This excludes the repayment of the near-totality of Algeria's foreign debt, estimated at $30 billion.

47 The explosion at Skikda's three out of six LNG trains claimed the lives of 27 people and injured dozens more. It followed a number of safety incidents at similar Algerian facilities over the previous year (*Gas Matters*, January 2004).

48 *MEES*, 27 October 2008.

49 *WGI*, 12 March 2008.

50 *MEES*, 7 July 2008.

51 MLE is now developed by Italy's ENI (75%) in association with Sonatrach (25%) following the former's takeover in September 2008 of struggling Canadian independent First Calgary Petroleum's MLE assets (*WGI*, 10 September 2008).

52 Hassi R'Mel, In Salah, In Amenas, Ohanet, Alrar, Hamra, Rourde Nouss and Tin Fouyé Tabenkort (TFT).

53 Gassi Touil, Tinhert, Ahnet, Touat, Timimoun and Reggane Nord.

54 Zérafa, Djebel Hirane, Hassi Mouina, Hassi Bahamou and Menzel Ledjmet Southeast.

55 Total estimates the costs of developing Timimoun at $1.3 billion (*MEES*, 10 November 2008). Touat and Reggane Nord are each expected to cost around $1.5 billion (*Arab Oil & Gas Directory* [AOGD], 2009, p.61).

56 The development plan of Sonatrach (51%), Total (37.75%) and CEPSA (11.25%) for the Timimoun field was approved by Alnaft in October 2009, following the earlier decision to give the go-ahead to a Sonatrach-GDF Suez joint-venture for the development of Touat. The approval of the development plan of the Repsol YPF-led consortium for Reggane Nord was due in January 2010. The gas production increment from the entire southwest project is expected to reach 14 Bcm at plateau level.

57 Aïssaoui, 'Algerian Gas', pp.52–53.

58 *BP Statistical Review of World Energy*, 2009.

59 *Commission de Régulation de l'Electricité et du Gaz*, 'Programme indicatif d'Approvisionnement du Marché national en Gaz, 2009–2018', 2009, p.11. CREG is Algeria's downstream gas and electricity regulator.

60 In September 2009, the Algerian government provided yet another financial lifeline to Sonelgaz to support its vast investment programme. See: 'L'État à la rescousse de la Sonelgaz: La BNA accorde un important prêt à la société', *Tout sur l'Algérie*, 29 septembre 2009.

61 Until 2007, power generation users paid half as much as industrial customers for gas feedstock.

62 H. Razavi, 'Natural Gas Pricing in Countries of the Middle East and North Africa', *The Energy Journal*, 30 (3) 2009, pp. 1–22.

63 The depletion premium is an indicator of the opportunity cost of consuming a unit of exhaustible resource now rather than in future.

64 CREG, 'Programme indicatif …', 2009.

65 In line with the heavy reliance of the power sector on natural gas mentioned above, the bulk of the planned new capacity will be gas-fired. Most plants with CCGT technology are developed as Independent Power Projects (IPPs), involving foreign investment.

66 Although In Salah produces 9 Bcm, 4 Bcm were committed early on to an existing supply contract with Italy's Enel.

67 *Gas Matters*, April 2009.

68 For more details, see: *Arab Oil and Gas Directory*, 2009, pp. 71–75.

69 *World Gas Intelligence (WGI)*.

70 The EPC contract for the Skikda reconstruction was awarded to American KBR in July 2007 for an estimated $2.8 billion, all of which is financed by Sonatrach.

71 This will mainly include Arzew's GL1Z and GL2Z units, which were last refurbished in the late 1990s, whilst GL4Z (Camel formerly) is likely to be decommissioned altogether (Figure 1.11).

72 As much as 12% of Sonatrach 2008 LNG sales were made on spot markets (*MEES*, 14 July 2008).

73 *World Gas Intelligence*, 6 February 2008.

74 For a detailed analysis, see: I. El Kadi, 'Le gaz algérien en passe de changer de religion', IFRI Notes, April 2009.

75 All but the four projects highlighted in Table 1.2.

CHAPTER 2

THE LIBYAN GAS INDUSTRY:
DOMESTIC ISSUES AND EXPORT POTENTIAL

*Waniss A. Otman**

Country Overview

Libya, known officially as the Great Socialist People's Libyan Arab Jamahiriya, is situated on the southern Mediterranean coast, being part of the African continent with a coastline of around 2000 km and a land area of 1,759,540 sq km, making it the fourth largest country in Africa by area. It shares borders with Egypt in the east, Sudan in the southeast, Chad and Niger in the south, Algeria to the west and Tunisia to the northwest. Despite its massive area, its population in 2008 stood at 6,310,434, mainly concentrated in the Mediterranean coastal belt.

Libya relies on oil and natural gas to drive economic growth and diversification. According to the IMF,[1] the country's real GDP grew from 5.9 percent in the period 2005–2006 to 6.8 percent in the period 2006–2007, while hydrocarbon exports accounted for 98.1 percent of total exports in 2007. Preliminary data from the IMF in June 2009 indicate that real GDP grew by about 3.8 percent in 2008, while GDP per capita stood at US$14,500. Real growth is projected to decelerate to about 2 percent in 2009. Generally speaking, the impact of the global financial crisis on Libya has been thus far limited to the decline in oil revenue, mainly due to the rather limited exposure of domestic banks to the global financial system.[2]

Libyan Gas Reserves in Global and Regional Terms

According to the BP *Statistical Review of World Energy*, Libya's global rank

---

* My initial gratitude is to both the late Professor Thomas Wälde and Dr. Shukri Ghanem for their support. For this I extend my deepest appreciation, not only for being largely in accord with the subject matter and my topic approaches, but also in promoting useful discussion and constructive analysis related to gas industry and its future. I wish to dedicate this work to Prof Thomas Wälde, whose untimely death in 2008 left his family and the world at large a sadder and emptier place. He was a dedicated teacher, mentor and leader, and an intellectual titan in his field.

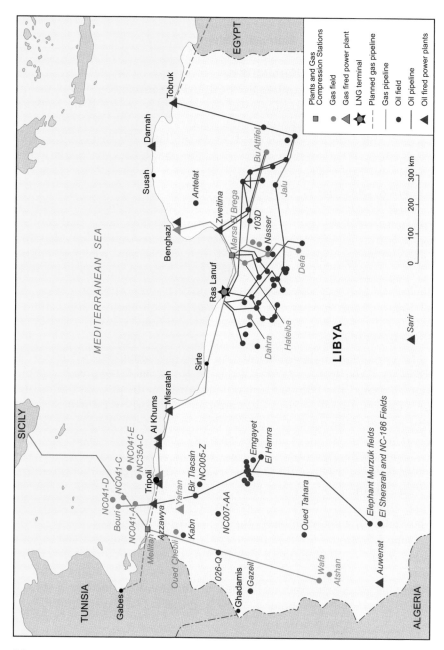

Map 2.1: Libya: Gas and Oil Fields and Transport Infrastructure

is 22nd in terms of proven gas reserves, with 1540 Bcm, or 0.8 percent of world reserves. This figure corresponds to that of another authoritative source, OPEC, which again puts Libyan proven gas reserves at 1540 Bcm, as at end 2008.[3] Both of these sources are relatively close to data made available to the author by the Libyan National Oil Corporation (LNOC), which puts Libyan proven gas reserves at 1612.6 Bcm (56.9235 tcf) as at mid 2009. Without doubt these will increase significantly as recent exploration activities by LNOC affiliates or International Oil Companies (IOCs) in the country's sedimentary basins, particularly the Ghadames basin, where mainly gas has been discovered, are factored in. These gas discoveries are summarised later in this chapter.[4]

Most researchers in the Libyan hydrocarbon industry are of the opinion that these reserve figures grossly understate the actual reserve potential of Libyan gas.[5] This is also borne out by the fact that the majority of gas reserves in the Sirte basin were discovered before 1970. Additionally, data held by the LNOC Exploration Division and its foreign partners, covering largely unexplored and unexploited areas in the deep horizons of the Libyan basins, and in the offshore sector such as the Sabratah basin, suggest that potential reserves could be as high as 3260 Bcm.

In the case of Libya, proven gas reserves more than doubled from 1980 to 2000, from 690 Bcm to 1310 Bcm. Although the US sanctions imposed in 1986 had a major negative effect on exploration, the activities of LNOC's Sirte Oil Company (SOC) in the Sirte basin in this period yielded some major discoveries, for example the As Sahel, Assumud and Attahadi gas fields, which contributed substantially to reserves in this period. After this, Libya's ability to increase its gas reserves, from 1990 to 2008, was seriously restricted, as the long-term effects of the US/UN sanctions began to kick in, both in terms of lack of funds for LNOC exploration and appraisal activities, as well as the denial of new technology for reservoir appraisal. Because of these factors, Libyan gas reserves registered a relatively small increase of only 1210 Bcm to 1540 Bcm in this period, or about 27.3 in percentage terms. This increase was mainly through discoveries in the offshore sector together with the availability of improved technology after the lifting of the UN sanctions in 1999 and the US sanctions in 2004.

Libyan Gas Production

Between 1981 and 2008, Libya's gross natural gas production grew from 12.7 Bcm/yr to 30.31 Bcm/yr (Figure 2.1). The gas utilisation rate for domestic consumption through the coastal pipeline increased from 2.6 million cm/d in 1991 to 11.7 million cm/d in 2008.[6] Marketed production increased from 5.2 Bcm in 1999 to 15.9 Bcm in 2008, an increase of over 200 percent in this period (Figure 2.1). This was largely due to the progressive build-up of output from the Western Libya Gas Project (WLGP), which exports large quantities of gas to the Italian market.

In terms of growth, Libyan gas production has been unspectacular and erratic. In general, in the early period, growth in associated gas production was linked to oil production levels, while the steady decline in production from the early 1990s onwards can be attributed largely to the effects of the US/UN sanctions which denied the country spare parts and technology for its gas processing and transportation sectors. Recent increases are due to the contribution of the WLGP, while in general gas production, even if only associated gas, will inevitably increase in line with Libya's ambitious plans to increase oil production capacity to 2 million b/d by 2010 and 3 million b/d by the middle of the next decade.

The total gross gas production in 2008 was 31.52 Bcm, with an average daily production of 86.35 million cm/d.[7] As can be seen from Figure 2.2, the breakdown of gas production by companies for the year 2008 showed Mellitah Oil and Gas Company heading the list, with a total production of 16.2 Bcm or 51.4 percent of production. This

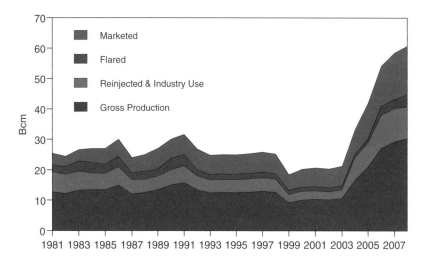

Figure 2.1: Gross Gas Production with Breakdown to Marketed, Flared and Reinjected/Industry Use, 1981–2008

Source: OPEC *Annual Statistical Bulletin*, 2009; BP *Statistical Review of World Energy*, 2009

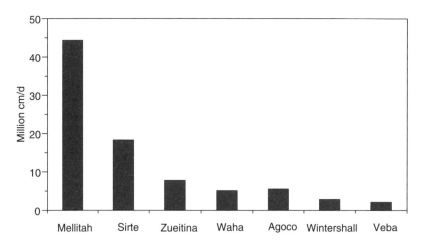

Figure 2.2: Breakdown of Average Daily Gas Production by Company, 2008

Source: LNOC, General Dept. for Exploration and Production, Gas Production
Report, May 2009.

was followed by the Sirte Oil Company with 6.7 Bcm (21.3 percent),
Zueitina with 2.87 Bcm (9.1 percent), Arabian Gulf Oil Company
(Agoco) with 2 Bcm (6.5 percent), Waha at 1.88 Bcm (6 percent),
Wintershall at 0.7957 Bcm (3.3 percent), and finally Veba with 0.796
Bcm (2.5 percent).

The domination of the Zueitina and the Sirte Oil Companies in
Libyan gas production is of course derived from their historical association with the highly prolific Sirte Basin, although Agip through the
WLGP is gradually eating into this domination to become the leading
gas producer. Both Zueitina and Waha (Oasis Consortium), through
the return of the US IOCs to their Libyan assets in 2005–2006, are
projected to become major producers of gas in future years, in view
of significant investment tied to the conditionalities surrounding their
return.[8] It can also be anticipated that the EPSA-IV rounds will produce
a gas bonanza, but this will probably not be realised until the next
decade.

The Growing Role of Non-Associated Gas

Libyan gas production is derived from both associated and non-associated gas (free gas), and Figure 2.3 shows the breakdown of these sources
for the last five years, and the coming four years as forecast by LNOC
Production Department from ongoing activities. In 2008 non-associated

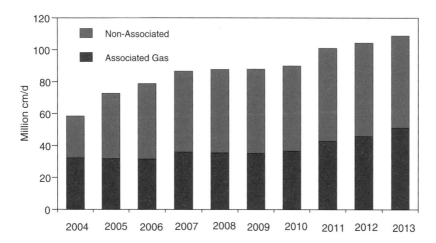

Figure 2.3: Total Natural Gas Production by Associated and Non-associated Gas, 2004–2008, with Libyan Government Official Estimates to 2013

Source: LNOC, General Dept. for Exploration and Production, Gas Production Report, May 2009.

Note: Figures from 2010 to 2013 estimated by LNOC Dept. of Production.

gas represented approximately 58.5 percent of the total production with the remaining 41.5 percent associated gas. This is mainly due to the large portion of free gas produced from the WLGP gas fields.

In 2004 associated gas accounted for 32.24 million cm/d which increased to 35.52 million cm/d by 2008, an increase of 10 percent. However, according to the LNOC this figure has risen dramatically to reach 51.133 million cm/d, an increase of 58.6 percent in the 2004 to 2008 period. The LNOC Production Department in 2009 also estimated that in 2013 non-associated gas production would reach 57.79 million cm/d, i.e. a significant 120 percent increase from 2004 production.

Figure 2.4 illustrates the contribution of gas production by each operator in the country in terms of associated/non-associated gas. As can be seen, Mellitah is leading in both categories with recorded outputs of 8.07 and 35.47 million cm/d respectively. Sirte Oil Company comes next with 12.72 million cm/d of non-associated gas and 3.654 million cm/d of associated gas. Zueitina produced 6.91 million cm/d of associated gas followed by Waha with an output of 4.645 million cm/d, Agoco with 3.31 million cm/d as well as 0.06 million cm/d of non-associated gas. Wintershall produced 2.776 million cm/d of associated gas, whereas Veba produced 1.33 million cm/d of associated gas.

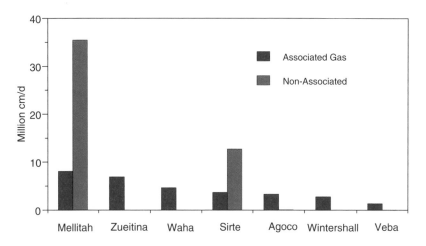

Figure 2.4: Breakdown of Average Daily Gas Production by Company as
Associated/Non-associated Gas, 2008

Source: LNOC, General Dept. for Exploration and Production, Gas Production
Report, May 2009

Note: Excluding flared gas

Libyan Gas Usage

Figure 2.5 identifies recent usage of the gross daily production of gas
by sector, and provides a snapshot as at 1 April 2009. The Western
Libyan Gas Project (WLGP) absorbs the largest portion, 42.5 percent,
mainly for export to the Italian market. This is followed by domestic
consumption through the coastal pipeline, which accounts for 13 percent of the total production. Reinjected gas accounts for 12.4 percent,
with 10 million cm/d or 97.4 percent of this figure due to the Zueitina
Oil Company and the rest to Waha Oil Company (2.6 percent). Gas
flaring amounts to 10.1 percent (the issue of gas flaring in Libya will
be discussed in detail later in this chapter). The fifth ranking for daily
usage is field operations in the oil and gas industry, and its value was
recorded at 7.74 million cm/d, or 9.6 percent of the country's total.

The sixth segment in the daily production of gas goes to the El
Brega industrial complex where gas is frozen for LNG and used as a
feedstock for petrochemicals, mainly for export. This amounts to around
7.08 million cm/d, at 8.8 percent. The LNG plant accounts for 4.05
million cm/d (57.2 percent) of the total El Brega requirement, while
the Petrochemical Complex takes up 3.03 million cm/d or 42.8 percent.

Finally, the last portion of total gross production of gas is used for

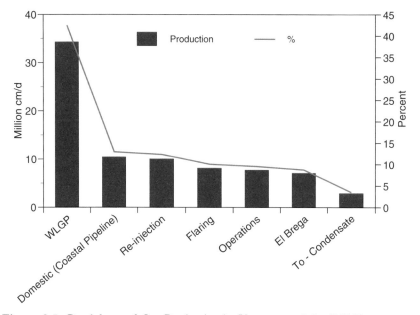

Figure 2.5: Breakdown of Gas Production by Usage, as at 1 April 2009.

Source: LNOC, General Dept. for Exploration and Production, Gas Production
    Report, May 2009

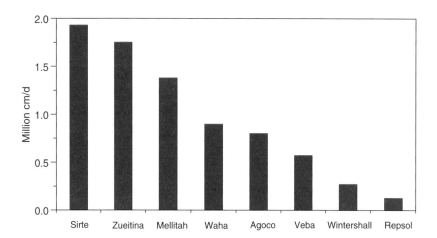

Figure 2.6: Breakdown by Company of Gas Usage in Oil and Gas Industry
    Operations, as at 1 April 2009

Source: LNOC, General Dept. for Exploration and Production, Gas Production
    Report, May 2009

condensate, accounting for 2.92 million cm/d or 3.6 percent. The largest condensate producer is Mellitah Oil and Gas Company with 2.38 million cm/d, 81 percent of the total condensate production from gas, while Wintershall is second at 0.29 million cm/d with 10 percent, followed by Agoco at 0.15 million cm/d with 5 percent, and finally Waha Oil Company with 0.10 million cm/d or 4 percent.

From Figure 2.6 it can be noted that the Sirte Oil Company is the leading consumer of gas for operational needs, with 1.93 million cm/d, or 25 percent, followed by Zueitina Oil Company with 22.7 percent, Mellitah Oil and Gas (the former name of Eni Agip) with 17.8 percent, Waha Oil Company with 11.6 percent, Agoco with 10.4 percent, Veba with 7.4 percent, Wintershall with 3.5 percent and Repsol with 1.6 percent.

Domestic Consumption Trends

As can be seen from Figure 2.7, the trend in Libyan domestic consumption of gas has been increasing steadily, from a relatively small usage of 2.6 million cm/d in 1991 to 11.7 million cm/d in 2008. This rise can be largely attributed to demographic factors, necessitating a massive

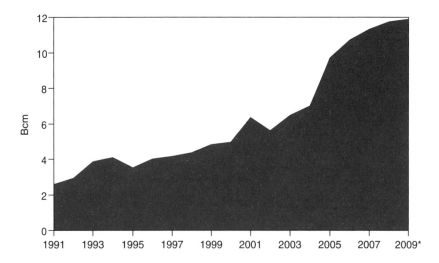

Figure 2.7: Average Daily Demand in Domestic Consumption of Gas through the Coastal Pipeline, 1991–2009

Source: LNOC, General Dept. for Exploration and Production, Gas Production Report, May 2009

* 2009 Figure estimated by the Author.

expansion of the infrastructure all over the country in the surveyed period, as well as residential construction in the main urban centres. The shift by GECOL (the General Electricity Corporation of Libya), the Libyan electricity utility which holds a monopoly, from oil- to gas-fired generating systems has undoubtedly also had a significant impact on gas usage. Demand has escalated by 350 percent in the period from 1991 to 2008.

This sharply rising trend demonstrates that looming issues will confront Libyan policymakers in future, as it is crucial to get the export/domestic balance for natural gas right. It also shows that the importance of projects such as the 2005 LNOC/Shell Libyan Sirte Gas Project – which aim to significantly increase exports of LNG from the El Brega plant – have not been adequately understood by policymakers, given future domestic gas shortages.

As shown in Figure 2.8, domestic demand supplied through the Coastal Pipeline was 9.83 million cm/d or 13 percent of total gas production for the first quarter of 2009. Generating electricity and desalination plants accounted for 65.7 percent of this at 6.46 million cm/d; the next major utiliser was the Misuratah Steel & Iron Plant at 17.6 percent, or 1.73 million cm/d followed by the Ras Lanuf Complex at 8.1 percent or 0.793 million cm/d and the cement industry, 7.5 percent at 0.74 million cm/d, with the residual amount of 0.11 million cm/d for others, representing 1.2 percent.

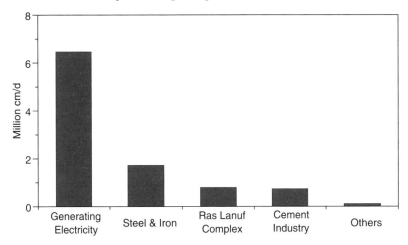

Figure 2.8: Libya: Average Domestic (Coastal Pipeline) Consumption for the First Quarter 2009

Source: LNOC, General Dept. for Exploration and Production, Gas Production Report, May 2009

Undoubtedly there is a massive domestic demand that has been held back by the rapid industrial and touristic diversification of post-sanctions Libya, and which poses a major challenge for GECOL which accounts for 65.7 percent of the total gas consumed within the country through the coastal pipeline (Figure 2.9). GECOL is, in point of fact, a prodigious loss-maker due to subsidised domestic energy prices, a major feature of the Libyan centralised and subsidised domestic economy. As will be discussed extensively in a later section, the crucial importance of satisfying rapidly growing domestic energy demand, and balancing this with Libyan gas reserves and gas exports, is a challenge which policymakers must not fail to address.

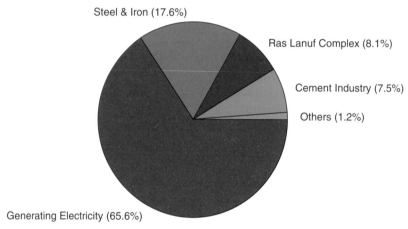

Figure 2.9: Percentage of Average daily Domestic Consumption of Gas by Sector, First Quarter 2009

Source: LNOC, General Dept. for Exploration and Production, Gas Production Report, May 2009

The Western Libya Gas Project (WLGP): Libya Emerges as an International Natural Gas Player

Examining the Western Libya Gas Project (WLGP)

After many decades during which its promising gas industry was sidelined, Libya finally emerged as a significant gas exporter in October 2004, when processed gas from the WLGP and its associated Greenstream pipeline to Sicily, connecting to an existing pipeline into Italy, started flowing. This project now positions Libya in the ranks of neighbouring Algeria and Egypt as a major gas exporter.

The natural gas for this project comes from two fields. The first, Wafa, is an onshore field close to the Algerian border while the second, Bahr Essalam, is an offshore field located 110 km off the Libyan coast. The Wafa gasfield is located in Block NC169a, in the south-west part of the Libyan side of the Ghadames basin, approximately 540km south west of Tripoli. The discovery in 1991 of the north Wafa gasfield by the Sirte Oil Company (SOC) typified the seemingly insurmountable infrastructure problems associated with developing a significant gas discovery in an extremely isolated area of Libya.

Although the southern part of the Wafa oilfield was discovered by Shell in 1964, it was SOC's discovery and extensive appraisal campaign in the northern part – conducted between 1991 and 1994 – that identified the field as being a giant one. As the crucial onshore supply component of the joint onshore/offshore project, its geological structure as the Libyan half of the Algerian Alrar field – discovered in 1961 and put into production in 1965 – effectively means that the Alrar gasfield depletion rate, over which Libya has no control, impacts pressure and therefore production of both gas and condensates over the Wafa field's production life.

Several concepts were envisaged for the development of Wafa, including export via the Hassi R'Mel pipeline in Algeria, but it was only in the late 1990s that ENI proposed its joint development with gas from NC-41 to produce an export stream to Italy which would effectively more than double Libya's gas production.

The offshore component of the WLGP is the Bahr Essalam field in Block NC-41, discovered in the late 1970s by Agip, who subsequently developed the highly productive Bouri oilfield there. The Bahr Essalam gasfield is situated in an area containing ten gas pools that were discovered during drilling operations in the Sabratah offshore basin by Agip when they were developing the Bouri field.

The Importance of the Western Libya Gas Project (WLGP)

In terms of Libyan gas projects, it is impossible to underestimate the importance, both real and symbolic, of the WLGP. It is equally important to appreciate that the project was conceived and, for the most part, implemented, during the period of US sanctions. As a landmark technological and financial undertaking, the WLGP demonstrated to the outside world that Libya was able to successfully conceive, implement and deliver a major hydrocarbon project without any US inputs. At the same time it permitted the Libyan downstream sector to have hands-on access to cutting edge gas and condensate production, collection and transportation technology, as well as the utilisation of current design

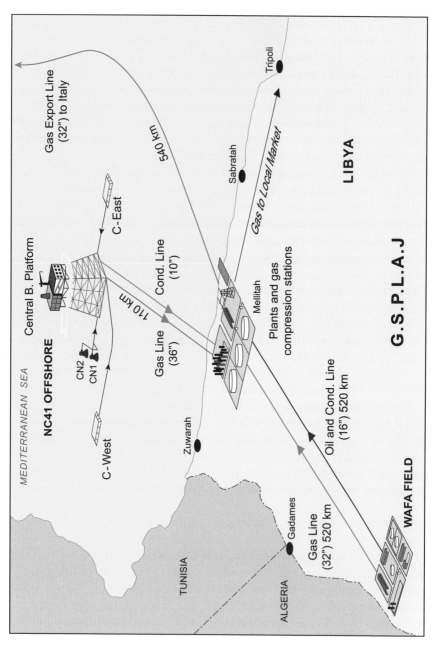

Map 2.2: The Western Libya Gas Project

and engineering. It also enabled negotiators in LNOC to understand the intricacies of co-financing a Joint Venture (JV) project which, with ENI of Italy, cost almost US$6 billion in total.

WLGP's design capacity is to produce 10 Bcm/yr, with 2 Bcm/yr earmarked for domestic consumption. The remaining 8 bcm/year will be exported by the Greenstream pipeline under the Mediterranean to Gela, Sicily. The company has successfully entered into contracts for selling its gas, based on take-or-pay deals. Energia Gas, a subsidiary of the Italian based conglomerate CIR, has contracted to purchase approximately 2 Bcm/yr over 24 years. Additionally, Italy's Edison Gas will buy 4 Bcm/yr, and Gaz de France 2 Bcm/yr. It can be said that the project was a time-driven one, since Agip, after the successful negotiation of these long-term contracts, had been under considerable commercial pressure to finalise the development of the project in order to meet its exporting deadlines.

Dealing with Future Gas Shortages in the WLGP

As stated earlier, the fact that Wafa and the Alrar field in neighbouring Algeria are part of the same reservoir means that the rapid Alrar gasfield depletion rate, over which Libya has no control, will impact pressure and therefore production of both gas and condensates over the Wafa field's production life. In fact it appears that the Wafa field can sustain a plateau rate of 13.45 million cm/d of gas (equivalent to 4.9 Bcm/yr of saleable gas) for only ten years from 2004. This will have serious implications for the contractual obligations of the 24-year supply contract to Italy. This deficiency is likely to place the LNOC and its partner ENI in considerable contractual difficulties. Fortunately, it is likely that the shortfall after 2014 can be met by tapping into the considerable remaining gas reserves contained in Block NC-41. These are detailed in Table 2.1.

It is clear from Table 2.1 that a massive amount of additional gas reserves, totalling approximately 577.41 Bcm are present and available for exploitation from Block NC-41, more than enough in fact to make up for any shortfall in the WLGP over its project life.

In connection with the production status of reserve depletion, a contract was signed in early September 2006 regarding the Wafa and Alrar Fields by Dr Shukri Ghanem, Chairman of the LNOC, and Mr Mohamed Mizyan, President of Sonatrach. The contract is the result of an agreement reached between the parties to study the links between the Alrar and Wafa fields.

In line with the contract both parties agreed to request the American

Table 2.1: Block NC-41 Offshore Basin, Gas Reserves

	O.G.IP. bcm	*RF %*	*Raw Gas Reserves bcm*	*IMPUR %*	*Net Reserves bcm*
A	28.89	69.3	20.03	5.7	18.89
C	316.90	60.7	192.5(3)	17.3	159.2(3)
D	598.58	49.0(1)	293.2(2)	80	58.64(2)
E	60.23	58.3	35.11	11	31.25
F	9.90	55.7	5.50	4.1	5.28
G	23.41	63.8	14.94	4	14.34
H	4.59	67.3	3.08	11.8	2.71
K	4.73	74.6	3.52	3.7	3.39
M	3.65	69.3	2.53	4	2.43
P	1.34	50	0.66	3.4	0.64
Q (4)	10.93	57.9	6.33	14.5	5.41
Total	1063.16		577.41	-	302.20
Total Without "D"	464.58		284.21	-	243.56

Notes: Reserves calculated assuming WHFP=350 Psia for "C" STR. and 1150 Psia for the remaining ones.
1. ECL estimate.
2. "D" structure gas producibility is badly affected by technical problems related to the quality of reservoir fluid.
3. Added "C" eastern area assuming R.F. equal to "C" central area.
4. Shared between NC-41 and NC-35 BLOCKS.

Source: LNOC, Libyan Gas Plan Report, February 2005

consultancy firm Degolyer and MacNaughton to provide a technical study of the two cross-border fields. The study is divided into two phases. In the first, scheduled to last six months, the consultants will conduct a study to determine the hydro-dynamics of the reservoir. The second part, which will last for 12 months, will determine the size of the reservoir, its precise location, reserves and production, in order to regulate its exploitation between both countries in accordance with international standards. Clearly the LNOC hopes that the results of the study can enable it, with Algerian cooperation, to meet its original offtake projections from Al-Wafa.

Additional sources of gas are expected to come from recent discoveries in the Ghadames Basin by IOCs such as Verenex and Woodside, and the gas from these discoveries will underpin the project's long-term commitment to export gas to the Italian market. Other major discoveries have been achieved by the LNOC and its affiliates Agoco, Sirte Oil Company and Woodside Oil Company. Table 2.2 summarises these discoveries and their estimated production rates.

Table 2.2: West Libyan Gas Discoveries, 2009

Operator	Block/Field	OGIP (BCM)	Reserves EUR (BCM)	Daily rate (MM CM)	Source of data
AGOCO	NC7A	70.651	54.674	N.A.	AGOCO Reserve Book
	NC7A (D structure)	56.657	48.158	N.A.	AGOCO and NOC Exploration Departments Reserve Calculations
	NC5	6.1756	5.609	N.A.	AGOCO Reserve Book
	NC8	10.736	7.592	N.A.	AGOCO Reserve Book
Sirte Oil	NC175	6.345	4.306	0.566	Reserves Calculation using Volumetric method
	NC180	5.807	4.362	0.566	Reserve Calculation using Volumetric method
	NC151A	11.983	8.356	1.133	Preliminary reserve calculation of NOC Exploration Department
LNOC	NC151 (Atshan)	26.062	16.997	2.0396	Woodside study, 2006
Woodside	NC210	26.742	18.725	2.2096	Woodside reserve calculation

Source: LNOC, General Dept. for Exploration and Production, July 2009, Apprising Onshore Gas Discoveries located West of Libya region. Also LNOC, April 2009, Oil and Gas Projects Targeted by Five Year Development Plan 2009 to 2013.

Figure 2.10 illustrates LNOC's forecasted production together with operating companies based on their existing reserves. The current production rate of Wafa is 15 million cm/d, to be increased to 16.43 million cm/d by the end of the year 2009. However, Mellitah Oil and Gas has recently submitted plans to invest $2.1 billion aimed at increasing production capacity to 22.662 million cm/d as highlighted in Figure 2.10. Other LNOC affiliates and Woodside will also participate in increasing gas production to WLGP from new discoveries, enabling Libya to maintain its long-standing contractual commitment to the project.

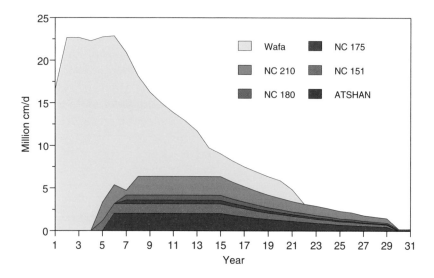

Figure 2.10: Long-term Production Forecast for the Western Libyan Gas
Discoveries, 2009

Source: LNOC, General Dept. for Exploration and Production, July 2009, Apprising Onshore Gas Discoveries located West of Libya region.

Gas Development in Libya: Fiscal Policy Concerns

Many gas industry researchers have suggested it would be logical
to assume that most governments in the world would have more
favourable fiscal terms for gas than for oil in order to stimulate gas
development.[9] This is due to a variety of factors which suggest that the
costs of developing and marketing gas are less economically attractive
than for oil. From the risk analysis approach, investors are concerned
about political and economic risks because of the considerable capital
expenditure that is required for the gas project cycle, including exploration, field development, gathering, processing and finally distribution
and marketing, whether by pipeline for domestic or transnational usage,
LNG facilities or more recently, GTL (Gas to Liquids) technology.
Under these conditions exposure to a project cycle period of 25 years
including exploration and production may be considered the norm,
but in more demanding environmental situations, this period is often
not enough to get a reasonable Return on Investment (ROI). Despite
these considerations, the fact is that, as revealed in Van Meurs' study
quoted above, the vast majority of countries still do not have separate
fiscal terms for gas developments.

In the thirty years spanning the use of the first three generations of the Libyan Exploration and Production Sharing Agreements (EPSAs), from EPSA-I in 1974 to EPSA-III in 2004, the failure of the LNOC to seriously address natural gas exploitation and development is very conspicuous. This has often been cited by analysts as one of the major reasons why the IOCs were reluctant to participate in Libya's gas industry. This is in stark contrast to how the Qatar government has successfully developed its massive gas resources, and to a more limited extent, Saudi Arabia in its development of the Saudi Master Gas System (SMGS), Sabic (Saudi Basic Industry Corporation), the Saudi Gas Initiative of 1998–2003, and Saudi Arabia's introduction of the Gas Supply and Pricing Regulations (GSPR) in 2003.[10]

For a variety of reasons, the gas sector in Libya has been regarded historically as the poor sister of oil, but now global trends in the increased usage of natural gas – because of its superior environmental credentials – as well as rapidly growing domestic demand in Libya itself, mean that policy, especially relating to the new discovery and development of free or non-associated gas, is due for a major overhaul.

In the following sections the author will appraise the terms in both EPSA-III and EPSA-IV in respect of developing gas discoveries. Although the latter contains promising changes with regard to exploitation of, in particular, non-associated gas, the Libyan policymakers must address this problem with much more urgency and focus. This is in view of existing and projected shortfalls in satisfying domestic gas demand in Libya, as well as major regional commercial opportunities for the sale of Libyan gas.

EPSA-III and the Gas Sector

In general terms EPSA-III, which was introduced in 1989, can be regarded as a major improvement over the earlier EPSAs, due basically to the critical state of Libya in general and the Libyan hydrocarbon industry in particular at the time of its introduction. The impact of the US companies' withdrawal in June 1986 had a major effect on the Libyan oil sector, since it effectively blocked any new US investment flow into the country's oil industry. Coupled with the low oil prices of the late eighties and its long-term financial commitments to major domestic infrastructure projects such as the Great Man-Made River Project, the Iron and Steel Complex at Misuratah and massive oil and gas downstream facilities and pipelines, the Libyan government found itself in a classic financial squeeze. The LNOC had somehow to boost the IOCs' participation in all phases of upstream activities in order to reverse this decline in oil production capacity, technically attributable to the age of the main production fields.

The answer was EPSA-III, in which the Libyan government tried very hard to ensure new exploration activity by offering IOCs more attractive returns and internationally competitive terms, guaranteeing them a rapid payback for investment in Libya. In this model LNOC adopted new and very flexible contractual terms. These included the guaranteeing of cost recovery to the second party, the potential to achieve a much better and earlier revenue flow from new investments compared to the previous EPSAs and importantly, for the first time, the exemption of shared production from taxes and royalties.

Unfortunately, however, scant attention was paid to the development of gas discoveries. In the entire 56-page EPSA–III, only a few articles/clauses refer to gas. The first refers to discovery of non-associated gas, and how this might impact on the termination period of the agreement, quoted in full in Appendix 1.

EPSA-IV and Monetising Gas

The calculation of the actual monetary value of the quantity of gas in the EPSA-IV belonging to the IOC is contained in article 12.3.2:

> For the purpose of determining the value of Natural Gas received by Second Party, the actual selling price according to the gas sales agreement shall be used.

However many other issues related to 'monetisation' of natural gas are poorly dealt with in EPSA-IV, as can be seen in Appendix 1. Probably the most contentious issue for IOCs considering investing in the Libyan gas sector is contained in Article 13.5.1.

> The Parties agree to give priority to supply the domestic market in GSPLAJ (Libya) from all or part of the Natural Gas produced under this Agreement.

In itself, this takes any decision-making power regarding the marketing of gas outside Libya completely out of the IOCs' hands. The situation is further exacerbated by Article 13.5.2, which states that

> The Parties (as sellers) and First Party or another local buyer (local buyer) shall proceed in good faith to negotiate a gas sales agreement incorporating the principles set forth in Article (13.4) and the price shall be stipulated in accordance with Article (13.4.3) less fifteen percent (15%).

Until these clauses concerning priority for the local market and subsidised pricing are considerably revised and ideally incorporated in a separate law containing a series of incentives specifically for gas, it is highly unlikely that there will be any foreign investment in developing gas discoveries. This has been borne out by the facts – apart from the WLGP and the Shell Libya Sirte Gas Project of 2005 there have been no major gas development projects announced in Libya since the implementation of EPSA-IV in 2004.

Additionally, the crucial linkage between the gas upstream and downstream sectors through access to infrastructure for transport and distribution of gas is dealt with very summarily in EPSA-IV. The reality is that, in many cases, the commercial success of upstream gas projects is based largely not only on having a relatively competitive market with regard to pricing, as touched on above, but also on having some type of guarantee concerning access to downstream infrastructure such as existing pipelines.

The virtual monopolistic position of the LNOC in terms of gas transport either through pipelines (Coastal Pipeline) belonging to its wholly owned subsidiaries such as SOC (Sirte Oil Company), or LNOC in majority-owned JVs with foreign companies such as Agip or Repsol, places a new investor in the Libyan gas segment in a particularly vulnerable position with regard to physical market access for its gas, whether for the domestic or export markets. Although Article 13.6 appears to guarantee access to such facilities owned or controlled by First Party (i.e. LNOC), on terms not less favourable than those granted to other shippers or users of the processing facilities (i.e presumably LNOC's subsidiaries/affiliates), it could have gone further by legislating for guaranteed third party access to plants and pipelines constructed for any future gas development projects by other companies.

The Fourth EPSA-IV Bidding Round (Gas Round)

On 4 September 2007, 56 companies were pre-qualified to bid, 35 as potential operators and 21 as investors (non-operators) in the fourth EPSA-IV round, known as the 'gas bidding round'. The result was declared through Public Announcement on Libyan TV on 9 December 2007. LNOC had received offers for investment in 12 areas from 13 IOCs of 11 nationalities.

The 12 areas offered included 40 blocks located in five different sedimentary basins. Five were offshore, two in the Sirte basin, two in the Ghadames basin, two in the Murzuk basin and one in the Cyrenaica basin, and details are provided in Table 2.3. All companies agreed to pay $10 million as signature bonus for each area, apart from Shell, which offered $103 million and RWE $5 million.

The total capital for minimum exploration commitments for the round was approximately $611 million, including 33 exploration wells, 8600 sq km 3D seismic and 13,100 sq km 2D seismic.

The breakdown of the minimum spending commitments during the initial exploration period ranged from $110 million for Gazprom, $108 million for Polskie (PGNIG), $95 million for Shell, $76 for RWE, $70 million for Occidental/Liwa, with Sonatrach/Oil India/Indian Oil Corp committing approximately $76 million for each area.

Table 2.3: Results of the 4th Exploration Bid Round, 9 December 2007

Basin	Area	Blocks	Size (km²)	Licensees	Operator Share
Sirte	89	1, 3	1790	Shell	15%
Sirte	103	1,2,3,4	4986	Occidental Petroleum/Liwa	18%
Ghadames	64	1,2,3	3936	Gazprom	9.8%
Ghadames	95–96	2 – 1,2,4	6934	Sonatrach/Oil India / Indian Oil Corp.	13%
Murzuk	113	1,2	5494	Polskie (PGNIG)	11.8%
Cyrenaica	58	1,2,3,4	10,289	RWE Dea	30%

Source: LNOC, 'Results of the 4th Exploration Bid Round, EPSA-IV', 2007.

Libya and Recent Oil and Gas Discoveries Resulting from EPSA-IV Rounds

Table 2.4 illustrates recent successful exploration activities achieved by IOCs as well as LNOC affiliates, and in particular highlights the aggressive exploration programme now rolling out across the country since the lifting of sanctions. Without doubt these will increase both oil and gas reserves, at the same time bolstering LNOC's plans to increase its target production to reach 3 million b/d. The contribution of these new discoveries to sustaining current gas production and providing additional capacity for pipeline exports to Italy or new LNG plants will be crucial for the growth of Libya's gas sector.

Libyan Gas Industry: Areas of Concern

Prioritising Domestic Requirements

A primary objective of an effective energy policy in any country is to ensure that domestic demand, to be supplied at affordable prices, is

Table 2.4: Oil and Gas Discoveries as a Result of Current Exploration Activities 2006–2009

No	Operator Company	Contract Area and Basin Name	Shareholders (interest)	Discovery date
1	SIPEX Libyan Branch	65/ Ghadames Basin	- LNOC as First party 75%. - SIPEX as Second party 25%.	13/4/2009
2	Repsol Exploration Murzuq	Block NC-202/ Offshore Sirte Basin	- LNOC as First party 65%. - Repsol Exploration Murzuq S.A. as Second party 25%. - OMV Oil and Gas Exploration GmbH. as Second party 14%.	9/4/2009
3	Woodside Energy	NC-210/ Ghadames Basin	- LNOC as First party 63%. - Woodside Energy as Second party 37%.	15/01/2009
4	Verenex Energy	47/ Ghadames Basin	- LNOC as First party 86.3 %. - Vernenx as Second party 13.7%.	25/10/2007
5	Amerada Hess	offshore Sirt Basin	- LNOC as First party 87.6 %. - Amereada Hess as Second party 12.4 %.	23/12/2008
6	Verenex Energy	47/ Ghadames Basin	- LNOC as First party 86.3 %. Vernenx as Second party 6.85%. - MEDCOas Second party 6.85 %	13/10/2008
7	Verenex Energy	47/ Ghadames Basin	- LNOC as First party 86.3 %. - Vernenx as Second party 6.85%. - MEDCO as Second party 6.85%	28/07/2008
8	Verenex Energy	47/ Ghadames Basin	- LNOC as First party 86.3 %. - Vernenx as Second party 6.85%. - MEDCO as Second party 6.85 %	10/12/2007
9	Verenex Energy	47/ Ghadames Basin	- LNOC as First party 86.3 %. - Vernenx as Second party 6.85%. - MEDCO as Secondparty 6.85 %	29/09/2008
10	Woodside Energy	NC-210/ Murzuq Basin	- LNOC as First party 63%. - Interests (37 %) in associated joint venture are: Woodside Energy (N.A.) Ltd. () Repsol Exploration Murzuq () Hellenic Petroleum S.A ()	N.A.
11	Verenex Energy	47/ Ghadames Basin	- LNOC as First party 86.3 %. - Vernenx as Second party 6.85%. - MEDCO as Second party 6.85 %	12/01/2009
12	AGOCO	Hamada Oil field/ Ghadames Basin	- LNOC – 100% - AGOCO as operator	N.A.

Table 2.4: continued

No	Operator Company	Contract Area and Basin Name	Shareholders (interest)	Discovery date
13	AGOCO	Hamada Oil field/ Ghadames Basin	- LNOC – 100% - Arabian Gulf Oil Company (AGOCO) as operator	12/01/2009
14	AGOCO	193/ Sirte Basin	- LNOC – 68% - Rwe Dea – North Africa 32%	10/12/2008
15	AGOCO	193/ Sirte Basin	- LNOC – 68% - Rwe Dea – North Africa 32%	29/09/2008
16	AGOCO	NC4/ Ghdames Basin	- LNOC – 100% - Arabian Gulf Oil Company (AGOCO) as operator	30/08/2009
17	Tatneft	82/ Ghadames Basin	- LNOC as First party 89.5%. - Tatneft as Second party 10.5%.	25/08/2009
18	Verenex Energy	47/ Ghadames Basin	- LNOC as First party 86.3 %. - Vernenx as Second party 13.7%.	12/01/2009
19	AGOCO	NC7/ Ghadames Basin	-----	15/12/2008
20	Sirte Oil Company	NC 216 A/ Ghadames Basin	- LNOC – 100% - (Sirt Oil Company) as operator	07/10/2008
21	RWE Dea-North Africa	NC 193/ Sirte Basin	- LNOC as First party 68 %. - RWE Dea 32%	10/09/2008
22	AGOCO	NC129/ Slouq Depression Basin	- LNOC – 100% - Arabian Gulf Oil Company (AGOCO) as operator	03/08/2008
23	RWE Dea-North Africa	NC 193/ Sirte Basin	- LNOC as First party 68 %. - RWE Dea 32%	29/09/2008
24	RWE Dea-North Africa	NC 193/ Sirte Basin	- LNOC as First party 68 %. - RWE Dea 32%	05/05/2008
25	Verenex Energy	47/ Ghadames Basin	- LNOC as First party 86.3 %. - Vernenx as Second party 6.85%. - MEDCO as Second party 6.85%	03/12/2007
26	RWE Dea-North Africa	NC 195/ Sirte Basin	- LNOC as First party 68 %. - RWE Dea 32%	24/09/2007
27	Zuetina Oil Company	NC 74A/ Sirte Basin	- LNOC – 100% - Zuetina Oil Company as operator	29/10/2006
28	RWE Dea-North Africa	NC 193/ Sirte Basin	- LNOC as First party 68 %. - RWE Dea 32%	29/10/2006

Source: LNOC, Department for Exploration, Discovery Report, 2009

catered for in the long haul. In this respect, the priority must be to strike a prudent balance between gas reserves, production for export (whether as raw pipeline gas or downstream products such as LNG) and production dedicated to long-term growth in the domestic consumer market. The unenviable and politically perilous situation when domestic energy subsidies are in place, faced by countries such as Indonesia in 2001, arose because policymakers had failed to get the export/domestic energy balance right.

For domestic energy power generation, in the past twenty years natural gas has undergone a global renaissance as the preferred energy feedstock, in view of its versatility and environmental credentials. In this connection, the SOE in Libya responsible for electricity supply and distribution, the General Electricity Corporation of Libya (GECOL) has gradually been converting its heavy fuel-powered generating system to a gas-powered one. The transfer to new gas conversion technology is deemed to be crucial in order to meet future demand and mitigate costs, as well as being more environmentally friendly.

GECOL proposes to implement this in two phases, the initial one from 2002 to 2006, and the second from 2006 to 2012. During the initial phase funding will be 100 percent Libyan government, but it is possible that for the period 2006–2012 external funding will be required, perhaps using some form of Independent Power Producer (IPP). Libyan domestic electricity demand is growing rapidly, estimated at around 7 percent p.a. based on the existing customer base and demographic trends, but this does not account for the inevitable upsurge in demand expected through Libya's current diversification programme, such as the expansion of the tourism sector where for the years 2010–2019 growth is expected to average 7 percent p.a.[11] To meet demand GECOL is working aggressively to expand its capacity, as can be seen from Table 2.5.

An analysis of the general expansion plan shows that, if GECOL proceeds with its gas conversion plans, as is currently the policy, it

Table 2.5: Development of Libyan Electricity Sector Capacity, 2003–2007

Units/Items	2003	2004	2005	2006	2007
Installed Capacity of Electricity Generation (Megawatt)	4556	4556	5125	5330	5541
Peak Electricity Load (Megawatt)	3303	3435	3857	4012	4167
Consumed Electricity Energy (Gigawatt/hour)	11342	11796	12900	13420	14303

Source: OAPEC, *Annual Statistical Report* 2008

is clear that over the next ten-year period, there will be significant shortfalls in the domestic supply of gas which will frustrate GECOL's plans. This is primarily due to the massive amounts of gas exported to Italy by the WLGP from 2004 onwards, and to a limited extent, the comparatively high rate of gas flaring in Libya, still around 16–17 percent on average, if the WLGP is excluded from the picture.

Addressing Existing Weaknesses in Gas Policy

In 1979 the LNOC closed down Gas Projects Administration, which was a major blunder in Libyan energy policy; essentially it led to a policy vacuum for gas development in the country in the succeeding 30-year period.[12] Others might argue that the successful development of major fields in the Sirte Basin by the Sirte Oil Company, such as As Sahel, Assumud and Attahadi, shows that an aggressive gas exploration and development policy was in place in the 1980s and 90s. In fact these fields were developed based on reservoir data derived from much earlier drilling, some of it going back to the 1960s.

Again, it can be argued that the successful implementation of the US$5.6 billion WLGP in 2004, as well as the more recently signed 2005 Libyan Sirte Gas Project Agreement between LNOC and Shell – to explore and develop gas in Blocks S6, S20, S12 and S25 and Block 6 in the Sirte Basin, subsequently linking these to the rejuvenation, upgrading and marketing of the output of the El Brega LNG plant – demonstrate that the Libyan policymakers are constructively dealing with gas developments in Libya.

But the author believes that on closer inspection, the existing general domestic consumption picture shows that LNOC has failed to deal with the fundamental issues relating to gas production in the country, which is to satisfy current and future domestic demand. In the WLGP, for example, of the total production of 10 Bcm/yr, only 20 percent of the produced gas or 2 Bcm/yr, is earmarked for domestic consumption while the remaining 8 Bcm/yr goes to satisfy demand in Italy and Southern Europe. As for the LNOC/Shell Libyan Sirte Gas Project, it is predicated on making the availability of discovered gas the basis for the Brega upgrade. Thus, in this case, any discovered gas will not be available for local consumption, but will be exported in the form of LNG.

These major projects have been highlighted because they demonstrate the uncoordinated way in which major decisions relating to gas development have been made, without addressing fundamental requirements based on domestic demand in line with long-term demographic factors, as well as Libya's present ambitious plans for industrial expansion and diversification.

The Need for a State Body for the Gas Sector

In order to co-ordinate future gas policy, Libyan policymakers should consider establishing a body, similar to the earlier Gas Projects Administration but much wider in scope, to include both the upstream and downstream sectors. Its remit would be to strategise, in a comprehensive and coordinated manner, the long-term future of the Libyan gas industry. An impressive example is the way in which Egypt, through the establishment of Egyptian Natural Gas (Egas), took control of the country's gas sector from the Egypt General Petroleum Corporation in 2001, and catapulted its gas industry into the global market. Again, in Malaysia, Petronas Gas, a separate and distinct entity under Petronas (Petroliam Nasional) is the body that deals with all matters pertaining to gas in Malaysia, both in the upstream and downstream sectors.

The author believes that such a body is necessary in Libya to deal effectively with the following key policy issues.

(a) The Importance of Expanding Libyan Proven Gas Reserves
The issue of increasing Libyan proven gas reserves needs to be seriously addressed. These have increased by only 1210 Bcm to 1612 Bcm in the period from 1990 to 2009, a figure which Egypt has achieved almost on an annual basis in recent years. The new body must define targets for increasing gas reserves within a planned time frame, and devise and propose fiscal mechanisms to overcome the existing barriers to investment in the Libyan gas sector in order to achieve these. The differential between domestic and export prices, as discussed in more detail later, needs to be urgently addressed by the Libyan policymakers, or Foreign Direct Investment (FDI) in the domestic gas sector will not be forthcoming, thus impacting the country's gas reserves.

(b) Defining the Gas Reserve/Production (R/P) Ratio
Gas reserves and production must be linked in order to ensure long-term sustainability. Although in terms of Reserve/Production (R/P) ratio, Libya can sustain existing gas production for more than 97 years according to the BP *Statistical Review of World Energy*, 2009, no policy currently exists in which these are linked.

As a practical example, in Egypt in 2003 the policy guidelines were that of total existing gas reserves there should be at least enough allocated for 20 years of domestic consumption, with the remainder to be split equally between the export market and strategic reserves. Any new reserves would be made available for export, although under government regulations, export commitments must not exceed one-third of total gas reserves at any one time.[13]

It is obviously important that for an orderly expansion of Libya's gas industry, whether for domestic or export markets, definite policy guidelines should be laid down and adhered to. The decision as to what the desired minimum R/P ratio should be – for example, 100, 50 or 25 years – will of course depend on Libya's long-term macroeconomic development plans.

(c) The Issue of Gas Pricing in the Domestic and Export Markets
The issue of foreign companies producing gas, and its sale and pricing in the domestic market, is one that the current EPSA-IV has attempted to resolve but, as discussed at length, has not succeeded in doing. This is because while CIF Europe gas prices have fluctuated between US$3.83 and US$12.61 per MMBtu in the period 1985–2008 (according to the BP *Statistical Review of World Energy*, 2009), the Libyan government-controlled price of natural gas for domestic consumption has been fixed at 208 Dirhams/MMBtu for the last ten years (i.e. between US$0.17 and 0.20/MMBtu depending on LD/US$ exchange rate). When this standstill domestic price is compared with Libya's gas export prices, as shown in Figure 2.11, the differential is again staggering.

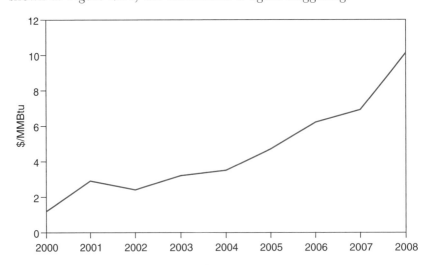

Figure 2.11: Export Price of Natural Gas, 2000–2008

Source: LNOC, Marketing Dept, 2009

Until domestic pricing issues are resolved to the satisfaction of foreign investors in the gas industry, they will continue to neglect gas development projects aimed at the domestic market, and this in turn will have a negative effect on the potential for increasing Libya's reserves.

(d) Dedicated Fiscal Terms for Gas

New and distinct fiscal terms, separate from those of EPSA-IV, need to be designed for the upstream gas sector to encourage investment. In other words, a new law for upstream gas developments needs to be drafted. In its drafting, the existing perceived barriers to IOCs investing in Libyan gas projects should be addressed, and incentives offered. Is there a case, for example, for decreasing royalty on gas production from the 16.67 percent presently paid on crude oil production?

Although of course under EPSA-IV all royalty and taxes are paid by LNOC on behalf of the Second Party (Article 19.1.12), the cost to LNOC of paying this is still factored into the agreed production split, for both oil and gas. Again, is there a case for extending the period of the EPSA beyond 25 years in the case of gas, in view of higher per-ceived investment costs and slower returns? Should the conditions and timing for declaring gas commerciality for gas discoveries be changed from those in EPSA-IV, to offer greater flexibility with respect to both of these key issues?

(e) Need for a New Policy to End Gas Flaring

Gas flaring in Libya still stands at around 10 percent, a very high figure in the light of industry experience in other gas provinces, whether in the MENA countries or Africa, and is an issue that needs to be urgently addressed by the Libyan policymakers.

The total amount of gas flared in Libya for the year 2008 is approxi-mately 7.337 million cm/d or 2.68 Bcm/yr. Figure 2.12 highlights the breakdown by company. The largest gas flarer is Agoco with 2.209 million cm/d or 39.6 percent of its produced gas, followed by Sirte Oil Company which flares 1.954 million cm/d or 11 percent of its output, and Zueitina with 0.935 million cm/d or 11.9 percent of company production. Veba currently flares 0.82 million cm/d which represents 12 percent of its production, Waha 0.51 million cm/d or 9.9 percent of its production, and Wintershall 0.085 million cm/d or 3 percent of its gas production. Worth noting is that the majority of these companies are LNOC owned.

Figure 2.13 demonstrates an even more alarming picture for Libyan gas flaring. Although it shows that this stands at around 10 percent, the fact is that if the WLGP's massive output had not been factored in to these national figures, the overall quantity of Libyan flared gas

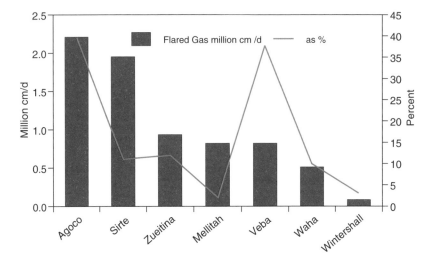

Figure 2.12: Average Daily Gas Production/Flaring by Value and Percentage by Company, 2008

Source: LNOC, General Dept. for Exploration and Production, Gas Production Report, May 2009

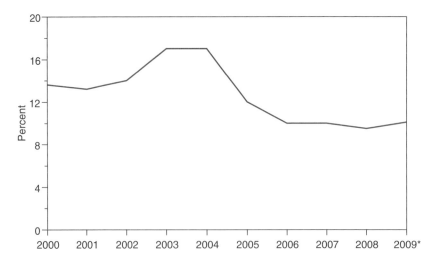

Figure 2.13: Percentage of Flared Gas from Total Production, 2000–2009

Source: LNOC, General Dept. for Exploration and Production, Gas Production Report, May 2009

Note: 2009 value taken from of 1 April 2009 as the daily production.

would increase to 16–17 percent. It is therefore timely that the Libyan authorities take some serious steps to end the flagrant waste of what is an increasingly valuable natural resource.

(f) Requirement for a Libyan Master Gas Plan
It is axiomatic that the upstream gas sector is focused on discovering and producing gas, while the downstream sector commercialises it. From its early encouraging start, the Libyan downstream gas market has entered into a long decline, largely due to the US sanctions, which the Libyan government now has the opportunity to rectify.

Because of the inherent tensions in present day Libya caused by the historical development of its centralised economy implemented in the early 1970s, and the current government's drive towards privatisation and decentralisation, it is difficult to envisage the rejuvenation of the Libyan gas sector without the introduction of a Master Gas Plan. However the design and implementation of this plan needs to be considered and structured very carefully, even conservatively.

This plan must link proven reserves with production, and allocate this between the demands of the Libyan domestic, the North African regional, and export markets in a long-term horizon, even for as long as 50 years. Critics may say this is too long, but as the Indonesian, Saudi Arabian and Malaysian experiences show, early emphasis on securing foreign exchange through gas exports from downstream gas projects such as LNG or petrochemical plants using gas as feedstock, invariably leads to shortages in the local market, at a point much sooner than anticipated.

As proposed in this section a window of opportunity exists for the formulation and implementation of a Libyan Master Gas Plan. Although Libya's policymakers have attempted to introduce more attractive terms for gas developments through the gradual evolution of the fiscal regime from EPSA-III to EPSA IV, it is doubtful if their efforts will succeed in securing major new investments in the gas sector, specifically for projects oriented towards the domestic market. In fact, this failure of the provisions in EPSA-IV might be turned to advantage, giving the policymakers breathing space to seriously consider an alternative long-term policy for the effective development of existing and undoubtedly considerable yet-to-be-discovered gas reserves.

LNOC and the Funding of Future Gas Mega-Projects, 2009

The Libyan government reacted swiftly to the lifting of the US sanctions in 2004, and the primary target for a major economic makeover was without doubt the hydrocarbon sector. Its strategy was two-pronged. The first approach was to immediately open new blocks for IOCs to explore under the introduction of a new petroleum fiscal model represented by EPSA-IV, the fourth generation PSC system utilised in Libya since the 1970s. This was aimed at increasing the country's reserves and production, as well as transferring the latest technology from IOCs, which was severely restricted during the sanctions era. The second strategy was aimed at the large-scale development of its oil and gas industry by pumping in massive capital injections to upgrade run-down oil and gas fields and increase their productivity, and also to overhaul the downstream industry including petrochemicals, refineries, storage depots, the domestic gas grid, and other processing facilities.

As can be seen from Table 2.6, LNOC, through its current five-year plan, is committed to invest US$46.333 billion in the hydrocarbon sector. This represents only LNOC's share and excludes the equity participation of the IOCs. Significantly, the highest share of this capital investment is the gas sector with approximately US$20,570 million, or 44.4 percent of total LNOC commitments. This capital for gas investment is targeted at both the domestic and export gas sectors.

Table 2.6: Hydrocarbon Industry: LNOC's Capital Commitment for Five-year Plan Projects, 2009–2013

No	Investment Type	Total cost of LNOC share (MMUSD)	%
1	Gas development, production and exploitation	20570	44.4
2	New refinery construction	5463	11.8
3	Development of undeveloped discovered fields	4465	9.6
4	Petrochemical development	3379	7.3
5	Work over and development of appraised fields	3166	6.8
6	Development of new discoveries	2892	6.2
7	Development drilling	2649	5.7
8	Exploration	1449	3.1
9	Upgrading of existing refineries	1400	3.0
10	Development of Storage capacity	900	1.9
	TOTAL	46333	100.0

Source: LNOC, April 2009, Oil and Gas Projects Targeted by Five Year Development Plan 2009 to 2013.

Despite the global financial crisis that has affected many IOCs, Table 2.7 provides a breakdown of the US$20,570 million shown in Table 2.6, emphasising the massive scale of developing existing major gas discoveries.

From a total of US$38,011 million, LNOC's share is US$20,570 million (representing 54 percent) while the balance is foreign capital. Table 2.7 shows that major increases in gas for export will be achieved through the NC 41 discovery development, Bahr El Salaam field development (Phase II), and development of the Wafa Field, jointly provided by the LNOC and Mellitah Oil and Gas (Agip Oil and Gas Libya). The table also shows that the LNOC has allocated US$12,000 million for existing exploration activities aimed at commercial discoveries, to be financed by both LNOC and its partners in the period concerned.

Also significant is the projected expenditure of the French firm Mabrouk (Total) in the D and C-NC137 discoveries. Here it will engage with LNOC in large-scale gas discovery appraisal and development, with a total capital investment estimated at US$2200 million, targeted at securing an additional 170 bcm of gas reserves and an average production of 3.116 million cm/d for 20 years.

In addition, LNOC and the Italian firm Mellitah Oil and Gas plan to develop the potential of the offshore Bouri field's associated gas, a project estimated to cost US$586 million to be split equally. This project is aimed at satisfying the 2.83 Bcm/d needs of the South Tripoli electricity station and will also be used to supply gas to the Tripoli cement factory and West Tripoli electricity station. As such it is considered to be a major utility project for the country's development.

There can be no doubt that in view of the relatively unexplored status of the gas sector in Libya, there exists considerable potential for its expansion. However, as discussed earlier in this chapter, the writer's view is that until a dedicated fiscal package for gas is put in place by Libya's policymakers, this is unlikely to happen because of a range of uncertainties related to subsidy issues and the monetisation of produced gas in the domestic sector.

Table 2.8 provides an analysis of LNOC's plans to invest US$2200 million for expansion of the domestic gas grid, a sum to be 100 percent funded by LNOC since there is currently no competition in the domestic gas market.

In Table 2.9 two other major gas projects are highlighted. The first is the 2005 Shell/LNOC Sirte Basin deal catering for the upgrading or rebuilding of the El Brega LNG plant, with the output destined for export. The total investment commitment for this project is US$667 million. The second major gas project is for Zueitina (Occidental) to develop re-injected gas; known as the Gas Cap Discharge of 103D Field, to date no capital has been allocated for this project.

To some observers, the sheer scale of the projected investments

Table 2.7: Investments in Gas Developments, Production and Exploitation (2009–2013)

Project	Target	Est. cost (MMUSD)	LNOC share (%)
Bahr El Salaam Field Development (Phase II) NC 41 (Mellitah Oil and Gas)	- To develop the second stage of the field to maintain the current production rates and develops the estimated reserves of 388 MM BOE.	1600	50
A1-NC151 Development (Phase I) (Sirte Oil Company)	- To evaluate the reserves, develop and produce gas and condensates.	63	100
NC 41 Discoveries Development (Mellitah Oil and Gas)	- To develop the offshore discoveries in NC41 block to produce reserves of 1205 MM BOE. - To achieve an exportable level of annual gas production of 0.316 bcm.	16300	50
Recovery Development of Al Wafa Field (Mellitah Oil and Gas)	- To increase the daily gas production from 14.16 million cm/d to 22.66 mm cm/d	2103	50
D and C-NC137 Discovery Development (Mabrouk Company)	- To develop the discoveries of 170 bcm of gas reserves - To achieve an average production of 3.116 million cm/d for 20 years	2200	50
Hateiba field gas plant Modification (Sirte Oil)	- To sustain the field productivity as per plant factory design and increasing the producible gas and condensate to 5.66 million cm/d and 0.142 million cm/d respectively.	720	100
Waha and Gialo fields Associated Gas Exploitation (AGOCO)	- To exploit the remaining associated gas which flared in the fields surrounding stations by gathering all the gas to one station along with the extracted condensate and pumping it to Nasser field of Sirte Oil.	119	59
Messla and Sarir fields Associated Gas Exploitation (AGOCO)	- To treat 1.416 mm cm/d which flared from Messla and Sarir fields to be utilised 126 MMBbls of condensate and 1.56 bcm of Gas.	120	100
Bouri field associated gas Exploitation (Mellitah Oil and Gas)	- To satisfy the needs of South Tripoli Electricity Station of 2.83 million cm/d - Gas supply to the cement factory, West Tripoli Electricity Station and Tripoli City Gas.	586	50
Domestic gas network	- To complete the coastal pipeline network	2200	100
Development of new discoveries	- New discoveries expected to be achieved through existing exploration programs	12000	50
Grand Total		**38011**	

Source: LNOC, April 2009, Oil and Gas Projects Targeted by Five Year Development Plan 2009 to 2013.

Table 2.8: Domestic Gas Project (Expanding Coastal Pipeline), 2009

Project	Target	Value (MM USD)
Gas Transmission Pipeline (Khoms–Tripoli) (Sirte Oil)	- To satisfy the needs of Zawia Electricity Station of 170 MMCFG/D. - To connect the coastal network extending from Benghazi to Tripoli.	210
Gas Pipeline from 103A field to El Brega (Sirte Oil)	- To pump a total of 1500 MM CFG/D to the coastal Network. - Usage of the natural gas as a substitute to the heavy fuel used in several factories along the Libyan Coast.	395
Completion and expansion of the Coastal Gas Network (Benghazi–Tobrouk)	- To expand the coastal network to include the Eastern region (Benghazi–Tobrouk). - To raise the capacity to comply with the expected local consumption in future.	1500
Gas Transmission Pipeline (Tripoli–Melita) (Sirte Oil)	- To satisfy the needs of Harsha Electricity Station of 170 MMCFG/D. - To support the gas local network by 200 MMCFG/D.	95
Total Domestic Pipeline		**2200**

Source: LNOC, April 2009, Oil and Gas Projects Targeted by Five Year Development Plan 2009 to 2013.

Table 2.9: Other Future Gas Projects Requiring Finance, 2009

Project	Target	Value (MM USD)
Upgrading El Brega Gas Plant (LNG)	To upgrade and develop the Brega Gas Plant and increase its capacity, Shell Gas project in Libya	650
Condensate Fixation Unit in El Brega Gas Plant (Sirte Oil Company)	To construct a condensate fixer unit as a substitute to the liquids Removal Unit during the annual overhauling.	17
Gas Cap Discharge of 103D Field (Zueitina Company), Oxy	*The project has still not been allocated any amount, also because the second party (Oxy) has just returned to Libya.	N.A
Total		**667**

Source: LNOC, April 2009, Oil and Gas Projects Targeted by Five Year Development Plan 2009 to 2013.

detailed in Tables 2.7, 2.8 and 2.9 might appear to be over-ambitious and unrealistic. However, the commitment of the Libyan government to upgrade and aggressively expand its hydrocarbon industry was underscored on 9 September 2009, when the Libyan Cabinet chaired by the Prime Minister, Dr Al-Baghdadi Ali al-Mahmoudi, approved a sum of Libyan Dinar 12,132 million (approximately US$10 billion) for new investment in the hydrocarbon sector.

This will go a long way to enable the LNOC to pay its way for its equity commitments to existing EPSAs and gas export projects. At the same time it will send a strong message to those IOCs who are second parties to these major investments: the LNOC will no longer tolerate any delays from them in meeting their financial commitments to existing EPSAs, which have in the past adversely impacted project feasibility and economic indicators.

Concluding Remarks

Although gas was traditionally regarded in Libya as the 'poor sister' of oil, increased global demand for cleaner fuels and the impetus provided by the WLGP has catapulted Libya into becoming a major gas producer and exporter. The pay-off to the country from the Fourth EPSA-IV gas round is already beginning to be felt, and GECOL's rapid gasification of the domestic power sector means that gas is firmly on the future energy agenda of Libya. Current technology advances such as Gas to Liquids (GTL) and Compressed Natural Gas (CNG) Transport will also mean that the future options for the country as a gas exporter will undoubtedly expand, whether in a regional or global context.

However grave doubts remain about domestic gas monetisation in the minds of foreign investors, which, as we have seen, have not been comprehensively addressed in the present EPSA-IV provisions for gas developments. These doubts mean that demand in the domestic sector will exceed supply at some point in the near future, depending on the success rate of existing upstream and appraisal projects, while commitments for gas export projects might, in the long term, mean that Libya is powering Italian domestic demand, but not its own.

In the author's view, a dedicated body for gas developments and a separate fiscal regime for gas are urgently required for the nation to realise its true potential as a gas producer. This proposed new body should not and cannot operate in a vacuum. It must be part of a comprehensive long-term strategic Libyan National Energy Plan (LNEP), to look far ahead, perhaps as far as 50 years, in order to safeguard the country's hydrocarbon/power resources and ensure their key role in developing the nation.

This is the responsible way to ensure that the country is adequately prepared and capable of seizing every opportunity for maximum economic benefit from its hydrocarbon resources. Within the architecture of such a plan, decisions of national importance such as investing in new LNG plants, as for example has been recently proposed by ENI and ExxonMobil, can be made within the context of the LNEP. This framework will ensure that such decisions will not be guesswork, but will effectively be made by the LNEP's long-term energy requirements and criteria.

With such a plan in place, uncertainty over the country's energy future will no longer exist, and an attractive investment regime in both the oil and gas sectors, upstream, midstream and downstream, will ensure even and sustained energy development and planning. This will guarantee Libya's long-term position as a key global energy player.

APPENDIX 1: GAS in EPSA III and EPSA IV

1. EPSA III

3.1 Term of Agreement

Subject to the terms and conditions of this Agreement (including, without limitation, Articles 3.2 and 3.3 below), the term of this Agreement shall be twenty-five (25) Contract Years commencing on the Effective Date.

3.2 Prior Termination

At the end of the Exploration Period, only the Exploitation Areas shall be retained under this Agreement, and this Agreement shall terminate in respect of all other parts of the Contract Area; provided, however, that if a discovery has been made but there has not been sufficient time to conduct adequate appraisal thereof prior to the end of the Exploration Period, then the Exploration Period shall be extended for the Block in which such Discovery was made for a period of time, not to exceed two (2) Contract Years, sufficient to conduct such Appraisal.

3.3 Termination in Case of Discovery of Non-Associated Gas.

The termination of this Agreement referred to in Article 3.2 above shall not have effect in respect of any part of any Block in which a Discovery of Non associated Gas has occurred. In the event of such Discovery, the Parties may agree (but shall not under any circumstances be obligated to agree) to proceed together with the Appraisal and development of the Field in which such Discovery occurred. If for any reason whatsoever the Parties do not reach such agreement before the date

which is the later of:
    (a) The end of the Exploration Period or
    (b) two (2) years after the date of such Discovery;
Then this Agreement shall terminate on such later date with respect to the part of such Block in which such Discovery occurred."

In effect this means that if the parties cannot agree on the terms for the appraisal and development of the field in which the non-associated gas discovery was made, then the agreement would end in the time frame as stipulated in (a) and (b) above, whereas in the case of an oil discovery, even if made right at the end of the 5 year exploration period, a further period not exceeding 2 contract years would be granted. In other words, development of oil is given more flexibility than development of non-associated gas.

The only other reference to gas in EPSA-III is Article 13, headed "Associated Gas", which states, "At its option, First Party (i.e. LNOC) may take and freely utilize, for its sole benefit and at its sole cost, all Associated Gas which is not used in secondary recovery, pressure maintenance or other Petroleum Operations under this Agreement. If First Party elects not to take such Associated Gas, then such Associated Gas shall be injected for storage or otherwise utilized or disposed of as may be determined by the Management Committee in accordance with the Petroleum Law."

In the context of its time, and considering the urgent agenda faced by the Libyan government at the time its introduction, it may be unsurprising that in view of LNOC's traditional preoccupation with oil in its dealings with the IOCs, gas is given short shrift in EPSA-III. Nonetheless, Libyan domestic SOE's such as the El Brega LNG plant, as well as the major Libyan ammonia, methanol and urea plants in the El Brega Petrochemical Complex, all of which used natural gas as feedstock, had demonstrated, even in the early period of the Libyan hydrocarbon industry, the industrial versatility and efficiency of gas.

2. EPSA-IV

Fundamentally the terms of EPSA IV were similar to those of EPSA-III, but designed to be more attractive. In summary they provided for exploration, appraisal, development and production costs to be recovered very quickly from a proportion of output, for development costs to be equally shared between the investor and LNOC, and for profit production share to be split on a sliding scale. The new EPSA IV covered all sizes of discoveries, with small discoveries still able to secure an acceptable return to the Second Party (IOC), as well as giving it a fair return in the case of major or giant discoveries. Management committee rules were similar to EPSA III, with the only changes made as to their composition - four members, two each from LNOC and the Second Party. Additionally no income taxes, royalties, rents or fees are levied on the Second Party's share of production.

Unlike the previous EPSA-III, exploitation of gas, whether associated or non-associated, is covered fairly extensively in Article 13, "Natural Gas". Again, on account of the generally poor accessibility to the EPSA-IV model contract, the author quotes below Article 13 in full.

13.1 General

The provisions of this Agreement applicable to Crude Oil shall apply (mutatis mutandis) to Natural Gas unless otherwise specified herein.

13.2 Excess Associated Gas

13.2.1 If the Proposed Development plan submitted to the Management Committee provides for the commercialization of Excess Associated Gas, then upon approval of such Development Plan:
a. The parties (as sellers) shall endeavour to conclude with buyers a long-term gas sales agreement (s) incorporating the principles set forth in Article (13.4).
b. When such gas sales agreement (s) is concluded, Operator shall commence implementation of the Development plan and construct the necessary facilities, such as, but not limited to, the gathering, treating, compressing, transporting and processing facilities required for the production and delivery to the delivery point of Excess Associated Gas as specified in the Development Plan or as may be otherwise agreed to in the gas sales agreement (s).

13.2.2 If the Management Committee does not declare a Commercial Discovery for a Discovery of Crude Oil containing Excess Associated Gas due to lack of a as utilization scheme, then First party shall have the option to take the Excess Associated Gas, free of charge, at the delivery point which is immediately after the gas oil separation plant (s). If the Management Committee then declares a Commercial Discovery:
a. Operator shall operate the separation facilities which will permit the delivery as aforesaid.
b. Costs of such operation shall be considered Exploitation Operations Expenditures.
c. First Party shall be responsible for the gathering at the delivery point specified in this Article (13.2.2), compressing and transporting of said Excess Associated Gas and shall bear all costs related thereto.

Any receipt and disposition of such Excess Associated Gas by First Party shall be carried out in accordance with Good Oil field Practices in a manner which will not unreasonably interfere with the Petroleum Operations regarding the said Commercial Discovery.

If First Party does not exercise the aforesaid option, the Parties shall meet to discuss an appropriate alternative.

13.3 Non- associated Gas

13.3.1 In the event of a discovery of Non-associated Gas, Operator shall prepare and submit to the Management Committee an appraisal program for review and approval.

13.3.2 If the Management Committee decides not to proceed with Appraisal

Operations, then the Exploration Period shall be extended with respect to such Discovery for a period of five (5) Contract Years, provided that Second Party shall submit to the Management Committee a bi- yearly assessment for a gas exploitation scheme.

After such extension, this Agreement shall terminate with respect to such Discovery unless an appraisal program is approved by the Management Committee.

13.3.3   If the Management Committee decides to proceed with Appraisal Operations, Operator shall without delay implement the appraisal program as approved by the Management Committee and prepare and submit to the Management Committee the final appraisal report according to Article (9.2), taking into consideration Article (13.4) below.

   a.   The Management Committee shall review the proposed Development Plan according to Article (10.1) and decide whether the development and production of the Non-associated Gas is feasible.
   b.   If the Management Committee decides that development and production of the Non-associated Gas is not feasible or Second Party decides not to proceed with the development Plan, then this Agreement shall terminate with respect to such Discovery.
   c.   If the Management Committee decides that development and production of the Non-associated Gas is feasible, then it shall declare a Commercial Discovery and adopt a development Plan. The Parties shall then execute the gas sales agreement pursuant to Article (13.4) below. Operations under the adopted Development Plan until such time as a gas sales agreement (S) has been executed.

13.3.4   If Second Party approves a Development Plan for a Discovery of Non-associated Gas but First Party does not approve such Development plan, then this Agreement shall remain in force for the remaining term of this Agreement with respect to the Exploitation Area as identified in the proposed Development Plan.

13.4   Gas Sales Agreement

In case of a Discovery of Non-associated Gas and/or availability of Excess Associated Gas, the Parties shall negotiate a gas sales agreement with buyer(s).

The disposition of Natural Gas under a long-term gas sales agreement with buyer(s) of such Natural Gas shall, unless otherwise agreed by the Parties incorporate the following principles:

13.4.1   The Parties (as sellers) shall have the obligation to deliver the Natural Gas to the delivery point specified in the gas sales agreement, where the natural Gas shall be metered.

13.4.2   The commencement of Natural Gas deliveries and the date by which buyer's facilities will be ready to accept deliveries of Natural Gas shall be specified in the gas sales agreement.

13.4.3   Pricing provisions shall be no less favourable than those applicable to gas sales into the same market and originating from competing sources, including, without limitation:

    a.   Base price reflecting the value of competing fuels in the marketplace which shall be in line with the level prevailing in the region for similar sales, taking into account appropriate location differential.

    b.   An adjustment formula based on acceptable indicators of competing energy fuels in the market place and/or other appropriate indices such as inflation.

    c.   An acceptable combination of a floor price and a (Take-or-Pay) commitment from buyer so as to ensure the economic viability of the Development Plan. and

    d.   A price revision clause to provide for regular review of the pricing provisions to ensure that the resulting contractual price remains competitive in the marketplace.

13.4.4   If the Natural Gas is marketed pursuant to Article (13.5), the (Take-or-pay) provision shall at least be applicable until the ration for determining the (A- Factor) according to Article (12.1.2) (B) (ii) exceeds (1.25).

13.4.5   Payment for Natural Gas shall be made by the buyer (s) at intervals provided for in the relevant gas sales agreement and shall provide for bank or other appropriate guarantees of amounts owed to the Parties hereunder.

13.5   Natural Gas for Domestic Use

13.5.1   The Parties agree to give priority to supply the domestic market in GSPLAJ from all or part of the Natural Gas produced under this Agreement.

13.5.2   The Parties (as sellers) and First Party or another local buyer (local buyer) shall proceed in good faith to negotiate a gas sales agreement incorporating the principles set forth in Article (13.4) and the price shall be stipulated in accordance with Article (13.4.3) less fifteen percent (15%).

For the purpose of determining the values of fuel oils referred to in the gas sales agreement for local market, the following shall be used:

    a.   Low sulphur fuel oil (1% sulphur) shall be valued as cargo CIF MED, basis Genova- Lavera monthly average (Platt's) high/low quotations as published in Platt's Oil gram.

    b.   High sulphur fuel oil (3.5% sulphur) shall be valued as cargo CIF MED, basis Genova- Lavera monthly average (Platt's) high/low quotations as published in Platt's Oilgram and

c. Gas oil (0.2% sulphur) shall be valued as cargo CIF MED, basis Genova-Lavera monthly average (Platt's) high/low quotations as published in Platt's Oilgram.

If Platt's as defined in Articles (13.3.3) and (13.5) ceases to be published or substantially changes the basis for pricing the products referred to in such Articles, either Party may request changes of the pricing quotes referred to in such Articles.

Second Party's share of the Natural Gas sold under the agreement referred to in Article (13.5.2) shall be paid by the local buyer in U.S. Dollars or other freely convertible currency or in kind from crude (S) and/or Liquid Hydrocarbon by- Products.

13.6   Transportation and Processing Agreement

The Parties shall enter into Natural Gas transportation and processing agreement with the owners of pipelines and, if necessary, processing facilities. First Party shall warrant that the terms and conditions of such agreement, to the extent such facilities are owned or controlled by First Party, shall not be less favourable than those granted to other shippers or users of the processing facilities, if any, according to the Petroleum Law.

3. COMMENT: EPSA IV AND GAS DEVELOPMENTS

With regard to field development scenarios, both for associated and free gas, the author believes that the provisions outlined in 13.2. and 13.3 are fairly straightforward, with regard to appraisal, commercialization and timing of gas developments, all of which hinge on the decision of the Management Committee (MC) which supervises operations in the contract area, as per Article 4.1. of the EPSA IV model as follows:

"Appointment of Management Committee"
"Petroleum Operations in the Contract Area shall be conducted under the control and supervision of a management Committee composed of four (4) members, two (2), including the chairman, to be appointed by First Party, and two (2) to be appointed by Second Party. The Management Committee shall be formed not later than one (1) month after the Effective Date. Each Party shall notify the other of the members of the management Committee it appoints."

The sequence of events for both development of both associated and free gas is illustrated in the following two figures:

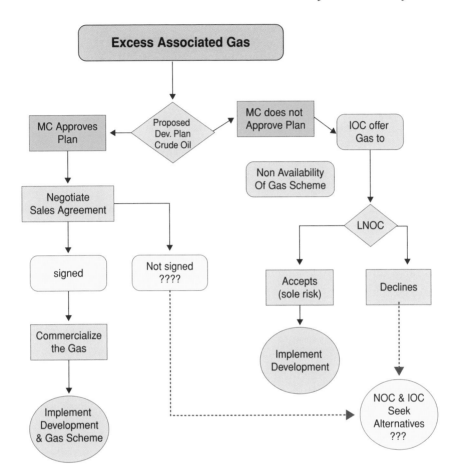

Figure A2.1: EPSA-IV: Development Scenario for Associated Gas

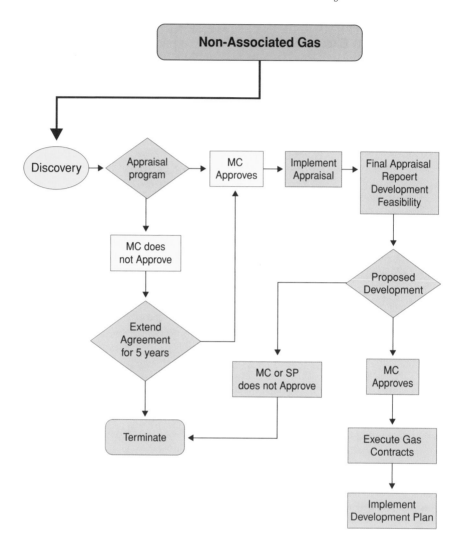

Figure A2.2: EPSA-IV: Development Scenario for Non-Associated or Free Gas

4. EPSA IV TERMS AND INVESTMENT RETURNS: THE A AND B FACTORS AND GAS

Under EPSA-IV the investment returns to the IOC are largely determined by three factors. The first is the Second Party Allocation, which is the percentage of production allocated to the IOC for cost recovery, offered in the bid document by the IOC in the competitive bidding for a given block (12.1.2). The second is the A factor which is defined as a negotiated figure set on the basis of the ratios of the cumulative value of the oil received by the investor from the production in such area over the cumulative petroleum expenditures incurred by the investor in respect of the area. The third is the B factor, which is a negotiated figure set at the indicated levels of average daily production from the area during the relevant calendar year and which, in the case of gas, is always 1, as defined in 2.1.2.b(i) below, regardless of production volume. Again, for reasons of clarity, and to understand the relevance of these factors to gas developments, it is worthwhile quoting in full the sections in the EPSA-IV model which cover these.

12.1   Allocation of Crude Oil and Liquid Hydrocarbon By-Products and Natural Gas

For any Calendar Year or part thereof, Crude Oil, Liquid Hydrocarbon by products and Natural Gas produced under this Agreement (Production) shall be allocated to the Parties as Follows:

12.1.1   First Party Allocation
100% of Production less Second Party allocation according to Article (12.1.2) below shall be allocated to First Party.

12.1.2   Second Party Allocation
a.   X% of Production shall be allocated to Second Party for Cost recovery until the cumulative value (determined in accordance with Article (12.3) of such allocation equals the cumulative Petroleum Operations Expenditures incurred by Second Party including its share of the Petroleum Operations Expenditures of such Calendar Year. Thereafter any excess of such allocation to Second Party, hereinafter referred to as (Excess Petroleum), shall be allocated as provided in Article (12.1.2 (b)).
b.   Second Party's allocations of Excess Petroleum shall be determined by applying the following formula:

(Base Factor) multiplied by (A Factor) multiplied by (Excess Petroleum) where:

i)   the Base Factor at the indicated levels of the average total daily production of Crude Oil and Liquid Hydrocarbon By-Product, in Barrels, for the relevant Calendar Year shall be:

Portion of average total daily production, (Barrels Per Day)	Base Factor
1- 20,000	B1
20,001- 30,000	B2
30,001- 60,000	B3
60,0010 85,000	B4
More than 85,000	B5

The Base Factor for Natural Gas shall always be equal to one (1)

ii) the A factor at the indicated ratios of the cumulative value (determined in accordance with Article (12.3) of Production received by Second Party over the cumulative Petroleum Operations Expenditures incurred by Second Party shall be:

Ratio	A Factor
Less than or equal to 1.5	A1
More than 1.5 but less than or equal to 3.0	A2
More than 3.0 but less than or equal to 4.0	A3
More than 4.0	A4

For purposes of this Article 12.1.2 (b) (ii), the ratio applied to each Calendar year shall be the ratio prevailing as of December 31 of the immediately preceding Calendar year.

c. Allocations made under (a) and (b) above shall be revised and adjusted each calendar Quarter during the current Calendar Year on the basis of the actual relevant data pertaining to the preceding Calendar Quarter.

Notes

1   IMF Country Report No. 08/301, 'The Socialist People's Libyan Arab Jamahiriya', 2008.
2   IMF Article IV Consultation Preliminary Conclusions of the IMF Mission, 2009.
3   OPEC *Annual Statistical Bulletin*, 2009.
4   LNOC; General Dept. for Exploration and Production, July 2009, Apprising Onshore Gas Discoveries located West of Libya region.
5   Hallett, D. *Petroleum Geology of Libya*, 2002; Otman, W.A. and Bunter, M.A., *The Libyan Petroleum Industry in the Twenty-first Century*, 2005.
6   LNOC; General Dept. for Exploration and Production. May 2009, Gas Production Report; also LNOC, Gas Projects Administration, Annual

Reports 1982, 1983, 1984 and 1985.
7 LNOC; General Dept. for Exploration and Production, May 2009, Gas Production Report.
8 Otman, W.A., November 2005, Legal and Economic Considerations of the Re-entry of US Oil Companies to their Assets in Libya, *Transnational Dispute Management* (TDM), Volume 2, issue No.05 -
9 Van Meurs, P., *World Fiscal Systems for Gas*, 1997.
10 Otman, W.A. and Bin-Dehaish, H., 'Unrealised Potential in the Saudi Gas Industry: Fiscal and Economic Considerations, 2006.
11 World Travel and Tourism Council, 'Libya Travel and Tourism', 2009.
12 Otman, W.A. and Bunter, M.A., Ibid, 2005.
13 Townsend, D. 'The Trillions Keep Coming', 2003.

CHAPTER 3

THE ROLE OF NATURAL GAS IN NORTH AFRICAN TRANSIT COUNTRIES

Waniss A. Otman and Hakim Darbouche

Introduction

The idea of transporting Algerian gas by subsea pipelines from the country's giant producing field Hassi R'Mel to southern European markets was first put forward in the 1960s. The concept had many attractions for the interested parties, but a number of challenges stood in its way from the outset. The proposed pipeline routes from Algeria to both Italy and Spain involved transit countries Tunisia and Morocco, as direct links to the southern European shores initially posed significant technical and investment challenges. The pipeline export option served obvious commercial and security considerations for Algeria's Sonatrach and its European customers, and also brought useful rewards for Tunisia and Morocco, which lack a generous hydrocarbon resource base and whose markets are too small to justify the construction of dedicated gaslines from Algeria.

Both the Trans-Mediterranean pipeline (Trans-Med) and Maghreb-Europe gasline (GME), as they became known,[1] were also credited with the potential to serve as catalysts for regional integration in the Maghreb, which had been a shared aspiration amongst peoples and elites in the region since the 1950s. However, the political task they were up against proved more difficult than anticipated. Indeed, besides the economic, commercial and technical challenges inherent in cross-border pipelines such as the Trans-Med and the GME systems, regional politics proved a determining factor in the conception and implementation of both projects. Political rivalry in particular between Morocco and Algeria, which led both countries into military confrontation in 1963 and 1976, was a structurally defining feature not only of the GME project, but also of broader regional cooperation ventures. Traditionally, the source of this bilateral animosity has been the conflict over the territory of Western Sahara – which has been illegally occupied by Morocco since 1975 and whose nationalist movement, the Polisario Front, has been supported by Algeria for the

94

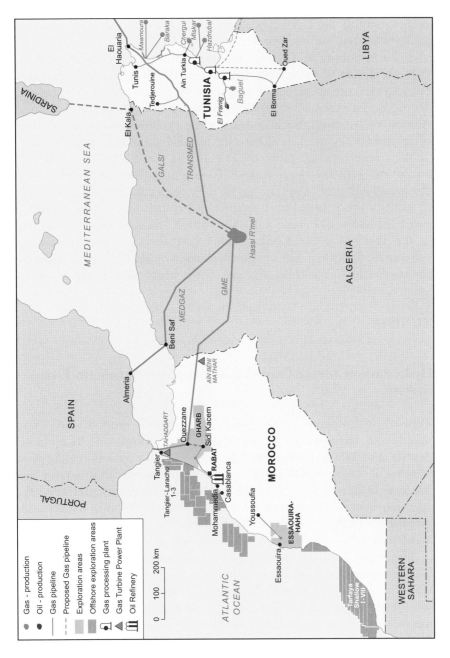

Map 3.1: North African Transit Countries: Gas Fields and Transport Infrastructure

achievement of the UN-advocated right to self-determination – as well as an unrelated border dispute.[2]

As such, politics and energy security concerns defined not only the implementation of subsea pipelines across the western Mediterranean, but also the corresponding development of gas markets in Tunisia and Morocco. This chapter examines the role of natural gas in the North African transit countries and assesses the evolution of its use in their respective energy markets against the parallel implementation processes of the transit pipeline projects. The aim of this study is to shed light on the different policy choices of Tunisia and Morocco in relation to the introduction of Algerian gas in their respective energy mixes, and to identify the political and security determinants of these dissimilar policy attitudes. The impact of these transit issues on the development of the Trans-Med and GME systems since their entry into operation will also be discussed. The chapter will begin by examining the Tunisian gas market followed by an analysis of the Moroccan energy scene.

TUNISIA

Hydrocarbon Sector Organisation and the Petroleum Fiscal System

Tunisia's hydrocarbon sector can be described as modest when compared with those of its prolific oil- and gas-producing neighbours Algeria and Libya. Dating back to 1894 with the first oil exploration licences, it was not until 1964 that the first commercial discovery was made in El Borma field in the deep south of the country, close to the Algerian border. Discovered by the *Société Italo-Tunisienne d'Exploitation pétrolière* (SITEP), a joint venture between the Tunisian Government and Italy's ENI, the field started production in 1965.

The main areas of hydrocarbon importance in Tunisia are the Mediterranean Gulf of Hammamet (Zinnia, Maamoura), the Gulf of Gabes (Hasdrubal, Chergui, Miskar, El Bibane, Ezzaouia, and Zarat), the Chotts region of Central Tunisia (El Franig, Baguel, Sabria) and the Paleozoic Ghadames Basin in the south (Oued Zar, ADAM, PDG, MLD, El Borma, Shurouq, Warda, BEK, Jenein Nord, Jenein Sud, and others).

As estimated by the country's state-owned oil company *Entreprise Tunisienne d'Activités pétrolières* (ETAP), Tunisia has proven oil reserves of 600 million barrels and recoverable gas reserves of 92 Bcm as at end of 2008.[3] In 2008, Tunisia produced around 89,000 b/d of crude oil, representing a 26 percent decline from the peak output of 120,000 b/d during the early 1980s.

Against the background of declining oil production, Tunisia's energy policy is now focused primarily on natural gas to meet its growing domestic energy requirements. The state-owned gas and electricity company, *Société Tunisienne de l'Electricité et du Gaz* (STEG) has promoted the use of natural gas through an incentive scheme that was introduced in 2005. According to STEG, natural gas represented a little over 45 percent of the total energy consumption in Tunisia in 2007, compared to just 14 percent in 2003.

Tunisia's drive for increased natural gas usage in its energy mix would appear, to some extent at least, to be optimistic. It is predicated on continuing supplies of natural gas from Algeria, through a royalty gas agreement for transport of Algerian gas across its territory through the Trans-Med gas pipeline, supplemented by contracted supplies of Algerian gas, and potential future supplies from Libya through the planned Mellitah-Gabes pipeline.

ETAP was set up in March 1972 by Law No. 72-22. Its remit was to manage oil and gas exploration and production activities for the Tunisian government. In August 1999, Tunisia reformed its hydrocarbon sector, issuing the Hydrocarbons Code under Law No. 99-93. This covered the entire E&P cycle and introduced new rates of royalty and taxation, which were reduced to encourage foreign participation in the sector.

Under Section 65 of the Hydrocarbon Code concerning the use of produced natural gas, 'the priority order for the natural gas utilisation' is as follows:

a) the Holder's own use on the extraction sites for the processing units and the production and/or reinjection operations in the Holder's fields;
b) the consumption needs of the local Tunisian market;
c) the export market, as is or after transformation into derivative substances.

Tunisia's energy deficit has effectively meant that all produced natural gas falls under priority (b) and must be sold domestically to STEG.

Recent changes to the Hydrocarbon Code (Amendment 2008-15) have enabled ETAP to spend risk capital for exploration, when this had hitherto been exclusively carried out by IOCs during the exploration phase. It is expected that this significant change in regulation will lead to increased exploration activity in future years and give ETAP more scope for the promotion of the hydrocarbon sector in Tunisia, with more investment in upstream activities as well as the development of marginal fields.

By end-2008, ETAP had awarded a total of 52 exploration licences to both international and domestic companies operating in the country, covering about 180,000 km^2.

Natural Gas Production

Tunisia has been a gas producer since 1966, producing associated gas from the El Borma oil field (see Map 3.1). However, production at El Borma has fallen sharply in recent years, amounting to 93.5 million cm only in 2008. Overall natural gas production increased significantly in 2008, rising to 2.97 Bcm, after dropping to 2.2 Bcm in 2007 from 2.3 Bcm in 2006 and 2.5 Bcm in 2005.[4]

The breakdown by field of domestic natural gas production can be seen in Table 3.1. ETAP-owned fields account for less than a third of total production, which is dominated by the Miskar field, which accounts for 69 percent of production, followed by the Adam field with 11 percent.

Table 3.1: Marketed Natural Gas Production in Tunisia by field, 2008

		Production in Bcm	*percent of total*
ETAP Fields			
1	Oued Zar/HMD	0.149274	5
2	Adam	0.328158	11
3	Djebel Grouz	0.032589	1
4	El Franig	0.187195	6.3
5	Baguel/Tarfa	0.045863	1.5
6	Sabria	0.020272	0.7
7	Ezzaouia	0.008316	0.3
8	Chergui	0.068601	2.3
Sub-total		0.840268	28
Other Fields			
1	Miskar	2.0320	69
2	El Borma	0.0935	3.2
3	Zinnia	0.0018	0.1
Sub-total		2.127323	72
Total		2.96759	100

Source: Arab Oil and Gas Directory, 2009

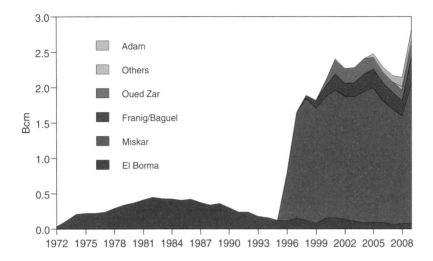

Figure 3.1: Tunisia's Natural Gas Production by Field, 1972–2008

Source: R. Mard (2009), 'Evolution de l'Exploration Pétrolière en Tunisie et Principales Découvertes'.

Figure 3.1 illustrates the historical production profile of the country since the early 70s.

The Miskar field is located on the offshore Amilcar concession in the Gulf of Gabes, and was discovered in 1975 by Elf. It was the largest field of non-associated gas in Tunisia, but was originally deemed non-commercial and as a result not developed because of the prohibitive costs of removing the high carbon dioxide/nitrogen content of the gas. It lies 225 feet below water about 125 km from Sfax and initially contained 47 Bcm of gas reserves.

Before the coming on stream of Miskar, Tunisia had no dry gas production and El Borma was virtually its only source of gas. A development agreement provided for British Gas Tunisia (BGT) to fully own and operate the Miskar field, whose commissioning in May 1995 dramatically changed Tunisia's energy balance. Gross natural gas production doubled in 1996 and has continued to increase since then, partly due to further increases in output from Miskar.

In 2005, output started to decline unexpectedly and BGT had to invest $500 million to restore production to the full capacity level. The development programme was originally designed to maintain a six-year peak rate of production of 2.48 Bcm/yr, yielding 4.5 million cm/d of sales gas after processing during the first five years of production, rising to 5.7 million cm/d in the second phase. BG Group net production in 2007 was 11.9 mboe from Miskar. Gas from the field is processed at the BGT Group-operated Hannibal plant, 21 kilometres south of Sfax, and sold into the Tunisian gas system. BGT Group has a sales contract with STEG for gas produced at Miskar, which gives it the right to supply up to 230 mmscfd on a long-term basis.[5]

By 2006, the development of Miskar had cost more than $800 million. Nationally, Miskar's share of Tunisian produced gas has been declining because of increasing production at the Oued Zar and the El Franig oil fields as well as the Baguel dry gas fields, which came on stream in 1998. Although in 1996 Miskar accounted for almost 90 percent of national output, between 2005 and 2008, its annual production averaged 1.8 Bcm, representing an average of about 73 percent of total production.

BGT is currently developing another important gas project, the Hasdrubal field, discovered in 1995 on the 2724 sq km offshore Amilcar concession, 25 km south of Miskar. BGT is the operator with a 50 percent interest together with ETAP. The field contains estimated recoverable gas reserves of 15 Bcm, and came on stream in the second quarter of 2009 with a production capacity of 1.022 Bcm/yr, 15,000 barrels per day of stabilised liquids (condensate and crude oil) and 400 tons/day of liquefied petroleum gas (LPG).

Tunisia's Trans-Med Transit Role

Historically good relations between Italy and Algeria as well as the troublesome experiences with the LNG industry of their respective national energy companies ENI and Sonatrach in the 1970s encouraged both sides to pursue the proposal of a 2500 km gas pipeline through Tunisia. The technical abilities of ENI's engineering and construction subsidiaries Snamprogetti and Saipem constituted additional assets for the project, as the underwater depths required for the Trans-Med pipeline necessitated pioneering technology at the time. Eager to diversify its gas supplies and satisfy its growing requirements, ENI was mobilised around the project and had the political and financial backing of the Italian government, which was necessary for the realisation of the Trans-Med gasline.[6]

Tunisia also stood to gain from the project, notably through the transit fees, and bore none of the costs involved. Its relative political stability and liberal economic outlook meant that, as a transit country, the risk it posed to pipeline gas flows from Algeria to Italy was deemed relatively limited, especially considering its friendly relations with both

countries. Nonetheless, from the outset, the Tunisian government opposed the participation of Algeria's Sonatrach in the transit section
of the Trans-Med for fear of giving the bigger neighbour additional
influence over national energy supplies.[7] As a result, Sonatrach and
ENI agreed to a contractual arrangement that provided for ownership
of the gas to be transferred to Italian offtakers at the Algerian border
with Tunisia. This configuration assuaged Tunisian concerns and paved
the way for the success of the first cross-border gas venture in the
Mediterranean.

In 1973, ENI signed an agreement with Tunisia for the construction
of the transit section of the pipeline, but by 1975 the project faced
its first major hurdle when the Tunisian government sought to wrest a
higher than initially envisaged transit fee rate of 10 percent from ENI
and, indirectly, Sonatrach. However, both companies rejected Tunisia's
demands and threatened to abandon the project, part of which had
already been under construction, and pursue the alternative LNG trade
option.[8] The move outmanoeuvred Tunisia, which was ultimately forced
to settle for around half of its initial royalty demand with an entitlement
of 5.25–6.5 percent of throughput in cash or in kind.

The settlement of the transit fee dispute permitted the signing in
1977 of a new agreement between ENI and the Tunisian government
for the construction and operation of the 370 km transit section of
the pipeline. The *Société pour la Construction du Gazoduc Trans-tunisien*
(SCOGAT) was set up for the construction of the transit pipeline.
SCOGAT was fully financed by the Trans-Tunisian Pipeline Company
Ltd (TTPC), which, in turn, was owned by ENI. After the construction phase, the ownership rights of the transit section were transferred
from TTPC to state-owned *Société tunisienne du Gazoduc Trans-tunisien*
(SOTUGAT), although TTPC has retained exclusive rights to transport
gas, including the right to conclude transportation contracts with third
parties.[9]

In the same year, ENI and Sonatrach concluded a separate contract
for the construction and management of the section of the pipeline
crossing the Sicily Channel. The agreement provided for the establishment for this purpose of the Trans-Mediterranean Pipeline Company
Ltd (TMPC), a 50/50 joint subsidiary of Sonatrach and ENI. Both
companies also signed their first sale and purchase agreement, which
priced the gas at 76.9 percent of the CIF price of Algerian LNG
supplies to France, indexed against a basket of fuel oil and gas oil.
However, the second oil shock and the coming into office of a new
management team at Sonatrach that was determined to review the price
of gas in its existing export contracts to achieve FOB parity with crude

oil, not only torpedoed this initial contractual price arrangement, but also delayed by two years the start-up of Trans-Med shipments until 1983. After arduous negotiations,[10] a new agreement set the final border price, which was to be indexed against a basket of crudes rather than products and crude, midway between Sonatrach's $5/MMBtu and ENI's $3.80/MMBtu at $4.41/MMBtu.

The Trans-Med pipeline is estimated to have cost $2.5 billion.[11] Given the financial commitment that ENI made to the project, either through direct equity or by guaranteeing the financing of the Algerian section of the pipeline, the Italian government threw its weight behind the company, notably by providing a 'political' subsidy of $0.40/MMBtu for the new price, allowing the commissioning of the line in June 1983. Since then, Trans-Med supplies of Algerian gas to Italy have flowed almost uninterruptedly,[12] encouraging the gradual expansion of the system's capacity up to about 33 Bcm/yr by early 2010.

Gas Supply and Domestic Consumption

The entire gas production of Tunisia is consumed domestically. Since the output of El Borma was not sufficient to meet demand from the early 1970s to mid 1990s, Tunisia was forced to satisfy its remaining gas needs with imports from Algeria via the Trans-Med gasline. Tunisia receives significant royalty gas in kind in lieu of transit fees from Algeria. Apart from royalty gas, Tunisia is also a major importer of gas from the same country. Figures 3.2 and 3.3 illustrate the contribution that royalty plus imported Algerian gas make towards the country's energy requirements.

A detailed analysis of Figure 3.2 reveals the dynamics of Tunisian domestic gas requirements vis-à-vis Algerian gas. In 1988, Tunisia produced 393 million cm, received 517 million cm Algerian fiscal gas (i.e. royalties from the Trans-Med pipeline) and purchased 548 million cm market gas, a total consumption of 1.46 Bcm.

By 1996, with the coming on stream of Miskar, the figures for domestically produced, fiscal gas and market gas respectively, rose to 838,962, and 1.039 Bcm, totalling 2.839 Bcm. By 2000 rising production from Miskar and increased fiscal gas, due to the increased capacity of the gasline, broke down to 1.966, 1.286 and .463 Bcm respectively, totalling 3.715 Bcm to meet domestic demand.

By 2005 these figures were 2.524, 1.295, and .567 Bcm respectively, a total consumption of 4.386 Bcm, again due largely to increases from Miskar and fiscal gas. For 2008, the decline in domestic production as

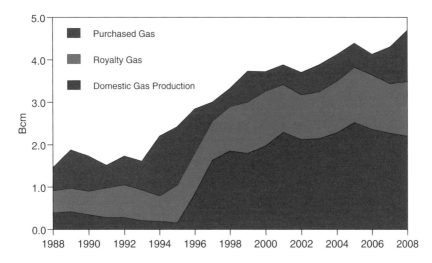

Figure 3.2: Tunisian Gas Supply, 1988–2008

Source: F. Bergaoui, 2009, 'Tunisia: Evolution de l'Offre et de la Demande du
　　　Gaz Naturel en Tunisie'.

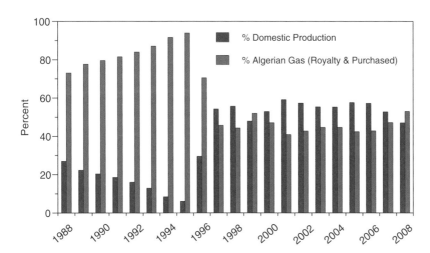

Figure 3.3: Share of Algerian Gas in Tunisia's Domestic Consumption,
　　　1988–2008

Source: F. Bergaoui, 2009, Ibid.

well as increasing domestic demand reveals figures of 2.202, 1.275 and 1.206 Bcm, in total 4.683 Bcm.

Significantly, Tunisia's direct imports of non-fiscal Algerian gas over the 2005–2008 period had increased from .564 to 1.206 Bcm, or 114 percent. Although the impact of the new Hasdrubal field production will be felt in 2009, adding a projected .607 Bcm/yr, it is clear that domestic production is hardly keeping up with rising domestic demand.

Similarly, it can also be noted that between 1988 and 1997, domestic consumption increased by 107 percent, from 1.46 to 3 Bcm, while in the ten-year period from 1998 to 2007 it rose from 3.3 to 4.3 Bcm, an increase of only 30 percent, and by 2008 it had risen by 9 percent to reach 4.7 Bcm.

Figure 3.3 shows that in 1988 Algerian gas provided over 70 percent of Tunisia's gas needs. By 1995 this dependence had increased to over 90 percent, although in 1996, when Miskar came on stream, it reverted to around 70 percent. From 1998–2008, as the effect of Miskar's increased production came into play, the percentage of Algerian gas varied between 44 percent and 52 percent. Despite the added contributions from the new Hasdrubal field in 2009, this high level of dependence on foreign gas to power the Tunisian economy is a key issue, the ramifications of which will be addressed below.

Gas Marketing

Tunisia is increasingly turning to natural gas to meet its growing domestic energy requirements. STEG and Independent Power Producers (IPPs) together accounted for around 74 percent of Tunisia's gas consumption in 2008.[13] From 2005, STEG has been promoting the use of natural gas for residential and commercial applications through an incentive policy, which provides loans and easy payment terms to finance installations. The Tunisian government has also encouraged the use of gas in all power generation projects. Most existing plants have been converted to gas, with only 5 percent remaining oil-fired plants relying on heavy fuel and diesel. Both STEG and IPPs, such as the Carthage Power Company (CPC), will only use gas for their future power projects.

The resulting growth in the use of gas is shown in Figure 3.4. According to STEG, natural gas represented 42 percent of the total primary energy consumption in Tunisia in 2008, compared to just 14 percent in 1988.

The country's total power generation capacity as at early 2009 was approximately 3320 MW/day and STEG plans to increase that to

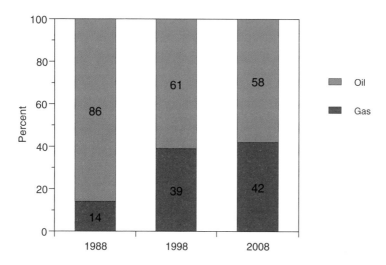

Figure 3.4: Share of Gas in Tunisia's Primary Energy Consumption, 1988–2008

Source: F. Bergaoui, 2009, Ibid.

between 3750 and 4000 MW/day by 2010, and then to 4500–5000 MW/day by 2015. Thermal power stations account for around 97 percent of total capacity, with the rest provided by hydroelectric plants. The largest new power station is the 400 MW CCGT one at Ghannoush, in the Gabes region, which became operational in 2009.

Over the years, Tunisia has imported small amounts of electricity from Algeria, when existing plants proved insufficient to cover peak demand. This has been made possible by the interconnection of the national power grid within the North African network with the Algerian and Libyan grids. The North African network is in turn connected to the European Union grid via a trans-Mediterranean link to Spain.

Natural Gas and the Role of IPPs in Electricity Generation

With the relatively high cost of converting existing power plants to gas and the growing need for new power generation capacity to keep up with economic development and demographic trends, government policy in Tunisia changed in 1996, ending STEG's state monopoly in the power generation sector. Under Article 66.3 (b) of the Hydrocarbons Code, the holder of an Exploitation Concession is authorised to valorise the gas produced from a given hydrocarbon field to produce electricity and sell it exclusively to a power distribution operator (e.g. an IPP) designated by the Granting Authority.

This provision was aimed primarily at developing gas discoveries and remote, marginal gas fields, which could then be used to generate electricity to overcome future power generation shortages. Under this scenario, STEG negotiates both power and gas purchase prices with ETAP, the concession holder, and the IPP investors. On the basis of an agreed price, the IPP operator can construct an IPP in line with STEG's plans for expansion of the power sector. In 2007, IPPs consumed around 14 percent of gas production in Tunisia.

The first IPP, operated by CPC and commissioned in 2003, was the 470 MW Radès combined-cycle power station. The project was financed by an international group under a 20-year BOOT (build-own-operate-transfer) contract signed in 1998 between the Tunisian government and overseas investors, including the Public Sector Enterprise Group (PSEG) of the United States (60 percent) and Japan's Marubeni Corporation (40 percent), with the consortium selling the output to STEG.

The second was on a more moderate scale, a 27 MW facility located at Zarzis, close to El Bibane, constructed by a 50/50 joint venture between Centurion Energy International (later Candax Energy) in 2005 and the US companies Caterpillar and CME (with 25 percent of the project each). The project aimed to use as feedstock flared associated gas from the Ezzaouia and El Bibane oil fields.

The Tunisian government through STEG in 2009 issued tenders inviting international investors to participate in constructing an additional CCGT power station as an IPP under the terms of a 20-year BOO (build-own-operate) agreement. This called for the investor to design, build, operate and maintain the plant, as well as arrange funding. This plant will be located in the city of Bizerte with a capacity of 350–500 MW and is scheduled for completion in 2014. A second plant under the same arrangement will be constructed in the city of Sousse, with a capacity of 380–450 MW single-shaft turbine, and is expected to start production in 2013.

Increased National Gas Coverage

In line with government policy, STEG intends to expand the gas distribution network to increase its country-wide coverage to consumers. Figure 3.5 illustrates the evolution of gas consumption by sector.

As the Tunisian government's ambitious policy for increased domestic gas usage rolls out, Figure 3.6 highlights the projected growth of gas usage by sector from 2007–2030.

In view of Tunisia's existing gas reserves and gas production profile, however, it is questionable whether its enunciated policy objectives on

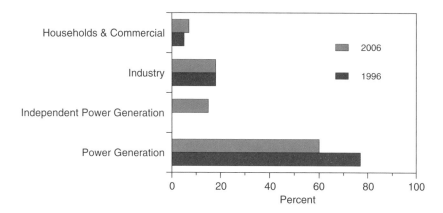

Figure 3.5: Evolution of Tunisia's Gas Consumption by Sector, 1996–2006
Source: STEG (2007), Natural Gas Statistics

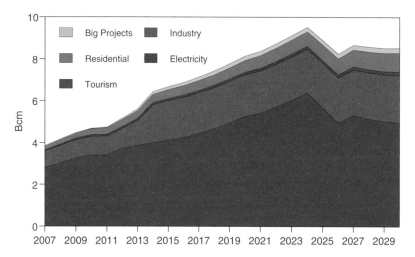

Figure 3.6: Projected Growth of Gas Development in Tunisia by Sector, 2007–2030

Source: F. Bergaoui (2009), 'Evolution de l'Offre et de la Demande du Gaz Naturel en Tunisie'

future gas usage are realistic. They are certainly not sustainable, given that the gas reserve-to-production ratio in Tunisia is almost thirty years and the data presented in Figure 3.6 show that domestic consumption, strongly supported by Algerian fiscal/contracted gas, is projected to more than double over the period 2007–2030.

In the following section the ramifications of the current gas policy and some key current/future issues of the Tunisian gas sector are analysed.

Future Issues in the Tunisian Gas Sector

The Changing Dynamics of Regional Cooperation

Because of a global rise in natural gas usage, producing countries with a deficit such as Tunisia have to deal with their finite resources and plan for long-term outside supplies. Alternatively, of course, they may plan to radically alter their energy mix by investing in, say, nuclear power or legislating for a gradual increase in the share of renewable sources of energy, such as wind or solar, in power generation.

As has been noted earlier, the amount of gas received from Algeria, whether as fiscal or purchase gas, depends largely on the supply situation in Algeria. An additional plan for the importation of gas from Libya, the Joint Gas Company (JGC), appears to be supportive of the Tunisian market, at the same time lessening Tunisia's dependence on Algerian gas.

The proposed Mellitah–Gabes project, a 50/50 Libyan–Tunisian JV consisting of a 265 km/24 inch pipeline, is planned to supply 1 Bcm/yr of natural gas from Mellitah in the western part of Libya to Gabes on the Tunisian coast. Planning started in 2003, and the estimated cost is approximately $300 million at current market prices.

Fiscal Policy and Foreign Investors

Undoubtedly, the Hydrocarbon Code of 2000 has been a major part of the Tunisian government's strategy to attract investment in its hydrocarbon sector, and in it there are definite incentives for gas production, as described in Chapter 3 of the Hydrocarbon Code, 'Special provisions for gaseous hydrocarbons'.

ETAP as an International Player

Another effective strategy to address the domestic gas deficit would be for ETAP to become much more active in bidding for overseas acreage, taking advantage of Tunisia's good relations with other African countries such as Chad, Sudan, Libya, Algeria, Mali, Mauritania, Niger, Egypt, and the Gulf of Guinea.

While its immediate neighbours Algeria and Libya have, since 2000, held seven and four bidding rounds respectively, ETAP has been conspicuously absent from the lists of bidders. Change might be on the horizon though – since 2006 ETAP has been legally enabled to participate in international projects, and an overseas arm, ETAP International, has been established and appears to be initially focusing on upstream acreage in Mauritania. Additionally a joint venture, Numhyd, owned 50 percent by ETAP and 50 percent by Algeria's Sonatrach, acquired acreage in Algeria and Tunisia in April 2008.

ETAP also has a 50 percent share in Joint Oil, a company established on 8 August 1988 between Libya and Tunisia, equally owned with Libya Oil Holdings Ltd. Immediately after its establishment, Joint Oil was granted the '7th of November' Block, a 3000 km^2 transboundary E&P unit located offshore in the Libyan Tunisian Continental Shelf. Seismic surveys and geological studies on this Block and surrounding areas, as well as recent exploratory operations, have led to the identification and mapping of several geological structures, indicating a number of significant leads and prospects.

Gas Pricing Issues

Monetisation of Gas. The transfer price of commercial gas produced in Tunisia and delivered to the main transport network (STEG) is regulated by the National Hydrocarbon Code of Tunisia and fixed by decree (Hydrocarbon Code 73.1) for gas delivered at the entry point to the main gas transportation network operated by STEG. The price is indexed to 80 percent of the previous nine-month average price of low sulphur heating fuel delivered to the nearest Tunisian port within the Mediterranean region (Miskar Gas) and 85 percent of high sulphur heating fuel delivered on the same basis.

As stipulated in Section 65 of the Hydrocarbon Code, gas producers must initially satisfy the Tunisian domestic gas demand, and monetisation at the above discounted prices can be seen as major impediments to investment in Tunisia's upstream gas sector.

Subsidised Domestic Gas Prices. As detailed above, the cost of gas to Tunisian consumers is effectively subsidised by the government. Thus, the domestic price of gas in Tunisia is substantially below its international value, resulting in a significant burden in subsidies to the government. This is undoubtedly constraining FDI in the upstream and downstream gas sectors. The implication is that the Tunisian government should perhaps reconsider the impact of domestic gas subsidies on FDI, as well as on achieving long-term and sustainable macroeconomic fiscal balance.[14]

Figure 3.7 illustrates the gap between cost of gas to the government (STEG) and sales price in the domestic market, and demonstrates how heavily subsidised gas has been in the Tunisian domestic market since the year 2000.

Prior to the year 2000, gas was being sold by STEG to Tunisian consumers at above its cost, and these prices were close to equilibrium from 2001–2002. But from 2003 onwards, the government began to heavily subsidise gas for the domestic market. In 2005 this subsidy for gas amounted to TD100/toe, in 2006 the gap widened to almost TD200/toe and by 2008 it had increased dramatically to TD300/toe (i.e. approx US$ 227).

In a regional context, Tunisia can be said to be fortunate since its neighbours Algeria and Libya are major gas producers. Therefore, it seems that long-term supply to Tunisia can be achieved from these sources.

Still, faced with dwindling gas reserves, increasing hydrocarbon imports and the issue of domestic subsidies, the long-term aim of the Tunisian government in achieving energy security, and switching electricity generation to gas, can be said to be challenging.

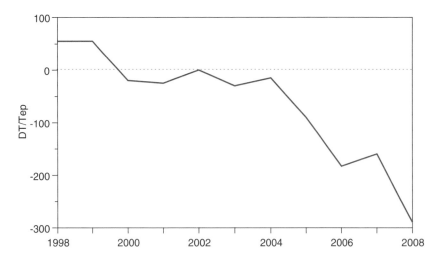

Figure 3.7: Gap Between Domestic Sales Price and Cost of Gas, expressed in Tunisian Dinar (DT) per Tonne Oil Equivalent (toe), 1998–2008

Source: F. Bergaoui, 2009, Ibid.

Note: 1Tep (Tonne équivalent pétrole) = 1 toe

MOROCCO

By regional standards, Morocco ranks on the lower end of the MENA gas reserves scale. In fact, the country holds limited reserves of fossil fuels in general, which has meant that imports of oil, natural gas and coal (as well as electricity[15]) account for over 97 percent of Morocco's primary energy needs. This overwhelming dependence on outside energy supplies has had a particularly burdensome effect on the Moroccan economy, which saw the country's energy import bill increase by 350 percent between 2003 and 2008,[16] driven by the upsurge in international energy prices over this period.

However, this structural dependence has not inhibited the growth of primary energy consumption in the kingdom, which more than tripled from 4.7 mtoe in 1980 to 14.7 mtoe in 2008 (Figure 3.8). In recent years, the pace of this growth accelerated on the back of higher demand for electricity, which increased at an average annual rate of 8 percent between 2003 and 2008. Despite these growing requirements, the rates in 2008 of Morocco's primary energy consumption per capita and per unit of GDP remained noticeably low at 0.46 toe and 0.17 toe/$1000 of GDP, respectively, relative to its Maghrebi neighbours Algeria (1 toe/capita; 0.24 toe/$1000 of GDP) and Tunisia (0.9 toe/capita; 0.23 toe/$1000 of GDP). As growth in energy consumption is expected to

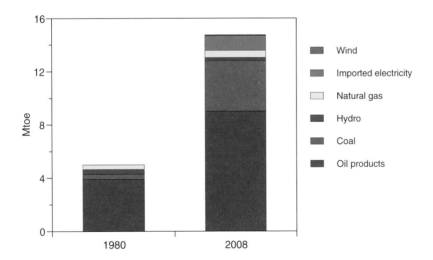

Figure 3.8: Evolution of Morocco's Primary Energy Consumption

Source: Moroccan Ministry of Energy and Mines, 2009, Energie et Mines: Des Chantiers en Marche

continue unabated to 2020, driven largely by sustained demographic expansion and economic development, the Moroccan government has devised a new energy sector strategy aimed at improving security of supply, promoting energy efficiency, and reducing dependence on imported petroleum products by pursuing greater diversification of the primary energy mix.

Alongside coal, natural gas is expected to play a more prominent role in Morocco's future energy balance and energy security policy. Until 2005, gas accounted for a negligible 0.3 percent of the country's primary energy consumption. The conspicuous absence of a gas market in Morocco had been the product not only of a poor resource base, but also of an instinctive political aversion to gas imports from neighbouring Algeria, either in the form of in-kind transit fees for the GME gas flows or contracted supplies. However, the expansion in 2005 of the capacity of the GME system from 8 to 11.5 Bcm/yr offered Morocco the opportunity to use its increased transit allowance and introduce natural gas in its energy mix, notably to fuel the country's first gas-fired power plants and satisfy more efficiently its growing energy requirements. Since then, Moroccan energy policy pronouncements have regularly referred to gas as a possible solution to the country's energy challenges, although it appears that political considerations continue to preclude the optimisation of this potential for the Moroccan economy.

Exploration Policies and Upstream Activities

Hydrocarbon exploration in Morocco dates back to the early 1900s with the first oil discovery in the Gharb basin, northeast of the capital Rabat, in 1923. The *Société Chérifienne des Pétroles* (SCP), set up in 1929 and tasked with an upstream mission, made further oil discoveries in the 1930s and 1940s but it was not until 1957 that the company made its first gas discovery in the Essaouira basin in the southwest of the country (see Map 3.1).

Since then, successive Moroccan governments have promulgated a string of hydrocarbon laws in the aim of stimulating exploration activity and accumulating more significant reserves. With each round of disappointing upstream results, the investment terms were liberalised further in order to attract still more foreign interest. The first legal framework, enacted in 1958, provided for foreign participation in the upstream on the basis of a 50/50 profit share with the state. By the late 1970s, up to 42 foreign operators were actively exploring in Morocco, but most of them ended up relinquishing their licences for lack of positive results.

In 1981, the government established the *Office national de Recherches et d'Exploitations pétrolières* (ONAREP) to oversee all upstream activities and to stimulate exploration activity. In the same year, ONAREP discovered Morocco's largest gas field, Meskala,[17] in the Essaouira basin, but by 1993 all 23 licences it had awarded to foreign companies were abandoned. In 1992, a new, more attractive hydrocarbon law was passed, but a number of onshore and offshore exploration licences awarded under the new framework yielded modest results only.

In March 2000, yet more incentives were introduced to the 1992 Law with a view to encouraging foreign investors to make longer-term commitments in Morocco. Under the resulting – and current – 'hydrocarbon code', there has been a manifest increase of exploration activity, particularly in offshore acreage, but disappointing results continue to militate against sustained foreign investor interest. The creation in 2003 of the *Office national des Hydrocarbures et des Mines* (ONHYM), merging ONAREP with its mining sector equivalent, led to a continuing interest of sorts in offshore basins, but a number of high-profile licence relinquishments in 2005 and 2006, notably by ENI, Shell, Wintershall and Tullow,[18] seemed to confirm that Morocco's upstream predicament is a quintessentially 'below-ground' problem.

Morocco's eagerness to redress its energy balance has led it to seek tapping into the hydrocarbon potential of offshore provinces on the Atlantic coast, reviving longstanding territorial disputes with neighbouring Western Sahara and Spain. The licensing in 2001 of offshore Western Sahara acreage to Total and Kerr-McGee was disapproved by the exiled Sahrawi government and the international community, and yielded nothing but renewed regional political tension, as both these and other companies eventually withdrew under mounting international pressure.[19] Exploration work in the Tarfaya offshore blocks between the Canary Islands and the Moroccan mainland also prompted mutually exchanged claims of territorial intrusion between Spain and Morocco (see Map 3.1). However, despite the existence of other disputes between the two countries in relation to Mediterranean offshore exploration zones, the issue has been less controversial than in the case of Western Sahara because of the nature of the ongoing conflict between the kingdom and the Sahrawi independence movement.

Gas Reserves and Production. Estimates of proven natural gas reserves in Morocco range between 1.48 and 1.54 Bcm.[20] However, Wood Mackenzie, a consultancy, estimates the remaining recoverable gas reserves in Morocco, as at 1 January 2010, at approximately 4.9 Bcm. Its assessment includes the reserves discovered in March 2009 by a

Repsol YPF-led consortium in the offshore Tangier-Larache blocks, and more specifically in the Anchois field, which is thought to hold about 2.8 Bcm of gas.[21] The commercial viability of this recent discovery remains uncertain, especially that neither ONHYM nor the Moroccan government have confirmed this – although officials in Morocco have been wary of hydrocarbon discovery announcements since what has been dubbed the 'Talsint debacle' in 2000.[22] Smaller reserve discoveries were also announced in 2009 by Irish independent Circle Oil, which operates mainly in the Gharb basin.

So far, natural gas production in Morocco has been concentrated in the Gharb and Essaouira basins (see Map 3.1). According to ON-HYM, overall production in 2009 stood at around 40 million cm, down from about 60 million cm in 2007 and 50 million cm in 2008. Over 60 percent of this output originated in the ONHYM-operated field of Meskala in the Essaouira basin,[23] while the remainder was produced in association with Cabre Maroc, a subsidiary of Caithness Petroleum, and Circle Oil in the Gharb basin (Figure 3.9). Circle Oil accounted for 63 percent of the 2009 gas production in the Gharb basin. Most of this gas is dry, whereas the gas produced from Meskala is wet. Unless more important reserves are discovered in Morocco, the outlook for gas production – even by extant standards – will remain bleak (Figure 3.10).

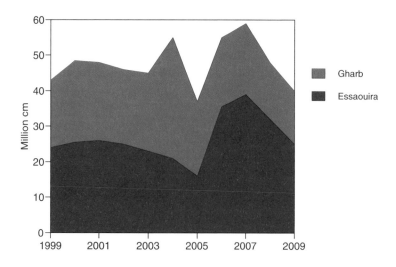

Figure 3.9: Natural Gas Production in Morocco, 1999–2009

Source: ONHYM website

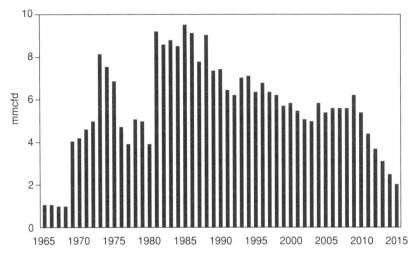

Figure 3.10: Natural Gas Production in Morocco, 1965–2013

Source: Wood Mackenzie, 2009, *Morocco Country Overview*

Natural Gas Consumption: Growing Requirements and Supply Dilemmas

The small volumes of gas produced in the Gharb and Essaouira basins are consumed by local industries, notably the refinery of Sidi Kacem and the *Compagnie Marocaine des Cartons et Papiers* (CMCP) in Kenitra for Gharb supplies, and the *Office Chérifien des Phosphates* (OCP) in Youssoufia for gas produced in Essaouira. Until 2005, gas consumption in Morocco was limited to these industrial end-users. However, the commissioning that year of the country's first CCGT power plant at Tahaddart, which has a nameplate capacity of 384 MW, resulted in the effective introduction of natural gas in Morocco's energy mix, with gas consumption jumping from 68 million cm in 2004 to 539 million cm in 2005.[24] As a result, from 0.3 percent in 2004, the share of gas in Morocco's primary energy consumption increased to 3.7 percent in 2008, accounting for 7.5 percent of the total installed power generation capacity (5352 MW).

Power generation has been the main driver of primary energy consumption in Morocco. As the government seeks to diversify its sources of energy, future demand for natural gas will be driven almost entirely by the power sector. According to the current government's energy strategy, anticipated growth in the use of gas for power generation alone would lead to an increase to 4.9 percent in 2012 and 14.1 percent in

2020 of the fuel's share in primary energy consumption (Figure 3.11). The coming online in May 2010 of another CCGT power plant in Aïn Beni Mathar, with a hybrid capacity of 472 MW (of which 20 MW is solar-powered), has led to an immediate increase in annual gas demand by around 350 million cm. Additionally, the planned conversion to gas of up to 900 MW of existing oil-fuelled power generation capacity in areas like Kenitra, Mohammedia and Tangier will reinforce the penetration of gas in the Moroccan energy market. Industry can also have an increasingly tangible effect on gas consumption in Morocco, as existing plants in the Kenitra-Mohammedia-Casablanca region as well as new projects, such as the Renault-Nissan car-assembling plant in Tangier, switch to and adopt gas as feedstock. Accordingly, from around 0.8 Bcm in 2009, gas consumption in Morocco would increase to 5 Bcm/yr by 2020.[25]

The gas requirements of the Tahaddart and Aïn Beni Mathar power plants have been supplied by in-kind transit fees to Morocco for the GME pipeline shipments from Algeria to Spain. Both these and other gas-fired projects were planned by Morocco in the 1990s, in anticipation of the coming online of the GME pipeline in 1996 and the potential spur this would give to the emergence of a gas market in the country.[26] However, it was not until 2002 that Moroccan decision-makers gave the nod to a final investment decision for the Tahaddart project, having

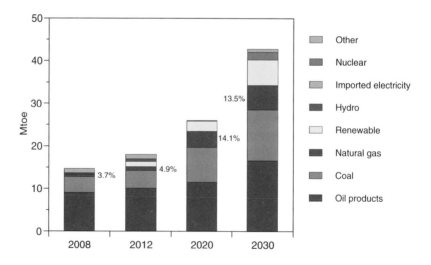

Figure 3.11: Projected Share of Natural Gas in Morocco's Primary Energy Consumption

Source: Moroccan Ministry of Energy and Mines, 2009, Des Chantiers en Marche

apparently come to terms with economic imperatives and overcome their political concerns vis-à-vis Algeria. Morocco's entitlement to GME supplies in the form of transit fees amounts typically to 7 percent of the gas actually transported through the pipeline.[27] As can be seen from Table 3.2, before 2005 the fees were paid in cash by the operators of the Moroccan section of the pipeline, Spain's Enagas and Portugal's Transgas, but since the expansion of the GME's capacity that year payment has been made in both cash and kind.

Table 3.2: GME Transit Data, 1999–2008

	Transported volumes (million cm)	In kind (million cm)	Transit fees In cash (million US$)	Average price ($/MMBtu)
1999	8,278	-	32	1.3
2000	7,801	-	61	2.7
2001	7,346	-	64	3.0
2002	8,578	-	60	2.4
2003	8,539	-	76	3.1
2004	9,682	-	94	3.3
2005	12,330	348	99	4.5
2006	10,900	423	81	5.5
2007	10,540	480	64	5.7
2008	11,480	477	126	8.6

Source: Moroccan Ministry of Energy and Mines, 2008, *Secteur de l'Energie et des Mines, principales Réalisations (1999–2008)*.

While current transit arrangements have permitted the construction of the country's first CCGT power plants, they will not be sufficient for future gas requirements. These can only be satisfied by additional supplies, which have to be contracted either from Algeria through the GME or from other sources. To this end, a regulatory gas framework (*Code Gazier*), aimed at providing for the development of a gas market in Morocco, has had a long gestation period but is still awaiting ratification. So far, it appears that Moroccan decision-makers have ruled out lifting additional gas volumes from the GME beyond their transit fee entitlement, especially because political relations between Morocco and Algeria have seen little or no improvement in recent years. Instead, they are considering commissioning a 3.7 mtpa regasification terminal, at an estimated cost of over $1 billion, to start importing LNG supplies from around 2014.[28] However, the project has faced a number of challenges not only owing to the lack of commercial viability,[29] but also as a result of disagreement within Morocco about the funding and eventual location of the LNG terminal.[30]

Morocco's GME Transit Role

The idea of laying a pipeline to supply the Iberian peninsula, France and possibly other countries in north western Europe with natural gas from Algeria dates back to the 1960s. However, a number of technical, commercial and political obstacles stood in its way.[31] It was not until the end of the 1980s that the main interested parties were able to overcome the most persistent of these stumbling blocks and move the project forward.

Politically, a return to a semblance of normality between Morocco and Algeria, following the resumption of diplomatic ties in 1988, paved the way for the less technically challenging possibility of routing the pipeline through Morocco and the Strait of Gibraltar. After 12 years of strained bilateral relations, this rapprochement became possible following the start of peace talks between Morocco and the Polisario Front of Western Sahara, which, with the backing of Algeria, had fought the occupation of the territory by the Moroccan army after the hasty withdrawal of Spain in 1975. These developments also allowed Morocco and Algeria to address their border dispute, which had plagued their relations since the early 1960s.

Political developments at the European level also contributed to the concretisation of the GME pipeline. The integration in 1986 of Spain and Portugal into the European Community not only helped dissipate the latter's political sensitivities with regard to becoming dependent on gas transiting through Spain, but it also inaugurated a new era for the EU's policies towards southern Mediterranean countries that has been characterised by increased European political and financial commitment to Euro-Mediterranean regional integration.

More fundamentally, the commercial viability of pipeline gas imports into the Spanish and, to a lesser extent, Portuguese markets improved markedly from the mid-1980s onwards, following the introduction of a string of policy shifts that encouraged the expansion of these markets. The success and stability of the Trans-Med pipeline from Algeria to Italy had convinced Spanish policy-makers that pipeline gas could supplement more problematic LNG supplies, helping expand the share of gas in the energy balance and reduce dependence on oil imports. As a result, the government persuaded the Spanish power industry to convert to natural gas more than 7000 MW of existing power generation capacity, leading to an increase in gas consumption from around 6 Bcm/yr in the early 1990s to 15 Bcm/yr by the end of that decade. Furthermore, in the case of both Spain and Portugal, funds from the European Commission helped the construction of gas transmission and distribution networks, which were crucial for the development and expansion of the gas markets in the two countries.

The official announcement of the 8 Bcm/yr,[32] 1620km pipeline project came after an intergovernmental agreement between Algeria, Morocco and Spain had been reached in April 1991. From the outset, it was decided that a contractual arrangement similar to that of the Trans-Med system, whereby ownership of the gas is transferred to the buyer(s) at the Algerian border, would be pursued. In the case of the GME, this was all the more pertinent given the political sensitivities involved. In 1992, Sonatrach concluded a long-term gas supply contract with Spain's Enagas, providing for plateau-level sales of 6 Bcm/yr, and in 1994 with Portugal's Transgas, stipulating a plateau level of supplies of 2.5 Bcm/yr. Both contracts run until 2020, contain take-or-pay, price review and international arbitration provisions. Deliveries of gas to Spain began in November 1996 and to Portugal in April 1997.

The cost of the GME pipeline was $2.2 billion. The pattern of financing was predicated on the project's ownership structure in that each section owner financed 15 percent of the section's cost, with the remaining 85 percent provided by multilateral agencies, export credit agencies and commercial banks. The fact that the European Investment Bank (EIB) underwrote around 50 percent of the overall project cost meant that securing funds from private sources was relatively easy (Table 3.3).

In 1992, the Moroccan government allowed Enagas to build, use

Table 3.3: Financing Structure of the GME in percentage

Section	Cost (US$ millions)	Self-equity	EU funds	EIB	Export credit agencies	Commercial banks
Algerian	675	15		37	48	
Moroccan	760	15		49	13	23
Strait of Gibraltar (split between Morocco and Spain)	145	15		49	13	23
Spanish coast to Cordoba	280	15	32	53		
Cordoba to Portuguese border	170	15	39	46		
Portuguese 1	220	15	39	46		
Portuguese 2	40	15	39	15		31
Total	**2,290**	**15**	**11**	**45**	**19**	**10**

Source: UNDP/World Bank, 2003, 'Cross-border oil and gas pipelines'.

and operate the Moroccan transit section of the GME pipeline. To this end, Enagas and Spain's state-owned National Hydrocarbon Institute (NHI) established Europe Maghreb Pipeline Ltd (EMPL), whose capital has been held by the pipeline users in proportion to their share of the system's nameplate capacity. Accordingly, Segane SA owned on behalf of NHI and Enagas 72.6 percent of EMPL, while Transgas owns the remaining 27.4 percent. State ownership of Segane was intended to be temporary and aimed at ensuring that the planned privatisation of Enagas would not undermine the Spanish government's commitment to the project. Enagas was acquired by Gas Natural in 1994, and as soon as the GME entered into operation in 1996 the latter exercised an agreed purchase option on NHI's shares, completing the transfer of EMPL ownership to Enagas/Gas Natural. Construction and operation of the Moroccan section of the GME have been handled by Metragaz, which is jointly owned by EMPL and Moroccan state-owned *Société nationale des Produits pétroliers* (SNPP).

The decisions regarding the corporate and contractual configurations of the GME project were made in a context of increasing political uncertainty in Algeria, as a result of the intensifying Islamist insurgency, and deteriorating relations between Morocco and Algeria, following the closure of the land border in August 1994. Yet, the construction and commissioning phases of the project witnessed no major incidents. The structure of the GME has meant that the contractual parties share not only an interest in the project (sales/market share, stable supplies, transit royalty), but also the potential risks associated with it. Alternatives to the GME available to Algeria, Spain and Portugal prior to the realisation of the project provided useful benchmarks for their contractual agreements and for the transit arrangement. These include existing LNG supply contracts between Spain and Algeria, the Trans-Med pipeline, other LNG markets, and the availability of other types and sources of energy supplies.

The rent available to Morocco as a transit country was defined by the difference between the known costs of existing LNG supplies from Algeria and the anticipated costs of pipeline shipments. As Morocco's transit fee is determined as a share of the overall project rent, it too shares in the price and volume risks of the pipeline. This has provided further stability to the contractual arrangement by reducing the chance for Morocco to forcibly provoke a renegotiation of its transit deal, especially given that the Medgaz pipeline, linking Algeria directly to Spain, is now complete. The concept of a direct line from Algeria to Spain is as old as the GME, but for the reasons cited above the latter was favoured by the interested parties in the late 1990s. However,

Algeria's decision to pursue the direct link option in the early 2000s despite the possibility of expanding the GME's capacity seems to have been driven by both commercial and political considerations. Market openings in Europe led Sonatrach to move away from its traditional FOB contractual preference and seek downstream access to European end-users, including for its LNG supplies. Moreover, Morocco's persistent refusal to commit to Algerian gas supplies beyond the transit fees seems to have swayed Algeria into considering more seriously the Medgaz option and denying its neighbour a higher transit rent.[33]

Conclusion

The role that natural gas plays as feedstock in various economic sectors in Tunisia has been far more important than it has in Morocco. This is reflective not only of Tunisia's larger, though in absolute terms modest, gas reserve base, but also and more importantly of the different political and energy security considerations of both transit countries vis-à-vis Algeria. Tunisia's decision to use its transit fee for Trans-Med shipments in kind and to contract further supplies from Algeria soon after the commissioning of the pipeline in 1983 allowed it to gradually expand the share of gas in its energy mix and to benefit from a source of relatively cheap, stable and flexible supplies of energy.

By contrast, Morocco was more hesitant to receive its GME transit allowance in kind and only began using part of its transit fee to supply its first gas-fired power plant in 2005, almost a decade after the coming on stream of the GME system. In view of its continuously rising energy bill and growing domestic requirements, Morocco soon decided to expand the introduction of gas in its energy mix by using the entirety of the transit fee in kind. However, despite the fact that the development of a natural gas market is now identified as an energy policy priority in Morocco, reliance on further supplies from Algeria is ruled out as a possible supply option.

Despite Tunisia's apparent initial concerns about the influence of Sonatrach on the transit section of the Trans-Med pipeline, relations between the two countries have been on a consistent friendly footing, reinforced by the in-built confidence of the gasline's contractual configuration. This has permitted all stakeholders to benefit from the expansion of the Trans-Med system's capacity, providing a benchmark of success for subsequent cross-border pipeline projects in the region.

Political relations between Morocco and Algeria, on the other hand, have been plagued by tension since the latter's independence in 1962.

This had for long hindered the materialisation of the GME project, especially given the fact that the option of a direct link from Algeria to Spain posed more significant technical challenges. Although by the time relations between Morocco and Algeria improved advances in gas pipeline technology had rendered the direct link option more feasible, the decision was still made to go ahead with the GME pipeline, in the hope that the project would help reinforce regional economic interdependence and cement more sustainable political cooperation.

However, this proved easier said than done, as Moroccan–Algerian relations reached new lows in 1994. Since then, Moroccan decision-makers have refused to take full advantage of the pipeline, invoking security of supply as their primary concern, notwithstanding the fact that the GME transit arrangement means that Algeria's Sonatrach has no influence on gas shipments beyond its border with Morocco. Furthermore, Algeria has no interest in risking damage to its reputation with its main customers in Europe by interrupting gas supplies through the GME. Thus, Morocco's decision on the lifting of gas from the GME pipeline – and its indirect negative impact on the expansion potential of the pipeline – appears to be more the expression of its intention to maximise its political leverage as a transit country than the product of genuine energy security concerns. Its aim ultimately seems to be to exert pressure on Algeria and drag European countries into the Western Sahara conflict.

Consequently, unlike the Trans-Med system, the GME has not been fully expanded to its design capacity potential of 18–20 Bcm/yr. Morocco's transit policy seems to have spurred Sonatrach and its Iberian customers to construct a new, direct pipeline even if at an economic cost higher than the expansion of the existing link through Morocco. The new Medgaz system has an initial capacity of 8 Bcm/yr, which is planned to be doubled by 2014. This means that Morocco will be left worse off as far as the development of its gas market is concerned, as it will be unable to benefit from a higher transit fee and will only have the option to consider more expensive supply options, such as through LNG imports – at least so long as its aversion to supplies from Algeria remains in place.

Notes

1   In 2000, the two pipelines were renamed Enrico Mattei Gas Pipeline and Pedro Duran Farell Gas Pipeline respectively. The traditional Trans-Med and GME appellations will be used here.

2   For more details, see: Zoubir, Y.H. (2000) 'Algerian-Moroccan Relations and their Impact on Maghribi Integration'.

3   ETAP, 2009, www.etap.com.tn

4   Arab Oil and Gas Directory, 2009.

5   BG Group website, 2009.

6   Hayes, M.H. 2006, 'The Transmed and Maghreb Projects: Gas to Europe from North Africa', p.59.

7   Tunisia was already dependent to some extent on electricity supplies from Algeria.

8   *MEES*, 27 June 1977.

9   Hayes, M.H. Ibid., p.65

10 On which, see Ibid., pp. 69–75.

11 $1.4 billion for the Algerian section, including gas processing installations at Hassi R'Mel; $500 million for the Tunisian section; and $600 million for the submarine Straits of Sicily portion (*PIW*, 31 October 1977; *MEES*, 31 October 1977).

12 Only in November 1997 were deliveries disrupted for 4 days by a fire described as a 'technical incident' (UNDP/World Bank, 2003, 'Cross-border oil and gas pipelines'). The resulting shortfall was covered by Italian storage.

13 Bergaoui, F. 2009, 'Tunisia: Evolution de l'Offre et de la Demande du Gaz Naturel en Tunisie'.

14 Achy, L. 2009, 'Fiscal Adjustment in Non-oil Producing MENA Countries'; IMF, 2009, Tunisia: 2009 Article IV Consultation.

15 Electricity imports from Spain and Algeria accounted for 17% of total electricity consumption in 2008.

16 The cost of energy imports rose from 21 billion Moroccan Dirhams (DH) (approx. $2 billion) in 2003 to DH71 billion in 2008 (approx. $9 billion). State subsidies for energy products amounted to an additional DH25 billion in 2008, representing almost 4% of GDP (Bank Al-Maghrib, 2009, *Rapport annuel*).

17 Recoverable reserves at Meskala were at the time estimated at 1 Bcm.

18 Wood Mackenzie, 2009, *Morocco Country Overview*.

19 The Texas-based Kosmos Energy and Irish independent San Leon (and partners) are the only international companies operating in Western Sahara – the former through its Boujdour offshore exploration licence and the latter in the onshore Zag block in the north of the territory (Wood Mackenzie, 2009, Ibid.).

20 *The Oil and Gas Journal*, 2009.

21 *MEES*, 6 April 2009.

22 In an important speech in August 2000, Moroccan king Mohamed VI announced an important oil and gas discovery by the American company Skidmore in the province of Talsint in the southeast of the country. But to the embarrassment of the Moroccan authorities it soon became clear that there were insignificant reserves in the area.

23 Production from Meskala began in 1987. Production from Toukimt, another field in the Essaouira basin, was stopped in 1998 after it had peaked at 65

million cm/yr.

24 *Arab Oil and Gas Directory*, 2009, p. 316.

25 Moroccan Ministry of Energy and Mines, 2009, 'Energie et Mines: Des Chantiers en Marche'.

26 Aïssaoui, A. 1999, 'Morocco to Introduce Natural Gas in its Energy Market by 2002'.

27 Elfetouaki, O. 2003, 'Le Gazoduc Maghreb–Europe'.

28 Moroccan Ministry of Energy and Mines, 2009, Ibid.

29 Shell is reported to have expressed doubts about the commercial feasibility of the terminal based on the current conditions of the Moroccan gas market.

30 Jorf Lasfar near the Kenitra-Casablanca area and Tangier-Med in the northeast of the country have been identified as two possible sites (*Le Matin*, 27/02/2008).

31 Hayes, M.H. 2006, 'The Transmed and Maghreb Projects', p. 77.

32 This was designed to allow for future expansion of capacity up to 18.5 Bcm/yr.

33 Aïssaoui, A. 2001, *Algeria: The Political Economy of Oil and Gas*, p. 144.

CHAPTER 4

EGYPT'S NATURAL GAS MARKET: SO FAR SO GOOD, BUT WHERE TO NEXT?

Hakim Darbouche and Robert Mabro[1]

Introduction

Petroleum exploration in Egypt dates back to the nineteenth century, with the discovery in 1869 of the country's first oil field, Gemsa, in the Gulf of Suez. Oil production, notably from this field, began in 1910 and expanded subsequently to the Western Desert area. However, limited reserves meant that Egypt was never able to become a major oil producer and exporter, unlike many other countries in the Middle East and North Africa (MENA) region, which developed their petroleum industries much later.

Despite being an oil industry pioneer, Egypt is a relative newcomer to the natural gas industry, especially as an exporter. It only saw the emergence of a domestic market for gas in the late 1970s, following the discovery in 1967 of the country's first non-associated gas field, Abu Madi, in the Nile Delta, which was brought on stream in 1975. However, domestic gas use remained modest until the early 1990s, when consumption began growing much more rapidly, reflecting both declining oil output and booming gas E&P activity. There has been sustained growth of natural gas production since the late 1970s, driven by the discovery of several prolific gas fields in the offshore Mediterranean area following the introduction of gas-dedicated upstream investment terms in the late 1980s. This expansion of gas supply has notably allowed the consolidation of the power generation sector in Egypt and satisfaction of the growing needs of the country's 80-million-strong population, as well as the development of large, competitive energy-intensive industries.[2]

With the firm consolidation of the natural gas reserve base, the prospect of developing an export industry became increasingly realistic towards the late 1990s in the eyes of Egyptian decision-makers, who were not only keen on having an additional source of foreign exchange revenue but also under pressure from upstream international oil companies (IOCs) to allow the monetisation of gas on more rewarding export

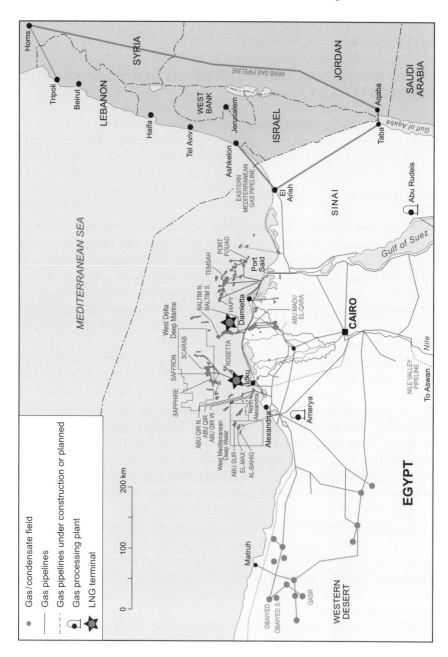

Map 4.1: Egypt: Gas Fields and Transport Infrastructure

markets. Although, initially, only neighbouring countries in the Mashreq and North Africa were considered as potential export markets through pipeline connections, from 2005 Egypt emerged as an important LNG supplier in the Mediterranean and, to a lesser extent, in the Atlantic and Pacific Basins, with overall annual sales in the range of 9–11 mtpa. However, no sooner had Egypt joined the ranks of gas exporters than doubts about its prospects began to emerge, especially following the announcement of a moratorium on new gas exports in June 2008.

Moreover, the rapid increase in Egypt's gas consumption over the last twenty years has given rise to renewed concerns over the impact that energy subsidies are having not just on the country's gas balance but also in broader fiscal and economic terms. It is evident that energy subsidies have become unsustainable in budgetary terms,[3] particularly in 2006–08 given the huge increase in the international prices of oil and gas, compared with the fixed prices of domestic supplies. In addition, subsidies cause economic distortions. They tend to benefit the rich at the expense of the poor, and increase the profits of energy-intensive exporters. Energy subsidies also lead to serious allocation problems by raising domestic demand for energy products above the levels warranted by their true opportunity costs. For gas, they give rise to a bias in favour of investments in export infrastructure and at the expense of the national grid. In short, the optimisation of resource allocation becomes difficult, if not impossible, to achieve.

Thus, despite a remarkable achievement in the development of a natural gas industry, which over a relatively short period of time has become one of the most dynamic sectors of its economy, Egypt has to grapple with issues of crucial importance to the future of its gas sector. Clearly the most pressing of these challenges are subsidies, in addition to export targets and strategy – (how) can Egypt deal with the thorny issue of subsidies, and what is the outlook for its gas exports after the expiry of the moratorium at the end of 2010?

This chapter deals with these two questions. In regard to subsidies, its aim is to assess the nature, extent and implications of the issue, and to propose, where possible, direct and indirect policy remedies. In terms of providing an assessment of Egypt's gas export policy and prospects, the chapter begins by examining the upstream gas segment's dynamics and policies, highlighting the government's recent coming to terms with the need to reconsider existing pricing terms and to respond to IOC concerns. It will also dissect recent trends in domestic demand and their main driver, the power generation sector. This will pave the way to dealing with the issue of subsidies, before delving into the export segment and its evolution since 2003. Finally, the chapter will end by providing an outlook for Egypt's gas exports, based on projections of supply and demand, concluding that, although Egypt is unlikely to experience a gas deficit in the short term, it has some tough decisions to make if it is to optimise the use of this resource over the longer term.

Upstream Dynamics and Policies: Grappling with Bottlenecks

The hydrocarbon industry in Egypt has since the early 1990s been increasingly focused on natural gas, reflecting the structural decline in the country's oil production and, concurrently, the growing prospects for gas. Indeed, official estimates indicate that proven gas reserves have grown six-fold over the last twenty years, reaching about 2160 Bcm in 2009 compared with 347 Bcm in 1989 (Figure 4.1).[4] This represents an annual average growth rate of 13.7 percent in the 1990s and 5.7 percent in the 2000s, largely satisfying the objective set by the Egyptian government in the early 1990s to accumulate new reserves to the order of at least 38 Bcm every year up to 2010, but falling short of the more ambitious 2006 target of adding 840 Bcm to the reserve base by 2011. This shortfall is the result of the declining rate of reserve expansion that has been observed since 2007, owing most certainly to the impact that the global economic crisis and government fiscal terms had on foreign upstream investment in Egypt.

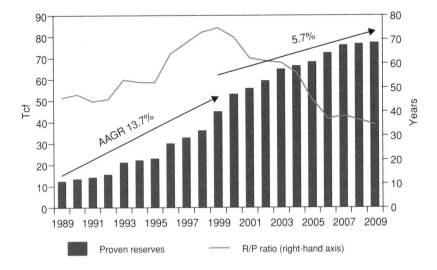

Figure 4.1: Egypt's Natural Gas Reserves and R/P Ratio, 1989–2009

Sources: Egypt's Ministry of Petroleum and BP (2010)

The overwhelming majority of additions to Egypt's gas reserves since 2000 are based in offshore fields in the Mediterranean, the Nile Delta and, to a lesser extent, the Western Desert. This is reflected in the geographical distribution of the country's overall reserve base, over 80 percent of which is located in the Mediterranean area east of Alexandria and northwest of Port Said (see Map 4.1), followed by the Western Desert, the Gulf of Suez and the Nile Delta (Figure 4.2). In May 2010, the US Geological Survey (USGS) estimated that the Nile Delta contained over 6200 Bcm of undiscovered, technically recoverable natural gas reserves, in addition to 5.9 billion barrels of NGLs.[5] The USGS' estimates tend to be overoptimistic, but if confirmed they can prove a game-changer for Egypt's gas industry, as it is certain that more gas needs to be found if this sector is to continue expanding in future at anywhere near the same rate as hitherto, and meet both the country's domestic requirements and export ambitions (Figure 4.3).

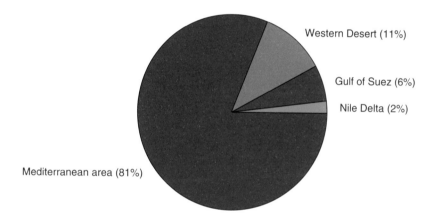

Figure 4.2: Geographical Distribution of Gas Reserves in Egypt

Source: EGAS

Production

Natural gas production in Egypt has grown consistently, not just over the last twenty years as shown in Figure 4.4, but since the mid-1970s. The development in the late 1990s and early 2000s of key upstream projects, mostly in the offshore Mediterranean and Nile Delta areas, such as Baltim, Ha'py, Temsah, Rosetta/Rashid and Scarab/Saffron has brought on stream significant supplies of gas that have been able to offset declining output from the country's oldest producing fields, Abu

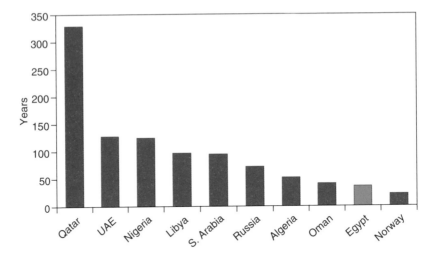

Figure 4.3: Egypt's R/P Ratio in 2008

Source: BP (2010)

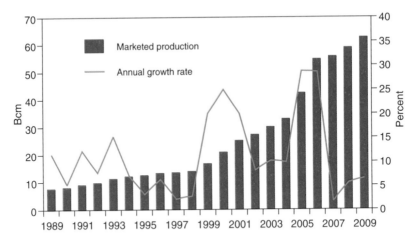

Figure 4.4: Egypt's Natural Gas Production, 1989–2009

Sources: BP (2010), Cedigaz and own estimates

Madi and Abu Qir, and meet the rapid increase in domestic demand and growing export commitments. However, since 2007 the average annual growth rate of gas production declined considerably to 4.7 percent, compared to the 18 percent recorded from 1999. This meant that, in 2009, Egypt's natural gas production stood at just over 62 Bcm, distributed geographically between the Mediterranean (76.8 percent), the Western Desert (16.9 percent), the Nile Delta (5.6 percent), and the Gulf of Suez (0.7 percent) (Figure 4.5). In addition to the above areas, other major gas-producing fields in Egypt include the Port Fouad fields offshore of Port Said, the Westani field in the onshore Nile Delta, the Obaiyed and Qasr fields in the north of the Western Desert.

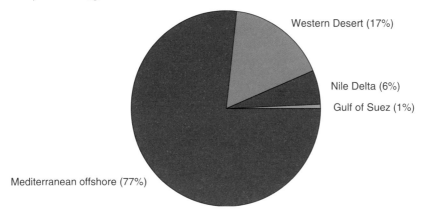

Figure 4.5: Breakdown of Egypt's 2009 Gas Production by Region

Source: Egypt's Ministry of Petroleum

These fields are operated by a number of IOCs, which have become central to Egypt's natural gas business. The largest operators include BG, ENI, BP, Apache Corporation, Petronas, Edison, Dana Gas, Shell, and Melrose Resources. The capital expenditure plans for the period 2006–2010, which were announced by the three largest investors alone, amounted to over $20 billion,[6] and while the financial crisis that emerged in 2007/8 and BP's oil spill predicament in the Gulf of Mexico will have forced a revision of these investment plans, they remain a strong indication of IOCs' long-term commitment in Egypt and their confidence about its upstream potential despite a number of structural bottlenecks. Foreign investors operate under joint ventures and production sharing agreements (PSAs) with state-owned companies the Egyptian General Petroleum Corporation (EGPC) and the Egyptian Natural Gas Holding Company (EGAS), which are also the main off-takers of marketed gas volumes.

Regulatory Framework and Pricing Policies

Mining legislation was first introduced in Egypt in 1953, shortly after independence. In 1956, the General Petroleum Authority (GPA) was set up by the Egyptian government to manage its interests in the oil business and undertake exploration on behalf of the state. In the same year, the General Petroleum Company (GPC), Egypt's first oil company, was formed and was granted exploration licences in the Gulf of Suez and in Egypt's Eastern Desert. GPC was later to acquire licences in Sinai also, and to become the most important operating company owned by EGPC, GPA's successor from 1962. EGPC has controlled and performed executive activities in all aspects of the Egyptian petroleum industry, namely licensing, exploration, production, refining, transportation and marketing. However, with the growing importance of the natural gas industry, EGAS was formed in August 2001 and given a mandate to drive forward the government's gas sector strategy, providing an opportunity for EGPC to focus on declining oil production. Besides being an equity partner alongside EGPC in all production joint ventures and downstream LNG projects, EGAS has also acquired joint authority with both EGPC and the government in the approval of work programmes and development plans.[7]

Since its creation, EGAS has organised four upstream licensing rounds, the most recent of which was completed in March 2009. The acreage on offer in the most recent bidding round was located in the deep offshore Mediterranean, and despite being adjacent to Egypt's largest producing gas fields, it attracted muted interest from IOCs, with only three of the seven blocks offered being awarded. After the poor showing in neighbouring Algeria's 2008 bidding round (see Chapter 1), this disappointing outcome came as no surprise to industry observers, but dealt a heavy blow to Egypt's hopes to spur offshore upstream activity and at least maintain gas output growing at a rate commensurate with domestic requirements. While the subdued results were partly imputed to the straitened global economic circumstances, which inevitably deterred smaller companies from bidding especially for costlier deepwater permits, there was also reason to believe that Egypt's gas pricing policies were to blame.

Egypt's current fiscal regime for hydrocarbon exploration and production, which was introduced through its 1973 Petroleum Policy, is based on production sharing contracts. The framework has provided relatively stable and attractive terms, albeit in a heavily bureaucratised environment, as the licensing process is notoriously protracted, with the examination and approval process of licences taking up to a year from award to ratification. Early licensing arrangements denied foreign companies the right to own the gas discovered in the course of drilling, which was to be automatically transferred to EGPC. But under pressure from the World Bank,[8] the Egyptian government introduced in 1986, and with retrospective effect, a 'gas clause' giving contractors sharing rights in associated and non-associated gas. Later in the early 1990s, improved fiscal terms were offered within offshore licences, leading to an increase in E&P activity in the Mediterranean from then onwards.[9] Consequently, gas presented the brightest prospect for future hydrocarbon export growth, with the assurance of rapidly increasing reserves. Nevertheless, gas regulation has dictated that only a third of proven reserves can be exported, while another third is earmarked for use on the domestic market and the rest is preserved for 'future generations', though this has not always been strictly implemented.

In the event of a commercial discovery a joint venture operating company, owned 50 percent by EGPC and/or EGAS and 50 percent by the contractor, is established. The joint venture operating company system allows Egyptian national oil companies (NOCs) to exert a significant level of control over field developments without requiring the state to fund any of the development, as all the exploration, capital and operating costs are borne by foreign investors. Bonuses, cost recovery ceilings, excess cost recovery and profit gas are all negotiable. The latter is shared between the investor and EGPC/EGAS on the basis of a sliding scale linked to production shares, and varies typically between 70–80 percent in favour of the government. Furthermore, foreign investors are required to sell part (up to two-thirds) of their share of gas (cost recovery + profit gas) to EGPC and EGAS for use on the domestic market. This is done through gas sales agreements between the Egyptian NOCs and contractors, committing the former to purchasing on a take-or-pay basis 75 percent of a given daily contract quantity (DCQ).

The price paid to foreign investors by Egyptian NOCs for these volumes has traditionally been capped, but it has been revised on many occasions as can be seen in Table 4.1. With the rising rig costs from the mid-2000s, the price cap of $2.65/MMBtu applied by EGAS and EGPC became untenable. IOCs saw their margins squeezed considerably and were unable to engage in fresh exploration, or even to justify capital spending on existing production facilities. As a result, the development of new offshore discoveries was put on hold in many instances and a number of IOCs were discouraged from participating in EGAS's 2008 bidding round.[10] Faced with spiralling domestic demand on the one hand and with a potential supply crunch on the other, the Egyptian government decided in 2008 to introduce higher price caps for supplies from deepwater fields, ranging from $3.70/MMBtu to $4.70/MMBtu depending on the requests of the companies, the concession agreements and the position of the acreage.[11]

The new price arrangement was introduced following the agreement reached in late 2007 between the Egyptian government and BP/RWE Dea for gas produced from their joint North Alexandria and West Mediterranean Deep Water concessions,[12] for which EGPC/EGAS said they would pay up to $4.70/MMBtu. More recently, both sides again agreed to amend the terms of the existing PSA, stipulating that the contractors will assume all investment costs, which are estimated at $9 billion, while Egyptian NOCs will have the right to buy all gas produced – instead of a limited share – at a price of $3/MMBtu at a floor of $50/bbl Brent, rising to a ceiling of $4.10/MMBtu at an oil price of $120/bbl.[13] The deal was hailed as a breakthrough in Egypt's struggle to come to terms with booming domestic demand, as it is expected to send a positive signal to investors and encourage more contractual flexibility within the PSA regime, which is likely to lead to more exploration in the Mediterranean. However, even with the 2008 price arrangement, selling volumes onto the domestic market at a heavily subsidised price – well below the price paid to IOCs, as discussed below – meant that Egyptian NOCs have on many occasions struggled to pay their dues to upstream contractors on time, leading to further frustration amongst foreign investors and to decision delays for key upstream projects.[14]

Table 4.1: The Evolution of Gas Prices Paid within PSAs by Egyptian NOCs to International Producers

---

	Price Formula
1993–2001	Gas price indexed to the Gulf of Suez Blend crude, subject to a 15 percent discount.
2001–2003	Gas price indexed to Brent with a ceiling of $2.65/MMBtu at $21/bbl and a floor of $1.50/MMBtu at $10/bbl. The floor and ceiling prices are not increased in line with any inflation factor; therefore there is no upside to high oil prices for sellers.
2004	Gas price indexed to Brent with a ceiling of $2.50/MMBtu at $22/bbl and a floor of $1.50/MMBtu at $10/bbl.
2006	Gas price indexed to Brent with a ceiling of $2.65/MMBtu at $22/bbl and a floor of $1.50/MMBtu at $10/bbl.
2007–2008	BP and RWE Dea negotiate a new price cap of $4.70/MMBtu. BG, ENI and other offshore producers obtain new price caps in the range of $3.70–4.70/MMBtu.
2010	BP and RWE Dea negotiate new terms and a new gas price of $3/MMBtu at a Brent floor of $50/bbl and a ceiling of $4.10/MMBtu at $120/bbl.

Source: Compiled by authors

Domestic Gas Consumption: Driving forward unabated

From the late 1990s, natural gas rapidly overtook oil as Egypt's main source of primary energy supply. Conscious of the declining oil output and of the growing potential of gas reserves, the government adopted early on a policy of encouraging the expansion of the domestic gas market by extending the national grid and promoting the conversion to gas of large parts of the industrial and power generation sectors. As a result, in 2009 gas accounted for 55 percent of Egypt's total primary energy supply (Figure 4.6).

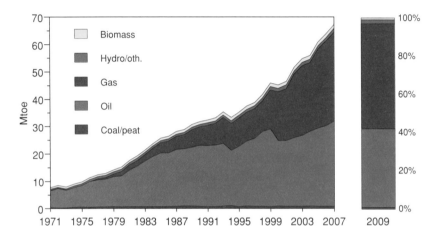

Figure 4.6: Egypt's Total Primary Energy Supply, 1971–2007

Sources: IEA (2009) and Egypt's Ministry of Petroleum

However, despite this growing gas penetration, demand for petroleum products – mainly LPG for residential use and diesel for use in the transport and agricultural sectors – has continued to grow at roughly the same rate as gas consumption. Furthermore, declining oil production and relatively limited refining capacity have meant that Egypt imports about 50 percent of its petroleum needs, at a cost of around $5 billion per year since 2005 – just under half of the country's entire oil and gas export revenue. To allay its petroleum needs, the Egyptian government has in recent years opened the refining sector to foreign investment, but poor economics and an unattractive taxation policy have deterred foreign firms from flocking into the country.

Over the last ten years, gas consumption has more than doubled in Egypt, growing at an average annual rate of more than 10 percent to reach 43 Bcm in 2009 (Figure 4.7). This makes Egypt the fourth largest

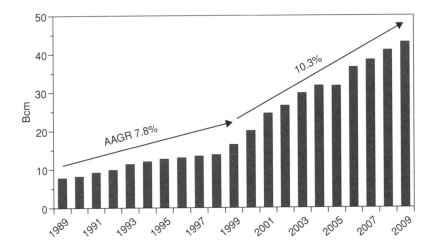

Figure 4.7: Natural Gas Consumption in Egypt, 1989–2009

Source: BP (2010)

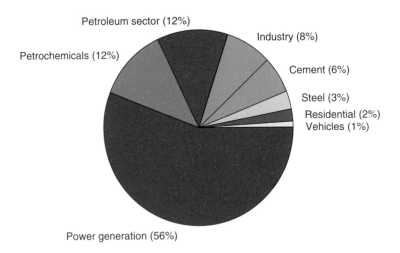

Figure 4.8: Breakdown of Egypt's 2009 Gas Consumption by Sector

Source: Egypt's Ministry of Petroleum

gas market in the MENA region, after Iran, Saudi Arabia and the UAE, and by far the biggest in Africa. However, with a relatively low energy intensity of 0.4 toe/$1000 GDP, the Egyptian economy seems to be more efficient than those of the top MENA gas consumers. Higher gas consumption growth rates in the 2000s, relative to the 1990s, were a reflection of the growing needs of the fledging gas sector and the government's ambitious petrochemical and power generation capacity expansion plans.

Indeed, these three sectors account for the largest share of gas consumption. The power sector has invariably been the single most important driver of demand for gas in Egypt, accounting for 56 percent of the country's gas consumption in 2009. Industrial users, for their part, represented 29 percent of demand, led by the petrochemical, cement and steel segments (Figure 4.8). ECHEM, Egypt's Petrochemicals Holding Company, has been forging ahead with its $10 billion, 20-year master plan that was launched in 2002 with the aim of expanding national production capacity to 15mt/yr, despite the effect of the global economic recession and local concerns about the availability of gas feedstock. Finally, residential users and transportation accounted for only a small portion of overall gas consumption, with just over 2.5 million households currently connected to the national grid and around 110,000 cars converted to compressed natural gas (CNG).[15]

Gas to Power

In 2009, over 80 percent of Egypt's electricity output was generated from gas-fired power plants, compared to around 30 percent in 1989 (Figure 4.9). By 2020, it is estimated that the share of gas will exceed

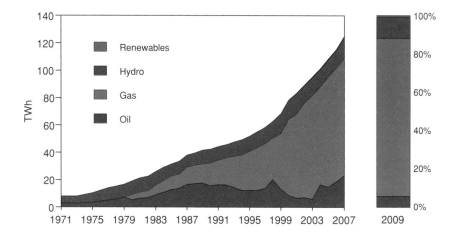

Figure 4.9: Egypt: Power Generation by Fuel, 1971–2007

Sources: IEA (2009), Egypt's Electricity Holding Company and own estimates

90 percent. Furthermore, demand for electricity has in recent years grown at an average annual rate of 7–8 percent, which meant that the government has had to plan to increase the country's generation capacity by 1500MW/yr to meet rising power needs. Indeed, Egypt's Electricity Holding Company (EEHC), the public power utility, is in the process of implementing the sixth in a series of successive five-year plans aimed at adding to the existing 23,500MW over 7700MW of mostly gas-fired generating capacity in the period 2007–2011. This is based on the anticipation that the average rate of increase in electricity demand over the corresponding period will be 6.4 percent. The next EEHC plan (2012–2016), which was finalised in 2009, is based on the assumption that demand will grow by 6 percent over the relevant period and will add 11,000MW of power generation capacity.[16] Residential/commercial consumption has been – and is likely to remain – the main driver of Egypt's surging power demand, as ownership of 'white goods', such as refrigerators, along with the rise in the use of air-conditioning and the growing penetration of personal computers increases.

Noticeably, Egypt's plans for power generation capacity expansion are largely based on the thermal power plant technologies of steam cycle and CCGT (Table 4.2). These are heavily reliant on natural gas for their fuel input, which means that renewable and hydro alternatives will remain relatively marginal in the short term, if important additions in the longer term, to the global capacity hike. Egypt's official target is that renewable sources (mostly wind and solar) should account for 20 percent of the country's total electricity generation by 2020, and there are also plans to develop nuclear energy in the long term. These are ambitious plans for the construction of new power generation capacity, which will remain subject to important planning and implementation provisos.

Most new capacity will continue in the short term to rely on concessional lending from multi- and bilateral donors, and to be developed by EEHC and its subsidiaries as engineering, procurement and construction (EPC) projects. Indeed, a currency crisis in the early 2000s forced the Egyptian government to abandon the build–own–operate–transfer (BOOT) model, following its successful introduction in the late 1990s for the award of the country's three existing independent power projects (IPPs),[17] and to revert back to the EPC arrangement. However, the improved economic outlook in recent years is likely to result in a return later in the forecast period to private financing through BOOT contracts, and a new electricity law, expected to pave the way for changes in this direction, is awaiting ratification, having been approved by the

Table 4.2: Egypt's Power Generation Capacity Expansion Plans to 2027, in MW unless otherwise indicated

	2009 Capacity	Share (%) Current	2008–2017	Share (%) 2008–17	2018–2027	Share (%) 2018–27	Total capacity in 2027	Share (%) Total
Thermal – steam cycle	13,099	55.7	9,472.5	39.5	13,447.5	43.6	34,491	44.9
Thermal – CCGT	7,178	30.5	8,227	34.3	11,002.5	35.7	26,594.5	34.6
Hydro	2,800	11.9	32	0.1	–	0	2,815	3.7
Solar/Thermal	–	–	150	0.6	–	0	150	0.2
Wind	425	1.8	5,100	21.3	2,400	7.8	7,725	10.1
Nuclear	–	–	1,000	4.2	4,000	13	5,000	6.5
Total capacity	23,502	100	23,981.5	100	30,850	100	76,775.5	100

Source: Adapted from World Bank, 2009, 'Project Appraisal Document on a Proposed Loan …'

cabinet in 2008.[18] The single most important barrier to both large-scale development of renewable sources of energy and meaningful private sector participation remains the issue of under-pricing and subsidies in Egypt's energy sector.

Price Subsidies: A Thorny, Burdensome Issue

Subsidies, not only of energy products (oil products, natural gas, and electricity) but of a wider range of basic goods also, are a structural feature of Egypt's political economy. Since 1977, they have been treated as a taboo subject by most government decision-makers. The widespread riots that took place then in reaction to a government announcement of price increases deeply unnerved Egyptian policymakers and left a legacy of government caution towards pricing and economic reforms.[19] However, under the effect of rising international energy and food prices, price subsidies have represented in recent years a growing fiscal burden on the government budget in Egypt, forcing decision-makers to consider revising domestic energy pricing policies.

Since 2007, the cost of energy subsidies, which on average account for 20–25 percent of government spending and represent 70 percent of total subsidies, has been in the range of $8–12 billion – about 8–10 percent of GDP. What's more, the economic value of the subsidies is much higher, because the oil and gas received by EGPC/EGAS as Egypt's share under PSAs are treated as 'free goods'. Their domestic sales at artificially low prices appear as an accounting profit. In reality, however, the Egyptian NOCs are incurring an opportunity loss equal to the difference between the domestic price and the prices at which oil and gas are purchased from foreign investors. Regardless of the accuracy of these estimates, the fact remains that the fiscal burden of energy subsidies is very heavy.

Faced with a worsening budget deficit, which stood at 8 percent in 2009, the Egyptian government launched a plan to bring energy prices close to actual costs by 2010. To this effect, electricity prices were increased for the first time in twelve years in 2004,[20] and have been rising since at the nominal rate of 7.5 percent per year. And in June 2008, the government decreed an immediate increase in gas prices for energy-intensive industries, from $1.25 to $3/MMBtu. At the same time, it was decided that the remaining industrial users would see their prices increase, more gradually and by July 2010, to $2.65/MMBtu.[21] However, these adjustments did not appear to extend to the power sector, as gas feedstock prices there are currently fixed at around $0.9/

MMBtu but should slowly rise to $1.6/MMBtu by 2013. Residential users were also to continue paying between LE0.1–0.3/cum of gas depending on consumption levels.

By late 2008, the decision to increase gas prices was delayed under the pretext of the global economic crisis, as the price for energy-intensive users was reduced from $3 to $1.7/MMBtu, while the rest of the industrial consumers continued to pay the same price. Yet, in the first half of 2010, the government seemed to have resumed the implementation of its subsidy-reduction plan, but promised to eliminate all energy subsidies by the end of 2011. This revised schedule is reflected in the 2010–11 spending budget, which provides for almost a $12 billion energy subsidy bill and confirms observers' prediction that the issue is too sensitive for the Egyptian government to tackle effectively before the presidential election of 2011.[22] Powerful lobbies of the energy-intensive steel, cement and ceramics industries are also likely to have sought to influence government plans in their favour.

Despite these efforts, the fact remains that the share of gas in the total energy subsidy bill sustained by the Egyptian government is relatively modest compared to other petroleum products, especially diesel, LPG and gasoline. Indeed, gas price subsidies accounted for just under 5 percent of total fuel subsidies in the last two years, though they have been projected to more than double in 2010–11.[23] However, on an opportunity cost basis, subsidies of natural gas are much higher, with up to two-thirds of gas sales revenue being generated by the export of only one-third of total marketed volumes (Figure 4.10). The prices of other petroleum products have remained unchanged for years, given that they are widely used by low-income consumers, but the government has recently confirmed its plans to eliminate these fuel subsidies by 2014 and to introduce a coupon scheme in September 2010 to improve the targeting of the LPG subsidy and reduce the numerous distortions it causes.[24]

Distributional Distortions

Subsidies also create numerous distributional distortions. Petroleum and natural gas subsidies to individuals and households benefit all consumers whether rich or poor. There is no reason based on equity or distribution to subsidise those who can afford to pay according to the economic opportunity cost of the fuel involved. In many instances, however, discrimination on the basis of income may be impossible, or very difficult, to implement. Gasoline, for example, cannot be sold in service stations at different prices depending on the income of the

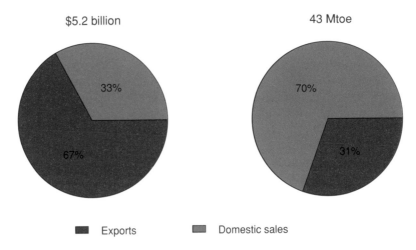

$5.2 billion

33%

67%

43 Mtoe

70%

31%

■ Exports　　■ Domestic sales

Figure 4.10: Egypt 2008 Gas Exports: Opportunity Cost

Source: EGAS

car owner or the driver who fills up the tank. The LPG cylinder is necessarily sold at the same price to all customers. The only way to introduce some discrimination between rich and poor is through some rationing device (as was established in Egypt during WWII for such necessities as sugar and cooking oil). Such a system is administratively cumbersome and open to abuse. It is always worth remembering that in the case of gasoline, diesel or LPG, the poorer Egyptians are in effect subsidising the rich. However, discrimination on the basis of income is possible to some extent in the case of household gas and electricity. A graduated tariff system could be implemented where those in a higher consumption bracket would incur higher tariffs. The concept is simple, based on the very plausible assumption that consumption correlates to the size of the accommodation, which in turn correlates to the income or wealth of the household. These correlations are not perfect, but are sufficiently close to reality to justify the graduated tariff policy.

Graduated tariffs are used in Egypt, but the system does not necessarily abolish all distributional distortions. Much depends on the structure of the scale (how many consumption brackets are involved and the levels at which the tariffs are set). Consider, for example, a scale in which the highest bracket, which by definition has no upper bound, starts at a fairly low consumption level. In such a scale, households with moderate fuel consumption will be paying for electricity or gas at the same tariff as rich households consuming very large amounts. An objective of equitable distribution will not be fulfilled in this case.

Subsidised fuels are not only supplied to households but to power stations, industry, the transport sector, and to the whole range of commercial, financial and other establishments. The aim is to make electricity, goods produced by industry and retailed by merchants, transport fares, services and so on, available to consumers at affordable prices.

Let us consider here the case of industry. Energy subsidies reduce production costs, which in turn are expected to reduce *pari passu* final prices. The significance of the cost reductions depends on the energy intensity of the production of the manufactured goods. Reductions would be fairly large in industries such as fertilisers, cement, metals or petrochemicals, but not very significant in light industries such as textiles, food processing and the like. Cost reductions are not always *fully* passed on to the final consumer. Much depends on the degree of market concentration for the good concerned (monopoly or competition), and in the case of monopoly much also depends on the efficiency of regulation. Some industries export part or all of their production.

Subsidised fuels reduce production costs across the board, whether the good is sold in the domestic or international market. The fuel subsidy will therefore increase the profits of the exporter or reduce losses. In the case of the former, it will provide a boost for further exports; in the latter it will delay the moment when a company ceases to export which inevitably happens if losses continue to be incurred. Of course, the increase in profits (reduction of losses) depends on the size of the subsidy and the energy input coefficient in the production of the exported good. Then again, the effect may be negligible for light-industry products, but would be more substantial for energy-intensive industries.

Allocation Distortions

Fuel subsidies naturally cause allocation distortions. We shall not dwell here on the familiar issue that subsidies stimulate consumption patterns that do not correspond to the structure of relative scarcities. We would rather focus on a specific problem: the allocation of gas production between domestic and export markets. In Egypt, both oil and gas are generally explored for, developed and produced by foreign investors under PSAs. The investor has a claim on two output shares: the first (CR) is to recover exploration, development and production costs over a certain period of time, and the second (PR) to provide a profit in compensation for the risks incurred, and a return on the capital invested. EGPC has a claim on another share (G) so that:

$$CR + PR + G = 1$$

In the case of oil, EGPC may buy from the investors either all or part of $(CR + PR)*Q$, where Q is the production of the field. For gas, the situation differs from that of oil in an important respect, as gas exports require a specific infrastructure: pipelines and/or liquefaction plants for LNG. And the use of gas domestically requires a pipeline network that links fields to consumption points such as power stations, factories and households. For oil, refineries are needed, but if their domestic capacity is smaller than the size of the national market a balance can be achieved by exporting crude and importing petroleum products. The development of gas resources by oil companies when new discoveries are made is only possible if the incremental output can be absorbed by the domestic or export market or both. But this depends on a domestic demand potential that is not constrained by the existing infrastructure, and/or on export markets that can be reached and supplied by the existing LNG and pipelines. The development of gas production in a situation where the domestic pipeline network is constrained and the LNG or export pipeline capacity is either non-existent or insufficient (always assuming that a demand potential does exist) will require investment in these installations and infrastructure, which could be done in joint ventures with foreign investors.

In Egypt, EGPC has a domestic monopoly in both oil and gas either directly or through subsidiaries and thus invests in the natural gas grid and all relevant connections. Sound investment decisions must take into account the opportunity costs of the fuels involved, *not* the cash costs, which determine cash flows but do not lead in the direction of an optimal allocation of resources. The oil/gas price structure in Egypt, presented in Table 4.3 in an ordinal scale, distinguishes between transactions made at administered or subsidised prices and transactions at international prices. The latter are the true opportunity costs of such highly tradable commodities as crude oil and petroleum products, and now in Egypt, natural gas.

We generally have: $[z] < [p]$ and $[y] < [c]$

And always: $b < v$

The opportunity cost of (1) is not zero, however. It is the international price, or its proxy, the price $[p]$ paid by EGPC for its purchases (2) from foreign investors. That of LPG is clearly v; and that of the range of fuels sold by EGPC domestically is clearly not $[y]$ or $[z]$, but their international price.

Table 4.3: Oil and Gas Price Structure, EGPC's Acquisition Prices

(1) from its share from PSA agreements	Free
(2) for its purchases from the share of foreign investors The price vector [p] is related to, but not necessarily equal to international prices. In gas contracts [p] is capped at $2.5/2.65/MMBtu, a level that may differ from international prices.	[p]
(3) Imported petroleum products at cost, insurance and freight (cif) prices [c] as given in international markets	[c]
(4) Imported LPG at international prices	v
EGPC's Sales Prices	
(5) Vary depending on the fuel. All petroleum products are sold domestically at fixed prices [y] lower than those in international trade. Gas is sold to households according to a tariff structure related to consumption levels. Prices can be represented by the vector [z]. Most of the elements of this vector are below the purchase prices [p], sometimes significantly.	[y] [z]
(6) LPG is sold at a heavily subsidised price	b

To illustrate with some numbers, for example, gas is purchased at the capped price of $2.50/2.65MMBtu from the foreign investors and there is a general view that it was initially sold in long-term export contracts at a bit less than $1.0/MMBtu in one case and $1.50 in another one. Spot export deals by EGPC usually bring prices comparable to those in the relevant international market. Natural gas is sold domestically at prices ranging between $0.48 and $1.44/MMBtu depending on consumption levels. A 12.5 kg LPG cylinder is sold at the official price of $0.43 per cylinder equivalent to $0.73/MMBtu.[25]

Considering opportunity costs instead of accounting prices has a significant bearing on the optimum allocation of natural gas between domestic consumption and exports. Gas used domestically displaces petroleum products: gasoline or diesel if CNG is used in taxis or buses; LPG if households are connected to the national gas grid; heavy fuel oil in power stations, and so on. The opportunity costs of the displaced petroleum products are to be compared with that of exported natural gas, more precisely with the netback obtained by EGPC at Egypt's border. The *actual* opportunity cost has to be computed as a weighted average.

The prices that a country or a company receives in gas sales may be lower than is warranted by international gas market conditions. Some will argue that the true opportunity costs are the warranted prices. In our judgment they are irrelevant if unobtainable under existing contracts. However, raising the point is important as a reminder that one should always seek to correct a flawed situation, and keep an eye on true opportunity costs in future deals or contracts.

Furthermore, the investment requirements in the domestic gas connection infrastructure and in the export installations (LNG trains and/ or export pipelines) need to be compared. These are not easy exercises but it is important to undertake them. Approximate results are better than no results at all. The heavy subsidisation of fuels in the domestic market and the peculiar institutional structure, which places a heavy burden on EGPC compelling it to sell fuels at lower than the purchase prices, inevitably distort the gas allocation decisions between exports and domestic use.

Other Policy Recommendations on Subsidies

Resolving EGPC's cash flow problem (to be distinguished from the fiscal burden on the country) calls for institutional reform. In essence, the functions of EGPC and the Ministry of Finance should be clearly separated. EGPC's role is to buy and sell fuels, and the Ministry's roles are (a) to obtain the value of the equity oil and gas as these belong to the state and not to EGPC, and (b) to disburse fuel subsidies. In practice this means that:

- EGPC would pay the Ministry of Finance a sum equal to [q]*[p] where [q] is the volume of equity oil and gas obtained and [p] the corresponding price vector of its acquisition from foreign investors. Then all oil and gas obtained both as equity or purchases from foreign investors are correctly accounted for in EGPC books;
- The Ministry of Finance would reimburse EGPC for the entire amount of implicit subsidies equal to [q]*[p] minus [q]*[z], and for LPG [m]*[v] minus [m]*[b] where m is the volume of LPG imported and sold domestically.[26]

This proposal would balance the books of EGPC, enabling it to work more efficiently and meet its payments obligations in a much easier and timely manner. It would also significantly increase transparency. The total amount of the subsidy will accurately appear in the state budget without the misleading subtraction of the proceeds from the sales of equity oil and gas assumed to be acquired at zero cost. The value of the rent accruing to Egypt from the PSA would also appear in the Ministry of Finance books. Another important advantage of this proposal is that the cash flow pressures, which influence EGPC/EGAS decisions on allocation between domestic gas consumption and exports, will be removed. The decisions will become freer of an exogenous factor that may cause distortions.

The subsidy problem, though transferred more clearly to the budget, would remain a heavy burden on the government and needs to be urgently addressed. There are no radical solutions, however. Mitigation can only occur through gradual, and in some cases, indirect, policies. To suddenly remove all fuel subsidies is not recommended although some economists advocate it on the grounds that a shock has immediate salutary effects, and that the pain initially felt tends to subside after a relatively short time. We do not belong to that school of thought.

The removal of all subsidies is politically dangerous and would cause hardship to low income groups. A solution of the Jordanian type – removing certain subsidies and making lump sum payments to those who are assumed to be affected – has theoretical merits, but its adoption in Egypt is likely to face difficult implementation problems.

The gradual approach is to increase domestic fuel prices over a period of five or six years by a small percentage, for example, 4 percent every year. The economic hardship would not be crushing and the risks of a political upheaval would be minimised. The tariff scales for gas and electricity should also be revised to ensure that those with high consumption (be it households or commercial, but not industrial establishments or power stations) are not lumped together with those with medium consumption.

Some indirect measures may remove the distributional distortions and generate some revenues to the government. Since automotive fuels (i.e. gasoline and diesel) cannot be sold at different prices to different customers (e.g. the wealthy and the less wealthy) an indirect approach is to impose a very high road tax on expensive cars according to cylinder capacity, price and age for example.

In addition, industrial plants, which export all or part of their output, could pay a fuel tax calculated as follows:

$$[s][f]x$$

Where [s] is the subsidy to the fuels [f] used, and x the ratio of exports to the total output of the company.

The LPG problem is more complex as it is heavily subsidised. The question is whether substitution with natural gas, which itself is subsidised, will reduce the fiscal burden. The answer to this question would have been straightforward if it only involved a comparison of the per Btu subsidy for the two fuels. The problem is that substitution requires investments for household connections to the gas supply network and changes in the domestic appliances that use LPG to enable them to burn natural gas instead.

A thorough study by Gerner and Sinclair (2006) of the World Bank, estimates the average LPG subsidy at LE57.8/MMBtu, and the natural gas subsidy at between LE14.3 and 18.5/MMBtu depending on the household consumption level. The total subsidy for LPG for domestic use was estimated at $1.5 billion in 2005.[27] It is likely to be higher now since crude oil prices, which lead butane prices, have risen compared to 2005, while domestic prices remain fixed. Assuming, however, that the international price of LPG will not change much compared to 2005, and that the natural gas subsidy will average LE15.6 (27 percent of the LPG subsidy), it is estimated that when completed, the substitution of LPG with gas will save EGPC/Egyptian government $1.095 billion in subsidies.

The investment required to achieve these savings is large. It is estimated at LE2500 ($439) per gas connection or a total of $2.6 billion for six million households. The Egyptian government requires households to contribute LE1500 toward the connection costs, which would reduce government investment to $1.054 billion. No sophisticated economic analysis is required to justify an investment that, once completed, will be recouped in one year.

However, poor households cannot afford to pay LE1500. Medium consumption households either cannot afford it or are not convinced of the benefits of gas since they accrue over the years while the contribution is paid up front. The rich can afford it but some will be reluctant to pay. As a result, only a proportion of the households will be connected even though, according to Gerner and Sinclair,[28] the National Bank of Egypt offers financing plans for the connection fees to some households.

In the case of partial connections, EGPC will recoup the investments made as the subsidy burden will be reduced (broadly speaking in the same proportion of the households connected) but the full savings on subsidies, which should be the objective, will not be achieved.

The bold proposal is that the government should undertake the entire investment without any contribution from connected households. Some revenues may then be obtained by raising gas tariffs by a modest amount to moderate consumers, and bringing them close to the gas opportunity cost to high consumers. It is beyond the scope of this paper to embark on a sophisticated economic analysis to justify the proposal. This requires assumptions on the time it takes to complete the investment, a forecast of future LPG prices that is bound to be uncertain, a view about the financing method used and its costs among other parameters. But the proposal deserves to be considered.

In all situations, Egypt will gain from promoting energy efficiency measures that reduce consumption of fuels without affecting economic development. Any such reduction means *ceteris paribus* a lower imports bill (when a net importer) or higher export revenues (when a net exporter) and in both cases a smaller subsidy budget. The introduction of energy efficiency measures often involves investment expenditures so their benefits must be carefully assessed in relation to costs.

Some policies can be easily recommended, however. Small gradual increases in prices as mentioned earlier can be effective after a relatively short period of time. The expansion of public transport networks is always worth looking at. And much can be achieved in industry, power stations and refineries by imposing energy audits that will inevitably reveal sources of waste and encourage owners to take remedial action. Some substitutes for electricity generated by oil or gas, such as solar and wind energy, have a good potential in parts of Egypt in a number of applications. This list can be further increased by conducting focused research on opportunities for energy substitution and efficiency.

Gas Exports: A Success Story so far

Egypt's plans for gas exports were formulated in the 1990s on the back of the convincing expansion of reserves that the country has experienced. Israel was initially regarded as the most likely market for Egyptian pipeline gas exports, in addition to Jordan and the Palestinian Territories. Furthermore, the possibility of trading Egyptian gas for Libyan oil was also mooted, though tentatively because of the costs the necessary infrastructure would have involved and the volatile preferences of the Libyan side. In terms of LNG, the most advanced option was to supply Turkey with up to 10 Bcm/yr from 2000, as stipulated in the memorandum of understanding (MoU) concluded between both sides in 1996.[29]

Although these plans did not all materialise, or only did so slowly and partially, it is safe to note that Egypt still made a laudable achievement in developing a promising gas export industry and becoming, over a reasonably short period of time, a key gas player and a potential hub in the Mediterranean (Figure 4.11). By 2006, it had successfully commissioned two phases of the Arab Gas Pipeline (AGP), which links it to the Mashreq markets (see Chapter 5), and three LNG trains with a total nameplate capacity of 12.7 mtpa. Egypt is now the EU's sixth largest natural gas supplier, and in 2009 it shipped over 18 Bcm of gas to customers in no less than twenty countries (Figure 4.12).

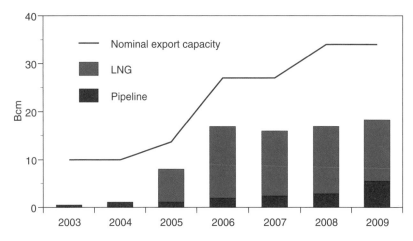

Figure 4.11: Egypt's Natural Gas Exports, 2003–2009

Sources: BP, Cedigaz and own estimates

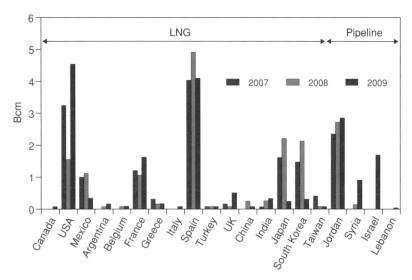

Figure 4.12: Egypt's Natural Gas Exports by Destination

Sources: BP (2010) and Cedigaz

Besides generating additional foreign exchange revenue for the Egyptian treasury (Figure 4.13),[30] gas exports helped attract sizable foreign investment flows into the country's upstream gas business and secure increased production. However, gas exports soon became a source of political controversy in Egypt, as well as a cause of uncertainty about the availability of sufficient reserves to meet growing export commitments over and above the booming needs of the domestic market. This has had far-reaching gas policy implications in Egypt, ranging from the revision of upstream and downstream pricing terms to the promulgation of a moratorium on new export projects until 2010.

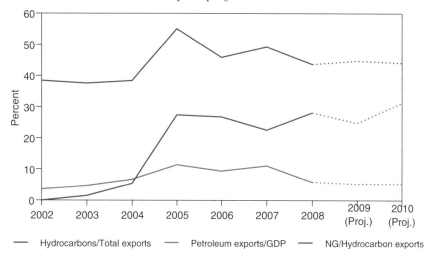

Figure 4.13: Hydrocarbons in the Egyptian Economy

Sources: Central Bank of Egypt, IMF and own estimates

Egypt's gas export success is partly the result of the marketing strategy it adopted early in the process. Pricing decisions within the supply contracts concluded with Unión Fenosa, Jordan and Israel were central to this strategy. It is said that the price to Unión Fenosa was initially very low. The highest number mentioned by observers of the Egyptian gas scene was $0.90/MMBtu. Lower numbers, such as $0.65/MMBtu are sometimes quoted. This is the price at the point of entry to the LNG plant. If these numbers are gross underestimates, EGPC/EGAS would be wise to publish the true figures in order to set the record straight. The government was for a long time reluctant to renegotiate on the grounds that it will have a negative impact on foreign companies' willingness to invest in Egypt. It seems, however, that some price adjustments were achieved.

It is true that in compensation for the low selling price EGPC/ EGAS have benefited from some advantages such as delayed payment of their equity share in the LNG plant and the right to use up to 50 percent of the facility for their own exports under a tolling agreement. But what is the value of these advantages compared to the assumed loss on every unit of gas sold?

The sale price to Jordan is said to be set at $1.50/MMBtu, which is a more reasonable number. Yet, one needs to keep in mind that Egypt purchases gas at the margin from foreign investors at a higher price depending on the concession and the position of the acreage. To say that it gets 60–70 percent profit gas at zero price and that the average cost of acquisition is therefore much lower than the purchase price is the wrong argument. As discussed elsewhere,[31] in the case of oil the equity oil is a rent for the state not necessarily a fund to subsidise domestic consumption or exports.

Furthermore, it is interesting to note a peculiarity in the agreement with BG for the development of gas fields dedicated to exports. There is a clause stating that if the netback revenue falls below the price at which the gas would be sold to EGPC for domestic use, EGPC would compensate the investor for the difference. Given that the investor was keen on the export option, the notion that they should be compensated whenever the domestic market becomes more attractive is intriguing, while the fact that the Egyptian government was prepared to make such concession is an indication of the thinking behind its early export strategy.

However, the fact remains that Egypt entered the world gas market at a time of expansion, and now has a share in it. The construction of the LNG trains was completed in record time. Furthermore, as mentioned earlier, the marketing of spot cargos has been competent. We also have to allow for the factors that may have influenced the negotiations of the initial contracts – a multiplicity of objectives that were to be achieved all at the same time. Hence, perhaps, certain concessions on prices were made which may not have been the case given other circumstances.

LNG

There are two LNG plants in Egypt; one in Damietta, west of Port Said and the other in Idku, east of Alexandria. Both operate as tolling facilities, whereby the contractor constructs, owns and operates the plants in return for a processing fee from the upstream suppliers who retain ownership of the gas through the liquefaction process. The plant at Damietta, developed by the Spanish-Egyptian Gas Company

(SEGAS) for $1.3 billion, is a single-train complex with a capacity of 5.5 mtpa. SEGAS is a joint venture between Spanish utility Unión Fenosa (40 percent), ENI (40 percent), and the Egyptian NOCs EGPC and EGAS (20 percent). Unión Fenosa is the main off-taker of output from Damietta, having under a 25-year tolling agreement with SEGAS committed to lifting 3.2 mtpa to supply its power plants in Spain. The remainder of the plant's capacity is booked by EGAS, which is also its main feedstock supplier from the grid.

As soon as the first train was commissioned in January 2005, an agreement was signed between BP and SEGAS' shareholders for the construction of a second 5 mtpa train based on the former's reserves.[32] However, the implementation of the MoU has been held up by concerns over gas supply issues, given that new reserves were considered barely sufficient to meet growing domestic demand. Yet, in early 2009, the Egyptian government seemed to have given its long-awaited approval for a second Damietta train, only to find that international economic and market conditions had led BP and ENI in particular to put their plans on hold.[33] The fact that the Damietta plant lacks dedicated equity gas supplies from its shareholders and relies on EGAS for the bulk of its feedgas was an issue at the project-financing stage of the existing train,[34] meant that the facility has been running at around 50–60 percent of its capacity, and is likely to remain a major hurdle for its expansion plans.

Unlike Damietta, the $1.9 billion plant at Idku is an integrated LNG project supplied by dedicated offshore reserves and has faced no such feedstock restrictions.[35] The facility consists of two 3.6 mtpa trains (ELNG1 and ELNG2), each with a slightly different ownership structure. ELNG1, which came online in May 2005, is operated by a joint venture between BG (35.5 percent), Malaysia's Petronas (35.5 percent), EGPC/EGAS (24 percent), and GDF (5 percent). Under a 20-year sales and purchase agreement concluded in 2002, GDF lifts the entire output of the first train. ELNG2, which is owned by BG (38 percent), Petronas (38 percent), and EGPC/EGAS (24 percent), started commercial operations nine months ahead of schedule in September 2005 and its production is committed in its entirety to BG Gas Marketing for delivery to Italy and elsewhere in the Atlantic Basin. Plans for a third train at Idku have been put forward by BG, but similar supply concerns to Damietta have so far precluded their realisation.[36]

The Arab Gas Pipeline[37]

The first section of the AGP project, running from El-Arish in the Sinai to the Jordanian port of Aqaba, was inaugurated in July 2003, marking the start of gas exports by Egypt. Initial deliveries of gas to Jordan's 650MW Aqaba power station through this 36in/250km pipeline were at a rate of 1.1 Bcm/yr. The gas sales agreement finalised by Egypt and Jordan in 2001 provides for preferential pricing for the latter, believed to be around $1.5/MMBtu, and a take-or-pay clause for 90 percent of the DCQ guaranteed by the Jordanian government for 30 years from 2003. The AGP has a design capacity of 10 Bcm/yr, and at full flow it is expected to deliver 4.2 Bcm/yr to Jordan.

The second phase of the AGP project extended the pipeline to the northern Jordanian city of Al Rehab, at the Syrian border, and was commissioned in January 2006. This section is operated on a BOOT basis for 30 years, and has allowed the supply of additional volumes of gas to other Jordanian power plants at Al Rehab and Al Samra, as well as to other industrial users. This was followed by a third phase, completed in early 2008,[38] which extended the AGP across Syria from the 750MW Deir Ali power station to Al Rayan gas compressor station near Homs. Deliveries to Syria began belatedly in July 2008 and are expected to increase from 900 million cm/yr to 2.2 Bcm/yr by 2013. More than a year later (in October 2009), Lebanon started receiving gas through a spur from Homs to the city of Tripoli and, under a 15-year swap agreement concluded in September 2009 between EGPC/EGAS and the Syrian Petroleum Company (SPC), it is expected to receive 600 million cm/yr of Syrian gas in lieu of Egyptian gas delivered to Syria.

There are plans to extend the AGP further north into Turkey and eventually supply the planned Nabucco gas system with 2–4 Bcm/yr, but it remains uncertain whether Egypt will have enough gas to achieve such an objective in the short term. It may be the case that the connection with Turkey would instead be used to transport gas into Egypt if and when it will need it. This is why it is also hoped that the AGP will in future be connected to the Iraqi gas grid, with a view to supplying Mashreq and European markets from Iraq's Akkas field.[39] These plans may seem far-fetched in the present circumstances, but regional governments and some IOCs are proceeding with the putting in place of framework agreements to help materialise these arrangements. This is the case of the Egyptian government, which in 2009 signed a MoU with Iraq,[40] and of Italy's ENI, which concluded a strategic framework agreement with the Egyptian government in August 2010, paving the way for the company to acquire transport capacity in the AGP and benefit from the eventuality of Egypt emerging as a possible gas hub in the Mediterranean.[41]

Exports to Israel and the Moratorium

Meaningful talks over an Israel–Egypt gas supply project began in early 2000, but by September they had all but collapsed following the eruption of the second Palestinian Intifada, which led to a strain in diplomatic relations between the two countries. However, East Mediterranean Gas (EMG), an Egyptian-Israeli consortium charged with the construction and operation of the subsea pipeline that would link Egypt's El Arish to Ashkelon in Israel, was successfully set up prior to the interruption of negotiations.[42] After a hiatus that lasted until 2005, when the Israeli withdrawal from Gaza eased somewhat the political logjam in the region, the project was back on track with the signing of both an intergovernmental agreement in June 2005 and a SPA between EMG and the Israel Electricity Company (IEC) for the supply of 1.7 Bcm/yr of gas for 15 years from 2008. The arrangements provided for Israeli imports of Egyptian gas potentially to reach 7 Bcm/yr.

EMG completed its 100 km gasline in 2008 and deliveries of Egyptian gas to IEC began on 1 May. The controversy that ensued soon brought to the fore the issue of the price paid for the gas by Israeli end-users, which was widely believed to have been below the Egyptian domestic gas price, let alone market levels.[43] The protests that followed, both public and within parliament, led the Egyptian government to announce in June 2008 a moratorium on new gas export deals, as well as a review of prices in all long-term supply agreements. Although international market conditions and the appraisal of domestic needs were invoked by the government, the move is widely believed to have been aimed at assuaging public anger over the Israel export deal. Public opinion in Egypt may be opposed to the principle of selling gas to Israel, but the government, under some pressure from the USA, was always prepared to proceed with export plans.

A year later, exports to Israel were resumed following the revision of contractual terms to provide for a higher price to Israeli buyers. Under the new pricing terms, these are said to be charged between $4–5/MMBtu for volumes delivered by EMG,[44] which in turn pays the Egyptian government $3–3.5/MMBtu.[45] Israeli gas demand is set to increase in the coming years, mainly as a result of the conversion to gas of a number of IEC power plants, but it is unclear how much of the 7 Bcm/yr capacity Israel will need to import in the medium term, given the potential of the Tamar field discovery to satisfy the country's future gas needs.

The moratorium, which is due to expire in 2010, in its current conception is almost irrelevant to Egypt's future gas exports. These depend, first and foremost, on the country's reserve base and the growth rate of domestic consumption. The current moratorium policy is of little effect on both fronts. What matters are the government's investment terms, its institutional efficiency and its ability to rationalise domestic demand. Furthermore, the Egyptian government says that the moratorium only applies to its share of production, but if it is to extend the PSA model based on the recent agreement with BP/RWE Dea to other concessions (old or new), then the policy becomes even more redundant because Egyptian NOCs' share of gas output will increasingly account for a small proportion of total production.

Outlook: Where to next?

There is no doubt that Egypt has made a remarkable achievement in developing its gas industry, from modest levels twenty years ago, into a flourishing and dynamic sector of the economy. It has succeeded in attracting the industry's main players, which have helped it consolidate a reasonably significant reserve base through long-term commitment and sizeable investments into the prolific offshore frontiers in the Mediterranean and Nile Delta. With the increasing output, the government was able to encourage the expansion of a domestic gas market, driven by the power generation sector and a large industrial base – both crucial to the country's economic growth and improved living conditions of the population. This has been complemented by an important gas-export industry, which has allowed Egypt to secure a timely share in the growing global LNG market, place itself as a potential pipeline hub in the eastern Mediterranean, and benefit from much-needed foreign exchange flows.

However, Egypt's gas market faces a number of challenges with a potentially defining impact on its future development. Chief amongst these is the booming domestic demand for gas and the concomitant issue of subsidised gas (and energy) prices for domestic users. Besides their fiscal and economic implications, Egypt's subsidy policies can have an increasingly constraining effect on upstream gas activities, especially if PSA terms and the price caps for the IOC supplies allocated to the domestic market remain unchanged. This is particularly pertinent in view of the fact that future production is expected to come from deep and ultra-deep offshore reserves, which involve significantly higher development costs and advanced technology. Besides subsidies, institutional efficiency and competence will have an increasingly direct bearing on Egypt's gas market, as important government decisions will need to be made and EGPC/EGAS will want to develop more expertise if they are to complement foreign input into the country's gas industry.

Tentative Projections to 2020

So far, the Egyptian government has shown a degree of flexibility in dealing with some of the challenges facing the country's gas market, but it has tended to do so in a reactive manner, usually when finding itself the subject of market or IOC pressure. Based on recent trends and current market conditions, projections of supply and demand can be put forward but with important provisos about policy (subsidies, PSA terms, exports), investment (upstream and downstream), and reserves.

Estimates of future gas demand in Egypt take into account the government's own projections for growth in the power generation, in-dustrial and other sectors. Changes in the subsidy policy would certainly affect these projections, but not only is it impossible to foresee what the government policy in this respect will be in future, it is also safe to assume that electricity tariffs are likely to be maintained at artificially low levels to avoid added inflationary pressure. With the population expected to increase to just under 100 million by 2020, demand for power is set to continue growing unabated. Thus, based on government plans for the expansion of the power generation and petrochemical industries, for the connection of households to the grid, and for the use of CNG in the transport sector, demand for gas is expected to reach 60 Bcm in 2015 and just under 80 Bcm in 2020, with the power sector's share increasing to 64 percent later in the forecast period (Figure 4.14).

In terms of supply, again based on the current government policies and market conditions, a field-by-field analysis suggests that production growth is likely to slow down until 2014/15 when a string of new fields in the Mediterranean and the Western Desert is expected to come on stream and compensate for declining output from existing fields. It is clear that changes in PSA terms and pricing policies would have a significant impact on investment in both existing and future concessions, but at the time of writing there is no visibility on the extent to which the Egyptian government may introduce new incentives for foreign investors. As a result, gas production in Egypt is expected to increase by an average annual rate of 4 percent over the forecast period, reaching 80 Bcm in 2015 and just under 100 Bcm in 2020.

If these projections of supply and demand prove accurate, there is unlikely to be any meaningful increase in *Egyptian* gas exports over the coming decade. Future production will at best be sufficient to maintain current levels of exports against growing domestic consumption and

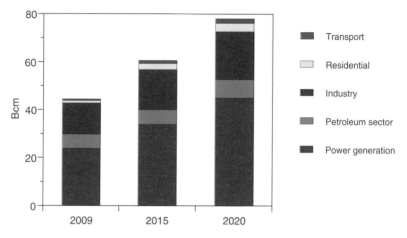

Figure 4.14: Egypt: Projected Gas Demand to 2020

Source: Cedigaz

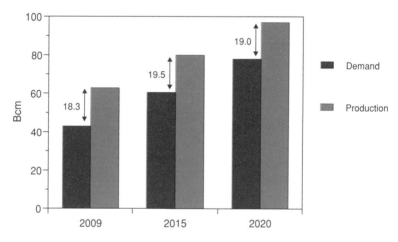

Figure 4.15: Egypt's Gas Balance to 2020

Source: Cedigaz and own estimates

at worst fall just short of meeting export and domestic requirements to 2014–15 (Figure 4.15), which may mean that external supplies of gas may be resorted to in Egypt over this period to offset a possible deficit. However, to reiterate, the potential for new discoveries in the offshore eastern Mediterranean and the underexplored Western Desert areas remains significant, and a great deal will depend on new reserves, government policies and foreign investment.

Conclusion

Having experienced significant advances over the last twenty years, Egypt's natural gas market is faced with rather more challenging times ahead. There are numerous questions about the impact of government policies on the optimisation of the exploitation of the country's gas resources. While there may be no 'gas crisis' in Egypt, there is certainly an acute fiscal problem and an even higher economic cost incurred as a result of government policies in the gas sector. Despite this, it is not clear whether the government will be able, any time soon, to come to terms in a meaningful way with the longstanding issue of domestic energy price subsidies. Politics and institutional inefficiency, which have been the main impediments to doing so since the 1970s, will continue to constitute the main obstacles in the face of the flickering will amongst decision-makers to deal with the issue. The onus is on the government to address Egypt's energy issues; to show political courage in dealing with foreign investors, domestic constituencies and the many stakeholders in the energy sector; and finally to reconcile the important objectives of helping the poor while ensuring a more efficient allocation of resources.

Even if gas prices are adjusted, it is not clear to what extent this will be extended to the power sector, and whether electricity tariffs will be affected as a result. Besides, regardless of pricing issues, it seems that demand for power will show no signs of abating owing to the expected economic and population growth. This means that gas consumption will continue growing too, putting ever more pressure on supply. In turn, this will translate into a more restricted room for the expansion of exports, despite the IOCs' exploration drive and the government's need for foreign exchange revenue. The moratorium will have had no impact on this situation, as it seems that the only purpose it served was that of assuaging the public outcry over the export of gas to Israel at a relatively low price. Whether or not it is lifted at the end of 2010, this policy will not in its current form have a meaningful impact on the prospects for Egyptian gas exports. These will continue to hinge on the country gas balance, which is intrinsically linked to the government's upstream and downstream policies over and above the size of the reserve base.

Notes

1   The section on subsidies is written by Robert Mabro and is based on and updates previous work by the author on the subject. See Mabro, R., 1998, 'The Pricing of Natural Gas: A Discussion of Pricing Policy in Egypt'.

2 For more details on the development of Egypt's domestic gas market, see Alami, R., 2006, 'Egypt's Domestic Natural Gas Industry'.

3 Like most food and other 'public good' products, energy products are heavily subsidised in Egypt. On average, energy subsidies account for around 70% of total subsidies and about 20–25% of government spending. In the fiscal year 2008/9, they amounted to $10 billion. See below for more details.

4 77.2 Tcf in 2009 and 12.4 Tcf in 1989. Other sources, namely the *Oil & Gas Journal* and Wood Mackenzie, a consultancy, have a lower estimate of 1638 Bcm for Egypt's proven gas reserves as at 1 January 2010.

5 *The Oil & Gas Journal*, 19 May 2010.

6 *Arab Oil and Gas Directory*, 2009, p.118.

7 Wood Mackenzie, 2009, *Egypt Country Overview*, p.36.

8 In 1987, Egypt had a serious foreign debt problem, which forced the government to sign a structural adjustment programme with the IMF. The World Bank had advised that gas could be used for domestic needs and free up petroleum products which can be used to earn foreign exchange through exports.

9 Wood Mackenzie, 2009, Ibid., p.43.

10 Production costs in offshore concessions at depths below 1000 meters are estimated to be in the range of $2–3.5/MMBtu.

11 *Middle East Economic Survey [MEES]*, 17 March 2008.

12 The fields are estimated to contain 140 Bcm of wet gas.

13 *World Gas Intelligence [WGI]*, 26 May 2010.

14 In 2009, delayed payments to only three of the largest international producers were estimated at over $2 billion (*MEES*, 9 March 2009; *WGI*, 10 February 2010).

15 GASCO, Egypt's grid operator, plans to deliver gas to 5.5 million households by 2015 (EGAS, 2009, Annual Report 2007–08).

16 EEHC, Annual Report 2008–09

17 These are the Sidi Krir, Port Said East and Suez Gulf plants. For more details on Egypt's experience with IPPs, see: Eberhard, A. and Gratwick, K., 2005, 'The Egyptian IPP Experience'.

18 *African Energy*, 8 May 2009.

19 Around 40% of the Egyptian population lives below or just above the poverty line ($2/day).

20 From an average of $¢2.2/KWh to $¢2.4/KWh (World Bank, 2009, 'Project Appraisal Document on a Proposed Loan …').

21 Within the same decree, electricity prices were hiked to $¢6.3/KWh, $¢4.6/KWh, and $¢3.8/KWh for ultra-high, high and medium voltage consumers, respectively.

22 This risks being a highly controversial election, as a frail Hosni Mubarak is not expected to run for office again, but is widely believed to have plans for his son Gamal to take over as president. Opposition movements are deeply resentful of this prospect and are attempting to form a united front ahead of the election.

23 Egyptian Ministry of Finance, 2010, 'Financial Statement on the State's

Draft General Budget for the Fiscal Year 2010–11'.

24 LPG (butane) canisters are widely used in Egypt, mainly for cooking and heating in poor households not yet connected to the grid. At just under $0.5/12.5 kg cylinder, their retail price is about a tenth of delivery cost, and Egypt is one of the world's largest importers of LPG.

25 Gerner, F. and Sinclair, S., 2006, 'Connecting Residential Households to Natural Gas'.

26 It seems that in line with this proposal, but entirely independently, Egypt has adopted an approach that records the implicit energy subsidies as an explicit item of public expenditure in the government budget.

27 Gerner, F. and Sinclair, S., 2006, Ibid.

28 Gerner and Sinclair, 2006, Ibid., p. 21.

29 *Arab Oil and Gas Directory*, 1998, p.105.

30 Between 2005 and 2009, the proceeds of natural gas exports averaged $3 billion per year, representing just under 30 % of total petroleum exports, with LNG sales accounting for the bulk of these revenues (Figure 4.13).

31 Mabro, R.,1998, Ibid.

32 The Damietta site can accommodate up to four trains of similar capacity.

33 *MEES*, 30 March 2009; *WGI*, 4 November 2009.

34 *MEES*, 18 August 2003.

35 Feedgas for the Idku trains comes from the BG-operated West Delta Deep Marine (WDDM) concession offshore the Nile Delta (see Map 4.1).

36 At some point, it was reported that BG considered using its gas find in the offshore Gaza field to supply part of the requirements for a third Idku train (*MEES*, 21 November 2005).

37 For more details on this, see Chapter 5.

38 The first two sections of the AGP were built by Egyptian companies at a cost of $530 million. The Syrians contracted Russia's Stroytransgaz to build the third section at a cost of $300 million.

39 Akkas is located in the Anbar province, northwest of Baghdad, close to the Syrian border and is thought to contain proven reserves of 60 Bcm, with probable reserves of around 200 Bcm.

40 *International Gas Report [IGR]*, 25 May 2009.

41 *WGI*, 4 August 2010.

42 EMG is now owned by Mediterranean Gas Pipeline Limited (28 %), Thailand's PTT (25 %), Ampal-American Israel Corporation (12.5 %), the US investors Samuel Sell and David Fischer (12 %), EGAS (10 %), Mehav Group (8.1 %), and Merhav Ampal Energy Holdings (4.4 %) (*AOGD*, 2009, p.124).

43 Estimates vary between $1.50 and $2.75/MMBtu.

44 *IGR*, 8 June 2009.

45 *MEES*, 22 June 2009.

CHAPTER 5

THE MASHREQ, ISRAEL AND
THE PALESTINIAN TERRITORIES

Andrew Cleary

Introduction

This study of the domestic and somewhat interrelated natural gas markets in Syria, Lebanon, Jordan, Israel and the Palestinian Territories will show that these countries have significant similarities – each suffers from a shortage of available gas, largely due to insufficient market incentives and an absence of energy strategies. Geology, though a factor, is not the most important explanation for natural gas shortages in these countries.

Challenges in the development of natural gas markets in each of the countries addressed in this chapter are diverse. In the case of Israel/Palestine, issues include complex politics and security matters, in addition to market players that have become accustomed to low-price natural gas.

Jordan, while having a record of political stability that sets it apart in the region, lacks significant indigenous hydrocarbon resources. Although the country produces a small amount of natural gas for use in electricity generation, Jordan's natural gas position in the region is primarily as a host to transit infrastructure.

Lebanon is more marginal to the regional gas picture. There is no shortage of talk in government and business circles as to the positive role natural gas could play in alleviating debilitating electricity shortages. However, in spite of its participation in the Arab Gas Pipeline (AGP) project to supply Egyptian gas to Syria, Lebanon and Jordan, Lebanon only commenced imports via a spur from the AGP in Syria to the northern city of Tripoli in October 2009.[1]

Syria is perhaps the most interesting subject for investigating the role and place of natural gas in the Levant. It has by far the largest population of the countries in this chapter, and a 25-year history of hydrocarbon exploration and production. Syria, however, is a difficult

*   The author offers his thanks and appreciation to Richard Kupisz, and particularly to Janet Brewer and Jim Deacons for their assistance and support throughout the research and writing of this chapter.

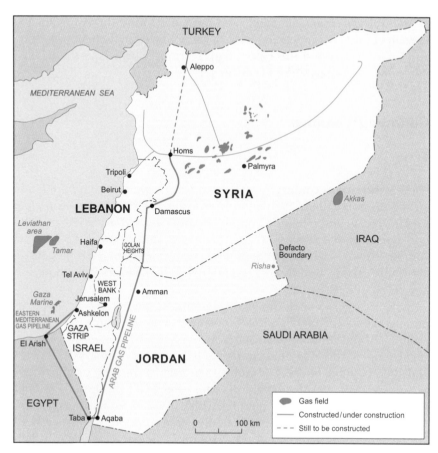

Map 5.1: The Mashreq, Israel and the Palestinian Territories: Gas Fields and Pipelines

analytical subject and due to a lack of consistent and reliable data can be something of a 'black box'. The country suffers from an under-performing bureaucracy, issues with corruption, and an absence of transparent legal structures. Basic statistics that are available in most countries are often absent or flawed. In relation to other countries studied in this chapter, Syria is unique in the extent of these difficulties.

Additionally, in all of the countries being addressed in this chapter, the most important source of demand for natural gas is electricity generation, demand that in all countries is growing rapidly. Expanding use of natural gas as fuel for electricity generation is consistently linked to electricity markets in the region.

This chapter is intended to provide a general overview of natural gas markets in each of these countries. It addresses the characteristics of natural gas supply, demand, and potential future directions for gas in each country, commencing with Syria, followed by Lebanon, Jordan, and finally Israel and the Palestinian Territories (which in the case of this study is primarily the Gaza Strip).

Country Dynamics

Syria

Syria is the largest country examined in this chapter. With a population of slightly more than 20 million, Syria has a larger population than Jordan, Israel, and Lebanon combined, and over a third of the population is less than 14 years of age.[2] A young and growing population, combined with sustained economic growth (measuring 4.8 percent in 2008[3]), is driving rapidly increasing energy demand. Supply, however, has failed to keep pace.

Syria is largely a state-directed economy, in spite of recent and continuing economic liberalisation. Consistent with the state's preeminent position in the economy, the state-owned Syrian Petroleum Company (SPC) and Syrian Gas Company (SGC) are the primary producers and interlocutors in the gas sector. The SPC primarily produces gas as a byproduct of oil production, while the SGC produces gas both independently and via joint ventures with private sector partners (IOCs).

Previously, the organisation of the state-sponsored hydrocarbons businesses placed the SGC in the position of being, technically, a division of the SPC. In February 2009, however, by presidential decree, a new body was established to supervise the preexisting state-company structure. The decree created the 'General Organization of Oil' (GOO), as well as the 'General Organization for Oil Refinery and Distribution of Petroleum Products' (GOORDPP). Most relevant for this chapter is the GOO, which was created with the aim of supervising upstream operations of the SPC and the SGC. Critically from the perspective of foreign firms, the GOO is meant to be the primary interlocutor for negotiating future Production Sharing Agreements (PSAs) with IOCs.[4] The newly formed GOORDPP is charged with supervising downstream activities in the sector, including construction of new oil refineries.[5]

Supply and Demand

BP's *Statistical Review of World Energy* reports that Syria's reserves of natural gas amount to 280 Bcm. In 2008, Syria produced 5.5 Bcm of natural gas,[6] which equates to a reserve to production ratio of just under 52 years. By the end of 2010, production had been projected to rise to 13.5 Bcm/yr,[7] though at the time of writing 10 Bcm/yr was a more likely figure.[8] This increase will be largely due to joint ventures with foreign companies. Table 5.1 shows Syrian production, consumption and imports of gas.

Table 5.1: Syrian Gas Production (not including vented/reinjected/flared gas), Demand, and Imports, 2000 (actual), 2008 (estimate/actual), 2015 (projected by author), Bcm

	2000	*2008*	*2015*
Production	5.5	5.5	12.0
Demand	5.5	6.0	16.0
Imports	0.0	0.5	2.2
Estimated unmet demand	0.0	1.0	1.8

Sources: BP *Statistical Review of World Energy* 2009; Albert Aji, 'Syrian Oil Minister: Egypt will begin exporting natural gas to Syria next month', Associated Press, 23 February 2008

Even with new developments coming online through the 2009–2010 period, a substantial gap between supply and demand is only likely to close for a period of 2–3 years. Some forecasts have suggested a supply-demand gap re-emerging by 2015, possibly rising to 20 Bcm thereafter.[9] Cumbersome state planning, an absence of energy strategy, difficulty attracting foreign investment (a 2007 offshore bidding round received bids for only one of the four blocks offered[10]), and a shortage of domestic capital, all contribute to ongoing energy shortages in Syria.

The EIA reports that the 2005 primary energy mix in the country was 69 percent oil, 26 percent natural gas and 4 percent hydroelectricity.[11] With declining (and low quality) crude oil production and an ongoing severe drought affecting hydroelectric production, natural gas' relative and absolute importance is increasing.

Half of Syrian natural gas production is associated with oil, with flaring and venting widespread in oil-related operations. A lack of collection and distribution infrastructure is a major hindrance to bringing additional natural gas to market. Additionally there is no residential natural gas distribution system in Syria. Home heating is accomplished either with electric heaters, or with small diesel-fueled furnaces common in most households. Cooking is largely based on locally produced LPG.

There is also a lack of pipeline infrastructure to bring associated gas from new oil plays to market. Primary generation and industrial facilities are connected directly or by spur to the main north–south and east–west pipeline axes, converging near the central city of Homs (site of a large petroleum refinery).

Syrian natural gas utilisation statistics are complex. Reports vary as to how much of Syria's natural gas production is flared, vented and/ or reinjected for enhanced oil recovery (EOR). The EIA estimates that venting, flaring and reinjection account for 25 percent of Syrian gas demand.[12] This is not included in the approximately 5.5 Bcm of annual Syrian production that BP reports (implying approximately 1.8 Bcm of reinjected gas).[13] Moreover, the use of gas for EOR is expected to increase as measures are undertaken to maintain oil production in the 380,000 b/d range, particularly if oil continues to enjoy a (per Btu) price premium.[14] A 2006 report quoted a Shell official as stating that Al Furat Petroleum Company (AFPC) could use 1 trillion cubic feet (28.5 Bcm) of natural gas for EOR if it were available.[15]

Of the 5.5 Bcm of production directed to non-EOR consumption, industrial customers account for approximately one-third (2 Bcm) of the total. The Homs oil refinery, a cement plant and fertiliser facilities are the primary sources of industrial demand. The remaining 3.5 Bcm of domestic supply is used for power generation, recently supplemented by 0.9 Bcm of Egyptian gas from the Arab Gas Pipeline (AGP). Electrical generation, therefore, accounts for approximately 75 percent of non-EOR consumption in Syria, and is the primary source of demand growth.

Increased domestic supply will go some way to alleviating chronic electricity shortages, but disequilibrium is expected to reemerge, with supply likely stagnating at around 15 Bcm/yr at best in the mid-2010s. This estimate is, however, highly contingent, and the gap could potentially be higher depending on policy choices made by the Syrian government. To reduce the projected supply-demand gap, policy changes, such as more attractive PSA terms for IOCs, would have to be dramatic.

Electricity

The EIA estimates that approximately half of Syria's generating plant is natural gas fired.[16] Electricity demand was growing by between 7 and 11 percent per annum in the years leading up to 2008,[17] and the Syrian government has embarked on a programme of converting heavy-oil plants to natural gas, and building new gas-fired facilities to meet growing demand. Insufficient natural gas to meet demand from the power sector is a major cause of power outages across the country.

Scheduled and unscheduled electricity cuts are common throughout

Syria, particularly in the coldest months of the winter and the warmest months of the summer. While not at the level of severity and regularity encountered in Lebanon (see below), power shortages and insufficient, dilapidated infrastructure are major brakes on the Syrian economy. In the first half of 2009, both scheduled and unscheduled power cuts lasting two hours per day or more were common.[18]

If electricity demand continues to grow rapidly, near or above double-digit rates, significant additional sources of natural gas will be necessary, as Syria lacks other viable options for large-scale electricity generation. Indeed, new natural gas-fired generating stations continue to be built[19] without any clear indication that sufficient natural gas will be available to fuel them.

IOCs

IOCs play a major role in the Syrian petroleum sector. The common perception of Syria as a country isolated from global commerce does not entirely match the realities of the oil and gas sector in the country. IOCs operating in Syria include Royal Dutch Shell, through its AFPC joint venture, CNPC, ONGC, Suncor (formerly Petro-Canada), Total, Russia's Stroytransgaz,[20] and several smaller (mainly oil-producing) companies.

Though, as detailed below, there are many international companies active in Syria, the country does not offer a transparent, efficient legal framework in which to operate. A lack of institutional capacity in the government, allegations of corruption and an absence of market signals, are significant obstacles to additional investment by IOCs in Syria (as well as effective independent analysis of the sector). There is neither a standardised approach to PSAs in Syria, nor an operational state strategy for natural gas (or other energy) exploration and production. Predictability for commercial operators in Syria is based solely on PSAs, and is not backed by robust domestic judicial and legislative structures. Investment risk is significant and the market is relatively small.

While the country is lacking in terms of rule of law and transparency, a strong police state does foster an environment where physical risks to corporate assets and individual security are less significant than in other countries in the region. Foreigners working in the oil and gas sector in Syria are not relegated to compound-only living, and have significant mobility and a reasonable quality of life if based in the capital, Damascus. Though regional and global politics often paint Syria as an insecure location, terrorism or other risks to physical security have historically been much greater in Yemen, Algeria, or even Egypt.

Strong interpersonal relationships with those in positions of authority are critical to successfully operating in Syria. The oldest, and by most accounts strongest, relationship between the Syrian government and an IOC is that forged by Shell over twenty years ago. AFPC is the oldest and largest of the joint ventures with foreign companies operating in Syria. AFPC was originally established in 1985 as a JV between the SPC (50 percent share), Shell (15.6 percent), Pecten Syria Petroleum (15.6 percent), and Deminex (18.8 percent). After purchasing the stake that then-independent Petro-Canada had come to own in 2002, ONGC of India and CNPC became significant players in Syria with a joint purchase of the Canadian company's 17 percent stake.[21] Al Furat is the largest producer of oil and gas in the country, with approximately 100,000 b/d of oil production[22] (down from 405,000 b/d in the mid 1990s)[23] and consequentially produces a large share of Syria's marketed associated natural gas.

Illustrating the idiosyncrasies of operating in the country, AFPC's production has been limited by a 1988 political decision to hurriedly expand production of the 400 million barrel Omar field, which had been discovered the year before. When Shell was compelled by the government to increase production from an initial rate of 55,000 b/d to 100,000 in short order, resulting in extensive reservoir damage, a 2008 article on the subject of the SPC's larger fields commented:

> Now, Omar produces less than 10,000 b/d from natural pressure (compared to about 15,000 b/d in March 2000), and about 20,000 b/d from pressure induced by water injection. By late 2005, it had been said that for every two barrels of water injected, one barrel of oil has been extracted.[24]

It should be noted by way of understanding the priority the state places on oil and gas extraction, that water is an extremely and increasingly scarce resource in Syria, particularly in the east where much of the hydrocarbons exploration and extraction takes place. Indeed, a February 2010 report in the *Financial Times* indicated that some Syrian farmers are so short of water that 'local sewage is the irrigator', and '40,000 to 60,000 families (have been) forced to migrate in search of alternative employment'.[25]

Processing capacity for associated gas production from Omar and the nearby Al Izba field is 2.4 Bcm/yr.[26] Sources indicate that this plant, as of mid-2009, is operating at full capacity. It is likely that Omar is operating at its maximum production rate in order to rapidly deplete the existing resources base, and thus have available future processing capacity should the nearby Akkas field, over the border in Iraq, be developed. Syria is eager to leverage its geographical position to become a regional transportation and processing hub, and using existing infrastructure to process Iraqi production is a key element of that goal.

Total is another major operator in Syria. Through its Deir Ez Zor venture with the SPC, Total operates a natural gas collection, treatment and gathering system in the eastern desert.[27] Additional production by Total amounts to 29,000 b/d of oil. In September 2008, Total CEO Christophe de Margerie accompanied French President Nicholas Sarkozy on a state visit to Syria, and signed an extension of the Deir Ez Zor licence through 2021.[28]

Suncor (which in 2009 bought Petro-Canada, including its Syrian operations) through its Ebla gas project, is projected to produce 0.8 Bcm/yr by mid-2010.[29] Ebla includes the Cherrife and ash-Sah'er fields, near the city of Palmyra, in the desert of east-central Syria.[30] The fields were originally discovered by Marathon in the 1980s, and Petro-Canada subsequently purchased Marathon's stake in a joint venture with the SPC in 2007.[31]

Stroytransgaz is also very active in Syria. In addition to its work on infrastructure related to the AGP,[32] it is responsible for the South and North Middle Area gas projects. Initial production from Abu Rabah, within the South Middle Area Project, commenced in early 2009, at an initial rate of 0.54 Bcm/yr.[33] The remainder of the South Middle Area Project will come online through 2010–2011. Including the Al-Faid and Qomqom fields, production from the project will total 1.8 Bcm/yr.[34] The North Middle Area Gas Project will eventually contribute an additional 1.1 Bcm/yr to Syrian gas production. Stroytransgas anticipates that the West Twinan, Twinan, Gal Gour, East Al Akram, and Al Harith fields will start production by the end of 2010.[35]

MOL (after its merger with INA of Croatia) is also active in the upstream Syrian gas sector, having produced 98 million cm in 2008 through its Hayan Petroleum Company venture.[36] The Hayan block, also near Palmyra, produces oil from the Jihar and Jazel fields, and additional gas production is anticipated when further infrastructure is completed. At present, natural gas is produced from two other fields in the block, Palmyra and Mustadira, which are expected to be expanded too, by 2011 with the completion of a new gas processing plant.[37]

Another smaller firm involved in Syrian E&P is Stratic Energy of Canada. Stratic is partnered with DualEx Energy International,[38] another Canadian firm, and KUFPEC (the Kuwait Foreign Petroleum Exploration Company)[39] in exploring its Block 17 concession, northeast of Damascus. The companies believe Block 17 contains a larger structure with gas-in-place of approximately 114 Bcm.[40]

Prices

Prices in Syria's natural gas market are consistently low relative to the cost of (AGP) imports, and the probable cost of future production. The role of the state, through its instruments – primarily the SGC and the SPC – is paramount. No comprehensive, reliable information on the hydrocarbons sector is available and without dramatic changes in information collection, processing and dissemination by official bodies, a market for natural gas – including functioning price signals – remains a distant prospect. In 2008 it was reported that the natural gas transfer price between the SPC and the Syrian Gas Company was between $1.10–1.20/MMBtu.

The role of the state in Syria's natural gas sector is hard to overstate. It directly or effectively controls the key consumers of natural gas in the country (industrial, refining, cement and power generation), as well as pipeline infrastructure, and a large share of the country's hydrocarbons production. Moreover, there is no third-party access to the pipeline network, which has insufficient geographic reach to capture the natural gas being produced at some oil concessions. The preponderance of state authority and control illustrates the extensive and complex changes that would be necessary for Syria to move towards a market-based structure that included price signals.

IOCs operating under PSAs have information on gas prices. However, these data remain largely private due to commercial confidentiality. Sources familiar with these contracts indicate that foreign producers operating under existing PSAs have received approximately $2.50/MMBtu for natural gas sold to the SGC. The author understands that by regional standards, IOCs have been operating under relatively generous terms. It is uncertain, though, whether or not future PSAs in Syria will contain fiscal terms that are sufficiently attractive to international operators. Given the government's desire to maintain and expand hydrocarbons production, the logic of extending relatively generous PSA terms is compelling.

Imports and Exports

Syria is situated in a strategically significant location, and its potential as a host for natural gas pipeline infrastructure serving the wider Middle East and onward to Europe has attracted attention. Adjoining major reserve-holder Iraq, and the potential transit-hub Turkey, on any likely route from the Gulf northward, and with underutilised ports on the Mediterranean, Syria's geography is a not insignificant asset. Taking advantage of its location though, will be an economic and political challenge for this still-isolated and under-resourced state.

From the perspective of the Syrian government, with insufficient indigenous energy resources to provide for its growing – but still small – economy, Syria needs to promote its place as a crossroads between the Near East and Europe.[41] The AGP has been the most significant manifestation of ambitions to host natural gas infrastructure, though Syria is host to other hydrocarbons transport infrastructure, such as the non-operational IPC pipeline between the oilfields of Kirkuk in Iraq and the Syrian port of Banyas.[42]

The AGP will be addressed in greater detail below but from a Syrian perspective, it is a pipeline system that runs from Arish in Egypt, to Taba on the coast of the Gulf of Aqaba, under the Gulf of Aqaba (to avoid Israeli territory) to Jordan, where it continues by land east of the city of Homs in central Syria,[43] linking by spur with the Deir Ali power station in the southern part of the country.[44] The system is eventually intended to connect with Turkey and onward to Europe.

The AGP is of huge importance, for the first time bringing imports to the natural gas market. In March 2008, Syria began to receive natural gas through the system. The contracted amount for the first year was to be 0.9 Bcm, an amount Syrian officials were keen to say would 'eventually' reach 2 Bcm/yr[45] (or 2.2 Bcm/yr, according to other accounts[46]). Regardless of the relatively small volumes involved, Syrian imports of Egyptian gas are critical to alleviating the electricity shortages noted above.

In 2008, Syria reportedly paid $5/MMBtu for AGP gas, plus $2/MMBtu for EGAS' transportation costs.[47] The price formula includes clauses that set a floor and a ceiling on what the buyer will pay. Natural gas from AGP is therefore extremely expensive in comparison to Syrian domestic gas.

Regional Ambitions

Syria is an important regional political actor. However, in economic terms it is less significant a country and its hydrocarbon resources are not substantial enough as to provide it with the capital urgently needed to modernise the country's industrial and transportation infrastructure, not to mention its massively under-resourced public services. These constraints led to regional economic aspirations within the Syrian leadership of making the country a hub for energy infrastructure, as well as taking advantage of relatively low labour costs to spur new industrial developments.

A primary ambition of the Syrian government and the SGC is leveraging Syria's geographical position between Iraq, Turkey and the Mediterranean to become a transport and processing hub for hydrocarbons.[48] While other countries in the region have pursued strategies of using inexpensive gas feedstock to develop gas-intensive industries, the lack of domestic resource base means that Syria is unable to execute a similar industrial strategy. What the country lacks in inexpensive or abundant feedstock it hopes to make up for, if only partially, in inexpensive labour and proximity to major markets in both Europe and the Middle East.

A May 2008 report in the government-owned *Syria Times* (translated by BBC Monitoring) commented:

> Syria enjoys a strategic position in the heart of the Middle East and is regarded as the link of three continents... The country's open position and its geographical location at the eastern end of the Mediterranean Sea provides it with an ideal channel to export refined oil and gas products to Europe via its northern neighbour Turkey.[49]

Similarly, Alexander's Oil and Gas Connections reported in October 2005:

> It is much more likely, they (foreign executives) say, that Syria will become a transit link to bring natural gas and oil from Iraq to the Mediterranean. '(Iraq's) Salah al Din field is only 80 km from Syria's (natural gas pipeline) network and it really is a huge field that Total would like to get access to,' a Damascus-based executive said.[50]

Given the proximity of the Salah al Din field (Akkas) to the Syrian border – and Syrian gas treatment and transportation infrastructure – Syrian officials have expressed enthusiastic interest in processing and transporting Akkas's potential production.[51] However, aside from the often-tumultuous Syrian–Iraqi relations, Iraq has options either to consume Akkas production domestically, or transit it to Europe via Turkey.

From the Syrian perspective, given the supply-demand disequilibrium that will likely worsen throughout the 2010s, Akkas is also an important potential source of new gas supply. However, with Iraq having reportedly committed the entire 5 Bcm/yr in potential production to supply European customers,[52] Syria would have to make a strong (and expensive) case to keep any of Akkas' production volumes for itself. This commitment, reported throughout 2008, seems somewhat premature given bidding on the field was only completed in mid-2009. Reuters reported on 30 June 2009 that Edison International was the only bidder (in conjunction with Korea Gas, Petronas, CNPC and Turkish Petroleum Corp.) to develop the field.[53]

Regional Politics

Politics constrain and define many of the gas sector dynamics in the region, particularly in Syria. American companies, for instance, are largely absent from the Syrian market due to US government sanctions and the stigmatisation of the country as a 'state sponsor of terror', in part due to its hosting the Palestinian Hamas party's leadership and Syria's ties to Lebanon's Hizbullah.

Moreover, Syria's relations with its larger, wealthier neighbour, Iraq, were fraught during the decades of Saddam Hussein's reign, and remain so to this day. Syria was a favourite target of Iraqi Prime Minister Maliki due to its alleged sheltering of militants responsible for perpetrating violent acts in Iraq.[54] Any relationship between the two countries that might lead to a partnership on the Akkas field would require a significant warming of the relationship between the governments.

Conclusions

Natural gas plays a significant role in the Syrian economy, and is poised to enhance its position as new production comes on-stream through 2010, and as the fuel is increasingly favoured for electrical generation. However, Syria has insufficient natural gas resources to use as inexpensive industrial feedstock, and attractive financial terms will be essential to ensure the necessary foreign investment to maximise the country's natural gas potential.

Natural gas serves primarily as fuel for electricity generation, and this is the sector that is expected to drive gas consumption over the course of the next decade. Enhanced reliability and availability of electricity is essential to Syria's economic development, and without sufficient natural gas supplies, chronic power shortages will continue to limit economic progress. Maximising imports of natural gas for use in power generation is thus essential for the Syrian economy.

Syria does have a role to play as a host to regional natural gas transit infrastructure. How great a role it will play depends not only on regional politics, but also on the extent to which Iraq and Egypt will wish to export natural gas by pipeline instead of as LNG.

Lebanon

Lebanon, a perennially complex country, is in many ways the most straightforward in this chapter. This is due primarily to the reality of energy scarcity in Lebanon, which has no indigenous oil or natural gas resources,[55] reserves or production. It is only connected to regional energy infrastructure by a small natural gas pipeline from Syria to Beddawi, a power generation facility near the city of Tripoli in the north of the country. The volume of natural gas from Syria to Beddawi – that started to flow from Egypt as a part of the Arab Gas Pipeline system in October 2009[56] – is small, at an estimated 0.35–0.6 Bcm/yr.[57] Table 5.2 shows details of production, demand and imports.

Table 5.2: Lebanese Gas Production, Demand, and Imports, 2000 (actual), 2008 (actual), 2015 (projected by author), Bcm

	2000	2008	2015
Production	0	0	0
Demand	0	0	1–5
Imports	0	0	0.5–2

Note: Demand figures assume dual-fired gas/oil power plants are only operated on natural gas after gas imports commence through the AGP spur from Syria.

Source: EIA Energy Profile – Lebanon

Natural gas in Lebanon, then, is on the surface a relatively simple story with no domestic production and only very small volumes being imported to a single location. There is no transmission or residential distribution network, and no major industry in an economy largely reliant on tourism, remittances from abroad, and a few key sectors such as banking.

Ironically, of the countries addressed in this chapter – countries that to varying degrees have both indigenous and imported sources of natural gas – Lebanon has, by some accounts, the most progressive potential legislative framework for energy.[58] Unfortunately though, a law formulated in a previous parliament has not been passed by the legislature. Given the characteristic uncertainty and drama of Lebanese politics, it is not certain if or when the previously proposed legislation – or something similar – might be adopted.

Electricity

Lebanon has an enormous appetite for energy, and its demand for electricity in particular is far in excess of supply. While importing oil for transportation is relatively straightforward, Lebanon relies on expensive fuel oil-fired power generation. Not only are these facilities expensive to operate, but their output is insufficient to meet electricity demand.

Previous Energy Minister Alan Tabourian commented to the Lebanese *Daily Star* in July 2009, that;

> Our power stations have a capacity of 1,500 MW while the actual need is 2,300 MW at least... We are going into an abyss. Our government has not taken any actions to improve electricity production. We need more power stations... I warned the ministers that the electricity problems will get worse if we fail to take action but no one listened.[59]

The expensive, imported fuel oil burned in Lebanon's generating facilities requires subsidies of approximately $1 billion per year,[60] a particularly enormous figure in the $28 billion Lebanese economy,[61] In 2007, for instance, state-owned Electricité du Liban (EDL) lost $1.2 billion, 70 percent of which was due to importing fuel oil for power generation.[62] EDL's finances suffer enormously from technical and commercial losses, in addition to the cost of importing fuel oil, and collection issues with customers. Building additional and more efficient generating facilities is therefore key to solving the country's energy crisis. More efficient generating plant would ideally be fired by natural gas,[63] however, aside from the aforementioned spur from Syria, Lebanon has no connections to import infrastructure.

LNG

LNG has long been discussed as an option for feeding Lebanon's power plants, both present and planned. An autumn 2006 article in the APS Review reported:

> Lebanon is to have a floating LNG receiving and regasification terminal to feed natural gas directly to the country's power stations, Energy and Water Minister Mohammad Fneish was recently quoted as saying: 'The Ministry of Energy is currently negotiating with a number of companies to establish a floating LNG plant which will convert liquified natural gas from tankers to fuel, which can then be piped to power plants.'[64]

Nearly three years later, nothing had come of this commitment, but in May 2009, it was announced that the World Bank would fund a feasibility study for an LNG import facility. The study is to be undertaken by an American company, Poten & Partners, which states the work 'will draw together a number of earlier energy plans for the Mediterranean nation that include LNG'.[65]

It is expected that this study will recommend the construction of offshore, floating regasification capacity for Lebanon. The complex interrelationship of business and politics in the country will likely lead to resistance from entrenched interests that may not benefit if LNG were to displace fuel oil in power generation. However, it is uncertain as to whether the Lebanese market is wealthy enough to afford LNG at international prices. Indeed the uncertain political and security environment in Lebanon may also lead potential export partners to question the viability of signing potential long-term supply contracts.

LNG is an attractive option for the Lebanese energy sector. Lebanon's contentious relationships with its only land neighbours – Syria and particularly Israel – makes unlikely the potential import of substantial volumes of pipeline gas (in addition to the uncertainty surrounding whether Egypt would even want to send additional volumes towards Lebanon through the AGP). For the efficiency of new CCGTs, if they were to be constructed, and for environmental reasons (particularly given recent comments by the Energy Minister favouring coal-fired generating capacity in the country[66]), natural gas in the form of LNG could be a major contributor to resolving Lebanon's energy challenges. However, the relatively higher price of LNG compared to coal may instead compel EDL – were it to make and implement strategic decisions on the future of power generation in Lebanon – to build coal-fired generating capacity. Additionally, it remains to be seen whether or not EDL and the government have the will and resources to compel strategic development in the energy sector.

Jordan

Though Jordan does not suffer from Lebanon's complete absence of indigenous natural gas resources, its resource base is very small. Currently, natural gas is produced at a single field, Risha, which feeds a 120 MW natural gas-fired electrical generation facility of the same name.[67] The producing field is located near, and indeed geologically crosses over, the Iraqi border, about 150 km from the Akkas field.[68] Production rates are so small as to merit no mention in BP's *Statistical Review of World Energy*, though EIA reports 2006 production of 0.3 Bcm from a reserve base of 6.2 Bcm.[69] The Economist Intelligence Unit indicates that 2008 production at Risha was approximately 0.2 Bcm/yr.[70] Table 5.3 shows Jordanian production, consumption and imports of gas.

Natural gas is consumed in Jordan, much like in the other countries in this study, primarily in the electricity generation sector. Also similar to the other countries featured in this chapter, the Jordanian government has prioritised natural gas for consumption in power generation. The government-owned Central Electrical Generating Company (CEGCO) has installed generating capacity of approximately 2000 MW. The

Aqaba facility in the south, with an installed capacity of 650 MW, consumes imported AGP gas (see below), as does the 360 MW generating facility at Rihab. The government has set the strategic goal of 80 percent of electricity to be generated from natural gas, but has also commenced discussions with hopes of a 2012 start for the construction of a nuclear power plant.[71]

Table 5.3: Jordanian Gas Production, Demand, and Imports, 2000 (actual), 2008 (actual), 2015 (projected by author), Bcm

	2000	*2008*	*2015*
Production	0.2	0.2	0.3
Demand	0.2	2.9	4–5
Imports	0	2.7	3.2

Sources: Economist Intelligence Unit, *Jordan Country Brief*, March 2009; BP *Statistical Review of World Energy*, 2009, 'Natural Gas: Trade Movements 2008 by pipeline'

Imports

Jordan was the first customer for natural gas from the Arab Gas Pipeline (AGP) that amounted to 2.72 Bcm in 2008.[72] Reportedly, the contract requires a minimum of 1.2 Bcm/yr of Egyptian AGP gas to be purchased by the Jordanians each year. Demand in the country is growing, and as such Jordan is likely to continue to purchase as much gas as it can secure through the AGP. The price of gas received through the AGP remains commercially confidential. However, prices are thought to be similar to those paid at the Syrian border.

Energy Strategy

In September 2008, reports surfaced that Jordan wished to expand production at Risha. The expanded production potentially would come both from inside the country, and also from the section of the field that is inside Iraqi territory. BP was the primary company interested in expanding Risha's output. Production at the field is expected to increase by 50 percent.[73]

Jordan also possesses significant resources of oil shale and in May 2009, signed exploration agreements with Royal Dutch Shell and Inter Rao of Russia. The Jordanian Energy Minister, Khaldoun Qutishat, stated his expectation that Shell should invest $500 million 'for exploration, assessment and designs on the project'.[74] In a paper submitted to a 2006 oil shale conference, Jamal Alali of the Jordanian Natural Resources Authority reported that Jordan has the eighth largest oil shale resources in the world, amounting to 65 billion tons.[75] Shale oil has the potential, in the next 10 to 20 years, to serve as a supplement to natural gas in electricity generation.

As noted above, Jordan has also expressed interest in developing a domestic civil nuclear programme.[76] While nuclear power may be a logical development given a lack of any significant and readily available indigenous energy source, Jordan remains a lower-income country (GDP per capita, PPP, $5,300).[77] It is not clear that a nuclear power sector in Jordan could survive without enormous state financial support, which may not be feasible.

Between shale oil, nuclear, limited domestic and some imported natural gas, Jordan, like many countries in the region, is pursuing a multifaceted approach to energy development. What is not clear, however, is any framework in which these elements might combine to form a strategic whole. As a lower income country with few energy resources, Jordan could benefit enormously from a comprehensive, strategic approach to energy, including natural gas. Conversely, it may have much to lose if energy strategy continues to be neglected.

Israel and the Palestinian Territories

It became clear in the late 2000s that Israel and the Palestinian Territories are endowed with substantial natural gas resources. While neither Israel nor the Palestinian Territories are mentioned in BP's *Statistical Review of World Energy*, the EIA cites numbers dating from 2006. In that year, the EIA estimated Israel produced 0.8 Bcm from total reserves of slightly more than 39 Bcm.[78] Neither EIA nor BP provides reserve estimates for natural gas in Palestinian Territories – or to be more precise, seas. Table 5.4 shows Israeli production, consumption and imports of gas.

Israeli Natural Gas Fields

Mari-B. Israel has long encouraged domestic hydrocarbon exploration. For decades, as one of the few countries in the region without significant oil or natural gas resources, and surrounded by often hostile neighbours, Israel has been intent on finding and exploiting any available domestic energy sources. It was only in 1999, that a significant discovery was

Table 5.4: Israeli Gas Production, Consumption, and Imports, 2000 (actual), 2008 (actual), 2015 (projected by author), Bcm

	2000	*2008*	*2015*
Production	0.01	0.8–1	6–8
Demand	0.01	2.5–2.7	6–10
Imports	0	1.7	0

Sources: CEDIGAZ 2009 *Natural Gas in the World 2009*, Tables 19, 21, 60, 65 and 66; EIA, Country Reports – Israel; *New York Times*, 'Egypt and Israel sign 15-year natural gas deal', 1 July 2005

made in close proximity to Israeli territorial waters (Gaza Marine, see below).

Soon after, in March 2000, Noble Energy discovered the Mari-B field, offshore Israel between Tel Aviv and the Gaza Strip.[79] The field has reserves of approximately 28 Bcm,[80] and production of nearly 1.5 Bcm/yr.[81] Interestingly, the 6 Bcm/yr capacity of offshore gas gathering infrastructure significantly exceeds the field's current production.[82] Additionally, Noble has rights to the undeveloped Noa field with estimated reserves of 5.7 Bcm, near Mari-B,[83] which may explain the small amount of the additional capacity that has been built.

Med Yavne. In November 1999, BG Group announced a natural gas find offshore Israel, in the Med Yavne concession. Adjoining Gaza Marine, in Israeli territorial waters, the find was made once again by BG as operator with a 50 percent share (along with Isramco Group with 42 percent and Delek Drilling with 8 percent).[84] Med Yavne was a relatively small find (no precise resource data are available), and BG has since announced its intention to relinquish its stake in the field. It has been reported that the cost of production was the main stumbling block to developing the field.[85]

Tamar. The most significant discovery in the short history of commercial natural gas in Israel came in 2008 when a consortium led by Noble Energy made a large natural gas find off the coast of Haifa, in the northern part of the country. Initially, reserves were estimated to be 180 Bcm;[86] an August 2009 assessment upgraded that estimate to 207 Bcm.[87]

Noble has stated that production from Tamar is likely to commence in 2012[88] at 5–6 Bcm/yr,[89] and continues exploring the area, including nearby offshore Cyprus. However, it is likely that full production rates will not be attained until nearer to 2014.[90] Its partners in the Tamar field are Avner Oil (16 percent), the Delek Group (16 percent), and Isramco Negev (29 percent).[91] Noble also reports that the Dalit prospect, near Tamar, has a resource estimate of 14 Bcm, and that further exploration and development in the region will be undertaken in late 2010 or early 2011.[92]

Mira and Sarah. In early February 2010, Bontan Corporation, a Canadian firm, announced additional offshore finds near Tamar. The Mira and Sarah fields are said to contain 'up to' approximately 170 Bcm of natural gas.[93]

Gaza Marine. In 1999, the Palestinian Authority, under then-leader Yassir Arafat, granted an offshore exploration block to BG Group (90 percent), in conjunction with their partners, the Greek-based Lebanese-owned Consolidated Contractors Company (CCC 10 percent). Together, CCC and the 'Palestinian Investment Fund', a Palestinian Authority (PA) investment vehicle, have the option of acquiring an additional 30 percent share, reducing that of BG to 60 percent.[94]

The Gaza Marine block, off the coast of the Gaza Strip, wedged between Israel to the north and east and Egypt in the south, is adjacent to the Israeli Med Yavne block.[95] BG estimates that Gaza Marine contains 28 Bcm of recoverable natural gas, though reports have suggested the figure could be as high as 40 Bcm.[96]

Marketing Gaza Marine gas has proven complicated. The Israeli government at the time had a goal of increasing the share of natural gas consumed in the country's energy mix. This goal would theoretically be accomplished both by constructing a natural gas distribution network for residential and industrial consumers, and by increasing the proportion of electricity generated by burning natural gas. From BG's perspective, Israel was the most desirable market for Gaza Marine's reserves both because of proximity, because of the relative wealth of the Israeli market by regional standards (GDP per capita, PPP, $28,400),[97] and because it already had a partner in the Israel Electric Corporation (IEC). IEC is effectively the monopoly buyer of natural gas in Israel, and in the absence of other major consumers, the prices it is willing to pay determine the viability of development.

In spite of some momentum for the development and marketing of Gaza Marine's reserves, the price IEC was willing to pay was insufficient for BG to justify the field's development. BG therefore commenced an investigation of alternate markets, in particular the viability of piping Gaza Marine's reserves to the south instead of east to Israel. The author understands that talks with Egyptian authorities, as well as technical assessments, showed that transporting Gaza Marine's offshore gas to the Egyptian network was viable. BG, already having a significant presence in the Egyptian gas sector, intended to transport its Gaza reserves to Egypt via sub-sea pipeline, where it could be swapped in exchange for feedstock for its Egyptian LNG production. This arrangement would provide a greater return than the prices IEC was offering, and thus was seriously considered by BG.

The Egyptian option, in addition to monetising the resource for the operator, BG, would be a very significant source of income for the Palestinian Authority. BG estimated that the PA's profit share, were the field to be developed, would be approximately 45–50 percent.[98]

However, in the summer of 2006 the Israelis approached BG, signaling that they were willing to provide similar price terms to the Egyptian route for Gaza Marine's gas. Eighteen months of negotiations were to ensue, through the end of 2007, but again ended with the parties unable to agree on price.

Meanwhile, political developments in the Palestinian Territories were gaining attention. In June of 2007, Hamas, a Palestinian party rival to Yassir Arafat's previously dominant Fatah, having won a majority mandate in the January 2006 Palestinian parliamentary elections forcibly took control of the Gaza Strip.[99] Hamas is classified by the United States,[100] the United Kingdom[101] and the European Union[102] as a terrorist organisation.

The Hamas takeover of Gaza, on the surface, appeared to add a further dimension of complexity to Gaza Marine negotiations. The *Jerusalem Post* wrote:

> The deal (to sell Gaza Marine gas to Israel) was further complicated last month when Hamas seized control of Gaza. Hamas wants to renegotiate the PA's 1999 contract with BG so it can get more money from any gas sold to Israel… Among the points reportedly being negotiated by partners in the deal is how to ensure that any money going to the Palestinians isn't used to finance terrorism. Negotiators are said to be trying to agree on a foreign trustee who would supervise distribution of the funds.[103]

To the outside observer, it may seem to be a critical turn of events that the Gaza Strip was suddenly controlled by a) a named terrorist organisation and b) an organisation that was dedicated to re-negotiating the original exploration agreement signed in 1999 with the PA. However, the industry view is that Hamas' takeover of Gaza is less consequential for Gaza Marine than headlines suggest. BG's contract was signed with the Palestinian Authority, which remains the dominant Palestinian force in the West Bank. BG, it is said, had and has no contract with Hamas. Hamas is not a contractual party to Gaza Marine and, according to this reasoning, has no authority – nor enforcement capacity – offshore. This said, the legitimacy of both Hamas and the Fatah-controlled Palestinian

Authority is far from unambiguous, and indeed any significant industrial development would likely require the consent of both parties, in addition to the Israelis.

Gaza Marine is likely to remain undeveloped for some time, as both uncertain politics and a changing Israeli natural gas market, with significant new discoveries, hold back progress on developing the field.

Imports

Israel's only option for importing natural gas at present is via a 100 km sub-sea pipeline from Egypt. Arriving at the southern port of Ashkelon, a consortium comprised of Egyptian, Israeli and Thai partners supplies IEC with a minimum of 1.7 Bcm per annum. Flows through the Egypt–Israel pipeline, itself a separate and distinct piece of infrastructure from the AGP, commenced in 2008 after a 15-year agreement was signed between the Israeli and Egyptian governments in mid-2005.[104] It has been reported that the price paid for this gas was previously as low as $1.50/MMBtu[105] but after revisions in the contract that took effect in June 2009, Israel is reportedly paying 'a bit more than' $3.00/MMBtu.

There has been some discussion over the course of the last several years of another pipeline project to diversify Israeli supply. The so-called 'Blue Stream II' project would potentially bring Russian natural gas – in addition to water, oil, electricity and even fiber optic cables – to Israel via sub-sea pipelines from Turkey.[106]

Additional diversification of natural gas supply to Israel was touted in an August 2009 report that Israel launched a tender for the construction of an LNG import terminal with a capacity of 5.6 Bcm/yr.[107] If resource estimates for Israel's recent offshore discoveries prove to be accurate, however, it is unlikely that the Israeli market will need these, or perhaps any, additional pipeline or LNG imports.

Electricity

As the effective monopoly buyer of natural gas in Israel, IEC is the consumer that will make or break natural gas developments. The willingness of IEC to pay what producers consider(ed) fair market prices for gas is presently the key variable in Israel's gas market development. BG's inability to conclude an agreement for Gaza Marine or Med Yavne indicated that the IEC was not willing to pay higher prices over much of the previous decade. With the (by Israeli standards) massive new Tamar find, the question of IEC's willingness to pay takes on enhanced importance. These potentially game-changing resources mean very little if producers and consumers – mainly the IEC – cannot arrive at a mutually agreeable accommodation on prices.

If Tamar – or any other – resources are to be monetised, the IEC is likely to be a (or perhaps *the*) key partner. This is no doubt known to Noble Energy, and on 29 December 2009, *Oil and Gas Journal* reported that Noble Energy had signed a letter of intent with IEC for 'at least' 2.7 Bcm/yr of gas from the Tamar field.[108]

There are also other, smaller entrants onto the consumer side of the Israeli gas equation. Dalia Power Energies is a private company with a licence to build a natural gas-fired power plant. Reportedly Dalia expects to begin operations in 2013, and has itself signed a letter of intent with Noble for Tamar gas. Volumes are approximately 5.7 Bcm over 17 years, as announced by Noble in December 2009.[109]

The Dalia and IEC volumes would only account for approximately half of the projected initial output from Tamar (5–6 Bcm/yr). Thus far, Noble has announced letters of intent with IEC and Dalia rather than signed contracts. Forward visibility for the successful monetisation of the Tamar resources, then, is uncertain. However, it is likely that due to the scale of the resource, and the strategic imperative of the Israeli government to promote more 'secure' (i.e. indigenous) energy sources, that the Tamar resource will make a significant impact on the domestic energy balance in the decade from 2012 through 2020, and indeed beyond.

This said, the Israeli gas market – which is to say largely the consumption of natural gas for electricity generation – could potentially use the natural gas that has been discovered offshore in the last decade. Particularly if the Israeli government decides to proceed with any power-hungry water desalination projects, increased demand for natural gas will drive the development of newly discovered resources. However, the question of whether there may have been too much gas discovered offshore Israel for the local market to absorb is unresolved. Recent indications that IEC is willing to pay higher prices for natural gas are a positive indication.[110] Diversifying consumption away from just IEC would be a first step in bringing gas to market, but given the lengthy delays that have been seen in commencing construction of a residential distribution grid, when such diversification might take place is another open question.

Energy Strategy

As is the case with the other countries addressed in this chapter – though to a lesser extent in Jordan – Israel suffers from the absence of a comprehensive energy strategy. Such a strategy in Israel would have to set out a long-term demand scenario in the country, including all potential or projected major industrial, desalination, and electricity generation projects. Critically, though, without a concerted and successful push to construct a national gas distribution network, it is the power generation sector that will remain the most important demand centre. Building LNG import facilities, and continuing to operate, let alone building new coal-fired facilities, all risk fatally undermining the game-changing scale of recent offshore discoveries, if they prove to be as large as reported.

Without a sound strategy that addresses all elements of Israeli energy demand and supply, Israeli policy makers' interest in 'going it alone' will not be fully realised. Offshore natural gas discoveries hold the potential to allow Israel to function as an energy 'island', but this will require policy decisions away from coal-fired generation. Perhaps as importantly, the IEC near-monopoly undermines the creation of an effective natural gas market in Israel. Without reducing its price-setting power as the most significant consumer in the country, natural gas producers will continue to struggle to sell gas at viable prices.

That said, the size of the resources reported to have been discovered offshore Israel are indeed of 'game-changing' scale. A March 2010 report by the United States Geological Service[111] is a further indication that substantial and commercial volumes of natural gas exist across the eastern Mediterranean. That said, even with an aggressive domestic market development programme, within the constraints outlined above, Israel is likely to find itself with more gas than it can plausibly consume domestically through 2020. This is of obvious consequence to the domestic market, as developing and utilising the newly discovered resource would serve to significantly displace coal in the power generation mix.

Internationally too, Israel's new natural gas wealth is of consequence. It is likely to mean that Israel no longer requires imports of natural gas (from Egypt in the future, and certainly not an LNG import facility). Indeed, the size of the resource suggests that, were Israel located in a different region, it might even be considering natural gas exports. However, given the tense relationship with Lebanon to the north and Syria to the northeast, Jordan's contracts and infrastructure linking it with Egyptian supplies, and Egypt's own domestic supplies, it is highly unlikely that Israel will develop pipeline natural gas exports.

Theoretically, LNG exports may be viable for monetising the resource base outside the limited domestic market. It is an open question as to how or from where such massive infrastructure investment would be financed, but should the resource base be confirmed to be as large as originally claimed, LNG would be the most logical large-scale export option for Israeli gas.

Further out in the realm of speculation, the course of action that may make most sense for Israel to monetise its offshore resource would be reversing the flow of the existing subsea pipeline from Egypt, and exporting Israeli natural gas via Egyptian LNG infrastructure.

Regional Dynamics – The Arab Gas Pipeline (AGP)

AGP is a 1200 km pipeline with a capacity of 10 Bcm/yr. Egyptian gas runs under the Gulf of Aqaba to Jordan and northward through Syria with a spur to Lebanon and (potentially) onward to Turkey. Flows commenced through the first phase of AGP, between Egypt and Jordan, in July 2003, with the connection between Aqaba and the north of Jordan (phase two) completed in 2005, and onward from Jordan to Homs in Syria (with a spur to the Deir Ali power station, phase three) becoming operational in July 2008.[112] A connection to Turkey is under construction, however as of mid-2010, a gap in AGP infrastructure between the north and south of Syria remains. These completed phases of the AGP system were constructed at a cost of more than US$1.2 billion.[113]

Construction of AGP phase two, which cost a total of $300 million, commenced in August 2002. An Egyptian consortium comprised of EGAS, Petrojet, Enppi, and GASCO was awarded a contract to build, manage, and operate the pipeline for a 30-year duration, with an optional 10-year extension, after which ownership of the pipeline will transfer to Jordan.[114] Financing came from a consortium including a Jordanian state bank, other regional financial institutions, and via a $100 million EIB investment to EGAS.

Gas transited through AGP is sold by the Arab Company for Marketing and Transporting Gas (ACMTG), established in 2003 by AGP founding governments. Originally, AGP was conceived as a project to catalyse the emergence of a regional market in natural gas. However, though AGP supplies much-needed gas to the Jordanian, Lebanese, and Syrian markets, its role as a potential supplier to Europe is in doubt.

The EU has a longstanding interest in AGP as a potential source of gas, for the long-hoped-for Nabucco pipeline project from the Caspian region to central Europe. Indeed, Energy Commissioner Andris Piebalgs expressed an expectation that 2 Bcm/yr of natural gas would be available for European markets from the AGP as early as 2010.[115]

Additionally, External Relations Commissioner Benita Ferrero-Waldner had stated that AGP opens 'important possibilities as a new transport route for gas to the EU, particularly for the Nabucco project'.[116]

The reality of growing demand in transit countries, growing demand in Egypt itself,[117] and the more attractive prospect of monetising gas resources through LNG exports to the Atlantic Basin makes exporting gas to Europe through AGP less attractive for Egypt, and thus highly unlikely. Indeed, at present, a best-case scenario would revise the 2 Bcm/yr that Commissioner Piebalgs envisaged flowing to Europe down to 1 Bcm/yr. Even then, though, following the global financial crisis, economic downturn, and resultant lower natural gas demand, it is difficult to envisage why Europe would need to secure additional volumes of natural gas prior to 2015 unless it is very attractively priced.

Rapidly growing regional demand makes it increasingly likely that not only will all available volumes be purchased by transit countries (Syria and Jordan) before they reach the Turkish border, but that additional volumes of natural gas may utilise the yet-to-be-completed Syria–Turkey link and be shipped southward, from Turkey, to meet Syrian, Jordanian and Lebanese demand. It is an open question as to whether Syria could buy natural gas on better terms from Russia via Turkey than from Egypt via AGP.

Even if these economic questions are resolved, there are technical hurdles to AGP supplying European markets with gas. AGP is better understood as a pipeline 'system' rather than a single 'pipeline' due to its modular construction. At present, for instance, the link to Turkey is being constructed from the northern Syrian city of Aleppo, while gas already flows from Egypt to southern Syria via Jordan. To the south of Aleppo, however, towards the industrial city of Homs, there is no capacity in the Syrian transmission system to ship gas northwards. Additional capacity would need to be created in order to transport gas northwards in the (increasingly unlikely) event that volumes became available to ship to Turkey and onwards to Europe.

AGP is therefore most likely to evolve into a bi-directional pipeline network, shipping gas to centres of demand growth in Syria and Jordan (and potentially additionally to Lebanon). Europe is not likely to be the most logical and accessible export market for Egyptian pipeline gas in the 2010–2015 period, and possibly through the 2020s. This is also assuming Egypt will be able to expand pipeline gas exports over the course of the next decade, a less than certain assumption given Egyptian domestic demand growth and the current moratorium on new export contracts.

The unlikely prospect of Egyptian gas transiting north of Syria is further confirmed by Iraqi interest in displacing Egyptian gas in Syria and Jordan in exchange for shares in Egyptian LNG cargoes:

> Egyptian oil minister Sameh Fahmy said in April that Iraq was interested in joining the Arab Gas Pipeline project and is negotiating with Egypt the possibility of shipping Iraqi natural gas by pipeline to Egypt's customers in Jordan and Syria in return for LNG cargoes from Egypt for export to Europe and the US.[118]

Though, as discussed earlier, the timeframe for Iraqi gas (probably from Akkas) to be marketed in Syria or Jordan is uncertain, should this happen, the potential for Egypt to be freed of the obligation to supply its AGP partners is not beyond the realm of possibility. As an investment banker in the region was quoted as saying in September 2008, in the context of a discussion on Egyptian export options:

> I doubt that under the current crunch in domestic supplies, we will see new volumes going to Turkey and Europe – unless there is a significant increase in future production of gas that will accommodate the increase in domestic consumption and export demands.[119]

The Arab Gas Pipeline, then, though serving at present as an important source of imports for Jordan and Syria (and, to a more limited extent, Lebanon), is unlikely to serve as anything more than regional transport infrastructure. It is highly unlikely that AGP will supply gas north of the Syrian border.

Conclusions

The countries addressed in this chapter could all utilise more natural gas. And indeed, most of them do have gas available, either from domestic reserves or imports. However, in each country there is a functional shortage of natural gas due to a variety of issues (Table 5.5). Israel's historical unwillingness to pay market-related prices for gas means that its newly found resources will likely remain under-utilised until attitudes of key domestic consumers change (a process that already appears to have commenced with IEC).

Lebanon pays a huge premium to keep its fuel oil-fired power plants running, yet has not established the basic infrastructure necessary to import cheaper natural gas. Lebanese officials have also balked at the cost of importing ostensibly expensive natural gas, despite the billions of dollars spent on purchasing almost certainly more expensive fuel oil.

Syria in the past has offered reasonably generous terms for IOCs to explore for and produce natural gas, and it is seeing the results

Table 5.5: Estimated Mashreq Gas Production, Consumption, and Imports, 2015, Bcm

	Syria	*Lebanon*	*Jordan*	*Israel*
Production	12	0	0.3	6–8
Imports	2.2	0.5–2	3.2	0
Demand	16	1–5	4–5	6–10
Supply/Demand (im)balance	(-)1.8	(-)0.5 – (-)4.5	(-)0.3 – (-)1.3	0 – (-)2

Source: Tables 5.1–5.4

of these terms over the course of 2010–2011, when substantial new production volumes will come onstream. Additionally, it has reportedly paid higher prices for imports than has much wealthier Israel. This said, it is not clear that Syria will offer sufficiently attractive terms to IOCs to develop the additional gas needed to minimise the supply-demand disequilibrium that is expected to worsen through the next decade.

Finally, Jordan, with its very limited natural gas resources, is almost entirely reliant on imports. How much Jordanian consumers are willing to pay for natural gas – primarily from Egypt and/or Iraq – will determine the energy resources it has available to fuel economic growth for its young, growing population.

In each of the countries addressed, a shortage of natural gas means a shortage of electricity. Each of the countries in question has growing populations. The largest, Syria, has a very young and very rapidly growing population. The availability of natural gas to generate sufficient electricity will have wide-ranging impacts on the social, political, and economic development of these countries over the course of the next decade. Supply can only meet demand if cost (and eventually market) related prices are paid for both gas and power, an outcome that is uncertain.

Additionally, there is an absence of energy strategy in the four countries in question. From Israel's plans to build-out several potential options for import in the context of potentially game-changing new domestic resource discoveries, to Syria's construction of power plants for which it has insufficient natural gas to fuel, governments are paying inadequate attention to developing a strategic energy policy.

Syria, Lebanon, and Jordan – in conjunction with Egypt, and potentially also with Iraq – are likely to remain an enclosed regional gas market for the next decade. Given the constraints identified in this chapter very little, if any, natural gas is expected to leave the region for export onward to Europe. However, there is the potential for gas entering the region from Turkey (including often-delayed or deferred Iranian exports to Syria).

Indeed, Syria, Jordan and Lebanon will all be in a highly precarious and potentially worsening position over the period up to 2020, especially if there is any fall in the deliveries of Egyptian gas (a possibility that cannot be ruled out). While the volumes presently flowing to Israel may provide for some cushion, it is not certain that Egypt would rather use these volumes for export to Mashreq countries than to supply its own (supply-constrained) domestic market – or indeed to export, almost certainly more profitably, as LNG. This latter point suggests that, in the ten-year period from 2010, Syria, Lebanon and Jordan are likely to be increasingly forced to compete with Egyptian LNG netbacks in order to secure their imports.

Iraqi exports to the region remain theoretical at present. With Akkas as the most likely source of exports from Iraq to the Mashreq, regional countries may once again find themselves in the position of competing with alternative buyers – this time potential European consumers – and therefore paying significantly higher prices than their governments would wish. This all assumes that Iraq does not decide to develop the infrastructure to use potential flows from Akkas to fuel its own energy-starved domestic market (see Chapter 7).

The final option for external supplies to the Mashreq regional market is potential imports of Russian gas from Blue Stream II via the Turkish pipeline system. As mentioned above, the final AGP section from Aleppo in northern Syria to Turkey could feasibly be operated as a north-to-south link, bringing supplies of Russian origin to Syria and onward to Lebanon and/or Jordan. With the reduction in European demand for Russian gas following the economic downturn of 2008/09, Gazprom may be interested in developing a new market for its pipeline gas. But, given the costs of delivery, it remains to be seen whether Mashreq gas markets will be sufficiently profitable.

Notes

1   'Lebanon receives Egypt gas to run Deir Ammar (Beddawi) plant', *Daily Star* (Lebanon), 20 October 2009.
2   CIA World Factbook – Syria. Available online at https://www.cia.gov/library/the-world-factbook/geos/SY.html.
3   Economist Intelligence Unit, Syria Country Report, April 2009.
4   'Syrian government restructures oil sector', Syria Report, 2 March 2009.
5   Ibid.
6   BP *Statistical Review of World Energy* 2009.
7   See: Ford, Neil, 'Damascus seeks to turn the tide of dwindling oil revenues', *The Middle East*, 1 March 2008; APS Review Downstream Trends, 'SYRIA

   – The Syrian Decision Makers – Ahmad Al-Mu'alla', vol. 70, No.13, 24 March 2008.

8   'Syria eyeing its gas hub potential', *World Gas Intelligence*, 13 January 2010.

9   Author's conversations with officials in Damascus.

10 *APS Review Gas Market Trends*, 'Syria – The Offshore Prospects' 8 March 2010.

11 Energy Information Administration, 'Country Brief – Syria', available online at www.eia.doe.gov

12 Ibid.

13 These statistics are corroborated at: 'Syria – The Gas Sector' – *APS Review Gas Market Trends*, 3 March 2008.

14 On 5 August 2009, for instance, the Henry Hub natural gas spot price was $3.61 per MMBtu at NYMEX, while oil traded $71.97 per barrel, or $12.41 per MMBtu, well above the traditional 2-to-1 ratio that has previously been common. Source: EIA, Natural Gas Weekly Update, 5 August 2009 available online at http://tonto.eia.doe.gov/oog/info/ngw/ ngupdate.asp.

15 *Middle East Economic Digest*, 'Al-Furat Petroleum Company: Arresting the decline', 25 August 2006, available online at http://www.meed.com. news/2006/08/alfurat_petroleum_company_arresting_the_decline.html.

16 EIA, Country Report, Syria.

17 The former datum is provided by EIA in its Syria country report, and the latter by Raphaeli, N. and Gersten, B., 'The Iran-Syria Alliance: The Economic Dimension', *The Middle East Review of International Affairs*, June 2008.

18 Author's experience.

19 Recently announced facilities include a 700 MW unit being constructed by a Greek company. Source: 'Greek-Italian venture wins Syria deal', Gulfnews.com, 8 September 2008, available online at http://www.gulfnews. com/business/Oil_and_gas/10243579.html.

20 'North and South Middle Area Gas Exploitation Project', Stroytransgaz, available online at http://www.stroytransgaz.com/projects/syria/gas- processing-plant-2, 11 September 2009.

21 *Middle East Economic Digest*, 'Al-Furat Petroleum Company: Arresting the decline', ibid.

22 Gavin, James, 'Syria comes out of the shadows', *Petroleum Economist*, August 2009, p. 40.

23 *APS Review Oil Market Trends*, 'Syria – SPC Fields', vol. 70 no. 11, 10 March 2008.

24 Ibid.

25 England, Andrew, 'Syria frets over drought's harsh harvest', *Financial Times*, 4 February 2010.

26 *APS Review Oil Market Trends*, "Syria – SPC Fields", ibid.

27 Total, 'Syria: Start-up of the Deir Ez Zor gas project', available online at http://www.stroytransgaz.com/projects/syria/gas-processing-plant-2, 11 September 2009.

28 'Total signs Syrian oil, gas deals', *International Gas Report*, 8 September 2008.
29 Suncor Energy, 'International and Offshore', available online at http://www.suncor.com/en/about/919.aspx
30 The city is also known as 'Tadmor', its Arabic name.
31 *APS Review Gas Market Trends*, 'Syria – The gas development background', Vol. 70 No. 11, 10 March 2008.
32 Stroytransgaz, 'Arab Gas Pipeline, Phase 1', available online at http://www.stroytransgaz.com/projects/syria/arab-gas-pipeline
33 Hunter, Catherine, 'Petro-Canada Prioritises Syria's Ebla Gas Project; Abu Rabah Gas Onstream', *Global Insight Daily Analysis*, 7 January 2009.
34 'Stroitransgas Plans Syria Gas Output Boost', *International Oil Daily*, 6 February 2009.
35 Ibid.
36 INA, Annual Report 2008, p. 35, available online at http://www.ina.hr/default.aspx?id=275
37 Ibid., pp. 15-17.
38 DualEx Energy International Inc., 'Operations', available online at http://www.dualexen.com/operations/overview.html
39 KUFPEC, 'Syria', available online at http://www.kufpec.com/KUFPEC/en-US/Operations/MiddleEast/Syria/
40 Stratic Energy Corporation, 'Operations – Syria', available online at http://www.straticenergy.com/operations/syria.html.
41 There are no shortage of references to Syria's 'strategic position' in the region in the context of geography and energy. See, for instance, 'Syria seen as future corridor for Arab gas; Looks to be link to European market', al Khayat, Faleh, *Platts Oilgram News*, 24 June 2008.
42 *APS Review Oil Market Trends*, 'Syria – SPC Fields', ibid.
43 Egyptian Natural Gas Holding Company (EGAS), 'Achieved Projects – Arab Gas Pipeline', available online at http://www.egas.com.eg/Business_Opportunities/Arab_Gas.aspx
44 'Contract News – Stroytransgaz Strikes Another Syria Deal', BMI Industry Insights – Oil & Gas, Middle East & Africa, 15 October 2008.
45 'Syrian Oil minister: Egypt will begin exporting natural gas to Syria next month', Aji, Albert, Associated Press, 23 February 2008.
46 'Contract News – Stroytransgaz Strikes Another Syria Deal, ibid.
47 'Syria begins importing Egyptian gas', Middle East North Africa Financial Network (MENAFN), 12 July 2008.
48 'Syria eyeing its gas hub potential', *World Gas Intelligence*, 13 January 2010.
49 'Report on Syria's efforts to increase oil, gas production', BBC Monitoring Middle East, [Report by Waad al-Jarf: "Syria's location ideal for export of gas and oil products to Europe", Syria Times website], 6 May 2008.
50 Sovich, Nina, 'Syria's drying wells have key role in oiling reforms' *Alexander's Oil and Gas Connections*, vol. 10 no. 20, 26 October 2005.
51 "Syria seen as future corridor for Arab gas; Looks to be link to European market", al Khayat, Faleh, Ibid.
52 'EU energy chief sees 7 Bcm/year gas imports from Iraq, Egypt', *EU*

Energy, Vol. 3 No. 183, 16 May 2008.
53 "CORRECTED – Iraq receives one bid for Akkas gas field", Reuters, 30 June 2009, available online at www.reuters.com
54 'Iraq PM challenges Syria to explain militant aid', Reuters, 30 September 2009, available online at http://uk.reuters.com/article/idUKANS349705
55 Though there is some speculation as to the potential for offshore gas resources, given recent discoveries immediately to the south in Israeli territorial waters, and exploration underway in nearby Cyprus.
56 'Lebanon receives Egypt gas to run Deir Ammar (Beddawi) plant', *Daily Star* (Lebanon), 20 October 2009.
57 EIA Country Analysis Brief – Syria, June 2009, available online at http://www.eia.doe.gov/cabs/Syria/Background.html
58 Author's conversations with executives in Damascus.
59 Habib, Osama, 'Lebanon again plagued by power rationing amid tourist influx', *Daily Star*, 3 July 2009.
60 Ibid.
61 *CIA World Factbook*, Lebanon, available online at https://www.cia.gov/library/publications/the-world-factbook/geos/le.html
62 'Siniora: Lebanon needs more power plants to meet demand; State-owned utility lost whopping $1.2 billion in 2007', Staff Writer, *Daily Star*, 6 February 2008.
63 Jaber, J.O., A. Al-Sarkhi, B.A. Akash and M.S. Mohsen, 'Medium-range planning economics of future electrical-power generational options', *Energy Policy*, vol. 32 (2004), pp. 357–66
64 *APS Review Oil Market Trends*, 'Lebanon to have floating LNG plant', 6 November 2006.
65 'LNG Unlimited: Poten & Partners to Run the Numbers in Lebanon', from poten.com, 8 May 2009.
66 Halawi, Dana, 'Diversity key to managing fuel price swings', *Daily Star*, 26 March 2009.
67 Hamarneh, Yousef, 'Oil Shale Resources Development in Jordan', Natural Resources Authority of Jordan, 1998, updated November 2006, available online at http://www.nra.gov.jo/images/stories/pdf_files/Updated_Report_2006.pdf
68 'Jordan views oil shale as key to greater energy self-sufficiency', *The Oil Daily*, 23 March 2009.
69 EIA Country Report, Jordan, available online at www.eia.doe.gov
70 Economist Intelligence Unit, Jordan Country Brief, March 2009.
71 "Jordan may build its first nuclear power plant at Aqaba", Xinhua, available online at http://news.xinhuanet.com/english/2008-12/22/content_10542636.htm, accessed 19 August 2009
72 *BP Statistical Review of World Energy* 2009, 'Natural Gas: Trade Movements 2008 by pipeline'.
73 Economist Intelligence Unit, Jordan Country Brief, March 2009.
74 Carlisle, Tamsin, 'Jordan signs oil shale agreements', *The National*, 17 May 2009.

75 Alali, Jamal, 'Jordan oil shale, availability, distribution, and investment opportunity', presented to the International Conference on Oil Shale, 'Recent Trends in Oil Shale', 7–9 November 2006, available online at http://www.sdnp.jo/International_Oil_Conference/rtos-A117.pdf

76 'S. Korea takes lead for Jordan nuclear plant deal – report', Reuters, 11 March 2009, available online at http://www.reuters.com/article/idUSSEO29770720090311

77 *CIA World Factbook* – Jordan, available online at https://www.cia.gov/library/publications/the-world-factbook/geos/jo.html

78 EIA, Country Reports – Israel, available online at www.eia.doe.gov

79 Noble Energy leads a five-member consortium with a 47 percent share in Mari-B. The consortium includes AVner Oil Exploration Partnership, with a 23 percent share, Delek Drilling Partnership, with 25.5 percent, and Delek Investments and Properties, with 4.4 percent. Source: 'Company News, Middle East: Noble Energy starts natural gas production offshore Israel', *Alexander's Gas & Oil Connections*, vol. 9 no. 1, 15 January 2004.

80 'Noble Energy Inc. announces startup of natural gas production from Mari-B field offshore Israel', Gulf Oil and Gas, 24 December 2003, available online at http://www.gulfoilandgas.com/webpro1/MAIN/Mainnews.asp?id=249

81 Noble Energy, 'Operations: Israel', available online at http://www.nobleenergyinc.com/fw/main/Israel-128.html

82 'Noble Energy Inc. announces startup of natural gas production from Mari-B field offshore Israel', Gulf Oil and Gas, 24 December 2003, available online at http://www.gulfoilandgas.com/webpro1/MAIN/Mainnews.asp?id=249, accessed 25 August 2009

83 'Noble Energy Inc. announces startup of natural gas production from Mari-B field offshore Israel', Gulf Oil and Gas, 24 December 2003, ibid.

84 BG Group, "Gas discovery offshore Israel", Press Release, 1 November 2009, available online at http://www.bg-group.com/MediaCentre/PressArchive/1999/Pages/pr-087.aspx, accessed 25 August 2009

85 BG Group, 'Israel and areas of Palestinian Authority', available online at http://www.bg-group.com/OurBusiness/WhereWeOperate/Pages/pgIsraelandAreasofPalestinianAuthority.aspx

86 Noble Energy, http://www.nobleenergyinc.com/fw/main/Israel-128.html

87 'Natural gas reserve in north Israel proven larger', China View, 11 August 2009, available online at http://news.xinhuanet.com/english/2009-08/11/content_11865506.htm

88 Noble Energy, http://www.nobleenergyinc.com/fw/main/Israel-128.html

89 'Gov't wants more gas from Tamar: Natural Gas Authority: We are interested in the Tamar prospect supplying added-value to the Israeli economy.', Globes – McClatchy-Tribune Information Service via COMTEX, 24 November 2009.

90 'Egypt raises gas supplies to Israel after reaching new price agreement', *Middle East Economic Survey*, vol. LII no. 25, 22 June 2009.

91 Harif, Tal Barak and Susan Lerner, 'Israel sees energy independence in

natural gas offshore fields', Bloomberg.com, 5 March 2009,.

92　Noble Energy, 'Operations: Israel"' available online at http://www.no-bleenergyinc.com/fw/main/Israel-128.html

93　'Canada's Bontan announces two more huge Israeli gas fields: Gas at the Mira and Sarah offshore prospects, adjacent to the Tamar field, could be worth up to $7.54 billion", Globes-McClathy-Tribune Information Services, 2 February 2010.

94　These details come from an October 2007 BP Group publication which is no longer publicly available. 'The Gaza Marine Project', BP Group, October 2007.

95　Bahgat, G., 'Energy Partnership: Israel and the Persian Gulf"', *Energy Policy*, vol. 33 (2005), p. 676.

96　EIU, 'Palestinian Territories: Country Profile – Main report' 1 December 2008.

97　*CIA World Factbook* – Israel, available online at https://www.cia.gov/library/publications/the-world-factbook/geos/is.html

98　'The Gaza Marine Project', BP Group, October 2007.

99　'Hamas takes full control of Gaza', BBC News Online, 15 June 2007, available online at http://news.bbc.co.uk/2/hi/middle_east/6755299.stm; McGeough, Paul, *Kill Khalid*, The New Press: London, 2009, p. 424.

100 'Chapter 6. Terrorist Organizations', United States Department of State, 30 April 2009, available online at http://www.state.gov/s/ct/rls/crt/2008/122449.htm

101 'Proscribed terrorist groups', United Kingdom Home Office, available online at http://security.homeoffice.gov.uk/legislation/current-legislation/terrorism-act-2000/proscribed-groups

102 'Council Common Position 2009/7/CFSP', *Official Journal of the European Union*, 27 January 2009, available online at http://eur-lex.europa.eu/LexUriServ/LexUriServ.do?uri=OJ:L:2009:023:0037:0042:EN:PDF

103 Ferzinger, Jonathan, 'BG Gaza gas deal may take months, Israel says', *Jerusalem Post*, 21 July 2007.

104 'Egypt and Israel sign 15-year natural gas deal', *New York Times*, 1 July 2005.

105 'Egypt: Energy provision', Economist Intelligence Unit – ViewsWire, 3 October 2008.

106 Naff, Andrew, 'Turkey, Israel agree to move ahead with Med pipeline; Gazprom near supply deal with Israel', *Global Insight Daily Analysis*, 18 July 2008.

107 'Israel tenders to bring LNG to east Mediterranean', *Petroleum Economist*, August 2009, p. 28.

108 Watkins, Eric, 'Noble Energy to sell gas to Israel Electric', *Oil and Gas Journal*, 29 December 2009.

109 'Noble Energy executes letter of intent for natural gas from Tamar', PRNewswire, 15 December 2009, available online at http://investors.nobleenergyinc.com/releasedetail.cfm?ReleaseID=430192

110 Baron, Lior, 'IEC to pay 40% more under new gas deal', globes-online.

com, 9 November 2009.

111 United States Geological Service, 'Assessment of Undiscovered Oil and Gas Resources of the Levant Basin Province, Eastern Mediterranean', March 2010.

112 'Contract News – Stroytransgaz Strikes Another Syria Deal', BMI Industry Insights – Oil & Gas, Middle East & Africa, 15 October 2008.

113 'Egypt begins pumping natural gas into Syria as part of giant pipeline project', Associated Press, 10 July 2008.

114 'Arab Gas Pipeline Agreement', *Gulf Oil and Gas*, 26 January 2004, available online at http://www.gulfoilandgas.com/webpro1/MAIN/Mainnews. asp?id=357

115 Watkins, Eric, 'Egypt struggles to meet demand growth for natural gas', *The Oil and Gas Journal*, 13 October 2008.

116 'Contract News – Stroytransgaz Strikes Another Syria Deal', BMI Industry Insights – Oil & Gas, Middle East & Africa, 15 October 2008.

117 Watkins, Eric, 'Egypt struggles to meet demand growth for natural gas', ibid. See Chapter 4.

118 'Arab Gas Pipeline link proposed for Europe', *Energy Economist*, issue 324, 1 October 2008.

119 'Egyptian, Iraqi gas maneuvers', *World Gas Intelligence*, 24 September 2008.

CHAPTER 6

THE SAUDI GAS SECTOR AND ITS ROLE IN INDUSTRIALISATION: DEVELOPMENTS, CHALLENGES AND OPTIONS

Bassam Fattouh

Introduction

Although the Kingdom of Saudi Arabia is mainly known for its massive crude oil reserves, which accounted for around 20 percent of the world's total proven reserves in 2009, it is also endowed with very substantial gas resources. While not playing in the same league as neighbours Iran and Qatar, Saudi Arabia holds currently proven reserves of natural gas of 7.92 trillion cubic metres (tcm), some 4.2 percent of the world's total in 2009 and the world's fourth largest proven reserves.[1] Despite Saudi Arabia's massive gas potential, the exploitation of these reserves has been exclusively aimed for domestic use. Natural gas has become the fuel of choice for the country's industrialisation and diversification efforts and hence lies at the heart of the Kingdom's overall economic development strategy. Natural gas is used in power generation, water desalination plants, the oil and refining industry and as a feedstock for the country's growing petrochemical industry.

The rising importance of natural gas in the energy mix raises key challenges for the Kingdom. These challenges relate to meeting the expected rapid increase in domestic gas demand, the rising costs and increasing complexity of developing domestic gas reserves, the entry of foreign players into the gas sector, the high investment requirements in key infrastructure projects such as power generation and water desalination, the type of fuel to be used in these projects, and the pricing of gas feedstock. At a broader level, it brings to the forefront the effectiveness and the long-term sustainability of Saudi Arabia's industrialisation path and development strategy.

Despite the fact that the Saudi gas sector has a large domestic dimension and currently there is a firm policy of not exporting gas, the development of the gas sector has wider implications on energy markets. By meeting domestic needs for fuel, the gas sector currently frees more than 1 million barrels per day (million b/d) of oil for export.[2] Thus,

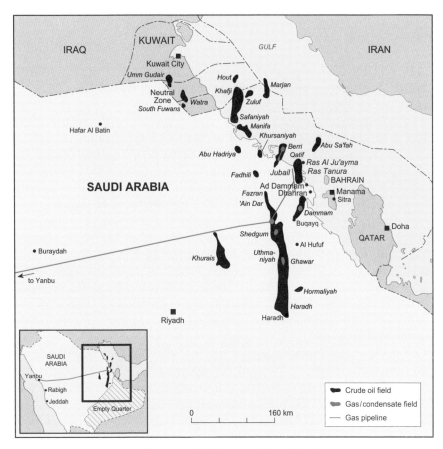

Map 6.1: Saudi Arabian Gas and Oil Fields and Gas Pipeline

the policy options currently pursued to meet the challenge of rapidly rising domestic consumption may have an indirect impact on global oil supplies and prices, especially in tight market conditions.

The purpose of this chapter is to discuss the recent developments in the Kingdom's gas sector and analyse their implications, both at the domestic and international levels. The chapter is divided into seven sections. Section 1 provides a basic overview of the Saudi economy and highlights the growing importance of gas in the country's development strategy. Section 2 discusses the Master Gas System, which constitutes the first building block of the Saudi gas industry. Section 3 analyses the key gas demand patterns and the future evolution of demand. Section 4 discusses the Kingdom's supply potential and assesses the challenges faced by Saudi Arabia in securing supplies to meet the rapidly rising domestic demand. Section 5 analyses domestic pricing issues. Section 6 evaluates the various options available for the Kingdom in confronting the 'gas challenge'. The last section concludes.

Saudi Arabia's Economy and the Role of Natural Gas

Despite continuous efforts to reduce oil dependency, the hydrocarbon sector still constitutes the largest sector of Saudi Arabia's economy accounting for almost a third of the country's GDP,[3] around 90 percent of export earnings[4] and almost 90 percent of government receipts in 2008.[5] The dominance of the hydrocarbon sector however extends beyond these direct contributions to economic activity. Government expenditure fuelled by oil revenues is the main driver of public and private consumption. Direct government services are the second largest contributor to economic output after the hydrocarbon sector accounting for 17 percent of GDP.[6] Government spending is also the main driver of private consumption as the public sector is a key employer of Saudi nationals. In 2008, the public sector employed around 20 percent of the Saudi national work force[7] with the number of employees in the public sector reaching 900,000, 92 percent of which are Saudi nationals.[8] This is in sharp contrast to the private sector where Saudi nationals account only for 13 percent of total private sector employment.[9] Government spending fuelled by hydrocarbon revenues is also the main impetus behind the growth in the private sector and non-oil output. Recent evidence suggests that apart from their effect on government expenditure, high oil prices do not exert an independent influence on underlying non-oil output in oil-rich economies.[10] This is especially true in countries such as Saudi Arabia where the oil sector accounts for a relatively large share of the economy.

Saudi Arabia has witnessed rapid expansion in its real GDP over the last few years making it the biggest economy in the Arab world. However, growth rates have been highly volatile mirroring volatility in oil output and prices (see Figure 6.1). Furthermore, rapid population growth during the last three decades resulted in real income per capita declining in the first half of the 1980s and then stagnating for most of the 1990s to rise slowly in the last few years. Population is expected to increase from its current level of around 24 million to almost 30 million in 2024 with the population growth among Saudi nationals remaining quite buoyant (see Table 6.1).[11] High population growth rates and a young population structure are putting pressure on the government to generate employment opportunities for the thousands entering the labour market each year.[12]

Given these challenges, the diversification of the economy has been

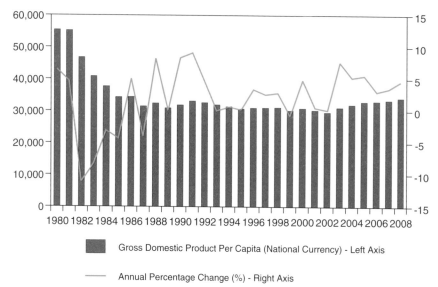

Gross Domestic Product Per Capita (National Currency) - Left Axis

Annual Percentage Change (%) - Right Axis

Figure 6.1: Gross Domestic Per Capita and Annual Growth, 1980–2008

Source: IMF World Economic Outlook Database

Table 6.1: Population Growth Projections (in Millions)

	2004	2009	2014	2019	2024	Average annual growth rate (2004–2024)
Total Population	22.67	24.39	26.52	28.26	29.86	0.87 %
Saudis	16.53	18.57	20.86	23.32	25.81	2.25%
Non-Saudis	6.14	5.82	5.66	4.94	4.05	-1.38%

Source: Central Department of Statistics and Ministry of Economy and Planning
    Estimates

a top priority for Saudi Arabia. This is clearly reflected in the Eighth Development Plan, which explicitly states that 'revenue from oil resources, which are non-renewable by nature, should best be invested in renewable assets that would contribute to diversifying the economic base and achieving sustainable development'.[13] For many Saudi policymakers, industrialisation is considered as a key strategy for achieving the goals of diversification, sustainable and stable growth, enhancing the role of the private sector in the economy, and generating employment. Industrialisation is also perceived as essential to enhance the Kingdom's integration into the global economy via channels other than the export of crude oil and petroleum products.

While the Kingdom's industrialisation efforts have followed an un-even path in the past, it is possible to identify a development paradigm based on the establishment of export-oriented industries that feed on relatively cheap energy sources (the main source for the Kingdom's competitive advantage) and that capture the value added of energy resources through extending the energy chain into downstream activities. Such a strategy is expected to have positive spill-over effects on economic growth, employment generation and over time should help reduce the economy's oil dependency.[14] This strategy is very capital intensive and involves heavy public and private investment in energy-intensive industries such as refineries, petrochemicals, and other sectors such as aluminium, fertilisers and steel. At the heart of industrialisation efforts are the large wholly or majority state-owned enterprises such as Saudi Aramco and SABIC and its affiliates which operate in economic cities or special economic zones, the two most important of which are Al Jubail and Yanbu'.[15] The major economic cities in planning or under construction, as well as a number of mega projects are either petrochemical or energy related and are estimated to cost in the region of $300 billion over the next 20 years with an additional $100 billion set aside for the mega cities.[16]

The natural gas sector is central to the Kingdom's current development strategy. In a recent speech, Saudi Aramco President and CEO Mr Khalid al-Falih highlighted the central role that the gas industry plays in shaping the Kingdom's economic competitiveness stating that 'the establishment of infrastructure for the gas industry by the Kingdom's government serves as the basis for achieving the goal of economic diversification and provides the vital life blood for the industrial cities of Jubail and Yanbu' cities and most recently Rabigh'.[17] Thus, any analysis of the gas sector should be positioned within the Kingdom's wider economic and development strategy. Furthermore, given the nature of the Saudi gas reserves, which are mainly associated with oil, it is not accurate to distinguish between a 'Saudi oil policy' and a 'Saudi gas policy'. Instead, the two policies should be analysed within an all-encompassing 'Saudi energy policy' which in turn should be placed within its wider political, economic, and social context.

The Master Gas System: The First Building Block of the Saudi Gas Industry

As oil production expanded rapidly during the 1960s and 1970s, large volumes of associated gas became available to Saudi Aramco. While some of it was used to fuel the company's operations, most of the associated gas was flared. In 1970, only around 11 percent of gas produced was used while the rest was flared or used for reinjection in oil fields.[18] In 1975, Saudi Aramco developed an integrated gas system that collects and processes associated gas in order to put an end to gas flaring and to capture this valuable energy source so it can be used as feedstock in the newly created petrochemical and chemical complex SABIC. The result was the establishment of the Master Gas System (MGS), which started operating in 1982. This represented a major turning point in the Kingdom's development and industrialisation path. As seen in Figure 6.2, while in 1980 more than 70 percent of the gas produced was flared, the ratio declined in the 1980s and by the 1990s it almost reached zero, enabling Saudi Arabia to fully capture this valuable and versatile resource over a relatively short period of time.

The MGS consists of a complex web of gas-oil separating plants, gas-processing plants, fractionation and Natural Gas Liquids (NGL) recovery plants and pipelines. At the heart of this system are the gas-processing plants, namely Berri, Shedgum, Uthmaniya, Hawiya, and Haradh.[19] At these plants, impurities are removed and the gas is prepared for domestic use. Since its establishment in the early 1980s, the gas-processing capacity witnessed a rapid expansion reflecting the increasing importance of gas in the domestic energy mix. When the system first started operation in 1982, its processing capacity amounted

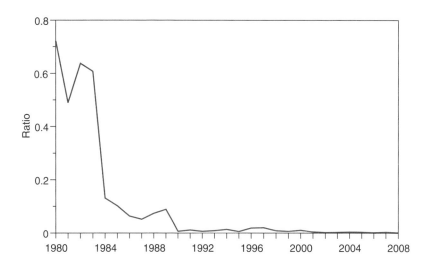

Figure 6.2: The Ratio of Gas Flaring to Total Gas Production

Source: OPEC *Annual Statistical Bulletin* 2008

to 99 million cubic metres per day. By 2009, the MGS had a capacity to process 312 million cubic metres per day of raw gas and to produce around 240 million cubic metres per day of sales gas.[20] In addition to increasing the capacity of gas-processing facilities, the MGS has been extended to deal with both associated and non-associated gas, reflecting the increasing importance of non-associated gas in the Kingdom's current gas strategy.[21] Most of the gas produced from these plants is methane and ethane, which are mainly used as fuels for power generation, water desalination plants, petrochemicals and other energy-intensive industries.

The NGL recovery plants and fractionation plants such as Juaymah, Yanbu' and Hawiyah are also integral parts of the MGS. NGLs are recovered and then piped into the fractionation units to produce ethane, propane butane and natural gasoline, which are used as feedstock for the petrochemical plants in Yanbu' and Jubail. In 2009, NGLs from hydrocarbon gasses amounted to 410.2 million barrels.[22] NGLs are then fractionated further to produce LPG for domestic use and export markets. Saudi Arabia is currently the largest producer of LPG in the Middle East with estimated production of more than 19 million tonnes/year in 2009, accounting for about 42% of the region's production.[23] Around 60 percent of the Kingdom's total production finds its way to export markets, mainly to South East Asia.[24] The rapid expansion of the gas sector is likely to increase the Kingdom's LPG capacity. However, the Saudi government's policy of promoting the development of a domestic petrochemical industry will result in a higher proportion of LPG being diverted for domestic use.[25]

Patterns of Energy and Natural Gas Demand

During the period 1980 to 2008, total energy consumption in Saudi Arabia grew at an average annual rate of 5.5 percent reflecting the rapid expansion in GDP. While in 1980 Saudi Arabia's total energy consumption stood at less than 700,000 barrels of oil equivalent per day (boe/d), energy consumption exceeded the 3 million boe/d mark in 2008 (see Figure 6.3).

In terms of sectoral shares, the transport sector accounted the largest share of crude oil consumption in 2004 followed by the services sector (which includes power generation and water desalination), then by industry and commerce (which include petrochemical and energy-intensive based industries) (see Figure 6.4). On the other hand, the shares of the agriculture and the residential sector are quite low.

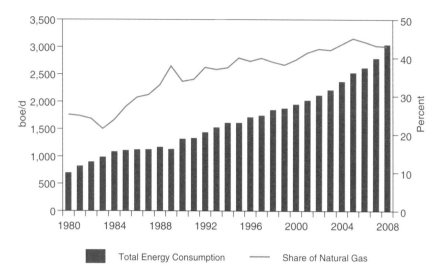

Figure 6.3: Total Local Energy Consumption (boe/d)

Source: SAMA *Annual Report* 2009

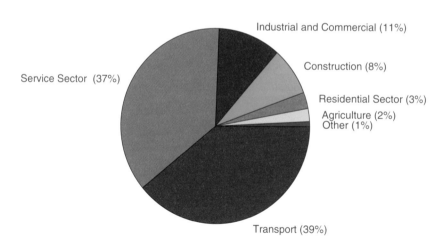

Figure 6.4: Sectoral Share of Total Crude Oil Consumption in 2004

Source: OAPEC *The Seventh Arab Energy Conference. Basics of Energy in the Kingdom of Saudi Arabia*, 2006, pp.59–60

However, the latter sector is an important indirect user through its consumption of electricity and water.

In terms of natural gas consumption, it is mainly used in power generation, water desalination and industrial cities Yanbu' and Jubail (the base for the petrochemical and energy-intensive industries) and Saudi Aramco which dominates the oil and gas sector.[26] The share of each of these sectors is shown in Figure 6.5. However, as discussed below, these sectoral shares are likely to change dramatically in the next few years reflecting the challenges faced by the Saudi gas sector.

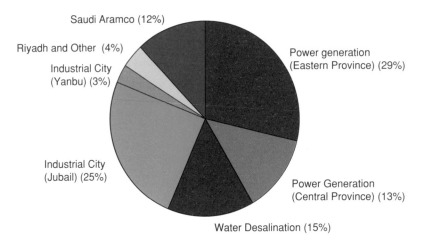

Figure 6.5: Sectoral Share of Domestic Use of Natural Gas in 2004

Source: OAPEC *The Seventh Arab Energy Conference. Basics of Energy in the Kingdom of Saudi Arabia*, 2006, p.87

With the MGS coming on-stream, the position of natural gas in the energy mix was transformed and gas became a primary source in domestic energy consumption. As seen in Figure 6.3, from around 25 percent in 1980, the share of natural gas in total domestic energy consumption continued to rise over the years reaching 45 percent in 2004 and declining slightly to 43 percent in 2008. One of the key objectives of the government is to increase the share of natural gas to more than half of total primary energy demand.[27] As seen from Figure 6.6, while in 1970 annual consumption of natural gas amounted to less than 2 billion cubic metres (Bcm), in 2009 Saudi Arabia consumed around 77.5 billion cubic metres. Between 2000 and 2009, the average annual growth of natural gas consumption stood at 5.37 percent. This rapid growth in domestic demand is likely to continue amidst rapidly growing population, general improvements in living standards and rapid industrial expansion.

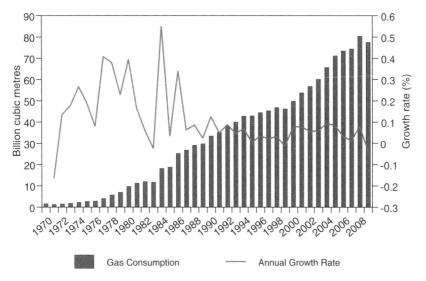

Figure 6.6: Consumption of Natural Gas, 1970–2009

Source: BP *Statistical Review of World Energy* 2010

Petrochemicals

The development of the petrochemical industry represents a major pillar in the Kingdom's development path. The underlying objectives of investment in petrochemicals are to promote industrialisation based on locally available raw materials such as oil and natural gas and to diversify industrial production and generate employment through more intensive development of downstream industries. While basic chemicals production does not generate large direct employment opportunities, there is substantial potential for job creation down the product chain and the associated services. So far, however, the petrochemical industry has had limited impact on employment generation. Despite its important contribution to GDP, the petrochemical sector currently employs around 90,000 employees who constitute only around 3.8 percent of the Saudi workforce or 1.2 percent of the total workforce. [28] While extending the energy value chain can in principle help develop more labour-intensive industries, the ability to exploit these opportunities would depend in large part on the dynamism and competitiveness of the private sector and the skill level of the domestic labour force. This could explain in part recent government efforts at reforming the education system and upgrading human capital with the necessary skills.

The foundation of the petrochemical industry can be traced to three key events in the 1970s and early 1980s, namely the development of the Master Gas System, the establishment of the industrial cities of Jubail and Yanbu' which provided the basic infrastructure for the petrochemical industry, and the establishment of SABIC as a national champion.[29] Since the mid 1980s the petrochemical industry has witnessed many transformations including the partial privatisation of SABIC, the entry of domestic and foreign private investors, the use of flexible feed crackers to increase the variety of petrochemical products, the acquisition of petrochemicals assets abroad and the development of projects outside the Kingdom, mainly in the Far East.

SABIC still accounts for the bulk of petrochemical production in the Kingdom but the government has been keen to promote private investment in this sector especially in plants that produce intermediate and finished products. This has led to the entry of many private sector ventures that operate alongside SABIC. Another important development in recent years has been the entry of Saudi Aramco into the petrochemical sector mainly through investment in integrated refining and petrochemical chemical projects. One such project is the Petro-Rabigh complex, a joint venture between Saudi Aramco and Sumitomo Chemical Company of Japan. Another project is the Ras Tanura complex, a joint venture with Dow Chemical. The completion of these two projects (and others under development) will help establish Saudi Aramco as an important player in the industry.

The petrochemical industry in Saudi Arabia has witnessed very rapid expansion accounting for 9 percent of the economy's output in 2008, the fourth largest contributor after the hydrocarbon sector, government services and finance.[30] Its transformation at the global level has been immense. From being a net importer in the 1970s, the Kingdom currently accounts for almost 7 percent of the global supply of petrochemical products.[31] This share is expected to increase to around 10 percent by 2015 as the Kingdom increases its production capacity from around 56 million tonnes/year in 2008 to 110 million tonnes/year in 2015.[32]

The main feedstocks used in petrochemical plants are ethane, methane, and by some distance NGLs.[33] All of these are derived from natural gas. Some petrochemical plants use light gasoline and naphtha as feedstock but these are used only in modest volumes. The reliance on natural gas resulted in an unbalanced mix of basic petrochemical products that are heavily tilted towards methanol and ethylene, accounting for almost 80 percent of the basic petrochemicals in the Kingdom.[34] To address this unbalanced mix of the petrochemical slate, there is an increasing trend towards using liquid feedstock in petrochemical plants but for the next decade, the petrochemical industry will predominately remain a gas-based industry.

The source of Saudi Arabia's global competitiveness in petrochemicals is ethane's substantial cost advantage. The policy of providing cheap feedstock at less than international prices is considered a key element to foster the Kingdom's petrochemical position in the global market and can largely account for the phenomenal growth of petrochemicals in the last two decades and the large domestic private and foreign investment flows into this sector. Natural gas prices for domestic use in Saudi Arabia have exhibited remarkable stability. In 1984, the government set the natural gas at the price of $0.50 per MMBtu. This price was maintained until 1998 when it was revised upwards to $0.75 per MMBtu.[35] Despite the sharp rise in gas prices in international markets during the period 1998–2008, the Saudi government did not attempt to revise the natural gas price upwards. The price stability provided an additional source of competitive advantage for the petrochemical industry in Saudi Arabia especially when compared to its Asian and European competitors. Most of the Asian and European ethylene producers rely on naphtha feedstock whose price is linked to the highly volatile crude oil prices. In addition, Saudi producers have a slight advantage over neighbouring Middle East petrochemical producers who also provide cheap ethane but at a slightly higher price range between $1.00 and $1.25.

As well as cheap ethane feedstock, local petrochemical plants also benefit from discounted prices of naphtha and NGLs. The pricing formula used to price the feedstock for domestic use is quite complex with NGLs receiving 30 percent discount to naphtha export prices and naphtha itself receiving an 11 percent discount to its price in international prices.[36] Thus, although naphtha prices are linked to crude oil prices and can be highly volatile, local producers still retain a substantial cost advantage.

While ethane seems to be the ideal feedstock for local producers, it suffers from two major disadvantages. The first relates to the increasing scarcity of ethane over the years. At the start of the industrialisation programme, ethane was in abundant supply relative to domestic demand, but this is no longer the case. This induces great uncertainty as to whether the government can maintain its policy of guaranteeing a regular flow of ethane at cheap prices in the long term. It may not have a big impact on petrochemical plants that have already secured their ethane allocation, but this will certainly be the key factor in determining the viability of new investments in the sector. The Samba financial group reports that SABIC has failed to receive any new ethane allocation since 2005 with the last ethane allocation awarded in 2006 to the Saudi International Petrochemical Company. This raises a broader issue as to whether the Kingdom's current strategy of diversification is sustainable in the long run. Views on whether the Saudi strategy produces a clear competitive advantage without domestic cheap feedstock differ. Luciani argues that while cheap feedstock prices in the GCC states' petrochemical industry played a major role in the past, they are less important today. He reasons that 'to conclude that the petrochemical industry in the GCC is not viable because it is based on cheap feedstock would be grotesque.'[37] Contrary to this, Aïssaoui argues that a change in the current dual pricing of Saudi energy for export and domestic use, and the subsequent increase in the prices for feedstock would have a 'dramatic impact on the competitiveness of the industry.'[38]

The second disadvantage relates to the fact that based on ethane, petrochemical plants can only produce low value and basic petrochemical products. As noted by a recent Samba report, encouraging the production of more sophisticated products needed to create jobs for the rapidly expanding labour force 'will require a more sophisticated feedstock mix involving both ethane and liquids such as naphtha, butane and propane'.[39] In this respect, naphtha has the additional advantage of being a much more versatile fuel and hence provides opportunities to produce more sophisticated petrochemical products that are needed to extend the value chain and generate employment opportunities. Furthermore, it is more abundant in supply given the Kingdom's massive oil reserves.[40]

Power Generation

The combination of a general improvement in the standard of living and a fast expansion of the industrial base has contributed to a rapid increase in electricity demand over the years. As seen from Figure 6.7, per capita electricity consumption in the Kingdom more than doubled from 2967 kWh per year in 1984 to more than 7000 kWh in 2007, an average annual growth of 3.7 percent during this period. Subsidised electricity prices also contributed to this high growth in demand. As seen from Table 6.2, for lower brackets, the tariff is 5 Halala/kWh for most sectors and 12 Halala/kWh for industry, which is quite low by international standards. Such tariff rates do not reflect the costs of production and encourage the inefficient use of energy. Furthermore, Table 6.2 also shows that the increase in tariff rate across the consumption brackets and across end users is minimal which raises a distributional issue. Since electricity demand increases with the level of income, these

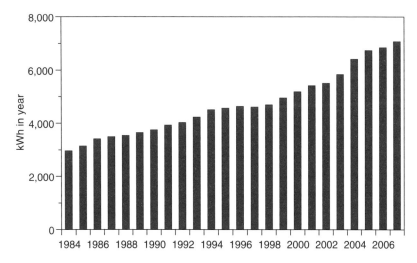

Figure 6.7: Per Capita Consumption of Electricity (kWh in year)
Source: Ministry of Water and Electricity

Table 6.2: Electricity Tariff from 2000 up to Date (Halala/kWh)*

Consumption Bracket (kWh/Month)	Residential	Commercial	Governmental	Industrial	Agricultural
1 – 1000	5	5	5	12	5
1001 – 2000	5	5	5	12	5
2001 – 3000	10	10	10	12	10
3001 – 4000	10	10	10	12	10
3001 – 5000	12	12	12	12	10
3001 – 6000	12	12	12	12	12
3001 – 7000	15	15	15	12	12
3001 – 8000	20	20	20	12	12
3001 – 9000	22	22	22	12	12
3001 – 10000	24	24	24	12	12
Over 10000	26	26	26	12	12

* 1 Halala is approximately US$0.003
Source: Ministry of Water and Electricity Website

subsidies are highly regressive in nature with households at the higher income brackets capturing the bulk of the electricity subsidy.

To meet the rapid rise in electricity demand, the last three decades witnessed a rapid expansion in power generation with capacity increasing from around 7 Gigawatts (GW) in 1982 to almost 33 GW in 2007 with the average annual growth between 2000 and 2007 exceeding 6 percent (see Figure 6.8). Interestingly, despite the robust expansion in the economy's industrial base, the share of industrial consumption has been declining and in 2007 accounted for less than 20 percent of total electricity generated. This indicates that the increase in electricity consumption has been mainly driven by the rapidly expanding population, which is expected to almost double in the next two decades.

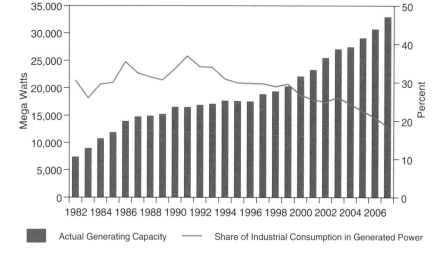

Figure 6.8: Actual Generating Capacity and Share of Industrial Use, 1982–2007

Source: Ministry of Water and Electricity Website

The fuel composition of power generation in Saudi Arabia consists of natural gas, heavy fuel oil, crude oil, and diesel oil. As can be seen from Table 6.3, fuel consumption for power generation has been growing at a fast rate, with heavy fuel oil being the fastest growing fuel between 2000 and 2008, followed by natural gas and diesel.

The power generation capacity is dominated by gas turbines and steam turbines with these two types of generating units accounting for around 90 percent of the total capacity (see Figure 6.9). The remaining 10 percent is accounted for by combined cycles and diesel engines. The Ministry of Water and Electricity expects the power generation capacity to double to 60 GW by 2023. In the original plan, natural gas and/or combined cycle were expected to drive this capacity expansion. However, there has been a change in policy and most of the newly created power generation capacity would rely on fuel oil. In 2006, the government issued a Royal Decree stating that the country's largest future power plants – which were initially planned to rely on gas – will

Table 6.3: Fuel Consumption in Power Generation by Type

Year	Diesel (tonnes)	Crude Oil (tonnes)	Heavy Fuel Oil (tonnes)	Natural Gas (million cubic metres)
2000	7,500,098	9,357,405	2,244,507	11,385
2001	8,300,947	7,124,777	2,258,160	14,733
2002	7,559,681	6,520,869	2,559,084	17,099
2003	8,220,198	5,723,823	3,803,219	18,367
2004	8,412,739	5,823,574	4,814,482	20,720
2005	8,797,885	6,565,087	4,855,595	23,097
2006	9,285,832	7,210,998	5,436,897	22,913
2007	9,287,591	7,566,051	6,233,075	22,779
2008	10,088,459	8,955,544	6,949,185	24,141
Average Annual Growth (2001–2008)	3.95%	0.38%	16.01%	10.22%

Source: OAPEC *The Eighth Arab Energy Conference. Basics of Energy in the Kingdom of Saudi Arabia*, 2010

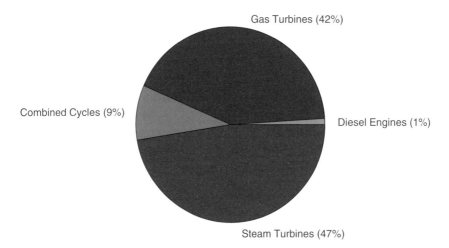

Figure 6.9: Generated Energy as Per Type of Generating Units, 2007

Source: Ministry of Water and Electricity Website

be fired by heavy fuel oil provided at a subsidised price of $0.46 per million Btu.[41] Thus, the volume of gas consumed in power generation is expected to remain unchanged reducing its share to less than 20 percent by 2023 as can be seen from Figure 6.10.[42] In this scenario, Saudi Arabia would be burning around 1.2 million b/d of liquids. A

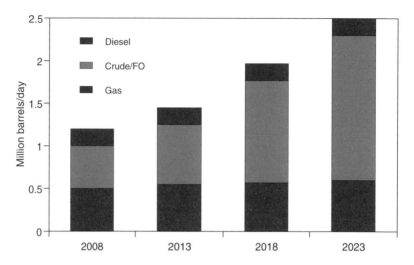

Figure 6.10: Fuel Used in Power Generation by type, 2008–2023 (Million barrels/day)

Source: Al-Khuwaiter, A. 'Solar Energy: an opportunity for Saudi Arabia', 3 June 2009

switch back to gas remains a possibility, but this will only materialise if large quantities of gas reserves are found. There are already some indications that Saudi Arabia has been forced to burn more crude oil for domestic power generation, especially at a time when it is sitting on a relatively large spare capacity. For instance, FACTS Global Energy estimates that crude oil being used for power generation could have reached as high as 470,000 b/d in 2009, up 62 percent from 2008.[43]

Water Desalination

Saudi Arabia is the global leader in water desalination with a production capacity of 3.6 million cubic metres per day.[44] Population growth, rapid urbanisation and wasteful consumption patterns for agricultural development have caused a dramatic increase in water demand. Although agriculture accounts for a small fraction of GDP, this sector was the major user of water resources in the Kingdom accounting for 88 percent of total consumption in 2000.[45] Water consumption patterns have been shaped by economic strategy in the 1970s and 1980s aimed at achieving self-sufficiency in food (especially in wheat). The cost of this strategy has been substantial in terms of depleting the Kingdom's scarce water resources and putting pressure on government finances as the cost of the subsidy programme inflated over time.

Furthermore, as in the case of electricity, water tariffs are low and this discourages the efficient use of water resources. Saudi Arabia has the highest per capita water consumption in the world consuming around 22 Bcm of water annually.[46] As in the rest of the region, water tariffs do not cover the production costs. The World Bank estimates that water subsidies amounted to around $3.2 billion in 2000 accounting for 1.7 percent of GDP and 7.0 percent of oil export revenues.[47]

Saudi Arabia has now abandoned the objectives of achieving food self-sufficiency.[48] The phasing out of Saudi wheat production in the next few years is expected to reduce the pressure on water resources. Despite this shift in strategy, Saudi Arabia's state-owned Saline Water Conversion Corp. (SWCC) has estimated that up to 2020, the country will need to spend at least $50 billion on water projects, many integrated with new power generation capacity.[49] This expansion in capacity is needed to meet the increase in water demand due to population growth, rising living standards and rapid urbanisation. The Seventh Development Plan projects an average annual growth in water demand of 1.4 percent between 2000 and 2020 with water consumption reaching 27.8 Bcm/yr in 2020 from its current level of around 22 billion cubic metres.

While part of this demand will be met by existing water reserves, desalination plants will play an important role in increasing water supplies. The IEA in 2004 estimated the desalination capacity would increase to 7.8 Bcm while the fuel requirements for desalination plants will more than triple from 11 mtoe in 2003 to 31 mtoe in 2030, accounting for around 11 percent of total primary energy supply. It is important to note that these fuel requirements include both gas and fuel oil and it is not clear how the shares of the two fuels would evolve over time. But as in the case of electricity, it is very likely that most of

Table 6.4: Fuel Consumption in Water Desalination, 1994–2014

	1994	2004	2010	2014
Diesel	686	804	730	730
	(0.98%)	(0.96%)	(0.38%)	(0.35%)
Fuel Oil	18519	36865	40462	40060
	(26.48%)	(44.07%)	(21.08%)	(19.01%)
Crude Oil	7665	0	68981	72517
	(10.96%)	(0%)	(35.94%)	(34.41%)
Natural Gas	43070	45990	81760	97455
	(61.58%)	(54.97%)	(42.60%)	(46.24%)

Source: OAPEC *The Seventh Arab Energy Conference. Basics in the Kingdom of Saudi Arabia* 2006

the additional capacity will be fuelled by crude oil reducing the relative share of gas in the water sector over the next decade. As Table 6.4 shows, although the volume of natural gas used in power generation will more than double between 1994 and 2014, its share will decline from 61 percent to 46 percent while the share of crude oil will increase from 0 to 34 percent by 2014.

The Oil and Refinery Industry

As seen from Figure 6.11, before the start of the Master Gas System, the oil sector accounted for more than 50 percent of the total natural gas consumed in the Kingdom. However, the share of the oil industry in total gas consumption has declined over the years (with some fluctuations) and now seems to have stabilised at around 20 percent. Natural gas is a key clean fuel for oil refining where it is used to produce refinery-based hydrogen to remove impurities such as nitrogen and sulphur from crude oil. Currently, existing refining capacity stands at around 2.1 million b/d but is expected to expand very fast in the next decade with much of the new additional capacity geared towards export markets. Refining projects under planning and development such as the Petro Rabigh, Yanbu', Jubail, Jazan and Ras Tanura could add as much as 1.8 million b/d of new refining capacity in the next five

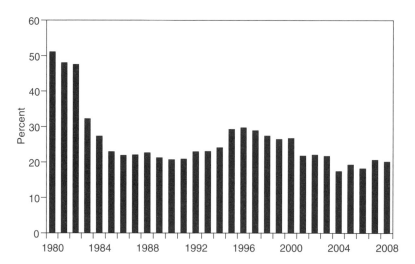

Figure 6.11: The Share of Natural Gas Consumed by the Oil and Gas Sector

Source: Saudi Arabia Monetary Agency, *Annual Report* 2009

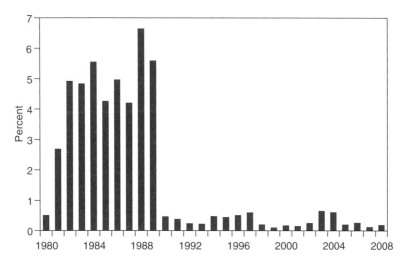

Figure 6.12: The Ratio of Gas Reinjection to Total Production

Source: OPEC *Annual Statistical Bulletin* 2008

years. It is not clear how such a rapid expansion in refining capacity would impact on gas demand.

Unlike some of its neighbouring countries such as Iran and the UAE, gas reinjection constituted less than 0.20 percent of total natural gas production in 2008. Figure 6.12 shows that while in the 1980s, the ratio of gas reinjection to total production averaged around 4.5 percent, the ratio declined during the 1990s and 2000s and in recent years has rarely exceeded 0.5 percent. This is unlikely to change in the near future as water injection is likely to remain the most prevalent form of oil recovery in Saudi Arabia.

Industrial Fuel

In line with its diversification strategy, Saudi Arabia has taken concrete steps to develop its minerals industry and there are plans to transform Ma'aaden from a small gold mining company into an integrated mining and minerals conglomerate. In 2009, the government unveiled a huge investment programme to build a phosphate/fertiliser export-oriented project to be completed in 2011. There are also plans to build a fully integrated aluminium project taking advantage of the Kingdom's baux-ite reserves. The aluminium project is very energy intensive with huge power requirements of 2.1–2.4 gigawatts. Most of these new projects will rely on liquid fuels reducing the sector's share in gas consumption over time. For instance, the dedicated power plant for the aluminium project will be fired by heavy oil provided by Saudi Aramco at the subsidised price of $2.46 per barrel.[50]

Evolution of Demand

The Ministry of Petroleum and Mineral Resources estimates that demand for natural gas will rise threefold between 2005 and 2030 reaching 150 billion cubic metres.[51] In the more immediate future, total energy consumption is expected to increase from around 3.8 million boe/d to more than 5.2 million boe/d according to the Ninth Development Plan (See Table 6.5) with natural gas accounting for around 45% of total energy consumption by 2014.

Table 6.5: Projections of Total Energy Consumption According to the Ninth Development Plan, 2009–2014

	Crude Oil (Direct Burning)	Refined products	Natural Gas (fuel)	Natural Gas (Feedstock)	Total Energy Consumption
2009	363.1	1667.3	942.1	893.9	3866.4
2010	403.0	1827.4	988.5	975.5	4194.4
2011	540.7	1986.8	1075.0	1050.0	4652.5
2012	569.9	2110.0	1161.1	1125.9	4966.9
2013	583.3	2191.9	1171.5	1119.5	5066.2
2014	624.5	2269.7	1186.8	1130.2	5211.2
Share in 2009	9.39%	43.12%	24.37%	23.12%	100.00%
Share in 2014	11.98%	43.55%	22.77%	21.69%	100.00%

Source: OAPEC *The Eighth Arab Energy Conference. Basics of Energy in the Kingdom of Saudi Arabia*, 2010

The rise in demand will bring substantial changes in the shares of the various sectors. There is a clear trend towards directing incremental supplies towards 'their most economic use in the petrochemical industry' which will have the effect of adding the 'highest possible value to the Saudi economy'.[52] This is already reflected in the share of petrochemicals in total gas consumption, which has been rising at the expense of power generation and water desalination as can be seen from Figure 6.13. Between 2003 and 2009, the share in power generation declined from 41 percent to 35 percent and water desalination from 17 to 13 percent while that of petrochemicals rose from 20 to 30 percent and industrial fuel from 8 to 10 percent. Given the challenges on the supply side (discussed in the next section), this trend is likely to consolidate in the next decade.

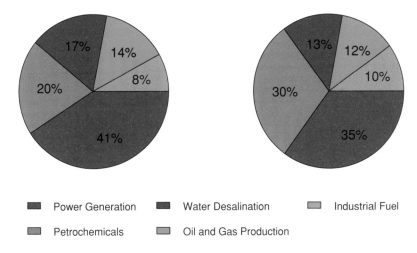

Power Generation Water Desalination Industrial Fuel

Petrochemicals Oil and Gas Production

Figure 6.13: Evolution of Sectoral Shares in Saudi Domestic Gas Market

Source: Al Falih, K.A., 'Saudi Arabia's Gas Sector ...' 2004, Figure 5.

The Supply Side: Patterns and Challenges

Given the strong pressures on the demand side, it is important to analyse whether Saudi Arabia is in a position to secure the necessary gas supplies to meet the expected rise in demand and evaluate the short-term and long-term options available to the Kingdom to deal with the 'gas challenge'.

Figure 6.14 shows the evolution of proven natural gas reserves over the period 1970 to 2009. In 2009, Saudi Arabia's proven gas reserves amounted to 7.92 tcm accounting for around 4 percent of the world's proven reserves. Although this is less than a third of the proven reserves of natural gas held by Russia, Iran, and Qatar, the world's three largest holders of natural gas, these reserves still make Saudi Arabia the fourth largest country in terms of proven natural gas. Some observers suggest that the potential for expanding gas reserves is quite large. For instance, the US Geological Survey estimates that Saudi Arabia may have around 19 tcm of undiscovered gas. Saudi Aramco claims that only 15 percent of Saudi Arabia has been 'adequately explored for gas'.[53] Interestingly, despite the rapid growth in the Kingdom's consumption of natural gas in the last four decades, proven reserves continued to increase with the rate of growth intensifying in the last few years. Between 2000 and 2009, the proven reserves grew at an average annual rate of 2.57 percent. This growth in reserves has been

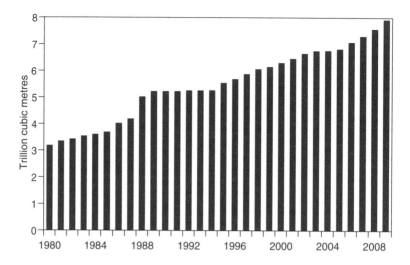

Figure 6.14: Proven Gas Reserves, 1980–2009
Source: *BP Statistical Review of World Energy* 2010

in part due to the expansion in the capacity of the oil sector since the bulk of Saudi Arabia's gas reserves are associated. According to the IEA *World Energy Outlook* 2005, around 60 percent of reserves consist of associated gas with the giant Ghawar oil field alone holding around one-third of the country's total gas reserves. In the past, the government has paid little attention to developing non-associated gas; however in recent years, efforts to increase its share in total gas production have intensified. Ali Al-Naimi, the Saudi Oil Minister, declared that between 1990 and 2008 Saudi Aramco has managed to increase the percentage of non-associated gas out of total gas production from 25 percent to about 58 percent. Many observers however doubt this figure, arguing that Saudi Arabia's use of associated gas represents at least 60 percent of its total supply.[54]

The current expansion in the Kingdom's capacity to 12.5 million b/d, which coincided with a decline in global oil demand, indicates that Saudi Arabia's spare capacity will stand above the official level of 1.5–2 million b/d for a few years to come. This implies that in the next few years Saudi Aramco will not heavily invest in the oil sector. Instead its main resources will be diverted towards the exploration and development of its non-associated gas reserves.[55] As Ali Al-Naimi puts it, 'Saudi Aramco's programmes for reserve development and gas production will continue unabated'.[56]

In order to meet its gas commitments, the Kingdom has pursued a strategy based on two main pillars. The first is to continue to expand the MGS capacity to process both associated and non-associated gas. The second is to initiate an aggressive exploration and development programme targeted at non-associated gas reserves. The latter is considered as key for the future development of the gas sector. In addition to providing secure supplies to customers and the general public, developing non-associated gas reserves increases the Kingdom's flexibility in oil production. It is important to note that there are no current plans to rely on imported gas, and as a result, Saudi Arabia is pursuing a policy of gas self-sufficiency.

The Saudi Gas Initiative

The future success of such a supply policy depends to a large extent on the prospects of discoveries in the Empty Quarter. In an unusual move, Saudi Arabia launched the Saudi Gas Initiative (SGI) in 1998 and opened up its gas sector to international companies. For the many oil companies that participated in the initiative, the initiation of the SGI signalled a shift in Saudi Arabian energy policy towards opening its oil and gas sector to foreign investment. However, the main purpose of the SGI from the government's perspective was much more limited in focus and was intended to attract foreign investment in upstream gas and downstream projects mainly in power generation, petrochemicals, and water desalination.

The SGI resulted in awarding contracts for three core areas to three consortia consisting of eight Western oil companies. The projected investment in these three core areas was estimated to stand at $25 billion. However, negotiations broke down and in 2003 Ali Al-Naimi announced the end of the SGI. Among the reasons cited for the collapse of the agreement was the high rate of return required by the foreign oil companies. But the problem is more fundamental and reflects the divergence of interests between international oil companies and the Saudi government. Through this initiative, the government wanted to achieve broad economic objectives including stimulating the growth of the economy, generating jobs, improving the infrastructure and freeing more oil for exports. For international oil companies, the objectives were rather different. In addition to achieving an acceptable rate of return, they considered the SGI as a first step towards gaining access to Saudi Arabia's enormous oil reserves. However, during the negotiations it became clear that the Kingdom would not allow oil companies to exploit its oil reserves and that access to upstream gas will be limited only to non-associated gas fields.[57]

The SGI was repackaged into a number of smaller projects that are much less ambitious in scope. Rather than pursuing a strategy of integrating upstream with downstream projects, contracts were granted for upstream non-associated natural gas reserves in an attempt to transform the Empty Quarter into a non-associated gas-producing region. The new initiative attracted a large number of foreign players. In 2003, the South Robh Al Khali company (SRAK), a joint venture between Royal Dutch/Shell, Total and Saudi Aramco, was formed to explore and develop natural gas in an area of more than 81,000 square miles in two separate concession blocks (Blocks 5-9 and 82-85). In 2004, Russia's Lukoil won a tender as part of a joint venture with Saudi Aramco (known as Luksar consortium) to explore and develop natural gas in an area of 11,000 square miles (Block A). Also in 2004, China's Sinopec won a tender as part of a joint venture with Saudi Aramco (the Sino-Saudi Gas consortium) for gas exploration and development in an area of 15,000 square miles (Block B). Finally, the Eni–Repsol YPF–Saudi Aramco consortium (known as the EniRepSA) was granted a licence to explore an area of 52,000 square km (Block C).[58]

Hopes of transforming the Empty Quarter into a non-associated gas-producing region seem to be fading. Despite drilling dozen of wells, the four consortiums have so far failed to make commercial finds of non-associated gas reserves. After drilling three wells between 2006 and 2007, Total decided to withdraw in 2008 and transferred its 30 percent share to the other partners. In 2008, Shell and Saudi Aramco drilled a new well, which has been described by MEES as 'the most expensive onshore well in oil industry history', but also failed to make a commercial discovery.[59] In August 2009, SRAK announced finding gas in one of the formations called Kidan (a field discovered by Saudi Aramco in the 1970s), but the tested gas is very sour and the reserves are very costly to develop. Nevertheless, the SRAK partners are preparing to submit a detailed plan to develop the field which signals a change in the Kingdom's gas strategy towards developing complex, challenging and costly gas fields.

A Shift in Strategy

Given these disappointing results, the Kingdom has reached a new phase where it is forced to turn to developing more challenging onshore and offshore fields. While in the early 2000s the development of the Empty Quarter constituted the cornerstone of the long-term gas development plan, this has been replaced by the development of Karan field, the first non-associated offshore gas increment in the history of the

Kingdom. The field has been fast-tracked to be completed in 2013 and is expected to hold more than 9 tcf of reserves and when completed to produce 1.8 billion scfd (18.6 Bcm).[60] The sense of urgency has also pushed Saudi Aramco to fast track the development of other offshore non-associated gas fields such as Arabiyah and Hasbah.[61][62]

One distinguishing feature from the past is that these offshore non-associated gas fields with high sulphur levels are more expensive to develop. The development of Karan is expected to cost around $3.50/MMBtu. The expected cost of developing the offshore gas fields Arabiyah and Hasbah is even higher at around $5.50/MMBtu as these fields contain high levels of sulphur and are generally more complex to develop.[63] By global standards, these costs are not especially high, but they are in comparison to the gas that Saudi Arabia has developed so far. Meanwhile, as discussed above, Saudi Aramco is committed to sell gas to its customers at a fraction of these development costs.

Pricing Issues

To many analysts, the provision of natural gas at a price below the international or regional price constitutes a classic case of a fuel subsidy intended to promote industrialisation and diversification of the Saudi economy. However, this issue is far from clear in the Saudi context. First, in order to identify whether a subsidy exists, it is important to compare the price charged to domestic consumers with some measure of cost. This is not straightforward as there is more than one concept of cost: the average cost, the marginal cost and the opportunity cost. The first refers to the overall cost per unit of output and is measured by the sum of average fixed costs and average variable costs. The marginal cost is the increment in total cost resulting from a unit change in output. In sectors such as oil and gas that require heavy capital investment, the average cost and the marginal cost are often very different. While the average cost in these sectors can be high, the marginal cost is comparatively very low. The opportunity cost on the other hand is not related to production costs. Instead, it measures the forgone value of the resource when that resource is not utilised in its best alternative use, e.g. its value in international trade if it can be exported.[64]

In the case of Saudi Arabia, it is not clear which of these three measures of cost to use. As discussed above, during the 1970s and early 1980s, most of the gas produced was in association with crude oil and NGLs. Given that crude oil was the most *sought-after* item, until very recently gas was treated by the government as a (free) by-product.

Consequently, one could argue that the cost allocated to gas production should be set to zero or at most the cost involved in construction and operating the infrastructure needed to capture, treat and distribute the associated gas. Thus, at the early stages of the development of the gas sector, the concepts of average and marginal costs were not relevant. The concept of opportunity cost for natural gas was also (and still is) irrelevant, as Saudi Arabia does not have the infrastructure to export its associated gas.[65]

As the demand for gas has intensified over the years, the Kingdom has been under pressure to expand its gas supplies by exploring and developing its non-associated gas fields. This implies that the concept of marginal cost (i.e. the cost of producing an additional 1 cubic metre of gas to satisfy the rising demand) is relevant. However, even in what seems to be a clear-cut case, it is possible to argue that the most *sought-after* item in the new projects is NGLs while the natural gas itself can be considered as a (free) by-product. In these circumstances, the concepts of average cost and marginal cost become irrelevant once more. Nevertheless, given the large spare capacity in liquids, the rapid increase in gas demand, and the recent development of non-associated fields, it is more appropriate to consider that the most sought-after product is natural gas. Hence, the cost of bringing additional gas supply from more difficult fields (i.e. the marginal cost or the average cost) should be the relevant concept of cost. The (long-term) marginal or average cost is expected to exceed the current gas price sold to domestic users.[66]

When it comes to power generation and water desalination, the issues are strikingly different and the concept of opportunity cost becomes relevant to our analysis. The rapid increase in energy demand has pushed the Kingdom to resort to burning crude oil or fuel oil in power generation and water desalination plants while diverting natural gas to the petrochemical sector where substitutes are limited. These potentially exportable fuels are provided at a fraction of international prices and hence using these liquid fuels domestically involves a substantial opportunity cost.[67]

Given that Saudi Arabia sits on large spare capacity, the crude oil used in power generation is not destined for exports. Thus, some would argue that the alternative uses of crude oil in the presence of spare capacity are either to leave it in the ground or use it in power generation and water desalination plants. According to this view, the benchmark that should be used in measuring the opportunity cost is not the export price. A natural extension of this view is that the existence of spare capacity implies that the domestic use of crude oil even at prices below international prices has no opportunity cost. On the contrary, since maintaining spare capacity entails a positive cost then all crude oil not sold internationally should be domestically utilised.[68]

This very short-term view however suffers from three major caveats. First, given that OPEC policy is set in terms of production quotas rather than export quotas an increase in domestic oil consumption reduces the country's oil export potential. Second, the availability of spare capacity fulfils a key role in stabilising oil prices in periods of disruption and sharp declines in oil demand. Thus, the cost of maintaining spare capacity should be compared to its benefits, which vary depending on many factors such as oil market conditions and the level of spare capacity. In certain circumstances, therefore, the reduction in spare capacity due to an increase in domestic consumption implies a positive (though difficult to measure) opportunity cost. [69] Third, the above analysis does not take into account inter-temporal choices. As argued by Hotelling,[70] the owner of the resource has two options: either to extract it today or to keep it in the ground for future extraction. Any amount extracted today is of course not available for extraction in the future. If the price of oil is expected to rise in the future, then the owner has the incentive to hold on to the resource and sell it at a higher international price in the future.[71] So the benchmark that should be used in measuring the opportunity cost in the presence of spare capacity is future price of oil or the long-term marginal cost of oil production.

In short, the gas pricing issue requires careful analysis that takes into account a number of factors including choosing the relevant concept of cost, the availability of spare capacity, and the phenomenon of joint products. However, regardless of the concept of cost used, it is clear that the current gas pricing policy involves a large opportunity cost and needs to be reconsidered.

Assessment of Available Options and the Current Strategy

It is clear from the above discussion that the environment surrounding the gas sector has evolved over the last two decades and accordingly the Kingdom's energy policy needs to adapt to the new realities. In effect, it needs to confront five interrelated challenges:

- Secure gas supplies to meet the rapid rise in domestic gas demand due to rapidly growing population, improvement in living standards and rapid industrialisation;

- Rely increasingly on non-associated gas reserves which are more complex and more costly to develop;
- Reassess its pricing policy to reflect the rising marginal cost and opportunity cost of utilising gas reserves;
- Ensure sustainable industrial growth; and
- Maintain the Kingdom's status as key global player in energy markets.

In dealing with these challenges, many options are available to the government. In what follows, we discuss the viability of some of these options.

Adjusting Domestic Prices

While low sale prices were justifiable during the 1970s and 1980s, with much of the new gas output in the Kingdom expected to come from more expensive non-associated reserves, including tight, deep, high sulphur reservoirs, such prices are increasingly untenable. Thus, one option is to encourage future supplies and investment in infrastructure and rationalise demand by adjusting the price of natural gas to reflect the true cost of the resource.

The decision to adjust domestic prices however is not an easy one. First, price adjustment may entail higher cost for basic services such as water and electricity, which is not politically appealing. Second, given the large sunk costs already incurred in energy-intensive projects, it would be difficult to see a reversal in government policy. The Kingdom's rapid industrial expansion is largely premised on the supply of cheap feedstock. Any change in this policy would indicate a u-turn in Saudi Arabia's long-term economic strategy with the effect of decreasing the Kingdom's competitiveness in global markets as well as increasing uncertainty in the business environment.[72] Furthermore, in an attempt to attract investment into energy-based projects, the government may have entered into legally binding contracts to provide cheap feedstock for a specified period of time. While the government has the power to revise contracts signed with domestic and foreign investors, this may come at a high cost in terms of legal proceedings and have the effect of decreasing the government's credibility as a reliable partner. Despite these factors, the gas pricing issue continues to receive high priority in the policy agenda where there are serious concerns about the economic and social impacts and the long-term sustainability of the current gas pricing policy. Furthermore, many of the contracts with industrial users are coming to an end in the next couple of years. This could induce the Saudi government to adjust its gas prices upward, though the revised price is likely to remain below what is paid by global competitors.

Dual Pricing Policy and the Option to Export

Despite the Kingdom's massive reserves, Saudi Arabia has no plans to export gas. This is unlikely to change even if massive gas reserves are found in the future and domestic demand is satisfied. The Kingdom will be reluctant to export gas as this will re-open the debate on dual pricing, an issue that Saudi Arabia has no interest in reviving.

The key factor that delayed Saudi Arabia's accession to the WTO was the pricing of natural gas for petrochemical companies.[73] The European Union was of the view that low gas prices for petrochemicals should be treated as subsidies and thus prices below international levels constitute an unfair advantage. Saudi Arabia's response rested on the fact that it does not export natural gas and hence the WTO members should take into consideration the cost of liquefying and exporting gas against the cost of using natural gas as feedstock for domestic industry.

Saudi Arabia extended this argument to the issue of discounts to naphtha and natural gas liquids. However, the issues surrounding these fuels are slightly different as Saudi Arabia adopts a dual pricing policy: a discounted price for domestic use and a price for exports.[74] The European Union insisted that dual pricing constitutes an unfair advantage and should be abolished. Saudi Arabia however stressed that discounts on NGLs and naphtha for domestic use are justified since these do not involve cost of liquefaction, storage and building new terminals, the lower costs of marketing domestically, the sale of NGLs and naphtha under long-term contracts which reduces the costs and risks associated with price volatility.[75] The European Union eventually dropped their demands for price reforms allegedly under US pressure and Saudi Arabia joined the WTO in 2005.

However, the above pricing issues did not die as recent events have clearly indicated. In June 2009, the Indian authorities issued an anti-dumping ruling against SABIC and another Saudi petrochemical company, Advanced Petrochemicals (APC) on their polypropylene products. Similarly, in 2009, China imposed anti-dumping taxes on methanol imports from Saudi Arabia. Given the cyclical nature of the energy-intensive industries into which Saudi Arabia is diversifying, the problems of anti-dumping are likely to persist, especially during downturns. In 2009, the WTO reported that during the period between 31 July and 31 December 2008, the number of initiations of antidumping investigations increased by 17 percent compared to the corresponding period a year earlier. Interestingly, the products most affected were base metal sectors and petrochemicals. During this period, there were four investigations directed towards Saudi Arabia's exports.[76] Thus, while the Kingdom may have achieved an initial success, the pricing issue is far from being settled.

The Option to Import

To secure future supplies, Saudi Arabia may consider the option of importing gas from regional producers with large non-associated gas reserves, mainly from Qatar. In fact, the two countries could enter in a swap deal with Qatar exporting gas to Saudi Arabia and the Kingdom exporting petroleum products to Qatar.[77] In the past, such options would not have been politically feasible. But in the last few years, relations between the two countries have improved. Saudi Arabia and Qatar agreed a final delineation of their land and sea borders in 2008, pledging to foster cooperation. This increases the chances of cross-border pipeline projects being undertaken in the future.

Despite the rapprochement between the two neighbours, relying on imported Qatari gas raises serious concerns about regional influence and energy security and this is likely to reduce the attractiveness of such an option. There is also the issue of pricing. To secure gas supplies from Qatar, Saudi Arabia needs to compete on prices with regional and international customers, which will create a large wedge between domestic prices and the cost of imported gas.[78] Experience from the region and the rest of the world suggests that concluding agreements on prices between regional neighbours is a lengthy and complex process that does not always result in success. However, with a shortage of gas in Saudi Arabia requiring increased consumption of domestic liquid fuel for power generation and a wider recognition of the high costs involved in such a strategy, there remains a possibility that Saudi Arabia may decide to import gas from Qatar, but this is likely to occur in the second half of the 2010s.[79] In the next few years, the no-import/no-export policy is likely to dominate Saudi Arabia's gas policy.

The Nuclear Option

Saudi Arabia may also consider the nuclear option to meet the increasing demand for electricity and water desalination. This will help free natural gas for use in the petrochemical industry to ensure sustainable industrialisation, reduce CO_2 emissions and increase energy security.

In conjunction with other GCC states, Saudi Arabia has expressed interest in nuclear energy.[80] In 2006 the 27th Supreme Council of the GCC announced that it was studying the possibility of establishing a joint nuclear energy programme, followed in 2007 by a feasibility study conducted by the International Atomic Energy Agency (IAEA) to study the feasibility of nuclear power in the region.[81] Although the nuclear option may change the entire dynamics of the energy scene in Saudi Arabia, it is unlikely to be relevant for our time horizon and hence will not be discussed further in this chapter.

The Renewable Energy Option

Renewable energy mainly in the form of power and wind can also help to meet part of the domestic demand. In terms of attributes, Saudi Arabia is one of the most productive solar regions in the world. The Saudi interest in solar energy is not new and dates back to the 1960s when the Kingdom in cooperation with foreign partners embarked on a number of solar projects.[82] However, the government did not build on the success of some of these projects and the utilisation of solar energy in Saudi Arabia did not make any reasonable progress due to a variety of obstacles, including the wide availability of oil which is superior to solar as a source of energy, the dust effect, the availability of governmental subsidies for oil and electricity generation but not for renewable energy.[83] Recently there seems to have been a revival of interest in solar energy. In 2009, Ali Al-Naimi, stated that the Kingdom has undertaken research efforts to make "'Saudi Arabia a centre for solar energy research" and, "a major megawatt exporter'".[84] It remains unclear how such an ambitious project will be achieved given that Saudi Arabia is not a technology leader in this field. Thus, while one cannot completely discount the possibility that solar energy may play a role in the energy mix sometime in the future, solar and renewable energy in general will not be relevant for our time horizon and hence are not discussed further in this chapter.

Leveraging on Oil Reserves

For the foreseeable future, Saudi Arabia's gas policy is unlikely to change and will be based on a programme of aggressive exploration and development targeted at non-associated gas reserves. According to its latest Annual Review, Saudi Aramco has set itself the target of discovering between 3 and 7 tcf of additional non-associated gas reserves annually.[85]

Unlike other countries, Saudi Arabia is in the fortunate position that it can rely on its oil reserves to hedge against the possibility of failure of such a strategy and if gas shortages ever emerge. Given the Kingdom's immense crude oil reserves and given that crude oil can replace gas in most sectors, such as power generation and water desalination, Saudi Arabia can use crude oil to fuel its utilities and free the gas for use in petrochemicals. This substitution is already taking place where additional power generating capacity will be fuelled by fuel oil rather than gas. Whether such substitution will intensify and extend to other sectors would depend on a number of factors including the level of available spare capacity at that time, the pace of industrialisation and the gas supply–demand gap.

The authorities are also increasingly encouraging the use of liquid feedstock in the petrochemical industry both in order to provide a viable alternative to ethane and to diversify the supply of petrochemical products to encourage extending the petrochemical chain.[86] In fact, the recent trend towards integration of refineries and petrochemical plants pursued by Saudi Aramco falls within this strategy. While the world's largest refineries are integrated with petrochemical facilities, this trend has just gathered momentum in the Kingdom. Long periods of low refining margins have discouraged Saudi Aramco from investing in increasing refining capacity. However, there is growing consensus among Saudi policy-makers that one of the solutions to the problem of feedstock availability is to integrate chemical facilities with existing refineries that produce naphtha and NGLs. Given that SABIC does not own any refineries, these large integrated projects are being implemented by Saudi Aramco and its foreign partners. For instance, the Ras Tanura petrochemical complex, the joint venture with Dow Chemical, will use naphtha as feedstock with the naphtha being produced from the Ras Tanura refinery. Similarly, the Petro-Rabigh petrochemical complex, the joint venture with Sumitomo Chemical Company of Japan, uses mixed feedstock produced from the Rabigh refinery. In 2008, Saudi Aramco and Total signed a Shareholders' Agreement and other core agreements for the establishment of a *Jubail Refinery-Aromatics Complex*. The contracts for construction were awarded in 2009 and are scheduled for completion during the second quarter of 2013. Saudi Aramco has also earmarked its Yanbu' refinery for integration.

Nevertheless, the option of leveraging on the Kingdom's massive oil reserves involves high costs. It also should not be treated in isolation of the Kingdom's general energy policy and its international role in oil markets. Thus, this option, though available, cannot be continuously relied upon in the long term and should only be used as a last resort.

Conclusion

From the margins, Saudi Arabia's gas sector has witnessed major transformations that have placed it at the centre of the Kingdom's energy policy and development strategy. While many milestones have been crossed in the past, the current challenges facing the sector are immense. Rather than widening its options to deal with the 'gas challenge', Saudi Arabia is likely to continue with its main energy strategy based on expanding its gas reserves to meet the expected growth in domestic demand. From the government's perspective, the provision of low and stable natural gas prices is central for the success of its industrialisation policy and for ensuring long-term political and social stability. Thus, changes in pricing policy seem remote but not impossible. On the other hand, due to energy security concerns and pricing issues, the options of gas imports and/or exports are not currently attractive and in fact these options may even create more problems than they would solve.

There are signs that the current strategy is facing some strains. The issues of allocation of scarce gas between sectors such as power generation and the petrochemical sector, the interaction between the gas sector and the oil sector and the ability of the Kingdom to maintain its key position in global energy markets, the centrality of natural gas in the country's long-term development strategy, the limited success of the petrochemical sector in creating jobs so far, and the domestic and international pricing issues are some indications of the challenges facing Saudi Arabia. The stated policy that the petrochemical sector has the top priority in obtaining gas supplies implies that in the absence of large gas finds, the requirements of any future expansion in power generation and water desalination will be met by liquid fuels and not gas, contrary to the general trend in the rest of the world. Unlike other countries in the region, the Kingdom is fortunate in that it can always rely on its massive oil reserves to continue with the current policies and to hedge against the potential failure of achieving self-sufficiency in gas. However, this would be far from ideal and such a policy would induce serious political and economic costs. It is the ability of the policy-makers to show a greater degree of flexibility and to make some hard choices today that will ultimately determine the evolution of the gas sector in the next few years and with it the country's economic path ahead.

Notes

1   BP *Statistical Review of World Energy*, June 2010.
2   Saudi Aramco, *Annual Report* 2007, p.22.
3   Calculation based on Saudi Arabian Monetary Agency (SAMA), *45ᵗʰ Annual Report*, 2009, p. 29, Table 2.2.
4   Ibid., p. 144 calculated from Table 10.1; Samba, 'Saudi Petrochemicals Sector: Current Situation and Future Prospects,' August 2009, p. 3.
5   SAMA, *45ᵗʰ Annual Report*, p. 132.
6   Calculation based on Table 2.2, Ibid., p. 29.
7   Calculation based on Table 18.6 and data from Ibid., p. 243.
8   Ibid,, p. 243.
9   Ibid., p. 246.
10 Husain, A.M., Tazhibayeva, K., and Ter-Martirosyan, A., 'Fiscal Policy and Economic Cycles in Oil-Exporting Countries', *IMF Working Paper* WP/08/253, 2008.
11 These projections are based on the assumption that the government is successful in reducing the number of non-Saudis, which is very challenging.
12 In addition to population growth, rising female participation in the labour force has increased new entrants into the labour market.
13 Kingdom of Saudi Arabia, *Eighth Development Plan* 2005–2009, Ministry of Economy and Planning, p.52.
14 However, it is not clear whether the current strategy of developing energy-intensive industries can really achieve the goal of diversification. After all, refining and petrochemicals are closely linked to the hydrocarbon sector. Development of energy-intensive industries such as petrochemicals and aluminium will only reinforce the dominance of the hydrocarbon sector. It is also not clear whether such capital-intensive projects can generate the jobs that are highly needed to alleviate the unemployment problem. Samba (2009), Ibid., p.5.
15 There are plans to build four such industrial cities by 2020: King Abdullah Economic City (KAEC) in Rabigh, the Hail Economic City in Hail, the Knowledge Economic City in Al- Madinah, and the Jizan Economic City in Jizan. There are also plans to build three additional cities but these are still at very early stages: Tabuk Economic city, Ras Az-Zawr Industrial Mining City and the Sudair Industrial City. These cities will not only contain real estate projects, but will also be the home for heavy industries such as petrochemicals and aluminium and other service-based industries.
16 Ramady, M.A., 'Saudi Petrochemical Industry: The Heart of Investment", *Arab News*, Monday 16 July 2007.
17 Al-Falih, K., 'Saudi Aramco's Role in Industrial Development', *Middle East Economic Survey*, 52:16, 20 April. 2009.
18 OAPEC, The Sixth Arab Energy Conference. Country Papers, Part 1. Cairo, Arab Republic of Egypt, 11–14 May 2002 (in Arabic).
19 OAPEC, The Seventh Arab Energy Conference. Energy Basics in the

Kingdom of Saudi Arabia. Amman, Kingdom of Jordan, 14–17 May 2006 (in Arabic); Al-Salamah, M., 'On the Natural Gas Production, Transportation and Consumption in Saudi Arabia: A 2000 Perspective', King Fahd University of Petroleum and Minerals, 2003.

20 Arab Petroleum Research Center, *Arab Oil & Gas Directory 2009* (Paris: APRC, 2009).
21 For instance, the Hawiyah gas plant brought on stream in 2001 exclusively processes non-associated gas.
22 Saudi Aramco (2010), *Annual Review-2009*.
23 Hart, W., R.Gist, K. Otto (2010) "Global LPG Market Begin Recovery from Recession", *Oil & Gas Journal*, June 7, p.62-68.
24 Arab Petroleum Research Center, *Arab Oil and Gas Directory 2009*.
25 The MGS system also enabled the recovery of sulphur dioxide at petroleum refineries and hydrogen sulphide at gas-processing plants such as Shedgum and Uthmaniyah. This enabled the Kingdom to become a major producer of sulphur with production expected to reach 3.2 million tons per year in 2013, making Saudi Arabia one of the key producers in the global market. Currently, the bulk of the sulphur is being exported. However, plans for rapid expansion in the fertiliser sector indicate that local demand is projected to increase in the next few years. Salamah, M., 'Sulfur Utilization Prospects in Saudi Arabia', Paper presented at the 2004 IFA Production and International Conference, 3–5 October 2004, Dubai UAE.
26 The category 'Riyadh and other' in Figure 6 stands for residential and commercial demand.
27 An interview with the CEO of Saudi Aramco Dr Khaled Al-Falih. *Al Hayat*, Tuesday 28 July 2009, p. 11 (in Arabic).
28 Samba (2009), Ibid., p.5.
29 Al-Sa'doun, A. 'Saudi Arabia to become major Petrochemicals hub by 2010', *Oil and Gas Journal*, 2 January 2006.
30 Samba, 'Saudi Petrochemicals Sector …' (2009), p.3.
31 Ibid., p.9.
32 Arab Petroleum Research Center, *Arab Oil and Gas Directory 2009*.
33 Al-Sa'doun, A. 'Saudi Arabia to Become Major Petrochemicals Hub by 2010', 2006.
34 Ibid.
35 OAPEC, The Seventh Arab Energy Conference 2006.
36 Samba 'Saudi Petrochemicals Sector … (2009), p.8.
37 Luciani, G, 'Domestic Pricing of Energy and Industrial Competitiveness', Al Jisr Research Paper, October 2009.
38 Aïssaoui 2004/05, The Likely Impact of Saudi Arabia's Accession to the WTO on the Saudi Petrochemical Industry, APICORP memo, p.10.
39 Samba, 'Saudi Petrochemicals Sector …' (2009), p.1.
40 Ibid., p.8.
41 EIA, Saudi Arabia. *Country Analysis Briefs*, August 2008, retrieved online at http://www.eia.doe.gov/emeu/cabs/Saudi_Arabia/NaturalGas.html (October 2009).

42 This is fundamentally different from IEA (2004) projections where it ex-
    pected the share of natural gas in power generation to rise from 46% in
    2003 to 66% in 2030. IEA, *World Energy Outlook. Middle East and North Africa
    Insight*, 2005.
43 Reuters, 'Saudi Burns more Crude for Power, Halts Fuel Oil Import", 27
    July, 2009.
44 Mukhtar, A., 'Saudi Arabia: Water & Waste Water in Saudi Arabia', US
    Commercial Service, United States of America, Department of Commerce,
    2007.
45 World Bank, 'A Water Sector Assessment Report on the Countries of the
    Corporation Council of Arab States of the Gulf' Water, Environment,
    Social and Rural Development Department Middle East and North Africa
    Region, Washington: World Bank, 2005, p.27.
46 Mukhtar, A. 'Saudi Arabia: Water & Waste Water … 2007.
47 World Bank, 'A Water Sector Assessment Report … 2005.
48 Reuters, 'Saudi Arabia Scraps Wheat Growing to Save Water', 8 January
    2008.
49 EIA, Saudi Arabia. *Country Analysis Briefs*, 2008.
50 'Saudi Arabia's Diversification Plans Take Shape as Ma'aden Receives
    Financing', *Zawya.com*, 17 June 2009.
51 EIA, Saudi Arabia. *Country Analysis Briefs*, 2008.
52 Al-Falih, K.A., 'Saudi Arabia's Gas Sector: its role and growth opportuni-
    ties', *Oil & Gas Journal*, 21 June 2004, p.21.
53 EIA, Saudi Arabia. *Country Analysis Briefs*, 2008.
54 'A New Chapter', *O&G Next Generation*, Issue 4, retrieved online at http://
    www.ngoilgasmena.com/article/A-new-chapter/ (October 2009). The rela-
    tive importance of non-associated gas receives special importance at times
    when Saudi Arabia is implementing oil output cuts as doubts are raised
    as to whether it can maintain production cuts for a long period of time
    without jeopardising local gas supplies. Ali Al-Naimi however dismissed this
    argument as a fallacy, arguing that Saudi Arabia has made it a priority
    to lower crude production at fields with heavy and medium crudes where
    little or no associated gas is produced. See *IHS Global Insight*, 'Associated
    Gas Demand No Longer Obstacle to Lower Crude Production—Saudi Oil
    Minister', 20 March 2009.
55 Interview with the CEO of Saudi Aramco Dr Khaled Al-Falih. *Al Hayat*,
    Tuesday 28 July 2009, p. 11 (in Arabic).
56 *O&G Next Generation*, Issue 4.
57 Simmons, M., *Twilight in the Desert: The Coming Saudi Oil Shock and the World
    Economy* (Hoboken, New Jersey: John Wiley & Sons, 2005).
58 *Gas Matters*, 'Is it Crunch Time for Saudi Arabia's Gas Development Pro-
    gramme?' April 2009, pp.14-17.
59 'SKAK's Kidan-6 Well Fails To Find Gas At Khuff Target', *Middle East
    Economic Survey*, 52:16, 20 April 2009, p.15.
60 'Is it Crunch Time for Saudi Arabia's Gas Development Programme?', *Gas
    Matters*, April 2009.

61 'Saudi Aramco Looks to Gulf Offshore for Gas Boost', *MEES*, 9 March 2009, p.2.

62 Another large non-associated offshore natural gas field is Durra, located offshore in the Saudi-Kuwaiti Neutral Zone. However, it is very unlikely that Durra will be developed any time soon. In July 2000, Saudi Arabia and Kuwait reached an agreement to share Durra output equally but 70% of the field is also claimed by Iran whose maritime border with Kuwait remains un-demarcated. Although there have been reports that Kuwait and Iran agreed to jointly develop the field, no production plans have yet been disclosed. See Aghdam, R.F., 'Why Invest in the Eastern Province', *ASharqia Chamber, 2008*, pp.26–7.

63 *Gas Matters*, April 2009, p.16.

64 For a detailed discussion of this, see Giacomo Luciani, 'Domestic Pricing of Energy and Industrial Competitiveness', October 2009.

65 This raises the issue of whether Saudi Arabia should aim at exporting gas, especially that the current policy of diverting gas to petrochemicals and energy intensive industries has had limited impact on diversification and employment generation. This requires a thorough cost-benefit analysis which is beyond the scope of this paper. See Mabro, R., 'Saudi Arabia's Natural Gas: A Glimpse at Complex Issues', *Oxford Energy Comment*, October 2002 for details on the arguments for and against such an option.

66 The availability of NGLs complicates the analysis as they play a fundamental role in changing the economics of the new upstream gas projects. However it is unlikely to alter the above point.

67 Luciani, G., 'Domestic Pricing of Energy and Industrial Competitiveness', 2009.

68 This raises a broader issue as to whether Saudi Arabia should invest in developing more costly gas reserves and building a more expensive gas infrastructure while sitting on large spare capacity and a cheaper source of energy.

69 Otherwise, if the opportunity cost of using spare capacity is always zero, then the Kingdom should aim to utilise all its spare capacity before developing any additional gas or oil reserves.

70 Hotelling, H., 'The Economics of Exhaustible Resources', *The Journal of Political Economy*, Vol. 39, 1931.

71 In fact, this inter-temporal dimension is recognised by Saudi Arabia's King Abdullah himself. Reuters news service reported that the King has ordered some new oil discoveries left untapped to preserve oil wealth in the world's top exporter for future generations: 'I keep no secret from you that when there were some new finds, I told them, "no, leave it in the ground, with grace from god, our children need it"' Reuters (2008), "Saudi King says keeping some oil finds for future", April 13.

72 Luciani, G., 'Domestic Pricing of Energy and Industrial Competitiveness', 2009.

73 Seznec, Jean-Francois, 'Saudi Arabia's Accession to the WTO: Is a "Revolution" Brewing?' *Middle East Policy Council Capitol Hill Conference Series on US*

Middle East Policy, Washington D.C., 13 January 2006.

74 The rapid expansion in the petrochemical sector however will render the dual pricing less important in the next few years as it is expected that most of the NGLs will be domestically consumed and hence the discounted price is the only one that will prevail.

75 Seznec, J.-F., 'Saudi Arabia's Accession to the WTO', 2006.

76 'WTO Secretariat reports increase in new anti-dumping investigations', WTO Press Release, 7 May 2009.

77 This might prove a less costly option than the current Gas-to-Liquid projects in Qatar.

78 When asked whether Qatar is under pressure to meet the gas deficit in the region, Abdullah bin Hamad Al-Attiyah, the Qatari Energy Minister responded that Qatar will direct the gas 'in judgment where we [Qataris] should use it. Then we will see what is the added value, what is the best for us to sell it in the region or convert it to LNG or GTL' asserting that Qatar is 'not in the social security game' but is 'business-oriented'. England, A., 'Middle East: Oil Rich Region Faces Gas Shortfall', *Financial Times*, 26 May 2009.

79 In case the Kingdom decides to import gas, the imported gas cannot be used in petrochemicals. With the current pricing policy, this would constitute a clear violation of WTO rules as the government would be buying gas at a higher price and selling it to petrochemicals at a lower price. One way to overcome this problem is to use all imported gas in power generation and water desalination. An alternative way is to adjust domestic prices upwards to levels in line with the cost of imports.

80 Saudi Arabia however has recently announced that it also considers going nuclear without the rest of the GCC. Husain, S., 'Saudi Arabia may go it alone on nuclear energy', *Maktoub*, 7 November 2009.

81 Al-Qaradawi, I., 'Setting up Nuclear Programmes in the Arabic Peninsula', Presentation at the World Nuclear University, Summer Institute, 2009.

82 For details see Alawaji, S.H., 'Evaluation of solar energy research and its applications in Saudi Arabia — 20 years of experience', *Renewable and Sustainable Energy Reviews* 5 (2001) 59–77.

83 Ibid.

84 'Saudi Arabia positioned to become solar power', CBS News, Friday, 29 August 2008.

85 Saudi Aramco (2010), Annual Review 2009.

86 Samba (2009), Ibid., p.17.

CHAPTER 7

NATURAL GAS IN IRAQ

Lorian Yacoub and Ian Rutledge

Introduction

A survey of the present state of the natural gas industry in Iraq presents special difficulties, which will no doubt be obvious to the reader. At the time of writing (January 2010) the country is still under US military occupation and although the security situation appears marginally better than a few years ago, government and administrative institutions remain weak and the infrastructure of the oil and gas sector has only begun to recover from the devastation of invasion, war and insurgency. For these reasons – as will be made clear in the text and Appendix A – there are very considerable difficulties in discovering and analysing even the most basic data about the natural gas sector of Iraq in its current state, let alone making reasonable forecasts of its future trajectory.

Nevertheless, within these very tight constraints, this chapter attempts to provide a basic outline of the industry. Sections 1, 2 and 3 examine the size, geographical distribution and chemical composition of the country's reserves of natural gas, underlining the fact that the majority consists of relatively sweet, associated gas in solution located in the southern governorates. Sections 4, 5 and 6 attempt to assess the size of natural gas production, its different components and its pattern of consumption. The great variability of public domain data with respect to production is underlined and in particular, the difficulties of coming to any reasonably certain estimate of 'marketed' production. The overall picture is one of relatively small quantities of gas being produced of which the majority is flared and wasted. Section 7 looks at the legal and contractual framework for hydrocarbon production in general and underlines the great and continuing uncertainties in this field. The particular problem posed by the serious disagreements between the Federal Government and the Kurdistan Regional Government are emphasised. Section 8 provides a brief survey of the major gas projects currently under development or consideration by the Iraqi and Kurdish authorities and the participation and role of international oil companies in these plans. Section 9 looks briefly at the controversy in Iraq regarding the

Map 7.1: Iraq's Oil and Gas Fields and Pipelines

Shell-led South Gas Exploitation Project and finally Section 10 situates this controversy within the wider one of Iraq's potential as a significant natural gas exporter. The authors conclude that in the near to medium term there seems little likelihood of Iraq playing such a role.

Reserves Data

Having increased fourfold since 1980, proven reserves of natural gas in Iraq remained roughly constant from 1990 onwards according to the principal public domain source on this subject, the *OPEC Annual Statistical Bulletin.*[1] Of the other three public domain sources, CEDIGAZ and BP appear to simply recycle the OPEC data, whereas the *Oil and Gas Journal* also seems to base its 'estimates' on the OPEC data, albeit with a few unexplained discrepancies in earlier years (Table 7.1).

Moreover, the most recent data on proven gas reserves from an Iraqi official source are almost identical to the figures given by the above-mentioned public domain sources – 3100 Bcm.[2] Using the BP data for total MENA proven reserves, Iraq's figure represents about 3.8 percent of the MENA total (81,290 Bcm).

Table 7.1: Iraq, Proven Reserves of Natural Gas, various data sources, selected years, Bcm

	OPEC/BP/ CEDIGAZ	OGJ	Iraq Oil Commission/ Ghadhban
1980	780	777	n/a
1985	821	821	n/a
1990	3107	2690	n/a
1995	3360	3101	n/a
2000	3109	3109	n/a
2005	3170	3170	n/a
2006	3170	3171	n/a
2007	3170	3170	3100

Sources: OPEC Annual Statistical Bulletin, various years; CEDIGAZ, 'Trends and Figures' various years; Oil & Gas Journal, various issues; IOC/Ghadhban, 'Iraq Oil Industry. Present Status and Future Outlook.

In addition to these proven reserves, it is believed that Iraq also has an additional 7500 Bcm of probable natural gas reserves.[3]

Breaking down the proven gas reserves according to reservoir source, it can be seen from Table 7.2 that by far the vast majority (around 80 percent) is found as associated gas in existing oilfields, either as gas in solution or cap/dome gas overlying producing oil fields.[4] However, according to the sources for Table 7.2, the percentage of associated gas has fallen somewhat since 1996 as some new reserves of free gas have been proven and cap gas reserves have depleted.

Table 7.2: Iraq, Proven Gas Reserves according to category, 2007 and 1996, Bcm

Type	Reservoir	Bcm 2007	% 2007	Bcm 1996	% 1996
Associated	Solution Gas	2200	71	2197	71
Associated	Cap Gas	280	9	459	15
Total Associated		2480	80	2656	86
Non-associated	Free Gas	620	20	428	14
Total (All Types)		3100	100	3084	100

Sources: Ghadhban, T. & Al-Fathi, S. 'The gas dimension of the Iraq oil industry', 2001, p.29 & IOC/Ghadhban, 'Iraq Oil Industry', p.8.

Analysis of the 78 oil and gas fields either producing (27) or awaiting development (51) listed in the Annexes to the February 2007 Petroleum Law (See Appendix B and Map 8.1), suggests that the share of associated gas reservoirs in the total is roughly the same as in Table 7.2 (82.8 percent) but with a smaller share for solution gas (64 percent) and a larger share for cap gas (18.8 percent). According to this data source the free gas share is 17.2 percent. (See Appendix C)[5]

When we turn to the probable reserves category, 4500 of the total 7500 Bcm are believed to be free gas with the remaining 3000 Bcm associated gas. Even so, it must be clear that, over the next few years, the bulk of Iraq's gas supplies will continue to be associated gas (predominantly in solution) and will therefore be largely dependent on the pace of expansion of Iraq's oil industry.

In addition it has been estimated that Iraq possesses around 4600 Bcm of undiscovered free gas reserves and a further 4646 Bcm of gas reserves associated with estimated probable oil reserves.[6]

Geographical Distribution of Gas Reserves

About 88 percent of Iraq's proven solution gas reserves (both developed and undeveloped) are located in Iraq's southern oil fields (Governorates of Al-Basra, Dhi Qar, Maysan) with the remaining 12 percent in the northern and central oil fields. This uneven distribution is due partly to the uneven distribution of Iraq's oil reserves (since about 75 percent of these are in the southern fields) and partly to the fact that the gas-to-oil ratio in the southern oil fields is, on average, nearly twice that of the northern fields.[7] The fields with the five largest proven reserves of solution gas are West Qurna, Nahr Umar, Majnun, North Rumayla and South Rumayla, all of them in the southern oil region and which between them contain 1349 Bcm (43 percent) of Iraq's total proven reserves of a natural gas (see Appendix B).

Apart from a small gas cap in the Ghar formation of the southern Majnun field, all the gas caps are found in the northern and central fields.

The free gas reserves, totalling around 620 Bcm according to the Iraq Oil Commission/Ghadhban (542.4 Bcm according to our breakdown of the Annexe data: see Appendix C), are located in ten fields of which two (Chemchemal and Kor Mor [formerly Anfal]), are in the Kurdish province of Sulaymaniya. The only significant free gas field in the south is at Siba, 30 km south of Basra, with 86 Bcm of proven reserves, while another free gas field, Akkas, with proven reserves most recently estimated at 129 Bcm, is situated in the Western Desert province of Al-Anbar close to the Syrian border.

Gas Specification

From Table 7.3 it can be observed that the solution gases produced by the southern oil fields are both richer in gas liquids and sweeter (less sulphurous) than those produced by the northern fields. With hydrogen sulphur levels on average more than 7 percent in gases from the northern fields, sulphur recovery is an essential part of processing. The example of a cap gas reservoir (Jambur) is – not surprisingly – dryer than the solution gases of the southern and northern fields, while also being 'sweet' like the gases from the southern fields. The example of free gas taken from an appraisal well at the Akkas field shows it to be broadly similar to the cap gas at the Jumbur field but containing carbon dioxide, albeit at a relatively low level.

Table 7.3   Composition of Gas Streams, %

Composition	Northern Fields	Southern Fields	Jambur Field	Akkas Field Well SA-2
	Solution	Solution	Cap	Free
Light Gases (C1 + C2)	75.4%	75.2%	89.5%	89.47%
Gas Liquids (C3 +)	13.1%	22.6%	10.5%	8.46%
H2S	7.2%	Trace	-	-
CO2	4.3%	1.5%	-	2.07%

Sources: Ghadhban & Al-Fathi, 'The gas dimension of the Iraq oil industry, p.34; Al-Shalchi, W., *Development of Akkas Gas Field in Iraq*, 2008, p.8

Production Data

The various sources of information on Iraq's production of natural gas are, at the time of writing, highly inconsistent. Conceptually, when analysing *any* natural gas industry we should be able to distinguish five categories of output. (1) 'Gross production' is the total output of raw gas at the well-head before any separation or processing takes place. From this 'gross production' three categories of gas are deducted before arriving at the net, 'marketed' production. These are (2) gas that is re-injected into oil wells to maintain or increase pressure; (3) gas that is wasted by flaring or venting into the atmosphere; (4) gas that is lost through 'shrinkage' (which is the volumetric loss resulting from gas processing operations, or any other loss or wastage). What remains is then (5) 'marketed production'. However, it should also be noted that because 'marketed' gas production is simply the residual after the deduction of categories (2), (3) and (4), it includes not only the gas which is traded in formal markets but also gas which is utilised in other industrial sectors such as petrochemicals or power generation where the transaction may be internal to a vertically-integrated economic organisation and the gas 'price' may be just a semi-theoretical transfer price.[8] Generally speaking our principal interest is to identify the size of this 'marketed' gas since it is the economically significant fraction. Ideally we should also like to be able to account for gas production in terms of energy (e.g. Joules, BTUs and so on) rather than volumes, given that identical volumes of natural gas may have different calorific values depending on the amounts of other, non-methane, gases they contain.

However, as acknowledged in a previous OIES volume on natural gas, published data on Middle East gas production rarely conform to the criteria laid out above or where it appears to do so, the appearance is often spurious:

> Data on gas production in Middle Eastern countries are often inconsistent leading to questions over their reliability. Variations occur because measurements are made using different units and the conversion factors depend on the quality of the gas. The way in which natural gas liquids and the gas used in treatment and compression are accounted for also varies between sources. Furthermore, in some cases gas re-injected into oil reservoirs to enhance production is included in the gas production data while in others it is excluded. The volumes of gas involved can be significant'.[9]

These and other data reliability problems – including some emanating from the Saddam period which may be little more than deliberate deception and others from commercial organisations purporting to offer business 'intelligence' which can only be described as seriously slip-shod 'research' – plague our understanding of just how much gas has been produced in Iraq in recent years and into which category this gas falls. And if we cannot accurately identify the historical base-line for these variables we have no means to assess whether any progress is being made with respect to the industry's contribution to sustainable economic growth and improved human welfare. Further elaboration of these measurement and data consistency problems is given in Appendix A.

At the time of writing, the most recent production figures available from official Iraqi sources are those of the Iraq Oil Commission/ Ghadhban and the Ministry of Oil (MOO) for the year 2004 presented at the 2007 Dubai Energy Conference. The former gives a figure for gross production (15.5 Bcm) and for flared gas (10.3 Bcm).[10] The MOO presentation states that 'current production' in the 'Southern region' is 1000 million standard cubic feet per day (mmscf/d) (10.3 Bcm/yr) and in the Northern region 500 mmscf/d (5.2 Bcm/yr), but that the volume which reaches the gas processing facilities 'does not exceed 300 mmscf/d (3.1 Bcm/yr) in the South and 200–250 mmscf/d (2.1–2.6 Bcm/yr) in the North.[11] However, these figures equate approximately to the same 15.5 Bcm/yr gross and 10.3 Bcm/yr flared as the IOC/Ghadhban figures for 2004. On the basis of both sets of data and those in the previous paragraph, we might, very tentatively, conclude that over the past few years 'marketed' gas production (i.e. gas production which has been processed and consumed by other sectors) has been somewhere between 2.2 Bcm/yr and 5.5 Bcm/yr bearing in mind that with respect to the latter figure, we have no data from either the MOO or IOC for any deductions due to reinjection or shrinkage. That is about the best we can do. And to put these figures into perspective they are roughly equivalent to 2.2 per cent to 6.7 per cent of 2006 UK net gas production.

Turning to specialist reports and trade journals offers little help in this respect. Suffice it to say, that one such source, published in the first quarter of 2009, gives 'historical' data for Iraqi gas production sourced to the BP *Statistical Review of World Energy*, when the BP *Review* has never published such figures. The same report was forecasting an increase for marketed production to around 8.0 Bcm in 2009, a prediction apparently based on the fact that the author of the report in question expected that Iraq would be 'exporting gas to Kuwait' by the end of 2008.[12]

Gas Processing and Utilisation

Although production of natural gas began with the commencement of oil production in 1927, the vast majority was simply flared. Even as late as 1970, with gross production at 6.1 Bcm, only 13 percent of it was actually utilised. Ten years later, this had only increased to 22 percent.[13] However, during the 1970s and 1980s, two modern gas-processing plants and gathering systems (North Area Gas Project and South Area Gas Project) were constructed to supplement two smaller existing ones.

The North Area Gas Plant design capacity was for a throughput of 536 mmscf/d of raw gas (about 5.5 Bcm/year).

The South Gas Project started in the mid 70s in two stages and was completed in 1985, but was not brought online until February 1990. Plant design was for a throughput of 1050 mmscf/d (10.9 Bcm/yr). Together with the throughput of two smaller plants, North Rumayla and Kor Al-Zubayr, before the US invasion, the gas-processing sector had a total raw gas throughput capacity of 2080 mmscf/d (about 21.5 Bcm/yr), a dry gas production capacity of 1560 mmscf/d (16.12 Bcm/yr) together with 5.5 million tonnes per year of LPG (butane and propane), 2.28 Million tonnes of natural gasoline and 500,000 tonnes/ yr of sulphur.[14]

Natural gas also used to be exported to Kuwait through a 40-inch, 105-mile pipeline. The gas was used to supply Kuwaiti power stations and LPG plants, but was halted following Iraq's invasion of the country in August 1990.

In addition, a 1775 km national gas transmission pipeline system, built and operated by the state-owned Oil Pipeline Company (OPC), was constructed extending from Basra in the south to Mosul in the north and connected to most of the industrial and power plants in the country.

During the 1990s, the dry gas produced by the processing plants together with dry natural (cap) gas from the Jumbur field was consumed by four main sectors, as shown in Table 7.4.

Table 7.4: Gas Consumption by Sector (%), 1995 and 1999

	1995	*1999*
Power Generation	25.45	35.2
Industrial feedstock	35.18	25.8
Industrial fuel	3.40	2.2
Oil industry (Fuel & Feed)	35.90	36.7
Other	0.07	0.01
Exports	0	0

Source: Ghadhban & Al-Fathi, 'The gas dimension of the Iraq oil industry', pp.40–1.

Currently the solution and cap gas operations in the north and central areas of Iraq (i.e. to the north of 32.5 degrees latitude) are controlled by the state-owned North Gas Company, itself a subsidiary of the North Oil Company, both companies being based at Kirkuk. The company's website reports that it operates 23 de-gassing stations at the following associated gas fields: Kirkuk (8), Bai Hassan (3), Jambur (2), East Baghdad (2) and one unit each at Khabbaz, Ajil, 'Ain Zala, Butma, Sufaya, Qayara, Naft Khana and Balad. There is also a gas production unit at the Kor Mor (Anfal) field. Twelve compressor stations collect the associated gas from the producing fields after which the gas is fed to a gas-processing plant at Kirkuk which produces LPG for household consumption, dry gas for industry, natural gasoline and sulphur.[15]

Although the focus of this chapter (and this volume) is upon natural gas (methane) it is worth noting in passing that liquefied petroleum gas (LPG) – around 90 per cent of which is derived from raw natural gas streams – plays a very significant role in the Iraqi economy as the preferred fuel for domestic cooking and heating and given the highly seasonal nature of the latter role, it is unlikely that natural gas will ever become a space-heating/cooking fuel as in northern Europe. During the 1980s and 1990s the production of LPG in Iraq rose from around 400,000 tonnes per year in 1980 to 1,600,000 tonnes per year in 1999 and, writing in 2001, Iraqi oil experts considered that LPG production and consumption might increase to around 2,800,000 tonnes by 2010.

Gas operations south of 32.5 degrees latitude are controlled by the state-owned South Gas Company itself a subsidiary of South Oil Company. Data published by the company in 2007 show that the oil company was then operating 12 oilfields, of which 11 had gas-separation units for initial gas separation and 3 had compressor stations. The gas separation stations are at South Rumayla (7), North Rumayla (7), Zubayr (7), West Qurna (3), Majnun (2), Abu Ghurab (2), and one each at Al-Luhays, Nahr Umar, Fakka, Amara and Halfaya. The compressor stations are at South Rumayla, North Rumayla and Zubayr.[16]

Gas Flaring

In reality much of the gas gathering, processing and transportation infrastructure described above is currently out of action, because of wartime damage, sabotage or general deterioration during the period of UN sanctions. Those same gas plants with a total raw gas throughput capacity of 2080 mmscf/d (21.5 Bcm/yr) in 1999, were only capable of processing 1270 mmscf/d (about 13 Bcm/yr) in 2004[17] while actual throughput of raw gas through these facilities was only around 500 mmscf/d (5.2 Bcm/yr).[18]

According to information given at the 2007 Dubai conference, the factors accounting for the small proportion of southern region raw gas reaching processing plants at North Rumayla and Kor Zubayr include inefficient compressors at the fields, lack of any gas transportation system from the East Qurna and Zubayr fields to the processing units, limited processing capacity and a decline in the primary gas pressure in some fields which has affected the performance of compressors.

In the northern region the problem is largely due to lack of repairs to the second gas line at the North Gas Complex and to inactive compressors. [19]

Consequently, as already noted, official Iraqi sources put the amount of gas flaring at around two-thirds of gross production. Indeed, according to a recent study prepared for the World Bank, Iraq has the third highest volume of flared/vented gas in the World after Nigeria and Russia and the third highest volumes of gas flared/vented per barrel of oil produced in the World after Cameroon and Equitorial Guinea.[20]

Not only is this contributing to global warming, it also represents a considerable loss of income to the Iraqi people. Estimates of the actual current loss of gas through flaring vary considerably as a glance at Appendix A Table A7.2 indicates. The most authoritative estimates emanating from the Iraq Oil Commission state that currently around 1 bcf per day (10.3 Bcm/yr) is flared.[21] Most recently this figure has been repeated by Luay Jawad Al-Khatib, advisor to the Iraq Parliament.[22] Another estimate puts the figure at 8.3 Bcm. Estimates of the financial losses incurred through flaring gas depend on the price per MMBtu and the proportion of the flared gas which it is reasonable to suppose can be utilised within the short to medium term, but on the fairly conservative assumption that (1) only the flared gas from the southern oilfields (600 mmscf/d) (6.2 Bcm/yr) is utilised and (2) the net price is $3/MMBtu, Iraq is losing $657 million per year. Approaching the problem from a different direction, it could also be said that 600 mmscf/d of gas could generate around 103 GWh of electricity in a modern combined cycle gas-fired power station (CCGT). This would be equivalent to an additional installed capacity of around 4GW at a time when installed generating capacity is 11GW but only 5.5GW is actually generating electricity.[23] Considerations such as these may partly explain why the proposed contract with Shell to gather, process and utilise all the 600 mmscf/d (6.2 Bcm/yr) of associated gas from the southern oilfields, initially appears to have met with favour by members of the Federal Government (see below).

Legal and Contractual Framework for Production of Hydrocarbons

Currently an ideological and economic struggle of almost epic proportions is being waged both inside and outside Iraq as to the appropriate form of law and fiscal regime for the country's long-troubled and only barely explored and developed oil and gas sector. It is impossible to determine the final outcome of this struggle; but for certain it will be of enormous importance to the people of Iraq. It will also be critical to the international oil companies for whom continual depletion of their hydrocarbon reserves as they extract and sell them means that they are remorselessly driven by a 'territorial imperative' to seek out new, replacement reserves in the few remaining regions which are relatively unexplored and undeveloped.[24]

It is beyond the scope of this chapter to engage fully with this fierce debate about the legal and contractual framework of Iraq's oil and gas industry, a debate which is already becoming embodied in a vast outpouring of relevant literature, much of it on the Internet. Instead, therefore, we aim to provide the reader with (a) a brief chronological outline of the main developments in the legislative and contractual field applying to the upstream sectors of both oil and gas industries, and (b) a closer look at the implications of these general developments for Iraq's natural gas sector, including an examination of the particular gas fields and groups of fields which were being offered by the Ministry of Oil (MOO) and the Kurdistan Regional Government (KRG) to the international oil companies in early to mid 2009 in various forms of contractual arrangement.

Two particularly important developments in the governance of Iraqi oil occurred under the Baathist regime. In April 1987, by a decree of the Revolutionary Command Council, the Iraq National Oil Company, which hitherto had been in charge of operating the nationalised Iraq oil industry, was dissolved and authority to sign contracts with third parties (e.g. international companies) was vested solely in the Ministry of Oil (MOO). Meanwhile day-to-day oil and gas operations continued to be conducted by state-owned entities (e.g. South Oil Company, North Oil Company) although these were now, in effect, subsidiaries of the MOO. Ten years later (1997), under the pressure of sanctions and growing US hostility, Saddam Husayn's regime took the first steps towards re-admitting international oil companies (IOCs) into Iraq by initialling production sharing contracts (PSCs) with Russia's Lukoil and the Chinese National Oil Company. The significance of these two developments under the Baathist regime will be underlined below.

Article 108 of the post-Saddam Iraqi Constitution (2005) declares that 'oil and gas are the ownership of all the people of Iraq in all the regions and governorates', while Article 109 states that the Federal Government with the producing governorates and regional governments shall undertake the management of oil and gas extracted from *current* fields provided that it distributes oil and gas revenues in a fair manner in proportion to the population distribution in all parts of the country ...'[25]

In June 2006, a three member Oil and Energy Committee began work preparing a draft hydrocarbon framework law, a version of which was approved by Iraq's Council of Ministers (Cabinet) in February 2007. The draft law and the accompanying annexes which allocated each of Iraq's proven oil and gas fields to 'current' and various 'non-current' categories (with the implication that the former would be the preserve of a newly established and centrally-controlled Iraq National Oil Company) were presented to an international conference in Dubai in April 2007. But a few days after the conference, the Kurdistan Regional Government (KRG) rejected the draft law and its annexes on the grounds that it attempted 'to allocate almost 93 per cent of Iraq's proven petroleum reserves to a new Iraq National Oil Company leaving barely 7 per cent for regions ...'[26] The KRG document also made a number of additional criticisms of the oil law.

On 3 July 2007, Prime Minister Nuri al-Maliki announced that the Council of Ministers had approved a final version of the framework law, which had been forwarded to the Council of Representatives (Parliament) for consideration. The KRG then withdrew its support for the legislation and coincidentally, the boycott of cabinet and parliamentary proceedings by various Iraqi political groups (and hence the lack of a quorum) prevented further discussion of the proposed oil law. Since then, there has been considerable criticism of the legislation from a variety of different sources and the draft legislation has undergone further changes.

However, this has not impeded the MOO or the KRG from pursuing contracts with international oil companies. In August 2007, the KRG enacted its own oil and gas law[27] and began signing PSCs with a number of small international oil companies. And in October 2008, the MOO announced that it would be holding its first licensing round (on 29–30 June 2009) at which pre-qualified international oil companies would make bids for production sharing contracts (PSCs) at eight fields, two of which are free gas fields (Akkas and Mansuriya). In the face of strong opposition from the Parliamentary Oil and Gas Committee which argued that legislation was required before such a step could be taken, the MOO justified its initiation of the licensing round without parliamentary approval by reference to the decisions of the Baathist regime referred to above. Nevertheless, many Iraqi oil and gas experts have continued to question the legality of contracts awarded solely by the 'Executive Branch' of government. According to one such expert, Ahmed M. J. Jiyad, formerly Senior Economist with the Iraq National Oil Company and the Ministry of Oil, currently based in Norway,

> The Council of Ministers and MOO are not constitutionally empowered to 'enter into force' such contracts and only the Parliament/Council of

Representatives (COR) has such authority. Legal opinion submitted recently, 4 June, 2009, to the COR on this matter by three Iraqi lawyers is in line with such understanding.[28]

The final versions of the MOO contracts in question, offered for both oil and 'dry' gas fields, took the form of service contracts, albeit with some unusual and unorthodox features. To date, the dry gas field contracts have failed to receive a bidder. Most international media sources attributed this to the fact that the terms of the contracts were 'too onerous' for the international oil companies; however, some Iraqi experts (and one international expert on petroleum fiscal regimes) have come to the opposite conclusion – that the contracts contained many features that were highly disadvantageous to the host government. For example, Jiyad, addressing his comments to the *Model Gas Service Development and Production Contract (GSDPC)* finalised in May 2009, commented adversely on (1) the duration of the contract (20 years compared with a typical service contract length of 9 years), (2) The fact that, in the face of disputes the English version of any contract prevails over the Arabic version, (3) exclusive rights given to the contractor to develop any undiscovered reservoirs within the contract territory, (4) 'Signature Bonuses' which are not 'signature bonuses' at all, in the conventional meaning of the term, but actually loans repayable at LIBOR + 1 percent; (5) restrictions of the right of government to curtail production – for whatever reason, (6) An over-generous (to the contractor) 'R' factor methodology in calculating the IOC's remuneration fee.[29]

Van Meurs[30] has also criticised a model MOO 'risk service contract' (although the contract in question included an exploration element not relevant to the 1st Round Licensing Regime). Lack of space prevents us from considering Van Meurs' criticisms in detail. Suffice it to say, for the present, that he concludes that (1) the contract does not achieve an optimal level of production with a maximum value of government revenues, (2) it seriously exposes the government to 'absurdly low' government takes if low oil prices would occur after development plans and remuneration rates have been approved, (3) It provides for overly generous conditions for the investors in the initial phases of the contract.

Van Meurs contrasts this MOO contract (on the whole, unfavourably) with the 'average' of thirty PSCs already signed by the KRG by 2008. The PSCs are broadly the same for oil and gas fields except for the differences noted in Table 7.5.[31]

Thus, it can be seen that the KRG PSC terms applying to non-associated gas fields are only marginally better for the IOC than those applying to oil fields.

Meanwhile, on 22 September 2008, a Heads of Agreement (HOA)

Table 7.5: Some Key Features of KRG Production Sharing Contracts

	Oil-related provisions	*Gas-related provision*
Exploration period	7 Years (3 + 2 +2) plus 2 years for appraisal	Additional 2 years for gas marketing work
Development & Production period	20 years + extension of 5 years if IOC requests it; further extension of 5 years if field is still producing after 25 years	Same as Oil
Maximum contact period	39 Years	41 years
Royalty	10% for oil and non-associated gas	0% for associated gas
Cost recovery	Cost cap of 45% for crude and associated gas	Cost cap of 55% for non-associated gas
Profit 'Oil'	Available crude less cost oil	Available dry gas less gas cost
Government Take of Profit 'oil'	R factor below 1.0: KRG take is 65–70%; R factor above 2.0: KRG take is 84–86%; between these R factors Govt. take increases linearly based on R factor	R factor below 1.0: KRG take is 55%; R factor above 3.0: KRG take is 82%; between these R factors Govt. take increases linearly based on R factor

Source: Van Meurs, P. 'Comparative Analysis of Ministry of Oil and Kurdistan Fiscal Terms as Applied to the Kurdistan Region'.

was signed between the MOO and Shell Gas and Power Developments BV, in effect, giving Shell the exclusive right to gather, process and commercialise associated gas produced at the oil fields of the state-owned South Oil Company which were currently being flared (see below). The HOA provided for the signing of a South Gas Development Agreement, which would set out the terms on which a joint venture company would be formed between South Gas Company (with 51 percent of the JV) and Shell (with 49 percent).[32]

Gas Projects and International Oil Companies, 2008–2009

In December 2008, the MOO announced that it would be holding a second licensing round, towards the end of 2009, for a further 16 fields, two of which were gas fields (Siba and Khashim al-Ahmar). Most recently, the two large European oil companies (OMV of Austria and MOL of Hungary) have farmed into a 2007 contract between the KRG and Crescent Petroleum/Dana Gas to expand production at a gas field in Sulaymaniya Governorate (Kor Mor) and to appraise another gas field in the same region (Chemchamel). The MOO has declared these agreements 'illegal'.

Table 7.6 and accompanying text provides some details on the gas fields and other gas-related operations which were proposed in 2008–9 for contracts with international oil companies either in the Federal licensing rounds or in bilateral negotiations with particular international oil companies.

Kor Mor: Known as 'Al-Anfal' before the overthrow of Saddam Husayn, this was the only free gas field actually producing before the US invasion. Kor Mor was operated by the state-owned North Oil Company and began production in May 1990. The gas was piped to the Jambur gas-processing plant near to the Kirkuk oil and gas field from where it was supplied to local petrochemical industries and Jambur power station.

In 1996 a Memorandum of Understanding (MOU) with Turkey was signed with the intention of developing Kor Mor and the four other free gas fields in the north of Iraq (Chemchemal, Jaria Pica, Khashim Al-Ahmar and Mansuriya) for a project to export Iraqi gas to Turkey. United Nations sanctions prevented the project going ahead.

In April 2007 Crescent Petroleum (of the Emirate of Sharjah, UAE) and its 21 percent owned affiliate, Dana Gas, signed a long-term service agreement with the Kurdistan Regional Government (KRG). The initial investment, reported to be around $605 million, is the largest private sector investment in Iraq at the time of writing. Dana Gas was appointed on a service contract basis to develop, process and transport natural gas from the free gas Kor Mor field in order to provide gas supplies to fuel two 625 MW electric power plants which were currently under construction near Irbil and Sulaymaniya. The contract also required the companies to concurrently appraise the potential of the free gas Chemchemal field (see below). The Kor Mor development has involved hooking-up, testing and re-commissioning five existing gas wells, appraisal of the reservoir including the drilling of an exploration well and two additional development wells, installation of raw gas separation facilities and an LPG extraction plant and laying around 180 km of 24-inch pipeline. It was originally anticipated by the companies that the field would have an initial production rate of 150 mmscf/d (1.55 Bcm/yr)[33] and by mid-2009 would be producing 300 mmscf/d (3.1 Bcm/yr); however it has been reported that production,

Table 7.6: Gas Projects offered for Contracts with IOCs under MOO First and Second Licensing Rounds, KRG Service Contracts and the Southern Gas Exploitation Project (Shell Agreement).

Field	Governorate	Proven Reserves bcm	Expected Production rate (plateau) bcm/yr	Companies involved	Notes
Kor Mor [Anfal]	Sulaymaniya	51(a) 39.6(b,c) 72.4(d) 39.2(f)	3.1(b,c) 2.6(d)	**Pearl Petroleum:** Crescent Petroleum (40%), Dana Gas (40%), MOL (10%), OMV (10%)	Began production in 1990. In 2003 only free gas field in production
Chemchemal	Sulaymaniya	59.5(a) 62.3(b) 55.7(d) 62(f)	2.1(d)	**Pearl Petroleum:** Crescent Petroleum (40%), Dana Gas (40%), MOL (10%), OMV (10%)	Free gas
Mansuriya	Diyala	90(a) 93(b,e) 88.2(d) 116.2(f)	3.1(a) 3.4(d)	No bidders in 1st Licensing Round, June 2009	Could produce 3.1 BCM/yr free gas Production with 10 wells
Akkas	Al Anbar	129(a) 60(b,e) 60.9(f)	1.0(a)	Bid received in 1st Licensing Round from consortium led by Edison S.p.A. Bid rejected	Could produce 1.0 BCM/yr free gas production with 10 wells
South Gas Exploitation Project	Al-Basra	1208(f)	6.2	SOC-Shell J.V.: South Oil Company (51%), Shell (44%) Mitsubishi (5%)	Solution Gas
Siba	Al-Basra	60(a) 87.8 (b) 86.4(f)	n.a	Recently removed from round	Free gas
Khashim al-Ahmar	Diyala	39.6(a) 50(f)	n.a		Free gas

Sources: (a) Al-Shalchi, W., *Development of Akkas Gas Field in Iraq*, Amman, 2008 and Al-Shalchi, W., *Development of Mansuriya Gas Field in Iraq*, Amman, 2008; (b) EIA, *Iraq, Country Brief*, 2009; (c) Iraq Oil Report, 'Iraq gas for Nabucco a tough deal', 19 May 2009; (d) Ghadban, T. & Al-Fathi, S., 'The gas dimension of the Iraq oil industry', 2001, (e) *Petroleum Economist*, 12 May 2009; (f) Petroleum Law Annexes, 2007

which commenced in October 2008, is currently running at only 90 mmscf/d (0.93 Bcm/yr).[34]

Chemchemal: The same service agreement between Crescent, Dana and the KRG also requires the companies to appraise the potential of this second large free gas field for development. The Chemchemal appraisal project includes acquiring seismic data, re-entry and re-resting of an existing well and drilling two appraisal wells. At the time of writing it is understood that work on the Chemchemal field has been frozen, partly as a result of the world financial crisis. Financial details of the service contracts for both the Kor Mor and Chemchemal fields are unknown.

Mansuriya: This undeveloped field was one of two gas fields included in the first MOO round of tendering for service contracts in June 2009 (the other was Akkas). However, no bids were made for this field. Hitherto it had been the object of considerable international interest including the Iraq–Turkey export plan in 1996 (see Kor Mor, above), a proposed production sharing agreement with AGIP and Gaz de France in 2000, and a MOU signed between the Oil Ministry and Bechtel in 2004 to develop the field and construct a 200 MW electricity generating station (cancelled because the US government was unwilling to provide funds for rapidly escalating security costs).

During the period 1979–1990 four wells were drilled, three of which located gas but with considerable inconsistency between the wells as to the amount of sulphur. The appraisal work at this time also indicated the presence of considerable quantities of condensates and possibly crude oil.[35] According to the MOU with Bechtel the company would have carried out 3D seismic, a work-over of the three existing gas wells and drilling two more wells, one exploration and one production. It was anticipated that initial production would be at 50 mmscf/d. After the US government withdrew funding, an amount of $US 39 million was exempted with a view to the exploration and work-over operations being carried on by Iraqi state-owned companies (North Oil Company, Oil Exploration Company and Iraq Drilling Company), but the whole project was subsequently cancelled after it was discovered that the funding allocated was insufficient to cover the proposed works.[36] Iraqi petroleum experts currently are of the opinion that Mansuriya could produce 300 mmscf/d (3.1 Bcm/yr) by drilling ten wells (eight for production plus two appraisal wells).

Akkas: Also known as the Saladin gas field, Akkas is an undeveloped giant free gas field in the northwest of Iraq 40 km from the Syrian border and about the same distance from a large industrial complex at the Iraqi city of Al-Qaim. It is 300 km from the city of Baiji where the main Iraqi gas grid passes.

In March 2008, the oil ministries of Syria and Iraq signed a MOU for natural gas from the 'Akkas field to be supplied to Syria. In October 2008, together with Mansuriya (see above), the field was included in the first round of tendering for service contracts.

A vertical exploration well was first drilled in August 1992 and although, for technical reasons, it did not reach its planned depth it confirmed the presence of gas at a depth of 4238 metres. In accordance with a 'Combined Cooperation Agreement' previously signed between Iraq and Syria, in 2001 the Syrian Petroleum Company drilled five new (horizontal) wells and worked-over the original well. As a result it was concluded that the 'Akkas field could support production of gas at the following rates/wells.[37]

50 mmscf/d (0.5 Bcm/yr) from the existing 6 wells
100 mmscf/d (1.0 Bcm/yr) from 10 wells
300 mmscf/d (3.1 Bcm/yr) from 30 wells
500 mmscf/d (5. 2 Bcm/yr) from 50 wells

Al-Shalchi[38] describes the different projects that might be developed according to these different scales of production. At 50 mmscf/d, the most likely use for the gas would be to fuel an onsite 225 MW electricity generating station which could be connected to the national grid by a 40 km high-voltage line to a transforming station at the Al-Qaim industrial complex. At 100 mmscf/d, the gas could be treated at a new, on-site gas-processing plant to produce dry gas, LPG and condensates and a 52 km 20-inch pipeline could be constructed to carry the dry gas to the T1 pumping station on the old Iraq–Syria oil pipeline from where it would be transported by another pipeline to the national gas grid. Alternatively the main gas-processing plant could be built at the T1 site with only partial treatment at the gas field itself. At 300 to 500 mmscf/d, the gas could be treated at an onsite gas-processing plant, as in the first option for 100 mmscf/d. However with this larger-scale operation, 100 mmscf/d would be transported by a new gas pipeline to pumping station T1 with the remaining 200 mmscf/d to be exported to the Al Malih site in Syria where the Syrian gas network ends by a new 99 km 22-inch gas pipeline (43 km of which would be on Iraqi soil). The natural gas could then be transported through the Syrian network to a connection point on the Arab Gas Pipeline for export to Europe. Al-Shalchi also considers the possibility of constructing a Gas-to-Liquids (GTL) plant but considers this option unlikely 'in the near future due to the shortage in [domestic] natural gas production'.[39]

In the MOO First Licensing Round on 30 June 2009, there was only one bid for this field. The bidder was a consortium led by the Italian energy company Edison S.p.A. and including the Malaysian state oil company (upstream operations) PETRONAS Carigali, China National Petroleum Corporation, Korea Gas Corporation and the Turkish Petroleum Corporation. The consortium proposed a development of the field which would have taken it to the maximum plateau production rate envisaged by Al-Shalchi (425 mmscf/d) and asked for a Remuneration Fee of $US/BOE of $38 as against the MOO's Maximum Remuneration Fee of $US 8.50. The bid was rejected.

South Gas Exploitation Project: In July 2005, the Ministry of Oil (MOO) signed an agreement with the Royal Dutch/Shell Group to conduct a Gas Master Plan for Iraq. Shell would carry out the research free of charge. The plan was completed in mid-2006 and its conclusions were presented at a seminar in August 2006. On 7 September 2008 the Iraqi Cabinet approved a preliminary agreement between the Royal Dutch/Shell Group and Iraq's state-owned South Gas Company (subsidiary of South Oil Company) and on 22 September 2008 a Heads of Agreement (HOA) was signed between MOO and Shell Gas & Power Developments BV. The broad objective of the agreement is to reduce gas flaring and gather the previously wasted associated (solution) gas from southern fields to new processing facilities where the gas would be separated into dry gas for industry and exports and LPG for local users. In February 2009, Japan's Mitsubishi Corp farmed into the project at 5 percent.

In pursuit of these objectives the HOA states that the parties to the agreement would form a long-term joint venture (for 25 years) initially covering the Governorate of Basra but with the option to expand the cover to other areas if agreed between the parties and/or their affiliates. In addition to developing the gas infrastructure, gathering and processing the raw gas, commercialising dry gas, LPG and condensate to both domestic and export markets, and developing LNG production and export facilities, the JV 'will pursue development of non-associated gas fields in southern Iraq'.[40]

The parties to the HOA would follow this up by establishing a South Gas Development Agreement according to which the state-owned South Gas Company and Shell would participate in a JV company with the former holding 52 percent of the equity and the latter 49 percent.[41]

Technical, safety, environmental, social and ethical standards adopted by the JV company would be 'similar to the ones applied by Shell in its worldwide operations'.[42]

All the raw gas produced in the South of Iraq would be purchased by the JV and compensation for that raw gas would be 'linked to international market prices through the following mechanism: ...as a fixed percentage of the revenues received by the JV for selling products ...that result from processing and treating the purchased raw gas. The products will be sold at prices linked to international market prices and therefore any change in international market prices will directly impact the raw gas compensation.' As to the 'mechanism' itself, the HOA merely states that 'the parties will determine the fixed price percentage based on an Economic Model developed by Shell and the Ministry'.[43]

The section on the Joint South Gas Development Agreement ends, with the statement that,

> The parties acknowledge that, in view of the economics of the gas industry, the long-term planning and optimisation required and the substantial investments to achieve an optimal solution for gas development, the JV will be the sole gas company engaged in business ...in the South of Iraq (Basra) and providing gas for domestic and export markets and generating revenues from gas marketing activities.'[44]

Criticisms of the Shell Contract

(i) Constitutional and Legal Issues

The Shell gas agreement has been criticised by a number of Iraqi oil and gas industry professionals and expatriate experts. For example, Secretary of the Parliamentary Oil & Gas Committee, Jabir Khalifa, who worked for more than 15 years at Iraq's Southern Gas Company, has argued that the contract is illegal because it did not pass through the Parliament. On the other hand, Oil Ministry spokesman Isam Jihad stated that the Ministry does have the right to form companies and joint ventures without a need for parliamentary approval; only agreements with other governments need parliamentary approval.[45] It would appear however that the Ministry's opinion is based on the Saddam Husayn decree of 1997.

As noted above, the contract indicates a 25-year monopoly on the associate gas in southern Iraq in addition to non-associated gas fields. Shell would purchase all the raw gas produced in the south and process it into products used in domestic and foreign markets with no competition from local or foreign companies. Many industry specialists criticised the lack of competitive bidding for the South gas project. However, according to an Oil Ministry spokesman,

> Contracts were negotiated with Shell instead of bidding processing because this is not an upstream development contract where IOC produces gas followed by a sales agreement; it is selecting a partner with South Gas Company to establish a joint venture'.[46]

However, industry expert Fuad Al-Amir stated that in September 2007 the Oil Ministry sent a letter to the Cabinet in order to win their approval for the HOA with a different argument. The letter justified the joint venture contract with Shell on the grounds that, 'Several companies studied the possibility of investing in the flared gas in the south and performing complete rehabilitation for the current gas projects; but because of the security problems they could not implement the projects.'[47]

Al-Amir questioned the idea that all the other companies abandoned the Basra gas project for security reasons but not Shell. He pointed out that the working environment in Basra is generally safer than the other areas in Iraq. He has also commented that the rehabilitation of the current south gas system in Basra does not need a long-term joint venture with a foreign company as simple service contracts with specialised companies could be enough to assist in working the project.

Additional criticisms of the Shell agreement focusing on constitutional and legal issues are made by Jiyad.[48]

(ii) Pricing Issues

A number of Iraqi economists have also raised questions about the likely domestic pricing policy of the Shell-controlled gas monopoly in southern Iraq.

According to the most recent data available to the authors, the price of natural gas in Iraq for power and industrial usages is $US 1.15/MMBtu.[49] This price is broadly equal to Egyptian domestic gas prices ($1.19 MMBtu) and it is higher than Saudi Arabia, UAE and Iran ($0.75, $1.05, $0.35 MMBtu respectively). However, prices for natural gas traded in the international market are far higher. For example, in 2006, average LNG sales prices varied between $4 US/MMBtu and $5 US/MMBtu.[50]

If the Shell project were to go ahead and assuming it sold its gas at internationally based prices, this could prove highly disadvantageous to Iraq's downstream petrochemical and power-generation industries.

In 2008 Al-Amir noted (p.56) that the Southern General Fertilizer Company reported that the price it paid suppliers for the gas it requires would soon rise to $3.00 – $3.50/MMBtu and suggests that this 300 percent price increase (to a level four and half times the current Saudi price) was the result of pressure from the Oil Ministry and might be in anticipation of the Shell contract.

The state-owned Fertilizer Company sells nitrogen fertilisers which are the pillar of the Iraqi agricultural industry. After losing its currently cheap gas supply (its competitive advantage), the company would not be able to compete with the other Gulf countries in the market for urea exports. Under the current gas prices ($1.15/MMBtu), the cost of gas purchased per tonne of urea was around $31.6 while if the gas price increases to $3.25, the cost of gas per tonne of urea will increase to $89.3 per tonne. The same scenario could be applied to other industries such as petrochemicals, cement, power and others.[51]

Muhammad 'Ali Zainy, a senior energy analyst and economist at the London-based Centre for Global Energy Studies (CGES), has also argued that by losing its competitive advantage (cheap gas supply) as a result of the Shell agreement, the Iraqi economy, during the coming 25 years, would be prevented from diversifying.[52] In response, Oil Minister Shahristani suggested that the price of gas sold to domestic power plants, petrochemical and fertiliser industries could be subsidised but, apart from the dubious economics which this would involve, Zainy has cast doubt upon whether such a policy would be compatible with WTO membership and IMF financial support.

At the time of writing (January 2010) there appear to have been no further developments with the Shell Gas Project. Shell sources report that no final agreement has, as yet, been signed and since the contract was first mooted four and half years ago, this would seem to tell us something about the likely pace of events.

Iraq as a Natural Gas Exporter?

The controversy over the Shell contract may be seen as part of a wider debate within Iraq over the role of gas exports because the Shell H.O.C. explicitly refers to the possibility of LNG exports from southern Iraq.

On 18 January 2010, a Memorandum of Understanding was signed between the Government of Iraq and the European Union. The MOU includes a number of clauses, which appear to envisage Iraq as an important source of gas exports to Europe. For example, in the preamble, the MOU states,

Recognising the ongoing activities of the Euro-Arab Mashreq Gas Market
in which Iraq participates as an observer, as well as the progress achieved
in the development of the Arab Gas Pipeline and the prospects for Iraq
of becoming a full partner in this project with a view to establishing Iraq's
role as a natural gas supplier to the EU market.

And continues,

Both sides will endeavour to enhance their cooperation in view to ...
identifying and putting in place additional sources and supply routes for
gas from Iraq to the European Union ... [and] With a view to the medium
and long term development of the natural gas sector in Iraq and with the
aim of providing security of supply and demand for Iraq and the EU, both
sides will endeavour to identify the scale of potential exports of natural gas
from Iraq to the EU with the full involvement of the EU Member States
and the private sector, taking into account Iraq's domestic market needs.[53]

However, many energy experts, both Iraqi and non-Iraqi, believe that
current and prospective Iraqi gas production may not be enough to
cover domestic consumption which is expected to rise in the coming
years. For example, Steve Peacock, Middle East head of exploration and
production for the UK's BP, has commented that 'in order of priority
for the Iraqis, it would be use of gas for enhanced oil recovery ... then
use of gas for local power generation, then for expanding the local
industrial sector'. He also says. 'It is not yet clear after satisfying all of
those things how much would be available for exports at this stage.'[54]

The present consumption of energy is not the relevant point of
comparison given the condition of the country's general infrastructure
as a result of decades of wars and sanctions. Al-Amir[55] points out that
National power producers claim that they provide half of annual peak
demand. If this were true then we could see twelve hours of electricity
per day during the summer but actually in July and August 2008 the
national power supply was available for only 3–4 hours. Moreover, in
2008 all cement factories were out of action and the production of
fertilisers and petrochemicals did not exceed 30 percent of their capacity. Amir concludes that if industry and power were fully restored it
would easily be possible to consume domestically all the current flared
gas and even double that amount.

Zainy believes that Iraq's domestic gas consumption could increase
to 3000 mmscf/d (31 Bcm/yr) by 2015, and if the domestic demand
increases thereafter at 5 percent per year then the demand would be
around 6000 mmscf/d (62 Bcm/yr) by 2030. Assuming that most of
the required domestic gas production would be associated gas, this
would imply 10 million b/d of oil production by 2030.[56] While it is just
conceivable that Iraqi oil production might reach this level by 2030,

it also seems clear that, along the way, there would be very little gas available for export.

A similar point is made by Al-Khatib. Taking the MOO's objective for expanded oil production (6–6.5 million b/d by c.2020) he calculates that the associated gas production (51.7 Bcm/yr), together with probable free gas production (18.6 Bcm/yr) might amount to around 6800 mmscf/d (70.3 Bcm/yr). Of this total, around 14.5 Bcm/yr would be required for reinjection in producing oil fields leaving 55.8 Bcm/yr available for processing and a dry gas production (after shrinkage) of 46.5 Bcm/yr. However by this time, assuming other sectors of the economy have expanded as planned, around 44.5 Bcm/yr would be required for electricity generation, industry and the petrochemicals sector leaving a surplus of only 2 Bcm/yr. And if, as intended, Iraq completely replaces oil by natural gas as its primary fuel for electricity generation, any surplus available for export will disappear: indeed by 2020 Iraq could have a deficit in its gas supply/demand balance.[57]

In spite of these doubts about the country's future export capacity, in mid-July 2009, the Iraqi Prime Minister, Nuri al-Maliki, announced that his government had 'offered to supply enough gas to fill half the proposed Nabucco pipeline' linking Central Asia with Europe.[58] In terms of volume, this would mean Iraq exporting 15 Bcm/yr via Turkey by 2015. It would appear that most, if not all, of this gas would have to come from the northern region, in particular from Kurdistan.

In May 2009, OMV, the partially state-owned international oil company of Austria and MOL of Hungary each acquired 10 percent of Pearl Petroleum, the company which holds Crescent's and Dana's interests in the Kurdish region. According to Helmut Langanger, OMV Executive Vice President for Exploration and Production, quoted in *Gulfoilandgas.com*,[59] the objective of the two companies was 'to participate in the appraisal, development and production of very large gas reserves as feedstock for the Nabucco pipeline' (in which OMV and MOL each own 16.67 percent).

The possibility of gas exports to Europe from Iraqi Kurdistan is based on the assumption that by around 2015 the Kor Mor and Chemchamel fields will be jointly producing 3000 mmscf/d (31 Bcm/yr) of gas together with substantial volumes of liquids. Such a high output level would be sufficient to supply 500 mmscf/d (5.16 Bcm/yr) for the KRG's domestic requirements including ambitious plans for a 'Kurdistan Gas City', leaving 1000 mmscf/d (10.3 Bcm/yr) for export to Turkey and 1,500 mmscf/d (15.5 Bcm/yr) to enter the 3300 km Nabucco pipeline planned to bring Central Asian gas to Europe.[60]

While a flow of 1500 mmscf/d (15.5 Bcm/yr) would be sufficient to justify the planned first phase of Nabucco, considerable doubts remain as to whether these two Kurdish fields could produce at such high rates without damaging the reservoirs. Moreover, some doubts remain about the size of the proven reserves at Kor Mor with quite widely different figures emanating from different sources as shown in Table 7.6. A further problem facing the project is that the Iraqi Oil Minister, Husayn al-Shahristani, has strongly criticised the KRG's 'go-it-alone' approach to contracts with IOCs and is quoted as stating that Baghdad, 'would not allow any side to export gas from the region without the approval of the central government and the Iraqi Oil Ministry'.[61]

In conclusion one might say that, whereas there may be very large quantities of *in situ* natural gas in Iraq, for the foreseeable future, the country's domestic energy requirements – in particular the need to rebuild a viable gas supply and infrastructure, essential for restoring Iraq's economy after decades of sanctions, invasion and virtual civil war – make it unlikely that Iraq will become a significant gas exporter for many years to come.

APPENDIX A

To give some idea of the kind of problems encountered consider the data in Tables A7.1, A7.2 and A7.3.

Table A7.1: Iraq, Gross Gas Production in 2004 (Bcm/yr): Different sources, different data

Bcm/Yr	Source	Issue no. Year	Year of Publication
3.66	OPEC	2004	2005
11.90	OPEC	2006(rev.)	2008
2.80	CEDIGAZ	2004	2005
15.50	Iraq Oil Commission	2007	2007
n/a	BP	n/a	n/a
n/a	EIA	n/a	n/a
6.20	OGJ	2005	2005
n/a	IEA	n/a	n/a

Notes: The 'Issue No.Year' is the latest year for which data are provided. The 'Year of Publication' is the actual date of publication. For example, in the above table the figure for 'gross gas production' in 2004 in the first line, is taken from the OPEC *Annual Statistical Bulletin 2004*, (where the latest figure available is for 2004) which was not published until 2005.

* The OGJ figure is the annualised figure for 'production capacity' at 14/9/2005.

The first thing to note about these three tables is that the normally ubiquitous BP *Statistical Review of World Energy* does not venture to give a figure for any of the three categories of gas production listed above; indeed, a glance back over the last twenty years or so of BP's *Review* shows that although BP has regularly published a figure for Iraq's proven gas reserves, they have never published a production figure: perhaps wisely – in the light of the substantial inconsistencies and omissions displayed by the other sources. At the other extreme the OPEC *Annual Statistical Bulletin* publishes a detailed break-down of Iraq's 'gross gas production' into its component parts and the residual 'marketed' gas production in a manner consistent with the 'good practice' described at the beginning of this section and CEDIGAZ has recycled this data until 2008; the only problem is that until the publication of the OPEC 2007 Bulletin in early 2009, the data must be considered absolutely spurious because the 2007 edition gives values for the five gas production categories (revised back to the year 2003) which are completely different from those published in the 2006 Bulletin,.

The scale of these revisions is amply illustrated by the data in

Tables A7.1 and A7.2. According to the 2004 OPEC Bulletin, Iraq's gross gas production in 2004 was 3.66 Bcm per year, whereas in the 2006 Bulletin (revised in 2007) it was stated to be 11.90 Bcm. Similarly the volume of natural gas flared or vented in 2004 was 0.855 Bcm according to the 2004 OPEC Bulletin but 7.70 Bcm (nine times as large) according to the 2006 (revised) Bulletin. However, it would be well to avoid drawing the conclusion that the new series of gas data for Iraq published by OPEC are now 'correct'. Firstly, when we compare these with another – and arguably more 'official' – source (Thamir Ghadhban, Chairman of the Iraq Oil Commission) the latter states that Iraq's gross gas production in 2004 was actually 15.5 Bcm, about

Table A7.2: Iraq, Gas Flared/Vented in 2004 (Bcm/yr): Different sources – different data

bcm/Yr	Source	Issue No.	Year	Year of Publication	
0.855	OPEC	2004	2005		
7.70	OPEC	2006(rev.)		2008	
0.850	CEDIGAZ		2004	2005	
10.30	Iraq Oil Commission			2007	2007
n/a	BP	n/a	n/a		
n/a	EIA	n/a	n/a		
n/a	OGJ	n/a	n/a		
n/a	IEA	n/a	n/a		

Table A7.3: Iraq, Marketed Gas Production in 2006 (Bcm/yr): Different sources – different data

bcm/Yr	Source	Issue No.	Year	Year of Publication	
3.50	OPEC	2006	2008		
1.80	OPEC	2006(rev.)		2008	
1.80	CEDIGAZ		2006(rev.)		2008
n/a	IOC/ Ghadhban	2007	2007		
n/a	BP	n/a	n/a		
1.81	EIA(i)	2009	2009		
2.90	EIA(ii)	2009	2009		
3.56	IEA	2009	2009		
1.75	OGJ	2008	2009		

Sources for Tables A7.1, A7.2 and A7.3: OPEC, *Annual Statistical Bulletin* 2005 and 2008; CEDIGAZ 'Trends and Figures', *Natural Year in Review* 2008; Iraq Oil Commission/Ghadhban, 'Iraq Oil Industry. Present Status and Future Outlook' 2007; EIA (i & ii), Iraq, Country Brief 2009; IEA, Statistics by Country/Region 2009; Oil and Gas Journal, 19 December 2009 and 22 June 2009.

30 percent higher than the revised OPEC figure; similarly, according to the Oil Commission, the volume of gas flared in 2004 was 10.3 Bcm compared to OPEC's 7.70 Bcm. A further problem with the revised OPEC data is the strange growth of the 'shrinkage' category (See Table A7.4) which has inexplicably risen from 0.8 Bcm in 2003 to 4.75 Bcm in 2007. It is possible that this is flared gas which has been wrongly categorised, but given that OPEC had already classified 6.62 Bcm of 2007 production as 'flared/vented' this would bring the total volume of gas which has been wasted in one form or another to 11.37 Bcm. This is not inconceivable but it is odd that this combined OPEC figure is more than a billion cubic metres greater than the most recently available Oil Commission's figure.

Table A7.4: OPEC (2007) Data on Gas Flaring and 'Shrinkage', 2003–2007, Bcm/yr

	2003	2004	2005	2006	2007
Flaring	7.14	8.0	7.9	6.6	6.62
Shrinkage	0.80	1.0	1.20	3.05	4.75

Source: OPEC, *Annual Statistical Bulletin*, 2007.

When we turn to 'marketed' production (Table A7.3) – we are left even more in the dark. For the year 2006 we can now draw the EIA, OGJ and IEA into the frame – but to little advantage. Only OPEC and CEDIGAZ publish figures explicitly identified as 'marketed' production, although the alternative terminology used by the EIA, OGJ and IEA seems to indicate that their own figures refer to *this* category and not to gross production. CEDIGAZ has now apparently broken free from its reliance on OPEC data, including its new 'revised' data and publishes a separate number. Curiously, the EIA gives two quite different figures for the same year on the same website! This means that for marketed Iraqi gas production (Bcm/yr) in 2006, we have six different figures, as follows: 3.50 (OPEC, 2006), 1.80 (OPEC, 2008 and CEDIGAZ, 2008), 1.81 (EIA(i)), 2.90 (EIA(ii)), 3.56 (IEA) and 1.75 (OGJ). Of greater concern is the fact that the only 'Official' Iraqi source (Iraq Oil Commission/Ghadhban) does not give any equivalent figure.

APPENDIX B

Table B7.1: Proven gas reserves of Iraqi oil/gas fields c.2007, Bcm

Field Name	Governorate	Total Gas (Bcm)	"Associated" (Bcm)	"Free" (Bcm)	Reservoir Type*
W.Qurnah	Basra, Maysan	387.60	387.60	0.00	S
Nahr Umar	Basra	348.92	348.92	0.00	S
Majnun	Basra, Maysan	276.43	272.46	3.96	S
North Rumayla	Basra	199.43	199.43	0.00	S
Jambur	Al-Tamim	187.65	38.96	148.69	C
South Rumayla	Basra	136.49	136.49	0.00	S
Ajil	Salah al-Din	131.19	7.59	123.60	C
Mansuriyah	Diyala	116.21	0.00	116.21	F
Bai Hassan	Al-Tamim	106.22	38.37	67.85	C
Balad	Salah al-Din	106.22	38.37	67.85	C
Zubayr: Shuayba, Rafthida, Safuan	Basra	99.96	99.96	0.00	S
Kirkuk,Khurmala, Avanah,Baba	Al-Tamim, Irbil	93.16	56.92	36.25	C
Siba	Basra	88.04	1.67	86.37	C
Sarjun	Ninevah	88.01	1.64	86.37	C
E.Baghdad, N.Exten. Rashdia S.Diyala	Baghdad, Wasit, Salah al-Din	82.49	82.49	0.00	S
Nasiriya	Dhi Qar	73.62	73.62	0.00	S
Chemchamel S. Dome	Sulaymaniya, Al-Tamim	61.96	0.00	61.96	F
Halfaya	Maysan	60.94	60.94	0.00	S
Akkas	Al-Anbar	60.94	0.00	60.94	F
Khashim Al Ahmar	Diyala	51.59	1.61	49.98	C
Khabaz	Al-Tamim	50.83	20.59	30.24	C
Ratawi	Basra	42.33	42.33	0.00	S
Khor Mor	Salah al-Din	39.22	0.00	39.22	F
Jeria Pica	Diyala	27.55	0.00	27.55	F
Buzurgan, N. Dome & S. Dome	Maysan	27.16	27.16	0.00	S
Himrin: Alas D., Nukhayla, Abu Fudul	Salah al-Din, Al-Tamim	20.56	14.72	5.83	S
Ahdab N. Dome & S. Dome	Wasit	19.93	19.93	0.00	S
Radifayn	Dhi Qar	19.20	19.20	0.00	S
Gharraf	Dhi Qar	18.46	18.46	0.00	S
Suba	Basra, Dhi Qar	15.55	15.55	0.00	S
Luhays	Basra	14.81	14.81	0.00	S
Abu Gharab, S. Dome & N. Dome	Maysan	11.16	11.16	0.00	S
Nur	Maysan	10.90	10.90	0.00	S
Qamar	Diyala	7.59	7.59	0.00	S

Table B7.1: continued

Field Name	Governorate	Total Gas (Bcm)	"Associated" (Bcm)	"Free" (Bcm)	Reservoir Type*
Fuqua	Maysan	7.39	7.39	0.00	S
Tel Ghazal	Diyala	5.80	0.40	5.41	C
Badra	Wasit	5.10	5.10	0.00	S
Amara	Maysan	3.96	3.96	0.00	S
West Butmah	Ninevah	3.68	1.10	2.58	C
Najmah	Ninevah	3.57	3.57	0.00	S
Naft Khanah	Diyala	3.31	0.62	2.69	C
Rachi	Basra	3.28	3.28	0.00	S
Gillabat	Diyala	3.28	3.28	0.00	S
Makhmour	Irbil	3.06	0.00	3.06	F
Qasab	Ninevah	2.58	1.61	0.96	S
Qayiarah	Ninevah	2.07	2.01	0.06	S
Huwaiza	Maysan	1.93	1.93	0.00	S
Judida	Al-Tamim	1.76	1.76	0.00	S
Alan	Ninevah	1.61	0.08	1.53	C
Kifl	Najaf	1.19	1.19	0.00	S
Kumait	Maysan	1.02	1.02	0.00	S
Dujayla	Maysan	0.99	0.99	0.00	S
Jawan	Ninevah	0.91	0.91	0.00	S
Nahrwan	Baghdad, Diyala	0.79	0.79	0.00	S
Qurra Chuq (S.Dome)	Irbil	0.74	0.68	0.06	S
Merjan	Karbela	0.71	0.71	0.00	S
Chia Surkh	Diyala	0.62	0.62	0.00	S
Abu Khaima	Al-Muthana	0.45	0.45	0.00	S
Dhaffria N. Dome & S. Dome	Wasit	0.45	0.45	0.00	S
Rifaee	Maysan	0.40	0.40	0.00	S
Demir Dagh	Irbil	0.37	0.31	0.06	S
Ain Zalah	Ninevah	0.34	0.34	0.00	S
Taq-Taq	Irbil	0.25	0.25	0.00	S
Bihaira	Ninevah	0.17	0.17	0.00	S
Tikrit	Salah al-Din	0.10	0.10	0.00	S
Sufiyah	Ninevah	0.08	0.08	0.00	S
Bulkhana	Salah al-Din, Diyala	0.08	0.08	0.00	S
Injanah	Diyala	0.03	0.03	0.00	S
TOTAL		3144.37	2115.12	1029.25	

Source: Ministry of Oil (2007), Petroleum Law, Annexes pp.1-8

*   Reservoir Types: S=Solution, C = Cap, F = Free

Note that, for reasons which remain unclear, in the original table, the column titled "Associated" refers only to solution gas, while the column titled "Free" includes both Free and Cap gas. The usual convention is to classify cap gas as associated. See also endnote 5.

APPENDIX C

Table C7.1: Proven gas reserves of Iraqi fields with predominantly solution gas 2007, Bcm

Field Name	Governorate	Total Gas (Bcm)	Solution (Bcm)
W.Qurnah	Basra, Maysan	387.60	387.60
Nahr Umar	Basra	348.92	348.92
Majnun	Basra, Maysan	276.43	272.46
North Rumayla	Basra	199.43	199.43
South Rumayla	Basra	136.49	136.49
Zubayr: Shuayba, Rafthida, Safuan	Basra	99.96	99.96
E.Baghdad, N.Exten. Rashdia S.Diyala	Baghdad, Wasit, Salah al-Din	82.49	82.49
Nasiriya	Dhi Qar	73.62	73.62
Halfaya	Maysan	60.94	60.94
Ratawi	Basra	42.33	42.33
Kirkuk:Khurmala, Avanah,Baba	Al-Tamim, Irbil	93.16	36.25
Buzurgan, N. Dome & S. Dome	Maysan	27.16	27.16
Ahdab N. Dome & S. Dome	Wasit	19.93	19.93
Radifayn	Dhi Qar	19.20	19.20
Gharraf	Dhi Qar	18.46	18.46
Suba	Basra, Dhi Qar	15.55	15.55
Luhays	Basra	14.81	14.81
Himrin: Alas D., Nukhayla, Abu Fudul	Salah al-Din, Al-Tamim	20.56	14.72
Abu Gharab, S. Dome & N. Dome	Maysan	11.16	11.16
Nur	Maysan	10.90	10.90
Qamar	Diyala	7.59	7.59
Fuqua	Maysan	7.39	7.39
Badra	Wasit	5.10	5.10
Amara	Maysan	3.96	3.96
Najmah	Ninevah	3.57	3.57
Rachi	Basra	3.28	3.28
Gillabat	Diyala	3.28	3.28
Qayiarah	Ninevah	2.07	2.01
Huwaiza	Maysan	1.93	1.93
Judida	Al-Tamim	1.76	1.76
Qasab	Ninevah	2.58	1.61
Kifl	Najaf	1.19	1.19
Kumait	Maysan	1.02	1.02
Dujayla	Maysan	0.99	0.99
Jawan	Ninevah	0.91	0.91
Nahrwan	Baghdad, Diyala	0.79	0.79
Merjan	Karbela	0.71	0.71
Qurra Chuq (S.Dome)	Irbil	0.74	0.68

Table C7.1: continued

Field Name	Governorate	Total Gas (Bcm)	Solution (Bcm)
Chia Surkh	Diyala	0.62	0.62
Abu Khaima	Al-Muthana	0.45	0.45
Dhaffria N. Dome & S. Dome	Wasit	0.45	0.45
Rifaee	Maysan	0.40	0.40
Ain Zalah	Ninevah	0.34	0.34
Demir Dagh	Irbil	0.37	0.31
Taq-Taq	Irbil	0.25	0.25
Bihaira	Ninevah	0.17	0.17
Tikrit	Salah al-Din	0.10	0.10
Sufiyah	Ninevah	0.08	0.08
Bulkhana	Salah al-Din, Diyala	0.08	0.08
Injanah	Diyala	0.03	0.03
TOTALS		2011.29	1943.44
Of which, Southern Governorates			87.60%

Source: As for Table B7.1

Table C7.2: Proven gas reserves of Iraqi fields with predominantly cap gas, 2007, Bcm

Field Name	Governorate	Total Gas (Bcm)	CAP (Bcm)
Jambur	Al-Tamim	187.65	148.69
Ajil	Salah al-Din	131.19	123.60
Bai Hassan	Al-Tamim	106.22	67.85
Balad	Salah al-Din	106.22	67.85
Khabaz	Al-Tamim	50.83	30.24
West Butmah	Ninevah	3.68	2.58
Naft Khanah	Diyala	3.31	2.69
Alan	Ninevah	1.61	1.53
TOTALS		590.71	445.02
Of which, North and Central Governorates			100%

Source: As for Table B7.1

Table C7.3: Proven gas reserves of Iraqi fields with predominantly free gas, 2007, Bcm

Field Name	Governorate	Total Gas (Bcm)	Free (Bcm)
Mansuriyah	Diyala	116.21	116.21
Siba	Basra	88.04	86.37
Sarjun	Ninevah	88.01	86.37
Chemchamel S. Dome	Sulaymaniya, Al-Tamim	61.96	61.96
Akkas	Al-Anbar	60.94	60.94
Khashim Al Ahmar	Diyala	51.59	49.98
Kor Mor	Salah al-Din	39.22	39.22
Jeria Pica	Diyala	27.55	27.55
Tel Ghazal	Diyala	5.80	5.41
Makhmour	Irbil	3.06	3.06
TOTALS		542.38	537.05
Of Which, Northern and Central Governorates			83.80%

Source: As for Table B7.1

Table C7.4: Total Gas Reserves

	Bcm	% share
Total Gas in predominantly solution fields	2011.29	64.0
Total Gas in predominantly cap gas fields	590.71	18.8
Total Gas in predominantly associated gas fields	**2602.0**	**82.8**
Total Gas in predominantly free gas fields	**542.4**	**17.2**
Total reserves	**3144.4**	

Source: As for Table B7.1

Notes

1 *OPEC Annual Statistical Bulletin*, 2007.
2 Iraq Oil Commission/T. Ghadhban, Chairman, 'Iraq Oil Industry. Present Status and Future Outlook', Paper presented at Iraq Oil, Gas and Petrochemical and Electricity Summit, Dubai, 2–4 September, 2007.
3 IOC/Ghadhban, 'Iraq Oil Industry.'
4 The definitions of the different types of gas reservoir follow Peebles, M., *Natural Gas Fundamentals*, (Shell International Gas Ltd., London,1992), pp.1–2.

5   This is a tentative conclusion because (a) contrary to conventional usage, the Annexes include cap gas fields in the category 'free' gas and although we have tried to break this down into separate 'cap' and 'free' categories using this and other data sources, it is possible that errors have been made; and (b) the proven reserves figures for individual fields in the Annexes frequently differ from those emanating from other sources (See also Table 7.6).

6   Ghadhban, T. and Al-Fathi, S., 'The gas dimension of the Iraq oil industry', *OPEC Review*, March 2001, p.31

7   Ibid., p.30.

8   See *OPEC Annual Statistical Bulletin*, 2007, p.1268.

9   Flower, A. 'Natural Gas from the Middle East', in Jonathan Stern (ed.), *Natural Gas in Asia. The Challenges of Growth in China, India, Japan and Korea*, 2nd ed. (Oxford: Oxford University Press, 2008) p.333.

   In all fairness, this problem of correctly identifying gas production volumes exists not only in other regions, but also in the data published in some companies' annual reports. For an attempt to unravel some of these discrepancies in oil company information see SERIS *Natural Gas Companies Worldwide Vol.6*, (Sheffield: Sheffield Energy & Resources Information Services, 2001), pp.93, 106–107.

10 IOC/Ghadhban, 'Iraq Oil Industry', p.14.

11 MOO, *Waqi' wa mustaqbal istighlal al-ghaz al-tabi'i janub wa shamal al-'Iraq li al-agrad al-sina'iyyya*, Paper presented at *Iraq Oil, Gas and Petrochemical and Electricity Summit*, Dubai, 2–4 September 2007, pp. 2–6.

12 Business Monitor International (BMI) *Iraq Oil & Gas Report* Q1 2009, p.49. The BMI chart which purports to show 'Iraq Gas Production, Consumption and Exports (2002–2013)' offers no definition of 'gas production' but it can be inferred that it is referring to 'marketed production' since production and consumption are shown to be equal for all years before 2009 (when exports are supposed to have begun). BMI's source for the chart in question is given as 'Historic data – BP *Statistical Review of World Energy*, June 2008.The BP *Review* has never published a figure for Iraq gas production or consumption. It appears that the author/s of the *Iraq Oil & Gas Report* have simply taken the 'other' category in the BP Review data and relabelled this as 'Iraq'.

13 Ghadhban and Al-Fathi, 'The gas dimension of the Iraq oil industry', p.40.

14 Ibid., p.37.

15 North Oil Company, 2009, Available at http://www.noc.gov.iq/english_ver/homepage_en.htm

16 South Oil Company (2007): available at http://www.socbasrah-iq.com/index.htm

17 IOC/Ghadhban, 'Iraq Oil Industry', p.14.

18 MOO, '*Waqi' wa mustaqbal…* , p.2. Note however, that the *Oil and Gas Journal* states that Iraq's four processing plants with a capacity of 2081 mmscf/d had an average throughput of 1550 mmscf/d in 2008 (OGJ, 22 June 2009). The journal seems to be confusing plant throughout with gross (raw) gas

production.
19 MOO, *'Waqi' wa mustaqbal ...'* , pp.7–8.
20 Gerner, F., Svensson, B. & Djumena, S. 'Gas Flaring and Venting', *Public Policy for the Private Sector* (World Bank, 2004) p.2. However it should be noted that these positions are based on the assumption that in 2003 Iraq was flaring around 14.5 Bcm/yr.
21 IOC/ Ghadhban, 'Iraq Oil Industry'.
22 Al-Khatib, L.J. 'Securing Iraq Gas Investment for Power and Industries' paper presented at the *Symposium for Reviewing Iraq Oil Policy 28/2/2009*, p.10, available at http://www.iraqenergy.org
23 Ibid.
24 See Rutledge, I., *Addicted to Oil: America's Relentless Drive for Energy Security*, (London: I.B. Tauris, London, 2005), pp.3–7.
25 Associated Press, 'Full Text of Iraqi Constitution, *The Washington Post*, 12 October 2005 (our emphasis).
26 KRG, Statement from Minister of Natural Resources, Kurdistan Regional Government, Iraq 27 April 2007, p.1 available at www.krg.org/pdf/MNR Statement 20070427.pdf.
27 KRG, Presidency of the Region, Oil and Gas Law of the Kurdistan Region – Iraq, Law no.22. available at http://www.krg.org/articles/detail.asp?rnr =107&lngnr=12&smap=04030000&anr
28 Jiyad, A.M., Preliminary assessment of the GSDPC, June 2009, p.1, available at http://www.iraq-enterprise.com/rep/jiyad61009.htm
29 Ibid, pp.1–6.
   The 'R' factor is an element introduced into traditional production sharing contracts (although in this case transplanted into a form of service contract) with the intention of making the regime more progressive (i.e. higher profits lead to proportionately higher government 'take' and visa-versa). The 'R factor' itself is the ratio of total accumulated revenues to total accumulated costs.
30 Van Meurs, P., 'Comparative analysis of Ministry of Oil and Kurdistan fiscal terms as applied to the Kurdistan Region' *Oil Gas and Energy Law*, No.3, University of Dundee, 2008.
31 For a good general description of how PSCs work and the concepts employed see Johnston, D., *International Petroleum Fiscal Regimes and Production Sharing Contracts* (Tulsa: Penwell Books, 1994), pp.39–71; and Bindemann, K., *Production Sharing Agreements: an Economic Analysis*, Working Paper WPM25, (Oxford: Oxford Institute for Energy Studies, 1999).
32 See MOO, Heads of Agreement, 2008, available at http://www.al-ghad. org/2008/11/22/shell-iraq-oil-agreement/; MOO, Dr Husayn Shahristani, *Ittifaq mabda'i hawl istighlal al-ghaz fi mintaqa al-busara*, 4 Sepember 2008, available at http://www.al-ghad.org/2008/11/22/shell-iraq-oil-agreement/
33 Crescent Petroleum, 'Crescent in Iraq', 2009, available at http://www.crescent.ae/html/crescent_iraq.html
34 IOR, 'Iraq gas for Nabucco a tough deal, 19 May 2009, pp.1–2.
35 Al-Shalchi, *Development of Mansuriya Gas Field in Iraq*, 2008, pp.3–4.

36 Ibid., p.8.
37 Al-Shalchi, *Development of Akkas Gas Field in Iraq*, 2008, p.6.
38 Ibid., pp.16–30.
39 Ibid, p. 28.
40 MOO, Heads of Agreement, p.3.
41 Ibid., p.4 and MOO, Dr Husayn Shahristani, *Ittifaq mabda'i hawl istighlal...* p.2.
42 MOO, Heads of Agreement, p.4.
43 Ibid, p.5.
44 Ibid., p.6.
45 Cocks, T., 'Iraq lawmaker says Shell deal lacks transparency', *Reuters*, 8 November 2008.
46 Zawya, 'Shahristani on Shell's Iraqi Gas Deal', available at: http://www. zawya.com/Story.cfm/sidv52n14-1TS01/Shahristani%20On%20Shell%20 s%20Iraqi%20Gas%20Deal/
47 Al-Amir, F., 'Mulahazat hawl "Al-ittifakiya al-ulya" bayna Wizarat al-naft wa sharika Shell li-mashrua' ghaz al-janub.' *Al Ghad*, 23 Dec. 2008, available at: http://www.al-ghad.org/2008/12/23/notes-on-the-draft-agreement-between-shell-and-the-iraqi-oil-ministry/ p.49
48 Jiyad, A.M., Iraq-Shell Gas Deal: Who occupies the driver's seat?, April 2009 available at http://www.iraqog.com/arabresults3.cfm?keywords=ahmed%20 Jiyad
49 Al-Amir, F., 'Mulahazat hawl "Al-ittifakiya al-ulya" ... p.56.
50 Rasavi, H., 'Natural Gas Pricing in Countries of the Middle East & North Africa', *Energy Journal*, vol. 30, no.3, 2009. The main theme of Rasavi's article is that domestic gas prices in the MENA area are too low, i.e. below LRMC plus a depletion rent charge. However his analysis appears to be based on the LRMC of non-associated gas production whereas in the case of Iraq, for the foreseeable future the majority of incremental gas supply will be associated (solution) gas where the supply price will be much lower than in many other countries. This also ignores the possibility of Iraq earning carbon credits for reducing flaring (See Al-Khatib, 'Securing Iraq Gas Investment for Power and Industries', 2009, p.14).
51 Al-Amir, F., 'Mulahazat hawl "Al-ittifakiya al-ulya" ... p.57.
52 Zainy, M.A., Istighlal al-ghaz al-'Iraqi mahaliya ajda min tasdirho, *Dar Babel* 2 Nov. 2008 available at: http://www.darbabl.net/show_derasat.php?id=25
53 MOU Iraq-EU, *Memorandum of Understanding between the Government of Iraq and the European Union on Strategic Partnership in Energy*, signed by Andris Piebalgs, 2010, pp.1–2.
54 Williams, P., 'Shell seeks to fast-track gas exports from Iraq'. *MEED* 16 Nov. 2008 available at: http://www.meed.com/news/2008/11/shell_seeks_ to_fasttrack_gas_exports_from_iraq.html
55 Al-Amir, F., 'Mulahazat hawl "Al-Ittifakya al-ulya"..., p.22
56 Zainy, M.A., Istighlal al-ghaz al-'Iraqi mahaliya ajda min tasdirho, p.1
57 Al-Khatib, L.J., 'Securing Iraq Gas Investment for Power and Industries', pp.15–16. It should be noted that the gas/oil production ratios used by

these two experts are different. According to Zainy, a production rate of 6 billion scf/d of dry gas would equate to 10 million bbl/d of oil (i.e. a ratio of 0.6:1). However using Al-Khatib's data a production rate of 4.5 billion scf/d of dry gas equates to 6.3 million bbl/d of oil (a ratio of 0.71:1). The difference is presumably because Khatib's figure of 4.5 bscf/d includes an estimate of non-associated gas production of 1.8 bcf/d gross).

58 *Financial Times*, 'Iraq offers to supply half of Nabucco's gas', 14 July 2009.
59 'MOL and OMV join Dana Gas and Crescent in Iraq' 17 May 2009, available at http://www.gulfoilandgas.com/webpro1/MAIN/Mainnews. asp?id=7938
60 *MEES*, 'Nabucco partners turn to Kurdistan region for gas supply; Baghdad says no', vol.52, no.21, May 2009, p.7.
61 *MEES*, 'Nabucco partners turn to Kurdistan region for gas supply; Baghdad says no', vol. 52, no. 21, May 2009, p.5.

CHAPTER 8

THE IRANIAN GAS INDUSTRY: UPSTREAM DEVELOPMENT AND EXPORT POTENTIAL

Siamak Adibi and Fereidun Fesharaki

In 2009, Iran's gas reserves were estimated at 29.6 trillion cubic metres (tcm).[1] Iran has the second largest gas reserves in the world after Russia, with roughly 16 percent of the world's total. As shown in Table 8.1 approximately 68 percent of these reserves are located offshore in the Persian Gulf (mainly in South Pars), with 32 percent onshore.

Table 8.1: Iran's Gas Reserves, 2009

Source of Gas	(tcm)
Offshore	
Associated Gas and Gas Cap	0.3
Non-Associated Gas	19.9
Onshore	
Associated Gas and Gas Cap	4.0
Non-Associated Gas	5.5
Total Gas Reserves	**29.6**

Source: *Iran's Hydrocarbon Balance 2008*, International Institute for Energy Studies (IIES).

Iran's largest gas field is the South Pars field, which is essentially the same resource as Qatar's North Field, but named differently. South Pars gas reserves are estimated at 13.1 tcm with a recovery factor of 70 percent. North Pars and Kish are the next largest gas fields in Iran, each holding around 1.4 tcm of gas. The North Pars and the Kish gas reserves are still undeveloped and have the potential to meet a major part of domestic gas consumption and/or export commitments.

Iran holds a unique position in terms of Middle East gas reserves and has great potential to increase current reserves by new discoveries. Since 2007, the National Iranian Oil Company (NIOC) has discovered several very large gas fields within the country. In late 2007, 0.3 tcm of new gas reserves (the Sefid Zakhour gas field) located in the southern Fars province were discovered. Early studies estimate at least 70–80 percent of recoverable gas.

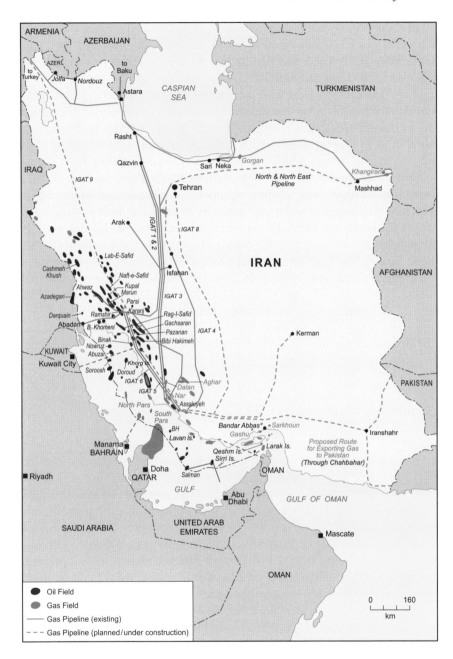

Map 8.1: Iran's Main Gas Lines

In 2008, Iran discovered a large gas field in the Farsi Block (the Farzad-B gas field) located in the Persian Gulf. The Farzad-B gas field, with an estimated 0.4 tcm of gas reserves, is one of Iran's largest gas discoveries in recent years.

The Halegan gas field with total reserves of 0.4 tcm of gas and 249 million barrels of condensate was discovered in February 2010. Then in late June 2010, NIOC confirmed large gas discoveries in the Persian Gulf. The Forouz gas field, which holds 0.7 tcm of natural gas and 280 million barrels of condensate, is located 30 km southeast of Kish Island.

Several of these huge gas fields, such as South Pars, Tabnak, Forouz, Nar, and Kangan, also contain significant condensate reserves. South Pars has the largest condensate reserves in Iran (17 billion barrels, of which 9.75 billion barrels are recoverable). In addition, Tabnak has 240 million barrels of recoverable condensate, Kish has 235 million barrels, Balal has 184 million barrels and Kangan has 135 million barrels.[2]

There is a strong possibility the country will find more gas in the new blocks, which are still open for exploration activities. However, utilisation of these huge reserves remains challenging for Iran as the country still faces many political and economic difficulties. Indeed, considering the opportunities for swift development, especially for export projects, progress has been extremely slow.

Regulatory Environment for Foreign Investment

Based on Iranian investment laws, foreign companies are not allowed to participate in upstream projects in the form of production-sharing agreements (PSAs). Working under service contracts (buyback) is the only available option in upstream involvement for international oil companies. In the buyback contracts, the engineering, procurement, and construction (EPC) contractors invest in the project, and the payback of the capital cost is deducted from oil and gas sales revenue. The rate of return on Iran's buyback contracts varies between 12–17 percent, and the payback periods are usually five to seven years. The buyback contracts generally have a strong incentive for contractors to keep costs down and there is limited flexibility in fiscal terms for the projects.

It should be noted that in recent buyback agreements, especially with Chinese and/or other Asian companies such as the Malaysian company SKS in the development contract of the Golshan gas field, more attractive and/or flexible terms have been offered to contractors. However, this may not necessarily translate into more international companies vying for Iranian projects. The political issues and risk of investment surrounding Iran have made international oil companies stay away from the country. Indeed, international companies are under increasing pressure to slow down work, and reduce any future investment in Iran. Statoil has articulated a clear policy that it will complete all ongoing projects but will not embark on new projects until further notice.[3] In February 2010, Italy's ENI officially ceased operations and announced that it will not embark on any new projects.[4] Total and Shell also cancelled their upstream agreements with NIOC to develop South Pars phases due to the recent sanctions.[5]

If the political problems are resolved, there will be some room for foreign investment in Iran's gas industry.

It is worth noting in June 2010, the United Nations Security Council approved the fourth round of sanctions against Iran over the country's nuclear programs. Following the UN, the USA also imposed new sanctions – the toughest ever passed by the US Congress – putting further pressure on Iran, especially the energy sector. The US sanctions target supplying refined petroleum products, as well as goods and services for the oil and natural gas sectors. However, the greatest impact came from the recent EU decision to set further sanctions on Iran's shipping, banking, and energy sectors. Indeed, the EU sanctions (approved in Brussels on 26 July, 2010 by foreign ministers of the 27 nation European Union) are a serious threat to Iran's new oil and gas projects and, in the worst-case scenario, might even interrupt standard oil and gas operations in the country for the near future.

Iran's Gas Organisations

The gas industry is controlled by two key organisations, National Iranian Oil Company (NIOC) and National Iranian Gas Company (NIGC). NIOC dominates all upstream activities such as exploration, development and production in oil and gas fields. It controls these activities through its key subsidiaries, such as National Iranian South Oil Company (NISOC), Iranian Central Oil Fields Company (ICOFC), Iranian Offshore Oil Company (IOOC) and Pars Oil and Gas Company (POGC).[6]

NISOC controls upstream activities such as associated gas production from Iran's oil fields in the south and southwest of the country, for example Masjed Suleiman fields. ICOFC controls all upstream activities in several oil and gas fields located mainly in the south and central areas of the country. The company produces non-associated gas from 13 key gas fields – Aghar, Dalan, Homa, Kangan, Khangiran, Nar, Qeshm, Sarajeh, Sarkhun, Shanoul, Tabnak, Tange Bijar, and

Varavi. IOOC controls all upstream activities in oil offshore companies and produces associated gas from offshore fields such as Salman, Sirri, Doroud, Balal and several other fields. POGC, a company established in 1998, is currently in charge of the development and production of non-associated gas reserves in the South Pars, the North Pars, the Golshan and the Ferdowsi gas fields.

In 2003, National Iranian Gas Exports Company (NIGEC) was established to handle all new pipeline and LNG projects in the country, assuming responsibility for NIGC's former activities. The company was working as a subsidiary of NIOC from 2003 to May 2010 when the Petroleum Ministry diversified responsibility for all new gas projects to NIGC. Under the new re-organisation, NIGEC was incorporated into NIGC and works under NIGC's control.

NIGC is the key company in charge of the country's gas downstream sector. The company processes and delivers gas and distributes it to domestic end-users. It controls all operations in gas-processing plants, pipelines and city natural gas networks. The downstream and upstream sectors in the gas industry are not integrated under the control of a centralised management and operation system and are handled separately by different organisations. The current structure may result in a mismatch between gas supply and demand causing delay and even cancellation of export projects.

Development of the downstream sector, such as expansion of the distribution system, needs less financial resources and time as compared with upstream development activities. Thus, NIGC can expand the downstream sector very fast. Development of the upstream sector, however, needs a large injection of funds and at least 3–4 years for each upstream project. It is therefore no surprise that NIOC faces an uphill task in developing the upstream sector. This imbalance between the downstream and upstream sectors and the consequent gas shortage will cause concern to international buyers about the ability to commit volumes to export projects.

Natural Gas Production

Iran's gross gas production enjoyed strong growth in the 2000s due to the development of non-associated gas fields (Table 8.2). In 2008, gross gas production stood at 180.4 Bcm,[7] representing an annual average growth rate (AAGR) of 5 percent for the 2000–2008 period.

Estimates indicate that as much as 80 percent of offshore associated gas volumes are being flared in the country mainly because of lack of

Table 8.2: Gross Gas Production, 2000–2008

Bcm	Marketed Production	Flaring	Gas Reinjection	Shrinkage and Loss	Gross Gas Production
2000	60.1	12.6	44.1	5.6	122.4
2001	69.1	7.4	32.4	5.3	114.3
2002	75.0	10.8	26.4	8.8	121.0
2003	81.5	14.8	28.4	7.2	131.9
2004	89.7	13.1	29.3	17.1	149.1
2005	103.5	12.0	30.5	15.5	161.5
2006	108.6	15.8	26.7	16.7	167.8
2007	111.9	15.7	28.5	18.1	174.2
2008*	116.3	16.8	27.4	19.9	180.4
AAGR (2000–2008)	8.6%	3.7%	-5.8%	17.3%	5.0%

* Estimated

Source: OPEC *Annual Statistical Bulletins*, 2004–2008.

infrastructure to deliver gas to the domestic market. The major volumes of flared gas are in the Kharg and the Bahregansar regions.[8]

In 2008, approximately 65 percent of gross production was delivered to the market and 15 percent of the total production was re-injected into the oil fields to enhance the oil recovery factor.[9] Gas re-injection volumes declined when the country was faced with a massive gas supply shortage in its domestic market and had to divert re-injection volumes to residential, commercial and power sectors.

Total gas shrinkage, loss, and flaring represented around 20 percent of gross production in 2008. Gas shrinkage increased with an annual average growth rate of 17 percent from 2000 to 2008 in line with greater liquids extraction from gas. It should be noted that in recent years, the country has tried to maximise its benefits from fractionation of high value liquids (such as LPG) from rich gas produced from different oil and gas fields. This has resulted in gas shrinkage increasing to 10–11 percent of gross gas production.

South Pars is the most important gas field in Iran, and in 2008 it produced 52.7 Bcm, approximately 35 percent of the total non-associated gas production in the country (Table 8.3). Two other important non-associated gas sources in Iran are the Nar and Kangan gas fields. In 2008, the Nar gas field produced approximately 12.4 Bcm, while the Kangan gas field produced 22.1 Bcm and the Khangiran non-associated gas field also delivered a total of 15.9 Bcm into the national grid for domestic consumption.[10]

Table 8.3: Gross Gas Production from Non-Associated Gas Fields, 2008, Bcm

Province	Gas Consumption (Bcm)	% of Gas Consumption
Tehran	22.9	18.4
Isfahan	15.0	12.1
Khuzestan	10.4	8.4
Khorasan-Razavi	9.1	7.3
Fars	8.2	6.6
Kerman	7.0	5.7
Eastern Azerbaijan	6.4	5.2
Mazandaran	6.0	4.9
Bushehr	5.7	4.6
Gilan	4.1	3.3
Markazi	4.0	3.2
Qazvin	3.8	3.1
Western Azerbaijan	2.7	2.1
Others	18.9	15.2
Total	**124.3**	**100.0**

Source: *Iran's Hydrocarbon Balance 2008*, International Institute For Energy Studies (IIES).

It should be noted that associated gas production from Khuzestan, Ilam, Booshehr, Lorestan, and Kermanshah Provinces, as well as off-shore oil fields are also playing an important role in the country's gas supply. It is estimated that Iran is producing around 30 Bcm/yr of associated gas. Gross gas production is expected to increase strongly by an AAGR of 6 percent from 2009 to 2015, increasing to 280 Bcm in 2015 (Figure 8.1).[11] This growth will be in line with the completion of new phases in South Pars (Phases 9–10, 12, and 15–18).

In recent years, Iran has introduced several new upstream projects especially for development of giant gas fields such as South Pars, North Pars, Kish, Golshan and Ferdowsi. Among these projects, the development of the shared gas field with Qatar, South Pars, is more politically sensitive for the Iranian government. Indeed, both countries are trying to maximise production of gas and condensate from their share of this field in the shortest possible time.

South Pars Gas Development

The South Pars gas field is designed to be developed in 26 phases. Currently, eight phases are in operation and seven phases are under

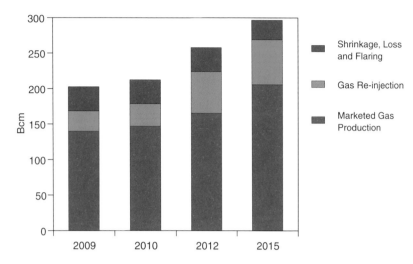

Figure 8.1: Gas Production Outlook in Iran

Note: 2009 preliminary, 2010–2015 forecasts

Source: FACTS Global Energy, 2010.

development and should be onstream by 2015. Other phases are likely to be completed in the late 2010s.

Phases in Operation

Phase 1 can produce plateau volumes of 10.2 Bcm/yr of gas (and 40 kb/d of condensate) for delivery to Iran's domestic market. Development of Phase 1 started in 1997 and was completed in 2004 by local contractor, Petropars Ltd.[12] However, since startup, actual output of this phase never exceeded more than 60 percent of its nameplate capacity due to technical problems at the gas processing plant. In March 2010, the gas production from Phase 1 was finally stabilised at around the nameplate capacity.

Phases 2 and 3 were completed by a consortium of Total (40 percent), Gazprom (30 percent), and Petronas (30 percent) in 2002. These phases produce 20.4 Bcm/yr of gas and 80 kb/d of condensate for delivery to the domestic market.[13]

Phases 4 and 5 were completed by a consortium of ENI (60 percent), Petropars (20 percent), and NIOC (20 percent) in 2004. Production includes 20.4 Bcm/yr of gas for the domestic market, 80 kb/d of condensate, 1.0 Mt/yr of ethane and 1.05 Mt/yr of LPG.[14]

Phases 6, 7, and 8 (see below) were assigned to Petropars in 2000.[15]

Phases 6 and 7 were completed in late 2008 and early 2009, respectively, while Phase 8 was completed after a long delay in late 2009. Phases 6 and 7 temporarily feed onshore facilities of South Pars Phases 9 and 10, where gas is sweetened for the domestic market while gas from Phase 8 is being delivered by a 512 km, 56 inch pipeline (IGAT-5) to the Agha Jari oil field for re-injection. The gas flows from these phases do not always correspond with the capacity of the onshore facilities and some times surplus gas has to be flared.

After completion of the Phase 9 and 10 offshore facilities, gas from Phases 6, 7, and 8 will be diverted by IGAT-5 for re-injection into the oil fields in Khuzestan province. Phases 6, 7, and 8 combined could produce plateau volumes of 38 Bcm/yr of gas, 158 kb/d of condensate, and 1.6 Mt/yr of LPG.

Phases Under Development

The development contract for Phases 9 and 10 was signed in September 2002 between Pars Oil and Gas Company (POGC) and a consortium of LG (South Korea), Oil Industries Engineering and Construction Company (OIEC), and Iranian Offshore Engineering and Construction (IOEC). Production of these two phases includes 20.4 Bcm/yr of gas for domestic consumption, 80 kb/d of condensate, 1 Mt/yr of ethane and 1.05 Mt/yr of LPG.[16] The project was due to be completed in late 2008 and the onshore facilities of Phases 9 and 10 started operation. However, US sanctions have caused difficulties for the upstream section because the well completion equipment was to be provided by Weatherford, a US company. As a result, the project was delayed and will be completed in 2011.

Phase 12 is expected to produce 31.0 Bcm/yr of gas to feed the Iran LNG project and the domestic market as well as 110 kb/d of condensate. The upstream part of Phase 12 is currently under development by Petropars, and is due onstream in late 2012 or early 2013.[17]

Phases 15 and 16 will produce roughly 20.4 Bcm/yr of gas, 80 kb/d of condensate, 1.05 Mt/yr of LPG, and 1.0 Mt/yr of ethane. The development contract of these Phases was signed between NIOC and a consortium of the Iranian company, Khatam Al Anbia Construction Headquarters (KACH) controlled by the Revolutionary Guard, the Iranian Offshore Engineering and Construction Company (IOEC), Saaf, and the Iran Shipbuilding & Offshore Industries Complex Company (ISOICO).[18] In July 2010, KACH pulled out from the project, which is now being implemented by ISOICO, IOEC and Saaf. Phases 15 and 16 are expected to come on stream in 2013/2014.

Phases 17 and 18 will also produce 20.4 Bcm/yr of gas and 80 kb/d of condensate and are expected to be developed by a consortium of IDRO, IOEC, and OIEC with a likely completion date of 2014/2015.[19] Although the Iranian government promised NIOC financing for the project from the special annual budget for development of South Pars, lack of adequate financial resources for completion of these phases is the main challenge to the project.

Recent Development Agreements for South Pars Phases

Phases 20 and 21 are expected to produce 20.4 Bcm/yr of gas, 75 kb/d of condensate, 1.05 Mt/yr of LPG, and 1.0 Mt/yr of ethane.[20] The condensate from these phases is to be desulfurised in Assaluyeh. In May 2009, NIOC and OIEC signed a contract worth over US$5.5 billion to develop Phases 20 and 21. According to the contract, these Phases were initially planned to be completed within 52 months. However, the contractor has not started the construction works yet due to lack of financial resources. Assuming additional delays (which are common for the South Pars development), the project is likely to come onstream in late 2015 or early 2016. OIEC is expected to bring in IOEC as its main local partner, as well as other foreign companies as contractors in order to complete the project.

The South Pars Phase 11 was initially allocated to the Pars LNG project. The designed production of this Phase is 20.4 Bcm/yr of gas and 80 kb/d of condensate.[21] Under the original plan discussed with Total for several years, Phase 11 (located near the Iran–Qatar marine border) was to supply gas to a joint venture of Total, Petronas, and NIGEC for liquefaction at Bandar Tombak. However, Total declared in 2008 that it could not proceed with the overall scheme until Iran resolves its disputes with the international community. Iran has been anxious to develop areas of the shared South Pars field closest to Qatar to minimise losses through gas migration in the reservoir. In June 2009, NIOC signed a new preliminary agreement with China's CNPC for the development of Phase 11 with a development cost estimated at US$4.7 billion.[22]

Phases 13 and 14 were previously allocated to the Persian LNG project, a joint venture comprised of Shell, Repsol, and NIGEC. However, talks with Shell and Repsol stalled because of a combination of tough fiscal terms and the US sanctions against Iran. In June 2010, Phase 13 was awarded to an Iranian consortium of Mapna, Sadra, and Petro Paidar.[23] Phase 14 was awarded to IDRO, National Iranian Drilling Company (NIDC), and IOEC.[24] Phases 13 and 14 are expected to produce a combined 41.3 Bcm/yr of gas and 154 kb/d of condensates.

In June 2010, Phase 19 was assigned to Petropars and IOEC, and is expected to deliver 18 Bcm/yr of gas, 77 kb/d of condensate, 1.05 Mt/y of LPG, and 1 Mt/y of ethane. [25]

In June 2010, the South Pars Phases 22, 23, and 24 were awarded to Petro Sina Arian and Sadra, and are expected to produce 20.4 Bcm/yr of gas, 77 kb/d of condensate, 1.1 Mt/y of LPG, and 1 Mt/y of ethane.[26] In 2007, Iran signed an MOU with the Turkish government for development of these phases and for the transportation of up to 30 Bcm/yr of Iranian and/or Turkmen gas via Turkey to Europe. However, the deal was not finalised.

It is worth noting that POGC mandates that contractors complete the recent South Pars projects within 35 months. However, considering technical delays, which are not uncommon in Iranian projects, the completion dates for recent phases are more likely to be after 5–6 years.

Development of the Kish Gas Field

The giant Kish gas field, located a few miles south of Lavan Island, is expected to produce up to 10.3 Bcm/yr in the first phase, with output rising to 31 Bcm/yr after the second phase. Iran estimates that the Kish field has 1.4 tcm of gas in place with up to 1.0 tcm of gas thought to be recoverable. The Kish field also has condensate reserves of 514 million barrels.

According to Iran's Petroleum Engineering and Development Company (PEDEC), NIOC expects the first phase of development of Kish to be completed by mid 2011. However, due to possible delays in the downstream activities, it is understood that the first phase of the project is likely to be onstream in 2014/2015 (at the earliest) as construction of gas treatment facilities may take at least four years

Iran and Oman are in negotiations to deliver a part of the Kish gas production through a 200 km subsea pipeline from Kish to Oman's Musandam Peninsula, but since 2007 sales negotiations have stalled over pricing.

Development of Golshan and Ferdowsi

Golshan and Ferdowsi are two large gas fields in the Persian Gulf near South Pars with roughly 1.4 tcm of gas in place. NIOC signed a US$6 billion buyback contract in December 2007 with the Malaysian company SKS for the development of these two gas fields.[27]

Development of North Pars

The North Pars field contains sour gas reserves. Apart from some initial offshore development work in the 1970s by Oil Services Company of Iran (OSCO), it remains undeveloped. The field is located in the Persian Gulf, in shallow waters 15 km offshore. The gas is lean and sour, with 6000 ppm of hydrogen sulphide and 4.96 percent CO_2. In December 2006, NIOC and CNOOC signed an agreement to develop the North Pars natural gas field and export 20 Mt/yr of LNG.[28]

Gas Re-injection into the Oil Fields

Gas re-injection plays a substantive role in oil recovery in Iran and as a result, political pressures are in favour of a gas re-injection policy. The exact volume of gas required for this purpose is unknown, but it is clear that massive volumes are dedicated to it. Iran's current oil recovery rate is approximately 20–25 percent. This means that approximately 20–25 percent of oil is recovered, with 75–80 percent remaining in the fields until enhanced oil recovery (EOR) methods are implemented. NIOC's reservoir engineers believe that gas re-injection into fractured carbonate reservoirs – which account for approximately 90 percent of the country's oil fields – are a better option than other methods such as water injection.

For this reason, NIOC is expected to inject massive volumes of gas into its oil fields – 63.8 Bcm/yr by 2015. Iran recently completed the construction of a 56-inch, 508 km gas pipeline from South Pars to Agha Jari. This pipeline is expected to deliver up to 40.3 Bcm/yr of gas for re-injection to the oil fields located in the south and southwest of the country (20.8 Bcm/yr for re-injection into the Agha Jari oil field and 19.5 Bcm/yr into other fields). The gas re-injection in Agha Jari is expected to be fully operational by 2010.[29]

Some Iranian reservoir engineers believe that the planned volumes of gas re-injection are not sufficient and are trying to push NIOC for further increases. The gas supply shortage has raised concerns of negative impacts on Iran's oil industry, as well as on the economy. For example, some engineers believe the shortage of gas for re-injection will seriously damage Iranian oil fields in the next few years. It should be noted that the current rate of decline in oil production is 8–11 percent annually[30] and gas reinjection is urgently needed to maintain current crude oil production.

It is believed that after 2010, roughly 207 Bcm/yr (approximately equivalent to 20 phases of South Pars production) is required to be re-injected into Iran's oil fields. But it is understood that this level of re-injection is completely unrealistic due to the lack of necessary infrastructure for transportation and the re-injection into the oil fields. The lack of financial resources means that NIOC is not expected to increase re-injection through 2015, but changes in government policy could have an impact on these plans.

The recovery factor of re-injected gas is usually 60–80 percent of injected volumes and therefore, after oil recovery, 60–80 percent of the gas will be available for recycling. This means that gas re-injection could be similar to large (albeit long-term) gas storage for the country.

Producing additional volumes of crude oil through gas re-injection as well as the availability of re-injected gas in the oil fields makes these projects attractive compared to exports of, for example, LNG. Gas re-injection projects also require lower investment costs than LNG exports. Based on available information quoted by NIOC,[31] one of the most expensive gas re-injection projects in Iran – re-injection of gas to the Agha Jari oil field – cost roughly US$2.1 billion. This represented roughly one-fifth of proposed investment costs of the PARS LNG project. The result of this has been strong opposition, especially among Members of Parliament, towards gas export projects. They believe that exports should be minimised and priority given to gas re-injection.

Gas Demand and Pricing

Iran is currently the third largest gas consumer in the world after the USA and Russia.[32] Since the early 1990s, the Iranian government has tried to expand the country's gas utilisation as part of its fuel substitution policy, which is aimed at boosting gas usage to free up more crude and petroleum products for export. As a result of this policy, gas demand has increased significantly in recent years. Indeed, consumption increased from 20.7 Bcm in 1990 to 62.7 Bcm in 2000. Posting a double digit annual average growth rate (AAGR) of 11.7 percent during the years 1990 to 2000.

Natural gas consumption has continued to grow since 2000 as shown in Figure 8.2. Gas consumption in the domestic market has shown an AAGR of 8.9 percent from 2000–2008. In 2008, Iran consumed approximately 124.3 Bcm of natural gas with the Tehran and Isfahan provinces representing roughly one-third of total gas consumption in the country (Table 8.4).[33]

In 2008, the residential and commercial sector represented the

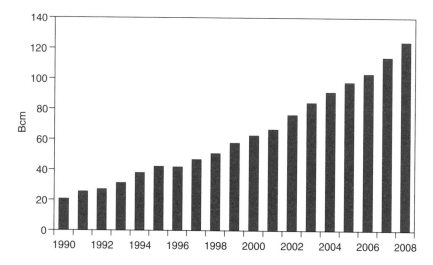

Figure 8.2: Natural Gas Consumption, 1990–2008

Sources: 1990–1997: *Energy Balances*, Iran's Ministry of Electricity and Watar.
1998–2008: *Iran's Hydrocarbon Balance 2008*, International Institute For
Energy Studies (IIES).

Table 8.4: Natural Gas Consumption by Province, 2008

Province	Gas Consumption (Bcm)	% of Gas Consumption
Tehran	22.9	18.4
Isfahan	15.0	12.1
Khuzestan	10.4	8.4
Khorasan-Razavi	9.1	7.3
Fars	8.2	6.6
Kerman	7.0	5.7
Eastern Azerbaijan	6.4	5.2
Mazandaran	6.0	4.9
Bushehr	5.7	4.6
Gilan	4.1	3.3
Markazi	4.0	3.2
Qazvin	3.8	3.1
Western Azerbaijan	2.7	2.1
Others	18.9	15.2
Total	**124.3**	**100.0**

Source: *Iran's Hydrocarbon Balance 2008*, International Institute For Energy Studies
(IIES).

largest share of gas consumption, with about 44 Bcm (35.4 percent of total consumption). This was followed by the power sector, which accounted for 43.2 Bcm (34.7 percent), while the industrial sector consumed around 26 Bcm (21 percent). Consumption in the energy sector, including natural gas in oil refineries and gas compressor stations stood at 9.2 Bcm (7.4 percent). Gas consumption in the transportation sector increased from 3 million standard cubic metres per year in 2001 to around 1.8 Bcm in 2008, a growth rate of 150 percent per annum during the period 2001–2008, but is still only around 1.5 percent of total gas consumption.[34] (Figure 8.3)

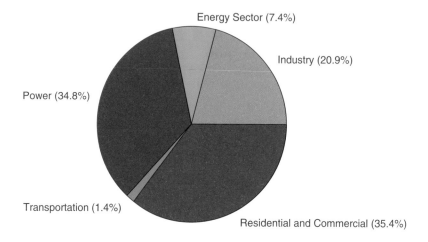

Figure 8.3: Natural Gas Consumption by Sector, 2008

Source: *Iran's Hydrocarbon Balance 2008*, International Institute For Energy Studies (IIES).

Despite the successful substitution of natural gas for petroleum products, the country has been facing a gas shortage that has become a serious threat to internal energy supply security. The key reasons for the shortage are fast growing gas demand caused by very low prices, and delays in upstream projects.

Gas prices in Iran are still subsidised[35] and are low compared with markets in other countries, let alone prices in international trade. In 2008, natural gas prices in residential and commercial sectors were estimated at US$0.33/MMBtu and US$0.74/MMBtu, respectively. Power plants paid the lowest gas price at US$0.15/MMBtu, while the price for industrial projects (including petrochemical projects) was estimated at around US$0.47/MMBtu (Table 8.5). As mentioned earlier,

Table 8.5: Natural Gas Prices, 2008

Sector	Iranian Rials/ Cubic Meter	US$/MMBtu
Residential*	112.5	0.33
Commercial	250.0	0.74
Industry	158.5	0.47
Powerplants	49.3	0.15

* Base Price

Source: NIGC

selling gas at these very low prices has resulted in rocketing demand, especially in the residential sector.[36]

In recent years, the gas shortage has become a major concern, especially for gas re-injection, gas export projects by pipeline, industrial projects, and power plants. A gas supply shortage would mean cutting gas exports and switching to other fuels such as gasoil and fuel oil for the power generation, residential and commercial sectors, and/or reducing re-injection volumes.

The impact of a gas supply shortage in Iran's oil economy is significant. Since 2006, power plants have experienced massive gas shortages during the winter, causing them to switch to burning petroleum products instead of natural gas. This has caused a growing demand for imports of gasoil within the country. Gasoil imports started from 18.2 thousand barrels per day (kb/d) in 2004 to over 40.4 kb/d in 2008.[37] Many industrial projects such as gas-based petrochemical plants at Assaluyeh and Bandar Imam also have a lower utilisation rate in the winter because gas supplies are temporarily cut off to meet increased demand from the residential and commercial sectors.

The Iranian government believes that cheap gas prices contribute to low efficiency and wasteful utilisation in the country's gas industry and have resulted in the rapid growth of consumption in recent years. Natural gas consumption in residential and commercial sectors is generally wasteful because of inefficient use. Most power plants in Iran also have low efficiency levels in power generation. Gas-fired plants usually produce only 3 kWh for each standard cubic metre of gas.

In an attempt to reduce wasteful natural gas consumption, the government has tried to increase domestic gas prices, especially for the residential and commercial sectors. Since 2007, the NIGC has introduced a pricing mechanism for residential users based on consumption, in order to control growing demand and decrease a part of the subsidies for high volume end-users. Using this mechanism, the gas price for some high volume end-users can increase to nearly eight times higher than the base price of US$0.33/MMBtu. However, applying a new gas pricing mechanism has not slowed down gas demand in the residential and commercial sectors where the number of end-users has significantly increased (as shown in Table 8.6).

Table 8.6: Natural Gas Distribution in Iran

Year	Natural Gas Network (Km)	Number of End-users		
		Residential	Commercial	Industrial
2000	7,945	4,301,302	172,246	2,600
2004	13,142	7,151,301	323,655	7,305
2008	13,252	10,497,120	572,220	42,119

Source: NIGC

In October 2009, the Iranian parliament finally approved the general outline for increasing energy prices and passed a bill to cut subsidies. Based on the recent approval, the price of petroleum products (including gasoline, gasoil, kerosene, and fuel oil) will be set near market prices within five years from the start of the reform plan from mid-2010. The natural gas price for the residential and commercial sectors is expected to increase from the current average price of US$0.5/MMBtu to nearly 75 percent of the average export price, which may translate into a huge jump in price of nearly US$6–7/MMBtu (on the basis of 2009 gas export prices to Turkey).

The impact of the new price reform on natural gas demand is still not clearly predictable. However, it is unlikely that consumption patterns will change dramatically especially in power and the residential sectors. Natural gas consumption is expected to increase at a rate of 5 percent during the next five years despite the price increase.[38] However, there could be a significant slowdown in gas consumption growth from 8–13 percent in recent years to 5 percent in the next few years.

Gas Export and Import Projects

Pipeline Exports

Iran's first gas exports started in 1965 when the country supplied gas to the former Soviet Union. The export contract was terminated in 1981 but was resumed when Iran signed a 15-year supply contract with Russia for possible resumption of gas exports from 1990. (Figure 8.4)

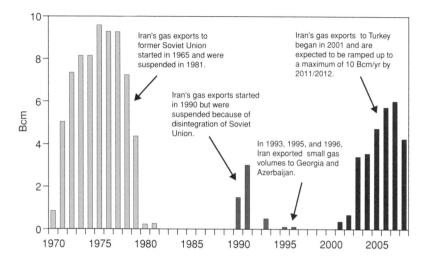

Figure 8.4: Iran's Gas Exports, 1970–2008

Source: OPEC *Annual Statistical Bulletin*, 2008.

Delivery of gas started at 1.5 Bcm and reached 3.0 Bcm in 1991. However, it was then suspended due to the breakup of the Soviet Union.

Iran–Turkey Gas Project[39]

In August 1996, the National Iranian Gas Company (NIGC) signed a contract with Turkey's BOTAS Company to export up to 10 Bcm/yr by pipeline for 22 years. Since the project started in December 2001, export volumes have been much lower than contractual volumes.[40] In 2008, Iran exported only 4.2 Bcm of gas to Turkey,[41] although it is expected that this will be increased to a maximum of 10 Bcm/yr by 2011/2012.

Iran exports its gas through a 40-inch pipeline connecting Bazargan in Iran to Dogubeyazit in Turkey. In recent years, Iran typically decreased and/or cut off its pipeline exports to Turkey in the winter due to gas supply shortages within the country. In addition, the Iran–Turkey pipeline has been sabotaged several times by the PKK terrorists.

Iran–Azerbaijan Gas Swap Contact

Azerbaijan has proven natural gas reserves of roughly 1.2 tcm and a current production of 14.7 Bcm/yr. Nakhchivan, a part of Azerbaijan, is surrounded by Armenia and has no access to Azeri gas. Due to disputes between Azerbaijan and Armenia during the 1990s and suspension of diplomatic relations between the two countries, Iran is the only country that can supply gas to Nakhchivan.

Iran signed a 25-year swap contract with Azerigaz in August 2004.[42] The new 16-inch pipeline from Jolfa (Iran) supplies 300–350 million standard cubic metres per year (mmscm/yr) to Nakhchivan, while Azerbaijan delivers the same volume of gas to Iran's northeastern Province of Astara. The swap project between the two countries started in November 2005.[43]

Iran–Armenia Gas Contract

In May 2004, Iran agreed to supply Armenia with 1.1–2.3 Bcm/yr of gas under a 20-year contract. The startup was targeted for January 2007.[44] Due to technical delays in the construction of the pipeline in Armenian territory, gas exports finally started in 2009. Armenia compensates Iran for the gas by supplying electricity. [45]

Iran–UAE Gas Contract

In 2001, National Iranian Oil Company (NIOC) and Crescent Petroleum signed a contract for the export of 5.2 Bcm/yr of gas from Iran's Salman field located in the Persian Gulf to the Emirate of Sharjah.[46] The Salman field is about 150 km south of Lavan Island and extends into the UAE offshore sector known as the Abu Al-Bukhoosh field. Initial plans were for Salman gas to be delivered by a 30-inch, 155 km pipeline to the Sirri platform and, after condensate extraction, sour gas would be exported to the Mubarak oil platform, operated by Crescent Petroleum in UAE waters.

In 2008, after a long delay, an Iranian contractor, PetroIran, completed the development of the Salman field and constructed an export pipeline to the Mubarak oil platform. However, serious price disputes between NIOC and Crescent Petroleum have prevented the start of gas exports. The main dispute lies in the agreed price formula with Crescent Petroleum, which translates into a gas price below US$1/MMBtu (even lower than initial Qatari Dolphin prices for the Abu Dhabi and Dubai emirates).[47]

The initial commencement date of the project was December 2005. Crescent Petroleum and its affiliate company, Dana Gas, invested in the construction of necessary gas pipelines and a gas processing plant (Sajgas) in Saja'a with a capacity of 6.2 Bcm/yr. The processing plant was completed in November 2005 but unless the price dispute is settled, it will never be utilised. Crescent Petroleum still hopes for a satisfactory resolution but a decision to divert Salman gas to the domestic market was approved by the government in summer 2008, and the construction of necessary infrastructure started immediately thereafter. NIOC has selected the Iranian Offshore Engineering and Construction Company (IOEC) to build a new 287 km, 32-inch pipeline connecting Sirri to Assaluyeh, which will deliver the Salman gas to the Iranian domestic market.[48] The total cost for the new pipeline is estimated to be US$750 million and the project is to be completed in 2010 after which the prospect of exports to Crescent Petroleum seem remote.

Iran–Pakistan–India (IPI) Pipeline

The Iran–Pakistan–India (IPI) pipeline has come a long way since the 1990s, when, after the easing of political tensions between India and Pakistan, the pipeline parties came to the negotiating table. However, serious negotiations between the three countries began only in 2005.[49] In 2007, India withdrew from the IPI negotiations as a result of political pressure, and many unresolved commercial issues, such as transportation tariffs through Pakistan.[50]

With India choosing to withdraw, the IPI pipeline became a deal between the two Islamic countries, Iran and Pakistan. The final gas sales and purchase agreement was signed between Iran's National Iranian Gas Export Company and Pakistan's Inter State Gas Systems in June 2009. Iran has agreed to supply 8 Bcm/yr of gas to Pakistan for 25 years starting in 2014.[51]

The main pricing related hurdle under discussion for around three years was finally overcome. In the previous 2007 agreement between Iran, Pakistan, and India, talks revolved around a 47 percent linkage to JCC.[52] But according to the new price formula, Iran and Pakistan have now agreed to a 79 percent linkage[53] which means that, at a JCC price of US$60/bbl, Pakistan will pay around US$8.2/MMBtu.

Iran is expected to export natural gas by extending a domestic transportation pipeline (the Iran Gas Trunkline 7 or IGAT-7) to Pakistan. The 900-km, 56-inch IGAT-7, which will span from Assaluyeh to Iranshahr in Iran's Sistan-Baluchestan Province, is currently under construction. The project also includes the construction of two compressor stations (totalling 150 MW) and is expected to be completed by 2010. Provided the number of compressor stations is increased to nine, the pipeline will be able to deliver up to 40 Bcm/year. IGAT-7 will also help meet domestic gas demand in the Sistan-Baluchestan Province in Iran. From Iranshahr, a pipeline that will initially deliver

8 Bcm/yr to Pakistan, will branch off from the IGAT-7 towards the Pakistani border. The pipeline may support up to 21.9 Bcm/yr of gas exports to Pakistan (and eventually possibly to India). However, as discussed earlier, this would require Iran to install more compressor stations, requiring an investment in excess of US$1 billion. In August 2010, NIGC awarded an EPC contract to KACH for the connecting pipeline from IGAT-7 to the Pakistani border. The 400 km pipeline is expected to deliver South Pars gas through Chahbahar, in the southeast of Iran, to the Iran–Pakistan border.

The gas will enter Pakistan from southern Balochistan and then enter Nawabhshah in Sindh Province, which is the pipeline hub in Pakistan. The pipeline length will be over 750 km and the construction cost is estimated to be in excess of US$1 billion. Financing will definitely be a concern and we believe that the pipeline will only be ready by 2015/2016. From Sindh, the gas will be placed into the existing network of Southern Sui Gas Corp.

Though the Iranian and Pakistani governments have approved an extension to India, it is unlikely that exports will materialise for a number of reasons:

- US objections: Though the present administration under President Barack Obama has yet to voice its opinion on the project, the previous Bush administration was clearly against it.[54] With the approval of the India–USA civilian nuclear agreement in 2008 and the strained relations between the USA and Iran, it will remain opposed to India's involvement in the project.
- Security has always been a concern as the pipeline will run through the troubled border areas and the Balochistan Province. Pakistan has made it clear that it cannot guarantee safe passage of gas to the Indian border. This, and the fact that the relations between the two countries are periodically strained, makes it a very risky proposition for India.
- An Iran–Pakistan border price of US$8.2/MMBtu would translate to a delivered price of around US$10.8/MMBtu in India. This is after taking into consideration transportation and transit fees through Pakistan (US$1.4/MMBtu), a pipeline tariff within India of US$0.60/MMBtu and interstate tax of US$0.60/MMBtu. This makes the IPI gas substantially more expensive than both LNG imports from Qatar under existing long-term LNG contracts and the KG-D6 gas for Indian consumers. Iranian gas will also be more expensive than current domestic gas prices in Pakistan. Currently the gas price in Pakistan for Independent Power Producers (IPPs) is about US$3.9/

MMBtu. It is understood that Pakistani fertiliser companies are currently paying between US$0.69 and US$1.2/MMBtu for their feedgas.[55]

- Shifting political sands could alter policy in Iran, which may lead to a further review of the project causing more delays.[56]

Other Pipeline Gas Export Projects

Iran and Syria signed an MOU for 3 Bcm/yr in October 2007,[57] but no final agreement has been reached between the two countries (see Chapter 5).

Iran and Oman signed several MOUs for the development of the Kish gas field and the export of 10–20 Bcm/yr of gas to Oman by a subsea pipeline.[58] However, the MOUs have not been finalised yet, mainly because of price disagreements (see Chapter 11).

In November 2007, Bahrain and Iran signed an MOU for the supply of 10 Bcm/yr of Iranian gas to Bahrain.[59] The recently discovered gas field, 'Farzad B', which is located in the Farsi block in the Persian Gulf near Bahraini territories, could be an ideal source of gas supply to Bahrain. The development plan for Farsi block would include two phases with each phase producing up to 5 Bcm/yr for the Iranian domestic market and/or exports to Bahrain. However, the negotiations between the two countries are at a preliminary stage (see Chapter 13).

Iran–Europe Gas Export Project

In late March 2008, gas exports to Europe became a reality for the Iranian government after it signed a contract with the Swiss company Elektrizitäts-Gesellschaft Laufenburg AG (EGL). Based on a 20-year contract between NIGEC and EGL, Iran will start gas exports to Europe with initial volumes of 0.5 Bcm/yr from 2011/2012.[60] The volumes will ramp up to around 5.0 Bcm/yr in 2015/2016. The gas would be available from the existing export pipeline to Turkey, which has spare capacity of 4–5 Bcm/yr and can support supply commitments to EGL.[61]

NIGEC is also looking at an ambitious export plan (up to 22 Bcm/yr) via the Nabucco pipeline to Europe.[62] Austrian company Econgas is in negotiation with NIGEC for the purchase of gas at the Iran–Turkey border.[63] However, due to the current political environment in Iran, growing domestic demand, and lack of necessary infrastructure, it seems unlikely that this project will materialise in the near term. It should be noted that if Iran wants to export greater amounts of gas to European customers, a new 1800 km pipeline (IGAT-9) from Assaluyeh to the Iran–Turkey border needs to be built and it is difficult to see how this can be done before 2020.

LNG Projects

The story of Iran's LNG exports goes back to the 1970s, when Iran decided to export LNG from the North Pars gas field with the participation of Japanese and US companies. Subsequently, a consortium called Japan Kalingas was created to export LNG to Japan and the USA. All these ventures were suspended in early 1979, following the Islamic revolution.

In the late 1990s, Iran started to re-develop the idea of LNG exports. In recent years it has introduced numerous LNG projects, such as Iran LNG, Pars LNG, Persian LNG, North Pars, Golshan, Lavan, and Qeshm. Map 8.2 shows the location of the terminals. The target was to supply 73 Mt/yr of new LNG into the market by 2015. However, the current political situation has created real difficulties for Iran's LNG projects, which have been heavily dependent on European

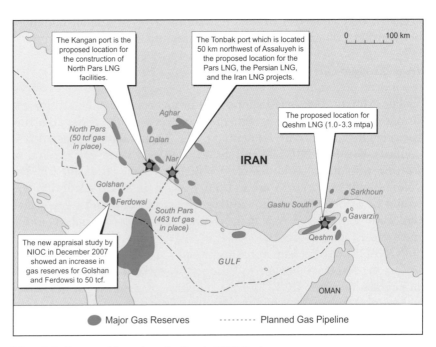

Map 8.2: Proposed Locations for Iran's LNG Projects

technologies and equipment. Shell and Total, two key players in these projects, are unlikely to go against the Western sanctions and this means the cancellation of two large LNG projects: Persian LNG (16.1 Mt/yr) and Pars LNG (10 Mt/yr). Table 8.7 gives details of recent LNG projects.

Iran LNG

This project includes the construction of two 5.4 Mt/yr trains, with gas from Phase 12 of South Pars. Despite several technical and commercial challenges, NIGEC has defined the Iran LNG project as one of its top priorities. It will be managed by NIGEC's subsidiary company Iran LNG Ltd. (ILG).[64]

Among the country's LNG projects, Iran LNG seems to be more advanced, as nearly US$1.3 billion has already been spent on this project. ILG has signed several EPC contracts through different packages, mainly with local and/or Asian contractors. In 2007, ILG signed an EPC contract with a consortium of Iran's Rah Sahel and South Korea's Daelim for the construction of LNG tanks and marine facilities.[65] Another EPC package was signed with Iran's Farab for the construction of gas sweetening units. They also engaged local contractors, such as Petro Sanat Maad and MAPNA, to build the offsite and utility segments.

Finally in 2008, ILG signed an EPC contract with a consortium of Iran's Pars International and Development Company (PIDECO), Farab, and China's HuaFu Engineering Company (HFEC) for the construction of liquefaction units.[66] In early 2009, ILG announced it had signed a new contract, worth US$500 million, for a partnership with South Korea's GS Engineering & Construction Corporation to construct the liquefaction unit.

The contractors are currently constructing LNG storage tanks for the project and the roofs of the first and the second storage tanks were successfully installed by a consortium of local and Korean companies. Meanwhile, the engineering and construction of the utility section are underway by Iranian contractor, MAPNA. The first phase of the utility section (including installation of two gas turbines with a capacity of 300 MW) is expected to be completed by summer 2010. Iran LNG Ltd. plans for the construction of a utility section with a capacity of 1130 MW.

However, construction of the liquefaction facilities, which is at the heart of the LNG plant, has made zero progress. Local and Chinese companies plan to construct the liquefaction units but none of the companies have any experience in LNG projects and it is certain that they will not be technically capable of building the facilities without help from an international EPC contractor.

ILG has signed a licensing agreement with German Linde to use the Linde Mixed Fluid Cascade (MFC) liquefaction technology, previously applied in Norway's Snohvit LNG (which had faced serious technical problems and delays). Despite this licence agreement and a FEED that has been based on European technology, under current European sanctions, there is a very slim chance that Iran will be able to procure key liquefaction equipment, such as main heat exchangers from European companies. Indeed, the EU sanctions would halt progress of the most serious LNG project – Iran LNG. Without any improvement in the political environment, the Iran LNG project would not be onstream in the near future.

The marketing for this project is still a big challenge. The 10.8 Mt/yr project has not yet finalised any LNG sales contracts. The contract for 5 Mt/yr starting from December 2009 with India was officially rejected by the Iranian High Economic Council some years ago and cancelled because of the low price. There was also a 10 Mt/yr preliminary agreement with Sinopec and a 2.2 Mt/yr MOU with the Austrian company, OMV, neither of which are expected to materialise.[67] In November 2009, ONGC and ONGC Videsh Ltd (OVL), the overseas investment arm of ONGC, in association with the Hinduja Group and Petronet LNG, signed two agreements with NIOC for participation in the development of South Pars Phase 12 and the Iran LNG project, in return for an assurance of 6 Mt/yr of LNG on a long-term basis.[68] However, these recent agreements with Indian companies are far from being finalised. Iran LNG does not yet have any commitment for its two trains.

The feedgas for Iran LNG will be provided from South Pars Phase 12, likely to be completed in 2013. With the delay and/or cancellation of Iran LNG, all gas from Phase 12 is expected to flow into the domestic grid, as there will be a dire need for this gas.

Pars LNG

In 2004, Total, Petronas and NIGEC agreed on a shareholding structure for development of South Pars Phase 11 and LNG exports. The Pars LNG project had aimed at a production capacity of 10 Mt/yr from two trains. Under the Pars LNG Shareholder Agreement, NIGEC could hold 50 percent of the shares, Total 40 percent, and Petronas 10 percent. This consortium was to finance the project, handle the EPC, and market the LNG.[69] However, due to the sanctions the project was cancelled in July 2010.

Persian LNG

Persian LNG production and export capacity was planned at 16.2 Mt/yr with two trains. A framework agreement signed in December 2004 declared NIGEC (50 percent), Shell (25 percent), and Repsol (25 percent) as shareholders of the project.[70] As with Pars LNG, Iran's domestic and international political issues resulted in the cancellation of this project.

Other LNG Projects

Over the past few years, Iran has signed a series of preliminary agreements, particularly with Asian companies, for the development of gas fields and LNG exports. These projects call for the construction of 35–38 Mt/yr of liquefaction capacity. However, since the signing of these memorandums of understandings (MOUs) no projects have been finalised and it is not expected that any will materialise in this decade, if ever. Indeed, the liquefaction facilities for these projects remain in the very early stages and it is more likely that the gas will be developed for the domestic market. It is worth noting that some of these agreements, such as MOUs for Lavan LNG and Qeshm LNG have already expired.

North Pars: NIOC signed an MOU in December 2006 with China National Offshore Oil Corporation (CNOOC) to develop Iran's North Pars gas field and export 20 Mt/yr of LNG. In 2008, NIOC announced that a buyback contract for the development of North Pars had been signed. However, there is no final agreement for liquefaction facilities and the project has no chance of going forward in the foreseeable future.

Golshan: In December 2007, NIOC signed a contract with the Malaysian company SKS, for the development of the Golshan and Ferdowsi gas fields. NIOC and SKS also agreed on an MOU for the production of 10 Mt/yr of LNG from the two fields. Based on their MOU, NIOC/NIGEC will be in charge of marketing 5.0 Mt/yr of LNG and the rest of the capacity is tentatively committed to SKS.[71]

Qeshm LNG: NIOC signed a heads of agreement (HOA) with Australian LNG Ltd in December 2006 for the development of gas fields for the production of 3.0–3.5 Mt/yr of LNG in Qeshm Island. However, there has been no further development. Australian LNG has never developed an LNG project anywhere and this project is no longer being seriously considered.

Lavan LNG: The Iranian Offshore Oil Company (IOOC), a subsidiary of NIOC, is considering a new plan to produce gas and construct

Table 8.7: Iran's LNG Projects, 2005–2010

Project	Number of Trains	Upstream Shareholders	Downstream Shareholders	Liquefaction Technology	Liquefaction Capacity (Mt/yr)	Latest Status
Iran LNG	2	NIOC (100%)	NIGEC (49%), The Pension Fund Organization (50%), The Pension Fund Investment Organization (1%)	Linde	10.8	Under Construction
Pars LNG	2	NIOC (100%)	NIGEC (50%), Total (40%), and Petronas (10%)	Axens	10	Cancelled
Persian LNG	2	NIOC (100%)	NIGEC (50%), Shell (25%), and Repsol (25%)	DMR (Shell)	16.2	Cancelled
North Pars	4	NIOC (100%)	NIGEC (50%) and CNOOC (50%)	N.A	20	Planned
Golshan LNG	2	NIOC (100%)	NIGEC (50%) and Malaysian Petrofield (50%)	N.A	10	Planned
Qeshm LNG	1	NIOC (100%)	NIGEC and Australian LNG Ltd	N.A	3-3.5	Cancelled
Lavan LNG	N.A	NIOC (100%)	NIGEC and PGNiG	N.A	2-3	Planned

Total Planned Liquefaction Capacity (Mt/yr) 72–73.5

Source: NIOC

liquefaction facilities at Lavan Island in the Persian Gulf. IOOC is negotiating with the Polish gas company, PGNiG to develop the Lavan gas field for the export of LNG. Meanwhile, NIGEC is in negotiation with PGNiG to setup a new joint venture for a liquefaction plant with a capacity of 2–3 Mt/yr. The project structure is still at a preliminary stage and it is unlikely that an agreement will be reached in the near future.

Will Iran Export LNG?

Iranian LNG exports and the participation of international players in these projects have been strongly tied with the domestic and international political environment. Without any improvement in the current political environment, such as the removing of sanctions, it is unlikely that Iran will be an LNG exporter in the foreseeable future. In a best-case scenario for the Iran LNG project, it is possible that LNG could be available by late this decade, taking into account technical and commercial delays. In this case, NIOC would need an experienced international partner to handle commercial and technical issues. Otherwise, bypassing sanctions for the procurement of necessary equipment and technology will not help the current contractors to finalise the project.

LNG projects in North Pars and Golshan are at an early stage and are not expected to be completed in the near future. As a result, it is more likely that the gas will be developed to meet requirements in the domestic market. Indeed, as the third largest gas consumer after the USA and Russia, Iran is more than capable of absorbing all gas produced from the new upstream projects in its domestic market.

Gas Imports

Iran has been importing gas from its northeastern neighbour, Turkmenistan, since 1997. In October 1995, the two countries signed a 25-year contract for up to 8 Bcm/yr via a 40-inch gas pipeline from Korpedzhe (Turkmenistan) to Kurd-Kui (Iran). In July 2009, Turkmenistan agreed to increase its exports from 8 Bcm/yr to around 14 Bcm/yr. In December 2009, Iran completed the construction of a new 48-inch, 35 km pipeline connecting Turkmenistan's Dauletabad and Iran's Hasheminejad gas-processing plant, which is located in the northeast of Iran near Sarakhs. With the completion of this pipeline, Iran is able to import an additional 6 Bcm/yr of Turkmen gas.[72]

Iran also plans to extend the new import pipeline from the Hashem-inejad plant to Sangbast, 40 km southeast of Mashhad city. The construction of the new 48-inch pipeline is expected to start in 2010 and may take one or two years to be completed. The length of the pipeline will be 120 km and will allow the Iranian gas network to absorb additional volumes of Turkmen gas.[73]

Historically, Turkmenistan has shown that it may not be a reliable gas supplier to Iran's domestic market, for there have been several disputes in the past few years. Turkmenistan cut the gas supply to Iran for more than three months in early 2008, when Iran's gas shortage increased to its maximum levels, and asked for a gas price hike from US$2.1/MMBtu to US$3.9/MMBtu.[74] Turkmenistan also claimed higher gas prices from Iran for 2009. The Iranian government tried to avoid Turkmenistan's supply cut and accepted a high price temporarily for the first half of 2009. Iran agreed to pay a recorded price of US$9.8/MMBtu (US$350/1,000 standard cubic metres) for gas imports during the first half of 2009.[75] In July 2009, Iran agreed with Turkmenistan on an oil linked price formula but at a lower gas price and also to increase gas imports from the initial contractual volumes.[76]

It should be noted that Iran is still highly dependent on the imports from Turkmenistan due to lack of the necessary infrastructure for delivering the domestic gas from the south and southwest of country to the north and the northeast where gas consumption is generally high. (Figure 8.5)

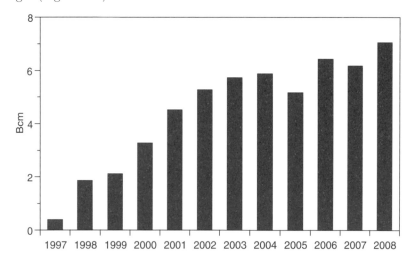

Figure 8.5: Gas Imports from Turkmenistan ,1997–2008

Source: National Iranian Gas Company (NIGC)

Conclusions

Iran has the second largest gas reserves in the world, and has continued to discover significant new reserves. The country has several super-giant gas fields that are capable of producing significant amounts of gas for domestic and/or international customers. Iran could therefore play an important role in the international gas market as a key exporting country; however, fulfilment of this role continues to prove challenging as the country faces significant domestic and international political and economic difficulties.

Over the past two decades, the government has tried to expand its gas utilisation plans in the wake of its fuel substitution policy, which is aimed at boosting domestic gas usage to free up more crude oil and petroleum products for export. Consequently, gas production and consumption have increased significantly and this trend is expected to continue in the future.

In recent years, the country has faced gas shortages especially during winter when consumption in the residential and commercial sectors increased significantly. Gas shortages occur mainly because of a disconnect between downstream and upstream operations. NIGC controls downstream development and is a separate company from NIOC, which operates upstream activities and has a separate management. The development of the downstream sector, such as expansion of the distribution system, needs less financial resources and time compared with upstream development activities, and can be expanded relatively quickly. This rapid expansion in the downstream and the availability of cheap gas for the domestic market have resulted in a strong growth in consumption. However, upstream development needs much larger revenues and a longer time to develop, at least 3–4 years for each project. It is no surprise then that NIOC faces an uphill task.

It is understood that international financial loans to Iran have dried up in the past few years because of sanctions, with the result that many projects, especially those in South Pars, have been delayed. This may result in the country postponing its export projects.

We believe that a realistic projection of Iran's gas exports is around 6 Bcm by 2010 and 12 Bcm by 2015. This represents only pipeline exports to Turkey, Armenia, and Nakhchivan. Exports to Pakistan are more likely to be post 2015. LNG exports are unlikely to start anytime in the foreseeable future. In a best-case scenario for the Iran LNG project, it is possible that LNG could be available by late this decade, taking into account technical and commercial delays. In this case, NIOC would need an experienced international partner to handle commercial and technical issues. Otherwise, bypassing sanctions for the procurement of necessary equipment and technology will not help the current contractors to finalise the project.[77]

From 1997 to the time of writing, Iran has been a net gas importer (because its imports from Turkmenistan exceeded its exports to Turkey and the Caucasus). It is expected that this will remain the case until and unless the Iran–Pakistan pipeline starts post 2015.

Notes

1   BP *Statistical Review of World Energy*, 2010.
2   Dizaji, Behrouz Esrafili, *Exploration of New Oil and Gas Fields in Iran*, University of Tehran, 2008.
3   *Reuters*, 'Norway's Statoil says still wary of Iran investment', April 2, 2009.
4   *Reuters*, 'Italy says firmly against new Iran energy deals', February 2, 2010.
5   *Financial Times* 'Iran struggles over its gas field riches', July 20, 2010.
6   NIOC Organization Chart, NIOC Official Website, http://www.nioc. ir/Portal/Home/Default.aspx?CategoryID=f398bd54-e170-44e9-a841-710c6c92b3a0&TabNo=4 (Retrieved May 2010)
7   OPEC *Annual Statistical Bulletin*, 2008.
8   FACTS Global Energy, 2009.
9   OPEC *Annual Statistical Bulletin*, 2008.
10 *Iran's Hydrocarbon Balance 2008*, Institute for International Studies, Iran, 2009.
11 FACTS Global Energy, 2010.
12 Pars Oil and Gas Company (POGC), http://www.pogc.ir/Default. aspx?tabid=142 (Retrieved May 2010).
13 Pars Oil and Gas Company (POGC), http://www.pogc.ir/Default. aspx?tabid=143.
14 Pars Oil and Gas Company (POGC), http://www.pogc.ir/Default. aspx?tabid=145.
15 Pars Oil and Gas Company (POGC), http://www.pogc.ir/Default. aspx?tabid=144
16 Pars Oil and Gas Company (POGC), http://www.pogc.ir/Default. aspx?tabid=146.
17 Pars Oil and Gas Company (POGC), http://www.pogc.ir/Default. aspx?tabid=149
18 Pars Oil and Gas Company (POGC), http://www.pogc.ir/Default. aspx?tabid=151.
19 Pars Oil and Gas Company (POGC), http://www.pogc.ir/Default. aspx?tabid=152, *Iran Oil and Gas Report*, Q3 2007, p.37
20 Pars Oil and Gas Company (POGC), http://www.pogc.ir/Default. aspx?tabid=153.
21 Pars Oil and Gas Company (POGC), http://www.pogc.ir/Default.

aspx?tabid=147

22 *World Gas Intelligence*, 'Iran's Turn to China For LNG Project', XX:23, June 10, 2009, p.4.

23 Pars Oil and Gas Company (POGC), http://www.pogc.ir/Default. aspx?tabid=150

24 Pars Oil and Gas Company (POGC), http://www.pogc.ir/Default. aspx?tabid=404

25 Pars Oil and Gas Company (POGC), http://www.pogc.ir/Default. aspx?tabid=284

26 Iran Shana News, http://www.shana.ir/154657-en.html

27 *Platts Oilgram News*, 'Iran's POGC in Ferdows oil agreement with SKS', 86:8, 11 January 2008.

28 *Platts Oilgram News*, 'Iran awards North Pars gas contract to CNOOC', 21 December 2006.

29 FACTS Global Energy, 2009.

30 NIOC.

31 Shana news website, www.shana.ir, Iran, 2009.

32 BP *Statistical Review of World Energy*, 2010.

33 *Iran's Hydrocarbon Balance 2008*, Institute for International Studies, Iran, 2009.

34 Ibid.

35 Based on the official statistics in Iran published by NIOC, total natural gas subsidies stood at US$ 27.2 billion (roughly US$6.1/MMBtu) in 2008. However, this figure was calculated based on average price of gas exports to Turkey. Some Iranian economists argue that the amount of gas subsidies may not be accurate as the real subsidies would be a weighted average of gas import prices and Iran's domestic gas production cost. Assuming a very low gas production cost in the country and also average gas import prices from Turkmenistan in 2008, the gas subsidies would be less than US$0.5/MMBtu.

36 Gas consumption in the residential and commercial sectors increased from 21.9 Bcm in 2000 to 44.0 Bcm in 2008. This represented an annual average growth rate of 9.1% during 2000 to 2008.

37 National Iranian Oil Refining and Distribution Company (NIORDC).

38 FACTS Global Energy.

39 For a comprehensive analysis of the Iran–Turkey gas project see, Kinnander, Elin, *The Turkish–Iranian Gas Relationship: politically successful, commercially problematic*, OIES, January 2010.

40 *World Gas Intelligence*, 'Iranian Gas Flows to Turkey at Last', XII: 40, December 12, 2001, p.4.

41 OPEC *Annual Statistical Bulletin*, 2008.

42 *International Gas Report*, 'Gazexport ups Azeri supply', No.507, 10 September 2004, p.6.

43 For more details of the Nakhichevan agreement see: Bowden, Julian, 'Azerbaijan: from gas importer to exporter', in Pirani, Simon (ed.), *Russian and CIS Gas Markets*, p. 225.

44 *Cedigaz News Report*, 44:1, January 7, 2005, 18
45 For more information on the Iran–Armenia gas contract see: Stern, Jonathan P., *The Future of Russian Gas and Gazprom*, 2005, pp. 84–5; Yeghiazaryan, Armen, 'Natural Gas Markets in Armenia', in Pirani (ed.), *Russian and CIS Gas Markets*, 2009, pp. 244–7.
46 *OPECNA Bulletin*, 'Iran, UAE sign two billion dollar gas deal', 20 April 2001.
47 *World Gas Intelligence*, 'New Mideast Price Reality', XVIII: 13, 28 March 2007, p.1; *Global Insight Daily Analysis*, 'Crescent Sees No Progress on Iran-U.A.E. Pipeline Gas Sales Agreement', , 16 April 2008; *International Gas Report*, 'Iran, Crescent talks break down', 16 June 2008.
48 *Platts Oilgram News*, 'Iran's NIOC drops delayed gas deal with UAE's Crescent', 86:117, 16 June 2008, p.7.
49 *World Gas Intelligence*, 'Iran Pipeline Gas to India Looking Pricy', XVI: 8, 23 February 2005, p.2; 'Iran-India Pipe Makes Headway', XVI: 21, 21 December 2005, p.3.
50 *World Gas Intelligence*, 'US-Allied India Drops Iran Pipe Plan', XVIII: 3 5, 29 August 2007, p.5.
51 *Argus Global LNG*, 'Teheran lines up gas deals', June 2009, p.7.
52 The Japan Customs-cleared Crude (JCC) is the average price of customs-cleared crude oil imports into Japan.
53 'Teheran lines up gas deals', Ibid.
54 For instance, see *World Gas Intelligence*, 'Politics Overshadow Iran-Pakistan-India Pipe', XIX: 34, 20 August 2008, p.3.
55 Oil and Gas Regulatory Authority (OGRA), Pakistan, 2010.
56 *World Gas Intelligence*, 'Iran's Great Gas Debate', XIX: 23, 4 June 2008, p.1; 'Iran Still Divided Over Gas Exports', XVII: 28, 28 June 2006, pp.2–3; 'Politics Overshadow Iran-Pakistan-India Pipe', XIX: 34, 20 August 2008, p.3.
57 *International Gas Report*, 'Iran, Syria pencil in supply deal', No. 583, 8 October 2007.
58 *Argus Global LNG*, 'Iran and Oman start new gas talks', August 2009, p.17.
59 *Oil and Gas Journal*, 'Iranian LNG, natural gas export plans outlined', 108: 13, 12 April 2010, p.48.
60 *Oil and Gas Journal*, 'Switzerland irks US with gas deal', 106:12, 24 March 2008, p.39.
61 *World Energy Intelligence*, 'Iran's Gas Export Ambitions Undaunted', XIX: 38, 17 September 2008, p.3.
62 *World Energy Intelligence*, 'Nabucco Backers Eye Iraqi, Iranian Gas', XIX: 47, 19 November 2008, p.3; *The Washington Times*, 'Gas pipeline looks to Iran; Proposed line hopes to use Iran as source despite worries of political risk, U.S. objections', 6 July 2009.
63 'Nabucco Backers Eye Iraqi, Iranian Gas', Ibid.
64 NIGEC Website, http://www.nigec.ir
65 *Reuters*, 'S.Korea's Daelim gets Iran deal for gas store tanks', 7 February 2007.

66 *Fars News Agency*, 'Iran LNG Liquefaction Deal Signed', 23 March 2008.

67 *Energy Economist*, 'No fear of sanctions: Sinopec enters Iran', 315, 1 January 2008; *World Gas Intelligence*, 'OMV Seeking Iranian LNG? Or Pipe Gas?' XVIII: 17, 25 April 2007, pp.2–3.

68 *Dow Jones International News*, 'ONGC, Hinduja May Invest $20B In India, Iran', 4 January 2008; *Petroleum Review*, 29 January 2010.

69 Pars LNG website, http://www.parslng.com

70 *Oil and Gas Journal*, 'Iranian LNG, natural gas export plans outlined', 108: 13, 12 April 2010, p.48.

71 *Petroleum Intelligence Weekly*, 8 December 2008.

72 *World Gas Intelligence*, 'Iran's Complex Azeri, Turkmen Options' XXI: 5, 3 February 2010, pp.2–3.

73 S.Adibi, 'Development constraints limit Turkmen gas export options', *The Oil and Gas Journal*, 108: 15, 26 April 2010.

74 *Tehran Times*, 16 September 2008.

75 Ibid.

76 *BBC Monitoring Middle East*, 'Iran, Turkmenistan fix gas transfer formula', 12 July 2009.

77 FACTS Global Energy, 2010.

CHAPTER 9

QATAR'S GAS REVOLUTION

Justin Dargin

Introduction

Qatar is positioning itself to take advantage of the worldwide increase in gas demand. The small nation is strategically placed in the Gulf at the tip of the Arabian Peninsula, where it straddles Bahrain and the UAE. Among the leaders in natural gas production, Qatar arrived relatively late on the scene, in part, because it has a population of 833,000, only 20 percent of whom are Qatari nationals.[1] Qatar also has one of the world's fastest population growth rates due to its unprecedented economic performance. It had a demographic increase of half a million over the period 2004–2008; most of the increase was due to a massive influx of foreign workers.[2]

According to BP, Qatar's proven natural gas reserves equal approximately 14 percent of total world reserves.[3] Its estimated 25.37 Trillion cubic metres (Tcm) plus 12–15 billion barrels (2009) of associated condensates are the third largest in the world, behind Russia and Iran.[4] Qatar's gas reserves exceed the entire reserves of the Americas, Western Europe and sub-Saharan Africa combined.

Qatar's reserves-to-production ratio is tentatively estimated at 100 years.[5] Most of the country's gas is located in the massive offshore North Field, which is the world's largest non-associated natural gas field. Qatar is ruled by a well-educated, ambitious and tolerant elite, which promotes a strong pro-market philosophy. Qatar became the world's largest exporter of liquefied natural gas production (LNG),[6] and also desires to be among the forerunners of Liquefied Petroleum Gas (LPG) exports by 2012, with a projected output of 12 Mtpa.[7] Qatar is now represented in every sector of natural gas trade, LNG, Gas-to-Liquids (GTL), pipeline gas, and Natural Gas Liquids (NGL).

At the time of writing, Qatar has the most successful economy in the Gulf Cooperation Council, with some of the highest economic growth rates per annum. Qatar's economy consistently outperformed its GCC neighbours. During 2002–2009 its economic growth proved resilient in the face of the global economic crisis because of its LNG sales. From

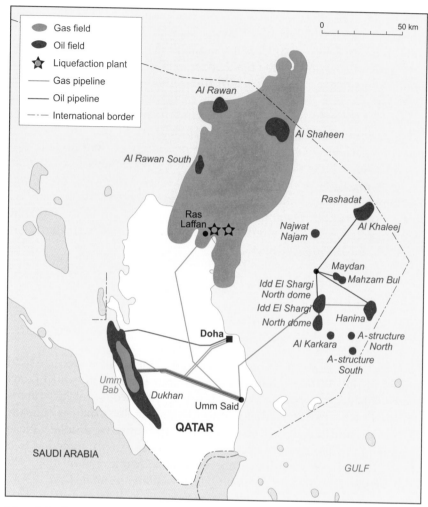

Map 9.1: Qatar's Oil and Gas Fields

being one of the relatively impoverished nations among the other GCC members, to its current status as one of the strongest economies in the Gulf, Qatar's rapid economic growth has been compared to the Saudi oil bonanza that took the world by surprise in the early 1970s.[8] Due to its hydrocarbon sales, the country is now one of the world's wealthiest nations with a per capita income of approximately $75,000, which is predicted to rise even higher in the coming years.[9] Qatari Energy Minister Abdullah bin Hamad Al-Attiyah estimated that, due to the energy boom, approximately $100 billion of development funds have been domestically invested during the first decade of the twenty-first century.[10]

Later recognised as the largest non-associated gas field in the world, the North Field, which covers 6000 sq. km off Qatar's coast, was initially discovered by the Shell Oil Company in 1971. The North Field has allowed Qatar to become a major regional gas exporter through the Dolphin pipeline, as well as a major international gas supplier through LNG exports. It is also the cornerstone of Qatar's quest to establish an independent foreign policy outside of Saudi Arabian political influence.

Qatar's previous Emir, Khalifa bin Hamad Al-Thani, had been far less innovative in the country's resource development than his son, the current Emir, Hamad bin Khalifa Al-Thani, who astutely foresaw that Qatar's natural gas resources were essential to its security and economic development and enhanced its global importance. As the far-sighted Hamad understood, Qatar's wealth was also its vulnerability, a fact that required reliance on the international community, and particularly on the USA, for its security needs.

The North Field

Reserves

The North West Dome Reservoir is a combined gas condensate field located in the Arabian Gulf, nestled between the Iranian and Qatari maritime border. Known as the 'Qatar Arch,' the geological structure is a Permian Khuff stratum that lies approximately 3048 metres beneath the surface, and runs north–south through the entire peninsula.[11] Near Qatar's tip the sub-stratum veers off into a northeasterly direction (see Map 9.1). It is estimated that the total recoverable gas of the field (both in the Iranian and in the Qatari sections) is 33.5 Tcm, 25.37 Tcm of which is in Qatar and approximately 8 Tcm in Iran.[12] This equals more than 95 percent of Qatar's recoverable gas reserves and 28 percent of Iran's.

Geologists have debated the actual size and reservoir composition of the field, with some contending that it is much larger than originally estimated, in that it spans the entire length of the 'Qatar Arch'.[13]

The 'South Pars' gas field delineates the portion of the joint field that sits in Iranian territory (see Map 9.1), while the North Field is located in Qatari waters. Qatar's portion of the joint North Field/South Pars geological structure comprises 62 percent of the reservoir, and the Iranian South Pars comprises 38 percent.[14] Both nations later increased the estimates to 11.32 Tcm/11,320 Billion cubic metres (Bcm), and subsequently to 14.15 Tcm. Although Qatar ultimately raised the estimate of its portion to 25.37 Tcm/25370 Bcm, Iran declined to follow suit. Many of these estimates were issued without the benefit of more detailed reservoir studies.

The only comprehensive North Field studies conducted were the partial Shell studies at the time of the North Field's discovery in 1971, a May 1980 evaluation of the German-based Wintershall concession, and the moratorium reservoir studies.[15] Although a large number of the wells have been sunk so far in the North Field appraisal study, the economic advisor to the Emir, Ibrahim Ibrahim, insisted that 'reservoir availability is not in question'. However, a senior Qatari official who wished to remain anonymous, contended that the 'North Field is overproducing because the multinationals want to cash it in today.'

Development of the North Field

The North Field covers an area equivalent to nearly half the surface area of Qatar (see Map 9.1). It is a carbonate reservoir with an approximate thickness of 457 metres, variable throughout the reservoir.[16]

When discovered, Qatar initially viewed the North Field as a 'disappointment', because of the difficulties in finding export markets for resources designated as 'stranded' natural gas reserves.[17] Because Qatar General Petroleum Company (QP) did not perceive its future potential, it initially earmarked the gas wholly for local consumption. Since it viewed gas so unfavourably in the early 1970s, Qatar flared approximately 80 percent of the 6.13 Bcm/yr (16.8 Million cubic metres) (mcm/d) of associated natural gas produced daily. As it became more cognizant of its gas wealth, Qatar reduced the percentage of onshore gas flared to 66 percent by 1974, and by 1979, to less than 5 percent.[18]

Even though Qatar nationalised the North Field in the late 1970s, the handover was so amicable that Shell remained as a contractor to provide technical and support expertise. In addition to the North Field, Qatar has other minor associated gas fields. A Khuff non-associated gas reservoir sits beneath the Dukhan oil field, but is considered relatively small when compared to other Gulf gas fields. The Dukhan field contains an estimated 141 Bcm of associated gas and 1.41 Bcm of non-associated gas. Until the discovery of the North Field, Dukhan produced nearly all of Qatar's non-associated gas. Minor amounts of gas were also produced by the Al Ghatta Al Ghazi cap gas deposits, located approximately 3048 metres below the Khuff region. Additionally, there are smaller associated gas holdings in the Maydan Mahzam, Id al-Shargi, Bul Hanine, and Al Rayyan oil fields. During Khalifa bin Hamad's reign, Qatar failed to pursue an aggressive production policy, largely because the preceding governmental approval process was so arduous that it required the Emir's personal involvement.

The 'Moratorium' on Additional Production

In March 2005, Qatar imposed a prohibition on new projects which would require additional gas production over and above developments that had already been agreed. After the initial 'pause' in new greenfield projects, this period was subsequently extended several times. It was initially only to last until 2006, but what was supposed to be a relatively short period to assess longevity potential and to develop a new reservoir model, turned out to be a prolonged hiatus. The international press designated the suspension on all further North Field capacity expansion as the 'moratorium.' However, the use of this term may be slightly misleading as there has not been any publicly available white paper, speech, or anything of an official nature that ever referred to the post-2005 period as a 'moratorium.' For instance, Saad al-Kaabi, director of oil and gas ventures at QP, designated the current period as a 'pause' when he announced at the 2009 International Petroleum Technology Conference that, '[t]his pause is our technical obligation to ensure the most prudent and optimal long-term development of the field for the country's best interest'.[19] The reader should bear in mind, that while this text will utilise the term 'moratorium,' and it is in general circulation, it is not typically used by Qatari officials.

Qatar's extension of the moratorium lengthened in July 2008, when the Chairman of Qatargas announced that further development of the gas from the North Field would be delayed at least for an additional five years, until 2013–2014.[20] Preliminary reports indicated that Qatari officials may be worried that the field is not as homogenous as previously assumed, which would increase extraction costs by necessitating enhanced production methods and additional wells.[21] Qatari officials also indicated that they will only expand production beyond levels required for currently sanctioned projects when they are satisfied that gas output can be further expanded without damaging the reservoir. However, Qatar strongly rejects any intimation that the natural gas moratorium is a result of potential North Field geological concerns, rather, as the director of Oil and Gas ventures at QP, Saad al-Kaabi contended, the production pause was, '...always meant to be in place until the last of the projects came on stream.'[22] Nonetheless, Qatar's concern is based on sound logic; it is not in the Emirate's long-term interest to simply produce without considering the ability for the North Field to sustain the rapid capacity expansion.

Comments by Qatari officials hinted at the new direction that Qatar would take. Al-Kaabi indicated that, 'If we go for grassroots projects, we'll have to set up new operating projects, we'll have new costs'. He continued that upgrading existing operations would be the 'cheapest and most efficient way to expand' for the future.[23] In addition to the North Field reservoir study, there appears to be a correlation between the moratorium extensions since 2009, and difficulties in identifying additional markets to absorb Qatari LNG exports. Both of these factors have been buttressed by concerns about the robustness of long-term LNG pricing being undermined by the growth of the spot market, which seemed to fragment the natural gas market into a two-tiered gas pricing framework.[24]

While officially, Qatar, along with Russia, during the Gas Exporting Countries Forum meeting in Oran, Algeria in 2010, refused to implement production cuts to support a price floor, at the same time the two countries took several unofficial steps that were widely interpreted as an attempt to combat the market oversupply.[25] Apparently, in order to counteract oversupply in the wake of the global financial crisis, Qatar idled 66 percent of its export plants, and at least eight LNG tankers in the Gulf of Oman, in 2010.[26] Qatar's significant shutdowns represent an effort to balance market oversupply by maintenance programmes, even as it increased its overall LNG capacity.

Meanwhile Qatar has proceeded quite cautiously in North Field exploitation and the moratorium studies are expected to clarify much of the mystique and uncertainty of the Field's reservoir characteristics. It appears that Qatar will not end the moratorium until all projects that have been allocated gas come online. The last sanctioned project pre-moratorium was the Barzan gas project, and its impact on the field may not be fully ascertained until 2015. During the latter stages of the moratorium, the dominant train of thought emanating from Qatar is that its end-2010 position in the global gas market is more than sufficient.

A stable unitisation agreement with Iran is also being reviewed by Qatari officials; both North Dome Field stakeholders are reportedly drilling quite heavily on either side of the maritime border separating the North Field from Iran's South Pars gas/condensate field, where Iran is increasing production.[27] A high-level bilateral negotiating team has been convened to bring both sides to agreement. However, as of the time of writing, a comprehensive agreement has not been forthcoming. Such an agreement would be in the interest of both stakeholders to prevent simmering conflicts over allegations of overproduction.[28]

Qatar's governing circles are not likely to seek to increase production beyond currently anticipated levels. In October of 2007, Qatargas CEO, Feisal Al-Suwaidi, announced that any new projects beyond those already commissioned may necessitate more technologically advanced and expensive compression methods to extract additional gas from the North Field.[29] He also suggested that the compression methods needed could render further monetisation of the field uneconomic by saddling future projects with significant additional cost, although he reasoned that the moratorium is useful because it can grant Qatar additional time to develop compression technology if needed. Qatar also reprioritised its natural gas monetisation strategy, and further gas exports are going to be predicated on Qatar being able to meet its domestic needs first, the long-term health of the field, as well as Qatar's overall strategic concerns. 2014 appears to be the key year when Qatar will sketch out the new direction for the field's exploitation. In 2009, al-Kaabi explained that, '[The] year 2014 is a decisive point – a time where QP will decide what is in the best interest of the country and the field,'[30] Al-Kaabi continued that, 'If after 2014 we take a decision to go ahead with new development then the priority will be to ensure that we have enough capacity available for electricity, water desalination in the long-term for the country, our local industrial needs and only then we will think about export'.

Other Gas Exploration

With the world's attention fixated on the North Field moratorium, Qatar encouraged International Oil Companies (IOCs) to conduct exploration and production outside of the North Field. Qatar's main efforts at expanded gas production focused on the pre-Khuff reservoir located just beyond the North Field. In November 2008, QP and Wintershall signed a 25-year oil and gas exploration and production sharing agreement for exploration in this area.[31] The area, block 4, was the first of four blocks available for exploration from the 544-sq. km. offshore field, which is located near the Al-Shaheen Field, northwest of the North Field, in water depths of up to 70 metres.[32]

Quite optimistic about its prospects, Wintershall committed to investing approximately $100 million on exploration and detailed seismic analysis for the period of 2008–2010. Exploration of the deepwater aspects of these blocks should not be difficult for the more experienced IOCs. Because some of the other blocks reach underneath the North Field, a number of IOCs could find it necessary to drill much deeper than would be required in the North Field. At the time of the award, Wintershall undertook the initial steps to reprocess and interpret the existing seismic data for the block over a two-year period. Relative to Wintershall's plans to drill the first two exploration wells in 2010, a company spokesperson explained that its optimism was based on the fact that, 'The [pre] Khuff formation, for which we have the rights to explore according to the license, is the same productive formation as the largest natural gas field in the world, the North Field. Block 4N is only 30 kilometres west of the North Field.'[33]

While QP granted Wintershall the licence for the first of the four-block offering, it attempted to encourage much broader IOC participation in its other offerings. By March 2009, QP gathered more than ten IOCs to auction off several blocks in the formation. While IOC interest may not be primarily in the production potential of these blocks in and of themselves, with the North Field moratorium extended to at least 2014, they prefer to have at least a foothold in Qatar. Although some IOCs were concerned that there appeared to be no seal to trap emergent gas in the offered blocks, they are still overall optimistic about the offerings.[34]

The Development of the Qatari Gas Industry

The Start of Qatari Gas Development

Upon discovery of the North Field, Qatar made it the centrepiece of its meteoric economic development programme. Historically, Qatar, as most Gulf nations, viewed itself through the narrow prism of an 'oil producer,' and did not readily discern the profitability of natural gas reserves. However, the call to diversify from oil into other economic sectors, especially into natural gas, was sounded as early as 1962, when Qatari officials commissioned the 1962 Arthur D. Little (ADL) study to examine the administrative effectiveness of governmental ministries. The ADL study expressed concern over Qatar's overwhelming economic and financial dependence on the oil sector, which it projected would be exhausted by 1982. The report, therefore, cautioned Qatar to develop other non-oil sectors, especially its natural gas wealth. The government subsequently relied upon the findings of the ADL study and planned a broad diversification into gas-based petrochemical industries.[35]

However, the geopolitical turmoil associated with the 1973 Organization of Arab Exporting States (OAPEC) oil embargo and the 1979 Islamic revolution in Iran significantly increased international oil prices and brought in such enormous revenue inflows to Qatar as to mitigate any impacts of oil field maturity. In spite of the ADL study's warnings,

Qatar gave natural gas production little consideration during this period. Because the country benefited enormously from the oil market upheavals in the 1970s, the government funnelled the increased oil revenue into massive social and infrastructure investments.[36]

After Qatar's oil production peaked in the 1970s, IOCs became convinced that the mature oil fields were not worth further investment. Furthermore, Qatar's service contracts made the prospect even financially less appealing. By the mid-1980s, the economy was still heavily reliant on the oil sector, but the economic diversification policy and falling oil prices meant that between 1979 and 1983 the percentage of government revenues derived from petroleum fell from 93 percent to 80 percent.[37]

Phase One of North Field development was interrupted several times prior to its planned start-up date in 1990. Not only did the Iraqi invasion of Kuwait upset most major regional development projects and force Gulf governments to be externally focused, Qatar faced numerous obstacles during this period as well. The evacuation of skilled personnel during Operations Desert Shield and Desert Storm measurably delayed North Field progress. Furthermore, progress was held back due to several infrastructure issues. Fourteen of the sixteen production wells in Phase One suffered from cement casing leaks. Additionally, a week prior to the revised start-up date of August 3, 1990, a chemical leak was discovered on an onshore pipe and the North Field had to be shut down.[38] September 3, 1991 marked the twentieth anniversary of Qatar's independence and of the North Field's discovery. It was also the date that the North Field commenced production. Up to this time, most of Qatar's natural gas came from a couple of onshore and offshore oilfields, from which associated gas was processed at the Umm Said complex.

After this date, Qatar took advantage of two events that significantly increased natural gas demand in the international and regional markets: first, the widespread use of combined cycle gas turbines in the 1990s in power generation; and second the cost reductions throughout the LNG chain.[39] These developments allowed Qatar to reverse course from its previous strategy, and reorient its gas resources primarily from domestic power generation and petrochemical production to global export markets.

Because most of Qatar's natural gas was associated with oil, periods of weak oil demand and stringent OPEC quotas obstructed many of the gas-reliant industries from maximum efficiency. Due to its great wealth, Qatar faced unique obstacles that other developing countries do not have. With its energy rich economy, it does not have impediments to capital-intensive investment; however, its small economy, with its limited absorptive capacity and the limited demographic base, are potentially economically disruptive.[40]

The Qatari leadership views economic diversification as key to overall economic sustainability. In the midst of the worst global economic downturn in decades, Qatar has scheduled an additional $130 billion of project investment for the period 2009–2014.[41] Even with these enormous strides, the Qatari economy is still overly dependent on gas and the hydrocarbon sector in general, since the diversification programme is in its infancy.

However, Qatar's much vaunted diversification efforts may not represent a substantive move away from hydrocarbon dependence, because most of its economic diversification is concentrated in the chain of downstream value-added industries, such as the petrochemical sector. Although the price of petrochemicals and other value-added products is much more stable and fluctuates less than crude oil and unprocessed gas, these products are still reliant on the hydrocarbon sector.[42]

In 2009, for the first time in the country's history, natural gas' share of the economy surpassed the oil sector. In 2008, Qatar's gas sector nearly doubled in size, based partly on higher LNG prices, but also because of increased output. In 2009, Qatar's gas sector increased a record 35–40 percent as many large projects came online.[43] The sector accounted for nearly 49.3 percent of the overall GDP growth of 59 percent in the first three-quarters of 2008. Given the sharp decline of Qatar's crude oil production, and the rapidly increasing LNG exports, the share of gas and its value-added products in the economy, appear poised to grow for the foreseeable future.[44]

Phased Development of the North Field

When the initial North Field production plans were developed, Qatari officialdom selected QP to spearhead development, and to construct LNG trains through joint ventures with major IOCs. Given the relative shallowness of the field, Qatar determined that field production development would not be arduous. During the 1982 negotiations for Qatar's first LNG venture (Qatargas), QP contracted US-based Fluor Company to develop an integrated production plan for the North Field, taking into account the field's sulphur content.[45]

Fluor initially prepared a North Field development plan that separated field production into three distinct phases, each respectively to produce 8.4 Bcm/year of natural gas: Phase One was designed to meet domestic gas demand for local power generation, industrial requirements and water desalination; Phase Two was designed to export North Field gas through regional pipelines, especially the still anticipated pan-GCC pipeline;[46] Phase Three was oriented toward producing significant quantities of LNG. At first Fluor estimated that Phase One would cost approximately $1 billion to develop. When the Qatari government received the recommendations, it resolved to finance Phase One North Field Development by four investment streams: 1) from the sale of 40,000 b/d of crude oil by QP; 2) the utilisation of export credit facilities by the home governments of the contractors; 3) from international bank loans; 4) from state budget revenue.[47]

Qatar began Phase One with an $80 million management contract to a Bechtel/Technip joint venture in May 1987.[48] Near the end, however, Qatar diverged slightly from the Fluor commissioned report and reduced the planned onshore processing plants from two to one. In August 1989, QP expanded the Phase One assessment to include a gas sweetening plant[49] and a sulphur-processing unit. QP incorporated the previous changes after weighing the needs of an increasingly pollution conscious public, and the profitability of sulphur export.[50] Phases Two and Three were combined into one integrated programme for pipeline export and LNG production known collectively as 'Phase Two.'[51]

Test production of Phase One started in early 1991; however, Saddam Hussein's invasion of Kuwait delayed final construction until September 3, 1991, when it was finally inaugurated. Phase One was developed for a wellhead production of 23 mcm/d, but actual output soon exceeded that to reach 25 mcm/d, and upwards of 40,000 b/d of NGL and condensates. To realise its industrialisation plans, Qatar initially allocated 14–16 mcm/d to domestic petrochemical and industrial plants. The remaining amount was reserved to bolster reserve capacity by reinjection in the Dukhan onshore field.

The offshore gas production facilities included six platforms, two wellhead platforms, and one flare platform. Gas was sent to Ras Laffan, where it was separated, and then sent on by two 140-km pipelines to Umm Said for further processing – much of it for the existing NGL plants and ancillary facilities – and export.[52] Approximately 9 mcm/d of production were initially reserved for expansion at existing fertiliser plants, aluminium smelters, and other associated petrochemical plants.

Phase Two: Regional Gas Export

The Failed GCC Pipeline. While Phase One of the North Field was to supply natural gas for Qatar's domestic consumption, Phase Two was to establish pipelines for export to the neighbouring GCC countries of Saudi Arabia, Kuwait, Bahrain, and the UAE (Dubai). The estimated $2 billion price tag was to be equally divided between the participating nations. Because of the cost of liquefaction technology and the short distance involved, Qatar's position in the 1980s was that the GCC gas export pipeline was substantially less expensive than LNG exports.[53] During a 1988 GCC ministerial meeting, the Gulf stakeholders agreed in principle to prepare for immediate pipeline construction. By the time the stakeholders convened at a December 1990 summit, all the project details were agreed upon except the pricing framework.[54]

In spite of an early wave of optimism, the GCC pipeline project collapsed because of border disputes,[55] political tensions, and minor diplomatic squabbles. There were also intra-GCC disputes connected with Qatar's increasingly close Israeli ties.[56] Saudi Arabia not only withdrew from the project, because it wished to promote its own substantial gas discoveries, but subsequently denied the stakeholders transit rights to enable the pipeline to pass through its territory to Kuwait and Bahrain.[57] Kuwaiti participation lagged, as its attention was focused on its massive reconstruction efforts after Operation Desert Storm.

The GCC pipeline, while conceived to promote regional cooperation, actually reactivated dormant boundary disputes. The early pipeline discussions were also spurred by a temporary abundance of very low cost natural gas supplies. Numerous other proposed pipeline extensions, to Pakistan, India, as well as a 'peace pipeline' to Israel soon collapsed, a victim of political realities, amidst the irrepressible optimism that spawned proliferating regional pipeline schemes during that era.[58]

The Development of the Dolphin Project

From the ashes of the GCC pipeline arose a proposal for a much reduced Gulf pipeline, known as Dolphin, to supply Qatari North Field gas to the UAE and Oman (see Map 9.2). Dolphin was designed by the UAE Offsets Group (UOG), which is a branch of the UAE Ministry of Defence.[59] Dolphin Energy Limited (DEL) was created in 1999 to administer the project.[60]

Qatar Petroleum processes the natural gas at the industrial city of Ras Laffan, for shipment to power and desalination centres in Oman and the UAE (see Map 9.2). The UOG agreed in 1998 that Qatar would serve as the exclusive supplier and marketer of Qatari gas in the UAE and Oman. With QP as the negotiating partner, the UOG completed initial Memoranda of Understanding (MOUs) with Qatar, Oman, and Pakistan, in June 1999. The MOU was a prelude to a long-term supply and purchase agreement that would allow UOG to

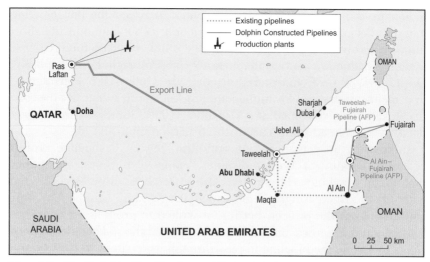

Map 9.2: The Dolphin Gas Pipeline and Related Infrastructure

obtain gas and condensate by-products from existing concessions, as well as grant UOG an option for gas purchase from Mobil Oil Qatar's Enhanced Gas Utilisation Project.

A statement of principle between QP and UOG allowed DEL to obtain its own concession from two blocks in the North Field over the project's term.[61] DEL successfully negotiated a 25-year development and production sharing agreement with QP in 2001.[62]

While much of the impetus behind Dolphin was to improve political integration of the GCC nations, the project also had crucial commercial aspects. The inescapable fact is that, (as discussed in Chapters 11 and 12) unless important reforms of marketing, rationing and domestic pricing are implemented, Oman and the UAE (Dubai and Abu Dhabi) will still experience substantial gas shortages, even with increased Dolphin imports from Qatar.[63] The implications of this situation for Qatar's Gulf leadership role in gas supply cannot be overstated..

As illustrated in Map 9.2, Dolphin connects Qatar's North Field to the national gas grids of the UAE, including those of Abu Dhabi, Dubai, and Oman. Dolphin transports gas from the North Field approximately 400 km, for processing at Qatar's Ras Laffan facility, where the gas is stripped of valuable condensates and liquefied petroleum gas and prepared for subsequent transport and sale. Dry gas flows through a dedicated 370 km offshore pipeline from Ras Laffan to the Al-Taweelah power and desalination plant in Abu Dhabi.[64] From Al-Taweelah, gas flows through existing domestic landlines for a distance of 182 km from Al-Ain to Fujairah on UAE's eastern coast.[65]

Managed by Emirates General Petroleum Corporation (Emarat) from January 2004 until DEL assumed control in January 2006, this pipeline delivered Omani gas directly to the desalination plant of Union Water and Electricity Company (UWEC) in the UAE. In 2008, the flow was reversed with gas coming from Qatar. DEL delivered its first gas shipment to Oman in January 2004, at the gas control station in Al-Ain, a truly historic moment in that it was the first ever cross-border gas transmission in the history of the GCC.[66] Dolphin began the transport of 11 mcm/d of natural gas to the UAE and Oman in June 2007, with the full allotment of 56 mcm/d of Phase One export reached in 2008.

Dolphin Expansion?

Dolphin's conception in 1998, to its successful birth nearly a decade later, overturned expectations and surpassed important regional benchmarks. Dolphin established that some form of intra-Gulf energy cooperation was not only viable, but that Gulf nations are able to overcome regional antagonisms. For the UAE, Dolphin gas was a veritable lifeline that saved it from even more extensive gas shortages in 2007. Yet, the benefits that Qatar derived from Dolphin were more intangible and were politically oriented. Since Sheikh Hamad bin Khalifa Al-Thani assumed power in 1995, Qatar sought leadership in Gulf affairs. Minister of Energy Abdullah bin Hamad Al-Attiyah asserted that the establishment of Dolphin provided 'the proper conditions that enhance economic and political ties among the GCC countries'.[67]

From its inception, however, Dolphin experienced very real difficulties that ranged from the pricing formula disagreements, to intra-GCC political difficulties, to rising demand for Qatari North Field gas in both domestic and international markets. Because international gas market conditions have changed radically since the development of Dolphin, Qatar now finds it extremely difficult to economically justify Dolphin's Phase Two expansion of 12.41 Bcm/yr (33.98 Million cm/d). Intuitively, regional sales would seem to be more practical than more remote markets, but regional customers are unwilling to pay anywhere close to international market prices, and therefore gas sales prices have been, and continue to be, one of the more prominent stumbling blocks for Dolphin. Differences over pricing strategies even delayed the Dolphin coming on-stream for several months while the stakeholders attempted to craft a satisfactory solution.

The pricing for the Phase One shipment of dry North Field gas to Oman and the UAE is for all intents and purposes a 'political price,' meaning it is a price that reflects political considerations instead of market realities. When the Qatari–Emirati negotiations stalled, the Qatari and Abu-Dhabi leaderships intervened, applied political pressure, and crafted a deal that, literally speaking, 'neither party could refuse.' QP agreed upon the relatively low sale price only after Dolphin granted QP the right to strip the valuable condensate from the gas to reap a greater profit.[68]

Dubai's price for North Field gas contains a built-in subsidy of $0.05–0.10/MMBtu, which at approximately $1.20–1.25/MMBtu, is slightly below the price that Dolphin and Abu Dhabi agreed, at $1.30/MMBtu (CIF at Al-Taweelah and subject to a 2 percent annual escalation). The Dubai subsidy is funded by the Abu Dhabi authorities and not Qatar or the Dolphin Project sponsors. The Dolphin agreement with the Dubai Supply authority (Dusup) provides for gas to be delivered at Jebal Ali in Dubai for 25 years beginning with a start date of 2007.

However, while the lack of a pricing agreement delayed Dolphin coming online for a few months, an even more significant revolution occurred in the international gas market that provided even less justification for Qatar to implement Dolphin's Phase Two increase. Since Dolphin was conceptualised, rising international gas demand and international prices of LNG have radically changed Qatari export price expectations. With Dolphin, Qatari officials recognised that to further their regional political ambitions they had to sell gas regionally for much less than the international LNG prices. After Qatar instituted the 2005 moratorium on North Field expansion, gas allocation proposals for similar regional projects came under the proverbial magnifying glass.

Exports to Kuwait

Dolphin's proposed expansion to Kuwait and Bahrain seems increasingly unlikely unless they are willing to pay substantially higher prices.[69] In March 2009, Kuwait and Qatar (RasGas) formally agreed that Kuwait would import nearly 1.6 Mtpa of LNG each summer for five years, beginning in June 2009.[70] Kuwait had initially hoped to import Qatari gas *via* a subsea extension of the Dolphin project, consistent with a memorandum of understanding signed in 2000. But the momentum for a subsea extension to Kuwait failed in the face of Saudi objections about the pipeline's route, as well as Qatar's reluctance to supply according to old pricing matrixes.

Due to difficulties in gaining Saudi approval and its own desire to avoid selling gas through the pipeline, Qatar negotiated to supply LNG to gas-starved Kuwait to start in the third quarter 2009.[71] But Kuwait was not happy with the Qatari LNG price terms and instead negotiated and concluded a purchase agreement with Shell in June 2009.

Exports to Turkey and the EU

During a joint press conference in an August 2009 State visit, Qatari Emir Sheikh Al-Thani affirmed that he and Turkish President Abdullah Gul would form a working group to explore pipeline construction and to promote energy cooperation.[72] While Sheikh Al-Thani stated, 'We hope a pipeline from Qatar to Turkey will also be realised,' President Gul revealed they had also discussed collaborative energy projects such as facilities, refineries and possible Qatari LNG export to Turkey.[73]

The Kuwaiti leadership also encouraged Qatar to agree to American–Turkish plans to construct a 35–40 Bcm/yr marine pipeline that will run from Qatar to Bahrain and Kuwait, and then run through Iraq and Turkey to connect with the planned Nabucco pipeline to supply the European Union.[74] Kuwait and Bahrain want this pipeline completed to satisfy burgeoning gas needs, and generate transit income.

However, despite optimistic Turkish and Qatari press reports about a pipeline, it is highly unlikely that Qatar will engage in further regional pipeline construction. Qatari reliance on LNG export has reduced the geopolitical uncertainties inherent in reliance on transit countries, and granted Qatar substantially higher financial netbacks. Unlike pipelines, tankers can be diverted at a moment's notice to alternative markets, consistent with market fluctuations. Because of a lack of immediate supplies for the Nabucco pipeline, European countries seeking to diversify away from Russian pipeline imports have increasingly turned to LNG.[75] The rapid expansion of Qatar's LNG export capacity, estimated to reach 104 Bcm by 2012 (see Chapter 10), means that Qatari LNG exports will vastly exceed, in both volume and price, regional exports while at the same time avoiding the political and commercial risks associated with the latter.[76]

Dolphin Phase Two?

In 2009, Dolphin Energy opened negotiations with Qatar to receive additional supplies of gas and fulfil UAE peak demand over the peak summer months. In a departure from its own corporate practices, Dolphin Energy, which has been structured as an integrated company that produces, processes, and transports gas from the North Field to the UAE, agreed to purchase third party gas on a contingent basis.

Dolphin and QP discussed the provision of an 'interruptible supply,' e.g., gas exported to the UAE when Qatargas' international customers required less gas during the season of low demand.[77] The original offer for 3.28 to 4.01 Bcm/yr (9 to 11 million cm/d) was formulated from the Qatari side. ADNOC leapt at the offer and announced the signing of the contract in July 2009.

The interruptible gas would be largely available during the summer, when Gulf consumer gas demand peaks, but falls in Europe and Asia. Dolphin understood that its assent to the Qatari proposition did not constitute a firm contract for gas supplies, as the UAE would only receive these additional supplies when QP's LNG customers did not want their fully allotted volumes.[78]

As the gas is already processed, the main issue will be additional front-end engineering and design (FEED) work, and the construction of extra compressors. At the time of writing, no price had been publically revealed, but it is likely to be in the range of the 'regional swing price', which in the past has been approximately $4–5/MMBtu. Another potentially contentious issue is that many parties in the UAE need gas, which will make allocation rights between Abu Dhabi, Dubai, Oman and Sharjah highly contentious. Nonetheless, third party gas will still be less expensive to utilise than fuel oil for power generation.[79]

Domestic Demand: GTL, Petrochemicals and Power Generation

Part of Qatar's strategy for diversification is to increase the revenue it garners from its natural gas (See Figure 9.1 for the sharp increase in production). As regional gas prices are very low when considered against the international price of oil, Qatar seeks to escape from this pricing conundrum and increase revenues by converting its natural gas into high quality, refined products such as GTL and petrochemicals. The Qatari leadership decided to foster domestic industrialisation and attract foreign direct investment in the energy-intensive industries with low-cost electricity and feedstock.

At the crux of the regional disagreements over new or expanded Qatari gas supplies is Qatar's new North Field Monetisation policy. During the 1990s, Qatar had not only achieved remarkable buyer diversification, but had adequately buttressed its economic growth with plans for domestic gas utilisation (see Table 9.4), LNG exports and GTL.

Qatar reoriented its gas prioritisation markedly, granting first

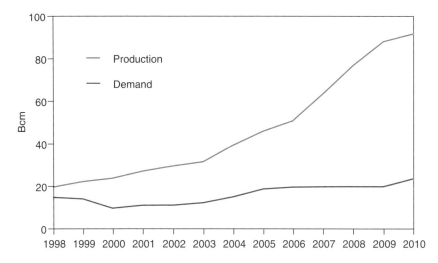

Figure 9.1: Qatar Natural Gas Production and Demand 1998–2010, Bcm

Source: BP *Statistical Review of World Energy*; author's calculations

allocation rights to domestic projects, followed by LNG export projects, pipeline exports, and GTL production.[80]

In fact, Qatar's domestic gas consumption, which has been rising steadily, reached 19.8 Bcm in 2008 and this is a primary concern.[81] 'We need the gas,' Qatar's Energy Minister Abdullah bin Hamad Al-Attiyah affirmed, 'The country is one big workshop. We cannot just export gas when [Qatar] needs it. We have to give domestic supply priority.'[82] From this statement it is apparent that Qatar is not just concerned about meeting current domestic demand. It does not want to bind itself to a multitude of long-term gas export contracts and risk the dire prospect that fast paced industrialisation may leave it unable to supply domestic needs.

Because of rapid industrial expansion, Qatari officials estimate that the country's gas demand will sharply increase over the next decade. Therefore, Qatar and Exxon-Mobil launched Phase Two of the Al-Khaleej project (AKG-2), which will deliver approximately 13 Bcm/yr for domestic markets in Qatar. It will also recover associated condensate of 15 million barrels a year, 1 Mtpa of natural gas liquids, and 870,000 tonnes annually of ethane for petrochemical feedstock.[83] Al-Attiyah hailed the AKG-2 project's potential to meet the country's spiralling domestic demand (see Figure 9.1).

In stressing the importance of AKG-2 for satisfaction of Qatari domestic demand, the Energy Minister announced that, '...AKG-2 today reflect[s] another major achievement toward meeting the increased domestic demand for natural gas. This project represents another important step under the ambitious vision...that aims to ensure the optimal utilization of the country's hydrocarbon resources.'[84]

Gas-to-Liquids Strategy

Not content to merely focus on global leadership in the LNG sector, Qatar forged ahead in the innovative field of gas-to-liquids (GTL), determined to leverage the gigantic reserves of the North Field into leadership status. GTL transforms natural gas into liquid fuel, which has environmental benefits as the diesel, naphtha or LPG has a low sulphur content, a low aromatic content, and a high octane number.[85] Proponents of GTL contend that the process is a superior diversification strategy as the resultant liquids do not need additional infrastructure investment in the sense that LNG does, e.g., specialised tankers, regasification and storage facilities.

There was an initial spurt of interest in the early 2000s, when QP signed a number of Letters of Interest and Memoranda of Understanding with several IOCs for the establishment of large-scale gas to GTL conversion projects for the manufacture of base oil stocks and synthetic fuels. Many of these projects either were cancelled or indefinitely delayed as Qatar implemented the North Field moratorium; QP and many IOCs questioned the economics of the projects in the wake of the ExxonMobil Palm GTL project cancellation, and as Qatar prioritised domestic gas supply over export projects.

Initially, Qatar viewed GTL as a favourable diversification to increase its presence in the value-added industries. However, as most of the GTL projects experienced extreme cost overruns, Qatar decided to limit GTL expansion, and instead focused on the two remaining GTL projects, the Oryx and Pearl projects.

Oryx GTL Project. Oryx GTL Ltd. was established at the end of January 2003 as a joint venture company between Qatar Petroleum (51 percent) and Sasol of South Africa (49 percent); it represents an investment of nearly $950 million and was the world's first new generation, commercial scale, GTL facility. Oryx GTL is able to process 3.39 Bcm/yr (9.3 Million cm/d) of lean natural gas from the Al-Khaleej field to produce 34,000 b/d of liquids. The output consists of 34,000 b/d of GTL diesel, 9000 b/d of naphtha and 1000 b/d of LPG.[86] Oryx came online in 2007 and made its first shipment of diesel in March of that year. The facility reached full capacity in January 2009, after problems with a superheater caused delays and cost $50 million to repair.[87] Since it came online, Sasol also sought to expand the facility's capacity to 100,000 b/d of GTL and also launch a separate 130,000b/d operation, in spite of the persistent cost overruns in the GTL sector. However, with the onset of the North Field Moratorium, the plant has not been able to secure additional gas volumes, and has since explored establishing GTL facilities in Nigeria, Algeria, Russia and Australia.

ExxonMobil. QP and ExxonMobil jointly announced in 2004 plans to construct a GTL facility, Palm GTL, for production of up to 154,000 b/d of GTL for export. ExxonMobil also sought to produce base oil stocks in addition to the synthetic fuels.

However, in February of 2007, cancellation of ExxonMobil's Palm GTL project illustrated that domestic gas demand has higher priority over export projects. Officially, Qatar cancelled the Palm GTL project because of soaring construction costs – the cost reportedly doubled from $7 billion to over $18 billion.[88] However, rapidly rising domestic gas demand, Exxon's basic strategy of risk mitigation and the concern for the reservoir health of the North Field, were all contributing factors to the project's cancellation.[89] Instead, Qatar granted to Exxon-Mobil the opportunity to develop the Barzan Gas Project in the North Field with the 15.51 Bcm/y (42.5 million cm/d) previously allocated for GTL production, immediately reallocated to provide gas to satisfy Qatar's rising domestic demand when the project comes online in 2012.[90]

Pearl GTL. In July 2004, Qatar Petroleum and Qatar Shell GTL Limited (Shell) signed a Development and Production Sharing Agreement for Pearl GTL. This integrated GTL project is located in Ras Laffan to develop 16.4 Bcm/yr (45.3 million cu m/day) of North Field gas to produce approximately 140,000 b/d of high quality GTL fuels, along with 120,000 boe of condensate, ethane, and liquid petroleum gas.[91]

When fully operational, it will be the largest GTL plant in the world, producing approximately 3 billion barrels of oil equivalent over the life of the project. The Pearl project will also be the first integrated GTL operation in the world, in that it will have upstream natural gas production integrated with the onshore conversion plant.

Pearl has two development phases: barring any unforeseen delays, the first phase will be commissioned by the end of 2010, with a planned production rate of approximately 70,000 b/d of various GTL products; the second phase is due to be operational by the end of 2011.

The project experienced significant cost overruns from its initial estimated construction costs in 2003 of $5 billion. By 2007, construction material and manpower costs increased to $19 billion.[92] The Pearl project has the potential to be extremely profitable. Based on $50 a barrel oil prices, it could have $4.5 billion in revenue per annum, with a full return on capital investment in four years.[93] However, some observers have questioned this calculation as being much too optimistic, pointing out that most of the GTL projects begun in Qatar have been plagued by extensive cost overruns.[94] Citibank analysts contended that the Pearl GTL project will achieve an internal rate of return of 9 percent, which is slightly below the standard firm return on invest target, if the facility costs no more than the conservative prediction of $15 billion.[95] Much of the ultimate profitability of the Pearl project depends upon the international price of oil. Pearl began when international oil prices were approximately $30 (July 2004). In a price environment of $70 and above at the time of writing (June 2010), even if the capital cost overruns are around $20 billion, investors should still have a sufficient, even if not exciting, rate of return.

The profitability of Pearl will determine future Qatari and IOC interest in GTL projects. Other IOCs considered entering the Qatar GTL sector, but gradually backed away because of technological and cost concerns, as well as questions regarding future gas availability when and if the North Field moratorium is lifted.

Project Cancellations. Other projects that were under negotiation during the early 2000s and subsequently cancelled included a 140,000 b/d plant with Marathon Oil, a 185,000 b/d plant with Ivanhoe Energy of Canada, an 80,000 b/d development with ConocoPhillips and a 120,000 b/d project with ChevronTexaco. All of the foregoing GTL initiatives were either cancelled or ultimately never left the drawing board.[96]

The cancellation of the Palm GTL project and the other GTL projects mean that Qatar's original goal of GTL leadership by 2011/2012 is under significant threat. The spate of GTL deals announced in the early 2000s represented a gamble that GTL would be a profitable and rational investment in a fuel that is less carbon intensive than regular gasoline. Furthermore, GTL offered an opportunity for Qatar to diversify into higher value fuel and lubricants, reducing its exposure to the volatility in the natural gas market. For the IOCs, it offered an opportunity for diversification as well. Qatar's rapid expansion in the GTL sector in the early 2000s has tapered off significantly as Qatar reprioritised and decided to focus much more on project upgrades and meeting future domestic demand.

Power Generation

The domestic power generation sector constitutes Qatar's single most gas-hungry sector. Table 9.1 shows details of the major power projects. Abdullah Al-Attiyah has estimated that generation capacity will increase to 13,000 megawatts (MW) by 2014, a quantum leap from a mere 1200 MW in 1997.[97] In 2010, Qatar experienced an additional 3200 MW capacity increase, at a projected cost of $2.2 billion and by 2015, a projected additional increase of 10,500 MW.[98] Qatar has also tapped international debt markets to partially finance a $30 billion expansion of the power and water sector. The transmission and distribution portion alone of this project is estimated to reach between $15–20 billion. As with many of the other Gulf countries, Qatar has been attempting to deal with summer blackouts by a two-pronged approach of increasing power supply and instituting a comprehensive grid renovation.[99]

Table 9.1: Major Qatar Power Projects

Power Projects	Generation Capacity MW
Independent Power Project II (IPP II) Mesai'eed (2009)	2000 MW
The Ras Girtas Power & Water Project (Est. 2011)	2730 MW at full operation.
Ras Laffan A (2003), B (2006) and C (est. 2011)	Combined 4500 MW
Ras Abu Fontas B (2007)	Phase One: 990 MW Phase Two: 570 MW

Source: Qatar Electricity and Water Company (QEWC)

As stated, Qatari per capita electricity generation is amongst the world's highest with demand rising by 12 percent a year.[100] In the first two months of 2009, Qatar's demand for electricity grew by an average of 15 percent compared to the same period last year, while desalinated water consumption rose by an average of 20 percent.[101] Business Monitor International estimated that from 2010 to 2018, Qatar's electricity generation will grow by 140.2 percent, the highest rate in the Middle East and Africa.[102] The successor to the Qatar General Electricity and Water Corporation (QEWC), the Qatar General Electricity & Water Corporation (Kahramaa) ruled against raising electricity tariffs, because the issue of power tariffs is politically sensitive.[103] Qatari citizens, who account for 25 percent of consumers and 40 percent of consumption, receive water and power free of charge, which is one of the main reasons why demand has been increasing rapidly. Fear of inflation factored in this decision, and Kahramaa is continuing to supply without charge.[104] Instead the government has set a monthly ceiling for household consumption for Qatari nationals, whereby if their power usage increases beyond the ceiling, end-user nationals are charged. Even without wholesale pricing reform, QEWC posted a robust 22 percent increase in net profits during 2009.[105] With its additional revenue, QEWC has sought to become a major power investor in other GCC member states, as well as a potential stakeholder in the European nuclear power sector, in order to diversify its revenue[106]

As with many of Qatar's other megaprojects, the principle reason behind its frenetic development of the power sector is to supply the enormous amounts of electricity needed to fuel the country's energy-intensive industries, which are undergoing significant expansion and require a consistent power supply. While Qatar does not face the regular blackouts plaguing the other GCC countries, its rapid expansion still places enormous pressure on its utilities and sometimes supply outstrips demand, or demand edges ahead of supply. The decision to separate generation from transmission and distribution has helped Qatar avoid the shortages suffered by its neighbours through facilitating prompt decisionmaking about new plant construction. However, by taking both a cautious approach to its future natural gas development, as well as a prudent stance towards power construction, Qatar is aiming to provide a cushion for its future industrial development.

Petrochemicals

Qatar's petrochemical industry is also growing at an extremely fast pace, which places additional demands on the country's gas reserves (for a detailed breakdown of the country's major petrochemical projects, see Table 9.2). Qatar's interest in petrochemical expansion is predicated on the need for a diversified, value-added downstream industry sufficiently stable to withstand the constant fluctuations of the international oil and gas market.[107]

By 2014, Qatar seeks to have the world's fourth largest petrochemicals output capacity of 29 million tonnes per year of 16 different products.[108] In support of this, it embarked on a $15 billion investment programme led by Qatar Petrochemical Company (Qapco), Qatar Chemical Co (Q-Chem), Qatar Vinyl Co (Q-Vinyl) and Qatar Fertiliser Co (Qafco), among others.[109]

Observers estimate that Qatar's rapid petrochemical expansion will

Table 9.2: Major Qatari Petrochemical Projects

Project	Capacity
Qatofin	450,000 mtpa/LLDPE
The Ras Laffan Olefins Company (RLOC)	1.3 mpta/Ethylene
Q-Chem	273,000 mpta/ high-density polyethylene (HDPE) 189,000 mpta/LDPE and 47,000 mpta/Hexane-1
Q-Chem II	345,000 mpta/alpha olefin 350,000 mtpa/polyethylene (PE)
Qatar Plastics Products Co (Qppc)	30,00 mpta/polyethylene
Qatar Fuel Additives Co (Qafac)	832,500mtpa/methanol and 610,000/mpta methyl tertiary butyl ethane (MTBE),

Source: Qatar Petrochemical Company (QAPCO) http://www.qapco.com/

comprise nearly three-fourths of Qatar's domestic energy consumption by 2030.[110] The rapid expansion of the sector was made possible by inexpensive natural gas feedstocks ($0.75–1/MMBtu; feedstock prices account for nearly three-quarters of production costs), robust state support of sector development, and the geographical proximity of major markets, such as China, the other East Asian countries and India, all of which are the fastest growing regions for petrochemical demand. However, with the breakneck sectoral expansion, many project plans faced delays originating from feedstock shortages, for example the ethylene cracker expansion at Ras Laffan.[111]

Qatar's petrochemical expansion has been focused mostly on growth in ethylene capacity, along with associated downstream industries. Qatar has a competitive advantage over other Gulf countries because of its relatively inexpensive upstream cost structure. As natural gas feedstock accounts for nearly 70 percent of petrochemical production costs, Qatar's production costs are quite competitive when compared with its neighbours. Technology, technical skill, and capacity give Qatar an unqualified advantage in petrochemical production. And its large non-associated production means that its petrochemical production is much less constrained than other Gulf States that produce the majority of their gas from associated gas fields and thus must adhere to OPEC quotas.

Conclusion: Outlook for 2015–2020

Production

Qatari gas production and demand will increase substantially over the next decade. Double digit GDP growth during the 2000s has been fuelled mainly by the development of the country's natural gas reserves. This economic growth has also propelled Qatar's diversification into the downstream value-added sectors. Assuming a scenario of several projects coming online within the 2010–2015 period, Qatar's natural gas production is expected to nearly double to 171.3 Bcm/yr by 2015, compared with approximately 89 Bcm/yr in 2009 (see Table 9.3). This includes AKG-1 and AKG-2, which together would add approximately 20 Bcm/yr and Barzan production of 15.3 Bcm/yr by 2012–2014.

Table 9.3: Qatar Production and Demand, 2000–2020, Bcm

Natural Gas	Production	Demand
2000	23.7	9.7
2008	77.0	20.2
2015 (est.)	171.3	35
2020 (est.)	175	53

Source: BP *Statistical Review of World Energy*

The present expectation is that by 2020, production will increase insignificantly to 175 Bcm/yr, mostly through upgrading of projects that are already under construction; but everything depends on the decisions of the Qatari leadership as to whether the moratorium will be lifted and, if so, to what extent and in what time frame. This in turn will substantially depend on the conclusion of the reservoir studies of the North Field currently under way.

Aside from the technical reservoir assessment, production decisions post-2014/15 will be based on a myriad of variables, such as the state of the global gas market, Qatar's strategic goals and other geopolitical factors. But even assuming a positive decision to increase to natural gas production at the earliest possible date of 2014, a four to five-year lead time for the development of any additional gas projects would mean no substantial increase until the end of the 2010s at the earliest.

Consumption

Qatari gas consumption has sharply increased since 1970. Excluding gas injected into the oilfields and gas allocated for export, consumption reached nearly 21.1 Bcm/yr average in 2009, up from 9.7 Bcm/yr in 2000, and from a miniscule 1 Bcm/year in 1970. For the forecast period, from 2010–2020, demand growth, driven by rapid expansion of the energy-intensive and the downstream value-added sectors, should experience an increase of approximately 150 percent, reaching 53 Bcm/yr by 2020.

Table 9.4 shows a projection of gas demand from power, gas to liquids and petrochemicals to 2020, with consumption predicted to increase from an estimated 21.1 Bcm/yr in 2009 to 35 Bcm/yr by 2015 and 53 Bcm by 2020. The basic assumptions underlying Table 9.4 is that the power sector will continue its robust double digit growth, tracking increases in GDP. The GTL sector is forecast to grow modestly as any increase will come from capacity upgrades, and not from new projects. The petrochemical sector is forecast to grow significantly as Qatar continues its overall development strategy to substantially expand its petrochemical sector. The country has the fastest growing economy in the Gulf, and the government and private companies are still injecting tens of billions of dollars into heavy industries that will transform natural gas into more advanced value-added exports. However, in 2008–09, each of the major industries into which Qatar poured its money and natural gas experienced a sharp downturn, e.g., petrochemicals, LNG and aluminium. Profits from petrochemicals are likely to remain weak until at least 2013–14 due to the perfect storm of overcapacity from the Asian and Middle Eastern suppliers and the global financial crisis.[112] Aluminium prices have slightly recovered from their lows of 2009, but are still forecast to remain relatively low; perhaps at least 20 percent below their 2007/08 levels of $2700–$3000 a tonne.[113]

If and when the moratorium is lifted, domestic demand is likely to be prioritised over new LNG or GTL export-related projects. For instance, the second phase of the Al-Khaleej Gas Project (AKG-2), which was officially inaugurated on March 11, 2010 was specifically mandated to provide gas for the local market.

Table 9.4: GTL, Power and Petrochemicals Demand 2010–2020, Bcm

Year	GTL	Power	Petrochemicals	TOTAL
2010	3.39 Bcm/yr (full operation of Oryx 2009)	4.65	13.06	21.10
2015 (est.)	5.08 Bcm	8.13	21.07	34.28
2020 (est.)	7.62	16.26	29.12	53.00

Source: Qatar Electricity and Water Company (QEWC)

Exports

Qatar will have 105 Bcm LNG export capacity by 2010 and, assuming it chooses to 'debottleneck' its existing LNG trains, may add an additional 20 Bcm/yr of capacity – given that additional production will be available when and if the moratorium is lifted.[114] In addition, Dolphin Energy will continue to produce its 20 Bcm/yr from its North Field concession for export by pipeline to the UAE and Oman. Small additional quantities of natural gas could also be made available for the regional markets on a seasonal or short-term basis (See Table 9.5). It is not likely that Phase Two of Dolphin exports to Oman and UAE will be implemented without a significant increase in price, and even then, it is not likely that Qatar will seek to lock itself into long-term contracts. Depending on the demand and price of LNG in international markets, as well as the regional pricing structure in the Gulf, additional interruptible or seasonal supplies could be sent to Dolphin downstream users each summer to help them deal with peak demand period.

Table 9.5: Qatar Pipeline Exports, Bcm

Natural Gas	Long-Term Export (Dolphin)	Potential Interruptible/Seasonal Summer Export (May-Aug.)
2000	NA	N/A
2008	15.4 (UAE) 2.0 (Oman)	N/A
2015 (est.)	15.4 (UAE) 2.0 (Oman)	1.31 (UAE/Oman)
2020 (est.)	15.4 (UAE) 2.0 (Oman)	1.31 (UAE/Oman)

Source: BP *Statistical Review of World Energy*

While the international community is focused on the prospects for increased Qatari exports of LNG, and the regional countries on exports of pipeline gas, both should recall that in 2009, QP's Director of Oil and Gas Ventures, Saad al-Kaabi, announced two strategic goals for Qatar's future gas allocation decisions. In terms of export, al-Kaabi warned that the world should not expect unlimited supplies from Qatar, and, 'If after 2014 QP decides to have new developments, the first priority will be given to securing sufficient reserves for our fast growing power and desalination sectors, our local industry development, and only then will we think about export.' In terms of Qatar's new pricing framework, al-Kaabi noted that natural gas consumers should be prepared to pay a 'fair value for hydrocarbon resources' and that IOCs must 'accept that fact that NOCs as resource holders, will give up less than in the past, and will be expecting to receive more value.'[115]

The statement made quite clear that even if and when the moratorium is eventually lifted export-led gas projects would be subordinated to domestic development post-2015. After its major projects come online during the period 2012–2015, Qatar will likely seek to maintain its position as the world's number one LNG producer, but it will not be likely to continue the runaway development of its resources that welcomed all suitors during the late 1990s and early 2000s. Qatar for much of the late twentieth century looked outward to export markets, which gave rise to an extraordinary period of export growth during the 1990s and 2000s. But it seems that in the future, the domestic market will be the most important priority, and almost irrespective of decisions taken about future projects, growth in the natural gas sector will become much more modest in the late 2010s and beyond.

Notes

1   Estimate from July 2009; *The World Factbook: Qatar*, The Central Intelligence Agency Website. Available at https://www.cia.gov/library/publications/the-world-factbook/geos/qa.html

2   Kawach, Nadim, 'Strong Economy Boosts Qatari Population', *Dubai Business News* (Dec. 7, 2008); Irish, John, 'Qatar's Population Doubles Since '04', *Arabian Business* (May 15, 2008).

3   BP *Statistical Review of World Energy*, British Petroleum (June 2010) Available at < http://www.bp.com/liveassets/bp_internet/globalbp/globalbp_uk_english/reports_and_publications/statistical_energy_review_2008/STAGING/local_assets/2010_downloads/statistical_review_of_world_energy_full_report_2010.pdf

4   The North Field's gas is approximately equivalent to 162 billion barrels of oil. Ibid. (January 2009) Available at < http://www.bp.com/liveassets/bp_internet/globalbp/globalbp_uk_english/reports_and_publications/statistical_energy_review_2008/STAGING/local_assets/2009_downloads/natural_gas_section_2009.pdf>;.

5   Previously, Qatar's Reserves/production (R/P) ratio was estimated to last for 200 years, however, with the completion of several LNG trains, its R/P ratio has narrowed to approximately 100 years. Hindley, Angus, 'Impact Assessment', *Middle East Economic Digest* (November 2006).

6   See Chapter 10.

7   Siddiqi, Moin, 'Exceptional Energy Prospects for Qatar', *Oil Review Middle East* (June 2007).

8   Romero, Simon, *Natural Gas Powering Qatar Economic Boom Growth Likened to the Saudi Oil Bonanza*, Red Orbit (Dec. 24, 2005).

9   Evans-Pritchard, Ambrose, 'Qatar Fashions Financial Oasis to go toe-to-toe with East and West', *Daily Telegraph* (May 22, 2009).

10   Romero, Simon, 'Natural Gas Powering Qatar Economic Boom,' *The New York Times* (Dec. 22, 2005).

11   For a detailed assessment of the Qatar Arch, see *Qatar North Arch Extension-Zagros Fold Belt Province*, United States Geological Survey. Available at http://energy.cr.usgs.gov/WEcont/regions/reg2/p2/tps/AU/au203021.pdf

12   Khaleghhu, Shahla, *Iran and Qatar: Bilateral Cooperation to Utilize Gas Market Opportunities*, Brazilian Institute of Petroleum (undated); BP *Statistical Review of World Energy*, *British Petroleum* (June 2010) p. 28.

13   El Mallakh, Ragaei, *Qatar: Energy and Development* (Routledge, 1985) p.32

14   For an account of the South Pars resource development see Chapter 10. *South Pars, Qatar North Field, Iran*, Offshore Technology. Available at http://www.offshore-technology.com/projects/southpars/;

15   There are presumably other studies that were carried out by the respective IOCs that operate in the North field; however, their results are not publicly available.

16   Within the main Khuff gas-bearing reservoir, four Khuff zones were defined. Of the four zones, K-4 is the most prolific and contains approximately 60 per cent of the gas reserves. *The Source: Qatar's North Field*, RasGas Homepage Available at < http://www.michaelpage.co.uk/minisite/3606/2137/the_source.html>; Perrodon, Alain, *Dynamics of Oil and Gas accumulations* (Editions TECHNIP, 1983) p.255.

17   Energy Minister Abdullah bin Hamad Al-Attiyah, reminisced that, 'I remember all the people who advised me and my country not to go into the LNG business.' Williamson, Lucy, 'Qatar's Fortunes Boom With Gas', BBC News (Feb. 2006).

18   Qatar was the first GCC member country to participate in the World Bank's Global Gas Flaring Initiative (GGFR) on January 25, 2009 program. The only other Middle Eastern country that is a member is Iraq. Qatar joined the GGFR because it seeks to reduce its flaring to zero, and thereby help positively impact climate change. As a result of its rapid development of its natural gas field, it has increased flaring from 1994–2006. Qatar's specific focus is to eliminate routine sources of associated gas venting that could be captured and conserved, and, eliminate or reduce the large sources of associated gas flaring, primarily the major sources of continuous production flaring, other than those related to emergency, safety, and operational problems. Malik, Talal, 'Gulf Eyes Use for Gas Flares', *Arabian Business* (March 11, 2008); *Qatar: First Gulf Country Joins World Bank-led Effort to Reduce Greenhouse Gas Emissions from Gas Flaring*, Global Gas Flaring Reduction Partnership Home Page (Jan. 25, 2009) Available at <http://web.worldbank.org/WBSITE/EXTERNAL/NEWS/0,,contentMDK:22044056~menuPK:34463~pagePK:34370~piPK:34424~theSitePK:4607,00.html>

19   *Pipeline Magazine*, 'Qatar Lengthens North Field Delay', (Dec. 18, 2009).

20   *Dow Jones News Wires*, 'Qatar May End North Field Moratorium in 2014', (May 15, 2009); Gavin, James, 'Moving Beyond the North Field', *Middle*

East Economic Digest (March 20, 2009).

21   Apparently, when ConocoPhillips drilled an unexpected dry hole in the North Field in 2005, that unanticipated event served as a partial catalyst for QP's revised perspective of the reservoir's structure and potential. Williams, Perry, 'An Inheritance Worth Protecting', *Middle East Economic Digest* (Sept. 14, 2007).

22   *MEES*, 'Doha Rules out New Gas Export Projects Post-Moratorium', (Dec. 14, 2009).

23   *Bloomberg News*, 'Qatar has No Plans for Further Natural Gas Plants', (Dec.7, 2009).

24   Amongst many LNG exporting countries, there is the fear that the spot market, as it developed in the course of the international financial crisis, threatened to undermine the long-term stability of LNG sales. In 2009 and 2010, many gas-importing countries were reducing their imports under multiyear contracts in favour of gas purchases on the spot market. Farey, Ben, et al, 'Gas OPEC Sends Prices Lower for Worst Commodity', *Bloomberg Businessweek*, (April 19, 2010); many national oil and gas companies, such as OAO Gazprom, warned that there was an 'abnormal' gap between spot fuel prices and long-term contracts that threatened investments in capacity upgrades, new fields and pipelines. Shiryaevskaya, Anna, 'Gazprom Says 'Abnormal' Gas-Price Gap to Undermine Investment', *Bloomberg Businessweek* (Apr. 14, 2010).

25   Ibid.

26   The combined output of the units being shuttered – for periods of roughly three weeks or longer – was 41 mta, out of the export capacity of 77 mta. Tuttle, Robert, 'Qatar, Russia Shutter Gas Supply', *Bloomberg Businessweek* (June 10, 2010). It appears that many LNG producers have taken steps to correct the glut by adopting corrective measures such as storage, maintenance and repair to attempt to alleviate the oversupply in the market. Nightingale, Alaric, et al, 'Qatar Idles LNG Ships as Year-End Gas 18 per cent More', *Bloomberg Businessweek* (June 3, 2010).

27   *MEES*, 'Doha Rules out New Gas Export Projects Post-Moratorium', (Dec. 14, 2009).

28   Khaleghhu, Shahla, *Iran and Qatar: Bilateral Cooperation to Utilize Gas Market Opportunities*, Brazilian Institute of Petroleum (undated).

29   Canty, Daniel, 'Qatar Matures, New North Field Projects Unlikely', *Arabian Oil and Gas* (Dec. 9, 2009).

30   *Pipeline Magazine*, 'Qatar Lengthens North Field Delay', (Dec. 18, 2009).

31   Wintershall already operates two other blocks in Qatar, block 11 since 2000, and block 3 since 2007. In Block 11, Wintershall conducted the initial appraisal work to assess the commerciality of a gas discovery. In block 3, Wintershall conducted joint exploration activities with Cosmo Energy of Japan and Indonesia's PT Pertamina. Klaus, Oliver, 'Germany's Wimtershall Signs a 25-yr Qatar Gas Exploration Deal', *Dow Jones Newswire* (Nov. 18. 2008); 'Wintershall Awarded New Exploration License in Qatar', Datamonitor (Oct. 29, 2007).

32   Gavin, James, 'Moving Beyond the North Field', Ibid.

33   Ibid.

34   A Wood Mackenzie analyst stated that, 'there is definitely a source rock, but from available data, no clear traps or structures.' Ibid.

35   Crystal, Jill, *Oil and Politics in the Gulf: Rulers and Merchants in Kuwait and Qatar* (Cambridge University Press, 1995) p.158.

36   For a detailed table of governmental expenditures pre-and-post 1973, see El Mallakh, Ragaei, *Qatar: Development of an Oil Economy* (Taylor & Francis, 1979) pp.59–65.

37   *The Middle East and North Africa 2004* (Routledge, 2004) p.943.

38   Victor, David G. et al, *Natural gas and geopolitics: from 1970 to 2040* (Cambridge University Press, 2006) p.244.

39   Modern combined-cycle power plants are able to produce 10,000MW with 1.58 Million cu m/yr, as opposed to 2.37 Million cu m/yr with traditional power plants. For costs in the LNG chain see David Lesdesma, 'Cost Increases for LNG projects', in Jonathan Stern, (ed.), *Natural Gas in Asia*: the challenges of growth in China, India, Japan and Korea, 2nd Edition, OIES/OUP, 2008, Appendix 1, pp. 402–4.

40   El-Mallakh, Ragaei, *Qatar: Energy & Development*, Ibid. p.68.

41   Evans-Pritchard, Ambrose, 'Qatar Fashions Financial Oasis to go toe-to-toe with East and West', Ibid.

42   Petrochemical prices generally are much higher than the primary products that make them, i.e., oil and gas. While petrochemical prices are relatively stable, they do exhibit some volatility; this is especially prevalent with the basic and intermediate petrochemicals. However, despite fluctuations, petrochemical prices lack the seemingly random sharp increases and decreases that characterise the natural gas and oil market. Nonetheless, one disadvantage of the petrochemical market is that producers may find their profit squeezed between the volatility of the feedstock inputs, which comprise 30–40 per cent of the production cost, and the relatively inelastic price of the end product. In the Gulf countries, this is not as much a concern because of the administrative pricing of natural gas feedstocks. Mercier, Claude, *Petrochemical Industry and the Possibilities of Its Establishment in the Developing Countries*, TECHNIP (1996) p.20; *The Shrinking world of petrochemicals*, American Chemical Society, (Feb 15, 2008) p.102.

   The Prebisch-Singer hypothesis argued that the long-term international prices of primary products, i.e., crude, and unprocessed natural gas (non LNG, GTL) present a secular, deteriorating trend, while the price of manufactured products, i.e., petrochemicals, fertilisers, etc., have a much more stable long-term pricing structure. Harvey, David et al, 'The Prebisch-Singer Hypothesis: Four Centuries of Evidence', *The Review of Economics and Statistics*, Vol. 92, No. 2, 367–77 (May 2010).

43   *Alexander's Gas and Oil Connection*, 'Qatar's Gas Sector Doubles in Size', Vol. 14, issue #10 (Aug. 7. 2009).

44   Kawach, Nadim, 'Qatar's Gas Sector Share of GDP More Than Oil Now', *Emirates Business* 24/7 (Sept. 15, 2009).

45   Approximately 5 per cent hydrogen sulfide.

46   Dargin, Justin, *The Dolphin Project: The Development of a Gulf Gas Initiative*, (Oxford Institute of Energy Studies,) (2008) pp.18–28.

47   *APS Review Gas Market Trends*, 'Qatar-North Field Development –Phase -1', (Aug. 14, 1995).

48   This initial contract covered the engineering schema, procurement, sub-contracting, construction and start-up assistance of first phase development. Ibid.

49   To extract hydrogen sulfide and carbon dioxide from the raw gas.

50   Sulphur utilised in the production of fertiliser has become increasingly valuable in the international market. The sustained increase in the international price of sulphur has made even previously unviable sour gas projects in the Gulf, such as the UAE's Shah Field, more economical. In 2008, the price of sulphur exported from Abu Dhabi surpassed $600 a tonne, which is several times more than the price of $20 where it was a few short years before. See 'UAE to Sign US$10bn Gas Deal', MidEast. Ru (Apr.30, 2008).

51   Qatar contracted Total in May 1991 to construct the upstream section of Qatar's first LNG project, Qatargas.

52   *Middle East Economic Digest*, 'North Field Inaugurated as Second Phase Progresses', (Sept. 6, 1991).

53   Barnett, Neil, 'Dolphin Project Surges Ahead', *The Middle East* (Feb. 2000); There were also numerous political considerations as well, as Qatar sought to extend its regional influence. See Dargin, Justin, *The Dolphin Project* Ibid., pp.13–31.

54   Ibid. *Dolphin Project.*

55   The Gulf Countries began to resolve their longstanding boundary disputes, replacing them with recognised borders. Although the GCC was set up in part to resolve disputes between members, this goal has been achieved not through the GCC, but through a combination of mediation, bilateral treaties, or international forums, such as the International Court of Justice. See Dargin, Justin, *The Dolphin Project*, Ibid., pp.23–8. Until 1971, the British maintained regional peace and acted as the ultimate arbiters for disputes. Many of the borders delineated by the British were never properly demarcated, and once oil was found, contention became rife. After the withdrawal of British forces, old territorial claims and tribal antipathy increased. The sudden importance of defining oil and gas deposits, while setting transit rights, enflamed these territorial disputes. See Wilkinson, J.C., *Arabia's Frontiers: The Story of Britain's Boundary Drawing in the Desert* (London: I. B. Tauris, 1991); Seddiq, Ramin, *Policy Watch/Peace Watch: Border Disputes on the Arabian Peninsula*, Washington Institute for Near East Policy (15 Mar. 2001).

56   In 1993, Qatar was the first Gulf country to have open diplomatic ties with Israel, and in 1995, initiated an economic relationship agreeing to supply Israel with natural gas. This caused some consternation with Qatar's neighbours, until Qatar eventually froze ties in 2001. The decision to seek

a *rapprochement* with Israel strained relations with other Gulf countries, and caused Egypt to send a diplomatic message to Qatari officials that it feared such an extreme stance with Israel might lead to assassination attempts against Qatari leadership. Egypt's warning seemed a bit overstated as Egypt began its own natural gas sales to Israel in 2005. See 'Threats against Qatar', *Arabic News* (21 June 2001); Morrow, Adam *et al*, 'Egypt: Govt Forced to Bend on Israel Gas Deal', *Inter-Press Service* (June 18, 2008).

57   Over the last decade, Saudi Aramco has added 2.03 Tcm/2030 Bcm of non-associated reserves. See Energy Information Administration, *Saudi Arabia: Natural Gas*,. Available at http://www.eia.doe.gov/emeu/cabs/Saudi_Arabia/NaturalGas.html

58   Dargin, Justin, *Dolphin Project*, Ibid. pp. 28–31.

59   It is interesting to see the involvement of a defence corporation in the development of a natural gas pipeline. To a certain extent it shows the importance that the Gulf pipeline has to the countries involved. Further, one of the driving forces behind the Dolphin project is reputedly Sheikh Mohammed bin Zayed Al Nahayan, the Chief of Staff of the UAE armed forces. Oil and gas issues generally fall under the province of the crown prince. The active involvement and oversight by Sheikh Mohammed may indicate the wider security/regional interest that the project holds. *See* the UOG mission statement available at *the Offset Program Bureau* http://www.offsets.ae/; see generally, Barnett, Neil, 'Dolphin Project Surges Ahead', *The Middle East* (Feb. 2000).

60   See the corporate website for general information at *Dolphin Energy* available at http://www.dolphinenergy.com/ The shareholders of DEL are the Mubadala Development Company (51 per cent) (which is a wholly-owned subsidiary of the Abu Dhabi government), Total (24.5 percent), and Occidental Petroleum (24.5 percent). The now infamous Enron had the initial (24.5 percent) stake that Occidental currently holds. After Enron's implosion, Occidental acquired those shares. Prior to the conceptualisation of the Dolphin project, there existed an earlier pipeline export project plan to deliver gas from Qatar to Dubai. This project was to be managed by an international consortium led by Arco, to deliver between .022 Bcm/d to .034 Bcm/d from Qatar's North Field to the Emirate. However, this project failed to gain sufficient momentum, and the regional actors turned to the UAE-supported Dolphin Energy. Cordesman, Anthony H., *The changing dynamics of energy in the Middle East, Volume 1* (Greenwood Publishing Group, 2006) p.275.

61   *Alexander's Gas and Oil Connections*, 'Mobil Partner in Dolphin Gas Venture', Vol. 4, No. 15 (9 Aug. 1999).

62   *Gulf Times*, 'Dolphin to Refinance $3bn of Debt Early Next Year', (28 June 2007). Under the terms of the DPSA, DEL will drill around 16 wells in the North Field, and build a production platform linked to an onshore gas gathering and processing plant at Ras Laffan to strip out the condensate. See *Middle East Economic Survey*, 'Dolphin officially announces CSFB as financial advisor,' Vol. XLV, No. 2. (14 Jan. 2002).

63 Much of the gas shortage is due to the Gulf pricing regime that places extreme disincentives for IOCs to invest in the sector. See Dargin, Justin, 'Trouble in Paradise – The Widening Gulf Gas Deficit', *Middle East Economic Survey*, (Sept. 29, 2008). Shortages of natural gas – hitherto the fuel of choice for electricity generation – have become a regular feature, forcing governments to consider alternatives such as coal, fuel oil, nuclear, and even imported gas. *Gulf News*, 'Gulf States Face Power Shortages amid Lack of Gas', (June 13, 2007); Rolling blackouts occur nearly every summer in the UAE, with disastrous consequences for local health facilities. See Al-Serkal, Mariam, 'Thousands Suffer in Three-Day Blackout', *Gulf News* (August 20, 2009).

64 The Taweelah Power and desalination plant is run by Abu Dhabi Water and Electricity Authority (ADWEA).

65 *Middle East Business and Financial News*, 'Dolphin Energy Project Defines New Era for Gas', (Jan. 2 2006).

66 'Initial Dolphin Gas Supplies Received in Al Ain Through Oman Pipelines', Dolphin Energy Website, (Jan. 25 2004). Available at http://www.dolphinenergy.com/press_news_releases.html

67 *Middle East Economic Survey*, 'Dolphin Makes Headway But Economic Currents May Rock Further GCC Integration', Vol.XLVIII No. 23 (June 6, 2005).

68 Butt, Gerald, 'Qatar to Break New Ground as Regional Gas Supplier and New Technology Developer', *Middle East Economic Survey* Vol. XLIV No.12 (Mar. 19, 2001).

69 Kuwait, for instance, sought to utilise a fixed price agreement for Qatari gas with unlimited upside for Kuwait during periods of elevated oil prices, while Qatar sought an indexed price system that would have incorporated a share in Kuwaiti savings for gas substitution.

70 Energy Information Administration, 'Kuwait, Natural Gas'; El Gamal, Rania, 'Shell to Supply Kuwait LNG Starting this Summer', LNGpedia (June 23, 2009). However, even while Kuwait is dealing with its own substantial natural gas shortages, it has intensified its search for domestic natural gas supplies and seeks to become a natural gas exporter in the near future. *Middle East Electricity*, 'Kuwait Seeks to Export Gas' (Mar. 17, 2008).

71 At the time of writing, the stakeholders did not release details about delivered volumes, price or contract duration.

72 Joshi, Mohit, 'Turkey and Qatar Discuss Energy Cooperation and Possible Pipeline' TopNews.in (August 18, 2009).

73 *Al Sabah (English)*, 'Emir Sheikh Al-Thani: We Want a Pipeline From Qatar to Turkey', (August 18, 2009).

74 *APS Review Gas Market Trends*, 'Betting On Qatar Link Up With Nabucco Pipeline Via Kuwait', (June 15, 2009).

75 However, if the EU wants to utilise Qatari LNG to offset Russian gas, it will have to compete on price with principally Asian importers. 'Qatari Gas to Reduce Russian Dominance', *Telegraph* (May 12, 2009).

76 Dargin, Justin, *The Dolphin Project* Ibid., p.32.
77 Williams, Perry, 'Dolphin Energy Holds Talks Over Gas Imports From Qatar', *Middle East Business Intelligence* (June 23, 2009).
78 Carlisle, Tamsin, 'UAE Dolphin Energy in Talks to Acquire Qatar Natural Gas', *The National* (June 23, 2009).
79 *Middle East Economic Survey*, 'Dolphin and Qatar in Talks About Additional Gas', Vol. LII No. 26 (Jun. 29, 2009).
80 GTL production has been given the last priority presumably because of the potential for cost overruns due to the nature of the new technology utilised in the plants.
81 'Natural Gas', *BP Statistical Review of World Energy* (June 2009) p.27.
82 *Iran Daily*, 'Mideast Seeks to Satisfy Domestic Gas Demand', (Apr.9, 2007).
83 *Arabian Business*, 'ExxonMobil Starts Second Phase of Al-Khaleej Project', (Nov. 30, 2006).
84 *Business Wire*, 'Qatar Petroleum and ExxonMobil Launch Al-Khaleej Gas Phase-2 (AKG-2)', (July 10, 2006).
85 Even though GTL has significant benefits in its end-use application in the transportation and aviation sector, there are concerns about the environmental impact during its production phase. Comparative Life-Cycle-Assessments of GTL production and conventional petroleum refining have found comparable levels of greenhouse gas emissions. Approximately 1/3 of the carbon on natural gas ends up emitted into the atmosphere during the GTL production phase. While the production phase carbon emissions tend to be offset by the lower greenhouse gas emissions during the use phase, the focus on the carbon reductions in its end-use may be slightly misleading. Several studies have indicated that conventional amine scrubbing utilised with carbon sequestration is able to capture the majority of carbon emissions during the production phase, giving it a significant advantage over standard petroleum refining. However, the use of amine scrubbing and sequestration add approximately 30 percent to the capital cost, posing serious questions about the incorporation of this carbon reducing technology by energy companies, and therefore, its overall viability to significantly reduce carbon emissions. See generally, O'Rear, Dennis, *Concepts for Reduction in CO2 Emissions in GTL Facilities*, Elsevier (2007).
86 Halstead, Kevin, 'Oryx GTL-A Case Study', *Petrochemicals*, (July 2006).
87 *Upstream Online*, 'Sasol Set to Open Qatar Taps', (Oct. 30, 2007).
88 Undoubtedly, this was a major factor. The 154,000 barrels per day approximation was originally estimated to cost $5 billion. When cost overruns reached $18 billion, both parties decided to cancel the venture. In spite of the cancellation of the Exxon-Mobil GTL venture, there are still several other major GTL operations in Qatar. It is estimated that more than 50 percent of the increase in the global GTL capacity from 2009–2015 will be created in Qatar. *AME Info*, 'Prices Rocket for Qatar's GTL Projects', (March 15, 2007); *The Peninsula*, 'Qatar: Rising Domestic Demand Poses Big Challenge to Gas Industry', (Mar.7, 2007).

89   *World Gas Intelligence*, 'Culprits in Qatar', Vol. XVlll, No. 10 (Mar. 7, 2007). Qatar allowed Exxon-Mobil a 10 percent stake, and participation in all future phases of the Barzan Gas Development Project. The initial phase of Barzan Project will supply about .0004 Bcm/d of Qatar's bourgeoning industrial and infrastructure growth, with a projected start date of 2012. *Business Wire*, 'Qatar Petroleum and Exxon-Mobil to Launch Barzan Gas Project', (Feb. 20, 2007); the placement of Exxon-Mobil in the lead position to develop the Barzan project was widely seen by analysts as a reward to Exxon for its years of loyalty, and as a reaffirmation to the market that Qatar's hydrocarbon's monetisation plan was on schedule. Williams, Perry, 'Doubts Surface Over Ras Laffan', *Middle East Economic Digest* (Sept. 12, 2008).

90   *Ibid.* 'Culprits in Qatar'. Qatar's strategy towards its GTL plants has been to focus on capacity expansion at existing plants.

91   Evans, Damon, 'Pearl GTL Set for Big Payback', *Upstream Online* (Mar. 11, 2008)

92   The Pearl project is a major undertaking. 500,000 cubic metres of concrete, 150,000 tons of structural steel, 100,000 tons of piping and 100,000 tons of equipment were needed to facilitate construction. 20,000 onsite workers were initially needed on the ground, but as the project neared completion, it peaked 35,000 and over 200 million man-hours will be needed to build the plant. Evans, Damon, 'Pearl GTL Set for Big Payback', Ibid.; For information about the increase in cost to $18 billion in 2007, see Reuters, 'Shell Says on Schedule with Qatar Pearl GTL Plant', (Oct. 30, 2007); *World Gas Intelligence*, 'GTL Approaching End of its Road', (Feb. 18, 2009); *Petroleum Economist*, 'GTL Investment Hits the Buffers' (Oct. 2009).

93   Ibid. Evans, Damon, 'Pearl GTL Set for Big Payback' (Mar. 11, 2008).

94   Cost overruns have been a commom problem in the Gulf energy sector. Typically, major energy and construction contracts were formulated under the lump-sum pricing framework, whereby the contractor delivered the project for an agreed price, while entirely assuming the risk of cost overruns. But the massive currency, labour, and commodity fluctuations of the late 2000s led many contractors to abandon the lump-sum pricing method in an attempt to manage sharp project cost escalations. Greer, Scott, et al, 'Middle East Constructing: Contracting in a Roller Coaster Market', *Oil and Gas Financial Journal* (Jan. 1, 2009)

95   *AME Info*, 'Prices Rocket for Qatar's GTL Projects', (Mar. 15, 2007).

96   *IHS Global Insight*, 'Qatar Eases Off the Gas: ConocoPhillips, Marathon GTL Projects Held Back', (Apr. 27, 2005).

97   'Culprits in Qatar', Ibid.

98   Irish, John, 'Qatar Looks to Finance $30bn Utility Expansion', *Arabian Business* (Jan. 23, 2008).

99   Sambidge, Andy, 'Qatar Aims to Cut Summer Power Blackouts', *Arabian Business* (Aug. 5, 2009); Qatar also instituted a comprehensive strategy to replace hundreds of old transformers with new high-voltage transformers. See *Arabian Business*, 'Pulling Power', (Aug. 16, 2008).

100 Siddiqi, Moin, 'Exceptional Energy Prospects for Qatar', *Oil Review* (Aug. 16, 2009).

101 Sambidge, Andy, 'Qatar Sees Large Increase in 2009 Power Demand', *Arabian Business* (May 7, 2009).

102 *The Peninsula*, 'Qatar-Power Generation to Take a Giant Leap', (Feb. 27, 2010).

103 Kahramaa took over the central planning and supervisory authority for the water and power sectors, as well as the managing authority of the transmission and distribution networks, from the Ministry of Electricity and Water in April 2000. .

104 Irish, John, 'Qatar Looks to Finance $30bn Utility Expansion', Ibid.

105 Attwood, Edward, 'Qatar Utility Eyes GCC Power and Water Projects', *Utilities-ME* (May 4. 2010).

106 At the time of writing, Qatar indicated interest in acquiring equity stakes in the French nuclear power producer, Areva SA. Bauerova, Ladka, et al, 'Qatar Leaders Confirm Interest in Acquiring Stake in Areva', *Bloomberg* (Mar. 25, 2010).

107 *AME Info*, 'Qatar: Diversification Efforts Real, But Hidden', (Mar. 22, 2006).

108 *MENAFN*, 'Qatari Petrochemical Production All Set for Expansion', (May 5, 2010).

109 Siddiqi, Moin, 'Exceptional Energy Prospects for Qatar', *Oil Review Middle East* (June 2007).

110 *Oil Review Middle East*, 'Exceptional Energy Prospects for Qatar', (June 2007).

111 Williams, Perry, 'Doubts Surface Over Ras Laffan', *Middle East Economic Digest* (Sept. 12, 2008).

112 Zhaoxia, Shu, 'Financial Crisis Impacts on Petrochemical Market Cycle', *China Chemical Reporter* (Apr. 16, 2009).

113 Stanton, Chris, 'Qatar Eases off on Gas-Fired Boom', *The National* (April 10, 2010). For LNG prospects see Chapter 10.

114 Farey, Ben, 'Qatar LNG Outlook May Rise After "Debottlenecking"', *Bloomberg* (Mar. 1, 2010).

115 al-Kaabi, Saad, Presentation at the 2009 International Petroleum Technology Conference, 'World Energy Challenges Endurance and Commitment' (Dec. 7, 2009).

CHAPTER 10

LNG IN QATAR

Andy Flower

Introduction

Qatar has made remarkable progress as an LNG producer since the first cargo of LNG was loaded at the end of 1996. Within ten years it had overtaken Indonesia to become the world's largest producer and it is now poised to strengthen that position as six of the world's largest LNG trains come on stream, taking annual production to around 105 Bcm/a (77.5 mtpa) by 2012, over three times the capacity of Malaysia, its closest competitor in 2009.

Qatar's success as an LNG producer is based on the North Field, part of which extends into Iranian waters where it is known as the South Pars field. Developing the resources to create an LNG business required the leadership of the Emir and Government of Qatar and the active involvement of many companies and individuals. Moreover, it took many years as is seen by the gap of over a quarter of a century between the discovery of the field and the start of LNG production.

The way in which Qatar has expanded its two LNG projects, Qatargas and RasGas, over the last decade has been impressive but the prospects over the next decade and beyond are uncertain. In 2005, the government announced a moratorium on further development of gas production from the North Field to allow the field's performance to be evaluated as total production rises to around 250 Bcm/a when all of its LNG, gas to liquids (GTL), pipeline gas exports and domestic gas projects under construction or in operation at the end of 2009 are producing at full capacity. The government wants to ensure that the rapid development of production does not put at risk the field's long-term performance and reduce the resources available to future generations. The moratorium, which was expected to last for two years when it was originally announced in 2005, is not now scheduled to end until 2014 at the earliest. Even if a decision is eventually made for further expansion of Qatar's LNG capacity, an outcome that is by no means certain, the pace of growth is likely to be slower than in the past and any new liquefaction capacity is unlikely to be on stream until around 2020 at the earliest.

The North Field

The North Field (see Map 9.1 in Chapter 9) was discovered in 1971 by Shell, who had been granted a concession covering Qatar's entire offshore continental shelf in 1952. The non-associated natural gas, which has a high condensate content, lies in four independent reservoir structures known as Khuff 1, 2, 3 and 4. Exploration and appraisal drilling has shown that the field covers an area of approximately 9700 square kilometres and extends into Iranian waters. Around 6000 sq km of the field is under Qatari territorial waters and 3700 sq km is under Iranian territorial waters.

It is estimated that the part of the field in Qatari waters contains 25.5 Tcm (900 Tcf) of recoverable natural gas reserves. A further 13 Tcm (460 Tcf) of recoverable reserves is in the Iranian part of the field. The total reserves of 38.5 Tcm represent just over 20 percent of the world's proved conventional gas reserves (i.e. excluding shale gas, coal bed methane, methane hydrates and other unconventional sources of natural gas). The Qatari section of the field is estimated to contain 10 billion barrels of recoverable condensate, the production and sale of which makes an important contribution to the economics of LNG and other gas-based projects.

It was clear soon after its discovery that the North Field contained very large reserves of natural gas but the full extent only became evident over time as appraisal and production wells were drilled. The current estimate of 25.5 Tcm was first announced in the early 2000s some 30 years after the field was discovered. Some observers question whether the recoverable reserves are really so large, pointing out that there has been no independent verification of the reserves estimate as, for example, would be required to meet US Securities and Exchange Commission (SEC) requirements. However, there can be little doubt that the North Field, together with South Pars, is one of the world's largest accumulations of natural gas and that it can support very high levels of production.

At the time of discovery of the North Field, the prospects for its development were limited. Qatar was a nation of less than 200,000 inhabitants and had a limited local demand for energy. Total energy consumption was marginally under 1 million tonnes oil equivalent (mtoe) per year, less than a twentieth of the level reached by 2008. Qatar already had a largely natural gas-based economy with 90 percent of its energy supply provided by natural gas produced in association with oil. Oil met the remaining 10 percent of energy supply. Natural gas consumption was divided almost equally between the industrial and power sectors.

There was no gas pipeline system in the Gulf region for the export of gas from the North Field and the limited demand for gas in neighbouring countries made the construction of export pipelines uneconomic. The LNG industry was in its infancy in 1971 with just three countries, Algeria, the USA (from Alaska) and Libya exporting LNG, and Brunei set to join them in 1972. Qatar's position in the Middle East put it at a competitive disadvantage to other potential producers who were closer to the growing markets in Asia and Europe and, therefore, enjoyed significantly lower transport costs.

The North Field was a stranded resource and no real progress was made in its development in the 1970s. The takeover of ownership and operatorship of Shell's concessions by the Qatar General Petroleum Corporation (QGPC), as Qatar Petroleum (QP)[1] was then known, in 1977 did nothing to enhance the prospects of the field being developed.

The Development of the LNG Option 1977 to 1984

Despite the expropriation of its assets in Qatar, Shell was still interested in participating in the development of the North Field and made proposals to QP for an LNG export project. By the late 1970s, Shell was well on its way to becoming the leading international oil company in the LNG business with the Brunei project, in which it was a major partner, in operation and plans for projects in Malaysia, Australia and Nigeria being developed. Its proposal was for a project in which QP would be the majority shareholder but Shell would be either the only, or the major foreign partner, with a share of up to 30 percent and would operate the liquefaction phase.

By the early 1980s, QP was actively planning the initial development of gas production for the domestic market followed by LNG production.[2] The LNG business globally was expanding rapidly, especially in Asia as demand grew in Japan and Korea was poised to become the second importer in the region. Indonesia had become an exporter with the start-up of the Bontang project in E. Kalimantan in 1977 followed by its second liquefaction plant at Arun in northern Sumatra, a year later. Abu Dhabi had become the Middle East's first LNG exporter with the start-up of the Abu Dhabi Gas Liquefaction Company (ADGAS) plant on Das Island in 1977 (see Chapter 12). The first of Malaysia's LNG plants, Malaysia Satu at Bintulu in Sarawak came into operation in 1983.

In June 1981, QP invited proposals from international oil companies to participate in the development of the North Field.[3] The companies were invited to make two separate but inter-dependent proposals.

i)   To provide technical support and advice to QP on the production, processing and transmission of about 2.4 Bcf/d (24.8 Bcm/a) of gas from the North Field to meet domestic energy requirements and to supply the gas required by the proposed liquefaction plant:

ii) To provide technical support for the development of a liquefaction plant capable of producing 6 mtpa (8.1 Bcm/a) of LNG and to participate in the joint venture company which would own and operate the plant.

The government's plan was that QP would own and operate the upstream part of the project, for the supply of gas for the domestic market and for the liquefaction plant. The government was prepared to allocate a 30 percent share in the liquefaction phase to foreign companies with QP retaining a 70 percent share. However, it wanted to divide the 30 percent allocated for foreign companies amongst at least four participants rather than follow Shell's proposal of having a single partner owning all, or the majority, of these shares.

BP and Total (then known as the Compagnie Française Des Pétroles or CFP) were selected as the preferred partners and entered into a Memorandum of Understanding (MOU) with QP in June 1983 setting out the main terms for the provision of services to QP and their participation in the liquefaction company, to be known as Qatargas.[4] The Joint Venture Agreement signed on 25 June 1984, expanded the MOU into a full contract amongst QP, BP and Total. BP and Total each had a 7.5 percent share in the liquefaction company with QP retaining an 85 percent share.[5]

The Joint Venture Agreement provided for 15 percent out of QP's 85 percent share to be allocated to one or more new partners. The understanding was that at least one new partner would be from Japan, which was expected to be the main market for the output. In September 1985, the Japanese Trading House, Marubeni, became the third foreign participant in Qatargas with a 7.5 percent share, which reduced QP's holding to 77.5 percent.[6] It was expected that a second partner from a country purchasing the output from Qatargas would be offered the remaining 7.5 percent share available for foreign partners at some stage in the future.

The Joint Venture Agreement established the principles of taxation and gas payments for the project. The basic tax rate was set at 55 percent of taxable income rising to 80 percent if the taxable income exceeded 30 percent of the capitalised expenditure of Qatargas less accumulated depreciation. There was no provision for a tax holiday at this stage.

QP committed that it, or a wholly-owned affiliate, would enter into a gas supply agreement to supply sufficient gas for the production up to 8.1 Bcm/a (6 mtpa) of LNG for customers. It was agreed that the price negotiations for the supply to the plant would be within a framework providing for a floor price, which would reflect 'the intrinsic value of the gas', and would take into account other relevant factors including the tax regime, the cost of the upstream gas production facilities and the liquefaction plant and the need for an acceptable rate of return on the investment in both the upstream facilities and the liquefaction plant. It was recognised that the aspiration of the participants in the Qatargas project was to earn a real after-tax discounted rate of return on the investment of 13 to 14 percent.

The structure of the project as envisaged in the Joint Venture Agreement is shown in Figure 10.1. The plan was for a three-phase development of both the upstream gas production and the liquefaction plant:

- ***Phase 1 – Conceptual Design***. The Statement of Requirements and the Project Definition Manual were to be prepared during this phase and the contracting strategy for engineering and construction were to be agreed. A survey of the LNG market would be carried out and letters of interest from potential customers would be received.

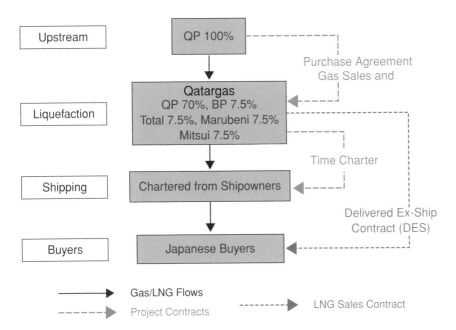

Figure 10.1: Qatargas I – Originally Planned Project Structure

The economics of the project would be evaluated and a finance plan developed.

- **Phase 2 – Basic Design and Tendering for Contracts**. The basic design, selection of the main processes to be used and the pre-qualification of contractors was to be carried out. On the marketing side, Letters of Intent with buyers were to be finalised. Agreements in principle for third party financing were to be approved and an Emiri tax decree obtained.

- **Phase 3 – Detailed Design and Engineering, Procurement and Construction**. In this phase, the main contract for the construction of the facilities was to be awarded, construction and pre-commissioning of the facilities would be carried out and the respective facilities handed over to the operators. Full Sales and Purchase Agreements (SPAs) with the buyers were to be in place, financing agreed and final agreements for the provision of shipping put in place.

The Joint Venture Agreement did not include target dates for the completion of the phases, probably because there was considerable uncertainty in 1984 about how quickly the project could be progressed. Qatargas would be the first LNG project developed in Qatar and there were questions over how long it would take to find buyers and what price they would be prepared to pay, making it difficult to evaluate the economics of the investment.

The twelve and a half year gap between the signature of the Joint Venture Agreement and the start of LNG production was longer than any of the individuals involved in negotiating the Agreement could have envisaged. However, the three phases of the development agreed in 1984 provided the road map for the project.

Early Stages of the Development of Qatargas 1984 to 1988

As is often the case with new LNG projects, good progress was made in the early stages on technical issues, including the basic design of the facilities, deciding their capacity and location and making initial cost estimates. However, progress on the marketing of the LNG and the negotiation of fiscal and gas supply agreements with the government was much slower and these issues began to determine the overall project schedule.

The initial plans were for the plant to be built at Umm Said (also known as Messaideed), 45 km south of the capital, Doha. Umm Said was first developed as an oil export terminal in 1949 when it was the only deepwater port in the country. Oil produced from the Dukhan field, in the west of the country, was piped across the country to Umm Said for export. Umm Said was also home to Qatar's oil refinery and fertiliser and petrochemicals plants. The plan was for a three-train LNG plant at Umm Said with each train having a capacity of 2 mtpa.

Finding buyers for the LNG proved to be difficult in the mid-1980s. Japan was the dominant force amongst LNG importers. It imported 73 percent of global LNG production in 1985[7] and it would have been impossible for Qatar to place all of its planned 8.1 Bcm/a (6 mtpa) output without a large share being sold to Japanese buyers. In the mid-1980s, Japan was recovering from the economic recession caused by the sharp rise in oil prices at the beginning of the decade (as a result of the Iranian crisis). Furthermore, in 1981, eight of Japan's largest LNG buyers had signed a Memorandum of Understanding (MOU) with Australia's North West Shelf (NWS) project for 7.8 Bcm/a (5.8 mtpa) of LNG.[8] By 1985 these buyers were deep in negotiation with the North West Shelf joint venture partners to turn the MOU into a full Sales and Purchase Agreement (SPA).[9] The 7.8 Bcm/a (5.8 mtpa) from the NWS project represented an increase of over 20 percent in Japan's annual imports compared with the level in 1985. There was very little room in the Japanese market for another 8.1 Bcm/a (6 mtpa) until the 1990s.

In 1985, when Qatargas's first marketing efforts were underway, Korea was on the point of emerging as Asia's second LNG buyer. Korea Gas had been established as the monopoly buyer of LNG and wholesaler of regasified LNG to city gas companies and to the Korea Electric Power Company (KEPCO). It was building an LNG terminal at Pyeongtaek in the north west of the country to receive imports from Indonesia. The Qatargas marketers considered that Korea had some potential as a supplement to Japan, but it was unlikely to be a core market.

Europe was the only other possible market for the output from Qatargas in 1985. The continent's four LNG importing countries at that time, France, Spain, Italy and Belgium, accounted for around a quarter of world LNG imports. One of the challenges for producers trying to sell LNG into Europe in the mid-1980s, was the competition from pipeline gas from the then Soviet Union and from Norway. The Qatargas marketing team made several visits to Europe between 1984 and 1988, to seek buyers who, while unlikely to be in a position to purchase a significant share of the planned output, might add to the sales to Asia. The USA, the only importer in the Americas until 2000, was not seen as a potential market for Qatargas in 1985. Natural gas prices there were low, it had a marginal 1.3 percent share of the global LNG market and three of its four receiving terminals had been mothballed because LNG imports could not compete with domestic gas production.

The collapse in oil prices at the end of 1985 put pressure on the economics of the Qatargas project. In 1984, when the Joint Venture Agreement was signed, the Brent crude oil price averaged $28.78/Bbl.[10] Japanese LNG import prices averaged $4.90/MMBtu and European gas prices $3.7/MMBtu,[11] prices that would have provided an acceptable rate of return for the partners in Qatargas. By 1987, the Brent crude oil price had fallen to $18.44/Bbl[12] and gas prices to $3.35/MMBtu in Japan and $2.59/MMBtu in Europe,[13] levels that made an investment in a new LNG project in Qatar look marginal at best.

Qatargas had started discussions with QP on gas supply and with the Qatari Government on the tax regime. However, it was impossible to enter into serious negotiations until more progress had been made marketing the LNG to provide a clearer indication of the potential revenues.

The Marketing Breakthrough 1988 to 1991

By 1988, four years after the signing of the Joint Venture Agreement, Qatargas had made progress on the technical aspects of the proposed project and the basis for the design of the facilities had been agreed. However, progress had been much slower on the commercial side of the project. The visits by the marketing team to Japan, Korea and Europe had indicated that there was some interest from potential buyers but none of them were prepared to move to the next stage of entering discussions on key issues such as price, volumes and timing. Qatargas's discussions with QP and the Government of Qatar were stalled awaiting progress on the marketing of the LNG.

The domestic gas phase of the project for which Total and BP provided technical support and advice was more advanced. Construction of the offshore facilities and a gas treatment plant at Umm Said had commenced by 1988.[14] The pipeline bringing gas from the offshore platforms to the plant at Umm Said made landfall at Ras Laffan in the north of the country and the onshore section by-passed the capital, Doha, on its way to Umm Said. This was the first, but certainly not the last, time that Ras Laffan featured in the development of Qatar's North Field gas reserves.

The breakthrough for the LNG phase came with the entry of the

Japanese trading house, Mitsui, as the fourth foreign partner in Qatargas. It took up the remaining 7.5 percent share reserved by QP for a new entrant in May 1989.[15] Mitsui brought with them the Japanese power company, Chubu Electric, based in Nagoya, as a potential buyer.

Mitsui is an experienced LNG company. It is the largest foreign shareholder in the ADGAS project (see Chapter 12) and it joined the North West Shelf project in 1983 when the Australian company, Woodside, reduced its share from 50 percent to 16.67 percent.[16] Chubu Electric is one of the main buyers of Indonesian LNG as a member of the so-called 'Western Buyers' consortium of six Japanese companies. It is also a member of the eight-company consortium that had committed to purchase 7.8 Bcm/a (5.8 mtpa) of LNG from Australia's North West Shelf project in December 1985.

In the late 1980s, Chubu was looking to increase its purchases of LNG largely for a new combined cycle gas turbine (CCGT) plant that it was planning to build at Kawagoe, near Nagoya. It wanted to be either the only buyer, or at least the dominant buyer, of LNG from a new project, mirroring the success it believed Tokyo Electric Power (TEPCO) had enjoyed as the sole long-term buyer from Abu Dhabi's ADGAS project. It felt that developing a close one-to-one relationship with a producer would give it more control and flexibility than was possible as a member of a consortium of buyers.

After initial discussions with the Qatargas marketing team and a visit to Doha, Chubu Electric indicated that they were interested in commiting to the 5.4 Bcm/a (4 mtpa) output from the first two trains and in taking an option on the 2.7 Bcm/a (2 mtpa) output from the third train. This was confirmed in a Letter of Interest from the Chairman of Chubu Electric in 1989.[17] Although the letter was not legally binding and, therefore, did not commit Chubu to anything more than entering into negotiations with Qatargas, coming from a Japanese buyer it was seen as a strong indication of Chubu Electric's intentions.

The Letter of Interest provided the partners with the confidence to increase their expenditure on the project by establishing a commercial and technical task force based in Doha to move the LNG project forward. The task force was led by a senior manager from QP and had representatives from all the shareholders. One of the main jobs for the team was to develop the Statement of Requirements which would be the basis for inviting contractors to bid to carry out Front End Engineering Design (FEED) for the liquefaction plant. The team also developed an economic model to provide the Joint Venture partners with estimates of the economics of the project. This provided the data needed by the teams negotiating with QP on the price of gas supplied to the plant and negotiating with the government on the fiscal regime for the project.

It was agreed that the base case economics would assume an oil price of \$20/Bbl in real terms which translated into an LNG price of \$3.45/MMBtu on a crude oil parity basis. The price of gas supplied to the LNG plant was assumed to be \$0.50/MMBtu escalating with the LNG price. This was based on indications from QP of the price they would be seeking. However, with the estimate of the capital cost of the plant having increased, the project was not economically viable with the tax regime included in the Joint Venture Agreement signed in 1984. It was clear that the tax regime, and probably the gas price, would have to be changed if the project was to go ahead.

The Government of Qatar recognised that Chubu's interest in committing to the output from the first two trains meant that, nearly two decades after the North Field was discovered, Qatar was positioned to earn revenues from the export of its gas. The project was offered a lower tax rate of 35 percent on its profits. The rate would be fixed and would not increase with the project's profitability as was originally proposed in the Joint Venture Agreement. The 35 percent tax rate has now been applied to all of Qatar's LNG developments. In addition, the government offered a ten-year tax holiday from the start of production. Qatargas's tax liabilities would still be calculated during the tax holiday and the assets would be depreciated but the Qatari Government would assume responsibility for the payment of the tax. The Joint Venture Agreement had stated that depreciation on capitalised expenditure would be charged on a straight-line, or other agreed basis, over ten years, which would have meant that the original expenditure would have been written off for tax purposes during the tax holiday. It was agreed to extend the period of depreciation to 15 years so that the project would still receive some tax relief from the depreciation of the assets after the end of the tax holiday.

The changes in the tax regime certainly improved the economics of the project but, at the assumed \$3.45/MMBtu LNG price, they still did not meet the aspiration of the partners for an after-tax discounted cash flow real rate of return of 13–14 percent, as was expressed in the Joint Venture Agreement. After some intense negotiations between QP and the foreign shareholders it was agreed that the price for gas supplied to the plant by QP would remain at \$0.50/MMBtu and would be indexed to the LNG price, i.e. the gas price would change by the same percentage as changes in the LNG price paid by buyers. However, up to 80 percent of the payment would be deferred until the cash flows from the project reached a level that would result in a real after-tax rate of return on the project of 12.8 percent or greater.

In parallel with the work of the Task Force in Doha and the negotiations with the Qatari authorities over the tax regime and gas payments, the marketing team was negotiating with Chubu Electric over the terms of a Letter of Intent (LOI) covering the sale and purchase of 5.4 Bcm/a (4 mtpa) of LNG with an option for Chubu to purchase a further 2.7 Bcm/a (2 mtpa). Meetings were held in the UK, France and Japan and the LOI was finalised in Nagoya on 15 January 1991, the day that the First Gulf War started. The plan was to initial the LOI that day but when news of the bombing of Baghdad came through the Qatargas team expected that Chubu would request a postponement. In the event, Chubu took the decision to go ahead with the initialling, an important sign of the buyer's commitment to Qatargas.

The LOI covered the main issues in any long-term LNG contract: duration, volumes, take or pay and downward quantity tolerance, and left the more detailed clauses for the full SPA. The LNG was to be sold on a Delivered Ex-Ship (DES), which meant that Qatargas took the responsibility for providing the ships and transporting the LNG to Japan. The clause on pricing was vague with wording to the effect that the price would be agreed before start-up of deliveries and would be 'in the range of prices for similar projects delivering to Japan at that time'. This is an approach to pricing that is unlikely to be repeated since, as will be discussed below, it took over three years from the start-up of deliveries for a price to be agreed.

The Restructuring of the Upstream Phase

Shortly after the LOI was finalised, QP approached each of the shareholders to inform them that it proposed to change the upstream arrangements. It had negotiated an agreement with the French company, Elf, for the latter to develop upstream production facilities in Qatar in return for a share of the condensate production. Elf would not receive any income from the production or sale of natural gas, which would remain the property of QP. Thus, the agreement with Elf was effectively an option for QP to call for the production of gas without linking it to a specific project. QP told its partners in Qatargas that it now proposed to implement the agreement with Elf to provide gas supply to the project.

The response of the Qatargas shareholders was that, if the Government of Qatar was now prepared to have foreign companies participate in the upstream development, they wanted to be involved themselves, since it would allow a closer integration between the two phases of the project, simplifying the structure and reducing the risks. They were also concerned that Elf's proposed upstream development was low cost and looked technically risky. The foreign partners did not consider this an acceptable basis for investment in a multi-billion dollar LNG project. Their position was that an LNG project requires a reliable and stable supply of gas for the 20 years or longer life of the project to remunerate the investment and to ensure that the contractual commitments with the buyer will be met.

BP, Mitsui and Marubeni favoured a joint proposal by the Qatargas shareholders to take over responsibility for the upstream development but Total, concerned that its main French competitor Elf was moving into the Middle East, which Total saw as being its sphere of interest, decided to approach QP separately and offer the same deal as had been agreed with Elf. QP accepted Total's proposal in mid-1991.[18] Total invited BP, Mitsui and Marubeni to participate in the Production Sharing Contract it had signed with QP. The other three foreign partners were concerned that Total was proposing the same low cost development as Elf, which they saw as involving unacceptable technical risks, especially when a multi-billion dollar investment in the liquefaction plant and ships depended on its performance. However, enhancing the design to reduce the risk would involve extra costs and lower the rate of return on the upstream investment to an unacceptable level.

BP's Withdrawal from Qatargas

Despite the progress that the Qatargas project was making by mid-1991, BP was beginning to review its continued involvement in the project. Its doubts about the investment in Qatargas were triggered by a combination of its own need to reduce capital investments and concerns about the direction the project was taking.

BP decided that it had to respond to the effect of low oil prices on its cash flows by withdrawing from some of the oil and natural gas projects in its portfolio, thereby reducing its future capital investment programme. As part of that process, it reviewed all of its planned projects to identify those that showed the lowest returns on investment and were not seen as being core to its long-term strategy. The Qatargas project had lower returns than many other of its projects and, at that time, BP did not give high priority strategically to LNG, especially in a country like Qatar, where it did not believe there would be an opportunity for either follow-on LNG investments or to participate in upstream exploration or downstream oil product marketing.

BP was also concerned at the lack of alignment amongst the share-holders in Qatargas, which was brought into focus by Total's decision to 'go it alone' in securing a position for itself in the upstream development rather than working with the other foreign partners. Support by Total for unproven French heat exchanger technology in the LNG plant, rather than the established Air Products and Chemicals Inc (APCI) process, which had been used in most of the world's operating LNG plants and was preferred by the other partners including QP, was another area of major disagreement amongst the partners.

A further uncertainty for BP was whether the fiscal and gas payment arrangements, which had been agreed with the government, would endure over the long term especially after the project came into operation and started to generate the large cash flows needed to remunerate the capital investment in the project. BP's perception of this risk had been heightened by an ongoing dispute with the Abu Dhabi Government over the tax and gas payments arrangements agreed at the time the ADGAS project was developed (see Chapter 12). Finally, BP felt that the project needed clear leadership, which was not being provided by the existing joint venture structure.

In November 1991, the decision to withdraw from the project was taken at the most senior level in BP and work began on an exit strategy that would minimise the damage to the project and to BP's relationships with the other partners. It was especially concerned over the effect of its withdrawal on Chubu Electric, with whom it had an existing relationship through the sales of LNG from the North West Shelf project in which BP was a 16.67 percent shareholder.[19]

In January 1992, the exit plan was activated. The Government of Qatar, the partners in Qatargas and Chubu Electric were all informed within the space of a few hours of BP's decision. They were told that it was final and not negotiable, a position which BP maintained despite high level attempts by some of the companies to persuade it to reconsider. BP had ensured that in all the agreements that had been signed over the years it had the option to withdraw from the project and that it would not break any contracts by withdrawing before a Final Investment Decision (FID) was taken for the project. The Joint Venture Agreement provided that any company withdrawing from the project before FID had to hand its shares back to QP without receiving compensation.

Mobil Replaces BP

Qatargas was left in a position in early 1992 where it was making progress towards FID around the end of the year or early in 1993. The Sales and Purchase Agreement (SPA) with Chubu Electric was close to completion, the award of the FEED contract was imminent and the agreements for tax and gas payments had been finalised. The withdrawal of BP raised doubts about the viability of the project and Qatar needed a major player with LNG experience to replace BP, if the project was not to be derailed.

The Qatar Government cast around for a new partner and found several companies interested. The company that stood out as providing the assurance that was needed was Mobil, an experienced LNG player through its involvement since the early 1970s in the Arun project in Indonesia. It would also bring a US company into the development of Qatari LNG, an important consideration for the government in the aftermath of the first Gulf War. Mobil was looking for a new LNG investment to replace its involvement in the Arun project, which was entering into a long-term decline as the reserves around the plant were depleted. A major exploration effort to find replacement reserves in northern Sumatra had been largely unsuccessful and Mobil had to find a new LNG opportunity if it was to maintain and expand its involvement in the business.

Mobil was not an easy catch for Qatar to land. Its starting position in the negotiations in many ways mirrored BP's objectives before it withdrew. It wanted the upstream development to be more closely integrated with the liquefaction phase, including a more robust technical design for the upstream facilities; it wanted clear leadership by one partner and guarantees that the fiscal and gas payment agreements would not be changed. It also sought a larger share in the project than the 7.5 percent on offer.

The Qatari authorities were prepared to make some concessions to meet Mobil's requirements but they were unwilling to unwind the arrangements that were already in place for Qatargas. They offered Mobil participation in a second project, which would be developed in a way that would largely meet its objectives. As a result, RasGas was born as a second Qatari project, which would have a fully integrated structure and in which Mobil would be the dominant foreign shareholder.[20]

Qatargas Restructuring and FID 1992–93

The Qatargas project underwent some restructuring when Mobil joined it. Mobil and Total's shares in Qatargas were increased from 7.5 percent to 10 percent each and QP's share reduced to 65 percent. Marubeni and Mitsui's shares remained at 7.5 percent each. The other partners agreed to participate in Total's upstream production sharing contract. QP took a 65 percent share and Mobil a 10 percent share, in line with their respective holdings in Qatargas. However, the Japanese participants were only willing to take a share of 2.5 percent each, leaving Total with a 20 percent share. The new structure of the project is shown in Figure 10.2. Mobil's shares are shown as being held by ExxonMobil (EM), the company formed after the merger of Exxon and Mobil in 1999.

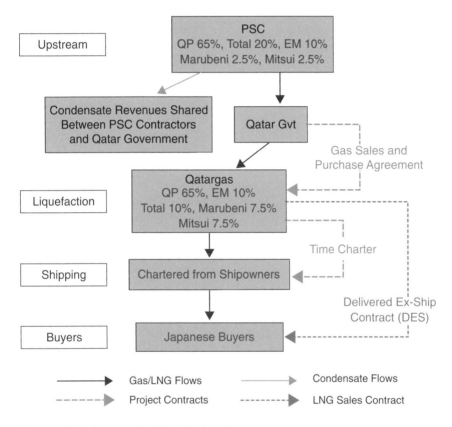

Figure 10.2: Qatargas I – Final Project Structure

The upstream facilities were redesigned to meet the requirements of the liquefaction project resulting in an increase in the estimated capital cost. However, the Government of Qatar agreed to reduce its shares of the condensate revenues in favour of the participants in the upstream development to provide the additional revenues needed to remunerate the increased capital cost.

Ras Laffan Industrial City

The Government of Qatar decided in 1990 that Ras Laffan, in the north of the country, would be the location for industries using gas from the North Field, including Qatargas and any future LNG developments. At the time the decision was made, Ras Laffan was a largely uninhabited and undeveloped part of Qatar. The government planned to allocate blocks of land for LNG plants, condensate refineries, petrochemical plants, natural gas treatment plants for domestic gas supply and power generation. It also planned the development of a large port for the export of LNG, condensate and other products at an estimated cost of close to $1bn.

The port facilities were designed to have four LNG berths, six berths for condensate and chemicals, a sulphur loading berth and berths for the receipt of materials. The project also included the dredging and blasting of a 5 km channel to deep water and a turning basin.

The foreign partners initially expressed concern that the transfer of the Qatargas plant to Ras Laffan could delay the project and add to the cost compared with building it at the Umm Said location with its existing infrastructure. They were also concerned about the possible interruptions to the use of the port because of weather delays or congestion in the channel linking it to deep water. These concerns proved to be unfounded and construction work on the port was substantially completed by September 1996, three months before the first LNG cargo was loaded and exported.

The development of Ras Laffan Industrial City and Port proved to be an inspired decision by the government since it provided the space needed to support the rapid expansion of LNG capacity and other gas-based industry that would not have been possible at Umm Said.

Construction and Start-up of Qatargas

With Mobil on board as a replacement for BP and the project restructured, Qatargas progressed to a Final Investment Decision (FID) in May 1993. The Sales and Purchase Agreement with Chubu Electric for 5.4 Bcm/a (4 mtpa) and an option for a further 2.7 Bcm/a (2 mtpa) was signed on 13 May 1992.[21] The Japanese company, Chiyoda, was selected as the Engineer, Procure and Construct (EPC) contractor in early 1993 and the EPC contract was signed in May 1993, at the time FID was taken.[22]

Qatargas did not want to invest in the ships required to deliver the LNG to Chubu Electric opting instead to charter them from a consortium of Japanese shipping companies, Mitsui OSK Line, NYK and K-Line. Seven ships were initially chartered to deliver 5.4 Bcm/a (4 mtpa) from the first two trains with a further three ordered subsequently for the output from train 3. The ships were constructed in the Japanese yards of Mitsubishi Heavy Industries, Mitsui Heavy Industries and Kawasaki Heavy Industries and were delivered into service between 1996 and 2000.[23]

The Qatargas project had become very much a Japanese project with the buyer a Japanese power utility, the EPC contractor Japanese, the ship-owners Japanese and the ships being built in Japan so it was not surprising that the financing for the onshore liquefaction plant came from commercial banks in Japan and the Export-Import Bank of Japan (now the Japan Bank for International Co-operation – JBIC). The ship-owners also financed their investment in the LNG tankers from Japanese sources.

Upstream production and the liquefaction plant were organised as two projects and were financed separately. The upstream development was the only part of the project that attracted non-Japanese financing. The revenues for this part of the project came entirely from condensate production, which was to be marketed internationally and it received funds from export credit agencies (ECAs) and commercial banks in several countries.

The total cost of the first 5.4 Bcm/a (4 mtpa) phase of the project was around $6bn, divided approximately $1bn for the upstream, $3bn for the two-train plant and $2bn for the seven ships. The separate financing of the upstream production and the liquefaction facilities made the financing more complex than for an integrated project since inter-creditor agreements were needed between the consortia of institutions financing each phase of the project. The financing of the Qatargas plant was finalised in late 1993.[24]

Chubu Electric decided in 1994 that it did not have the demand to justify committing to the output from the 2.7 Bcm/a (2 mtpa) third train and it brought together a consortium of six other Japanese utilities to purchase the LNG on the same terms as it had agreed with Qatargas for the output from the first two trains. The volumes of LNG each of the seven utilities committed to purchase are shown in Table 10.1.

The sales and purchase agreement for the train 3 volumes was signed on 31 December 1994 and commitment to the construction of the train was made in 1995 by exercising the option in the original EPC contract with Chiyoda. The timing allowed the construction of the plant to take place as a single project avoiding the cost of demobilising and remobilising the workforce.[25]

Table 10.1: Qatargas Train 3 Contracted Volumes

Company	Volume	
	in Bcm/a	in mtpa
Tokyo Gas	0.47	0.35
Osaka Gas	0.47	0.35
Toho Gas	0.23	0.17
Tohoku Electric	0.70	0.52
Kansai Electric	0.39	0.29
Tokyo Electric	0.27	0.20
Chugoku Electric	0.16	0.12
Total	**2.70**	**2.00**

Source: Author's research

The construction of the facilities progressed on schedule and the first train started to produce LNG in late 1996 with the first cargo being loaded at the end of December.[26] It arrived at Chubu's newly constructed receiving terminal in Nagoya in early January 1997 having completed the 6400 nautical miles (11,800 km) voyage in around two weeks. Train 2 was commissioned in the second half of 1997 with train 3 following in 1999.

The commissioning and build up from the three trains went relatively smoothly and they quickly showed that they could sustain production at levels significantly above their design capacity of 2.7 Bcm/a each. By mid-2001, the capacity of the three-train plant was being estimated at 10.1 Bcm/a (7.5 mtpa), some 25 percent above Qatargas's contractual commitments with its Japanese buyers. The capacity of the plant was further enhanced by the debottlenecking of all three trains taking their capacity to around 4.4 Bcm/a (3.3 mtpa) each and the total capacity, at what is now known as Qatargas I, to close to 13.5 Bcm/a (10 mtpa).

The increase in capacity allowed Qatargas to diversify the markets for its output. In May 2001, it signed an agreement with Gas Natural of Spain for the supply of 1 Bcm/a (0.7 mtpa) for eight years.[27] Supplies under the contract commenced in 2001 and the contract has since been extended to 2012. A second contract for the same volume of LNG but this time on a DES basis started in 2002 and will also run through to 2012. In January 2004, a third contract with Gas Natural was signed, this time for 2 Bcm/a (1.4 mtpa) for 20 years from 2005 to 2025.[28] In late 2002, an agreement was signed with BP for the supply of 1 Bcm/a for three years commencing in the third quarter of 2003.[29]

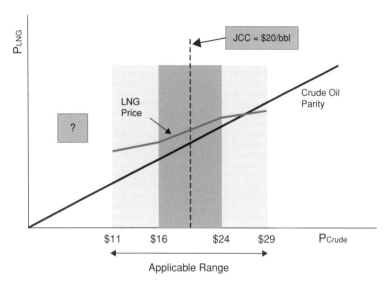

Figure 10.3: The Japanese "S"-curve

A major issue for Qatargas in the relationship with its Japanese buyers has proved to be pricing. The wording in the LOI that the price would be agreed three months before start-up and would be in the range of similar projects supplying LNG to Japan at that time was carried through into the full Sales and Purchase Agreement. The parties did meet as agreed before start-up but it quickly became clear that they had very different interpretations of what the clause meant. They failed to reach agreement before the first cargo was loaded and deliveries began on the basis of provisional prices, which continued for over three years until agreement on the price was reached in 2000.

The pricing approach that was eventually agreed was an 'S'-curve which had been adopted by 2000 for most of the projects supplying Japan. Figure 10.3 illustrates the traditional 'S' curve used in the 1990s and early 2000s. The price of the LNG is linked to Japanese Custom Cleared Crude Oil Price (JCC), often referred to as the Japanese crude cocktail, which is the average price of crude oil imported into Japan each month. In the mid-range of oil prices, which in the 1990s and early 2000s was seen as being from around $16/Bbl to $24/Bbl, for every $1/Bbl increase in the oil price the LNG price went up by $0.1485/MMBtu. From $11/Bbl to $16/Bbl and from $24/Bbl to $29/Bbl the relationship between the crude oil price and the LNG price was halved i.e. the LNG price changed by around $0.07/MMBtu for each

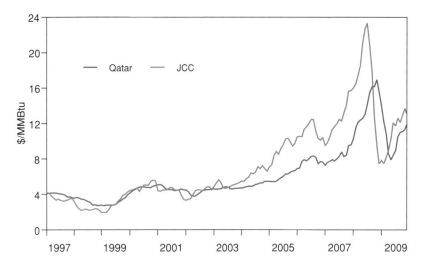

Figure 10.4: Monthly Price of LNG from Qatar Delivered to Japan and the JCC Price, January 1997 to January 2010

$1/Bbl movement in the oil price. This approach mitigated the effect of low oil prices on the seller and gave the buyer some compensation at high oil prices.

In 2000, when Qatargas reached agreement with its Japanese buyers on the pricing formula, a JCC price of $20/Bbl was seen as the long-run average price of crude oil and prices below $11/Bbl and above $29/Bbl were seen as 'exceptional circumstances'. It was agreed that the parties would meet and discuss how to price the LNG should the oil price be outside the $11/Bbl to $29/Bbl range.

JCC went above $29/Bbl in November 2003 and remained above that level into 2010, leaving Qatargas without an agreed price with its buyers. However, deliveries continued using provisional pricing as the parties entered into discussions on how to respond to the new pricing environment. A partial agreement was eventually reached in 2009, which fixed the prices for the period 2004 to March 2009 but left some unresolved issues regarding future prices. Figure 10.4 compares the average price of LNG from Qatar delivered to Japan with the average JCC price in $/MMBtu over the period from start-up of deliveries in January 1997 to February 2010 as reported in monthly data issued by the Japanese Ministry of Finance.

The price of Qatari LNG delivered to Japan was over $4/MMBtu when deliveries started but declined to $2.75/MMBtu by end 1998 as oil prices fell. By the beginning of 2000 they were back above $4/

MMBtu and continued on an upward trend peaking at $16.95/MMBtu in 2008 before falling to $7.90/MMBtu in June 2009. By January 2010, they were back up to $11.92/MMBtu. For a project that was planned assuming an average LNG price of $3.45/MMBtu in real terms, the prices realised in the first 12 years of operation, together with the higher than expected output, suggest that it has proved to be a good investment for its shareholders.

RasGas

A key part of the agreement between the Government of Qatar and Mobil in 1992 was the establishment of a second liquefaction company, Ras Laffan Liquefied Natural Gas Company Limited, which is commonly referred to as RasGas.[30] The joint venture agreement was signed in 1993 with QP taking a 70 percent share and Mobil 30 percent. RasGas was given the right to drill for and produce gas within a specified block in the North Field and to produce and export up to 13.5 Bcm/a (10 mtpa) of LNG.

RasGas I

RasGas I, as the project is now known following the addition of more trains from 2004, is structured as an integrated project with RasGas owning and operating the upstream production facilities, the pipeline to shore and the liquefaction plant (Figure 10.5). It pays a royalty on the natural gas produced and supplied to the liquefaction plant and on the condensate sales.

The initial plan was for a two-train plant with each train having a capacity of around 3.2 Bcm/a (2.4 mtpa). The target markets were Korea and Japan since Europe was still not paying prices that would remunerate the investment. Indeed a planned liquefaction project in Qatar to supply the Italian market had been abandoned after it became clear that it was not economically viable because of prices in Italy.[31]

The RasGas I project saw Japan as a potential market even after Qatargas's success in selling 8.1 Bcm/a (6 mtpa) to Japanese buyers. In 1996, the Japanese trading houses, Itochu and Nissho Iwai (whose shares were subsequently transferred to LNG Japan, a joint venture between Nissho Iwai and Sumitomo) signed a Heads of Agreement to purchase 4 percent and 3 percent respectively in the RasGas I project.[32] As part of the deal, the trading houses agreed to assist the project in

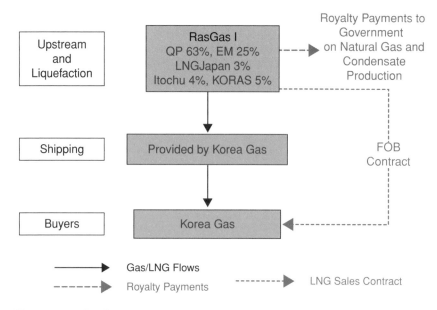

Figure 10.5: RasGas I – Project Structure

marketing its LNG in Japan and to provide QP with a loan facility to assist it in funding its equity share of the investment. In the event, RasGas I did not find any buyers in Japan and the output from the first two trains was committed to Korea Gas. As part of the deal with Korea Gas a consortium of Korean companies, under the name of KORAS, was given the right to purchase a 5 percent share in RasGas I. KORAS, which is led by Korea Gas and includes Hyundai, SK Energy, Daewoo and Samsung, eventually secured its position in RasGas I in September 2005.[33] The participation of the Japanese trading houses and of KORAS resulted in QP's share in RasGas I being reduced to 63 percent and ExxonMobil's to 25 percent (Figure 10.5). In October 1995, RasGas I signed its first long-term agreement with Korea Gas for 3.2 Bcm/a (2.4 mtpa) of LNG from the first of the planned two trains.[34] The sale was on an FOB basis and the duration was 25 years from the date of first delivery, which was expected to be in 1999. 90 percent of the price escalated with the JCC oil prices and the remaining 10 percent escalated at 3 percent per annum. The agreement was unique at that time in having a floor price, which was set at $2.50/MMBtu and was to be increased by 3 percent at the beginning of each contract year until the debt raised by RasGas I to fund the project had been repaid.

The floor price was seen by the RasGas I shareholders as being important in providing assurance to lenders. However, it was not liked by Korea Gas who turned to Oman LNG rather than RasGas I for its next long-term LNG purchase, signing an agreement to purchase 5.5 Bcm/a (4.1 mtpa) of LNG for 20 years from 2000. The contract with Oman LNG did not have a floor price, sending a clear message to RasGas I that it would have to agree to remove its floor price if it wanted Korea Gas to increase its contract volumes. In June 1997, a second agreement was signed with Korea Gas increasing the contract volumes to 6.4 Bcm/a (4.8 mtpa) and dropping the floor price entirely.[35] By that time the financing for RasGas I was in place and Mobil had to give assurances to the financiers that it would provide support for the project should the LNG price fall below the level of the previously agreed floor price.

The estimated cost of the project was $2.5 billion for a single train development and $3.4 billion for two trains. The project successfully raised $2.55 billion of finance in December 1996, which included $1.2 billion of bond financing, a first for an LNG project, $0.9 billion from Export Credit Agencies and $0.45 billion from commercial banks. The financing was completed before the planned output from the second train had been sold.[36]

RasGas I entered into a lump sum contract with a joint venture of JGC and Kellogg for the construction of a single train liquefaction plant with a nameplate capacity of 3.5 Bcm/a (2.6 mtpa). The expectation was that it would be able to produce at 115 percent of that level, i.e. at 4 Bcm/a (3 mtpa). The contract with JGC and Kellogg had an option for a second train of the same design and capacity, which RasGas I was able to exercise when Kogas doubled its contracted volumes. Output from each of RasGas I's trains reached 4.5 Bcm/a (3.3mtpa), 27 percent above their nameplate capacity, soon after start-up and has remained at that level.

Production from train 1 commenced in April 1999, before the start date in the contract with Korea Gas, and the first cargoes were delivered on a spot basis to the USA.[37] The first cargo for Korea was loaded onto the Korea Gas chartered tanker, the *SK Summit*, in August 1999. The second train came into operation in March 2000 and output built up quickly thereafter. By September 2001, the first loan repayments were made and the first dividends were paid to shareholders.

At the end of 2001, Qatar had five LNG trains in operation with a total capacity of around 18.9 Bcm/a (14 mtpa) and the country produced 18.3 Bcm/a (13.6 mtpa) of LNG in 2002 (Figure 10.6), making it the world's fourth largest LNG producer, only six years after operation commenced. However, Qatar's ambitions did not stop there. Before RasGas I came into operation QP and ExxonMobil were already

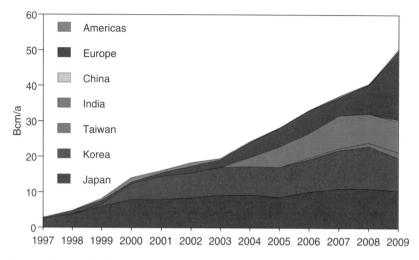

Figure 10.6: LNG Exports from Qatar, 1997–2009

planning further expansion of the plant's capacity, taking advantage of the enormous reserves of the North Field and the infrastructure that had been developed at Ras Laffan.

RasGas II

In July 1999, RasGas agreed to supply the Indian company Petronet, which was planning to build an LNG receiving terminal at Dahej in Gujarat State, with 6.75 Bcm/a (5 mtpa) of LNG.[38] The agreement provided for the possibility of increasing the volume to 10.1 Bcm/a (7.5 mtpa). This represented Qatar's first diversification of long-term supply from the Japanese and Korean markets, where prices had supported the construction of new, greenfield facilities. A combination of falling LNG construction costs globally, the lower unit costs of an expansion compared with a greenfield plant and the economies of scale through constructing larger LNG trains, helped underpin the economics of sales to India, which, at the time the agreement was signed, was seen as being unlikely to be able to pay prices at the levels of those in Japan and Korea.

RasGas II was established in March 2001 to develop three more trains at the RasGas site, each with a nameplate capacity of 6.3 Bcm/a (4.7 mtpa). The shareholdings in RasGas II were the same as for RasGas I when it was originally established in 1993, i.e. QP 70 percent and ExxonMobil 30 percent.[39]

RasGas II is an integrated project covering the upstream facilities and the liquefaction plant. It was agreed that all the trains on the site, including any future developments, would be operated by the RasGas Company Limited on behalf of RasGas I, RasGas II and RasGas III, which was established in 2005 to own trains 6 and 7 on the site (see below).

FID for train 3 was taken in late 2001 and the EPC contract awarded to a joint venture of Chiyoda and Technip.[40] The train commenced production in early 2004 and the first cargo was delivered to the Dahej terminal in February of that year.[41] The sales were on an FOB basis with Petronet chartering two ships on a long-term basis to transport the LNG. After several rounds of negotiation and various proposals on price, RasGas II agreed to a fixed price of $2.53/MMBtu for five years from the start of deliveries. The estimated transport cost from Ras Laffan to Dahej is $0.27/MMBtu resulting in a delivered price of $2.80/MMBtu for the LNG. The relatively low price compared with those paid by Qatar's Japanese and Korean buyers helped Petronet develop the downstream market for regasified LNG. The period of fixed prices ended in December 2008 and the following month a five-year transition to a 100 percent linkage with crude oil prices commenced. When that is complete at the end of 2013, the RasGas FOB price with Petronet, at an oil price of $80/Bbl, will be around $10/MMBtu.

In June 2001, RasGas II signed a long-term agreement to supply 4.7 Bcm/a (3.5 mtpa) to Edison in Italy,[42] providing further evidence that the economics of expansion could support sales to markets where prices were lower than in Asia. At the time the agreement was signed, the start-up of deliveries, which were to come from train 4 at the RasGas site, was scheduled for 2005. Delays in progressing Edison's planned terminal in the northeast of Italy resulted in the start-up of deliveries being deferred and in November 2003 the agreement was amended to increase the contracted volumes to 6.2 Bcm/a (4.6 mtpa) and delay start-up until 2008.

The opposition in Italy to an onshore terminal led Edison to opt instead for a gravity-based structure positioned around 15km offshore the Veneto coast in the north east of the country. However, progress continued to be delayed until ExxonMobil and Qatar Petroleum stepped in each taking a 45 percent share in the terminal, leaving Edison with a 10 percent share. However, Edison retained 80 percent of the capacity to import the LNG it had contracted from RasGas (the remaining 20 percent had to be offered to third parties as required under Italian regulations).[43] The terminal eventually received its first cargo in August 2009.[44]

The sale was on a DES basis, the first time that LNG from RasGas had been sold in this way, requiring the project to acquire shipping capacity. RasGas II's first time-charter was signed in July 2002 and was followed by charters for a further twelve ships. They were all built in Korean shipyards and were delivered into service between 2004 and 2007.

RasGas II's marketing efforts continued to show positive results through agreements with CPC in Taiwan in March 2003 for 4 Bcm/a (3 mtpa) from 2008,[45] with Endesa in Spain for 1.1 Bcm/a (0.8 mtpa) from 2005 in July 2003,[46] and with Distrigas in Belgium in February 2005 for 2.8 Bcm/a (2.1 mtpa) from 2007.[47]

In addition, in June 2004, RasGas committed to 4.6 Bcm/a (3.4 mtpa) of capacity in the expansion of Fluxys LNG's terminal at Zeebrugge in Belgium.[48] This agreement gave RasGas the right, but not the obligation, to deliver LNG to the terminal, effectively providing a flexible outlet in Europe for LNG cargoes that were surplus to the needs of its long-term buyers. In June 2007, RasGas transferred its capacity rights at Zeebrugge to EdF Trading and signed an interruptible contract to deliver up to 4.5 Bcm/a of LNG to EdF Trading at the terminal for four and a half years.[49] The agreement maintains RasGas's option to deliver LNG to the terminal without the need to develop a trading and marketing function.

RasGas II's success in marketing its planned output enabled it to commit to trains 4 and 5. The EPC contract for train 4 was awarded to a joint venture of Chiyoda and Technip in October 2002 and production commenced just over three years later. FID on train 5 followed in July 2004. Its start-up in December 2006 took the total capacity of RasGas's five-train plant to 28 Bcm/a (20.7 mtpa) and Qatar's total capacity to over 40 Bcm/a (30 mtpa). In 2006, with all eight trains at the Qatargas and RasGas plants in operation, Qatar produced 33.1 Bcm (24.4 mt) of LNG and in the process it overtook Indonesia to become the world's largest LNG producer.[50]

As Table 10.2 shows, the long-term commitments secured by RasGas II exceeded the capacity of the three-train facility. However, some of the commitments will be met from spare capacity in RasGas I and through the diversion of RasGas III cargoes from the US market. The delays in the start-up of the contract with Edison Gas in Italy and the flexibility of the arrangements to supply EdF Trading at the Zeebrugge terminal positioned RasGas II to trade LNG on a short- and medium-term basis, including entering into a medium-term contract to supply a total of 5.18 Bcm (3.84 mt) of LNG to Korea Gas from late 2004 to April 2008.

Table 10.2: Contracted LNG from RasGas

Buyer	Market	Basis	Volume in Bcm/a	in mtpa	Duration
RasGas I					
Korea Gas	Korea	FOB	6.5	4.8	1999–2024
RasGas II					
Petronet	India	FOB	6.8	5.0	2004–2029
Edison Gas	Italy	DES	6.2	4.6	2009–2033
Endesa	Spain	DES	1.1	0.8	2005–2024
Distrigas	Belgium	DES	2.8	2.1	2007–2026
EdF Trading**	Belgium/Europe	DES	4.6	3.4	2007–2011
RasGas III					
Korea Gas	Korea	DES	2.8	2.1	2007–2026
Petronet Expansion	India	FOB	3.4	2.5	2009–2029
CPC*	Taiwan	FOB	4.1	3.0	2008–2032
QP & ExxonMobil***	USA	DES	18.3	8.0	2010–2034
Total RasGas			**49.0**	**36.3**	

*   Initially supplied from RasGas II
**   Interruptible Contract
***   Actual volumes will balance deliveries to other markets

Source: Author's research

The design of the RasGas II facilities included two technical innova-
tions for Qatar. Firstly, the trains extract LPGs (propane and butane)
from the LNG and export them as separate products. Both Qatargas I
and RasGas I leave the LPGs mixed in with the LNG, which increases
the heating value and meets the specifications for natural gas in the
Korean and Japanese markets. However, with some of the output from
RasGas II and future trains expected to be sold to Europe and the
USA, where the requirement is for LNG with a lower heating value,
the extraction of LPGs was a necessary addition to the plant design.
Secondly, the Ras Laffan Helium project to produce liquid helium from
all the trains at Qatargas and RasGas was implemented in parallel with
RasGas II and it came into operation in August 2005.

Qatargas II

The RasGas II project was developed in a conventional way with the
LNG being sold on long-term contract to gas and power companies

who were responsible for providing receiving terminal capacity and for marketing the regasified LNG or the power downstream of the terminal. The only commitment made by RasGas II that did not fit with that model was the booking of capacity at the Zeebrugge terminal in Belgium, and even there a decision was made to transfer the commitment to EdF Trading albeit on a medium-term basis.

The plans for Qatargas II, which were announced by QP and ExxonMobil in October 2002,[51] broke new ground. The LNG was to be supplied to the UK through a terminal at South Hook near Milford Haven in south west Wales, which would be owned and operated by QP and ExxonMobil with ExxonMobil Gas Marketing Europe (EMGME) as the buyer of the regasified LNG. No third party would be involved in the purchasing of the LNG or the marketing of regasified LNG downstream of the terminal. This was made possible by the liquidity of the UK natural gas market.

Natural gas is widely traded in the UK with the price set at the National Balancing Point (NBP), a virtual point in the UK's natural gas network. Any gas entering the system is deemed to be at the NBP, where it is bought and sold both on a prompt and on a forward basis. At any point in time, the NBP price is the level at which natural gas supply with demand is in balance. Lower supply will result in prices moving upwards to increase supply and reduce demand while a reduction in demand will cause prices to fall reducing supply and increasing demand until they move back into balance. In this type of market, a seller can find a buyer for its regasified LNG provided it is sold at a price netted back from the market price, which, in the case of the UK, is the NBP. This means that LNG sellers are 'price takers' and their revenues will depend on the level of prices in the market, which can be very volatile since they are influenced by events such as temperature, supply of natural gas from other sources and market demand, over which the seller has no control.

LNG producers selling into this type of market need to ensure that costs are kept as low as possible to minimise the risk of making losses when prices fall. In the LNG business, the principal way of reducing costs has been to take advantage of the economies of scale, i.e. increasing the capacity of the facilities to minimise unit costs. QP and ExxonMobil used this approach in deciding to build the largest ever liquefaction trains and LNG ships of up to twice the capacity of those already in operation at the time the decision was made. When the Qatargas II project was announced the capacity of each train was put at 9.5 Bcm/a (7 mtpa) but the eventual design capacity is 10.5 Bcm/a (7.8 mtpa), over 50 percent larger than the RasGas II trains. Two sizes of ships were selected, 210,000m^3 to 217,000m^3 capacity, designated as Q-flex ships, and 263,000m^3 to 267,000m^3 capacity, designated as Q-max ships. The term Q-max comes from the fact that these ships are the largest that can be built with a draft that allows them to enter the Ras Laffan port. The channel linking the port to the sea had to be dredged to allow access to LNG ships and there are restrictions on the draft of ship that can use it. The Q-flex ships are smaller giving them more flexibility to unload at receiving terminals around the world, although in many cases terminals have had to be modified to allow this to happen.

Qatargas II was planned as a two-train, 21 Bcm/a (15.6 mtpa) plant and the South Hook terminal was designed with the capacity to receive the entire output. Fourteen ships, eight Q-flex and six Q-max, were ordered from Korean yards to transport the LNG. FID was taken in December 2004 and the EPC contract was awarded to the joint venture of Chiyoda and Technip. Start-up was originally scheduled for late 2007.[52]

The structure of the Qatargas II project, as initially planned by QP and ExxonMobil, is shown in Figure 10.7. It is the first project to use what has been called the 'integrator model' in which shareholders are involved in all phases of the project, from natural gas production through to the delivery of regasified LNG into the market. The only facilities not owned by the partners are the ships, which, in the case of the Q-flex ships, were chartered from joint ventures of the Qatar Gas Transport Company (known locally as Nakilat), which was formed in 2004, and independent ship-owners. The Q-max ships have been chartered from the Qatar Gas Transport Company.

Raising finance for the project, which was successfully completed in 2004, involved some major challenges. Firstly, the financing covered the upstream production facilities, the liquefaction plant and the regasification terminal, the first time these three phases of an LNG project had been financed together. The total estimated cost was $10.15 billion, $9.4 billion for the facilities in Qatar and $0.75 billion for the receiving terminal in the UK. The entire output was to be sold in the UK, where it represented around 20 percent of market demand. The price was linked to the NBP price, the first time that a project had been financed on the basis of hub-based pricing rather than an oil-linked price formula. The liquefaction trains were the largest ever built and used many items of equipment that had never been used before in a liquefaction plant, including the APX heat exchangers designed by the US company, APCI, to provide the required level of production. Although the ships were financed separately, the fact that they would

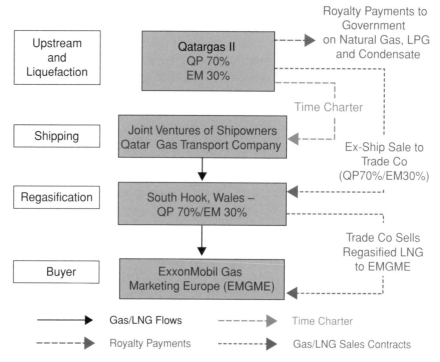

Figure 10.7: Initial Structure of Qatargas II

be the largest ever built was another risk factor that had to be taken into account by financiers.

The success that Qatar had had in developing and operating the Qatargas I and RasGas I projects was a major factor in Qatargas II being able to raise 50 percent debt from the commercial banks and the Export Credit Agencies. ExxonMobil lent the project around 20 percent of the cost and the remaining 30 percent was provided as equity from the shareholders.

Total, who had played an important role in the development of Qatargas I, was left out of the expansion of the project despite its Chairman having announced at the Gastech Conference in Doha in October 2002 that his company would commit to underwrite and market the output from a 5 mtpa fourth Qatargas train.[53] Target markets would be Europe and the USA, including Total's own gas systems in Europe. He indicated that Total would also consider an option on providing similar support for a fifth train, but said he wanted to take it one train at a time. Despite seeing their proposals rejected in favour of ExxonMobil's more ambitious plans, Total continued to press for participation in Qatargas II.

Eventually, in February 2005, after FID had been taken and construction of the two trains had commenced, agreement was reached for Total to take a 16.7 percent share in the second train of the Qatargas II project. ExxonMobil's share of train 2 was reduced to 18.3 percent and QP's to 65 percent. Total agreed to take delivery of 7 Bcm/a (5.2 mtpa) from the output from the train at terminals in the UK, France, Mexico and USA;[54] 2.5 Bcm/a (1.85 mtpa) out of these volumes were to be delivered to the South Hook terminal in the UK and Total became an 8.35 percent partner in the facility. QP's share was reduced to 67.5 percent and ExxonMobil's to 24.15 percent as a result of the deal. Figure 10.8 shows the final structure of Qatargas II and the flow of output for the two trains as was expected at the time the structure was finalised. However, as is discussed below, a strategy of diverting LNG to alternative markets has been adopted by Qatar and, hence, the actual delivery of cargoes will almost certainly vary from the original plans.

Following Total's participation in the project, Qatargas II signed a contract for the supply of 0.95 Bcm/a (0.7 mtpa) of LNG to the Altamira terminal in Mexico, in which Total is a shareholder. Qatargas has also signed a contract with CNOOC in China for 2.7 Bcm/a (2 mtpa).[55] Initial deliveries under this contract, which came into operation in late 2009, were from the Qatargas II trains but it is understood that Qatargas III will be the long-term source of the LNG after it comes on stream.

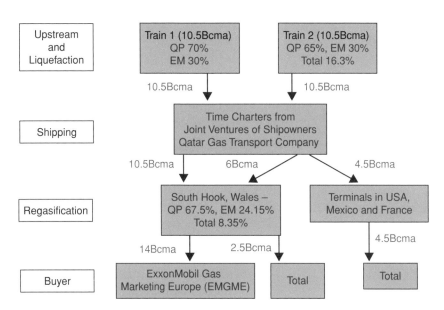

Figure 10.8: Final Structure of Qatargas II

The commissioning of the first of the Qatargas II trains started in the third quarter of 2008 but with many pieces of equipment never used before in a liquefaction plant having to be tested, progress was cautious and first production was not until March 2009. However, it was almost immediately closed down again and production did not restart until June 2009. Output built up rapidly and the train was operating at design capacity by September 2009. The Q-flex ship, the *Tembek*, delivered the first cargo to the South Hook terminal in March 2009[56] but the LNG was sourced from older trains rather than Qatargas II. Nevertheless, after the start-up of the new train a regular flow of cargoes began arriving at South Hook and a total of 5 Bcm (3.7 mt) was delivered in 2009. The commissioning of the second of the Qatargas II trains commenced in September 2009. Progress was much smoother than for the first train and by October it was operating at full capacity.

RasGas III

The next phase of the expansion of Qatar's LNG capacity was back at RasGas where QP (70 percent) and ExxonMobil (30 percent) agreed to build two 10.5 Bcm/a (7.8 mtpa) trains, taking the total capacity of the plant to 49 Bcm/a (36.3 mtpa). The project was launched in October 2003 when the two companies signed a Heads of Agreement to supply 21 Bcm/a to the US market.[57] The proposed project structure was essentially the same as the initial structure for Qatargas II (see Figure 10.7), with the LNG delivered to a purpose built receiving terminal, in this case Golden Pass, to be located on the Texas side of the Sabine River.

FID was taken in September 2005[58] and the first train was scheduled to start-up in late 2008 and the second train around nine months later. The project suffered some delays with the first train eventually starting commissioning in August 2009, followed by the second train in February 2010. The Golden Pass terminal, which was originally scheduled to be commissioned in mid-2009, was badly damaged by Hurricane Ike in 2008, causing a delay of at least 12 months. RasGas entered into agreements to deliver LNG to Chevron at the Sabine Pass terminal in Louisiana, to Sempra at the Cameron terminal also in Louisiana and to Statoil at the Cove Point terminal in Maryland over the period from 2009 to the end of 2010, by which time Golden Pass was expected to be in operation.

As discussed above, commitments to the output from RasGas II exceeded the capacity of the three trains and some of the contracted volumes will be delivered from RasGas III, releasing capacity at the Golden Pass terminal. As a result, it was decided that some of the output from the Qatargas III project (see below) would be delivered to the terminal and ConocoPhillips, QP's partner in Qatargas III, became a shareholder in the facility. However, by early 2010, all of the Qatargas III output had been fully committed or provisionally committed to alternative destinations in China and Poland and, hence, the main flow of cargoes into Golden Pass will probably be from RasGas.

RasGas II and RasGas III were financed jointly in 2005. A total of up to $10 billion was raised through a combination of bonds, bank debt and shareholder loans. $4.6bn were made available immediately with a further $5.4bn to be drawn down as the construction progressed. The interest rates on the bank debt were amongst the lowest achieved for an LNG financing, demonstrating the confidence of the finance community in Qatar's ability to develop major projects and their acceptance of both the Indian market risk, which represented around 25 percent of the output, and prices linked to Henry Hub for sales to the USA, which was planned to be the destination for around 50 percent of the output from the five trains at the time the financing was completed.

Qatargas III and IV

ExxonMobil was the main participant in the expansion of Qatar's LNG capacity, as the only foreign participant in RasGas II and RasGas III and in Qatargas II, until Total became a partner in the second train of the latter project. However, there are risks in being dependent on one partner and the Government of Qatar looked for new partners to participate in further expansion of the Qatargas plant.

ConocoPhillips was the first new participant in LNG in Qatar when, in July 2003, QP and ConocoPhillips announced that they would develop Qatargas III, a 10.5 Bcm/a (7.8 mtpa) train to supply the US market.[59] Shell followed in February 2005 with its agreement to develop Qatargas IV, a 10.5 Bcm/a (7.8 mtpa) train, jointly with QP, the seventh at the Qatargas site.[60] The original plan was for QP to have a 70 percent share and ConocoPhillips a 30 percent share but, subsequently, QP reduced its share to 68.5 percent through an agreement for Mitsui to take a 1.5 percent share.

Shell's agreement with QP also covered the development of the Pearl project, a 140,000 barrels per day gas to liquids plant to be built in Ras Laffan and supplied with gas from the North Field. The output from Qatargas IV was intended to be delivered to the US market through capacity at the Elba Island terminal for which Shell had made a long-term commitment.

It was decided that Qatargas III and IV would be constructed under a single EPC contract, which was awarded to the joint venture of Chiyoda and Technip in December 2005.[61] Start-up of the two trains was originally scheduled for late 2009 and 2010 but it slipped by around one year with Qatargas III expected to start commissioning in late 2010 and Qatargas IV following about three months later.[62]

The Diversion of Cargoes from the UK and the US Markets

Asia provided the markets for 83 percent of Qatar's LNG production between 1997 and 2008. However, in 2009 the start-up of the first three of the mega-trains together with the impact of recession on the demand for LNG in Japan and Korea had a significant impact on the regional shares of Qatar's LNG sales as is shown in Figure 10.6. Asia's share declined to 60.5 percent in 2009 as an increasing number of cargoes were delivered to the South Hook terminal in the UK, the Zeebrugge terminal in Belgium and in the last few months of 2009, the Adriatic LNG terminal in Italy, taking Europe's share to 38.2 percent with the Americas (USA and Canada) accounting for the remaining 1.3 percent.

The diversification of Qatar's export markets is expected to continue. In the early days of the expansion of Qatar's production capacity, it appeared likely that approximately one-third Asia, one-third Europe and one-third the Americas would be the likely outcome. However, the decision to anchor the sale of the output from the six mega-trains in the flexible UK and US gas markets has positioned Qatar to divert cargoes on a short-, medium- or long-term basis to alternative markets for strategic reasons or to take advantage of higher prices. By the end of 2009, a number of full Sales and Purchase Agreements and Heads of Agreement had already been signed with buyers in China, Thailand, Poland and Mexico and discussions, which had the potential to lead to further diversions, were ongoing.

It is not always clear which trains will supply each of the new sales commitments. Furthermore, there have been transfers amongst phases and between Qatargas and RasGas to meet commitments in advance of the start-up of trains. Tables 10.2 and 10.3 summarise the apparent position in terms of the contractual commitments by RasGas and Qatargas respectively in the first half of 2010.

China has been the main market for diverted volumes with 6.8 Bcm/a (5 mtpa) of Qatargas volumes already diverted from the US

Table 10.3: Contracted LNG from Qatargas

Buyer	Market	Basis	Volume in Bcm/a	in mtpa	Duration
Qatargas I					
Chubu Electric	Japan	DES	5.4	4.0	1997–2021
Japanese Consortium	Japan	DES	2.7	2.0	1999–2021
Gas Natural	Spain	FOB	1.9	1.4	2001–2012
Gas Natural	Spain	DES	1.9	1.4	2005–2024
Total Qatargas I			**11.9**	**8.8**	
Qatargas II					
QP and ExxonMobil*	UK	DES	12.4	9.2	2009–2033
Total	UK	DES	2.6	1.9	2009–2033
Total	France and USA	DES	3.6	2.7	2009–2033
Total	Mexico	DES	0.9	0.7	2009–2033
Chubu Electric	Japan	DES	1.6	1.2	2008–2012
Total Qatargas II			**21.1**	**15.6**	
Qatargas III					
QP and ConocoPhillips*	USA	DES	5.1	3.8	2010–2034
PGNiG**	Poland	DES	1.4	1.0	2014–2033
PTT**	Thailand	DES	1.4	1.0	2011–2021
CNOOC**	China	DES	2.7	2.0	2009–2033
Total Qatargas III			**10.5**	**7.8**	
Qatargas IV					
QP and Shell*	USA	DES	5.5	4.1	2011–2035
Dubai Suppy Authority***	Dubai	DES	0.9	0.7	2011–2021
PetroChina	China	DES	4.1	3.0	2011–2031
Total Qatargas IV			**10.5**	**7.8**	
Total Qatargas			**53.9**	**40.0**	

*   Actual volumes will balance deliveries to other markets
**   Source of supply not confirmed
***   Shell has agreed to supply 0.65 to 1.5mtpa to Dubai from its portfolio including
  at least 0.65mtpa from Qatargas IV. Excludes volumes under preliminary
  agreements between Qatargas and CNOOC and PetroChina for upto
  9.5Bcm/a (7mtpa) signed in November 2009. If agrements are finalised for
  the full 9.5Bcm/a (7mtpa) the LNG is expected to be supplied from Qatargas
  III and Qatargas IV reducing the maximum volume available for the USA to
  1.1Bcma (0.8mtpa)

Source: Author's research

market through SPAs finalised in April 2008.[63] The LNG to meet these commitments will come from the Qatargas III and Qatargas IV projects and these sales have been included in Table 10.3. In November 2009, it was announced that Qatargas had made a preliminary agreement to supply 4.1 Bcm/a to CNOOC from 2013 and 2.7 Bcm/a to PetroChina, with supply in this case expected to start by 2015.[64] The agreement with CNOOC said that the supply of a further 2.7 Bcm/a (2 mtpa) is also being contemplated. It is likely that, if these preliminary agreements are confirmed, the deliveries to CNOOC will be from Qatargas III and those to PetroChina from Qatargas IV, which would be in line with the sources of supply for the SPAs signed in April 2008.

If these preliminary agreements are turned into full SPAs then Qatar would be supplying 16.3 Bcm/a (12 mtpa) to China by around 2015, which would overtake the contracted volumes to Japan and make China the country's largest LNG market in Asia. Qatar appears to be on course to have a sales portfolio by the mid-2010s of around 50 percent supplied to Asia, 35 percent to Europe and 15 percent to the Americas but this could change if further deals with Asian buyers, or indeed buyers elsewhere in the world, are concluded. In March 2010, the Indian Oil Secretary said that India was in negotiation to purchase an additional 4 mtpa of Qatari LNG by 2013.[65] The Qatari Deputy Prime Minister and Energy Minister, Abdullah Al-Attiyah confirmed that discussions were underway adding that he sees China and India as the most important markets for Qatar.

The Effect of the Moratorium on the Development of New Projects Based on North Field Reserves on Qatar's LNG Projects

In the early 2000s it seemed there was no limit to the expansion of Qatar's gas-based industries. Construction started on six mega-trains at the RasGas and Qatargas LNG sites, the Oryx gas-to-liquids (GTL) plant was also under construction and plans for the Pearl GTL plant, in which Shell is a partner with QP, were well advanced and further production of gas for the local market was being planned. There was talk of Qatar becoming the 'GTL capital of the world' as at least a further four GTL projects were being discussed. In April 2005, Qatar's Energy Minister surprised the gas world by announcing a moratorium on further development of gas production from the North Field to allow an analysis to be made of its performance as production increased to around 250 Bcm/a[66] by 2012.

When the moratorium was announced the expectation was that it would last for two years. At the end of 2009, Qatari officials indicated that 2014 was the earliest date that the studies could be concluded and a decision made on whether and how rapidly to allow further development of production from the North Field.[67] The decision to impose a moratorium appears to have been triggered by concerns that the performance of some of the wells already drilled on the North Field had not lived up to expectations. The government sees the gas reserves in the North Field as the country's heritage, which it is duty bound to develop in the optimum way to ensure that future generations derive maximum benefit. No indications have been given on the progress of the studies of the field's performance nor has there been any indication about the possible outcome in terms of future development if and when the moratorium is lifted.

The moratorium has had a much greater impact on Qatar's plans for GTLs than on its LNG projects. In April 2005, the RasGas III and Qatargas III and IV projects were still at the planning stage but their progress towards FID continued without any delays. GTL projects proposed by ConocoPhillips, Marathon and Sasol Chevron, involving the production of a total of 330,000 bbl/day, were immediately put on hold for three years and eventually dropped. Work on ExxonMobil's project to produce 154,000 bbl/day of GTLs continued for nearly two more years but in February 2007 it was announced that it would be replaced by the Barzan project to produce gas for the domestic market.[68] Plans to expand QP and Sasol's Oryx GTL plant, the first phase of which started production in 2006, have also been put on hold.

The Long-term Outlook for LNG in Qatar

The future development of LNG production is uncertain as a result of the moratorium. The six 10.5 Bcm/a (7.8 mtpa) liquefaction trains will be in operation by 2011 taking total LNG capacity to 105 Bcm/a (77.5 mtp/a) but there are no firm plans for further trains despite sites in Ras Laffan Industrial City being allocated for future LNG developments. Foreign companies are queuing up to partner QP in the next LNG project but they will have a long wait since the only reasonably firm plans to expand capacity are through the debottlenecking of the six mega-trains.

At the World Gas Conference in October 2009, Faisal Al Suwaidi, Qatargas Chairman and Chief Executive Officer, announced that the capacity of each of the mega-trains could be increased by 2.7 Bcm/a (2 mtpa) through debottlenecking.[69] He said that the 16.2 Bcm/a (12 mtpa) of additional capacity would only be developed after the moratorium has been lifted.

Debottlenecking is a relatively low cost and effective way of adding capacity to an existing LNG plant. It is impossible to say at this stage what the potential cost would be in Qatar or how long it will take since it will depend on the modifications to the trains that will be required. The debottlenecking of plants in other locations has cost as little as 10 percent of the cost per tonne of annual production capacity for the original plant. Implementation is likely to be on a train-by-train basis with the main changes being made during the maintenance shutdown of individual trains. If this is the case, the 14 mtpa of additional capacity would probably be brought on stream over the period 2015 to 2017 or 2018.

It is premature to speculate on whether Qatar will embark on further expansion of its LNG capacity. Even if a decision was made in 2014 to construct further LNG trains, it would not be until around 2020 that they could come into operation, after taking into account the time needed for FEED and construction.

Conclusions

Although it took Qatar 25 years from the discovery of the giant North Field to the export of its first LNG, the story since then has been one of rapid expansion, which has established the country as the world's leading LNG producer by a wide margin with exports set to reach 105 Bcm/a (77.5 mtpa) by 2012. Qatar has left behind other major producers such as Algeria, Indonesia and Malaysia, who took much longer to build-up their exports and who are all now facing a levelling off and decline of production because of limited gas reserves and a policy of prioritising domestic gas consumption over LNG exports. Only Australia amongst the world's current and potential LNG producers has the potential to challenge Qatar's leadership in the future, but that will not happen for many years since Australia's LNG projects are based on a number of gas fields located around the country with their development depending on the decisions of many companies.

Qatar's emergence as an LNG exporter was not easy. It took many years for a clear strategy for LNG production and exports to be developed and for Qatar to convince potential buyers that it would be a reliable source of LNG supply. It would not have been possible without the strong leadership of the Emir and senior government ministers, who ensured that key decisions were taken and implemented quickly. The decision in 1990 to locate the first liquefaction plant, Qatargas, at Ras Laffan rather than Umm Said was one of the most important since it positioned the country to embark on a major expansion of capacity after the first projects were implemented.

The government also recognised the importance of partnering with major players in the LNG industry who could bring expertise and experience to the development of the projects. It was prepared to adapt project structures to make them more attractive to foreign investors and it changed the fiscal regime to improve the economics and encourage investment. The agreement to integrate the upstream gas production with the liquefaction plant was particularly effective in producing project structures that aligned the interests of Qatar and its foreign partners.

However, first Shell and then BP withdrew from Qatari LNG. Shell, who discovered the North Field, did not pursue participation in the first project, Qatargas, when it was unable to achieve its target of being the only, or the leading, foreign shareholder. However, Shell made its comeback into Qatar in 2005 when it signed an agreement for a 30 percent share in Qatargas IV, part of a deal which included participation in the Pearl Gas-to-Liquids project. BP withdrew in 1992 after nearly ten years participation in the development of the first Qatargas project and at a stage where the project was on the verge of being launched. BP's reasons were partly its own cash flow problems in the early 1990s but its senior management lacked the vision to recognise the potential that Qatar offered as a major LNG exporter as they focused on the relatively modest returns the first project offered rather than the longer-term opportunity. BP's loss was Mobil's (and subsequently ExxonMobil's) gain as it replaced BP and became the main foreign partner in the rapid expansion of Qatar's LNG industry.

By 2011, Qatar will have 14 operating LNG trains with a capacity to produce 105 Bcm/a (77.5 mtpa) of LNG, a port capable of loading at least ten LNG ships simultaneously and a fleet of 69 owned and long-term chartered LNG ships. It has adopted a flexible marketing strategy to optimise the value of this portfolio while ensuring that it meets the obligations to supply its long-term customers around the world. Its geographic location distant from the world's major gas markets was a disadvantage in the 1980s when it was attempting to secure its first customers but in 2010, with transport cost having been reduced, in part by its fleet of Q-flex and Q-max tankers, it is well positioned between the main markets in the Atlantic and Pacific Basins.

There is considerable uncertainty over the future expansion of

Qatar's LNG production. The moratorium on the further development of production from the North Field, which was announced in 2005 and is not expected to be lifted until 2014, has called a halt to any further increases in capacity. The outcome of the ongoing studies of the North Field's performance will be an important factor in determining the government's strategy for LNG after the moratorium ends. The debottlenecking of the six mega-trains, which will add around 14 mtpa of capacity is likely to be the first addition to capacity if the decision is made to continue the expansion of LNG production. It is less certain whether the government will agree to the development of new LNG trains. Even if the outcome is to continue to invest in LNG production, it will be around 2020 before the next expansion of output can come into operation.

Notes

1   The current company name Qatar Petroleum (QP) will be used in the remainder of this chapter.
2   'Liquefied Natural Gas from Qatar – the Qatargas Project' by Kohei Hashimoto, James Elass and Stacy Eller is part of the Geopolitics of Natural Gas, a joint project of the Program on Energy and Sustainable Development at Stanford University and the James Baker III Institute for Public Policy at Rice University, published in December 2004.
3   *World Gas Report*, 'CFP seeks Qatar LNG partnership', 20 July 1981, p. 6.
4   'The Qatar government has signed a memorandum with BP and Compagnie Française des Petroles' subsidiary, Total', Lloyd's List International, 22 June 1983.
5   Dixon, A. and Lawson, D., 'Qatar concludes deal to develop world's biggest known gas field', *Financial Times*, 28 June 1984.
6   *Financial Times*, 'Marubeni of Japan is to have a 7.5% stake in a gas project offshore the state of Qatar', 6 September 1985.
7   'LNG trade and Infrastructures', Cedigaz, Paris February 2004.
8   *World Gas Report*, 'Japan, Australia gas deal moves much closer', 6 July 1981, p. 6.
9   'Nearly 6m tonnes of liquefied natural gas is to be bought by Japanese power and gas companies from the Australian North West Shelf project', Lloyd's List International, 3 August 1985.
10 *BP Statistical Review of World Energy 2009*.
11 *BP Statistical Review of World Energy 2002*.
12 *BP Statistical Review of World Energy 2009*.
13 Ibid.
14 *Middle East Economic Digest (MEED)*, 'North Field drilling proceeds as firms bid for procurement', 19 August 1988.

15 *Reuters News*, 'Mitsui buys 7.5 pct share in Qatargas', 18 May 1989.

16 Stern, Jonathan P., *Natural Gas in North America and Asia*, Gower: 1985, pp. 184–5.

17 *Reuters News*, 'Japanese reported interested in buying Qatar gas', 18 December 1989.

18 Dow Jones Newswires, 'Total-Compagnie Française in Pact for Qatar Project', 29 May 1991.

19 *Oil and Gas Journal*, 'BP withdraws from Qatar North LNG project', 20 January 1992, p.31.

20 *Dow Jones Newswires*, 'Total-Compagnie Française in Pact for Qatar Project", 29 May 1991.

21 *Financial Times*, 'Chubu signs up Qatar LNG', 15 May 1992.

22 *International Gas Report*, 'Chiyoda lands $1.4bn Qatar Contract', 11 June 1993, p.4.

23 *MEED*, 'Qatargas signs vessel chartering agreement', 25 October 1993.

24 *MEED*, 'Finance fixed for Qatargas downstream works',, 20 December 1993.

25 *MEED*, 'Japan to sign up for Qatargas supplies', 12 December 1994; Lloyd's List International, Special Report: 'Japan shares big LNG deal', 27 December 1994.

26 *Oil and Gas Journal*, 'Qatar ships first LNG to Japan, signs accord', Vol. 94, No. 53, 30 December 1996, p.28; and Vol. 94, No. 53, 24 January 1997, p.28.

27 *MEED*, 'Spain signs for Qatar LNG', 18 May 2001.

28 *Gas Matters Today*, 'Gas Natural Signs for Another 2Bcm/yr of Qatar LNG', 15 January 2004.

29 *World Gas Intelligence*, 'Qatar LNG's Mega Growth', Vol XII, No 42, p.1, 16 October 2002.

30 '*MEED*, Qatar General Petroleum Corp establishes Ras Laffan Liquefied Natural Gas Co', 16 July 1993.

31 *International Gas Report*, 'Italian Mid-East gas projects plunge into turmoil', 21 January 1994, p.1; *Platt's Oilgram News*, 'News Briefs: Qatar/Italy', 17 February 1994, Vol. 72, No. 34, p.6.

32 *Gas Matters*, 'Trading companies to take equity in Ras Laffan', December 1996, p.31; *Energy Alert*, 'Itochu, Nissho Iwai Buy Shares In Qatar Firm', 10 December 1996, Vol. 28, No. 50.

33 *Energy Argus Gas and Power*, 'Korea Gas Takes RasGas Stake', Vol. V, No. 19, 28 September 2005.

34 *International Gas Report*, 'Rasgas clinches KGC deal', 27 October 1995, p.12.

35 *Reuters News*, 'Qatar, South Korea sign deal to double gas supply', 30 June 1997.

36 *Reuters News*, 'Qatar's Rasgas raises $1.2 billion via two bonds', 12 December 1996; Energy Alert, 'Qatar's Rasgas Secures $2.25 Bln Financing', 30 December 1996.

37 *API News*, 'RasGas LNG plant receives first gas from the offshore complex', 22 April 1999.

38 *International Gas Report*, 'Qatar's RasGas seals Indian Petronet deal', 6 August 1999, p.4.
39 *Middle East Daily Financial News*, 'Qatar's USD2bn third LNG JV', 27 March 2001.
40 *International Gas Report*, 'Technip JV to boost Qatargas', 29 October 2001, p.23; *Gas Matters Today*, 'Construction of third Ras Laffan train now under way', 15 January 2002.
41 '*Gas Matters Today*, Dahej LNG Shipment Sets Sail from Qatar', 27 January 2004.
42 *Oil and Gas Journal*, 'Edison Gas', 2 July 2001, p.9.
43 *International Gas Report*, 'Exxon/Qatar take Italy LNG stakes', 21 November 2003, p.10.
44 *International Gas Report*, Adriatic LNG sends gas to the grid', 28 September 2009, p.27.
45 About RasGas, Milestones pages on RasGas website: www.rasgas.com
46 *World Gas Intelligence*, 'Endesa Goes Shopping', 6 August 2003.
47 *Reuters News*, 'Qatar to sign final LNG supply deal with Distrigas', 28 February 2005.
48 *Oil and Gas Journal*, 'Fluxys agrees LNG supply', 12 July 2004, p.9.
49 'EDF Trading Takes RasGas Volume and Capacity at Zeebrugge', Heren LNG Markets H.L.M 3.6.4, 22 June 2007.
50 BP *Statistical Review of World Energy* 2007
51 *World Gas Intelligence*, 'Qatar LNG's Mega Growth', Vol. XII, No. 42 p.1, 16 October 2002.
52 *World Gas Intelligence*, 'QP, ExxonMobil Finalize UK Supply Venture', Vol. XV, No. 51, p.2, 22 December 2004.
53 *World Gas Intelligence*, 'Qatar LNG's Mega Growth', Vol. XII, No. 42, p.1, 16 October 2002.
54 *Gas Matters Today*, 'Total Buys 5.2mtpa from Qatargas II and Takes a 16.7% Stake', 28 February 2005.
55 'CNOOC and PetroChina Join the Ranks of Qatar's Asian LNG Customers', Heren LNG Markets, HLM 4.4.2, 11 April 2008.
56 *Platts LNG Daily*, 'UK's South Hook Terminal Receives First Cargo', Vol. 6, no. 54, 20 March 2009.
57 *Gas Matters Today*, 'Qatar Petroleum Sign Deal to make RasGas II Largest Exporter of LNG to USA', 16 October 2003.
58 *World Gas Intelligence*, 'Qatar Contracts Flow', Vol. XVI, No. 39, 28 September 2005.
59 *World Gas Intelligence*, 'Conoco's Qatari Partnership', Vol. XIV, No. 29, 16 July 2003.
60 *Gas Matters Today*, 'Qatargas-4 Deal with Shell Takes Qatar's Planned LNG Output to 77mtpa by 2010', 29 February 2005.
61 *Gas Matters Today*, 'Qatar Petroleum, ConocoPhillips and Shell Sign Multi-Billion Dollar LNG Deals', 21 December 2005.
62 ICIS Heren Global LNG Markets, 'Qatargas-3 Slips Back to Q4', Vol. 6.14, 7 May 2010.

63 *World Gas Intelligence*, 'Qatar in China', Vol. XIX, No. 16, 16 April 2008.
64 ICIS Heren Global LNG Markets, 'Qatargas Diversions Reset Supply, Demand', Issue No 5.45, 20 November 2009.
65 *Platts LNG Daily*, 'India Plans to Lift Qatari LNG Purchases to 11.5mt/year by 2013', Vol. 7, Issue 54, 22 March 2010.
66 *World Gas Intelligence*, 'Qatari Delays', Vol. XVI, No. 18, 4 May 2005.
67 ICIS Heren Global LNG Markets ,'Qatar Rolls Back North Field's Moratorium Decision', Issue No 5.25, 19 June 2009.
68 *Gas Matters Today*, 'ExxonMobil Cancels Qatar GTL Project but Wins Share in North Field Barzan Project', 21 February 2007.
69 ICIS Heren Global LNG Markets ,'Qatar to Nudge 90mtpa After Debottlenecking – Al Suwaidi', Issue No 5.39, 9 October 2009.

CHAPTER 11

NATURAL GAS IN OMAN

David Ledesma

Introduction

The development of oil and gas in Oman led to the commercialisation of gas in the 1990s and the development of LNG export projects. Gas in Oman is a key energy source providing valuable LNG export revenues and a fuel to drive economic growth through power generation and industrial development. This chapter will show how moves to commercialise gas in the 1990s led to the development of Oman LNG, and later Qalhat LNG. Since 2006/07, with the growth of domestic demand and limited increases in production, Oman has become short of gas. This has resulted in some new projects being deferred and LNG export volumes curtailed so that gas can be used domestically. In parallel, Oman has sought to expand overseas through the government-owned Oman Oil Company (OOC) and to import gas from neighbouring countries. The country is currently seeking to grow its gas production through increased exploration, but new reserves are more costly to develop and do not contain as high a level of natural gas liquids as the older fields did.

The country is located strategically outside the Straits of Hormuz, has seen considerable economic growth over the period 2005–2009.[1] The economy is still dominated by oil and gas despite government policies to diversify away from energy. In a press conference on 2 January 2010 Minister of National Economy and Vice Chairman of the Financial Affairs and Resources Council Ahmed Macki said that in 2010 oil and gas exports would represent 76 percent of total Omani revenues (down from 78.8 percent in 2005), with gas contributing 12.5 percent, or $2.08 billion (a 19.4 percent increase over 2009), and oil 63.5 percent.[2] The gas sector is therefore an important revenue earner for the Sultanate.

---

* The author would like to thank his friends in Oman, UK and around the world who assisted with this research. I would also like to thank *Middle East Economic Survey* for providing access to their publication.

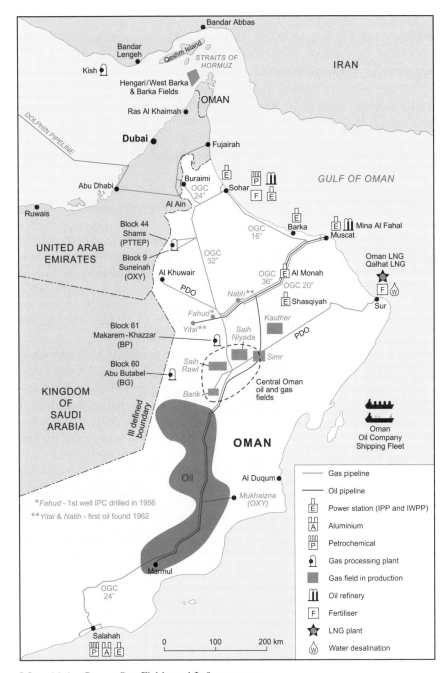

Map 11.1: Oman Gas Fields and Infrastructure

Oman is not a member of OPEC or the Gas Exporting Countries Forum (GECF). It joined the World Trade Organisation (WTO) in 2000 and as a country has historically operated a more free market approach in its energy sector and economy than some other Middle East Countries, with privatisation programmes in power, communications and transport sectors.[3] In 2004 the Authority for Electricity Regulation was established for the electricity and water sectors. This signals the process of fair competition in the Sultanate with respect to the power sector. There is no gas regulator at present, this role being carried out by the Ministry of Oil and Gas.

History of Oil and Gas in Oman

Oman's growth into a successful oil- and gas-producing nation started in 1925 with a geological survey of the country which found no oil (as with all exploration at that time oil was the target not gas). In 1937 a 75-year concession was awarded to the Iraq Petroleum Company (IPC) with the exploration and production operations being run by Petroleum Development (Oman and Dhofar) Ltd (Shell 23.75 percent; Anglo-Persian Company – later BP – 23.75 percent; Compagnie Française des Pétroles (CFE) – later Total – 23.75 percent; the Near East Development Company – ExxonMobil 23.75 percent; and Partex 5 percent).

IPC drilled its first well in Fahud (see Map 11.1) in early 1956 followed by further dry wells and in 1960 most of the partners withdrew from the venture with only Shell and Partex opting to remain in Oman. Then in 1962 they struck oil in Yibal. Further oil was found in the Natih and Fahud fields, which led to the investment in pipelines to move the oil 275 km to the coast and export infrastructure at Saih al Maleh (later re-named Mina al Fahal) with the first export of crude in July 1967. The availability of oil also led to the development of power and industrial projects. In June 1967 CFE rejoined the partnership, renamed Petroleum Development (Oman) with the revised shareholding of Shell 85 percent; CFE 10 percent and Partex 5 percent.

On 23 July 1970 His Majesty Sultan Qaboos took over from his father as ruler of the country and the early 1970s saw new oil fields and oil infrastructure being developed, including Saih Nihayda and Saih Rawl in 1975 (later to be the associated gas fields that were to supply Oman LNG).

In January 1974 the Government of Oman acquired a 25 percent shareholding in Petroleum Development (Oman) increasing its share six months later to 60 percent, resulting in the shareholding that we see today – Government of Oman 60 percent; Shell 34 percent; CFE-Total

4 percent and Partex 2 percent. The company was renamed Petroleum Development Oman (PDO) when it was registered by Royal Decree.

In the 1970s PDO developed the Government Gas System, which started operation in 1979 to move gas to industry located on the coast. PDO's gas exploration programme in the early 1990s proved up more reserves and, working with Shell, the government decided to develop a gas export project as a means of earning and diversifying export earnings away from oil. Three projects were under consideration, a pipeline to the UAE, the Oman–India Pipeline (promoted by Transworld Oil) and LNG exports (promoted by Shell). In 1996 PDO signed an agreement with the government to develop the central Oman gas fields (Saih Nihayda, Barik and Saih Rawl) and to construct a new gas processing plant at Saih Rawl and a new 352 km pipeline to Qalhat (a second processing plant was added in 2005 at Saih Nihayda). At the same time the government contracted to supply gas to the LNG plant for 25 years and the Oman LNG partners signed agreements to proceed with a two-train 6.6 mtpa LNG export project. The Saih Rawl Central Processing Plant and the pipeline were dedicated in November 1999 and the first cargo of LNG was shipped to Korea in April 2000.

Oil production in 2009 averaged 812,500 barrels per day, an increase of 7.3 percent on 2008, of which 81.9 percent is exported, with sales primarily to Asian buyers and the balance refined domestically in the two refineries at Muscat and Sohar. Condensate represents 12.3 percent of oil production[4] and forms an important part of its oil exports. PDO is the country's major producer of oil and condensate. In addition Oman produces liquid petroleum gas (LPG), which is both used domestically and exported.

The Economy

The Omani economy has seen considerable growth over the past five years as shown in Table 11.1. Real GDP growth averaged 7.8 percent from 2005 to 2008 but also saw a sharp rise in inflation, in part due to the Omani Riyal being pegged to the US Dollar. The Minister of National Economy has said that Oman will remain pegged to the US Dollar and does not intend to join the single currency that the Gulf Cooperation Council is planning to introduce in 2010.[5] Lower oil prices and the 2008/09 global economic slowdown caused further problems with economic growth estimated at 4.0 percent in 2009, although the country still managed to maintain positive growth during the period of global economic turmoil. The main impact of the world recession on Oman was a fall in the value of its hydrocarbon exports.

Table 11.1: Oman Key Economic Indicators, 2005–2010

	2005	*2006*	*2007*	*2008*	*2009**	*2010**
Real GDP Growth						
(percent change)	6.0	5.9	6.5	12.9	4.0	4.5
Nominal GDP ($ billion)	30.0	35.7	41.6	60.2	49.6	55.8
CPI (average percent change)	1.9	3.4	5.9	12.5	3.5	4.0
Budget Balance (percent GDP)	12.1	14.2	13.7	13.0	2.0	7.0
Current Account Balance						
(percent GDP)	16.0	14.2	4.8	9.1	0.0	3.0
Population (Millions)	2.5	2.5	2.6	2.7	2.7	n/a

* Estimates

Source: *Middle East Economic Survey* (MEES), various.

The primary energy balance for Oman is set out in Table 11.2. It shows that domestic oil and gas are the main energy sources for the country with, in 2009, 18 percent oil and 56 percent gas produced in the country consumed locally (gas export volumes are as LNG).

Table 11.2: Oman Primary Energy Balance, 2005–2009

	2005	*2006*	*2007*	*2008*	*2009*
Oil kb/d					
Crude Oil	715	677	651	671	713
Condensate	60	61	59	88	100
Total Oil	774	738	710	759	813
Export	718	639	608	594	666
Domestic	56	99	102	165	147
Gas Bcm/yr					
Domestic Production	25.9	30.2	30.3	30.2	30.3
Imports					0.3
Total Gas	25.9	30.2	30.3	30.2	30.6
Export	11.5	14.9	14.8	13.3	13.0
Domestic	14.4	15.3	15.5	16.9	17.6

Source: Oman Government, Ministry of Oil & Gas and Author Analysis

The government is keen to reduce Oman's reliance on oil and gas, but income from these sectors still represents some 75 percent of total government revenue as shown in Table 11.3.

In March 2009 Standard and Poor's reaffirmed Oman's credit rating at A long term and A-1 short term, adding that the outlook of the Sultanate is stable. In making this rating Standard and Poor's stated 'The ratings in Oman are supported by the government's strong fiscal

Table 11.3: Oil and Gas Revenue as a Percentage of Total Government Revenue

2003	*2004*	*2005*	*2006*	*2007*	*2008*	*2009*	*2010Est*
72.7	78.1	78.8	77.1	75.8	78.6	74.6	76.0

Source: Oman Government Ministry of National Economy *Monthly Statistics*, Minister of National Economy Budget Statement (2 January 2010) and Author Analysis

position, together with the country's solid external finances and increasing wealth levels'.[6] This was reaffirmed in August 2009 by Moodys, stating that the outlook for Omani banks is stable reflecting the 'relative resilience of Oman's non-oil economy to global recession' and 'adequate capitalisation ratios in the banking sector'.[7] Oman's sovereign ratings were further raised in February 2010 based on the strength of the public finances. Moody's reported,

> Over the years, the [Omani] government has accumulated a deep cushion of net financial assets which now imparts considerable fiscal flexibility relative to similarly rated countries. Moody's considers Oman's economic strength to be high based on the country's relatively high level of GDP per capita (notwithstanding volatility stemming from a heavy reliance on oil and gas exports) and robust international investment position.[8]

Gas Production

Overview

At the end of 2009 Oman's gas reserves were 34.6 Tcf (905 Bcm), 0.5 percent of global gas reserves[9] with the majority of these reserves in the PDO concession area. Production in Oman has remained stable at just under 30 Bcm/yr since 2006 and in 2009 was 30.7 Bcm, slightly up on the previous year. Over this period however the amount of condensate has increased as new fields have started production and 2009 condensate production averaged 100,000 barrels/day.

Figure 11.1 shows Oman gas production from 2000 to 2015. It shows how production increased between 2000 and 2001 as Oman LNG started operations, increasing again in 2006 with the start-up of Qalhat LNG. The period 2007–09 saw limited growth, despite gas-consuming projects being approved by the government. This has led to a shortage, hence the moves by the government to import gas and encourage new exploration in Oman. Government figures estimate

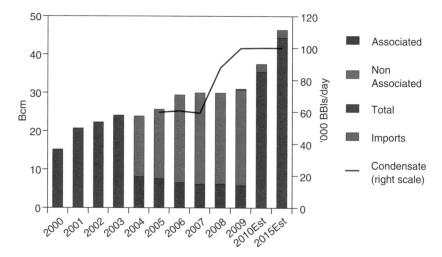

Figure 11.1: Oman Gas Production and Imports, 2000–2015Est

Source: Oman Government Ministry of Oil and Gas, Author Analysis (Condensate
2010 & 2015 estimates from author)

that gas production will increase from just under 30 Bcm in 2006 to
an estimated 44.3 Bcm in 2015.

The question is whether Oman can achieve this large increase in gas
production. With the increased effort by the government on domestic
production and recent exploration successes by PDO and BP, this target
is viewed as achievable but there is always the possibility of delays. If
that happened the gas gap would have to be managed through demand
management measures.

In Oman, gas is owned by the government and is either produced
under a service contract (e.g. Oman LNG and Qalhat LNG gas supply
from PDO central Oman fields) or the government purchases the gas
from the companies who are producing it under newer production
sharing contracts which are specifically related to gas (e.g. BP and
Oxy).

Oman is aggressively seeking to increase gas production as, along
with other Gulf countries, it is facing rising domestic demand from
the petrochemical sector and the power sector – which is itself endeav-
ouring to keep pace with rapidly growing industrial demand – from
water desalination projects, as well as population growth. Gas is also
required to feed the LNG projects and importantly to feed PDO's
gas-intensive enhanced oil recovery programme. In 2009, 19.5 percent
of domestic gas was used for oil field reinjection, a figure that is likely
to increase with more gas needed to meet demand from enhanced oil

recovery (EOR) projects. These are high cost projects increasing the oil breakeven price for PDO (the biggest oil and gas producer in the country) to $40–50/bbl.[10]

Omani Companies and New Entrants

Oman Oil Company (OOC)

The Omani government has sought to use energy-intensive industries as a means to diversify the economy and to develop domestic skills and experience. Their intention, therefore, is to keep investment in-country and one company that has been a focus of this strategy is Oman Oil Company, a commercial company wholly owned by the Government of the Sultanate of Oman. The company was incorporated in 1996 to pursue investment opportunities in the energy sector both inside and outside Oman. Through participation in energy and energy-related projects, the company plays an important role in the Sultanate's efforts to diversify the economy and to promote Omani and foreign private sector investment. OOC also provides commercial support to the government. CEO Ahmad al-Wahaibi said the company's strategy is to be 'a vertically integrated oil and gas company, going from upstream, to exploration, transportation, logistics and downstream, such as refineries, petrochemicals, fertilizers, and other energy related operations'.[11] OOC's portfolio already includes assets from across these diverse sectors and it seeks further global expansion. These investments give valuable local input and involvement in domestic as well as overseas developments.

Appendix III sets out details of OOC's portfolio of investments which are all energy-focused and seek to bring employment as well as business opportunities to the country. OOC has further investment plans across a number of industries including a new refinery (Al-Duqm), a new petrochemical complex and an aluminium project with IPIC.[12] The pace of OOC's acquisitions slowed with the 2008/09 financial crisis; the only transactions concluded during that period were:

1. The signing of a strategic cooperation agreement with MOL Plc[13] for the purchase by OOC from Gazprom of 8 percent of MOL shares in exchange for certain international assets of OOC[14] (including OOC's share in the Caspian Pipeline Consortium) and
2. An increase in OOC's shares in an Indian refinery from 2 percent to 26 percent.

In June 2009 it was announced that, as part of the asset disposal plan agreed between the Spanish regulator and Gas Natural when it acquired Union Fenosa (March 2009), OOC had purchased a 5 percent interest in the Spanish gas system operator Enagas.[15] This builds upon OOC's other investments in Spain – 10 percent shareholding stake in CLH (Compañía Logística de Hidrocarburos), a 7.5 percent interest in Sagunto Regasification plant (SAGGAS) acquired in November 2004 and a 6 percent shareholding stake in La Seda de Barcelona (power). It must be said that OOC's investments in Spain are likely to be linked to the Oman government's close relationships with Union Fenosa Gas (UFG), specifically the inclusion of UFG as a shareholder in Qalhat LNG and government-to-government relations between Oman and Spain. Under the terms of the original agreement with UFG, as part of the QLNG project development, OOC was expected to take a 15 percent stake in the Sagunto import terminal near Valencia; the final percentage was 7.5 percent.

OOC also has plans to invest $2 billion in the Kish field incorporating the joint development of the offshore Hengam/West Bukha gas and condensate field in Iran (see the section on imports below). This field straddles the two countries' territorial waters and is estimated to contain 1.8 tcf (47.09 Bcm) of gas and 400 million barrels of condensate. The field is operated by the UAE based company Rak Petroleum (40 percent), in association with LG International (50 percent) and Eagle Energy (10 percent); it started flowing in February 2009 and is expected to reach 0.4 Bcm/yr by 2010.[16] The gas is currently piped to the UAE and is sold to the Ras al Khaimah Gas Commission (RakGas).

Petroleum Development Oman
PDO faces a formidable set of challenges to achieve the government's goal of having a 100 percent reserves replacement ratio. Execution of its EOR projects and expansion of gas production are important targets and the discoveries of new fields such as the Simr gas field near Saih Niyayda and an extension to the Burhaan gas field, will help it maintain its position in the forefront of the country's oil and gas business. PDO has had some new gas fields start operation. The Kauther field, discovered in 2001 was fast tracked by the government and in October 2007 the Kauther Gas Plant came on stream, able to process up to 7.3 Bcm/yr of gas for domestic supply. The gas is supplied to the capital Muscat and the industrial Sohar area in the north east of the country (via a 85 km pipeline).[17] In 2009, gas production from the field was not operating at capacity due to the high hydrogen sulphide content of the gas, but this constraint should be removed by 2011 when production should reach full capacity and also produce 90–100 million barrels per day of condensate. In 2009, associated and non-associated

gas production from the PDO concession was 410,000 barrels per day oil equivalent[18] (approximately 24 million cubic metres/day), an increase of 5.1 percent over 2008.

The PDO block 6 concession is almost 100,000 sq. km. in size and the company continues to explore for new oil and gas within this area. It has reported that three new oil fields and one gas field have recently been discovered. The gas discovery at Khulud in the north of PDO's concession area has potentially large gas volumes at a depth of more than 5000 metres in very tight reservoirs with low permeability and at very high temperatures. PDO is planning to drill two wells in 2010 to help evaluate the discovery.[19] The report also notes that oil and gas exploration activities will increase significantly, indicating the government's urgency to increase its available oil and gas resources.

PDO has implemented new technology in order to reduce operating costs and access new gas at an economic cost. At Saih Rawl for example a state-of-the-art plant is being installed containing four gas-compression units and 120 MW of generation.[20]

PDO is a major employer in the gas business in Oman and many employees of other related companies in Oman have started their careers in the company. Its employees are well trained, have a good understanding of business processes and ways of working and take these skills to other Omani companies. This does put a strain on PDO which is having to continually hire new Omani staff while the size of the talent pool in Oman is limited.

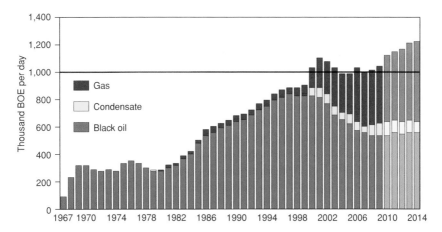

Figure 11.2: PDO Oil and Gas Condensate Production

Source: *PDO Media Briefing 2009*, 15th February 2010

New Entrants

In the early 2000s PDO experienced problems in maintaining its oil and gas reserves replacement and production growth. Reservoir water flooding, natural oil production-rate decline and the fact that the new fields being found were smaller than planned – all meant less oil and increased costs. A full review in 2000 led to wide-ranging changes in PDO with ambitious production-recovery plans, including enhanced oil recovery (EOR). Meanwhile, these production problems led the government to reduce its reliance on PDO (and Shell) and to diversify the number of companies operating in Oman's upstream to bring new technologies and experience.

Confronting the growing shortage of gas, the Omani government has put pressure on PDO to increase gas production, use new technologies while keeping costs as low as possible. The government is also seeking to expand the number of companies operating in the country in order to reduce PDO's (who some still see as Shell) dominant position in the country and to bring in new technology and experience. Similar pressure was exerted on the company to reverse the downward trend in condensate production. PDO's activities are constrained by human and financial resources, so bringing in new companies can relieve these pressures. In the case of gas developments by PDO, the government has to pay for 100 percent of the costs and therefore bears exploration risk. However, using third parties under production sharing contracts (PSCs) means that the government can pass on the exploration risk to another party. Under the terms of these contracts the government has the right to a 20 percent stake in the concession on declaration of commerciality. It can therefore manage its risks while being able to access part of the upside. Smaller companies, including local Omani ventures are also gaining a position in the upstream. In April 2010 the Ministry again tendered new fields out to third parties from the PDO concession.

The Ministry of Oil is confident that it has sufficient gas supplies through to 2018–2020 (though some commentators believe that shortages could become apparent as early as 2010–12). New companies are starting to invest in Oman.

Notable new finds are the Khazzan and Makarem tight gas prospects, west of Saih Rawl, which are being developed by BP and could contain 20–60 tcf (520–1570 Bcm) gas in 4500–5000 metre deep complex structures (tight, deep reservoirs with poor porosity of the rock). The fields will require stimulation/fracturing in order to produce the gas. Small volumes of gas production should commence through an extended well test scheme in the second half of 2010. If all goes well, output from these prospects should be as large as 20 Bcm/yr (2000 MMscf/day) by 2020, with some liquids. BP is targeting a declaration of commerciality in mid 2012 and first production three years later, but due to the complex nature of the reservoirs there is always a risk of delays that could mean a small gas shortfall in 2015/16. Either way, the production cost of the gas is expected to be quite high. The BG Group was developing the onshore block 60 in Wusta region, which contains the 5–10 tcf (130–260 Bcm). In November 2009 it renegotiated the price the government will buy the gas upwards from less than $1.00/MMBtu to $2.50–3.00/MMBtu Despite this renegotiated price, in June 2010 BG announced that it had informed the government of Oman of its decision to exit Block 60 and therefore Oman. BP will also be able to use existing facilities for its early gas and will be likely to seek a higher price from the government, who some believe may find it difficult to give a price higher than the new BG level.

A third company producing gas in Oman is PTT Exploration and Production Public Company Limited (PTTEP) with a 100 percent interest in the Shams gas field on block 44. The field produces at 0.5 Bcm/yr (50 MMscf/day) gas and 4000 barrels/day condensate (2007 data). Production is expected to rise in the future.[21]

In November 2008 the Minister of Oil and Gas signed an Exploration & Production Sharing Agreement (EPSA) with Occidental for block 62, saying that the concession award represented another successful breakthrough in the ministry's ongoing efforts to bring in new players to develop and explore for new gas reserves. The minister added: 'This is in continuation of the strategy that ended up bringing into the country British Gas and BP. We sliced off three blocks which were under PDO's exploration on behalf of the government. The first lot of these blocks was signed away today. By January (2009), we hope to be able to sign two more concession agreements specifically for gas'. This is further evidence of the government's wish to diversify operating companies.[22]

A factor that potentially holds back international and domestic companies from exploring and developing gas reserves is the price paid for gas in the domestic market. Producers say that while industries were able to purchase gas at $0.80–1.50/MMBtu, the newer non-associated reserves are in more complex reservoirs (and therefore do not enjoy a liquids 'credit') costing in the range of $2.50–5.00/MMBtu and will need higher gas prices. As with other Gulf producers, the Omani government will have to accept higher prices in order to commercialise these higher cost reserves. The agreements between the government and producers, which are not disclosed, follow a formula that covers operators' expenditure and profit. 'The ministry is realistic and realizes that the days of cheap gas are over and it is not fair to ask companies to subsidize our industries for ever,' one government source has admitted,[23] It is interesting to note how views have changed. In an interview with *MEES* in March 1998, Dr. Mohammed Hamed Saif Al-Rumhy, Oman's then Minister of Oil and Gas, said 'Between $0.60 and $1.00/ MMBtu is the kind of range that companies should expect from Oman' but added 'If the added value is to the benefit of Oman rather than to another country (i.e. brings jobs) then the government will try to encourage these projects through favourable gas pricing'.[24] showing that, even at the inception of Oman's gas business, the intention was always to generate jobs in the Sultanate.

The government therefore accepts that potentially it will have to buy gas at a higher price than it can sell it in the domestic market. The difference could be structured as a formal 'subsidy' as in the power sector (see below) or set off against any equity interest that the government may hold. The government will have to balance the need to get a competitive price for the gas from the concession holders, versus paying a higher price in order to attract new gas exploration and production.

Government spending on oil and gas developments is increasing, as more difficult gas reserves are being developed. The ministry's 2010 budget includes $3.77 billion spending on the oil and gas sector. Such a large spending programme is necessary because 'oil and gas production is the engine room of the economy and we therefore need to keep it healthy', the Director General, Planning and Studies, at the Ministry of Oil and Gas told *MEES* in an interview in April 2008.

Domestic Gas Consumption and Pricing

As mentioned earlier, the growing availability of low-cost gas, together with government encouragement, led to an increase in domestic gas demand. Demand for the power and industrial sectors has increased at an average of 15 percent a year over the period 2000–2009, with gas supply to the LNG sector increasing by 30 percent over the same period while the use of gas in oil production has fallen (see Table 11.4).

In 2009, 42.8 percent of gas was used as feedstock for LNG, while 19.9 percent was used in the power sector, 17.7 percent in the industrial sector and 19.5 percent as fuel for oil production and reinjection into oil reservoirs. This percentage is expected to rise to over 30 percent by 2015 as new complex fields start production (an increase of 6 Bcm from 2006). New technologies are being used to reduce the amount of gas required

Table 11.4: Oman Gas Usage, 2004–2015

Bcm/yr	*2000*	*2001*	*2002*	*2003*	*2004*	*2005*	*2006*	*2007*	*2008*	*2009*	*2010**	*2015**
Power Sector	2.94	3.23	3.48	4.02	4.20	4.48	4.87	5.11	5.43	6.04	6.72	7.77
Industrial Sector	0.27	0.30	0.30	0.36	0.41	1.40	1.98	2.56	3.36	5.37	7.88	8.47
LNG Sector	3.96	8.64	9.48	10.32	10.16	10.32	13.59	13.87	13.29	12.96	13.47	13.65
Export to UAE	-	-	-	-	0.65	1.16	1.32	0.88	-	-	-	-
Oil Fields Flared and other	8.04	8.53	9.06	9.38	8.61	8.59	8.45	7.84	8.06	5.91	7.37	14.45
Total	**15.21**	**20.71**	**22.32**	**24.08**	**24.03**	**25.94**	**30.21**	**30.26**	**30.15**	**30.28**	**35.44**	**44.35**
Percentages												
Power Sector	19.35	15.62	15.60	16.69	17.48	17.27	16.13	16.89	18.01	19.95	18.95	17.53
Industrial Sector	1.78	1.46	1.33	1.51	1.69	5.38	6.55	8.46	11.16	17.72	22.25	19.09
LNG Sector	26.00	41.73	42.48	42.84	42.28	39.78	45.00	45.83	44.09	42.80	38.00	30.78
Export to UAE	-	-	-	-	2.72	4.46	4.35	2.91	-	-	-	-
Oil Fields, Flared and other	52.87	41.19	40.58	38.96	35.82	33.11	27.97	25.91	26.75	19.53	20.80	32.59

* Estimates

Source: Oman Government Ministry of Oil and Gas, Author Analysis

for EOR, for example PDO has located a power station on top of a heavy oil field to utilise the power by-product steam in oil production.

Table 11.4 gives details of demand for gas in Oman in volume and percentage terms. It shows how demand from industrial projects has increased from 6.55 percent of total gas demand in 2006 to an estimated 22.25 percent in 2010, falling back to 10.09 percent by 2015. Power sector demand increases in volume terms but remains at 16–19 percent of total gas demand. The share of gas used for LNG export has fallen from 45 percent in 2006 to an estimated 30.8 percent in 2015 despite remaining fairly constant in volume terms. This reflects the prioritisation of gas for domestic use, specifically the substantial increase in gas for use in the oil fields to enhance oil production

The power sector gets priority access to available gas, but if Oman cannot increase gas supplies, then expansion in all the sectors will be deferred or cancelled. In 2007 gas shortages and high capital costs (construction costs have quadrupled from first estimates) were the fundamental reasons why the Oman Petrochemical Industries Company's (OPIC)/Dow Chemicals olefins complex was cancelled. At the end of 2009 Oman LNG's 0.8 Bcma LNG sales contract with BP was not extended so that gas could be used in the domestic market.

Power and Water

In December 1999, the Council of Ministers approved the introduction of government policy designed to facilitate the wholesale restructuring of, and further private sector participation in, the electricity and related water sector in Oman. As part of this policy, the government tendered the Al Kamil, Barka and Sohar projects and awarded them to private sector participants. In addition, it began the process of preparing a new law to facilitate the restructuring, privatisation and regulation of the electricity and related water sector. The Sector Law came into force on 1 August 2004.

Prior to 2005, all generation, transmission and distribution assets were owned and maintained by the Ministry of Housing, Electricity and Water (MHEW), other than the generation and desalination assets of the incumbent independent power (and water) producers and the privatised concession in Salalah. Royal Decree 92/2007 established the Public Authority for Electricity and Water (PAEW) on 10 September 2007. It also transferred to PAEW all of MHEW's functions, assets and responsibilities concerning the electricity and related water sector (and other water-related functions). Royal Decrees 92/2007 and 58/2009 prescribe PAEW's system and the management of its affairs. The later Royal Decree 59/2009 amended certain provisions of the Sector Law to give effect to the matters described above regarding PAEW's responsibilities.

The Authority for Electricity Regulation, Oman (AER), was established by the Sector Law in 2004 to regulate the electricity and water sectors. The regulator reports annually to the Council of Ministers by publishing an open annual report that includes details on the electricity and power sector in Oman.[25] The appointment of a regulator has signalled a process of fair competition in the Sultanate with respect to the Omani power sector. The regulator examines different technologies that can be used for the generation of electricity and in May 2008 issued a report on potential renewable energy resources in Oman.[26] The report recommended the immediate implementation of several pilot projects including solar, solar/diesel hybrid and wind and a feasibility study for a large-scale solar project.

In comparing new I(W)PP projects, even though the cost of gas to power is $1.50/MMBtu, the regulator assumes an economic cost of natural gas of around $5.00/MMBtu. By so doing, it ensures that the correct decisions are made when choosing the optimum technology for power generation and appropriate gas technology is referenced to the economic cost of gas not to its price.

In its annual report,[27] the power regulator also sets out the case for further market liberalisation and concludes that this may be possible within four years in some parts of the sector, but it is likely that the current structure will remain in place for several years to come. At the time of writing it is not clear what is the status of discussions on the appointment of an independent gas regulator, a role that is currently being carried out by the Ministry of Oil & Gas.

Power in Oman consists of two separate grids, 'MIS', covering the centre and north of the country and 'Salalah' to the south. Both distribute power generated from gas. In addition, areas that cannot access power from the grids are covered by the Rural Areas Electricity Council (RAEC), which generates power from diesel.

Demand for power in Oman is very seasonal with ~ 70/30 spread between the summer (April–September) and winter (December–March). This seasonality can lead to some constraints. The Ministry of Finance provides a subsidy to power supplied by four licensed suppliers[28] so that consumers do not pay the full cost.

Oman has been examining alternative sources of energy to meet its growth in power demand. A 1000 MW IWPP using coal was planned at Al Duqm in the south of the country. In an independent report, commissioned for the Oman Power and Water Procurement Co, it was

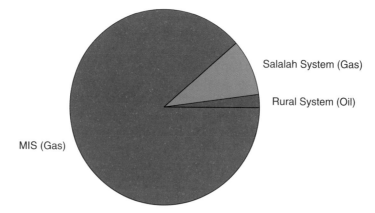

Figure 11.3: Power Generation by Fuel, 2008

Source: Authority for Energy Regulation Oman, p.12

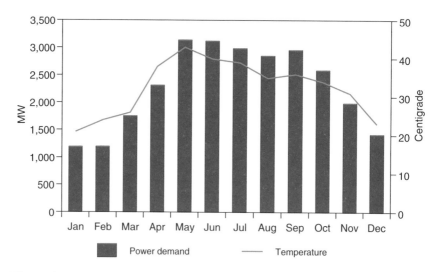

Figure 11.4: Monthly Power Demand on the Main Interconnected System (MIS)
2008 and Temperature

Source: Authority for Electricity Regulation Oman, *Annual Report 2008*

stated that coal ranks second to natural gas as a low cost fuel resource
in power generation in the Sultanate.[29] It was further argued that adding
coal to Oman's generation portfolio would provide a valuable hedge
against oil and gas price movements. Coal would have to be imported,
however, as domestic reserves are not of the correct quality. Security
of supply concerns, together with domestic environmental pressures,

has meant that coal-fired power plant has been deferred in favour of using new higher cost domestic gas for power generation. Gas will be supplied through a new 48 inch gas pipeline from central Oman to Duqm, with a delivered cost potentially exceeding $5/MMBtu.

In addition, renewables are being examined as a source of energy and solar power and wind generation trials are ongoing. As part of a wider initiative with the GCC, Oman is also examining nuclear power though at the time of writing there seems to have been little progress.

Petrochemicals

In the late 1990s, Oman decided to establish a petrochemical and fertiliser industry as a means of developing jobs in-country, based on the higher volume of domestic gas that had been discovered. There are six plants in operation with one due to start production in 2010 (see Appendix IV). Approval for these plants was given in a period when there was surplus gas available in Oman. The likelihood of more high gas use petrochemical plants being constructed is low, though feedgas supply will be found for the existing plants even at the expense of LNG exports.

Aluminium and Mining

The Omani Government has for many years sought to develop an aluminium production industry in the country. There is one plant in operation in Sohar and the government has plans to expand it utilising aluminium produced by Sohar Aluminium Company as feedstock. A feasibility study is being undertaken.

Power (and Water Desalination Joint Projects)

As part of the government's privatisation plans, since the mid 1990s all new power projects are being developed as independent power projects (IPPs) or independent water and power projects (IWPPs). Oman's power generation capacity is approximately 3800 MW, and consumption approximately 3000 MW (2008). Five I(W)PPs have been completed, bids for two 750 MW IPPs are under evaluation and competition for a further IWPP (700 MW and 40 million gallon/day desalination plant) is expected to commence during the first half of 2010. The intention is that all new power projects will be gas powered and domestic gas will be prioritised to ensure sufficient feedgas.

Water Desalination Projects

A reverse osmosis plant, rather than a seawater distillation, is in operation in Sur. Smaller similar plants are in operation around Oman
serving smaller coastal and inland communities. In November 2009 a
commercial plant using manipulated osmosis desalination technology
was opened at Al Khaluf.[30] As with power projects, all water desalination projects are intended to be gas powered and domestic gas will be
prioritised to ensure sufficient feedgas.

Gas Transmission

The transmission of gas for domestic public use is managed and operated by Oman Gas Company (OGC). If gas is for its own internal use
then PDO builds and operates the pipeline.

Established in 1999 OGC is owned 80 percent by the government
and 20 percent by OOC. In 1999 OGC was awarded a 27-year concession and tariff agreement to operate the Government Gas Transmission
System (GGTS).[31] OGC is a cost centre not a profit organisation, with
gas used in transmission being metered but not charged to OGC. This
means that the company does not buy and sell the gas, but provides
pipeline capacity, with costs paid by the government. OGC also constructed the oil pipeline between Oman's two refineries in Mina Al
Fahal (Muscat) and Sohar, which is managed by OOC. These pipelines
enabled the development of power plants and industry in the north of
the Sultanate at Sohar and in the south at Salalah as well as industrial
zones along the pipeline routes.

A further pipeline in the north of the country, the Northern Oman
Gas Pipeline, inaugurated in March 2005, supplies gas from the Oxy-
Mitsui Block 9 E&P Northern Oman Gas Project (NOGP) to Al-ain and
Fujairah. The pipeline transports non-associated and associated gas and
is part of the Sultanate's strategy to reduce flaring[32] and commercialise
4.1 Bcm of gas and 1.9 million barrels of crude oil. The 1.3 Bcm/yr
of gas supplied from the NOGP is sold to the government in a sales
and purchase agreement (SPA) dated 29 April 2003.

LNG

Despite some internal political statements arguing that Oman should
have used its gas only to develop domestic industries, a topical argument

in times of gas shortage, LNG has enabled Oman to rapidly commercialise its gas and generate substantial foreign exchange earnings
(revenues in the region of $3.5–4.0 billion in 2009). However, although
LNG earns considerable income, it does not create a large number of
jobs, and the Sultanate has therefore used this income to develop domestic infrastructure and local industry as well as a shipping company.
Thus, LNG has benefited Oman considerably since the first cargo was
loaded in April 2000.

Oman LNG

Following the discovery by PDO of considerable volumes of gas in
commercial quantities in the Saih Nihayda, Barik and Saih Rawl fields
in central Oman, the government sought to commercialise this gas
for the benefit of the population. Shell proposed the development of
an LNG export project, which was supported and sponsored by the
Ministry of Petroleum. Oman LNG was established by Sultani Decree
in 1994 to develop, construct and operate the LNG project at Sur, 150
km south-west of the capital, Muscat. This location was selected as it
has deep water close to the shore and favourable ocean conditions, with
no need to build a breakwater, so keeping capital costs down. Since
the plant is located outside the Strait of Hormuz, its LNG shipments
are less vulnerable to regional conflicts than those of other GCC LNG
producers. This was an important selling point when the LNG was
being marketed.

Final investment decision was taken in November 1996 following
the signing of the LNG sales and purchase agreement with Korea Gas
Corporation (Kogas), plant construction contract, gas supply agreement
with the government of Oman, and other key contractual documents
(the final agreements had been signed during the preceding weeks). The
first cargo of LNG was shipped to Korea in April 2000.

The development of the Oman LNG project was not without its
problems. Securing a creditworthy offtaker who was willing to underpin
the LNG projects was not easy, especially as the preference was for the
anchor buyer not to be a greenfield venture (for financing reasons). Also
discussions by a separate company on the possibility of an Oman–India
pipeline raised doubts in the minds of the LNG buyers about the
seriousness of the project. Oman LNG was also in direct competition
with RasGas of Qatar.

The major Japanese buyers expressed interest in Oman LNG but
the timing of the start of supplies did not fit well with demand from
the major utilities. The plan therefore was that Oman LNG's first core

buyer would be Kogas. Discussions were also ongoing with other Asian and Southern European buyers, including the Petroleum Authority of Thailand (PTT) with whom negotiations were completed. PTT later decided that it did not want to import LNG as large volumes of domestic gas were found in Thailand. This led to a complete review of all aspects of the project, especially cost. Kogas became the foundation customer and with the purchase contract of 4.1 mtpa it meant that shareholders could commit to a two-train 6.6 mtpa LNG project, providing confidence in attractive future LNG sales before project completion. A decision to sell the LNG FOB[33] indicated that the project did not have to incur the shipping capital costs; also Kogas preferred an FOB purchase as Korea was keen to develop its own LNG ship building capability. Falling contractor prices for plant construction and reduced project specification meant that the plant costs were cut to around $1.5 billion (which was low in relation to comparable projects).

In October 1996, the sales and purchase agreement was signed between Oman LNG and Kogas for 5.6 Bcm/yr (4.1 mtpa). As part of the agreement Korean companies received 5 percent of the equity in Oman LNG. In February 1997 a consortium of Kogas, Samsung, Hyundai, Daewoo and Yukong secured this 5 percent stake. Under the restructuring, the Omani government retained its 51 percent share, Shell reduced its share from 34 percent to 30 percent, Total reduced from 6 percent to 5.54 percent, Mitsui and Mitsubishi cut their equity from 3 percent to 2.77 percent each and Itochu reduced from 1 percent to 0.92 percent. Partex retained its 2 percent equity (Table 11.5). The large number of shareholders in Oman LNG did however impact on the speed of shareholder decision-making during the development phase of the project.

Following final investment decision in November 1996, Oman LNG worked hard to sell the balance of the capacity and in October 1997 it signed an MoU with Osaka Gas for 0.96 Bcm/yr (0.7 mtpa) LNG with an SPA being signed a year later.

Both the sales to Kogas and Osaka Gas were made on an FOB basis. The Government of Oman was keen to sell the LNG ex-ship, (in which case Oman LNG would arrange the shipping,) but Kogas was not willing to accept such an arrangement. Later this led to some tensions in the government and Oman Oil Company chartered two LNG ships which were then chartered back to Oman and Qalhat LNG some years later (see later section on OOC Shipping).

Oman LNG entered discussions with the Enron-led Dabhol Power Co (DPC) in Maharashtra, India, for the sale of 2.4 Bcm/yr (1.7mtpa) LNG, with first cargo targeted for December 2001. The collapse of

Table 11.5: Oman LNG Shareholder Position

	Shareholders	*Start-date*	*Plant capacity Bcm/yr*	*Upstream gas supply*
Oman LNG (OLNG)	Government of Oman 51.00%; Shell 30.00%; Total 5.54%; KOLNG* 5.00%; Mitsubishi 2.77%; Mitsui 2.77%; Partex 2.00%; Itochu: 0.92%	2000	10.1 (7.4 mtpa) Two trains Note: Initial design was for 9.05 (6.6 mtpa)	Barik, Saih Nihayda & Saih Rawal Fields, 100% owned by the government. PDO is paid a fixed fee by the government to operate the upstream. Gas is sold to OLNG. Government sells the condensate with the crude oil.

*   KOLNG = Kogas 24%; Samsung 20%; Daewoo 20%; Hyundai 20%; SK Corporation 16%

Source: Author research

Table 11.6: Oman LNG Contractual Position (as at January 2010)

	Volume BCMA	*Primary Destination*	*Start Date*	*End Date*	*Delivery*
Kogas	5.55	Korea	2000	2024	FOB
Osaka Gas	1.00	Japan	2000	2025	FOB
BP	0.80	Spain & trading	2004	2009**	Ex-ship
Itochu*	1.00	Japan & Trading	2006	2026	FOB***

*   Volume initially from QLNG, transferred prior to FID and is on-sold to Chugoko Electric

**   Expired 31 December and not renewed

*** The ship to transport the LNG is chartered by Oman Shipping Company to Itochu

Source: Author research

the Dabhol projects, followed by the bankruptcy of Enron (which had a 65 percent stake in DPC) left the future of the contract in doubt. In the event this contract was never honoured and no cargoes were sold to DPC. Oman LNG sold the spare volumes initially short-term, then later on a long-term basis.

As at January 2010 the Oman LNG plant is producing 7.5 Bcma LNG to meet its contractual obligations with Kogas, Osaka Gas and Itochu (Table 11.6). The current capacity of the OLNG plant is 10.1 Bcma, which means that it is operating at 74 percent capacity – due to shortage of feedgas. High LNG prices however mean that the company is delivering good revenues to the government and shareholders, well in excess of what was planned at the outset of the project. The key question is what will happen during the period 2010 to 2024/26 when the long-term LNG sales and purchase agreements expire; will there be enough gas to meet contractual requirements and in 2024/26 will the contracts be renewed? The government has stated that contracts will be honoured, albeit probably at the minimum volume allowed under the SPAs. Certainly, the contracts will only be renewed if new gas reserves are found over and above domestic gas requirements.

Qalhat LNG[34]

In March 2002 the Government of Oman decided to develop a third LNG train adjacent to the Oman LNG Plant. Shell acted as technical adviser to the government and in January 2003, together with Chiyoda-Foster Wheeler the government signed an engineering procurement and construction (EPC) contract. The project was designed using the same specifications and similar technical design and construction as Oman LNG's two existing liquefaction trains with a nameplate capacity of 3.3 mtpa and the ability to increase to at least 3.7 mtpa after 18 months from the EPC plant acceptance. Construction started in March 2003. LNG ships were also chartered to deliver the LNG to the buyers (see below section on OOC Shipping).

Qalhat LNG's shareholding structure is different to that of Oman LNG with the Government of Oman taking a larger direct equity position, initially 55.84 percent (in addition to its share of the 36.8 percent held by Oman LNG) (Table 11.7). In May 2006 the government reduced its direct interest to 46.84 percent when Mitsubishi Corporation, Osaka Gas Co. Limited, and Itochu Corporation each acquired an additional 3 percent share in Qalhat LNG.[35] The involvement of Union Fenosa Gas (UFG) – 50 percent Union Fenosa, 50 percent ENI – in the project[36] is a good example of a utility moving upstream into LNG production as a means to secure gas for its domestic market. LNG lifted by Union Fenosa Gas is destined for Spain, but many of the cargoes have been diverted by Qalhat LNG to higher value markets of Asia, while Union Fenosa Gas have covered the LNG requirements from their supply from Egypt or the spot market. As part of the contractual terms agreed with QLNG it is understood that any upside gained as a result of cargo diversions is shared between QLNG and the offtaker.

In Oman, QLNG is seen as a local company, fully staffed by Omanis. The company has achieved a good reputation internationally and developed creative diversion schemes to access new markets and optimise returns for its shareholders. QLNG manages the commercial aspects of its operations, with all plant operations carried out by OLNG on an arms-length operations and maintenance contract basis. The two companies jointly optimise production and LNG cargo operations.

Table 11.7: Qalhat LNG Shareholder Position

	Shareholders**	Start-date	Plant capacity Bcm/yr	Upstream gas supply
Qalhat LNG (QLNG)	Government of Oman 46.84%*; Oman LNG 36.8%; Union Fenosa Gas 7.36%; Itochu 3%; Mitsui 3.00%; Mitsubishi 3.00%	2006	4.45 (3.3 mtpa) nameplate rising to 5.07 (3.7 mtpa) One train	Saih Rawl, Saih Nihayda and Barik fields (the same as gas supplied to Oman LNG) or from any other reservoir located in Oman

* The Government of Oman's share was reduced from 55.84% to 46.84% in May 2006 when 3% equity was transferred to each of Mitsubishi, Mitsui and Itochu

** Taking into consideration the OLNG shares, the shareholding of each company in QLNG is, Government of Oman 65.60%; Shell 11.04%; Union Fenosa Gas 7.36%; Mitsubishi 4.02%; Mitsui 4.02%; Itochu 3.34%; Total 2.04%; KOLNG 1.84%; Partex 0.74%

Source: Author research

The 3.8 tcf (107 Bcm) gas required to provide for the plant over 25 years is supplied from government gas from Saih Rawl, Saih Nihayda and Barik fields or from any other reservoir located in Oman. The gas is transported using the same pipeline as gas supplied to Oman LNG under the terms of a tripartite agreement between the government, Oman LNG and Qalhat LNG, which was signed in September 2004.

With the success of Qalhat LNG's marketing efforts, the available cashflows together with the common use of infrastructure, the company was able to borrow US$612 million third party limited recourse debt to finance the expansion project on the basis of a debt/equity ratio of 90:10.

In December 2005 Qalhat LNG and Malaysia LNG signed a co-operation agreement to swap cargoes (thus potentially saving shipping costs), exchange technical information and staff and to work together to arrange alternative supply arrangements and optimise LNG supplies.[37] This move shows how the government is increasingly looking to other government companies for expertise and support, rather than relying on international energy companies. The company has also signed over 30 mt LNG sales with different international LNG buyers.

Table 11.8: Qalhat LNG Contractual Position (as at January 2010)

	Volume BCMA	Primary Destination	Start Date	End Date	Delivery
Union Fenosa Gas	2.26***	Spain	2006	2025 + 5 year extension option	Ex-ship**
Mitsubishi*	1.08	Japan & USA	2006	2020 + 5 year extension option	FOB**
Osaka Gas	1.15	Japan & Trading	2009	2026	FOB**

*   Mitsubishi and Tokyo Electric signed a JV in January 2004 to jointly market the LNG
**   Ships to transport the LNG are chartered to Mitsubishi and Osaka Gas
*** Equivalent of 2.33 Bcma FOB

Source: Author research

Qalhat LNG is currently operating at 88.5 percent capacity. With shortage of feedgas it is unlikely to make any spot sales.

The two projects have a total maximum capacity of 15.8 Bcma with term sales of 12.1 Bcma. The LNG facility is therefore operating at 76.4 percent capacity with 3.7 Bcma of spare capacity. There are no plans at present to expand LNG capacity and in March 2010 Oman LNG stated that the utilisation would remain around 80 percent.[38] Both Oman and Qalhat LNG sell all their production on a term basis, with little or no spot/short-term cargoes available due to shortage of feedgas and LNG cargoes.

LNG Shipping

As part of the development of Oman's LNG industry, the government was keen to have an involvement in LNG shipping. The initial volumes from Oman LNG were sold on an FOB basis as the buyer (Kogas) sought to develop its own LNG shipbuilding capability and to use its own vessels for transportation. Because there was a surplus of supply on LNG markets and buyers were able to secure advantageous terms, Oman LNG accepted Kogas' requirement to arrange the shipping since this also reduced the capital cost of the OLNG project.

However, Oman is traditionally a seafaring nation, building and trading dhows in the region, and has always wanted to own vessels and be involved in the shipping part of the LNG chain.[39] In 2003, Oman Shipping Company (OSC) was incorporated – OOC 20 percent,

Oman Government Ministry of Finance 80 percent. At that time the government said OSC was established

> with the goal of reviving the Sultanate's illustrious seafaring past through the establishment of a modern ocean-going shipping fleet encompassing a diverse variety of shipping vessels from LNG carriers and crude oil tankers to product carriers and other commercial transport ships. The company initially focused on developing an LNG tanker fleet that would add value to the Sultanate's LNG industry by extending the business chain to include LNG shipping.[40]

The importance of involvement in shipping for Oman cannot be overestimated.[41]

OSC also owns chemical, crude oil, methanol and oil product tankers as well as other multi-purpose vessels and there are reports that it is planning to supply oil tankers to Iranian National Transportation Company under long-term charters.

Gas Imports

When Oman came to realise that it was facing a gas shortage, it looked to pipeline imports to meet the shortfall. 2008/09 saw Oman examining all potential sources of gas imports from neighbouring countries and swops with other countries as a means of securing additional gas.

There are two main import projects.

Gas Imports from Qatar via UAE

Qatar's Dolphin project signed a long-term gas sales agreement in September 2005 committing Qatar to supply an average of 2 Bcm/yr of gas to Oman for 25 years from 2008 (approximately 10 percent of Dolphin's phase I capacity). At the signing of the agreement the Chairman of Dolphin Energy Shaikh Hamdan bin Zayid Al Nuhayyan said 'With the signing of this agreement, we can celebrate the creation of a true GCC gas grid – linking Qatar, the UAE and Oman'.[42] Gas from Dolphin is to be used in the Oxy operated Mukhaizna heavy oil project, which is planned to increase oil production from 21,000 barrels per day to 150,000 barrels per day by 2012.[43]

Most of Dolphin's customers, including Oman, have been pushing for an increase in supplies,[44] but additional volumes of gas have not been available due to the Qatari moratorium on developing new gas projects (see Chapter 9 on Qatar's gas revolution). First gas was supplied to Oman on 31 October 2008 when the final part of the

Qatar–UAE–Oman pipeline was completed. Since 2004 Oman had been supplying 1.4 Bcm/yr (135 MMscf/day) of gas to Fujairah's Union Water and Electricity Company (in the Northern United Arab Emirates) before the Dolphin pipeline started operation. This meant that Qatar could commence supply to all customers before all sections of the Dolphin pipeline were on stream, and demonstrated cooperation between Oman and Qatar.

As part of the supply arrangements for Dolphin gas, Ras al-Khaimah will take gas from Oman, up to the full contract volume of 2 Bcm/yr (200 MMscf/day) during the Omani winter when gas demand is low. It is understood that the price for this gas will be $5/MMBtu.[45] This is considerably higher than the price for the first phase gas from the Dolphin pipeline which is reported to have been contracted at around $1.30/MMBtu with a 1.5 percent annual escalator CIF Omani border.

Oman has been seeking additional gas volumes from Qatar without success. If more gas were made available to the Dolphin pipeline buyers by the Qataris, which is unlikely before 2016/17, then Oman would probably only be able to secure a share of the extra gas as other potential buyers are seeking additional volumes. If the pipeline was expanded from 2 Bcm/yr to 3 Bcm/yr then this could mean an additional 100 MMscf/day for Oman.

Gas Imports from Iran

Since May 2007, when Iran and Oman signed a Memorandum of Understanding (MoU) on broad cooperation across the oil and gas sector, the two countries have been in discussions about gas cooperation. The 2007 MoU covered the development of Iran's Kish gas field, joint exploration of the West Bukha/Hengam gas and condensate field, technology sharing, working together on petrochemical projects and the establishment of a joint venture company to develop gas opportunities. This relationship deepened in April 2008 with the signing of a framework agreement for the development of Kish field (estimated gas reserves 50 tcf (1310 Bcm) hopefully by July 2009, but this did not happen. In August 2009 Sultan Qaboos Bin Said, with a delegation including Omani Minister of Oil and Gas visited Tehran[46] in an attempt to advance the project.

The relationship is politically sensitive and the close governmental links with Britain and pressure from the USA could well put the Omani government in a difficult position – whether to move ahead and upset its western friends or to delay gas developments with Iran and face potential shortages. Iran however is seen as a close neighbour with whom it will continue to have discussions in the future. With these political tensions a fast conclusion to the negotiations is unlikely.

The cost of the Kish project varies depending on who is making the statement; in July 2008 Iranian Offshore Oil Company (IOOC) managing director Mahmoud Zirakchianzadeh said 'Oman says the cost will be $12 billion, others say $8 billion'.[47] The investment cost is significant partly because of the need for a 500 km, 42 inch pipeline running from the central Persian Gulf island to Oman. 'The gas is sweet and the pressure is very good', Zirakchianzadeh added. The pipeline would land in the Musandam Peninsular. The two-phase field project should give gas export capacity of 10 Bcm/yr increasing to 20 Bcm/yr with development of the third-phase (at a cost of an additional US$ 5 billion). It is planned that half of phase 1 gas would be used in Southern Iran and the other half would be split 70 percent to Oman and 30 percent to Iran (which would also be sent to Oman as LNG feedgas). Phase II gas could be used for export to Pakistan. Under the buyback deal, Oman would recover its investment and an agreed rate of return until all costs have been recovered.[48] Reports however say that one of the sticking points has been Tehran's insistence on having different prices depending on how Oman intends to use the Iranian gas.

There has been a proposal that gas supplied from Iran could be used as feedstock for Oman LNG and Qalhat LNG; a joint company could be established that would market LNG produced from the Iranian gas. This would give Tehran valuable marketing experience for its own LNG export projects, but it may be difficult to achieve.

By the end of 2009 the message from the Iranians to Oman was that Iran has several export options, to Europe via Turkey, to India and Pakistan as well as to Oman. The Iranians were of the view that these exports could yield prices of $6–7/MMBtu (at $70/bbl oil) and that is what Oman would have to pay for the gas. Since Oman would not be able to secure gas from Iran at a discount price, at the prices being offered, it would be cheaper to develop its own domestic gas reserves, which would also provide greater supply security. In February 2010, the press reported[49] that a $10 bn contract to finance and develop the Kish gas field had been signed between the National Iranian Oil Company and an Iranian consortium headed by Bank Mellat. However, a month later the Omani Minister of Oil and Gas announced that the negotiations with neighbouring countries on gas supply were still ongoing.[50] It is therefore not clear whether Iran wants to export its gas and, if it does, whether Oman will be the buyer.

Energy Challenges and Gas Strategy

As with other Gulf countries Oman has huge challenges facing its energy sector. After some years of declining oil and gas exploration, including being embroiled in the Shell reserves downgrade in 2004,[51] oil production started to rise again in 2008 and this trend continued in 2009. Government policy has been to establish gas-intensive industries as a means to develop the economy and increase jobs. The real issue is gas availability. Currently there is enough gas to meet growing domestic demand, but gas is being diverted away from the LNG export plants to meet local requirements. This results in underutilised capacity in the LNG plants (3.7 Bcma or 24 percent of capacity as at January 2010). The government insists that the country has sufficient gas until 2018–20, but some industry observers believe that real shortages could appear nearer to 2010[52] if no new gas is discovered. Thus there could be a short-term shortage of gas if new gas fields do not start production as planned by the government. Most long-term LNG contracts expire in 2024 and in order for these to be renewed substantial volumes of additional gas will need to be found.

New gas reserves are however more complex to develop and produce and domestic gas prices of $0.80–1.50/MMBtu are not sufficient either to support the high cost of developing the tight gas or sour gas projects or to compete with international LNG market prices; new domestic gas will cost $2.80–5.00/MMBtu. The dilemma facing the government is therefore how to stimulate the development of new gas reserves in an environment of low domestic gas prices with gas demand expected to grow at 5–10 percent per annum. Concerns over gas availability have already forced the cancellation of new petrochemicals plants and trials on alternative sources of power generation. The government has stated that the strategic priority for domestic gas will be the power sector.

The last seven years have seen the government implement positive initiatives in order to develop more gas reserves. These include attracting new companies into the country to bring new technology and to diversify the development away from PDO. The government has also pushed PDO to operate more efficiently and to discover more reserves. New gas developments are being undertaken by BP, Occidental (Oxy) and small Omani independents. The start-up of some smaller gas fields in Oman and imports from the Dolphin pipeline in October 2008 have provided welcome relief. As described above, the government has considered imports of gas from Iran. However, as at early 2010, the conclusion reached is that Iranian gas will potentially cost $7–8/MMBtu and the Qataris are unlikely to make substantial volumes of additional gas available. Hence the focus has turned to the development of domestic gas reserves, which can be produced at price levels similar to the cost of importing from Iran. The government has reported that expenditure on oil and gas production in 2010 is expected to be $3.77 billion, a 5.8 percent rise from 2009 levels.[53]

The strategy for use of gas produced in Oman has changed over the last ten years. In the mid 1990s, commercialisation of gas was new to the country, and it regarded the development of an LNG export project as a means to generate foreign exchange revenues, which could be used to diversify away from oil and grow the Omani economy. The expansion of LNG exports, through the development of Qalhat LNG, together with the extensive expansion of domestic power, industrial and petrochemical projects has left Oman short of gas with LNG projects operating below full capacity and new domestic gas projects delayed or cancelled. In 2009 19.9 percent of gas produced in the country was used for power generation, 42.8 percent for LNG production and 17.7 percent in the industrial sector. Oman also needs gas to produce its oil (currently approximately 20 percent of domestic production) and this percentage is expected to rise with increased demand from enhanced oil recovery (EOR) projects. To meet this rising domestic demand, gas supplied to the LNG projects was reduced in 2008 vs. 2007 and further in 2009. Most of the LNG contracts expire in 2024–26 and without the discovery of new gas reserves they are unlikely to be extended – even though this would leave the LNG facilities under-utilised and reduce hydrocarbon export earnings.

Gas is currently sold into the domestic market at fixed prices – the power sector pays $1.50/MMbtu, industry $1.50/MMBtu and metha-nol/fertiliser $0.80/MMBtu.[54] The cost of new gas depends on whether any condensate revenues or government shareholding is taken into account, with estimates as low as $2.50 and as high as $5–6/MMBtu. It is unlikely that gas prices to existing domestic projects will increase, so the difference between the gas price and the cost of gas will be borne by the government, either as a formal declared subsidy (as with the power sector) or simply absorbed by the budget. By signing agreements with companies to purchase new gas at higher prices, the government has effectively accepted that such financial support must be given.

The government has restricted the sale of LNG to long-term commit-ted volumes only, not agreeing to any new short- or long-term contracts, in order to push back to 2018/2020 the time when gas supply cannot meet demand. In parallel new gas developments have been encouraged and the use of new technology to increase production – for example PDO has been developing new sources of government gas to use in its EOR projects, thus freeing up gas for domestic use. Domestic gas is prioritised first for power and new projects will be sanctioned based on economics, gas usage and the number of jobs that they generate.

New domestic projects will come under pressure to pay market prices for gas, perhaps linked to oil. The sentiment is that although domestic gas prices will have to increase over time, if they increase too high or too fast then industry may decide not to invest in Oman. Therefore the government may decide to offer a discount from the cost of production to attract industry and consequently jobs. Ironically, expansions to existing projects may be able to pay a higher price for gas (as they will enjoy economies of scale and can 'blend' the initial lower cost with the new higher cost gas). On the other hand it is new projects that can offer greater employment.

Coal has been considered for power and water projects, but plans have been deferred for environmental, economic and strategic reasons. There are pilot projects underway for power from solar and wind.

Oman is not in crisis, but without new domestic gas production the country will obviously be unable to develop new gas-based industry or gas-fired power generation. LNG exports are unlikely to increase and may fall further, but the government will meet its existing long-term LNG supply obligations. The dilemma is likely to be whether to use gas for production of oil, for domestic industry, or for export as LNG. It is probable that economics will dictate that the use of gas for EOR would be a more efficient use of its resources.

Conclusions

Increased domestic gas demand, driven by power and the development of gas-intensive petrochemical and fertiliser projects, together with lower volumes of domestically produced gas has led to a shortage of gas in Oman. The LNG projects are operating below full capacity and new domestic projects have been deferred which could have had a positive impact on the country's economic growth. The priority for domestic gas is power followed by EOR; and increased demand for power means that new power and water projects have to be built. These are likely to be gas-fired, as coal is not a preferred option for environmental and security of supply reasons.

It is true that a considerable amount has been done over the past 5–7 years to address current and future gas shortages. Pressure has been put on PDO by the government and new companies bringing technology and resources exploring for gas has led to new gas being found, leading to increased production by 2015. Oman has also closely examined importing gas from neighbouring countries but, with the exception of the gas from Qatar via the Dolphin pipeline, it is unlikely that large volumes of reliable gas will be available at attractive prices. The Omanis are therefore not going to rely solely on incremental imports from its GCC neighbours and the focus is on finding more gas in the country. To that end, the author believes that the government will agree to realistic pricing and fiscal terms with investors that will encourage exploration. Oil and condensate production has increased and in 2009 a record 100,000 barrels/day of condensate was produced.

In the short term exports of LNG have been maintained at a level that only meets long-term contracts, which means that the plants are operating below 80 percent capacity. It is unlikely that the spare capacity will be contracted, or the existing long-term contracts extended, unless considerable new volumes of gas are discovered in Oman. However, with the current focus on exploration new gas discoveries are possible.

While the economic cost of developing new gas increases, domestic prices are low and are likely to remain so. The difference will be borne by the government, either in the form of a formal subsidy or set against its oil and gas revenues. Another possibility is setting the cost of new higher cost gas against older cheaper gas, with the result that the average price of domestic gas could be affordable to some new industries. Over the past five years Oman has taken considerable steps to maintain its gas supply position and it is likely that the government will continue with its current policies to ensure additional production is maintained in the future.

Appendix I – Oman Domestic Gas Pipelines

a. Owned by OGC

From/To	Size	Comments
Fahud production and processing centre to the Sohar industrial zone	305 km, 32 inch 3.65 Bcm/yr (353 MMscf/d)	Completed in 2002 and owned by OGC. Capacity increased to 805 Mcf/d with the installation of new compression facilities at Buraimy.

From / To	Size	Comments
Saih Rawl production processing centre in central Oman to Salalah, capital of Dhofar province in the south	670 km, 24 inch 2.77 Bcm/yr (268 MMscf/d)	Completed in 2002
Yibal to Muscat 20 inch	324 km, 20 inch 1.28 Bcm/yr (124 MMscf/d)	Completed in 1978
Yibal to Muscat 36 inch	297 km, 36 inch 5.11 Bcm/yr (494 MMscf/d)	Completed in 1986
Murayrat to Sohar	226 km, 16 inch. 1.8 Bcm/yr (177 MMscf/d)	Completed in 1981
Saih Rawl to Sadad commissioned September 2009	252 km, 32 inch. 2.55 Bcm/yr (247 MMscf/d)	Completed in 2009
BVS 07 of 32" P/L (Fahud to Sohar) to Mahadha	45 km, 24 inch.	Completed in 2003

Source: OGC

b. Owned by PDO

From / To	Size	Comments
Yibal to Muscat	331 km, 20 inch 1.28 Bcm/yr (124 MMscf/d)	Expanded in 1986 and 1989 with an additional 120 km 26 inch section between Izki and Murayat. Owned by PDO
Saih Nihayda to Sur (LNG plant)	355 km, 48 inch line	48 inch loop installed to supply the third LNG train (Qalhat LNG). Owned by PDO
Spur line from Yibal to Muscat pipeline to Rusail industrial zone.		Owned by PDO
Mureirat to Sohar	250 km 16 inch	Owned by PDO
Saih Nihayda to Ghaba	30 km	Owned by PDO

Source: Author research

Appendix II – Oman Shipping Capacity

a) *Vessels chartered by Oman*

Vessel Name	Size (m³)	Ownership	Use
Sohar LNG (formerly LNG Lakshmi)	138,000	OSC (50 percent); Mitsui OSK Line - MOL (50 percent)	In 2001 Oman LNG chartered the LNG Lakshmi, an LNG vessel that was on long-term charter hire to the defunct Dabhol Power Company (DPC). It is now chartered to Oman LNG for ex-ship LNG sales
Muscat LNG	145,000	OSC (75 percent), MOL (20 percent) and Mitsui and Co (5 percent)	Chartered by Oman LNG for 17 years, currently sub-chartered to Shell

b) *Vessels constructed for Oman Shipping Company*

Vessel Name	Size (m³)	Ownership	Use
Nizwa LNG	145,000	OSC (60 percent), MOL (20 percent), Itochu Corporation (20 percent)	Chartered to Itochu Corporation for 20 years (as part of the arrangements whereby Itochu purchases LNG from Oman)
Ibri LNG	145,000	OSC (60 percent), MOL (20 percent) and Mitsubishi Corporation (20 percent)	Chartered to Mitsubishi corporation for 20 years (as part of the arrangements whereby Mitsubishi purchases LNG from Qalhat LNG)
Salalah LNG	145,000	OSC (80 percent) and MOL (20 percent)	Chartered to Qalhat LNG to transport LNG to Union Fenosa Gas
Ibra LNG	145,000	OSC (80 percent) and MOL (20 percent)	Chartered to Qalhat LNG
Barka LNG	153,000	OSC (40 percent) and Osaka Gas (60 percent)	Chartered to Qalhat LNG

Source: Oman Shipping Company website www.omanship.com

Appendix III – Oman Oil Company Operating Investments

Upstream

Investment	Country	Oman Oil Company Share
Abraj Energy Services	Oman	100 percent
Oil Exploration and Production in Mukhaizna Concession	Oman	20 percent
Oil Exploration in Caspian Offshore Concession ('Pearls')	Kazakhstan	20 percent
Oil Exploration in Dunga Concession	Kazakhstan	20 percent
Service Contract in Karim Small Fields	Oman	25 percent
Service Contract in Rima Small Fields	Oman	25 percent

Source: Oman Oil Company

Energy Infrastructure

Investment	Country	Oman Oil Company Share
China Gas Holdings (10,000 km + pipeline)	China	7.45 percent
Compañia Logística de Hidrocarburos S.A - CLH (3,200 km + pipeline)	Spain	10 percent
Oiltanking Odfjell Terminals & Co. (OOT)	Oman	25 percent
Oman Gas Company - OGC (2,000 km + pipeline)	Oman	20 percent
Planta de Regasification de Sagunto (150,000m³ capacity)	Spain	7.5 percent*
Qingdao Lixing Logistics	China	30 percent
Enagas (gas pipelines)	Spain	5 percent

*   Under the terms of the original agreement with Union Fenosa Gas as part of the QLNG project development, OOC was expected to take a 15 percent stake in the Sagunto import terminal near Valencia

Source: Oman Oil Company & author research

Shipping

Investment	Country	Oman Oil Company Share
Gulf Energy Maritime - GEM (ownership vessels)	UAE	30 percent
Oman Shipping Company (OSC)	Oman	20 percent

Source: Oman Oil Company & author research

Power

Investment	Country	Oman Oil Company Share
GS EPS (1075 MW power plant)	South Korea	30 percent
Orient Power Co. Ltd - OPCL (450 MW power plant)	Pakistan	49 percent

Source: Oman Oil Company & author research

Petrochemicals

Investment	Country	Oman Oil Company Share
Aromatics Oman (AOL)	Oman	70 percent
La Seda De Barcelona	Spain	6 percent
Oman India Fertilizer (OMIFCO)	Oman	50 percent
Oman Polypropylene (OPP)	Oman	40 percent
PTT Chemical (PTTCH)	Thailand	1.12 percent
Qingdao Lidong Chemical	China	30 percent
Salalah Methanol (SMC)	Oman	100 percent

Source: Oman Oil Company

Refining and Marketing

Investment	Country	Oman Oil Company Share
MOL	Hungary	7 percent
Oman Oil Marketing Co. S.A.O.G Oil products marketing and sales	Oman	49 percent
Oman Refineries & Petrochemicals Co. (ORPC) (two refineries in Oman, one in Mina Al-Fahal and another in Sohar)	Oman	25 percent
Oman Trading International (OTI is a publicly listed company)	UAE	51 percent
Takamul Investment Co. (investments in the resources sector)	Oman	90 percent
UAE Gas Sales	Oman	100 percent

Source: Oman Oil Company & author research

Metals

Investment	Country	Oman Oil Company Share
Sohar Aluminium Company (SAC)	Oman	40 percent

Source: Oman Oil Company

Appendix IV – Major Gas Users in Oman

Petrochemicals

Plant	Location	Size	Ownership	Comments
Methanol	Sohar	1 million MT/year (3000 MT/day)	Oman Methanol Company - Methanol Holding Trinidad & Tobago: 50 percent, OOC: 30 percent, MAN: 20 percent	Started production in first half 2007. There are plans to double capacity in the second phase.
Polypropylene terephthalate	Salalah	300,000 MT/year (3000 MT/day)	Octal Holding	Started production in October 2008. A second phase is scheduled to be completed in 2011 with an additional 200,000 MT/year capacity
Methanol	Salalah	1 million MT/year (3000 MT/day)	Salalah Methanol Company a subsidiary of OOC	To start production in 2010. The project includes power and seawater de-salination and waste water treatment facilities.
Paraxylene and benzene aromatics complex	Sohar	I million MT/yr (3000 MT/day)	Aromatics Oman LLC – OOC: 60 percent, Oman Refinery Co: 20 percent, LG International: 20 percent	Production started in November 2009. The plant runs on naphtha from the Sohar refinery.
Polypropylene	Sohar	Ammonia: 340,000 MT/year (1000 MT/day) Urea: 1.3 million MT/yr (3500 MT/day)	Oman Polypropylene LLC – OOC: 40 percent, Gulf Investment Corp: 20 percent International Petroleum Investment Co: 20 percent,* LG International: 20 percent)	Started production in October 2006

Plant	Location	Size	Ownership	Comments
Ammonia & urea	Sohar	700,000 MT/yr (2000 MT/day)	Sohar International Urea and Chemical Industries	Started production in 2008.
Ammonia & urea	Sur	Ammonia: 1.3 million MT/yr (3500 MT/day) Urea: 1.7 million MT/yr (4700 MT/day)	Oman India Fertiliser Company – OOC: 50 percent, Indian Farmers Fertiliser Cooperative: 25 percent, Krishak Bharati Cooperative: 25 percent	Started production in 2005.

* OOC sold 20 percent to International Petroleum Investment Company (IPIC) two months after the plant started up

Note: Oman Petrochemical Industries Company's (OPIC)/Dow Chemicals olefins complex was cancelled in 2007 due to increasing costs (from $2 billion to over $3 billion) and shortage of gas feedstock. The Liwa Petrochemicals ethylene dichloride plant that was to be developed in Sohar, was also cancelled in 2007 for the same reason.

Aluminium and Mining

Plant	Location	Size	Ownership	Comments
Electrolysis	Sohar	360,000 MT/yr	Sohar Aluminium Company - OOC 40 percent, Abu Dhabi Water and Electricity Authority: 40 percent, Alcan: 20 percent	Production started in June 2008, full production reached by February 2009

Power and Water Desalination Projects

a. Private Sector IPP and IWPP

Plant	Location	Size	Ownership	Comments
Al Manah IPP	All Manah (supplies Nizwa, Barka & Irki)	90 MW expanded to 280 MW	MENA Infrastructure Investment Limited, Omani investors and 40 percent public shareholding	First IPP in region, stage one COD in 1996
Al Kamil IPP	Sharqiyah	275 MW	International Power, 35 percent public shareholding	Build own and operate BOO project
Salalah I IPP	Salalah	196 MW	Dhofar Power Company - Omani Founder Group, 35 percent public shareholding and Electricity Holding Company SAOC	The company is also responsible for transmission, distribution billing and collection in the Salalah Concession Area
Barka I IWPP	Barka	427 MW and 20 million gallons/day water desalination	AES, Multitech, 35 percent public shareholding	BOO IWPP project
Sohar 1 IWPP	Sohar	585 MW and 30 million gallons/day water desalination	Sohar Power Company – GDFSuez and four local companies – 35 percent equity was sold to the public in 2008	BOO IWPP project. The power plant supplies Sohar refinery, polypropylene plants and other industries
Al Rusail IPP	Barka	690 MW	Suez, Mubadala, NTC Oman	Privatised in 2007
Barka 2 IWPP	Barka	678 MW and 12,000 m³/hour water desalination	Suez, Mubadala, NTC Oman	Early power 2008, full power May 2009 full water production commenced Q4 2009

b. *Government owned Production Facilities*

Plant	Location	Size	Ownership	Comments
Al Ghubra	Muscat (supplies the capital Muscat)	523 MW and large desalination plant	Ghubra Powerand Desalination Company (100 percent government owned)	Government of Oman
Wadi Jizzi	Wadi Jizzi	295 MW	Wadi Jizzi Power Company (100 percent government owned)	Government of Oman

c. *IWPP Under construction*

Plant	Location	Size	Ownership	Comments
Salalah 2 IWPP	Salalah	400 MW and 15 million gallons/ day water desalination	Sembicorp, Oman Investment Corp (OIC)	Start-up expected H2/2012

In addition PDO owns its own power generation facilities.

Water Desalination Joint Projects

Plant	Location	Size	Ownership	Comments
BOO Water desalination	Sur	80,200 m³/ day	Veolia Water Solutions and Suhail Bahwan Group	

Notes

1   Minister of National Economy Oman, 'Monthly Statistics'. www.moneoman. gov.om
2   Minister of National Economy Budget Statement on 2 January 2010 and MNE statistics. Assumes Omani Rial/US$ exchange rate of OR1 = $2.60.
3   *Petroleum Argus*, 2 March 2009, 'Oman Special Report'.
4   Ministry of Oil and Gas, 'National Economy Monthly Statistics', www. moneoman.gov.om

5   *Arab Oil & Gas Directory 2007*, 'Oman'.
6   www.alacrastore.com/research/s-and-p-credit-research-Oman_Sultanate_of-708625, 12 March 2009.
7   *MEES*, LII:32, 10 August 2009, p.17, 'Moody's sees stable outlook for Omani banking system'.
8   Moody's Global Credit Research.
9   BP *Statistical Review of World Energy*, June 2010.
10   *Petroleum Argus*, 2 March 2009, 'Oman Special Report'.
11   *MEES*, 23 June 2009, Vol LI No 25, 'Oman Oil adds to upstream assets'.
12   International Petroleum Investment Company, Abu Dhabi.
13   http://www.molgroup.hu
14   www.oman-oil.com press release 10 March 2008, 'Oman Oil Company SAOC and MOL Plc. Sign Strategic Cooperation Agreement'.
15   www.gasnaturalyunionfenosa.com/en, press release 1 June 2009, 'Gas Natural sells its 5 percent stake in Enagas to Oman Oil'. From this press release the CEO of OOC said, 'We are proud to announce this latest acquisition by Oman Oil Company, which comes in line with the Company's strategy to grow its investments internationally... The acquisition of a stake in Enagas is in line with our efforts to diversify our investment portfolio between Omani and international assets'.
16   *Petroleum Argus*, 2 March 2009, 'Oman Special Report'.
17   There are four gas processing plants in Oman with a total capacity of 35 Bcm/yr: 1) Kauther (7.3 Bcm/yr) 2) Saih Nihayda (7.3 Bcm/yr gas and 80,000 b/d condensate) 3) Saih Rawl (14.6 Bcm/yr) 4) Yibal (6 Bcm/yr).
18   *PDO Media Briefing*, 15 February 2010, p. 3.
19   *PDO Media Briefing*, 15 February 2010.
20   PDO *Annual Report* 2008.
21   www.zawya.com/story.cfm/sidZAWYA20070221032834/Hanover percent-20set percent20to percent20expand percent20Oman percent20operations
22   http://www.zawya.com 'Block 62 concession awarded to Oxy', 23 November 2008.
23   *MEES*, 21 April 2008, Vol LI No 16, 'Oman becomes first frontier in Gulf battle for difficult oil and gas'.
24   *MEES*, 16 March 1998, Vol XLI No 11, 'Industrial players get priority as Oman allocates growing gas reserve base'.
25   See www.aer-oman.org
26   'Study on Renewable Energy Resources', Oman, Authority for Electricity Regulation, Oman. Final Report. May 2008.
27   http://www.aer-oman.org/about us/annual reports
28   Subsidy is defined as the difference between the economic cost of supply (including financing costs) and permitted tariff – see Authority of Electricity Regulation, *Annual Report 2008*, p.33 (www.aer-oman.org)
29   Seminar on 'Using Coal for Electric Power Generation in the Sultanate of Oman' was held January 24–25, 2010 in Muscat, organised by the Ministry of National Economy.
30   The plant is run by ModernWater; see website for details (www.modernwater.

co.uk).

31 For details of individual pipelines see Appendix I.

32 *APS Review Downstream Trends*, 30 January 2006, 'Oman – The Local Market'.

33 FOB = Free on Board where the LNG buyer arranges the shipping.

34 The main source for this section is www.qalhatlng.com

35 Qalhat LNG Press Release, 27 May 2006, www.qalhatlng.com/pdf/qal-hat_lng_02.pdf

36 In 2009 Gas Natural purchased Union Fenosa.

37 http://www.zoominfo.com/

38 *Muscat Daily*, 13 March 2010.

39 The LNG value chain is made up of four elements: upstream, liquefaction, shipping and regasification.

40 http://www.zawya.com/story.cfm/sidZAWYA20051129055126, 29 November 2005, 'Oman Shipping Co acquires interest in new LNG carrier'.

41 A list of OSC's LNG vessels can be found in Appendix II.

42 http://www.dolphinenergy.com/Public/media-center

43 http://www.mubadala.ae/en/about-mubadala/investments/mukhaizna-oil-field.html

44 *MEES*, 10 August 2008, LII:32 p. 17, 'Oman and Iran continue to discuss gas cooperation'.

45 *MEES*, 21 April 2008, Vol LI No 16, 'Oman becomes first frontier in Gulf battle for difficult oil and gas'.

46 *MEES*, 10 August 2009, LII:32 p. 16, 'Oman and Iran continue to discuss gas cooperation'.

47 *Upstream*, 11 July 2008, 'Oman and Iran close to deal on Kish gas for LNG scheme'.

48 *World Gas Intelligence*, 23 April 2008, 'Oman, Iran in unique gas buyback deal'.

49 http://www.shana.ir/151721-en.html

50 *Muscat Daily*, 13 March 2010.

51 Reserves downgrade means that the amount of gas reserves declared by a company is reduced in their annual accounts and with the statutory agencies. Source: *Alexanders Gas & Oil Connections*, 5 October 2004, vol 9, issue #19, 'Chinese Oil in Oman'.

52 *MEES*, 30 March 2009, Vol LII No 13, 'Oman sidesteps credit crunch as liquids output rises'.

53 Minister of National Economy Budget Statement on 2 January 2010.

54 Author's estimates.

CHAPTER 12

THE UAE GAS SECTOR: CHALLENGES AND SOLUTIONS FOR THE TWENTY-FIRST CENTURY

Justin Dargin and Andy Flower[1]

Brief History of the UAE

The UAE was formed from a group of tribal Sheikdoms organised along the southern coast of the Arabian Gulf and the north-western coast of the Gulf of Oman. The area was a heavily trafficked trade route and had fallen prey to periodic piracy. Britain initially began what turned out to be a long involvement in the area, minor actions to suppress brigandry and piracy on the open seas that were threatening its valuable India trade. In 1820, the principal sheikhs of the region concluded a general peace with British authorities pledging to halt all piracy and to protect trade. In 1853, the various sheikhs signed a treaty with the United Kingdom, under which the sheikhs (the 'Trucial Sheikhdoms') agreed to a 'perpetual maritime truce'. This peace was enforced by the United Kingdom, and disputes among sheikhs were referred to the British for arbitration and settlement. For the next hundred years, Britain and the UAE had an extremely close relationship.

However, by 1968, the UK announced its decision to withdraw from all of its commitments 'east of the Suez'. The UK reaffirmed its decision in March 1971 to withdraw by the end of that year. The Trucial Sheikhdoms had been, together with Bahrain and Qatar, the Gulf States formally under British protection. During 1971, just prior to the British withdrawal, the nine states – the seven Sheikhdoms, along with Bahrain and Qatar – negotiated to form a unitary state. However, as the date of British disengagement rapidly approached, they were unable to resolve their differences and negotiations collapsed.

Bahrain became independent in August and Qatar in September 1971. When the British–Trucial Sheikhdoms treaty expired on 1 December 1971, Bahrain and Qatar became fully independent. On 2 December 1971, six Trucial Sheikdoms, Abu Dhabi, Dubai, Ajman, Sharjah, Umm al Quwain and Fujairah, entered into a union

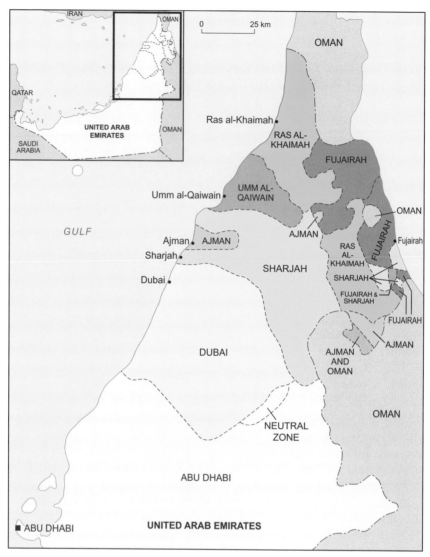

Map 12.1: UAE Domestic Border Map

designated, the United Arab Emirates (See Map 12.1). The seventh, Ras al-Khaimah, joined in early 1972.

In contemporary times, the UAE is characterised by a flexible federalism that enables the various Emirates to keep their own unique form of governance. Each Emirate has its own ruler, who thereby sets the tone for the pace of modernisation within his territory.

Overview of the UAE Domestic Gas Sector

Domestic Reserves

After the Russian Federation, Iran, Qatar, and Saudi Arabia, the United Arab Emirates (UAE) holds the fifth largest proven gas reserves in the world, i.e., 3.5 percent of the global total. Estimated at 6.43 Trillion cubic metres (Tcm) at the end of 2009, Emirati reserves should last another 85 years at 2009 rates of production.[2] The bulk of Emirati gas is located in the capital of the UAE, the Emirate of Abu Dhabi, which holds more than 90 per cent, approximately 5.62 Tcm of the UAE's total reserves (see Table 12.1).

Table 12.1: UAE Gas Reserves, 2009

	TCM	*Share of Total (%)*
Abu Dhabi	5.98	92.58
Dubai	.11 (113 Bcm)	1.87
Sharjah	.303 (303 Bcm)	4.99
Ras Al Khaimah	.03 (34 Bcm)	.56
Ajman		0
Umm Al Quwain	.01 (14.16 Bcm)	0
Fujairah		0
Total	6.43 (6070 Bcm)	100

Sources: BP *Statistical Review of World Energy*, 2010

The Emirate of Dubai holds 2 percent (113.3 Billion cubic metres (Bcm), while the Northern Emirates of Sharjah[3] and Ras al-Khaimah contain the remaining amounts of 303 Bcm and 34 Bcm, respectively.[4] Because the gas fields in the Northern Emirates have matured, their respective production rates have fallen in recent years.

In Abu Dhabi, the non-associated Khuff natural gas reservoirs that sit beneath the Umm Shaif and the Abu Al Bukhush (see Map 12.1) oil fields are some of the world's largest gas reserves. Since most Abu Dhabi gas is 'sour', extraction and processing are significantly more costly compared to the early associated gas fields that traditionally provided most Emirati gas.

UAE Production

However, natural gas is perhaps the UAE's most important domestic energy source; it produced 48.8 Bcm in 2009, or 1.6 percent of global natural gas production for that year.[5] But more indicative of the regional energy challenges, it consumed 59.1 Bcm, which exposed it to a shortfall of 10.3 Bcm.[6]

During 2009, the UAE imported, through the Dolphin natural gas pipeline, 17.25 Bcm (approximately 47.3 Million cubic metres per day (million cm/d))[7] of natural gas from Qatar, and exported 7.01 Bcm of natural gas in the form of LNG that same year.[8] Because much of the UAE's gas is associated with oil reservoirs or is 'sour' gas in non-associated fields, Emirati authorities have focused primarily on increasing production capacity by simultaneously advancing their technical expertise on sour gas treatment technology, and development of technology that separates oil from gas. Even before Qatar became the dominant gas producer in the Gulf, Abu Dhabi was one of the first Gulf nations to recognise the inherent value of monetising natural gas that other oil-producing states were wastefully flaring. In 1977, The Abu Dhabi Gas Liquefaction Company (ADGAS) constructed the first LNG plants in the Gulf at Das Island to process associated gas from the Umm Shaif, Lower Zakum, and Bunduq oil fields[9] (see Map 12.2).

Even though the UAE increased its gas production slightly in the mid-to-late 2000s, since late 2006, gas demand continued to steadily outstrip incremental production increases (see Figure 12.1). One reason Emirati natural gas demand is so high is because of the disproportionate role it plays in power generation, where it accounts for 98 percent, with fuel oil comprising the rest.[10]

As discussed below, energy shortages have wreaked havoc in the domestic economy, and reversed some of the Federation's most ambitious

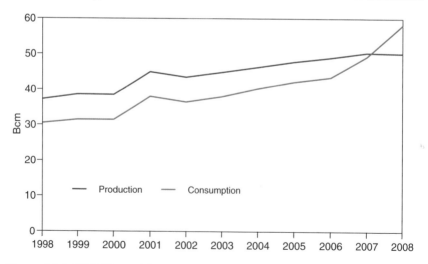

Figure 12.1: UAE Natural Gas Production and Consumption

Source: BP *Statistical Review of World Energy*, 2009

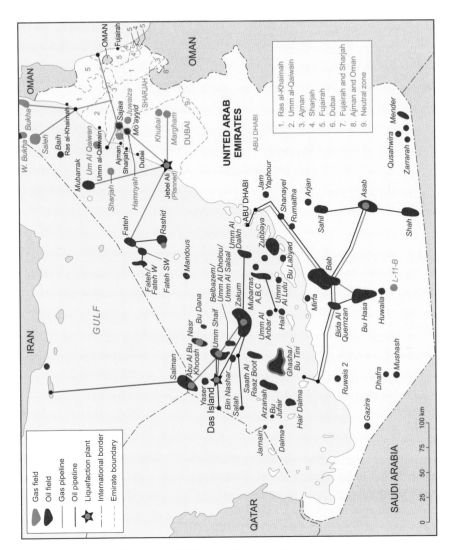

Map 12.2: UAE Oil and Gas Fields and Related Infrastructure

industrialisation plans. Demographic increases, burgeoning electricity consumption, real estate growth, and an expansion in the petrochemical industry have combined to increase demand significantly, putting pressure on the UAE's ability to provide sufficient gas for the domestic market. Emirati gas demand has increased at an annualised 10 percent for the past 34 years.[11] In addition to demographic factors, the large demand increase in natural gas reflects the petrochemical industry's preference for natural gas as a feedstock, as well as for natural gas in power generation and water desalination projects.

Table 12.2: UAE Natural Gas Imports and Exports, 2009, Bcm/yr

Exports (LNG)		Imports	
Japan	7.41	Qatar (Dolphin) (Dubai and Abu Dhabi)	17.25[14] (additional 'interruptible' supply) 0.91–4.12
India	0.13	Qatargas and Shell LNG (Dubai)	0.9
		Oman (West Bukha) (Ras al-Khaimah)	1.09–1.4

Source: BP *Statistical Review of World Energy*, 2010

Table 12.3: Gas Flows Between the Emirates, 2008, Bcm/yr

Domestic Imports/Exports	Dubai (Import)	Ras al-Khaimah (Import)
Sharjah (Export)		1.02 (2.8 million cm/d)
Abu Dhabi (Export)	5.16 (14.1 Million Cu m/d)	
Umm al-Quwain (Export)		.80 Bcm/yr (.0227 Million Cu m/d)

Source: Author's research

The UAE also consumes approximately 18 Bcm/yr of natural gas for re-injection in mature oil fields, a practice that places even more pressure on its ability to satisfy domestic demand. Stringent OPEC oil production quotas, increased domestic gas consumption, and the reluctance of regional suppliers – Iran and Qatar – to supply low priced gas, motivated the UAE to develop its own significant non-associated gas reserves.[12]

Reluctance to develop Abu Dhabi's sour gas led the UAE to seek gas imports from neighbouring countries, i.e., Iran's Salman gas field, and even more so, Qatar's enormous North Field gas reservoir. For much of the late 1980s the UAE and Qatar negotiated the development of a pan-Gulf natural gas pipeline. After the negotiations ultimately collapsed, the UAE, Qatar and Oman focused on their own individual needs and in the late 1990s collectively negotiated an agreement to construct a natural gas pipeline that would supply the UAE and Oman with relatively inexpensive Qatari gas.[13] The brainchild of Dolphin Energy Limited (DEL), the Dolphin Natural Gas Pipeline Project was constructed primarily for the express purpose of relieving some of the

UAE's – then minor – gas shortfalls, and, secondly, to support Gulf energy coordination.

Although gas imported through Dolphin became a vital economic lifeline for the UAE, nevertheless, starting in 2007, a period of severe gas shortages developed. Dolphin gas imports are neither a permanent, nor a viable solution to the Emirate's gas deficit, rather they represent a holding action until the UAE's own formidable reserves can be brought into production. In 2009, the UAE imported 17.25 Bcm (57.3 million cm/d) of natural gas from Qatar through the Dolphin pipeline (see Table 12.2).

The Dolphin imports were much needed as the UAE's gas supply shortage reached 7.9 Bcm in 2008 and 10.3 Bcm in 2009.[15]

Not only do rolling blackouts spread through the various Emirates, but the gas shortages, having a decisive impact on power production, precipitated major project delays and cancellations.[16] To mitigate this crisis, the UAE undertook several innovative approaches, from the promotion of nuclear energy to energy conservation campaigns in order to mitigate the economic fallout. In the absence of a thorough review of the domestic gas and electricity tariff structures, many policy modifications will have only a cosmetic impact and ultimately leave the major structural problems unresolved.

The UAE Energy Crisis

Like many of the other Gulf countries, the UAE confronts a potentially sustained and far-reaching energy crisis. Despite increased energy production and imported Qatari gas through the Dolphin project, UAE domestic gas demand substantially exceeds supply. This created a shortfall that is filled by meeting power generation requirements with fuel oil, natural gas liquids, and in certain circumstances, coal. Because the UAE is almost totally reliant on natural gas for power generation, its total gas consumption is expected to reach 90 Bcm/yr by 2018, a significant increase from the 2009 rate of 59.1 Bcm.[17]

The UAE's rapid economic and demographic growth caused it to have the second highest consumption rate in absolute terms, e.g., after Saudi Arabia, amongst members of the Organization of Arab Petroleum Exporting Countries (OAPEC).[18] In 2010, The UAE National Human Resources Development and Employment Authority (Tanmia) announced that the UAE population doubles approximately every 8.7 years as compared to 55 years for the world population.[19] In 2010, the population reached 8.19 million and was continuing to grow at a robust rate, despite the global economic crisis. This population growth will increase the demand on scarce natural gas reserves.[20]

In a stark illustration of its rising natural gas demand, Emirati consumption overtook that of Egypt, a major consumer of natural gas in 2006.[21] Because the majority of the UAE's gas production is associated with oil production, the production limits attached to OPEC's quota system make future gas production difficult to predict as associated gas production is determined by oil output, and thereby dependent on the health of the global economy.[22]

On 8 February 2008, Khaled al-Awadi, the gas operations manager at Emirates General Petroleum Company (Emarat), made perhaps the first official acknowledgement of the UAE energy crisis, when he warned that unless decisive action was undertaken to increase gas supply and the efficiency of the UAE's gas grid, gas shortages could reach 20 Bcm/yr by 2025.[23] Al-Awadi stressed the need to find a resolution to the gas crisis, by stating: 'We need new gas supplies. The alternatives for gas are nuclear power in the long-term, and further sourcing of gas from Qatar and Abu Dhabi.'[24] Al-Awadi urged that power stations in the Northern Emirates be upgraded from open cycle to a combined cycle, which would potentially increase by 25 percent the power generation for a given quantity of gas.[25]

Yet, it must be kept in mind that the UAE official gas demand figures, which are limited to power generation and industrial use, exclude both volumes earmarked for enhanced oil recovery and LNG exports.

The UAE's energy situation has interrupted the industrialisation, modernisation and environmental plans of the government. The peak demand season of the summer of 2006 required deliveries of more than 300 trucks daily, laden with heavily polluting diesel fuel for Abu Dhabi's gas deficient power plants.[26] Before the Dolphin gas imports came online in 2007, it appeared that the UAE was heading for an economic implosion, as it was not able to meet its basic energy and power requirements.

However, officials at the Dubai Electricity and Water Authority (Dewa) disputed the use of the term 'energy crisis', and instead contended that Dubai did not experience any type of electricity shortage, primarily because, as in 2009, Dewa was able to fully satisfy the peak demand while holding approximately 1200 MW in reserve. Other analysts conclude that the main issue may not be a gas shortage per se, but rather a distribution bottleneck largely located in the Northern Emirates.[27] These contentions are justifiably disputed, since they focus merely on meeting peak demand, while neglecting the fact that fuel oil and coal, which in an Emirati context are much less economical fuels for electricity generation, were used to meet the significant repressed demand.[28]

The UAE incurred one of its worst gas shortages during the summer of 2007, when fuel oil and coal met the 10.25 Bcm/yr (28.1 million cm/d) shortfall.[29] For the summer months from calendar years 2006–2008, gas demand regularly surpassed the annual average by approximately 40 per cent, which, while peak seasonal demand is a common occurrence in many countries, significantly strained the UAE's ability to supply sufficient gas to the power utilities.[30] To mitigate the crisis, Abu Dhabi diverted some of its associated gas from its enhanced oil recovery (EOR) projects to local power plants, which resulted in a near-immediate drop in oil production.[31] Approximately 17 million cm/d (6.20 Bcm/yr) of gas, nearly a third of Abu Dhabi's EOR requirements, was diverted to power plants for electricity generation.[32]

Dubai and Abu Dhabi were spared the brunt of the gas shortage because Dolphin imports enabled them to avoid utilising significant amounts of expensive fuel liquids. While these two emirates were able to escape crippling blackouts, the gas shortage was most glaring in the Northern Emirates which were, in fact, in the worst position, and had to burn liquids even during off-peak demand.[33]

Even with the utilisation of liquid fuels as part of the energy mix, the Northern Emirates were not able to forestall rolling blackouts. It is not predicted that Dubai and Abu Dhabi will have to grapple with blackouts during the period up to 2015, despite the threat of runaway gas demand. Dolphin gas imports will be able to spare the two emirates that fate, but it does mean that the relatively less wealthy Northern Emirates will probably face continued blackouts. Dubai and Abu Dhabi have the financial resources to burn expensive fuel liquids and import LNG, while the Northern Emirates do not have that luxury.

The Northern Emirates may be symptomatic of the fate that awaits the rest of the UAE if a rational gas development strategy is not pursued. Chronic and unrelenting energy shortages in Sharjah, and the Northern Emirates of Ajman, Fujairah, Ras al-Khaimah and Umm al-Quwain, have posed a grave economic and ecological threat that illustrates the paradoxes at the crux of the crisis. Substantial adverse economic consequences resulted from the twin adversities of chronic electricity shortages and the global recession. Essentially, the real estate market dried up because investors and banks stopped funding new projects.[34]

During September 2009, Sharjah, which is home to approximately 40 percent of UAE-based businesses, witnessed extensive power interruptions that severely impacted more than 20 percent of its population and threatened its economic reputation.[35] This industrial centre, five times the size of Monaco, incurred a sustained power blackout for more than 12 hours per day, lasting over a month. At the beginning of the disruption, economists initially estimated that the power outages in Sharjah would cost the economy between $20 to $30 million dollars over a three-week period. When the blackout continued and was later found to impact the Sharjah Airport International Zone and the Hamriya Free Zone, economists revised the estimated losses sharply upward to approximately $136 million.[36] It appears that there is no end in sight, as Sharjah Electricity and Water Authority (SEWA) officials warned of recurrent blackouts as 'the gap between power production and consumption increase and power shortages worsen.'[37]

A 2009 government study carried out by the Federal Electricity and Water Authority (FEWA) painted a grim picture of the Northern Emirates' situation.[38] The Northern Emirates lack their own electricity and water authorities, and thus are dependent on FEWA to provide their basic power.[39] Because of the chronic power shortage, approximately 1000 commercial buildings waited to be connected to the power grid, some to no avail, after waiting many years.[40]

For calendar year 2008, gas demand in the north of the country reached around 31 million cm/d, but supply was well below this amount. In 2008, Ras al-Khaimah's gas demand was approximately 3.1 Bcm/yr (8.5 million cm/d), with the industrial sector (i.e. cement factories) accounting for 60 percent of the total.[41] The Northern Emirates met the shortage by burning diesel, fuel oil, and even coal during the peak demand periods. British Petroleum produces approximately 2.08 Bcm/yr (5.7 Million cm/d) from the Mo'ayyid, Sajaa, and Kahaif fields in Sharjah. Ras al-Khaimah receives some volumes diverted from these fields when Sharjah demand drops during the winter months (see Map 12.2). Ras al-Khaimah Petroleum supplies approximately 2.08 Bcm/yr (5.7 million cm/d) (and 900 b/d of condensates) to Ras al-Khaimah from the mature Bukha field. However, Bukha production is falling, and 2009 output was a mere .0365 Bcm/yr (0.5 million cm/d).

Because of the long delay to get their buildings connected to the grid, many in the Northern Emirates resorted to private and environmentally polluting diesel-powered generators to make their buildings habitable.[42] Generators are increasingly the only alternative for developers who have waited years to be connected to the grid. As a sign that many are becoming resigned to the lack of grid access and consistent power supply, developers began to build permanent generator enclosures to protect them from the elements. The construction of permanent enclosures signifies that residents and developers are intending to use generators for the long term, resigned to insufficient power supply and grid access.[43] However, because of the negative externalities, local authorities have sought to limit their use, while simultaneously guaranteeing that they will have the ability to meet the power, water, and gas demand from property investors.[44]

In a bid to increase power generation in 2007, authorities in the Northern Emirates recruited the private sector to help fund power projects.[45] The gas shortage also reversed many economic development plans of the Northern Emirates. The local authorities sought to transform the industrial area of al-Hayl into a vital industrial centre, but the lack of available power to fuel the energy-intensive industries and the increasing environmental pollution from the heavy industrial sector led some of the smaller Emirates, such as Ajman, Fujairah and Sharjah, to focus on reorienting their industrial base to produce higher technology offerings such as computers and related products.

The natural gas shortfall and the resultant lack of power, leaves rows of buildings empty and vast areas vacant. Federal officials attribute the energy crisis in the Northern Emirates to the lack of adequate city and residential planning.[46] These power problems are not only confined to the Northern Emirates; areas of Sharjah managed by the FEWA have also been hit by punishing power cuts throughout 2009.[47]

The Electricity Sector

As described above, gas demand in the UAE is driven by the strong growth in electricity demand, which itself is buttressed by economic growth, especially in the industrial sector, and population growth. There is almost a direct correlation between UAE electricity production and natural gas consumption; a slight change in one, invariably impacts the other. A 2009 Nomura Group 'Middle East Energy and Power' report illustrated that the UAE power market is extremely tight, especially during the peak summer months. The analysis estimated that in worst-case scenarios, there is only a 6 percent surplus spread unevenly across the UAE.[48] The report also cautioned that the UAE will require power sector investments of $12 billion annually until 2020 to confront rising electricity demand.[49]

UAE gas demand for power generation and water desalination is expected to double over the next decade. An important cause behind the consumer demand for power was the often-overlooked factor of increased wealth of individual citizens. At both a micro and macro level, increased wealth drove up demands on the power sector. Furthermore, economic growth is predicted to regain its tempo by 2011–2012.[50] The

UAE is also facing rapid population growth that will further complicate the country's ability to supply power to a populace that has no tradition of energy conservation. Both demand and supply side initiatives are necessary in order to prevent excess strain on the power and natural gas sectors. As long as the UAE's population continues to increase, power sector challenges will remain. Demand side strategies, as a means of reducing excessive electricity consumption, should be emphasised to achieve a balance in electricity requirements.

The establishment of marginal pricing before 6 pm – which means that the price of electricity increases with higher usage – is another way to reduce electricity over-consumption, encouraging consumers to introduce electricity conservation. Supply side investment in electricity generation such as thermal power production is required as well; this should be augmented by increased investment in electricity distribution systems. In addition, alternative energy sources could be developed to reduce reliance on natural gas for domestic power production. Nevertheless, in the absence of a political will to rationally increase electricity tariffs to send market signals to the end-users, the overall effect is likely to be simply cosmetic.

However, due to the onset of the global financial crisis in 2009, the prognosis may not be so dire. The Emirati government expects that the 2008 global recession will have an impact on long-term electricity demand and has accordingly revised downward its ten-year forecast by approximately 16 percent, with projections for 2020 reduced to 33.5 GW from the earlier forecast of 40 GW, which would still be an increase in generation capacity of 81 percent. The readjustment is likely to be a result of lower demand in Dubai, as ADWEA previously predicted a three-fold increase in capacity in the period 2010–2020.

Emirati electricity generation, however, still lags considerably behind demand, faces many obstacles, including an extremely low tariff structure, inefficient usage, significant investment requirements, insufficient peak load management, and limited interregional grid integration. UAE gas demand is buttressed by the rapid expansion of the cement and fertiliser sector, by aluminium, steel smelters and other industrial users. The sustained rise in the international price of oil from 2001 to 2008 increased industrial and development projects, and caused the UAE to shift more of its power generation to natural gas. The price rise also encouraged the UAE to utilise more natural gas in EOR operations to squeeze out additional barrels of oil to gain additional revenue.

UAE officials and regional analysts have warned that electricity tariffs must rise to better reflect the market realities of the rising cost of gas feedstock. The electricity tariff, hovering around 2 US cents per KWh for the UAE, has been largely left in place and unchanged for the past decade. The relatively low price has failed to account for the increased cost of gas production, which is the dominant fuel for power generation.[51]

One of the consequences of the low tariff rate has been to encourage extremely high consumption. Because the financial health of the local electricity companies is often uncertain, they tend to rely upon government subsidies.[52] The various Emirati electricity and water authorities agitated for government approval to increase power and water tariffs to cover expansion and runaway costs, with the federal authorities responding by introducing minor tariff increases in certain areas.

Frequently, increased costs reflect the demographic growth including an influx of expatriate workers, as well as inefficiency and the higher cost of using fuel oil instead of natural gas.[53] Future availability and cost of natural gas will also be influenced by two factors: OPEC oil quotas which have cut into the government's ability to autonomously increase its associated gas production, and the relatively high cost of producing domestic sour gas, which is estimated at between \$4–5/MMBtu.[54]

The Abu Dhabi power generation authority was able to limp along as well as it did without complete collapse because of the inexpensive associated gas it could pump alongside its prodigious oil reserves. Both Abu Dhabi and Dubai were rescued, seemingly at the last moment, from the fate that befell the Northern Emirates, by the extremely inexpensive imports (\$1.50/MMBtu) from the Dolphin project.[55] When Dubai and Abu Dhabi contemplated the Dolphin project in the mid-to-late 1990s, natural gas was indexed to the price of oil, then hovering around \$0.50/MMBtu; in 2009, the regional price was converging around \$4.00–\$5.00/MMBtu, with no regional gas sales contracts contemplated below that level.[56]

Fuel oil for power generation is much more expensive than natural gas, costing approximately \$12.51/MMBtu.[57] When peak power production is met by the relatively expensive fuel oil, the discrepancy between the electricity tariff and the cost of power generation becomes stark. At a natural gas price of \$5/MMBtu, the cost of producing electricity increases to nearly \$0.11 per KWh; using fuel oil, the figure increases to \$0.20.[58] As of 2009, the UAE tariff structure was constructed so that UAE nationals would receive electricity at the extremely low price of \$0.02/KWh, noncitizens pay \$0.04–0.05 KWh and industrial consumers pay \$0.06–0.08 KWh.[59]

The low regional natural gas prices that prevailed through the early 2000s with the advent of the Dolphin pipeline, allowed Dubai to produce electricity at a cost of less than \$0.05 per KWh. But once

Dubai has to contract for new supplies, the price will be at least $4–5/ MMBtu, and perhaps even higher. The cost of electricity production has risen steadily over the years, but the electricity tariff has not risen in tandem. This forces the unsavoury proposition of either the government directly subsidising electricity generation or power generation entities becoming bankrupt. Since Dubai and the Abu Dhabi government already subsidise electricity prices by around 10 percent during the peak summer season, this can cushion the 'real' demand and cause it to increase by up to 40 per cent above average levels. In Sharjah and the Northern Emirates, government subsidies have been even higher, sometimes reaching 300 per cent.[60]

With Qatar declining to implement Phase Two of the Dolphin project under the previous pricing framework (and perhaps under any framework which does not yield a return on investment equal to LNG exports), and Iran refusing to export Salman gas unless 'European Prices' are paid, significant additional imports, if they happen at all, will only happen at substantially higher prices.[61] Although it is unlikely that Dubai and Abu Dhabi will allow blackouts to become regular, it is unclear who will pay for the increased electricity cost.

Sheikh Ammar, the ruler of Ajman, answered that question when he warned that citizens must expect an imminent electricity rate increase. In short, he cautioned that, '[Emiratis] have to expect the price of energy to go up because FEWA just can't provide us with the energy that we need.'[62] Undoubtedly, nearly all of the options to increase gas supply will entail added costs, which will either be borne by the Emirati consumer or the state. The increased use of generators has resulted in consumers paying electricity bills that typically surpass $200 per month. Arguably therefore, some consumers have already been socialised to higher power prices.[63] The widespread use of small-scale generation, while a short-term solution, may also have the unintended consequence of pushing up the demand for limited feedstock, thereby exacerbating the price situation in the mid-to-long term. With so much uncertainty about future energy security, Ajman decided to place its hopes in coal import to meet its increasing power demand.[64]

The energy crisis renewed calls for federal authorities to complete the Emirates National Grid Project begun in 2001, which was initially designed to integrate the power generation transmission and distribution networks of the seven emirates into a unified national grid. This grid was also to pave the way for a fully unified pan-GCC grid, consistent with the construction of the Gulf Cooperation Council Interconnection Project to link the electricity grids of all the GCC members. The Emirates National Grid Project has been neglected in the years since its optimistic announcement in 2001. As of this writing, the UAE remains divided into four separate grids: one in Abu Dhabi, a second in Dubai, a third in Sharjah, and a fourth federal grid that manages the other four Northern Emirates.[65]

However, while the idea of a unified grid is an adequate start, the substantive pricing issues that underlie much of the power crisis will probably go unresolved. To remedy this systemic flaw, pricing directives must emanate from the highest responsible levels. Currently, the four respective power authorities produce electricity from government-owned gas, for which they pay below-market rates. The power authorities then sell the power to their commercial and private customers at officially controlled, largely subsidised tariffs. Even if it were possible to effectively coordinate the cooperation between the four disparate grids, the most difficult issue would be the price for the sale of electricity from grid to grid.

While there is enormous confusion surrounding what constitutes an energy subsidy, the narrowest and most commonly used definition is where prices fail to cover short-run production and delivery costs.[66] In the UAE, the price at which natural gas is granted to domestic industries is approximately \$1/MMBtu; this is approximately equivalent to the cost of production. Therefore, under this definition, Emirati natural gas prices would not constitute a subsidy.

Emirati natural gas disbursements to the local utilities and energy-intensive industries are instead an opportunity cost, which economists conclude is the value of expenditure in its highest alternative use, e.g., LNG sales to the Asian Pacific market.[67] Opportunity costs also apply to those domestic prices that are significantly less than long-run marginal cost (LRMC), which is defined as the expected cost of future domestic production or pipeline/LNG imports. The LRMC of gas production in the UAE is likely to approach \$5–6 per MMBtu because of the costs associated with the production of domestic gas. Future prices of internationally traded pipeline gas and LNG are unlikely to fall below \$5 per MMBtu. Regional gas suppliers, i.e., Iran and Qatar, have so far refused to sell natural gas at anything less than \$5–6, while current LNG sales to Dubai from Qatar will reportedly exceed \$8 per MMBtu.[68] When considered against the price that the UAE could sell its LNG on the open market, or the cost of LNG imports, it is clear there is a significant opportunity cost.

The development of the GCC Interconnection Grid should serve to increase energy efficiency between the Gulf nations and make the construction of trans-border natural gas pipelines obsolete, as the neighbours are able to simply wheel electricity to each other. The first phase of a joint power grid for GCC countries linking the grids of Saudi Arabia, Qatar, Bahrain and Kuwait was completed on 26 July 2009. By 2011, the United Arab Emirates and Oman will be linked to the grid. When the final link is completed in 2011, the GCC countries will have a joint power grid that guarantees an adequate and consistent supply of power, even in emergencies, and reduces the cost of power generation in the respective member countries. However, at the time of writing, the Gulf countries had little excess capacity to sell to their neighbours. It is much too early to speak of significant power trades through the grid as all of the GCC members, with the exception of Qatar, are facing natural gas shortages, which contributed to the power shortfalls. They all have similar patterns of power consumption, which sees demand peak in the summer as air conditioners are operating almost continuously to combat the soaring temperatures.

In 2010, the UAE declined to consider a pledge to provide extra power to its neighbours. The Emirati priority is first and foremost to meet the exponential domestic demand, before it would even consider exports through the Gulf grid. However, in the future, it is possible that sales of excess capacity on the grid may be exactly what the UAE desires as a future revenue stream. With the increased capacity from the planned nuclear plants, projected to start in 2017, the UAE could very well become a major regional electricity exporter.

Alternative Domestic Gas Supply Options

To deal with the gas shortage, the UAE launched a comprehensive process to systematically develop alternative (both nuclear and renewable) energy, expand production of domestic gas, import natural gas from Iran and Qatar, reduce gas flaring and utilise alternative methods for enhanced oil recovery,[69] and also to engage in a coordinated energy conservation campaign to reduce the rapidly expanding domestic use of energy.[70] In a sign of the UAE's determination to have renewable energy take a larger slice of its power demand burden, and in line with its commitment to have 7 percent of electricity generation by renewable electricity by 2020, in June 2010, a consortium composed of the Spanish company, Abengoa Solar, and French Total, partnered with Abu Dhabi's Masdar to build the world's largest concentrated solar power plant, Shams 1.[71]

Additionally, in a bid to transform its fragmented energy policy into a coherent whole, Dubai enacted an August 2009 law that created a Supreme Energy Council, essentially a regulatory body that will ensure a comprehensive strategy to meet Dubai's energy and power supply.[72] Related to the issues that the Supreme Energy Council was created to deal with, Khaled al-Awadi, the gas operations manager at Emarat, argued that the main predicament of the UAE's gas sector was the lack of cohesive and comprehensive natural gas legislation and the absence of an integrated, high pressure gas network across the UAE.[73] Al-Awadi argued that to ensure the success of mega gas development projects, legislation should be promulgated to cover all aspects of the gas industry and trade, whether imports, exports, contracts and distribution, commissioning of pipelines and networks, or other operations. A readily foreseeable obstacle in the UAE gas sector is that the natural gas system operates in several different legal jurisdictions, which are subject to different laws and different operators in each Emirate.

Most of the Emirates have funnelled enormous investment sums into their local power authorities to expand capacity and develop a more efficient system. Yet, on the macro-level, the UAE is a member nation linked to the GCC Interconnection Project (GCCIP), which explicitly promises to provide efficient power generation security for the GCC by establishing a pan-GCC electricity sector.[74]

To mitigate the impact of the power crisis and the debilitating blackouts on the country's industrial base, an arrangement has been made for natural gas pipelines to be connected directly to strategic sites for onsite power generation. In 2008, Emirates Aluminium (Emal) and Gasco constructed a natural gas pipeline to the site of the world's largest aluminium smelter providing an uninterrupted source of natural gas, which is converted into onsite power. [75]

Sharjah-based Dana Gas has also conceived of specially constructed 'gas cities' in the UAE established to enable large-scale industrial complexes to utilise economies of scale for their energy-intensive plants. These cities will also promote the placement of several natural gas dependent industrial and petrochemical complexes in the same area.[76] Gas cities will plausibly attract international investors, who would seek to shield themselves and their investment projects from the power shortages prevalent throughout the UAE. Investors could reasonably consider government guarantees of secure gas supplies to the key industrial sectors as a significant inducement to invest in these new gas zones.

Abu Dhabi also embarked on a massive campaign to reduce gas demand by substituting carbon, nitrogen or water for the substantial 18 Bcm/yr of gas that it reinjects into its mature oil fields to increase production as part of its extensive EOR programme. Water injection has worked successfully in the region, even though it has some detractors. Still, it is a plausible option to free up more of the UAE's precious gas reserves. Another alternative is to use nitrogen (with air as a feedstock) for reinjection purposes.[77] The main obstacle to this project is the upfront capital costs for the air separation facilities, which are significant.[78]

Reinjection of captured carbon dioxide is also being reviewed for feasibility. However, there are conflicting reports about the expense and feasibility of CO_2 utilisation for EOR.[79] Some studies indicate that reinjection of captured CO_2 may be an even more challenging and expensive endeavour than nitrogen reinjection, but others seem to suggest that CO_2 based EOR is superior to nitrogen injection for maximisation of oil production. It appears that the argument that CO_2 is superior to nitrogen for oil extraction purposes is based primarily on the special attributes of CO_2, especially its relative tendency towards miscibility.[80]

The global financial crisis slowed down the runaway energy and power demand growth in the Emirates of Dubai and Abu Dhabi. Anecdotal evidence suggests that Emirati demand eased to such an extent, as to encourage ADNOC to issue a rare export tender in April 2009 for low sulphur gas oil.[81] Generally, this is sold to fuel retailers in Dubai when demand in Abu Dhabi is low. However, Dubai had no need for low sulphur gas oil as it appeared most of its demand was being met for the interim.

After a 2008 gross domestic product (GDP) surge of 6.8 percent, the UAE economy had nearly zero GDP growth in 2009, which was the weakest since 1993.[82] The UAE did not allocate funds for diesel purchases in the fiscal year that began 21 March 2009, since it expected new gas output to meet local power needs. There is no certainty that the gas equilibrium will endure once the global economy limps back to health. For the interim, however, it appears that Abu Dhabi and Dubai were able to barely satisfy local demand for the calendar year 2009. Yet, the UAE experiences uneven growth demands, as different emirates have different demand cycles. While Dubai underwent a noticeable slowing of energy demand, Northern Emirati gas demand had greater resiliency in the wake of global financial upheavals because of their dependence on large-scale energy-intensive industrial projects. Dubai focused much more upon the financial services industry for its economic growth, whose demand principally arises from the retail sector.

Expansion of Domestic Production

The Abu Dhabi National Oil Company (ADNOC) launched a major plan to boost the UAE's gas production. Over a five-year period from 2003–2008, the UAE increased its natural gas production by nearly 8 Bcm/yr to meet rapid growth in local consumption and export commitments. During that period UAE production grew steadily from 44.8 to 50.2 Bcm (see Figure 12.1).[83]

By 2008, the UAE utilised approximately 18 Bcm of gas for EOR. Because the UAE still views itself primarily as an oil-producing country, it earmarks massive amounts of gas for its large-scale EOR programme. With official oil reserves at 98 billion bbl, the gas reinjection programme is certain to continue for the long term. ADNOC forecasts that peak oil production will occur over the next decade; therefore, the 2008 injection rate of 18 Bcm/yr is estimated to increase at 8 per cent annually through the year 2020, if alternative EOR methods are not utilised, such as nitrogen or carbon.[84]

With virtually zero economic growth in 2009, the UAE suffered from both the loss of liquidity in the international market, and the drop in the international oil price from its high in the summer of 2008. These two events impacted and weakened the international appetite for Gulf gas development projects. The severe oil production quotas that OPEC instituted to contain the oil price freefall also constrained its ability to produce associated gas. However, the UAE leadership remained committed to increasing its gas production, and directed ADNOC to continue its gas development programmes and to award tenders for integrated gas projects to link onshore and offshore activities worth up to $50 billion in 2009, regardless of any budgetary weakness or liquidity shortage.[85]

Such a massive surge of funding directed toward gas production allowed the UAE to maintain its position as the fourth largest Arab gas producer after Qatar, Algeria, and Saudi Arabia. Because many of its gas reserves are associated, the UAE prefers to increase production from new non-associated fields to avoid a breach of strict OPEC quotas.

Concurrently, the Northern Emirates embarked on their own ambitious gas production programme to meet rising demand. In 2008, Sinochem began production at its Atlantis field in Umm al-Quwain (one of the few Emirates with spare gas export capacity), from which it exported .80 Bcm/yr (2.2 million cm/d) to its neighbour, Ras al-Khaimah. Atlantis production could potentially reach .94 Bcm/yr (2.6 Million cm/d), because the Atlantis processing plant is able to process up to 1.53 Bcm/yr (4.2 million cm/d) of gas, producing up to 20,000 b/d of condensate and 120 tons/day of LPG as well. In August 2008, Rak Petroleum initiated production in the West Bukha field offshore Oman. The initial volumes were 1.09–1.46 Bcm/yr (3-4 million cm/d), with a planned increase to 0.36–0.40 Bcm/yr (1–1.1 million cm/d) (alongside 12,000 b/d of natural gas liquids), all to be exported to Ras al-Khaimah.[86]

RakGas also has a contract to import 1.02 Bcm/yr (2.8 million cm/d) from Sharjah-based Dana Gas. [87] Ras al-Khaimah presently seeks a coordinated exploration programme around the mature Saleh field. Located 42 km offshore Ras al-Khaimah, the Saleh field may also have the potential for commercial wet gas production.[88] Rak Petroleum, which bought a stake into the Saleh field in 2007, acquired a 40:60 partnership with RakGas, and developed a coordinated plan to revive production. RakGas declared that 3D seismic data supported the proposition that production decline at the Saleh field was primarily an issue of pressure depletion and encroaching water.[89] Increased exploration at one of the major Saleh production areas, Prospect C, which potentially could hold up to 141.5 Bcm of reserves, was stalled because of simmering border disputes between Ras al-Khaimah and Umm al-Quwain.[90] At the time of writing, it is unclear whether there will be an amicable resolution to free up production.

Rak Petroleum discovered the Hafit prospect (with potential reserves of 99 Bcm) in Block 31, on the Omani side of the UAE–Oman border. Even though the UAE is in dire need of the gas, if significant reserves are discovered in Hafit, Oman would be likely to monopolise it for its own use. However, Oman and the UAE have been able to amicably resolve the issues of joint fields previously. In 2005, Oman signed an agreement with Ras al-Khaimah to allow RakGas to purchase and process gas from the West Bukha offshore field.[91] Even though Oman's nearby Bukha field has been producing and exporting gas to Ras al-Khaimah since 1994, Ras al-Khaimah sought to extend the existing pipeline to the joint West Bukha/Hengam (Oman and Iran) gas field. The gas will be sent to Ras al-Khaimah through a subsea pipeline that links to Oman's Bukha field. RakGas expects that the field will supply up to 0.40 Bcm/yr (1.1 Million cm/d) by late 2010. RakGas concluded that the easiest method was simply to drill on the Iranian portion of the field, Hengam, and pipe the gas directly to Ras al-Khaimah. However, a pricing framework agreement with the Iranians proved to be a major stumbling block.[92]

As discussed above, pricing is always a significant issue in gas negotiations with Iran. Another complication is that decisions must emanate from the highest levels. For example, the lower level Iranians who signed the initial contract with Dana Gas for gas imports from the Hengam field, were prosecuted in Iran.[93] Ras al-Khaimah is the UAE's largest cement producer, an energy-intensive industry that is the crux of the emirate's industrialisation. However, many of the cement companies have complained since the shortages began in 2007 that their financial growth is being hampered as they are increasingly forced to substitute natural gas with expensive coal and fuel oil for power generation.[94] Rak

Gas has engaged in a massive gas development and investment strategy, putting aside $100 million for investment in the emirate's natural gas infrastructure. Ras Al-Khaimah requires (as of 2009) 2.5 Bcm/yr (7.08 million cm/d)–3.6 Bcm/yr (9.91 million cm/d) to stay afloat. However, with only 1.86 Bcm/yr (5.09 Million cm/d) of production, there are significant shortages that Ras al-Khaimah officials hope to rectify with the production and import strategies discussed above.[95]

While it is important to note that all of the Northern Emirates' exploration and production efforts can only be realised over a five- to ten-year period, the North will still be drastically short of gas even when these projects are completed. However, Sharjah's Western Offshore concession, which includes the Zora gas field, has potential for immediate development. In March 2008, Dana Gas (an affiliate of Crescent Petroleum) was granted a 25-year concession and a 50 per cent interest in the project. Dana plans to bring the first phase production online by early 2010. [96]

In the Northern Emirates, Sharjah has been the traditional natural gas hub because of the Sajaa, Mo'ayyid and Kahaif onshore fields and the offshore Zora and Mubarak fields[97] (see Map 12.2). Since Amoco Sharjah discovered the Sajaa field in 1980, the field has maintained a relatively high output and become the backbone of Sharjah's gas production with approximately 48 producing wells.[98]

A portion of Sharjah's gas is exported by pipeline to Dubai, while the federal energy entity, Emarat, transports gas to the other northern Emirates. After years of ongoing political disputes with Dubai, in April 1985, Sheikh Sultan Bin Mohammed Al-Qassimi and Dubai's Sheikh Muhammad bin Rashed negotiated and concluded a wide-ranging political accord.[99] This ended years of intense border disputes between the two emirates in what had formed one of the most intractable boundary conflicts in the UAE.

As Dubai and Sharjah settled their dispute in 1985, the leaders of the two emirates allied themselves and cemented their new found alliance with a major long-term gas deal in 1986. A gas supply pipeline was built to transport gas, an initial amount of 4.45 Bcm (12.17 Million cm/d) from the Saghyah field to the power and desalination plant of the Dubai Electrical Company at Mina Jabal Ali. From 1992 to 2005, Sharjah exported 4.45 Bcm/yr (12.17 Million cm/d), then in 2006, export volumes dropped to 3.1 Bcm/yr as Sharjah directed more of its gas to satisfy its rising domestic demand.[100]

When gas exports from Sharjah completely dried up, Dubai began to depend much more upon Qatari imports through the Dolphin pipeline to meet its needs.[101] Because of the rapid development in Sharjah, the

Emirate now only has enough domestic fuel to power its gas and fuel oil generators for roughly half of the year, and is seeking imports from regional suppliers, such as Iran, for its import needs. Sharjah, in fact, depended upon Dubai for natural gas imports from the Dolphin pipeline. In April 2008, Dolphin began to export some gas to Sharjah through its pipeline connection in Dubai, granting the Emirate some relief from its gas shortages.[102] Sharjah is negotiating with Dolphin Energy to secure additional supplies through the Dolphin pipeline. However, with no firm Qatari commitment on expansion of Dolphin supplies to the UAE, Sharjah sought to obtain additional supplies from the Qatari 'interruptible' exports (see section on Import Options below).[103]

In June 2010, Russian-based Rosneft joined with Crescent Petroleum in a gas concession in Sharjah. This joint venture is the first collaboration between the two companies. Rosneft will help develop Crescent's existing onshore gas concession in Sharjah.[104] The companies will drill two wells in the 1243 sq. km concession with an initial investment of $59.91 million. At the time of writing, there has been no production on the concession. However, the two companies hope to jointly produce gas reserves of approximately 68 Bcm and gas condensate of approximately 117 million barrels that they estimate to lie in the concession. If gas is found, it would go to satisfying domestic Emirati demand, while the condensates would be sold on the international market. Crescent and Rosneft desire to use this first joint venture as a template for potential expansion of gas production and sale opportunities in the wider GCC. The Rosneft–Crescent collaboration signified quite an evolution in thinking about Middle Eastern gas reserves. While the region was viewed previously as a potential supplier for global gas consumers, it is increasingly considered to be a significant gas market.

Despite the administrative pricing framework in Sharjah, as in the other Emirates, Crescent and Rosneft considered the return on investment for the domestic gas sales to be healthy enough to sustain their involvement. In a notable contrast to the ConocoPhillips withdrawal from the Shah Field, Crescent viewed the Sharjah gas development strategy as being so remunerative, that the investment did not depend upon the sale of condensates at international prices to global consumers to be viable. Badr Jaafar, the Executive Director of Crescent, contended that, 'We've done our economics based on the prevailing gas prices and they satisfied our hurdles for economic investment.'[105] He continued that, 'Based on estimated reserves, the project is economical.'[106]

Overall, growth of the UAE gas demand has averaged approximately 10 percent per annum during the first decade of the 2000s, and is projected to grow into the next decade (see Table 12.4). The indigenous gas fields, most of which were discovered during the 1980s, are declining and no longer able to meet the increasing demand; therefore, deals with either regional gas importers, such as Iran, or increased collaboration with internationally recognised gas companies, such as Gazprom, will be necessary for future supply increases.

Shah Gas Development Plan

Sour gas production is the centrepiece of Abu Dhabi's energy strategy. The Shah Gas Development plan (SGDP), previously known as the Sour Gas Development Plan, was established with the aim of producing more than 10.32 Bcm/yr (28.3 Million cm/d) of raw gas from Abu Dhabi's onshore Shah gas field (see Map 12.1), with 5.18 Bcm/yr of processed gas available for use, based on a project start-up date of 2015.[107] AD-NOC shortlisted several major international oil companies (IOCs), but in July 2009 ultimately chose to partner with ConocoPhillips under a joint venture framework. Sour gas development had traditionally been considered too costly an undertaking, but ADNOC was confident that it would be able to reduce the cost of the $10–12 billion project by approximately 30 per cent. In an attempt to lower the production costs, ADNOC issued tenders for four large construction packages to various construction firms before it signed the ConocoPhillips joint venture.[108]

However, in April 2010, ConocoPhillips withdrew from the project citing a change in corporate priorities, but it is also likely that the $5 MMBtu price agreed upon to develop the field may have been too low for them to recoup what the company viewed as an acceptable return on investment.[109] The ConocoPhillips withdrawal was the second major energy company to retreat from an Emirati energy project over profitability issues in as many years. In 2009, the oilfield services company, Petrofac, withdrew its bid for ADNOC's $12 bn Ruwais oil refinery upgrade in Abu Dhabi. As with ConocoPhillips, the Petrofac withdrawal represented a perception amongst a portion of the energy companies that some of the major Emirati energy projects involve overly optimistic projected rates of return.[110] In the wake of the surprise withdrawal of ConocoPhillips, ADNOC vowed to pursue the Shah development with or without an IOC as partner. However, autonomous development of the Shah gas field without the collaboration of an IOC seems to be an unlikely prospect as the sulphurous quality of the gas requires specialised technology and skills that the national oil company may not possess.

There are also environmental risks associated with the project, because sour gas is both extremely toxic and flammable.[111] Sour gas development requires processing plant that adds substantially to the cost. Even prior to the withdrawal of ConocoPhillips, however, certain factions in the UAE leadership believed that the SGDP does not need the advanced technology and expertise held by the IOCs, and that ADNOC can develop the project in participation with a contractor.[112]

The SGDP incorporates substantial development of wells, gas plants, and pipelines with corrosion-resistant material to handle the 23 percent hydrogen sulphide and 10 percent carbon dioxide components of Shah natural gas. The sulphur and condensates are to be removed and exported through the port at Ruwais, while the treated lean gas would be supplied to the domestic market.[113] The investments associated with the SGDP imply a production cost of approximately $4/MMBtu. The potential sulphur to be produced from the project is estimated to be more than 4.2 Mt/yr and ADNOC intends to export sulphur to recoup some of the production costs.[114]

Integrated Gas Development

Abu Dhabi Gas Industries Company (Gasco) and Abu Dhabi Gas Liquefaction Company (Adgas) instituted the $7–8 billion Integrated Gas Development (IGD) project amid expectations that it will generate an additional 10.34 Bcm/yr of natural gas production via construction of a 38 km pipeline from the offshore Umm Shaif field and onshore Bab Field to Das Island, where the gas will be partially processed.[115] From the preliminary processing at Das Island, the gas will be shipped to an onshore plant at Habshan and Ruwais for final processing and delivery to the domestic market. The IGD project is due to come on-stream in 2014 with an initial phase of 5.18 Bcm/yr (14.20 Million cm/d) from the Bab field, followed by a second phase of 5.18 Bcm/yr (14.20 Million cm/d) from the Umm Shaif field. As evidence of the accentuated importance of supplying domestic demand, the offshore production will limit the potential gas reserves available for future LNG production from Das Island in the near to mid term, demonstrating a clear preference for domestic consumption.

Hail Gas Development Project

In addition to the IGD and SGFD projects, Abu Dhabi seeks to develop the Hail gas field, located in the shallow waters halfway between Abu Dhabi and Ruwais to the west. This field is estimated to have a production potential of nearly 5.18 Bcm/yr (14.20 Million cm/d.)[116]

Abu Dhabi Company for Onshore Oil Operations (ADCO) officially launched the multi-billion-dollar offshore Hail gas field development project by inviting a multitude of companies to express interest for the marine works project.[117] ADCO first explored potential sour gas production at the Hail field in 2001, but delayed production because an environmental assessment indicated that severe environmental damage would likely result. ADCO also concluded that gas imports from Qatar through the Dolphin project provided a better and less expensive alternative. As with the Shah gas field, the Hail development presents its own set of production related challenges as much of the field is difficult to access because the bulk of it lies below the sandbanks.[118]

Abu Dhabi LNG Exports – The ADGAS Project

Abu Dhabi became the first LNG exporter in the Middle East when the Abu Dhabi Gas Liquefaction Company (ADGAS) plant commenced production in 1977. It is located on Das Island, about 160 km offshore Abu Dhabi, and is supplied with gas from offshore fields operated by ADMA-Opco (Abu Dhabi Marine Areas Operating Company), a joint venture comprising ADNOC (the Abu Dhabi National Oil Company), BP, Total and JODCO (Japan Oil Development Company).

ADGAS was originally developed as a two-train facility with a total design capacity of 2.06 mtpa to utilise natural gas produced in association with crude oil and which, in the early 1970s, was being flared. At the time plans for the project were developed, Japan had just emerged as an LNG importer and buyers there were seeking additional supplies to fuel the rapid growth in consumption that had followed the introduction of LNG in 1969. The Tokyo Electric Power Company (TEPCO), which was one of the first two importers of LNG into Japan (Tokyo Gas was the other), was prepared to commit to purchase the entire output from the planned project and in December 1972, it signed a Heads of Agreement (HoA)[119] to purchase 2.8 Bcm/a (2.06 mtpa) for 20 years on a Delivered Ex-Ship (DES) basis.

The agreement between the partners for the development of the project was signed in September 1971.[120] The partnerships eventually included BP and Total, two Japanese companies (Mitsui and Bridgestone Liquefied Gas) and ADNOC, representing the Abu Dhabi national interest. The ADGAS Company was initially registered in Bermuda with ADNOC holding 20 percent of the shares. However, as the interest of the Government of the Emirates in LNG production and export grew, ADNOC's shareholding was increased to 51 percent in 1975. Immediately before start-up in 1977, ADGAS's registration was moved from Bermuda to Abu Dhabi.

The participation of BP and Total in ADGAS is based on their long-term involvement in the offshore oil concessions that are the source of natural gas supply to the liquefaction plant. A BP subsidiary, D'Arcy Exploration, was first awarded a concession to explore for oil offshore Abu Dhabi in 1953. Two years later, the agreement was widened to give BP:

> the sole and exclusive right to explore for, drill for, develop, produce, transport and dispense of oil within an area of the seabed and subsoil lying beneath the high seas of the Arabian Gulf contiguous to the territorial waters of Abu Dhabi and which were proclaimed on 10th June 1949 to fall within the jurisdiction of the Ruler of Abu Dhabi.[121]

In 1955, D'Arcy Exploration assigned its rights, specified in the concession agreement, to a new company ADMA Ltd (Abu Dhabi Marine Areas Limited), in which BP had a two-thirds share and the Compagnie Française des Pétroles (now Total) a one-third share. In December 1972, at the time ADGAS was being formed, BP sold a 45 percent share in ADMA to JODCO, a consortium of Japanese companies. In 1973, ADNOC, which had been established in 1971, took a 25 percent share in ADMA, which was subsequently increased to 60 percent in 1974. Three years later, a new company, ADMA-Opco, was created to operate the concessions. The current shareholders in the company are: ADNOC 60 percent, BP 14.67 percent, Total 13.33 percent and JODCO 12 percent.

The participation of Japanese companies in ADGAS is related to the marketing of the LNG and LPG produced by the project rather than JODCO's participation in ADMA-Opco. The trading house, Mitsui, which has a long-term relationship with the buyer, TEPCO, became the largest Japanese shareholder with Bridgestone Liquefied Gas, who provided the transportation for the LPG produced by ADGAS, taking a minor shareholding. In the early 1970s, TEPCO's objective was to secure the supply of LNG for its power plants in Japan on a delivered basis and it had no interest in participation in either the liquefaction plant or the transport of the LNG. TEPCO's policy has now changed and, by the early 2000s, it began to purchase an increasing share of its LNG supply on an FOB basis and to take a minority share in the liquefaction plants from which the LNG was produced and in the upstream gas production.[122]

ADGAS Project Structure 1975 to 1994

The structure of the project for its first phase from 1975 to 1994 was established after ADNOC's share was increased to 51 percent. The remaining 49 percent was divided on a 50/50 basis between the European and the Japanese shareholders. BP and Total split the European 24.5 percent share on the same basis as their original holdings in ADMA, i.e. two-thirds (16.33 percent) to BP and one-third (8.17 percent) to Total. Mitsui had a 22 percent share in ADGAS and Bridgestone Liquefied Gas (which eventually became Mitsui Liquefied Gas) a 2.5 percent share. The voting arrangements required major decisions to be approved by ADNOC plus one European partner and one Japanese partner, which mitigated the risk of ADNOC using its majority position to push through decisions opposed by the foreign partners.

The ADMA-Opco concession gave the foreign partners the right to lift oil but the natural gas produced in association with the oil, or from non-associated fields, remained the property of the Abu Dhabi government, with ADNOC acting on its behalf. ADGAS negotiated an into-plant sales agreement to purchase the gas supply required by the plant with ADNOC. The pricing formula included a fixed element to cover ADNOC's costs for the development and operation of the gas production facilities and the pipelines to Das Island. In addition, it was agreed that ADNOC would have a 50 percent share in ADGAS profits after an agreed threshold on the rate of return had been exceeded.

The Government of Abu Dhabi contributed to the economic feasibility of the project by agreeing to a five-year tax holiday, during which the project would not be required to pay tax on any profits, plus accelerated depreciation of the investment over an eight-year period (four years at 15 percent per annum and four years at 10 percent per annum) rather than the ten years for investments in oil production. The tax rate on profits from the project after the end of the tax holiday was set at 55 percent, the same as for oil production in Abu Dhabi. Both the gas payments agreement and the fiscal agreement were drafted in a way that left some of the key clauses open to differing interpretations by the parties. The consequence was a dispute over tax and gas payments between the Abu Dhabi government and the foreign shareholders in the late 1980s, which, after several years of negotiation, was eventually resolved with ADGAS making a payment of over US$0.5 Bn to the government.

The contract with TEPCO was unique since it was for the sale of liquefied gas rather than LNG. The buyer committed to take delivery of all the LNG and LPG produced by the plant. Since associated gas was ADGAS's main source of supply, the plant produced significant volumes of LPG, which TEPCO agreed to purchase on the same terms and conditions, including price, as the LNG. The LPG is used to fuel some of the units at TEPCO's Anegasaki power plant, which is located close to the Sodegaura LNG receiving terminal in Tokyo Bay. The ADGAS plant also produces and exports condensate (light oil) and, since the early 1990s when a separation unit was installed, sulphur.[123]

Sales of LNG and LPG were on a DES basis requiring ADGAS to provide shipping capacity to transport both products to Japan. The shareholders did not want to incur the cost of owning ships so they opted to charter them from the Norwegian shipping companies, Gotaas Larsen and Leif Hoegh, who had ordered ships on a speculative basis. Three ships were originally time-chartered[124] from Gotaas Larsen, the *Hilli, Gimi and Khannur* (named after villages in Abu Dhabi) and a fourth ship, the *Golar Freeze*, was added when the project found it required additional shipping capacity, in part because one storage tank had been taken out of service (see below). Leif Hoegh provided the *Norman Lady*. The Gotaas Larsen ships each had a capacity of around 126,000m^3 while the Leif Hoegh vessel was smaller, with a capacity of 87,600m^3.

The ships for the transport of the LPG were provided by Bridgestone Liquefied Gas on a Contract of Affreightment basis, under which Bridgestone provided the capacity to transport the LPG from within

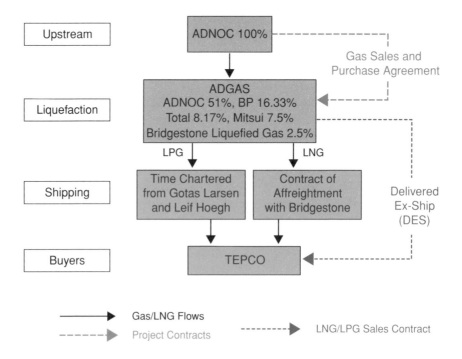

Figure 12.2: ADGAS – Original Project Structure, 1977

its fleet but did not dedicate specific vessels to ADGAS. The structure of the ADGAS project when it started up is shown in Figure 12.2.

Construction and Operations 1973 to 1994

The contract for the construction of the Das Island liquefaction plant was awarded to a joint venture of the US contractor Bechtel and the Japanese contractor Chiyoda in March 1973 and the foundation stone was laid by the then ruler of Abu Dhabi in December of the same year. The project was built as a two-train facility, with each train designed to produce 1.4 Bcm/a (1.03 mtpa) of LNG. It included two 100,000m^3 storage tanks and a single jetty and berth able to accommodate ships up to around 135,000m^3 capacity, at the time the largest ships in operation. The first cargo from the plant was loaded onto the *Hilli* in April 1977 for delivery to Japan. However, the unloading at the Sodegaura terminal in Tokyo Bay had to be stopped when a large metal bolt was found in the LNG. The remaining cargo was unloaded through strainers and the ship freed of gas to allow full inspection of the tanks, which revealed a number of items that had been left in the tanks during construction.

This incident was relatively minor compared with a crack that developed in one of the two 100,000m^3 storage tanks. The tank had to be taken out of service and after inspection it was determined that the crack was the result of distortion to the floor of the tank caused by the freezing of the ground under the tank ('frost heave') when it was filled with LNG. The government was not prepared to allow ADGAS to bring the tank back into operation after it was repaired and ships were used as floating storage until new tanks were built and commissioned in the early 1980s.

The washing away of the sub-soil under the plant after unusually heavy rainfall required major work to underpin the foundations and in the early 1980s, the concrete used in the construction of the plant started to deteriorate, which was determined to have been due to the use of sea-water during construction. Additional expenditure was incurred in remedying these problems, the largest of which was the cost of new tanks, which, in total, exceeded the original cost of the plant. These problems also affected the build-up of production from the project and the design capacity of 2.80 Bcm/a (2.06 mtpa) was only reached five years after start-up (Figure 12.3).

One of the consequences of the uncertainty in the level of output during the build-up period was the failure of ADGAS and TEPCO to turn the HoA, signed in 1973, into a full Sales and Purchase Agreement

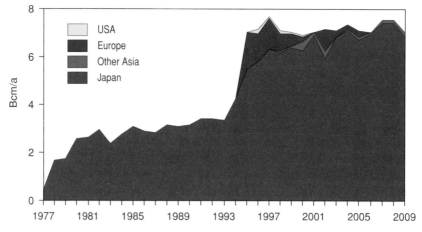

Figure 12.3: LNG Exports from Abu Dhabi, 1977–2009

Source: Cedigaz and Author's Estimates for 2009

(SPA). It was not until 1990, that an SPA with TEPCO was signed covering the output from the two existing trains and the planned new train. For 17 years LNG was sold and purchased under the terms of a non-binding HoA and during that time the price was renegotiated a number of times including moving from a fixed price to oil price indexation. With the exception of two cargoes on small ships delivered to the Fos Tonkin terminal in the south of France in 1977 and 1979,[125] the entire output from ADGAS was delivered to TEPCO over the period from 1977 to the start of production from the third production train in 1994. During that period, TEPCO received a total of 46 Bcm (34 mt) of LNG. It is a testament to the strong relationship that developed between buyer and seller, and which is a feature of many LNG contracts involving buyers in Asia, that deliveries were maintained despite the lack of a legally binding contract. Furthermore, major external events, including the Iran–Iraq war from 1980 to 1988 and the first Gulf War in 1991, did not result in the cancellation of a single cargo.

Project Expansion

By the late 1980s, ADGAS's technical problems had been overcome, replacement tanks were in operation and the plant was producing at levels consistently above design capacity. Production from the two-train plant peaked in 1991 at 3.45 Bcm/a (2.6 mt), some 23 percent above design capacity. A price renegotiation, triggered by the collapse in oil prices at the end of 1985 had been resolved with the introduction of a new price formula, which included, for the first time in an Asian LNG contract, an 'S'-curve reducing the linkage between LNG and the oil price below agreed thresholds of around $16/Bbl and above $24/Bbl.

TEPCO demonstrated its confidence in the project by proposing to ADGAS an expansion of the plant to double its capacity and offering to buy the entire output from the expanded plant. The ADGAS partners responded to the proposal by commissioning technical and economic studies to evaluate the feasibility of an expansion. The construction of a third liquefaction train with a capacity of 3.1 Bcm/a (2.3 mtpa) was identified as the preferred option and negotiations commenced with TEPCO on a contract for the entire output from the original two trains plus a new, third train. A 25-year agreement was signed by ADGAS and TEPCO in October 1990 providing for TEPCO to purchase 7.3 Bcm/a (5.4 mtpa) of liquefied gas (LNG plus LPG) commencing in 1994. TEPCO committed to take delivery of a minimum of 5.8 Bcm/a (4.3 mtpa) of LNG, with a best endeavours undertaking for 6.3 Bcm/a (4.7 mtpa) and a reasonable endeavours for 6.6 Bcm/a (4.9 mtpa). Effectively, TEPCO agreed to give preference to taking delivery of LNG and vary LPG off-take in the event of a downturn in its demand. This reduced the downside risk on ADGAS revenues since, at the time the agreement was negotiated, there was a spot market for LPG but very limited spot and short-term trading of LNG. ADGAS could sell any LPG not required by TEPCO on the international market whereas it was uncertain whether markets could be found for surplus LNG cargoes.

The contract for the construction of the new train was awarded to Chiyoda in 1990 and the first cargo was loaded in July 1994. Production built up quickly, as is shown in Figure 12.3, and in 1995, the first full year of operation of the third train, output reached a total of 7.03 Bcm (5.2 mt), an increase of 3.38 Bcm (2.5 mt) over the production in 1993, when only the first two trains were in operation. However, there were limits to the rate at which TEPCO could increase its off-take from ADGAS and it negotiated an agreement for Chubu Electric, Japan's third largest power utility, for the latter to take delivery of up to 0.95 Bcm/a (0.7 mtpa) of ADGAS LNG over a three-year period from start of production from train 3.

With train 3 producing above capacity and the commitments to TEPCO and Chubu Electric building-up over three years, ADGAS had uncommitted LNG available at a time when LNG buyers in Europe required extra supplies to overcome a shortfall in availability from their main source, Sonatrach in Algeria, as it revamped its LNG trains. In 1995, 1.5 Bcm of LNG was delivered by ADGAS to buyers in Spain, Belgium and France.[126] Deliveries to France and Belgium had stopped by 1997, when the revamped Algerian trains were back in service and commitments to TEPCO had ramped-up. However, with the third train producing above capacity, ADGAS had cargoes available over and above its contractual commitments with TEPCO and, with the short-term trading of LNG increasing, it has continued to sell LNG to third parties on both a DES and a Free on Board (FOB) basis. Spain has been one of the main destinations for the surplus LNG with buyers there purchasing a total of 5.39 Bcm (4 mt) over the period 1995 to 2005. Italy (in 1998 and 1999), South Korea (1998 to 2007), the USA (1996 to 2000) and India (2006 to 2009), have been the other destinations for ADGAS's LNG.[127]

Japan, through the contract with TEPCO, has remained ADGAS's main market by a wide margin accounting for 94 percent of deliveries between 1977 and 2009 and 91 percent since the plant expansion in 1994. TEPCO has also purchased a significant proportion of the uncommitted LNG that ADGAS has had available, accounting for a total of 2.9 Bcm (2.1 mt) above its 6.6 Bcm/a (4.9 mt) reasonable endeavours undertaking between 2004 and 2009.

The relationship between ADGAS and TEPCO has remained strong except on the price issue, where the two sides have often found it difficult to reach agreement, and this has led to lengthy negotiations. The price has been reopened on several occasions since the start of the expansion in 1994, and each time the deadline for agreeing a new price before the old price expired has been missed. The most recent renegotiation has been the most prolonged. The pricing formula that applied in the early 2000s had a provision for the parties to meet and discuss how to respond if the Japanese custom cleared crude oil price (JCC), which is the oil index used in the price formula, exceeded $29/Bbl. JCC went above $29/Bbl in early 2004 and the price has remained above that level, leaving ADGAS and TEPCO without an agreed price. Six years later in early 2010, still no agreement had been reached on a new pricing formula. ADGAS has been billing TEPCO at one price and TEPCO has been making payments using a lower price. TEPCO has put nearly US$1 Bn in an escrow account[128] pending resolution of the 'price out of range' issue.[129]

LNG Shipping

The four additional ships required to transport the output from the third train were ordered by ADNOC from a consortium of Japanese yards and were delivered into service in 1994 and 1995. After extensive inspection and analysis by BP Shipping, the five ships that had been transporting LNG from the first two trains since 1977, were determined to have at least another ten years of useful life left and the project's initial plan was to extend the time charters. However, ADNOC decided that the ships should be replaced by new-builds and it ordered four more ships from the Kvaerner yard in Finland.[130] They came into service between 1995 and 1997 and the time charters on the older vessels were terminated. The four ships chartered into ADGAS by Gotaas Larsen, are now owned by Golar LNG (which Gotaas Laresen became after several takeovers). In 2010 the *Golar Freeze* was being converted to a floating storage and regasification unit (FSRU) for employment in Dubai and the *Gimi, Hilli and Khannur*, were being held by Golar LNG for conversion.[131]

The eight new ships were bareboat chartered by ADNOC into the National Gas Shipping Company (NGSCO), which was established by the ADGAS shareholders in 1993 to provide transportation capacity for ADGAS. NGSCO appointed Gotaas Larsen (subsequently Golar LNG) to operate four of the ships and BP Shipping to operate the other four. However, in 2004, NGSCO commenced taking over the management of the ships and it completed the process in 2007.

Project Re-Structuring

The Abu Dhabi government decided that it wanted a larger shareholding for ADNOC in the expanded project and in 1997 a new structure was put in place with ADNOC holding a 70 percent share. The shares of the foreign partners were reduced pro-rata leaving BP with a 10 percent share, Total 5 percent and Mitsui (which had earlier taken over the shares held by its subsidiary Mitsui Liquefied Gas) 15 percent. The new structure of the ADGAS project is shown in Figure 12.4

The Future of ADGAS

The 15 years since the plant was expanded have seen Abu Dhabi producing between 6.95 Bcm (5.1 mt) and 7.81 Bcm (5.8 mt) per year but there have been no attempts to expand the plant further. One constraint is the lack of space on Das Island, which is only about 1.2 km wide and 2.4 km long, although that constraint could probably be overcome by reclaiming land.

Speaking at the Gastech Conference in Abu Dhabi in May 2009, Hamed Al-Marzouqi, acting Head of Market Research for ADGAS, said that the company is considering its production options when the contract with TEPCO comes to an end in 2019. He said that the

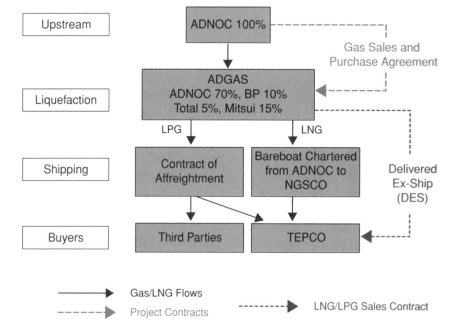

Figure 12.4: ADGAS – Project Structure from 1997

company could choose to increase production but it also has the option of reducing output, since Abu Dhabi has a rapidly growing need for gas to meet both domestic demand and for reinjection into the oil fields. The country's total natural gas requirements are forecast to increase at 8 percent per annum through to 2020. He added that ADGAS has to do a feasibility study to determine whether the demand for LNG is there, whether the reserves are suitable for increased production and what are the costs of extending capacity.[132]

Import Options

The Salman Field

To increase the available gas for the domestic market, the UAE has attempted to develop several import plans, in part because increased domestic output from existing fields and developing new fields have long lead times before the gas will enter the Emirati market. In addition to Qatari gas, Iranian gas imports represent the only viable import option to rapidly increase gas supplies.

Key among the UAE's import plans was the Crescent Petroleum strategy to pipe 6.2 Bcm/yr of gas to the UAE from the Iranian offshore Salman field. After several years of negotiations, Crescent and the National Iranian Oil Company (NIOC) signed a 25-year contract in 2001, which was Iran's first contract for a southern export route, with deliveries to commence in 2005. However, several disputes between the parties stalled the contract. As of fourth quarter 2009, the 231 km undersea jointly constructed pipeline from the Salman field to Lavan Island sat empty. Crescent alleged that the NIOC had breached the agreement by its failure to construct production facilities for the Salman gas field, and by its declaration that it wished to revise the pricing agreement, and introduce 'European gas prices'.

When the international oil price rallied in the years following 2001, many Iranian political factions became upset at what they concluded was an indefensibly low gas price offered to Crescent when considered against its subsequent increase in the international market. The original price was agreed upon when gas prices hovered around $.50/MMBtu. Iranian auditors claimed that unless gas prices were modified to reflect current market realities, Iran could lose as much as $21 billion over the life of the 25-year contract.[133]

In an attempt to move beyond the impasse, Crescent offered approximately $5/MMBtu, the highest price ever for a Gulf regional natural gas sale, but Iran rejected this historic price as still much too low, and contended that Salman gas should be closer to the price paid by Turkey for Iranian gas. Iranian President, Mahmoud Ahmedinejad, alleged that corruption had been behind the original low price, but added that the deal could be concluded if based on the 'current market price.'[134] The CEO of National Iranian Gas Company, Seyyed Reza Kasaeizadeh, announced in 2008, that Iran should sell its gas for $12–$13/MMBtu in the Crescent contract. Kasaeizadeh stressed that a gas price in that range was quite generous, because Turkey was willing to pay even more for its imports from Iran.[135]

Crescent alleged that despite its higher offer, Iran failed to construct the specialised pipelines or other common facilities as it was contractually bound. NIOC, for its part, has defended itself, and affirmed that it had been ready to begin exports in August 2009.[136] After several years of delay, Crescent became extremely impatient since the gas was contracted to be delivered in 2005, and finally initiated international arbitration proceedings in July 2009 against NIOC. Ultimately Crescent seeks a determination of NIOC's legal obligation for gas delivery and wants indemnification against damages arising from potential customer lawsuits.[137]

In 2009, Reza Kasaeizadeh argued that contractual problems such as a 'fair price' and a 'proper formula for price revision' had not been resolved. He vowed that, unless an agreement was reached soon, NIOC would redirect the gas to the Iranian domestic market.[138] Despite the Iranian intransigence over the pricing formula, as late as 2009 officials in Sharjah were still optimistic that they would be able to import 'cheap' Iranian gas, such that there would be no need to subsidise local electricity production. Omer Khougali, SEWA planning design and project manager stated affirmatively that, 'Iranian gas will be very cheap, with power at 4 to 5 fils, ($ 0.011 to $ 0.014) per MWh to produce, we won't need a subsidy.'[139] However, it is not likely that the Iranians view subsidisation of Emirati power generation as a viable use of their natural gas reserves. While the Iranians desire a higher price for their natural gas, Crescent is also constrained from purchasing Iranian gas at substantially higher rates. Crescent purchases of Iranian gas would be funnelled to the Sharjah market at administrative prices, i.e., below market rates; therefore with government mandated low electricity and gas prices for the domestic sector, Crescent would not be likely to have a viable return on investment with substantially higher Iranian prices.

The two stakeholders, Iran and Crescent, find themselves in an extremely difficult situation with limited ability to adopt a flexible position. Unlike in many Western countries where the energy company could have simply acquiesced to higher prices and passed on the price increases to the end-user, energy companies in the Gulf are administratively prohibited from doing so.

While the Crescent–NIOC negotiations stalled, three other Emirati companies moved in and offered to purchase Salman gas. In particular, Abu Dhabi-based Mubadala Petroleum Services Company offered to import Iranian gas. The NIOC and Mubadala reached a preliminary agreement in August 2009 to import 3.6 Bcm/yr (10 Million cm/d) to the UAE three years after details have been finalised.

In a surprise statement in September 2009, Iran announced that it had signed an agreement with an as yet unnamed UAE company for Salman gas import rights. At the time of writing, the identity of the UAE Company has remained anonymous, with Mubadala declaiming that 'Neither Mubadala nor any of its subsidiaries is involved in discussions with NIOC.'[140] Many observers concluded that the agreement referred to the long-awaited breakthrough in Crescent–NIOC negotiations.

Another potential gas supply source for the UAE would be through the offshore joint Iranian–Omani Hengam gas field, located in the Hormuz Strait about 20 km south of Qeshm Island between Iran and

Oman. The reserves in Hengam are estimated to be in the range of 14–15 Bcm, and could potentially produce at approximately 3.1 Bcm/yr (8.5 Million cm/d.) In 2008–2009 Ras al-Khaimah Gas Company (RakGas) negotiated with Iran to secure supplies. However, the project, even if eventually agreed upon by both parties, would require significant development before it is brought online.

Dolphin Interruptible Supply

In an effort to avoid or mitigate a power crisis, the UAE has repeatedly asked Qatar to institute Phase Two of the Dolphin Project, which would export an additional 12.41 Bcm/yr (34 Million cm/d) to the UAE, above the contractual amount of 18.61 Bcm/yr. However, the 2005 Qatar export moratorium was provisionally extended to 2014, and Phase Two expansion seems increasingly unlikely at least before 2014/15, if at all.

Qatar undertook a surprising move when it approached Dolphin Energy in June 2009 and offered an 'interruptible supply' of Qatari gas between .91–4.12 Bcm/yr.[141] ADNOC leapt at the offer, and announced the signing of the contract the week of 20 July 2009. The offer was contingent on a provision that maximised the seasonal fluctuation between the gas demand of Qatar's European and Gulf customers. Essentially, the UAE could purchase much needed gas quantities if Qatar's international customers did not want all of their allotted volumes.

Gas import based on the divergence between regional energy usage is not new to many of the Emirates. Ras al-Khaimah signed a contract with Oman to take .51 Bcm/yr (1.4 Million cm/d) of Oman's contracted volume of 2.08 Bcm/yr (5.7 Million cm/d) Dolphin gas during the winter. The mountainous Ras al-Khaimah is quite cold during the winter season and needs gas for heating, a time when Omani demand is low.[142] Dolphin gas is also being delivered to the SEWA on an interruptible basis via its new Qatar–UAE export pipeline connection to Dubai.[143] For Dolphin Energy, the purchase of third party gas was quite a departure from its corporate mission, since it has consistently fashioned itself as an integrated company that produces, processes, and transports Qatari North Field gas.[144]

Because the gas offered to the UAE would already be processed, the main issue would be the Front-End Engineering and Design (FEED) work and the installation of extra compressors to deal with the additional volume. Given that this is a preliminary agreement, the parties have not yet established a price. It is estimated that they will agree to a figure in the range of the regional swing price of $5/MMBtu.[145]

Yet, even at a price several times more than the contracted price for the original Dolphin Phase One export of 18.61 Bcm/yr (51 Million cm/d) to the UAE at between $1.19–1.32/MMBtu, $5/MMBtu would still be substantially less expensive than burning fuel oil in the UAE's power plants. The prospect of increased Qatari gas imports sparked intense competition as the energy-starved Emirates of Abu Dhabi, Dubai, and Sharjah, as well as Oman, all vied with each other for the additional gas allotment.

Dubai LNG

To find further sources of gas, in April 2008 Dubai contracted to purchase LNG from Shell and Qatargas for 15 years to cover the peak summer months from 2010. Shell announced that it planned to supply Dubai with 650,000 tonnes per year. The LNG may be sourced from the Qatargas IV project, a 70:30 joint venture between state-run Qatar Petroleum and Shell.[146] LNG imports will help Dubai immensely to deal with power and water (desalination) demand, growing at approximately 20 percent annually.[147] Dubai Supply Authority (Dusup), a governmental entity, has the sole rights to supply gas through Dubai's gas pipeline network and is building a floating LNG regasification facility at Jebel Ali port.

The *Golar Freeze*, an existing LNG ship, is set to be chartered by Dusup from the Golar LNG company and converted into a floating storage and regasification unit offshore of the Jebel Ali Terminal. The *Golar Freeze* has an LNG storage capacity of 125,000 tonnes and a regasification capacity of 4.9 Bcm/yr (13.6 Million cm/d) (equivalent to the regasification of 3 Mt/yr of LNG).[148]

On arrival, LNG ships will moor alongside the *Golar Freeze* to offload the cargo. The *Golar Freeze* will then pipe the gas through a sub-sea pipeline into the Dubai natural gas pipeline network. Dusup will operate the jetty and the high pressure export line which will supply gas during the peak demand months between May and October.[149]

While the prices were not made publicly available, it is certain that Dubai will have to pay market rates for LNG shipments. Dubai for its part is following Kuwait's strategy of LNG importation to cover peak demand shortages.[150] In recent years, Dubai has not discovered any gas fields, and its associated gas production is collapsing along with its oil production. The lack of domestic supplies is a major reason why the Emirate faces a fuel shortfall for power production, and faces a difficult choice between importing LNG and generating electricity with oil products.

Dubai is paying a heavy premium for the lack of viable Emirati alternatives in the near term. Its supplementary summer gas supply may not be arriving from a nearby country such as Qatar or Iran, but could instead be shipped from Shell's gas portfolio, which includes Australia and Sakhalin Island off the Pacific coast of Russia.

Balancing the Dilemma: Emirati Gas Supply and The Way Ahead

Given the UAE's massive gas reserves, it appears that the major gas deficit predicted by 2017 is almost entirely self-inflicted.[151] Gas is supplied to the domestic market at close to the wellhead price of $1/MMBtu. Artificially low domestic prices make the import of gas through the Dolphin pipeline a more attractive proposition than developing domestic reserves. Selling North Field gas at $1.30/MMBtu while international LNG prices range from $6–10/MMBtu, Qatar incurs a significant opportunity cost which indirectly cross-subsidises the UAE's industrialisation. Thus while the UAE imported gas at low prices through Dolphin in order to feed the rapidly increasing consumption of its fast growing Emirate, Dubai, Abu Dhabi continued to export LNG to both its long-term contract customers in Japan, as well as spot cargoes to Atlantic Basin countries.

The Emirati government is extremely concerned that its prodigious natural gas reserves will not be able to provide for its future power needs. Even though the UAE has increased its electricity generating capacity by 24 percent per annum over the last 30 years, this frenetic pace has not been sufficient.[152] On 20 April 2008, the Emirati government released a white paper, entitled, 'Policy of the United Arab Emirates on the Evaluation and Potential Development of Peaceful Nuclear Energy,' outlining the national energy challenges. The white paper concluded that national annual peak demand for electricity is likely to rise to more than 40,000 MW by 2020, from the current level of around 15,000 MW in 2010, reflecting a cumulative annual growth rate of roughly 9 percent from 2007.[153] The four 1400 MW nuclear plants are planned to provide 25 percent of the country's electricity demand by 2020. These four plants, to be built by a consortium led by Korea Electric Power Co. (KEPCO), have an estimated construction cost of $20.4 bn.[154] As with the Abu Dhabi solar project, Shams 1, there are enormous subsidies involved with building these plants.[155] Nuclear power plants are notoriously expensive compared with gas-fired plant.[156] However, while the financial burden will still be quite large,

Emirati officials have allowed for risk allocation with the development of a Public-Private Partnership where KEPCO is in charge of designing, building and operating the nuclear power plant.[157]

The primary driver behind UAE plans to establish its civilian nuclear programme is the expected shortfall of natural gas production.[158] Although the first nuclear plant is expected to come online by 2017, there will be an interregnum when the UAE will still be highly vulnerable to supply disruptions. Mohamed al-Hammadi, chief executive of the Emirates Nuclear Energy Corporation (ENEC), promised that even more nuclear plants could be forthcoming if Emirati electricity demand continues to rise. He announced that, 'The more demand we have for electricity the more power plants we'll have to build.'[159] A secondary consideration for the UAE in its nuclear drive is the conservation of its oil for export, as opposed to its inefficient use in power plants. By approximately 2018, the UAE could substantially increase its oil export volumes when it no longer has to burn it to meet peak power demand. By reliance on nuclear and other alternative energy sources for power generation, natural gas would also be conserved and be available for the petrochemical sector.

The UAE has shown interest in Turkmenistan's gas fields to supply its own needs.[160] Mubadala allied to ConocoPhillips to bid for Turkmen gas fields. The two companies are also planning to jointly drill in the Kazakh portion of the Caspian Sea in the third quarter of 2010. In an effort to diversify its energy imports, the UAE seeks to develop linkages with energy-rich Central Asian countries to help supply its own significant energy needs. However, without a comprehensive gas swap agreement with Iran (which would encounter the same obstacles as Iranian gas supply) going as far afield as Turkmenistan for natural gas would make little economic sense. Deliveries from Turkmenistan would be just as, if not more, expensive as domestic UAE gas production.

Production and Demand Estimates 2015–2020

Even though the global economic crisis weakened natural gas demand growth in the UAE, as the global economy seems poised to return to growth by 2011–2012, it is likely that robust Emirati natural gas demand growth would return at the same time. Paradoxically, global economic recovery would increase global oil demand, which in turn would cause OPEC to increase its production quotas to allow the UAE to drastically increase oil and associated gas production.[161] Even without global economic recovery, the broad infrastructure development projects planned in the UAE would still serve as a driver of natural gas demand.[162] The global economic crisis acted as both an obstacle and a catalyst for sectoral evolution. While there were significant liquidity challenges for natural gas companies as the international credit market dried up, the many energy project cancellations caused commodity and construction costs to decline precipitously.[163] In the scenario that the global economic crisis deepens and spreads due to economic difficulties in the Eurozone, it is possible that the drop in UAE gas consumption from 2008 to 2009 of .4 Bcm could expand if European and global oil, steel and petrochemical demand weakens.[164]

While the massive governmental stimulus measures and infrastructure plans could be a major consumer of already scarce natural gas supplies, governmental funds could also be directed to natural gas development. In 2009, the UAE developed a comprehensive plan to pump nearly $1 trillion into the Emirati economy, building roads, power plants, and the metro system.[165] However, it is extremely likely that Emirati gas demand only temporarily diminished during the peak of the global economic crisis of 2008–2009, and that natural gas demand growth will have the same unrestrained increase that typified the Emirati gas sectors during the hydrocarbon 'boom' years of 2002–2008, when natural gas demand grew by 20.2 Bcm. It is estimated that the natural gas demand will continue to increase at approximately 7 percent per annum due to the growing power and industrial sectors, the increase in global oil demand, government investment in strategic industrial sectors and the Emirati stimulus plans.[166]

Emirati associated gas production is likely to remain constrained, at least until the predicted return to economic growth by 2011–2012 or until OPEC loosens its strict oil production quotas for the UAE to increase production from its associated gas fields.[167] ADNOC's strategy is to increase oil production by 14 percent by 2014, and although it is uncertain what the OPEC quotas will be at that time, such an increase would boost associated gas production significantly.[168] However, non-associated natural gas reserves projects are expected to gradually come online from 2012 to 2016 (see Table 12.4), especially the smaller natural gas reserves in the Northern Emirates (discussed above), and the IGD and Hail Gas Development projects. The exit of ConocoPhillips from the Shah field in May 2010 is likely to result in a two-year delay, with production starting up around 2016–2017, under the most optimistic scenario. Until 2014–15, the UAE may still be in a precarious position in terms of gas supply, with blackouts continuing to plague the Northern Emirates during the peak demand summer period (May–August).

If the UAE continues its robust industrialisation drive over the next decade with a 7 percent annual demand growth, it is likely to face a serious gas shortfall in 2015 (see Table 12.3) despite non-associated gas production, Dolphin natural gas imports and Shell/Qatargas LNG.[169] Even under the most optimistic scenario that the various domestic non-associated gas fields will come online as planned, there would still be a 29.4 Bcm/yr shortfall. If the UAE is able to utilise nitrogen or carbon for its EOR operations, that would liberate approximately 18 Bcm/yr for domestic consumption. Furthermore, since 2007, the UAE had been developing a nascent carbon trading platform, with the expectation of an eventual cap-and-trade system. However, the onset of the global financial crisis in 2008, combined with the lack of a binding global compact at the Copenhagen climate negotiations in 2009, decisively constrained its realisation. If the UAE were to develop a cap-and-trade system, the carbon caps would forge a type of darwinistic environment, whereby the energy-intensive industries would be forced to incorporate energy efficiency measures.[170] The gains that would result from binding carbon limitations would translate into enormous gains in the natural gas sector, as gas would be utilised more effectively in the industrial and retail sectors.[171]

All the above measures, in addition to demand-side energy efficiency and peak demand imports from regional suppliers, should be sufficient to allow a razor thin margin for the UAE to escape from crippling blackouts. If the UAE nuclear plants do come online by 2017 (an extremely optimistic scenario), and the various energy efficiency and renewable energy projects are able to exert significant downward pressure on natural gas demand, then the prognosis will not be as dire. Incorporating a robust gas sector rationalisation plan would mitigate the future gas shortages. Nonetheless, the foregoing would have a significant impact in only the most optimistic scenarios.

Conclusions

Between 2015 and 2020, the UAE will continue to import 15.4 Bcm/yr of Dolphin gas under the Phase One contract and since these exceed exports of LNG from the ADGAS plant, the country is already a net gas importer. As discussed above, no additional long-term pipeline supply contracts are to be expected from Qatar (i.e., Phase Two Dolphin) without a significant reformulation of the pricing schedule, and even then, Qatar is not likely to want to remain locked into an additional long-term export relationship. However, much of Qatar's reluctance depends upon whether there is a sustained downturn of the global economy and whether a global gas glut continues to drive down gas prices. In the scenario of a protracted downturn in natural gas prices, that could be the very development that would push the UAE and Qatar into a mutually agreeable contract for additional long-term gas sales.

By 2015–16, natural gas production in the UAE is predicted to increase significantly, by an estimated 14.4 Bcm/yr when several non-associated fields start producing. But this increase will be accompanied by a huge jump in gas demand over the same period (see Table 12.4). In spite of gas allocation issues, the UAE's state-owned companies are pressing ahead with diversification into petrochemicals. Abu Dhabi National Chemicals (Chemaweyaat) is currently building a petrochemicals complex in Taweelah, the first phase of which is expected to produce 7 mtpa of products, such as olefins and aromatics. Additionally, from 2013, Abu Dhabi Basic Industries (ADBIC) announced plans to build another such complex in Abu Dhabi by the end of 2010.[172] However, in order to alleviate the burden on natural gas supplies, the petrochemical producers are researching the viability of other feedstocks in the production process.[173]

It is likely that the UAE will be in dire need of 'interruptible' gas supplies from Dolphin or additional LNG imports during the peak demand periods of the summer months, and perhaps significant imports during the off-peak season as well. If the UAE is successful in its quest to replace the massive amounts of natural gas for EOR (18 Bcm/yr), with nitrogen or carbon, additional gas supplies should be liberated for domestic consumption in the industrial and retail sector.

Table 12.4: UAE Production and Demand, 2000–2020, Bcm

Natural Gas	*Production*	*Demand*
2000	38.4	31.4
2008	50.2	58.1
2015 (est.)	64.6	88.5
2020 (est.)	78.1	107.5

Source: BP *Statistical Review of World Energy*, 2010

As far as LNG exports are concerned, the outlook for the period to 2019 looks to be a continuation of the last 15 years with production remaining in the 7.0–7.8 Bcm range and most of the output being delivered to TEPCO in Japan using the existing eight LNG ships. The question of ADGAS's future beyond 2019, when the current contract with TEPCO expires, will have to be addressed by 2014 or 2015 to allow investment to be made in extending the life of the plant and if it is decided to increase output. Furthermore, with ADGAS being its largest supplier of LNG, TEPCO will need to know ADGAS's plans by 2015 at the very latest to allow it to line up replacement supplies should the decision be made not to extend production or if Abu Dhabi decides to reduce the commitment to TEPCO from 2019 to allow it to diversify its sales portfolio rather than continue to rely on one major buyer.

Gas import from Dolphin is likely to remain stabilised at its Phase One commitments of 18.61 Bcm/yr until the contract expires in 2032. Additional 'interruptible' or seasonal supplies through Dolphin, as well as short-term LNG supplies on the spot market, may be purchased to help offset peak demand. Therefore, the current expectation is that UAE's current net import position will not only continue but increase over the next decade.

Emirati strategies to increase its natural gas supply and reduce demand will likely be cosmetic unless power and natural gas prices are increased substantially. The ConocoPhillips withdrawal from the Shah sour gas project is a harbinger of events to come unless structural pricing reform is undertaken. To be consistent with WTO provisions of the Agreement on Subsidies and Countervailing Measures, the Emirati authorities should adopt a dual pricing formula for its industrial and retail sectors. The retail sector does not contribute as much to economic modernisation as the industrial sector. Therefore, in terms of gas allocation, the industrial sector should be given preferential pricing, perhaps cost-plus, to encourage the development of the horizontal and vertical value-added industries e.g., petrochemicals, fertilisers, steel and aluminium smelting, and so on. The retail sector should be brought as close as possible to market-based pricing to discourage overconsumption of the UAE's natural gas patrimony.

However, judging by the lack of a political commitment to a comprehensive restructuring of the natural gas and power sector, it does not seem that the UAE will be able to effectively rationalise natural gas supply and allocation within the next decade. A fragmented natural gas and power policy focusing on the promotion of nuclear and renewable energy, gas imports, coal plant construction and energy efficiency measures, rather than full natural gas price liberalisation, is the probable reality until at least 2020.[174]

If the UAE desires to truly liberate itself from its natural gas impasse, it will need to proactively create a viable strategy to increase natural gas production, while moderating demand for electricity. If it does not undertake a comprehensive restructuring of its fragmented energy policy, the UAE could find enormous challenges in the coming decades to its hitherto successful economic growth model.

Notes

1   Andy Flower is the author of the Adgas LNG section and Justin Dargin is the author of the rest of the chapter.

2   Natural Gas: Proved Reserves, *BP Statistical Review of World Energy* (June 2009) p.22; Kawach, Nadim, 'UAE Gas Output Rises by 10 bcm in Five Years', *Emirates Business 24/7* (Dec. 15, 2009).

3   Sharjah's most important gas deposits are at the offshore Mubarek field and the onshore Sajaa, Moveyeid and Kahaif fields. 'Country Profile: Emirates Sharjah', Oxford Business Group. Available at http://www.oxfordbusinessgroup.com/country.asp?country=59

4   There are other smaller amounts spread out in the other Emirates.

5   This figure excludes gas which was flared or reinjected. Reinjected gas accounts for an additional 18 Bcm/yr. Natural Gas, *BP Statistical Review of World Energy* (June 2010) p.24.

6   Ibid. p. 27.

7   The UAE contracted for Dolphin gas at 18.61 Bcm/yr, however because of a series of maintenance and inspection programmes at a Qatar Gas facility in Ras Laffan during 2009, the exported quantity dropped below its contractual amount. *Zawya Dow Jones*, 'Qatar's Gas Supply to the UAE will be Down 25 Pct', (Feb. 10, 2010).

8   Ibid. p.30. Most of the LNG is shipped to Japan, with a lesser quantity exported to South Korea and India.

9   See section on Adgas LNG below.

10 *Emirates Business*, 'Demand for Electricity to Increase 6%', 24/7 (March 2, 2009).

11 Webb, Simon, 'Update 2-Adnoc Aims to Double Domestic Gas Supplies in 2009', Reuters (Feb. 19, 2009).

12 OPEC oil production quotas significantly impact Emirati gas production as most of the gas produced in the UAE is from associated wells. *Middle East Economic Digest*, 'OPEC Faces Up to Cost of Output Cuts', (Mar. 12, 2009).

13 See Chapter 9.

14 Due to maintenance on the gas processing facility at Ras Laffan, export quantities declined during 2009 and 2010, often by as much as 25 percent below the contractual amounts. DiPaola, Anthony, 'Dolphin Plans U.A.E Gas Pipeline Work in Mid-June', *Bloomberg Businessweek* (May 27, 2010).

15 The shortage is computed by the difference between production in 2009, i.e., 48.8 Bcm, and the consumption for 2009, i.e., 59.1 Bcm. See Natural Gas, *BP Statistical Review of World Energy* (June 2010) pp.24, 27.

16 Dargin. Justin, 'Trouble In Paradise – The Widening Gulf Gas Deficit'. *Middle East Economic Survey (MEES)*, September 29, 2008.

17 *Oil and Gas Journal*, 'Poten: Abu Dhabi Gas Demand Could Limit Sour Gas for LNG', (July 27, 2009).

18 Saudi Arabia's gas consumption in 2008 was 78.1 Bcm vs. 58.1 Bcm by

the UAE. Natural Gas: Consumption, *BP Statistical Review of World Energy* (June 2009) p.27; see generally, Kawach, Nadim, 'UAE Gas Output Rises by 10 bcm in Five Years', *Emirates Business 24/7* (Dec. 15, 2008); Natural Gas: Consumption, *BP Statistical Review of World Energy* (June 2009) p.27.

19   *UAE Interact* 'Population Leaps to 8.19 Million', (May 30, 2010).

20   Ibid.

21   Egypt's gas consumption was 40.1 in 2008. Ibid.

22   For a discussion on the impact of OPEC production cuts on Gulf associated gas production, see Salisbury, Peter, 'OPEC Faces Up to Cost of Output Cuts', *MEED*, (March 12, 2009).

23   *APS Review Gas Market Trends*, 'UAE Gas Shortage to Triple by 2025', (May 26, 2008).

24   Ibid.

25   Ibid.

26   James, Ed, 'Gas Shortfall Leaves a Sour Taste', *Middle East Economic Digest*, (Aug. 31, 2007).

27   Remo-Listana, Karen, 'Alternative Energy is an Answer to Dwindling Natural Gas Supplies', *Arabian Business 24/7* (Apr. 6, 2009). The power demand in Ajman is driven by rapid GDP growth, estimated at 27 percent annually, with demographic increases reaching 18 percent per annum. A senior official at the Federal Electricity and Water Authority deflected responsibility, and instead blamed the lack of adequate development planning on Ajman officials. See 'Utilities Supply Crunch in the Northern Emirates', *Emirates Business 24/7* (July 10, 2008). Hassan Abdullah al-Ghasyah, FEWA's executive director of supply, seconded this assessment with the statement that, 'local government authorities have not coordinated on precise water and power requirements with FEWA.' As a result of the lack of coordination, al-Ghasyah stated that poor planning was the primary cause for the shortages and for the need for independent generating capacity. See 'UAE Private Supply', Oxford Business Group (Oct. 8, 2008).

28   Maree, Karen, 'Coal is Dubai's Best Option to Meet Rising Demand', *Middle East Business Intelligence* (Feb. 22, 2008); 'UAE Cement Firms Turn to Coal', *Arabian Business* (June 24, 2007).

29   Many companies saw their profits drop when they had to switch from below market price natural gas, to higher cost oil. Natural gas is not only 'greener' but much more efficient. Natural gas is almost 30 percent less carbon intensive than oil, and approximately 45 percent less than coal. See Mackenzie, Kate, 'Coal Die-off, NatGgasBoom are Already Reducing US Emissions', *Financial Times*, (May 6, 2010).

30   *Gulf News*, 'UAE Gas Supply is 20% Below Peak Demand', (Feb. 21, 2008).

31   Remo-Listana, Karen, 'Gas Shortage to Double Cost of Electricity', *Emirates Business 24/7* (March 17, 2008).

32   James, Ed., 'Gas Shortfall Leaves a Sour Taste', Ibid.

33   Fuel liquids can refer to diesel, medium fuel oil, crude oil, kerosene, or LPG. Dargin, Justin, 'Trouble In Paradise – The Widening Gulf Gas Deficit', *MEES*, Ibid.; Ghazal, Rym Tina, 'Ajman Hopes to be Next Mini

Dubai', *The National* (May 17, 2008).

34 In the Northern Emirates, the local banks understand that any new projects will not be attached to the grid, and, therefore, they refuse to fund many otherwise viable projects.

35 Carlisle, Tamsin, 'Victim of its Own Success, Emirate Seeks New Option', *The National,* (Aug. 25, 2009).

36 Al-Baik, Duraid, 'Sharjah Power Crisis Could Hurt Economy', *Gulfnews* (Sept. 7, 2009); Al-Baik, Duraid, 'Why is Sharjah Suffering?', *Gulf News* (Sept. 21, 2009).

37 Ibid. 'Why is Sharjah Suffering?'

38 It is beyond the scope of this study, but the UAE and the wider Gulf also face a significant challenge to their ability to adequately desalinate water due to the rising cost of energy. The increased use of desalination increases the quantity of brine in the Arabian Gulf, and may create diminishing returns for further desalination efforts. Todorova, Vesela, 'Desalination Threat to the Growing Gulf', *The National* (August 31, 2009).

39 Only Abu Dhabi, Dubai and Sharjah have their own water and electricity authorities, Fujairah and the other Emirates depend primarily on the Federal Electricity and Water Authority (FEWA) for their energy.

40 Naylor, Hugh, 'Emirates Left in the Dark', *The National* (Aug. 26, 2009); in 2008, there were many more real estate projects under construction that once completed would desire to be connected to the grid, causing further supply strains. *Utilities Supply Crunch in the Northern Emirates*, http://www.za-wya.com/story.cfm/sidZAWYA20080710035054/Utilities%20supply%20crunch%20in%20Northern%20Emirates

41 http://books.google.com/books?id=9DRRsjkk8UgC&pg=PA64&lpg=PA64&dq=gas+demand+and+ras+al+khaimah&source=bl&ots=y8_GXTm8y5&sig=hD_J-okBYsHRg_Rrr97EfTmN2ik&hl=en&ei=9W_9TN7oKIa8lQfBycicBQ&sa=X&oi=book_result&ct=result&resnum=2&ved=0CBsQ6AEwAQ#v=onepage&q=gas%20demand%20and%20ras%20al%20khaimah&f=false

42 While generators are often the only alternative for building owners to power their high rises, they are expensive, noisy, and polluting. In Fujairah, the exhaust and jarring roar have convinced local authorities to curtail their use in many circumstances.

43 Naylor, Hugh, 'Off the Grid: No Power, No Business', *The National* (Aug. 26, 2009).

44 In 2008, Ras al-Khaimah offered an official guarantee to new property investors that their investments would have a stable and uninterrupted supply of gas, power and water. See *Gulf News*, 'RAK to Develop 2,740 MW Power Generation Capacity for New Residential Communities', (July 15, 2008).

45 Maree, Karin, 'Emirates Turn to Private Sector, as the Construction Boom Continues', *Middle East Economic Digest* (Dec. 14, 2007).

46 A Federal National Council (which functions much as a legislature) member from Ras al-Khaimah, Yousef Neaimi, posited that the energy problem

was because of the low interest rates given developers several years ago to help build the region. Subsequently, many rates went up, and the loans provided by local banks are threatened with mass defaults because the owners have not been able to recoup their financial outlays. Mr. Neaimi placed the blame squarely on the electricity authorities, who had to approve each building before it could be built. Naylor, Hugh, 'Emirates Left in the Dark', Ibid.

47   Al Serkal, Mariam M., 'Residents Battle Heat while Sharjah Blackout Continues', *Gulf News* (Aug. 19, 2009); Al Serkal, Mariam M., 'Thousands Suffer in Three Day Blackout', (Aug. 20, 2009), http://gulfnews.com/news/gulf/uae/general/thousands-suffer-in-three-day-blackout-1.536267.

48   *Emirates Business 24/7*, 'Demand for Electricity to Increase 6%'.

49   In a 2010 RNCOS report entitled, 'Middle East Power Sector Analysis', Emirati power demand was forecast to increase approximately 10 percent from 2010 to 2013. (Apr. 2010).

50   Kawach, Nadim, 'UAE to Grow by More Than 3% in 2011, Says Report', *Emirates Business 24/7* (April 14, 2010).

51   Where there have been modifications, the changes were so minute, with a myriad of exemptions to essentially nullify the intention of the tariff increase. Maree, Karin, 'Dubai Power and Water Tariff Hikes too Limited in Scope to Cut Consumption' (Feb. 22, 2008). The rate increase authorised in Dubai utilises the Slab tariff rate, which is widely used in the developing world. The sliding scale slab rate does not impact 80 per cent of the users who fall into the first category. The average Dubai citizen has an electricity consumption rate of 20,000 KWh per annum, a per capita rate that far exceeds that of many major cities in the USA, Europe and Japan. See *Eye of Dubai*, 'Dewa Restructures Tariff For More Responsible Electricity and Water Consumption', (Feb. 19, 2008). For an in-depth discussion on the role of electricity tariff setting and the developing metropolis, see Mohan, Rakesh, *Understanding the Developing Metropolis* (Oxford University Press USA, 1994), pp.259–73.

52   Shaikh, Abdul Hafeez, 'Privatization of Energy in the Gulf: Selected Issues and Options' in (ed.) *Privatization and Deregulation in the Gulf Energy Sector* (I.B.Tauris, 1999) pp.28–9.

53   The cost of using fuel oil – as opposed to natural gas for energy generation – is approximately three times higher. For a concise discussion on energy management and the role of liquid fuels versus natural gas in electricity generation, see Turner, Wayne C., *Energy Management Handbook* (The Fairmont Press, Inc., 2006) pp.116–19.

54   *Gulf News*, 'Dubai Eyes First Power, Water Tariff Hike Since '98', (Nov. 6, 2007).

55   Two years before Dolphin imports arrived, Dubai suffered through an infamous blackout on June 9, 2005. See Krane, Kelly, 'Dubai Hit by Major Power Cut', *Gulf News* (June 10, 2005).

56   During the late 1990s, when oil prices were depressed at around $18 per barrel, Gulf natural gas sold between $.50–1.40 MMBtu. See *Alexander Gas*

and Oil Connections, 'Crescent-Iran Negotiations Stalled Amid Corruption Allegations', volume 13, issue #20 (Nov. 12, 2008).

57 The cost structure is predicated on a West Texas Intermediate (WTI) crude oil price of $72.54 per barrel. See 'Natural gas Weekly Update', Energy Information Administration (Aug. 27, 2009).

58 *Arabian Business 24/7*, 'Gas Shortage to Double Cost of Electricity', (March 17, 2008).

59 *Middle East Economic Survey*, 'Northern Emirates Look to Neighbors for Gas Salvation', (Apr. 21, 2008).

60 'Gas Shortage to Double Cost of Electricity', Ibid.

61 By 'European Prices,' Iran typically has in mind a price range of $9–13/ MMBtu.

62 Sheikh Ammar did not indicate how much electricity prices could increase, but he suggested that it would reflect inflation, as 'life is getting more expensive.' However, he reassured the citizenry that the rulers will not allow energy prices to become too high. Ghazal, Rym Tina, 'Ajman Hopes to be the next Mini Dubai', *The National* (May 17, 2008). However, the lack of electricity services has caused hardship for many low-income Emiratis. There have been several instances where subsidised housing built in Ras al Khaimah under the Sheikh Zayed Housing Programme has sat vacant due to the lack of grid access.

63 Naylor, Hugh, *Off the Grid: No Power, No Business*, Ibid.

64 In October 2008, Ajman signed a $2 bn deal with the Malaysian power company MMC to construct the Gulf's first coal plant. The 1 GW plant is scheduled to come on-stream in early 2012. However, because the lignite feedstock will be sourced from several thousand miles away – most likely South Africa – there is the potential that Ajman may have merely substituted one problem for another. See 'UAE Private Supply', Oxford Business Group (Oct. 8, 2008).

65 The grids of Dubai and Abu Dhabi have been linked since April 2006.

66 Von Moltke, Anja (ed.) et al., *Energy Subsidies: lessons learned in assessing their impact and designing policy reforms*, (Greenleaf Publishing, 2004). The Agreement of Subsidies and Countervailing Measures has an alternative definition for subsidies which may include the natural gas market in the UAE. The ASCM loosely defines subsidies as government grants or outlays that have a direct impact on the production of goods. For example, a prohibited subsidy is either dependent upon export performance or upon the favoured use of domestic goods over imports. The UAE has been a member of the General Agreement on Trades and Tariffs (GATT), and then the WTO, since 1994. While many Western petrochemical firms allege that below market pricing in the Gulf countries constitutes a WTO illegal trade subsidy, as of yet, it has not been subject to suits under the Dispute Settlement Body.

67 The UAE sells LNG in the Asian Pacific market, which typically pays crude oil-related prices. Henni, Abdelghani, 'Gas Crunch Dominates UAE Summit', *Arabian Oil and Gas* (Mar. 15, 2010).

68   *Oil and Energy Trends*, 'Dubai and Qatar Agree to World's Shortest LNG Route', Volume 33, Issue 5, pp. 7–8 (May 12, 2008).

69   The UAE has substantially reduced flaring from the period 1995–2006. See Kerr, Simeon, 'Gulf States Target Gas Flares', *Financial Times* (Mar. 11, 2008); Carlisle, Tamsin, 'Gas Flaring fuels Environmental Fears', *The National* (July 5, 2008). Many of the UAE's energy companies have instituted a zero-flaring policy and most have substantially met that goal. See *UAE Interact*, 'Adnoc Boosts Output by Injecting Gas', (Apr. 9, 2001).

70   The UAE has instituted a conservation campaign entailed, 'Heroes of the UAE,' formulated to encourage people to be conscious of their energy use, since the UAE has one of the largest per capita carbon footprints in the world. Dargin, Justin, 'A model in preparation for a "post-oil" world', *The National* (March 20, 2009); Due to encouragement from the government, many of the UAE's ubiquitous hotels rushed to install energy efficient lighting. Lighting accounts for 30–40 percent of the electricity consumption in the country's hotels. Landais, Emmanuelle, 'Energy Efficient Lighting Cuts Bills by 80%', *Gulf News* (Sept. 18, 2009).

71   At the time of writing, construction of the plant was to begin in the third quarter of 2010 and be completed by 2012. The plant would have a 100 megawatt capacity, with expected costs of approximately $600 million dollars. Masdar will have a 60 percent equity stake, while Total and Abengoa will hold 20 percent each. *Saudi Gazette*, 'Abu-Dhabi to Build World's Largest Solar Plant', (June 10, 2010); *Renewable Energy World*, 'Abu Dhabi Sets 7 Percent Renewables Target', (Jan. 19, 2009).

72   Rahman, Salfur, 'Dubai Enhances Energy Security', *Gulf News* (Aug. 31, 2009).

73   *Alexander's Gas and Oil Connections*, 'UAE Needs Gas Network and Law', Vol. 11, Issue #11 (June 8, 2006).

74   At the time of writing, Phase One of the $1.4 bn GCC Interconnection Project has been completed, whereby Qatar, Saudi Arabia, Kuwait, and Bahrain, have joined their respective power sectors. Oman and the UAE will link up in 2011/2012. Power trading on the grid will initially be limited as Qatar is the only stakeholder with additional power to spare. *Arabian Business*, 'Gulf Arab States Link Up to Foil Power Crunch', (July 23, 2009. For a detailed look at the capacity upgrades across the Emirates, see *Arabian Business*, 'Energise the Emirates', (June 10, 2009).

75   *Arabian Business 24/7*, 'Emal and Gasco Open Gas Pipeline to Power Smelter', (Aug. 24, 2009); Reuters, 'Dana, Crescent to Build Yemen 'Gas City,' (Sept. 9, 2009).

76   Kawach, Nadim, 'Dana Gas to Develop 'Gas Cities', *Arabian Business 24/7* (May 8, 2007).

77   The quest to utilise nitrogen in Abu Dhabi's enhanced oil recovery scheme advanced with the announcement of a joint venture between the German-based Linde Group and ADNOC for the construction of an $800 million facility named the Ruwais. The joint venture, known as Elixir, is to produce nitrogen from the air. The plant became operational in January 2010. See

Carlisle, Tamsin, 'Adnoc Finds Elixir for its Oil Finds', *The National* (May, 8, 2008).

78 Nitrogen is considered to be quite an effective means to improve oil production. It is environmentally safe, non-corrosive, and chemically inert, meaning that it does not combine with the oil to create sludge. While the upfront capital costs to build the air separation facilities are relatively costly, the marginal cost of nitrogen injection is approximately $0.06/ MMBtu or less. See, generally, Calvin, James et al, 'An Evaluation of Nitrogen Injection as a Method of Increasing Gas Cap Reserves and Accelerating Depletion-Ryckman Creek Field, Uinta County, Wyoming', SPE Annual Technical Conference and Exhibition, 23–26 September 1979, Las Vegas, Nevada, American Institute of Mining, Metallurgical, and Petroleum Engineers, Inc. (1979).

79 Robin Mills argued that CO_2 is an extremely effective recovery process which could potentially recover 5–10 per cent of the original oil in place, and if used judiciously, could perhaps increase to 20 percent. The Japan Oil Company in Abu Dhabi envisaged recovery rates of 25–35 percent with gas floods. Use of CO_2 would increase the recovery rates to 40–50 per cent. See Mills, Robin, *The Myth of the Oil Crisis* (Praeger, London 2008) pp.88–90.

80 Both the Masdar Initiative's Abu Dhabi Future Energy Company and British Petroleum conducted CO_2 injection feasibility studies for a project that they argue would not only save valuable natural gas reinjected into oil wells, but would also enhance oil-well output, use hydrogen for power generation and provide a safe repository for carbon, Mortished, Carl, 'BP Offers Abu Dhabi Green Solution to Chronic Gas Shortages', *The Times* (Oct. 31, 2007).

81 The tender to sell the 223,200 barrel parcel of 0.05 per cent sulphur gas oil. See *Gulf News*, 'Rare UAE Gas Oil Tender Highlights Demand Fall', (Apr. 2, 2009).

82 Ibid.

83 Natural Gas: Production, *BP Statistical Review of World Energy* (June 2009) p.22; Kawach, Nadim, 'UAE Gas Output Rises by 10 bcm in Five Years', *Emirates Business 24/7* (Dec. 15, 2009).

84 *The Oil and Gas Journal*, 'ADNOC Eyes 50% Boost to Drilling', Upstream Online (Mar. 8, 2010); *The Oil and Gas Journal*, 'Poten: Abu Dhabi Gas Demand Could Limit Sour Gas for LNG', (July 27, 2009).

85 *Alexander's Oil and Gas Connections*, 'ADNOC plans Investment of $50 bn into Projects', volume 14, issue #10, (Aug. 7, 2009); Although given the fall in oil prices since Fall 2008, the UAE has embarked on a cost cutting drive, therefore the scope of many projects may be reduced or delayed. Salisbury, Peter, 'Emirates Press Ahead with Expansion', *Middle East Economic Digest* (March 20, 2009).

86 '*Northern Emirates Look to Neighbors for Gas Salvation*', Ibid.

87 Reuters, 'UAE Short of Gas in Summer Heat', (June 25, 2007).

88 The Iranian Ministry of Petroleum has initiated a regional campaign to

prioritise exploration and development of oil and gas structures that extend into neighbouring countries. A prime example of this strategy has been the Iranian interest in developing the South Pars gas field, which extends into Qatari maritime territory and combines with the North Field, and the Hengam/West Bukha offshore discovery shared with Oman. In 2008, Iran was interested in the development of the Saleh extension project. Iranian Offshore Oil Company (IOOC) is drilling wells to determine whether the UAE's offshore Saleh gas field extends into Iranian territorial waters. The IOOC claimed seismic data acquired around the year 2000 under its Persian Carpet 2000 Seismic Program, showed an extension of Saleh into Iranian waters. See *Middle East Economic Survey*, 'Iran Plans Well to Prove Up Extension of UAE's Offshore Saleh Gas Field', (Apr. 21, 2008).

89   Ibid.

90   *Northern Emirates Look to Neighbors for Gas Salvation*, Ibid.

91   The West Bukha field, shared by Oman and Iran in the Gulf off Oman's Musandam Peninsula, has production potential from the Mishriff-Maudud and Thamama reservoirs of about .29 Bcm/yr (0.8 Million cm/d). *Pipeline Magazine*, 'Oman Starts Pumping Gas for RAK', (Feb. 16, 2009); *Scandinavian Oil and Gas Magazine*, 'Heritage Produces First Oil from West Bukha Field', (Feb. 19, 2009).

92   Ras al-Khaimah Keen on Iran Gas, Press TV (Feb. 20, 2008).

93   'The Report Ras Al Khaimah', Oxford Business Group, (2008) p.62.

94   Ibid.

95   Ibid.

96   The agreement covers a total offshore area of over 1000 square kilometres, and includes the Zora gas field in Sharjah, which was discovered in 1979. See *Gulf Oil and Gas*, 'Dana Gas Moves Ahead with Plans for Offshore Concession in Sharjah', (Jan. 27, 2009). The UAE's two largest non-associated gas fields, the Shah and Bab fields, have extremely high concentrations of sulphur, with a content level of approximately 30 percent. For comparison, Qatar's North Field, which is considered a sour field, has a sulphur content of approximately 5 percent. See Canty, *Preview Sogat* (March 13, 2009).

97   Even though it has substantial gas reserves, Sharjah lacks a national oil or gas company. The Sharjah Petroleum Council has a purely regulatory function. From the beginning of energy production, Sharjah has had a liberal stance towards participation from local and international oil companies.

98   'Emerging Sharjah 2007', Oxford Business Group (2007), p.46.

99   *APS Review Gas Market Trends*, 'Sharjah's Decision Makers', (June 5, 2006), p.122.

100   *The Report: Dubai 2008*, Oxford Business Group (2008).

101   Al-Abed, Ibrahim et al, *United Arab Emirates Yearbook 2005* (Trident Press Ltd, 2004) p. 154. Dubai has only one onshore gas field, the Margham Field, which can deliver approximately 1.46 Bcm/yr. of natural gas and condensates for domestic utilisation.

102 *The Report Sharjah 2008*, Oxford Business Group (2008) p.67.

103 Ibid.

104 49 percent of the initial investment will come from Rosneft and 51 percent from Crescent, who has held the 25-year gas concession in Sharjah since February 2008. Webb, Simon et al, 'Russia's Rosneft Joins Crescent in UAE Gas Venture', Reuters (June 5, 2010).

105 Carlisle, Tamsin, 'Sharjah Gas Deal Shreds Red Tape', *The National* (June 6, 2010).

106 Crescent does not publish financial statements or details of its oil and gas reserves and production, but it considers this joint venture to have the potential to be a major development. Ibid.

107 Several IOCs declined to bid for the project. The UK's BG Group stated that company concerns over project viability and safety made it determine that the plan was not viable. James, Ed, 'Gas Shortfall Leaves a Sour Taste', *Middle East Economic Digest* (August 31, 2007).

108 The tenders covered gas wells, pipelines, and a processing plant, off site facilities, sulphur recovery, and utilities.

109 Karrar-Lewsley, Tahani, 'Conoco to Exit Abu Dhabi Gas Project', *Wall Street Journal* (April 28, 2010).

110 Baxter, Kevin, 'Petrofac Drops Bid for $12bn ADNOC Refinery Job', *Arabian Oil and Gas* (Oct. 25, 2009).

111 Just one error in extraction or procession could cause a major explosion; this has added significance as the Shah field is located near population centres, especially the oasis of Liwa.

112 'Poten: Abu Dhabi Gas Demand Could Limit Sour Gas for LNG', Ibid.

113 Ibid.

114 The sulphur can be granulated and shipped, either piped or trucked, to the Habshan gas-treatment plants in Ruwais.

115 'Abu Dhabi Assess Bids for Gas Development', Alrroya (July 19, 2009).

116 'Gas Shortfall Leaves a Sour Taste', Ibid.

117 'Adco Launches Hail Gas Field', Projects, No. 7 (Sept. 2007).

118 One potential solution would be to build a causeway to service the well-heads, as was done with the Manifa offshore development in Saudi Arabia. James, Ed, 'Gas Shortfall Leaves a Sour Taste', Ibid.

119 ADGAS History and Evolution, ADGAS website www.adgas.com/default.aspx?tabid=132

120 Ibid.

121 ADMA History, ADMA Website, www.adma-opco.com/AboutADMA/History/tabid/65/Default.aspx

122 As was first seen in its deal with ConocoPhillips for LNG from the Darwin project in Australia and the deals the company struck with Chevron in 2009 for both the purchase of LNG and the participation in the Gorgon and Wheatstone projects in Australia.

123 In a paper entitled 'The future of ADGAS in the LNG Business' presented at the Gastech Conference in Abu Dhabi in May 2009, Hamed Al-Mazouqi, Acting Head of Market Research for ADGAS said that in

2008 ADGAS's total revenues of US$7.2 Bn were made up of LNG US$5.2 Bn (72.2%), LPG US$1.3 Bn (18%), condensate US$0.5 Bn (6.9%) and sulphur US$0.2 Bn (2.8%).

124 Under a time-charter arrangement the ship-owner provides the ship and the crew and operates it on behalf of the charterer, who controls how the ship is used. The time charters for the ADGAS ships were on a long-term basis with ADGAS paying an agreed daily fee to cover both the operating costs and the capital cost of the vessel. The charterer pays for the vessel provided it is available to trade which means that the ship-owner only takes technical and nautical risks, leaving the charterer to take volume and price risk on the LNG.

125 LNG Log 25, Published by the Society of International Gas Tanker and Terminal Operators Ltd (SIGGTO) in 2000.

126 'LNG Trade and Infrastructures', Cedigaz, Paris, February 2004.

127 Ibid. and the BP *Statistical Review of World Energy* 2004 to 2009.

128 An escrow bank account is one into which funds are placed by a party and can only be released when certain pre-agreed conditions are met. The account is normally operated by trustees who are independent of either the party placing the funds into the account or the party that will receive the funds when the conditions are met.

129 'Japanese Redouble Efforts to Finalise Price Reviews', *LNG in World Markets*, February 2010, Poten and Partners, New York.

130 National Gas Shipping Company Website, www.ngsco.com/profile/index. aspx

131 Presentation of Fourth Quarter 2009 Results, 26 February 2010, Golar LNG website, www.golarlng.com

132 *Platts LNG Daily*, 'Abu Dhabi Considering Options for LNG After 2019', Vol 6, No 101, 28 May 2009.

133 *Emirates Business 24/7*, 'UAE Company Signs Deal to Transport Gas from Iran', (Sept. 17, 2009); although it must be added that 'current market realities' in terms of energy investment in Iran has a significant political risk which bears on any price negotiations.

134 *Alexander's Gas and Oil Connections*, 'Crescent-Iran Negotiations Stalled Amid Corruption Allegations', Vol. #13, Issue #20 (Nov. 12, 2008).

135 *Iran Daily*, 'Crescent Making New Gas Offer', (Oct. 8, 2008).

136 *Shana News*, 'First Train of Salman Gas Field to Inaugurate in a Month', (July, 4, 2009).

137 Crescent customers did not have contractual clauses compensating them for non-fulfilment of the contract. Many who suffered heavy monetary losses burned expensive diesel for power generation thereby incurring enormous financial burdens.

138 *The National*, 'Iran: Crescent Petroleum takes NIOC to International Arbitration', (Jul. 16, 2009). This is the course of action which Iran appears to be following, see Chapter 8.

139 'The Report Sharjah 2008', Oxford Business Group (2008) p. 67.

140 *Emirates Business 24/7*, 'UAE Company Signs Deal to Transport Gas from

Iran', (Sept. 17, 2009).

141 Carlisle, Tamsin, 'UAE Dolphin Energy in Talks to Acquire Qatar Natural Gas', *The National* (June 23, 2009).

142 The parties negotiated a contract that incorporated the highest regional price for gas at $5/MMBtu. 'Northern Emirates Look to Neighbors for Gas Salvation', Dow Jones Wire.

143 *Arabian Business*, 'Dolphin Energy Takes Gas to All Seven Emirates', (May 5, 2008).

144 *Middle East Economic Survey*, 'Dolphin and Qatar in Talks about Additional Gas', Vol. LII, No 26 (June 29, 2009).

145 'Swing' price in this chapter refers to the overall price floor and price ceiling at which gas is sold within a particular region or country. Swing may also refer in other contexts to the flexibility embedded within a gas supply contract to supply gas to the buyer over the peak demand. See generally, 'The Benefits of Gas Swing', Shepherd and Wedderburn Law Firm (Jan. 4, 2006); see also, Barbieri, Angelo et al, 'Understanding the Variation of Swing Contracts', Financial Engineering and Associates (undated).

146 *Dow Jones Newswire*, 'Update: Dubai Floating LNG Terminal Work On Schedule-Shell', (Mar. 30, 2010).

147 *Upstream Online*, 'Shell Signs on for Dubai LNG Supply', (Apr. 21, 2008).

148 *AME Info*, 'Dubai Signs Shell, QP LNG Import Deal, as Yet Another Gulf Market Tries to Escape Gas Crunch', (Apr. 27, 2008).

149 Dipaola, Anthony, 'Golar Says Dubai Floating LNG Terminal May Start in 2010', Bloomberg (June 1, 2009).

150 Kuwait in 2008 contracted for imports between 1.4 Mt/yr and 1.7 Mt/yr of Qatari LNG, starting in the summer of 2009. After the signing of the contract, Kuwait immediately began construction of the necessary regasification and receiving facilities.

151 *Alexander's Gas and Oil Connections*, 'Greater Supply Deficits Force Middle East to Focus on Domestic Needs', Vol. 12, Issue 9 (10 May 2007).

152 *US Energy Information Administration*, Country Analysis Briefs: United Arab Emirates, Electricity available at < http://www.eia.doe.gov/emeu/cabs/UAE/Electricity.html>

153 See 'Policy of the United Arab Emirates on the Evaluation and Potential Development of Peaceful Nuclear Energy', UAE White Paper Policy Document (Apr. 20, 2008) available at: http://www.carnegieendowment.org/publications/index.cfm?fa=view&id=20070

154 The consortium comprises KEPCO, Samsung, Hyundai and Doosan Heavy Industries, along with US firm Westinghouse, Toshiba of Japan and KEPCO subsidiaries, Coker, Margaret, 'Korean Team to Build U.A.E. Nuclear Plant', *The Wall Street Journal* (Dec. 28, 2009).

155 Reportedly, the cost of producing electricity at the Shams1 solar thermal plant at Madinat Zayed in Abu Dhabi would be about three to five times higher than the average cost of producing electricity from natural gas. The government would provide a direct subsidy by paying the difference

between the average costs of power generation and the actual costs of generation at Shams 1. Stanton, Chris, 'Green Subsidy for Solar Power', *The National* (June 9, 2010).

156 Crane, Agnes et al, 'Nuclear Power at Bay', *New York Times* (May 22, 2010); Muthiah, Shanthi, 'Generation Asset Valuation: Are We at the Nadir for Gas-Fired Power Plants?', *Electric Lights and Power* (Nov/Dec. 2004).

157 Patel, Kamal, 'Challenges and Prospects for the UAE Power Sub-Sector', *Zawya* (Mar. 18, 2010).

158 'Energy Expert: Supply of Gas in the Market Exceeds Demand', In the News, The Dubai Initiative, November 11, 2010.

159 *The Peninsula*, 'Power Demand to Dictate More N-Deals in the UAE', (Jan. 9, 2009).

160 Bierman, Stephen et al, 'U.A.E. Bid for Caspian Gas May Test Russian Dominance', *Bloomberg Businessweek* (May 5, 2010).

161 *UAE Interact*, 'Adnoc to Lift Curb on Oil Output', (Mar. 9, 2010).

162 Additionally, under the 'Plan Abu Dhabi 2030: Urban Structure Framework Plan', Abu Dhabi pledged to spend upwards of $15 billion until 2012 in massive urban construction.

163 McGinley, Shane, 'Abu Dhabi Construction Costs Down by 30%-TDIC', *Arabian Business* (Apr. 17, 2010); Kawach, Nadim, 'Abu-Dhabi Says Oil Project Cost Slashed 20 per cent', *Emirates Business 24/7* (Jan. 27, 2009); *CityScape Intelligence*, 'Building Materials Decline in Cost in UAE', (Nov. 24, 2009).

164 *BP Statistical Review of World Energy* (June 2010) p.27.

165 Singh, Timon, 'Abu Dhabi Invests $1 Tn into Infrastructure', *Mena Infrastructure* (Nov. 3, 2009).

166 Kumar, Himendra Mohan, 'UAE Gas Demand to Touch 15 bcf/day by 2020, Says Expert UAE Gas Demand Rises 7% Annually', *Gulf News* (May 18, 2010).

167 The Institute of International Finance predicted that the UAE would have probably 3.3 percent economic growth by 2011. However, the report indicated that under optimistic scenarios, UAE's 'growth could reach 2.7 percent in 2010 and 4.2 percent in 2011' if debt-laden Dubai successfully resolves its debt issues and accelerates reforms. *Agence France Press*, 'IIF Expects 4.4 pct Gulf Economic Growth', (May 18, 2010).

168 *Maktoob*, 'Adnoc to Press Ahead with 5-Year Plan', (June 2, 2009).

169 The most pessimistic forecast was announced by Khalid al-Awadi, Gas Operations Manager at Emirates General Petroleum Corporation (Emarat), who calculated that in 2020, Emirati gas demand would reach 155 Bcm/yr. However, al-Awadi was optimistic that increased imports, domestic capacity expansion, nuclear plans and renewable energy would be able to meet the demand increase. Kumar, Himendra Mohan, 'UAE Gas Demand Rises 7% annually', Ibid.

170 See generally, Dargin, Justin, *The Development of a Gulf Carbon Platform: Mapping Out the Gulf Cooperation Council Carbon Exchange*, Harvard Kennedy School, Working Paper No.1 (May 2010).

171 Dargin, Justin, 'A Carbon Solution for the Gulf's Energy Deficit' *Petroleum Economist* (November 4, 2010).

172 *Business Monitor*, 'Second Phase of Al-Khaleej Launched as Domestic Demand Grows', (May 11, 2010).

173 One such feedstock being explored as an alternative to ethane is liquid petroleum gas condensate. Shamseddine, Reem, 'Gulf Petrochemical Firms Seek Alternatives to Gas', *Arabian Business* (June 9, 2010).

174 The UAE has made some attempts to reform the electricity tariffs and gasoline prices. In April 2010, the UAE attempted to liberalise gasoline prices. These incremental movements, combined with the increase in price for Qatari gas and the refusal of IOCs to produce Emirati gas fields for a less than adequate return on investment, i.e., ConocoPhillips will likely have some impact on the overall budgetary burdens and spur greater pricing reform, *Gulf Daily News*, 'UAE Planning to Increase Petrol Prices', (Apr. 19, 2010).

CHAPTER 13

NATURAL GAS IN BAHRAIN AND KUWAIT

Randa Alami

Introduction

In spite of their relatively small sizes, Kuwait and Bahrain are an important part of the regional gas picture in at least three ways. Firstly, gas has been central to the development of their domestic economies for three decades, since the construction of the first pipelines linking gas production facilities to refineries and industries. Secondly, both countries are involved in infrastructures being developed in the region to meet the growing demand for gas and power, such as the Dolphin project and the Gulf Co-operation Council (GCC) electricity grid. Thirdly, for the last few years they have been looking to their neighbours to secure future import needs.

In both Bahrain and Kuwait, domestic demand for gas was created in the 1970s and 1980s. Since then, gas has been channelled to three main uses: oil and gas production, power and electricity, and petrochemicals and heavy industry. Critically, rising demand has been sustained by significant underpricing of gas. Subsidised domestic gas prices helped the power sector not only to grow, but also to shift to gas. They also encouraged energy inefficiency and a 'wasteful consumption of electricity'.[1] Electricity tariffs are nominal in Kuwait, and have yet to reach cost recovery levels in Bahrain. Price increases are a sensitive political issue, as subsidies have been provided under a long-prevailing social contract.

Gas was used in both countries to establish what have become significant petrochemical and heavy industry sectors, particularly in terms of job creation and diversification. Bahrain now boasts the largest steel plant in the world, which accounts for 3 percent of GDP. Kuwait is also an important regional producer of ethylene.[2] Its competitors complain of the unfair advantage given by feedstock priced at one-half to one-third of world levels. Others point out that despite being assisted, they may face supply shortages.

In the context of rising oil prices and revenues in the last few years, a gas 'demand bubble' was created driven by several factors – strong economic growth and a concomitant construction boom,[3] continued

486

emphasis on industrialisation, and a phenomenal rise in electricity and power consumption.[4] As with other countries in the region, the combination of growing consumption and stagnating – if not peaking – production levels led to a situation of conflicting demands for gas uses. This conflict is more pronounced because the previous market configuration assumed available supply at subsidised prices. As a result both countries

- have intensified their upstream efforts, and
- explored the securing of supplies from Iran, Iraq, and Qatar, with LNG being the only interim solution.

As Dargin puts it, the crux of the supply problem is the gap between domestic prices on the one hand, and import prices and upstream and activation costs on the other.[5]

This chapter first considers the case of Bahrain, where natural gas is a key component of energy consumption. Bahrain's low R/P ratio means it may be heading towards a crisis due to a need to import much of its gas within ten years. Section 2 examines the Kuwaiti natural gas sector. As in Bahrain, natural gas has been used to develop Kuwait's industrial and petrochemical ambitions. However, Kuwait has not witnessed a switch to gas; rather, rising demand for gas, fuelled by electricity needs, has raced ahead of production, creating a shortage. Both sections consider the medium-term prospects for gas, making simple extrapolations in light of recent growth trends for supply and demand. The current outlook for gas demand has been affected by the global recession that began in 2008. It is assumed that while the rapid pace of the last decade has been curbed, there will be no significant destruction of demand. The final section draws some conclusions.

Bahrain

The Bahraini Gas Sector

At the end of 2007, Bahrain had only 85 billion cubic metres (Bcm) of natural gas reserves, giving it a very low R/P ratio of 6.3 years.[6] Reserve levels reflect the fact that the country is struggling to keep up production of oil and gas from its maturing fields. Most of the gas is not associated with oil production, and is produced from the Bahrain and Arab (low and high pressure gas) fields. Bahrain has been offsetting a 14 percent annual rate of natural decline mainly through active drilling, exploration and development programmes, and by enhanced

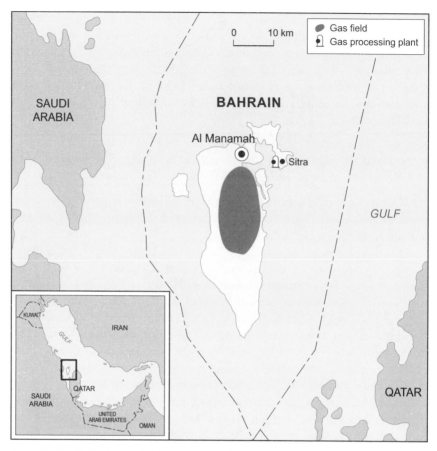

Map 13.1:   Bahrain Gas Field and Processing Plant

recovery techniques, which involve re-injecting gas. Hence, between 2005 and 2008, increasing Khuff gas production helped to supply additional feedstocks to local industries.

Figure 13.1 plots Bahraini natural gas consumption and marketed production since 2000. Data for the former are taken from the official Bahraini data for distributed gas published on ministerial websites, while the latter is from BP. The figure shows that production and consumption have tracked each other up from 8.6 and 8.8 Bcm in 2000 respectively, to 12.5 and 13.4 Bcm in 2008. Bahraini gross production in 2008 was some 2.6 Bcm higher at 15.1 Bcm because of the use of gas for re-injection. Both consumption and production more than doubled between 1990 and 2000, growing at a similar pace of some 4 percent per annum since then. However, as in the rest of the region, growth has accelerated in the last few years: 2007 levels were 24 percent

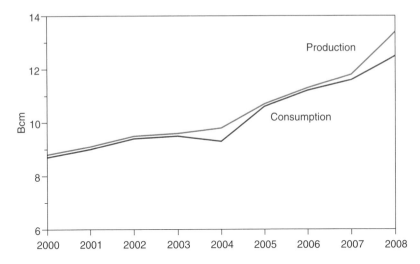

Figure 13.1: Bahrain's Natural Gas Balance

Sources: Production – BP *Statistical Review of World Energy 2009*; Consumption –
　　　　Ministry of Finance, 'Gas, Production and Distribution According to
　　　　User', August 2009

higher than in 2004 in the case of consumption, and 21 percent in the case of production. Post-2008, the global recession may well have slowed down this momentum, but it is still the case that in the medium term, Bahrain has to meet at least 13 Bcm/year of gas demand from dwindling reserves.

Bahrain does not have a national grid. In 2007, it had only four pipelines of 10–18 inches in diameter, with a total length of 185 km with seven compressor stations, which deliver the gas to a central gas processing plant.[8] This plant delivers 7 million cm/d of processed gas (25 percent of daily local consumption) to Bahrain's refinery and the Aluminium Company of Bahrain (ALBA). It also produces LPG and naphtha, which are stored in Sitra port for export and local distribution.[9] The throughput of the processing plant stands at 7.8 Bcm. However, there is an ongoing investment programme to increase gathering and processing capacity, which should also double the plant's capacity to 14 Bcm by 2020. Bahrain's new power station of Al-Dur will also be supplied with gas through a new 10 km pipeline.[10]

Industry Organisation

The natural gas sector is dominated by state companies. While BAPCO is in charge of the upstream, Banagas, which was established in 1979 by Royal or Amiri decree, is in charge of production and is the main domestic supplier. The government controls 75 percent of the company, the rest being owned by APICORP (12.5 percent) and Chevron Bahrain (12.5 percent). Banagas supplies LPG and exports natural gas liquids, with residue gas forwarded to ALBA and power stations. It is largely a midstream and downstream company. However, it is BAPCO who signs feedstock agreements to supply local industries and power plants.

Up to 2005, the Ministry of Oil organised the sector and determined its legislative framework. In September 2005, the Ministry was replaced by the National Oil and Gas Authority (NOGA), the idea being to corporatise the sector so as to give it more flexibility and independence. The Authority launched a US$20 billion sectoral development plan, including the aforementioned $200 million plan to expand gas processing facilities. It was hoped that the authority would revitalise exploration prospects, following the resolution of the dispute with Qatar, which freed major offshore blocks. Since gas is so central to the country's energy mix, boosting gas reserves has been a key aim of the upstream strategy since 2005/2006. Aside from developing fields such as Khuff and drilling new gas wells, this strategy meant introducing the latest advanced technologies and techniques, and more financial input from IOCs. By 2007, NOGA was re-offering blocks under new PSAs.

Additionally, in November 2008, the Authority launched an initiative for deep onshore gas exploration of pre-Khuff formations (15,000–20,000 feet), offering a new Development and Exploration PSA (DEPSA). Unfortunately, the initial interest of dozens of companies evaporated in the face of the world recession and falling natural gas prices: only two bids were received in July 2008 with only three IOCs shortlisted. The tender was won by a consortium comprising Mubadala – a UAE group – and Occidental. The DEPSA gives a dominant share to the consortium (48 percent to Occidental and 32 percent to Mubadala), leaving NOGA with a minor share of 20 percent. Should these developments be successful, oil production should reach 102,300 b/d by 2016, peaking in 2019. Gas production should double from 13 Bcm to 25–27 Bcm by 2020, which would mean that Bahrain would be able to meet domestic needs beyond 2015.[11]

While NOGA defines Bahrain's upstream gas policy, allocation and pricing issues are under different management. With gas being used for power, desalination, industry and residential consumption, since 2005/06 all the relevant ministries are involved with strategic decisions – particularly regarding pricing – being made by the National Gas Committee. Finally, gas policy is also influenced by environmental policy, including the fact that Bahrain is a signatory to the Kyoto

Protocol. The country's environmental commitments have combined with dwindling reserves to encourage energy-saving measures throughout the economy. Since 2006, an Energy Conservation Committee directs and co-ordinates such measures, which are mainly technical in nature. Examples given in NOGA's 2007 *Annual Report* include energy auditing and linking industrial networks to the national grid. As discussed below, significant energy price increases are yet to be contemplated.

Markets for Gas

Main Patterns. Like the rest of the Middle East and indeed many developing countries, Bahrain has witnessed a seemingly unrelenting rise in energy consumption. This growth has been particularly strong in the last five years, because of a growing population, strong economic growth and the completion of major energy-intensive industrial projects. Table 13.1 indicates that energy consumption grew at 7 percent per year between 2002 and 2007 to reach 13,803 tonnes of oil equivalent (TOE), 87 percent of which was natural gas. It is this underlying pattern that has sustained such strong growth in domestic demand for gas. However, natural gas has been a dominant source of energy in Bahrain for the last two decades or so. Bahrain's limited crude oil reserves were only ever sufficient to meet local demand for refined products.

Table 13.1: Bahraini Total Energy Consumption, Thousand tonnes of oil equivalent (Toe)

	2002	*2003*	*2004*	*2005*	*2007*	*Composition in 2007*
Oil	1,235	1,312	1,419	1,643	1,743	13.2%
Gas	8,500	8,658	8,820	9,630	12,060	86.9%
Total	9,735	9,965	10,239	11,273	13,803	100%

Source: ESCWA, *Status of Energy Statistics and Indicators in the ESCWA Region*, 2009

The structure of demand for gas in Bahrain has changed only slightly in the last decade. The two main changes are a reduction in the share of re-injected gas, and a noticeable expansion in the electricity sector. This rise is hard to discern after 2005 as the gas consumed by privatised plants and/or Independent Power Plants (IPPs) is categorised under 'Others'. Hence, as can be seen in Table 13.2, by 2008, gas consumed by the power sector rose to at least 4 Bcm, accounting for some 34 percent of total gas consumption. The shares of industries have weakened, reflecting absolute levels that have risen *vis-a-vis* the 1990s, but which tended to stagnate recently. Similarly, according to NOGA, in 2007 gas consumed by the Electricity and Water Authority absorbed 33 percent of domestic gas production (including 17 percent by the privatised power companies). ALBA, BAPCO and the Gulf Petrochemical Industries Company (GPIC) respectively used 27 percent, 18 percent, and 8 percent of gas consumed, BAPCO's share being largely for re-injection operations. Other industries consume the remaining 14 percent.[12]

Table 13.2: Bahraini Gas Demand by Sector, Billion cubic metres

	1997	2000	2001	2003	2005	2008	2015*
Electricity	2.0	2.8	3.0	3.6	4.0	2.1	2.1–2.5
Others	0.5	0.5	0.6	0.6	0.6	3.6	3.6–4
Alba	3.1	3.0	3.1	3.2	3.7	3.8	3.8
Industry	2.4	2.4	2.5	2.3	2.4	3.0	3.6
TOTAL	7.9	8.7	9.1	9.9	10.6	12.5	12.5–13.5

Source: Ministry of Finance (2009), Economic Bulletin, Table 11

Notes: 1. As of 2006, consumption by privatised power station is now included in "Others"
2. Industry consists of GPIC, GIIC and the refinery
3. Total excludes the 2.5 BCM of gas used for reinjection each year.

* Expected value under most likely scenario

Bahrain's residential energy sector based on LPG has remained small. Consumption has moved from 1100 b/d in 2003 to 1300 b/d in 2008. This is amply supplied by the LPG plant, which exports the rest of the output of 2600 b/d (naphtha and butane). These levels have fallen since the 1990s [13]

Industry. The shares of segments constituting Bahrain's gas market are illustrated in Figure 13.2. This clearly shows that put together, Bahrain's industries and ALBA comprise the largest component of demand for natural gas. In most of these industries the rise in capacity has been small and largely gradual. The consequent requirements for additional feedstocks have added to the pressure to sustain production increases. Hence the refinery now consumes 1.3 Bcm compared with 1 Bcm in 2000, while the petrochemical complex of GPIC at Sitra uses 1.4 Bcm *vs* 1.1 Bcm in the earlier year. GPIC produces about 1.4 million tonnes of urea, ammonia, and methanol. The Gulf Industrial Investment Company (GIIC) has an iron pelleting plant at Hidd that has

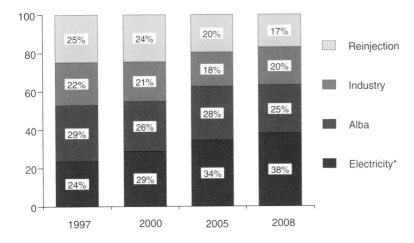

Figure 13.2: Bahraini Gas Demand by Sector, percent

Source: Ministry of Finance, 2009, Economic Bulletin, Table 11

been using 1.1 Bcm.[14] The current recession may well mean changes to plans, apparently under way, to more than double the capacity as neither regional nor world demand for steel is rising.

However, by far the biggest and most important industry is ALBA. In its third decade of operation, it now accounts for 3 percent of GDP, and 9 percent if the hundred or so local companies using its output are included.[15] As its fifth potline came on stream in 2005, it became the largest smelter in the world.[16] Its gas use rose accordingly, from 3 Bcm in 2000 to 3.7 Bcm since 2005. Plans to introduce a sixth potline have been put on hold because of the lack of additional gas supplies. This underlying tightness of supplies, together with the large share of operating costs being spent on energy, have created an openly expressed concern for energy conservation. In its *Annual Review 2008*, ALBA says that power constitutes 30 percent of operating costs, and that it is considering importing gas from neighbouring countries.

Power Generation. Underpinning the growth in energy consumption in Bahrain has been a phenomenal rise in demand for electricity. According to the Ministry of Electricity and Water, electricity demand doubled from 5041 MWh in 1997 to 10,689 MWh in 2007. Similarly, EIA data indicate that at 8.7 billion KWh, electricity consumption in 2006 was already 61 percent higher than in 2000, with both data sets indicating an annual growth rate of less than 7 percent. In response to this pressure, Bahrain has been racing to add additional capacity, and generating capacity has struggled to keep ahead of peak demand, as is clearly depicted in Figure 13.3.

Installed capacity rose by 54 percent between 2000 and 2004, and another 50 percent by 2007, when it reached 2767 MW. Given the costs of continuous expansion, Bahrain has opted to add capacity through privatisation. The al-Hidd power station was privatised in 2004/05 and Bahrain's two new power stations, namely Al-Ezzel and Al-Dur, are IPP projects costing some $500 million and $2.6 billion respectively. Such is the demand pressure that both were designed so that capacity is delivered in two consecutive phases. Hence Al-Ezzel provided 470 MW of generating capacity in April 2006, with another 480 MW made available in May 2007. The plant sells electricity to the ministry under a 20-year power purchase agreement, and buys natural gas from BAPCO under a long-term sales agreement. Likewise Al-Dur is expected to add some 1200 MW to Bahrain's generating capacity in mid 2010.[17] Prior to that, the country relied on four power stations, but also on ALBA's plant, which provides up to 275 MW to the national grid.

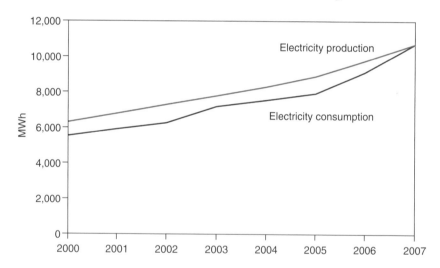

Figure 13.3: Bahraini Electricity Production and Consumption

Sources: ESCWA database; Ministry of Electricity and Water, 'Electricity', *Annual Report 2007*

Bahrain also contributed $134 million toward the $1.2 billion interconnection project linking Bahrain, Kuwait, Qatar and Saudi Arabia. In March 2009 it signed an agreement allowing it to import up to 600 MW a day. On 21 July 2009, the first cycle of undersea cable linking Al-Jasra in Bahrain and Ghunan in Saudi Arabia as well as overhead lines were commissioned. This marked the completion of the first phase of the interconnection, linking the four countries through spur lines and back-to-back HVDC interconnections. The 400 kV double circuit comprises overhead lines and a submarine link from Ghunan to Al-Jasra and associated substations in Bahrain.[18] The main benefits would be to reduce the size of the capacity used for reserves (150 MW instead of 300 MW currently used), and the possibility of relying on being able to import up to 1200 MW during emergencies.[19]

For over two decades, Bahrain had organised its electricity sector to use gas turbines. With technological advances and pressures to add capacity, it seemed only logical for the country to opt for combined cycle turbines. Figure 13.4 illustrates the fact that CCGT plants doubled their share of electricity production from 33 percent to 63 percent at the expense of gas and steam turbines.

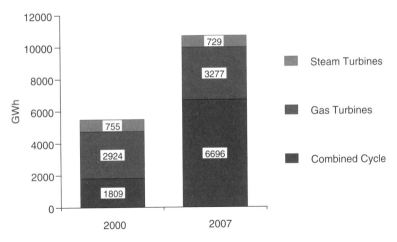

Figure 13.4: Bahraini Electricity Production by Source, GWh

Source: ESCWA database

Much less change can be detected in the structure of demand for electricity.[20] Between 2000 and 2007, the residential sector was the largest consumer of electricity expanding its share marginally from 52 percent to 58 percent at the expense of industry, whose share retreated from 19 percent to 15 percent. Electricity demand by the commercial sector also expanded in absolute terms, but accounted for 28 percent of electricity demand for the same years. The rapid rise in power generated and electricity consumed led to large increases in natural gas used – a 30 percent increase between 2004 and 2007.

Cost and Price Levels

Pricing. As in much of the developing world, Bahrain operates a framework of subsidised energy prices, despite occasional price increases. With respect to domestic gas feedstock prices, a tariff schedule (Table 13.3) had been in place between 2000 and 2007, whereby gas was supplied at a price range of Bahraini Dinar BD0.117–0.754/MMBtu, corresponding to $0.33–$2/MMBtu.[21] In April 2007, a new pricing structure was announced and has since been implemented, whereby existing customers will be charged $1.1/MMBtu, while new users should pay $1.50. The price for the former will be increased gradually also to reach $1.50 in 2011. The move should bring in $40 million in additional revenues for the government.[22]

Table 13.3: Bahraini Domestic Gas Prices by customer, 2000–2007

Client	Price in BD	Price in US$
Water and electricity	0.117	0.311
Darlafa Aluminium	0.188	0.500
Alba, GIIC, GPC, Others	0.282	0.750
Refinery	0.263	0.699
Banagas	0.754	2.005

Source: OAPEC, 'Bahrain', 7th Arab Energy Conference, p.99

In the absence of data on costs of production and delivery, the extent of subsidies is unclear. But because Bahrain is investing heavily in advanced recovery methods and expanding processing facilities, short- and longer-run marginal costs can be guessed to be in the region of $2–$5/MMBtu, with $5–$6/MMBtu being the least Bahrain could expect to pay if it had to import gas. As such, domestic prices are only 20 percent of the probable long-run marginal cost.

A similar pattern exists with respect to electricity. In 2005, tariffs were lowered for smaller residential consumers, giving a current schedule of $0.08/KWh for up to 3000 KWh, $0.16 for the next band of 3001–5000, and $0.43/KWh for 5001 and above. All other customers are charged $0.43/Kwh.[23] Previously (between 1992 and 2005), commercial customers faced tariffs of $0.159, $0.319, and $0.43/KWh for consumption levels of up to 2000, 5000, and over 5000 KWh.[24] Industrial customers have paid a flat rate of $0.43/KWh since 2000.

The prevailing tariffs for the higher bands exceed the published costs of production. According to the Arab Union of Producers, Transporters and Distributors of Electricity (AUPTDE) 2008 *Statistical Bulletin*, the average costs of production have come down to an impressive

$0.229 /KWh. However, this average masks a significant rise in energy prices, including offtake prices paid by the ministry for the new IPP projects. It seems that while it secured an impressive $0.213/KWh for Al-Ezzal plant in 2004, it faced $0.373/KWh for Al-Dur IWPP in August 2008.[25] If this rate is taken to be the current cost of production, current prices to residential, industrial and power stations cover 43, 85 and 115 percent of this cost respectively.

Ministerial attempts in 2008 to charge full costs or to get tough on tariff recovery were not welcome, though no major political disturbances were reported. By 2009, poor families were given time to repay bills.[26] Given that tariffs were lowered in 2005, and given the requirement to go to parliament for any tariff increase, eliminating or reducing subsidies is currently a no-go area. Political opposition also explains the gradual approach to increasing domestic gas prices, which remain at less than half the prices of internationally traded gas.

Prospects

Bahrain is fast approaching a critical point in its energy needs: its limited reserves indicate it may have to import part or all of its gas requirements by 2017. Its environmental and industrial strategies have led to an energy balance entirely dependent on natural gas. The former may have encouraged energy conservation, but energy intensity in the country remains alarmingly high. ESCWA stresses the familiar point that Bahrain and the GCC countries have unsustainable energy consumption levels: in 2006, it stood at 1.2kgoe/$1000 of GDP, compared to a world average of 0.32 kgoe/$1000 of GDP.[27] These levels reflect demand that has been fuelled partly by the aforementioned price subsidies. Even before the recession, there were calls to raise prices so as to curtail demand for environmental reasons.

A continuation of current trends would see gas demand rise to 1617 Bcm by 2015. A more likely scenario is a slowdown in energy consumption caused by the world recession. In this context, the Economist Intelligence Unit expects the growth rate of regional gas demand to fall from the highs of 5–7 percent per annum to 3–4 percent.[28] Should economic activity wind down, demand for electricity and for gas could either stagnate, or fall back to 2004/05 levels. This is not unlikely: in the 1990s demand for gas stagnated, with increases only due to ALBA's expansion.

The big unknown in the Bahraini case is production capacity. Bahrain has succeeded in keeping up gas production by heavy upstream investments, but output is suspected to have peaked and certainly cannot continue to grow as in the past. Hence, since 2000, Bahrain has been staring at the possibility of having to import part, if not all, of its gas needs. Only the success of the current DEPSA will postpone this possibility.

Under a best case scenario of constant flat production, Bahrain will postpone having to import if demand stabilises or falls. A more likely scenario would be for production to fall by 1–2 Bcm by 2015 with largely constant consumption, creating an import requirement equivalent to 1–2 Bcm. A third possibility, made less likely by the recession, is for demand to grow to 15–16 Bcm by 2015, while production weakens to 2004/05 levels of 10–11 Bcm. This would require some 5 Bcm to be imported (see Table 13.4).

Table 13.4: Scenarios for Bahraini Consumption, Production and Imports, 2015, Bcm

	Baseline	*Worst*
Production	12	11
Consumption	13	16
Imports	1	5

Source: Author's estimates

Bahrain has been looking at alternative supply sources for some time, forming a special committee in 2003 to explore the possibilities of importing gas from Iraq, Iran and Qatar. Discussions of imports have focused on two main difficulties. Firstly, despite their ample reserves, importing from neighbouring states has involved a protracted negotiating process: no supply contract has been secured. In a nutshell, neither Iraq nor Iran is in any position to deliver gas in the medium term, even setting aside the political row between Iran and Bahrain in 2009.[29] Qatar had been Bahrain's best hope, particularly in view of the advantageous prices offered by Qatar for the Dolphin project. Ironically, in 2005, the Dolphin price of $1.5/MMBtu was seen as way above the $0.75 paid by Bahraini industry.[30] That possibility has now ended because of Qatari price ambitions and its moratorium on committing new supplies. Shell is currently studying other import options. As no possibilities of pipeline imports exist at present, these will probably focus on LNG. In either case, Bahrain will be paying market prices, which are at least five times higher than the domestic price.

Secondly, importing gas at market prices will almost inevitably mean a major shock to the economy, particularly for the government budget. Passing on rising feedstock prices will undermine the profitability of local industries. But given their importance for the domestic economy and for employment, industries will not be starved of gas. In terms of the residential sector, passing on rising energy costs in any rapid or significant way is a political no-go area in the short term.

Kuwait

The Kuwait Gas Sector: Overview

While Kuwait has 8 percent of world crude oil reserves (excluding its share of the Neutral Zone at its borders with Saudi Arabia), its estimated gas reserves rose to 1.78 Tcm in 2009, up from 1.48 Tcm in 2005, i.e. 1 percent of world reserves.[31] As this is mostly associated, gas production levels have fluctuated with oil production, with current gas levels linked to a crude output of 2.6 million b/d (including the Neutral Zone). Due to Kuwait's quota limits as an OPEC member, production is now lower than in the 1980s or 1990s. In 2006, there was an important discovery of non-associated gas fields at Sabriya and Umm Niga, which are said to have 991 Bcm of gas, as well as light oil and condensates.[32] However, this potential has yet to be translated into production, which only inched up from 12.1 Bcm in 2007 to 12.8 Bcm in 2008.

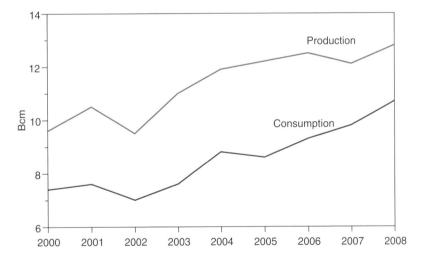

Figure 13.5: Kuwaiti Natural Gas Balance

Sources: BP *Statistical Review of World Energy 2009*; Ministry of Oil, 'Gas (MMSCF, Petroleum Products Refinery Output. LPG, 1990–2008', 2009

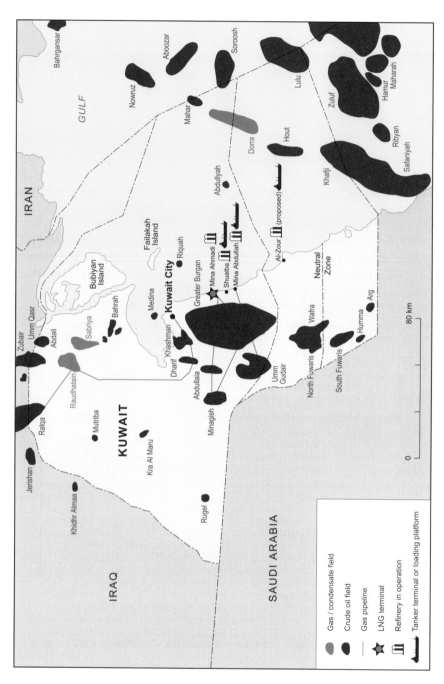

Map 13.2:   Kuwait: Gas and Oil Fields and Transport Infrastructure

Figure 13.5 traces Kuwaiti gas production and consumption since 2000. Data for the former are from BP's 2009 *Statistical Review of World Energy*, and exclude gas flared or re-injected. Data for consumption, provided by the Ministry of Oil, are taken to be marketed or distributed gas. Having hovered around 10 Bcm in the 1990s, marketed gas rose mildly and erratically in the 2000s from 9.6 Bcm to 12.8 Bcm. In the first half of the decade, consumption moved unsteadily upwards, but since 2004/05 it has risen more quickly and much faster than production, to 10.8 Bcm in 2008. At least 1.5 Bcm of gross production are lost to shrinkage, flaring, and possibly reinjection.

This apparent market balance masks the fact that Kuwait's overall energy needs are much higher. Indeed, as can be seen in Table 13.5, Kuwaiti energy demand jumped up by 75 percent between 2002 and 2007. This phenomenal growth led to an equally impressive 61 percent rise in gas consumption for the same period. Because of limited availability, the share of gas in total energy consumption has remained around 45 percent. The largest growth has been in electricity and desalination, which account for 52–55 percent of total energy consumption. As a result, gas demand by electricity rose by 9 percent per annum compared to 5.6 percent for gross production between 2002 and 2007.

Table 13.5: Kuwaiti Total Energy Consumption, Thousand Tons of Oil Equivalent (Toe)

	2002	2003	2004	2005	2007	Composition in 2007
Oil	7,271	10,097	11,443	13,944	13,695	55.2%
Gas	7,200	8,200	8,700	8,700	11,600	44.8%
Total	14,471	18,297	20,143	22,644	25,295	100.0%

Source: ESCWA, Status of Energy Statistics and Indicators in the ESCWA Region, 2009

As with Bahrain, Kuwait's energy consumption levels have led to one of the worst energy intensity ratios in the region.[33] Yet, Kuwait signed the Kyoto Protocol. It has also expressed interest in Clean Development Mechanism (CDM) projects, particularly carbon-related enhanced oil recovery schemes. Likewise, a Code of Practice for buildings and the use of air-conditioning systems was established in 1983. According to Hajiah,[34] substantial savings were achieved, but by 2001 demand for power for air conditioning was still growing at 6.9 percent per annum. Initiatives such as time-of-day control for air conditioning systems reduced daily demand for power by 55 percent in some locations, but consumption growth has not been tamed at the national level.

Before 2006, Kuwait had anticipated a shortfall in domestic gas supplies and explored import options accordingly. In the meantime, Kuwait hit a real gas supply crisis in summer 2008, leading to a power cut. Refineries and petrochemical plants were shut down in order to ease demand for electricity.[35] That experience not only re-focused efforts on implementing gas development plans, but led the country to construct a $150 million LNG import terminal which can receive 14 million cubic metres a day. The terminal, built by Excelerate Energy between January 2008 and August 2009, features a rented Energy Bridge Regasification Vessel stationed at the Mina Al-Ahmadi refinery, with an innovative shuttle tanker berth that provides for ship-to-ship LNG transfer and boil off gas management capabilities between a conventional LNG carrier and the ship. Thus, the ship is kept on station while LNG deliveries are received from conventional carriers, resulting in a flexible terminal.[36] This configuration will be of interest to all potential importers in the region because it is cheaper and quicker than a conventional land-based LNG terminal. In the period August–October 2009, 0.9 Bcm of LNG was imported, of which nearly half came from Russia and the rest from Australia, Oman, Malaysia and Trinidad.[37] Hence, Kuwait is now importing a small part of its gas (around 10 percent) from the region, but not from either Qatar or Iran.

Before then, the Kuwaiti supply chain was really about linking oil fields to two facilities: the oil refinery at Al-Ahmadi and a dedicated fractioner at Shuaiba, which together can process 14.6 Bcm. This capacity was designed in the 1980s, when Kuwaiti crude output was at 3 million b/d compared with 2.7 million b/d in 2008/09. There are six gas pipelines of 10/40 inches in diameter, totalling 150 miles in length. Some 41 miles of these pipelines serve Shuaiba, while the rest link Al-Ahmadi to the Burgan, Ruwaidathain, and Magwa fields.[38]

The new gas finds have led to plans for an eventual processing capacity of 24 Bcm/year (10 Bcm/year by 2015), but so far only 1 Bcm has been achieved. Work is under way to meet the more modest targets of first doubling output to 2.4 Bcm, and then reaching 6 Bcm by 2012. Plans for a new gathering centre in the northern fields (CG24) are going ahead. A new gas train at Sabriya, with a capacity of 0.8 Bcm, is due to come on stream in 2011. Similarly a new 140 km pipeline costing some $540 million was tendered in 2008 to link a booster station in the new fields to al-Ahmadi.[39] Bids were also issued in August 2009 for a massive increase in the pipeline system servicing the western fields, and for an additional gas train and a dehydration unit, with a capacity of 1.2 Bcm. This project is expected to cost some $800 million.[40] Such figures tally with Razavi's estimates that $2 billion are needed in upfront investment up to 2012, and another $4 billion to increase production to 18 Bcm in 2020.[41]

It was expected that the liquids produced from the new fields would help the financing of the project. However, it seems that the quantity had been underestimated, and was running ahead of the evolving gas-processing facilities. Another problem has been 'unconventional geological formations, difficult reservoir conditions and complex gas compositions'.[42] These two reasons explain the current delay in reaching the targets. While it was increasingly clear that resources were being frontloaded to finance the project, in February 2010, a new direction was taken when KOC signed a five-year deal (Enhanced Technical Service Agreement) with Shell to help it develop the fields, including training for Kuwaiti personnel.[43] Clearly, all is being done to complete gas development as quickly as possible.

End to Years of Impasse?

In terms of institutional organisation of the sector, gas policy is the responsibility of Kuwait's national oil company, the Kuwait Petroleum Corporation (KPC). Its upstream arm is the Kuwait Oil Company or KOC, which is in charge of production, distribution and feedstock supply. In the context of tight supply, KOC has been balancing the demand for gas between domestic sectors. The summer power outages have forced it to prioritise power stations, and also led to a major re-statement of priorities. Thus, in November 2008, KOC stated that developing gas production is now central to its upstream strategy, and that it is crucial to double gas output.[44] This refocusing was somewhat overdue as the new reserves have proved difficult to develop, and billions of dollars are needed just for the basic production and processing facilities.

However, the crisis in the gas sector reflects an on-going crisis of widespread administrative problems. Projects and contracts in Kuwait are constantly retendered, delayed, or cancelled, taking years to start or to be completed. They are subject to a convoluted process and to political wrangling: there are constant disputes between parliamentary opposition on the one hand, and ministers and the ruling family on the other. To ensure transparency, and as a way of maintaining democratic supervision over the executive, parliament is involved in all contracts and projects; tenders go through a central committee. In reality, contract awards are closely followed; they may be blocked or passed for political favours, or in exchange for approval of other contracts. Such are the difficulties that only 32 percent of all foreign investment applications since 2004 have been approved.[45]

Near paralysis has characterised the oil sector for the last few years, particularly since 2007, when parliament won the right to scrutinise each contract under the ministerial plan to revamp the sector. Hence the $8.5 billion Project Kuwait (launched in 1997) and $18 billion Clean Fuels Project were dropped.[46] Project Kuwait was intended to expand crude production capacity to 4 million b/d, and recognised the fact that Kuwait is now a mature province.[47] Moving from producing accessible light oil to more difficult heavy oil is a challenge, in terms of production, capital costs, and marketing. Likewise, Kuwaiti refineries need upgrading, are polluting, and cannot meet export and petrochemical ambitions.

In the upstream, a key issue is to entice IOCs while retaining Kuwaiti ownership and control of its crude reserves. KOC has little experience in heavy oil or in non-associated gas. In a constantly evolving industry, going it alone means foregoing advanced techniques, with costs impacting the country's foreign reserves or the Future Generation Fund.[48] In the downstream, contracts to upgrade existing refineries and build a new one at al-Zour, agreed to in December 2008, were cancelled by parliament in January 2009. Objections included failure to go to Central Tenders Committee (CTC), failure to demonstrate viability in light of the world recession, accepting prices that were too high and/or exceeding previously agreed budgets, and suspicions about the dominant role of a local contractor and the fee agreed with the South Korean contractors.[49]

KPC officials and ministers rebuffed these objections, arguing for example that the cost-reimbursable principle was already approved, precluding the need to go to the CTC and that the CTC was not sufficiently qualified to assess the best offer technically. But the main result has been frequent resignations – the sector has witnessed over five ministerial changes in 2006–2007 alone.[50] By 2009, IOCs were not renewing their short-term contracts, with Chevron leaving in July 2009. While other countries (like Mexico) also have parliamentary scrutiny over oil executives, in the case of Kuwait the sector was almost paralysed.

In June 2009, a new five-year development plan was approved. More modest targets are in place, and a relatively quick activation of the aforementioned projects for the new gas fields.[51] More crucially, in February 2010, the National Assembly passed a four-year national development by a majority of 53 to 56. The plan includes all the previously stalled energy projects including clean fuel and new non-associated gas developments.[52] While old rivalries and previous acrimony may resurface, there seems to be a will to move ahead.

Markets for Gas

Main Patterns. Like its neighbours, Kuwait moved from flaring its associated gas in the mid-1970s to channelling it towards domestic use. At that time, Kuwait crude capacity was at some 3.5 million b/d, and gas plans were set out on that basis. It built a gas supply system from the fields to the country's first refinery at Al-Ahmadi, and to an industrial and LPG/NGL plant complex at Shuaiba. By the 1980s, power generation and desalination also became important gas markets.

From modest beginnings, these three components grew substantially, taking total consumption from 4.5 Bcm in 1990 to 7.5 Bcm in 2000, and 10.7 Bcm in 2008. Table 13.6 details this evolution by sector. The oil sector refers to oil and gas production, the three refineries,[53] and the LPG plant. Petrochemicals refers to the industrial complexes operated or owned by the Petrochemical Industries Company (PIC). PIC is KPC's petrochemicals, chemical and fertiliser arm. Power generation reflects the use of gas by Kuwait's few gas-turbine plants, the bulk of the installed capacity consisting of dual-purpose plants.

Table 13.6 shows that the oil sector has had a dominant share of gas consumption, with levels rising almost steadily from 3 to 4.9 Bcm by 2008 or 45 percent of total consumption. The amount of gas consumed by power stations has been more erratic: levels in 2007–2008 were higher than in 2000, but essentially the share of the sector remains unchanged at 37 percent. Lastly, gas demand by petrochemicals expanded from 0.9 Bcm in 1997 to 1.5 Bcm in 1998 when the main petrochemical plant started operating. Since then, gas consumed by the industry inched up to 1.8 cm, its relative share shrinking from 22 percent in 2000 to 17 percent in 2008. These changes are illustrated in Figure 13.6.

The Ministry of Oil explains that natural gas is the only fuel

---

Table 13.6: Kuwaiti Natural Gas Consumption by Sector, Bcm

	1997	2000	2001	2003	2005	2008	2015*
Power Station	4.1	2.8	2.7	2.1	2.5	4.0	6
Oil Sector	3.1	3.1	3.2	3.8	4.2	4.9	6
Petrochemical Industries	0.9	1.6	1.7	1.7	1.8	1.8	3
Total Consumption	8.1	7.4	7.6	7.6	8.6	10.7	14

Source: Ministry of Oil, 'Gas (MMSCF, Petroleum Products Refinery Output. LPG, 1990–2008',2009.

* Expected value under most likely scenario

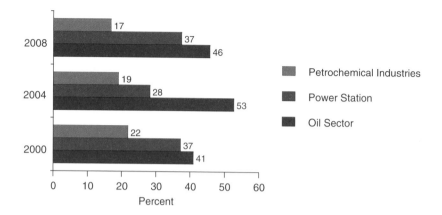

Figure 13.6: Kuwaiti Gas Demand by sector

Source: Ministry of Oil, 'Gas (MMSCF, Petroleum Products Refinery Output, LPG, 1990–2008', 2009

consumed in the oil and petrochemicals sector.[54] Therefore, in allocating feedstocks it seems that the priority is to satisfy the needs of the oil sector. The second sector to be prioritised is power: while fuel oil is now the dominant source of energy, how much is used is decided upon once gas supplies are secured. That in turn explains why the levels of gas consumed by industries have fluctuated and their share has shrunk: the supplies they can secure are only a residual of what other sectors do not consume.

Kuwait's LPG market has not changed much. Production increased from 100,602 bbls in 2003 to 114,770 bbls in 2008. Exports accounted for 96 percent of that output, the rest being adequate to cover local needs.[55]

Industry. In its attempt to diversify the economy and build on its oil wealth, Kuwait began to consider using gas as feedstock for a petrochemical industry in the 1960s, with plans taking shape in the 1980s. The sour and poor quality of much of the associated gas led the KPC to plan an ethylene business that mostly uses naphtha. Eventually, petrochemical venture EQUATE was established by Amiri decree in 1995 as a joint venture between PIC, Union Carbide and Boubyan Petroleum Company (BPC). EQUATE's other shareholders now include Dow Chemicals and two locally listed industrial holding companies, the Qurain Petrochemical Industries Company and BPC. EQUATE started operating in 1997 and has grown enormously since then, as PIC drew up ambitious downstream plans in 2001 for five projects.[56] Dubbed

EQUATE II, PIC embarked on a project to produce aromatics, and styrene (joint venture with Dow Chemicals); and to further develop its Olefins II project.

The main ethylene project started operating fully in 2008, at which stage its ethane cracker had a capacity of 850,000 tons per year (t/y) and a 600,000 t/y ethylene glycol unit. In June 2009, the polyethylene expansion project was concluded, allowing an additional 225,000 t/y of polyethylene. In spring 2009, the aromatic plants started operation, while the styrene complex (part of the Olefins II project, 450,000 t/y) was completed in August 2009. The aromatics plant should produce 370,000 t/y of benzene, 820,000 t/y of paraxylene. Its benzene output is to be fed to the styrene plant.

As already mentioned progress was marred by political disputes, the global recession, and the gas shortage of 2008, when the plants worked at 50 percent of capacity. EQUATE argues that petrochemicals should be given priority in obtaining domestic gas. The derivatives produced from ethane have high value added; and the region has a cost advantage, particularly in key Asian markets, where ethylene spot prices easily top \$1,000/ton.[57] Power stations on the other hand are burning gas on the basis of subsidised prices of \$0.5–2.5/MMBtu, with a consequent huge opportunity cost.

The PIC also operates fertiliser plants at the Shuaiba Complex, producing ammonia and urea. Polypropylene is another important chemical output of the company. According to Eltony, as a result of this significant growth petrochemicals rose from 0.9 percent of GDP in 1982 to 1.3 percent in 2005.[58] By that year, the share of manufacturing stood at 7 percent of GDP and 14.4 percent of non-oil GDP. Thus, petrochemicals now account for a significant share of the economy, but their survival depends on the availability of gas supplies at subsidised prices. After significant growth in the late 1990s, domestic gas demand by this sector can be expected to grow from the current level of 1.8 Bcm if the new plants are fully operational. That in turn depends on additional domestic production coming on stream, and on the impact of the current recession.

Consequently, it can also be expected that industrial demand for gas – i.e. including the LPG plant and other industries – will grow by 3–4 Bcm in the next few years. As documented by Eltony, the share of natural gas in industrial (including power and desalination) energy consumption fell from 79 percent in 1980 to 52 percent in 2004.[59] Gas will remain the dominant fuel used in the petrochemicals sector only. Other industries will continue to consume mostly oil or electricity. Feedstock availability is not the only reason: gas prices charged to industrial customers have changed almost monthly, and are higher than electricity prices, which have been fixed at token levels for decades.[60]

Power Generation. As with Bahrain, electricity consumption has grown phenomenally since 2000, putting the country in a crisis by 2008. Tabors calculates that installed capacity grew by 3.7 percent annually between 1997 and 2005, while consumption raced ahead at 6.3 percent.[61] This trend is depicted in Figure 13.7, where ESCWA data indicate a 51 percent rise in consumption vs. a 48 percent rise in production between 2000 and 2007. More significantly, the maximum peak load has grown by 36 percent compared to 28 percent in the case of installed capacity between 2000 and 2006. For the same years, peak load rose from a comfortable 77 to 90 percent of generating capacity. It is in this context that a power cut took place in 2008, when power consumed and generated stood at 45.2 GWh and 51.7 GWh.[62] No significant change can be detected in terms of sectoral distribution. In 2007 the largest electricity consumer was the residential sector at 48 percent of the 42.6 GWh consumed. The industrial and commercial sectors accounted respectively for 33 percent and 7 percent of that total.

Unlike Bahrain, Kuwait's power plants are mostly oil-based. Kuwait has eight power plants, consisting of older and newer units. Because of gas shortages and irregularity of supplies, most can run on gas or fuel oil. The latest additions were in 2000 at Sabiya and in 2004/05 at Al Zour South II, which expanded capacity by some 2000MW and

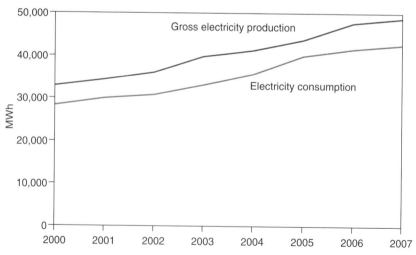

Figure 13.7: Kuwaiti Electricity Production and Consumption, 2000–2007
Source: ESCWA database

1000 MW respectively. It seems that, operating as single open cycle, the installed turbines could be better utilised.[63]

In 2008, CCGT accounted for 16 percent of installed capacity according to OAPEC's 2008 Annual Bulletin, and only 3.4 percent of electricity production in 2007 (ESCWA's ESIS database). Otherwise, most installed capacity is simple turbines that can run on oil or gas. As previously shown, gas consumed by Kuwaiti power plants has risen from 2.8 Bcm in 2000 to some 4 Bcm in 2008, a level previously reached in the late 1990s. At present, gas accounts for 25 percent of total energy consumption for the sector,[64] and it seems that current gas demand levels will prevail in the medium term.

In 2008, Kuwait's generating capacity stood at 11.3 GW, an addition of 5 GW compared with the 2000 level of 6.5 GW. In light of this pattern, it is not surprising that Kuwait agreed to finance its part (36.5 percent or $438 million) of the GCC grid, which may allow it to import up to 1200 MW i.e. 10 percent of current capacity. According to Tabors, at peak load, the marginal cost of production in Kuwait is $188/KWh compared with an average of $150/KWh for the GCC grid, allowing room for trading.[65] The first phase of the grid was commissioned on 20 July 2009, and links Kuwait to Qatar and Saudi Arabia. These links include a double-circuit 400kV, 50Hz line from Al-Zour in Kuwait to Ghunan in Saudi Arabia.[66]

Kuwait has plans to add 16 GW by 2014, essentially by adding gas turbines and new power plants. Four projects have been under discussion since 2006: 2000 MW in combined-cycle gas turbine units at Subiya; a new 4700 MW power plant in Al-Zour North by 2011; a 800 MW plant at North Shuaiba by 2010; and extending the gas turbine at Al-Zour South by 560 MW. The Subiya contract, retendered four times and costing $2.6 billion, and the Al-Zour North, costing $1 billion, were moving ahead in September 2009, the latter being Kuwait's first IWPP.[67]

Such phenomenal growth has led to energy conservation campaigns, including a government awareness campaign in June 2007. Consumption levels fell a little, but not enough to avoid the 2008 crisis. As long as tariffs are next to nothing, such campaigns will have a limited effect.[68] Indeed, there seems to be a consensus in the literature and press[69] that much of this growth in demand has been fuelled by electricity being sold at token prices. In turn, this has been possible partly because utilities have used subsidised fuel. The underpricing of energy has led to a reliance on inefficient power plants on the production side, and wasteful consumption patterns on the demand side. Hence, it is commonly remarked that major price corrections are needed, particularly in electricity, if demand growth and pollution are to be limited. Some commentators call for privatisation as a way to end a culture of non-payment of tariffs.[70] Clearly there are expectations of some tariff corrections.

Costing and Price Levels. The Kuwaiti gas price structure has evolved significantly over the last decade. The Ministry of Oil has increased domestic gas prices, but these remain well below cost and international market levels. Essentially, between 1997 and 2000, prices rose to US$0.401/MMBtu and $0.615/MMBtu respectively. Prices then dipped slightly, rising again to $0.65/MMBtu in 2003 and $0.837/MMBtu in 2004.[71] [72] Others report a fixed price of $0.86/MMBtu[73] and $0.6/MMBtu.[74]

The fixed price structure was abandoned in 2006, when an indexed price formula began to be used. According to the Ministry of Oil, domestic gas prices charged to power stations and most industrial consumers are now indexed to Kuwaiti crude oil prices as shown in Table 13.7.

Table 13.7: Kuwaiti Domestic Gas Prices Charged to Power Stations and Industry

Up to $46 per	$1.0
$47–60	$1.3
$61–80	$1.5
$81–100	$1.7
$101–120	$2.0
$121–140	$2.2

Source: Ministry of Oil, 'Gas (MMSCF, Petroleum Products Refinery Output, LPG, 1990-2008' (Excel Worksheet), Economic Affairs (internal publication), 2009b.

This price formula largely explains the variation in energy bills and unit prices paid for by industry as reported by Eltony.[75] Yet another price formula applies to petrochemicals. Under an agreement with the KPC, for the first eight years EQUATE was charged $1/MMBtu. However, currently, EQUATE and PIC are charged a flat rate of $2.50/MMBtu for the lean gas they buy.

At present, the authorities have not expressed any intention to increase prices, although it is widely argued that more serious price corrections are needed to curb demand growth. In 2010, these domestic prices were less than half of world levels and before the 2008 recession, internationally traded gas prices (based on oil prices) exceeded $10/MMBtu. Razavi argues that domestic gas prices in the Middle East are below the price at the point of delivery, i.e. they cannot cover the costs of investment, production, transmission and distribution. For Kuwait, Razavi estimates the netback values of gas at city gate and at power use to be $6.15 and $5.82, which were six times the 2006 domestic price of $1/MMBtu.[76] In other words, domestic prices in Kuwait are way below the cost of recovery, and at less than half the price it would have to pay for imports.

Indeed, it is widely believed in Kuwait that energy demand will not be controlled *until and unless much higher prices are charged*. Current demand levels and spectacular growth rates are not inevitable, as numerous studies have shown. In particular, Eltony shows that the growth of energy consumption by industry could fall to 1.5–1.9 percent if subsidies were reduced or removed.[77] Under a baseline scenario of unchanged prices, natural gas consumption could rise to 7.9 Bcm in 2005 and 8.8 Bcm in 2015. If subsidies are removed the 2005 and 2015 levels of gas consumption would be 6.6 Bcm and 7 Bcm. Similarly, residential energy demand is projected to fall by 29 percent by 2015 if prices increased by 200 percent.[78] Lastly, Eltony shows that there may be little harm to industries as a result of price hikes, while efficiency in energy use may improve.[79]

Another widespread belief is that subsidised gas feedstock prices have led the substantive growth in petrochemical production capacity in Kuwait and throughout the GCC. Ethane for example, is supplied to their industries at US$0.75–$2/MMBtu, compared to $9–12/MMBtu elsewhere. This difference creates doubts about their competitiveness. On the other hand, global petrochemicals based on oil-feedstocks have higher costs. Thus, local industries may well retain their strategic advantage, even if they were made to pay higher feedstock prices.[80]

The underpricing of domestic fuels has had major consequences for the government's purse. The IMF estimates that 9.5 percent of GDP and 25 percent of government spending are spent on subsidies for fuel, electricity and water.[81] Electricity is a key concern: astonishingly, tariffs have not changed for 30 years, and remain negligible (US$0.35–0.7 cents or KD0.01–0.02), even if we accept the current average production cost to be in the range of $0.02–0.04/KWh. The Ministry of Electricity and Water admits that consumers only pay $692 million (KD 200 million), whereas the authorities spend about $5.5 billion on producing electricity ($6.57 billion including desalination).[8283] This suggests an annual direct subsidy of $4.8 billion a year. Clearly, in a high income country, there is room for the public to pay more towards the power bill. However, people have become accustomed to the nearly free provisions by the state.

Prospects. In 2009, Kuwait imported nearly 0.9 Bcm of LNG. Although this accounted for only a small part of domestic consumption, it was critical for the power and petrochemical industries, which is why Kuwait is willing to pay a premium for imports. In the absence of rapid production increases and pipeline imports, LNG imports are likely to be a defining feature of Kuwait's gas sector by 2015. The sector's immediate outlook and the size of forthcoming gas imports depend on demand and supply developments.

On the demand side, it is unclear how much, if at all, gas demand will fall as a result of the economic recession. Over the last few years, Kuwaiti energy consumption has been racing ahead on the back of a strong economic boom, including in the residential and industrial sectors. Much of that growth was met by oil: gas supply shortages had already caused many users to either shut down or use fuel oil.

Consequently, it is unlikely that the current size of the domestic market will shrink, as the bulk of any downward adjustment in energy demand is likely to be in oil consumption. Further, since no major increases in domestic gas or electricity prices are planned, there will be no downward pressure on demand from pricing. On the contrary, if the EQUATE II ventures and the four new power plants come on stream, demand could increase. Using the increases in demand resulting from previous increases, the former could add 1.5–2 Bcm, and the latter 2.5–3 Bcm.

On the supply side, the magnitude of LNG imports will depend on how quickly Kuwait manages to bring on additional supplies from its north fields. Current plans aiming to add 10 Bcm by 2015 would double current production, and would meet increases in demand. But delivering these supplies will depend on continuing costly investments and on timely implementation of development, processing, and distribution projects. No specific budget for the gas sector has been published, but the 2009 budget for the oil sector allows for $82.5 billion over the next five years.

Looking ahead to 2015, a likely baseline scenario would be for production increases to remain weak, so that levels would only rise by 2–3 Bcm and demand growth would slow because of the world recession. Consumption levels rise mainly because of new power plants, and in line with the slower pace of the 1990s, i.e. by 4–5 Bcm. The best-case scenario would combine steeply rising production levels, and the same moderate to weak demand growth. The worst case would be a continuation of the current situation: significant production increases fail to materialise, while demand races ahead at the same speed as between 2004 and 2008. Under this scenario, production levels would rise by only 2–3 Bcm, while consumption levels would rise by 6–7 Bcm (see Table 13.8).

These scenarios show that only in the unlikely situation of a very successful and rapid growth in production can Kuwait avoid imports. The more likely prospect is for the country to import at least 2–3 Bcm by 2015, and double that amount if power and petrochemicals expand as foreseen. Hence the Kuwaiti preoccupation with import options, which are now limited to LNG. Pipeline imports from Iran are still at the exploratory stage: Kuwait and Iran are far from either building the infrastructure or agreeing on the price.[84] The same applies to Iraqi gas supplies. Qatari LNG prices were said to be too high, and pipeline imports are blocked by the Qatari moratorium and Saudi objections. Consequently, Kuwait will be importing anything between 1 Bcm to 6 Bcm in LNG at international prices.

Table 13.8: Kuwait: Scenarios for Consumption, Production and Imports, 2015, Bcm

	Baseline	*Worst*
Production	13	14
Consumption	14	18
Imports	2	6

Source: Author's estimates.

Note: In 2009, Kuwait imported 0.44 Bcm of LNG when production and consumption were at 12.5 Bcm and 10.7 Bcm respectively.

The scenarios also show that recession carries a silver lining in the form of slowing demand growth. But unless plants are mothballed and economic activity shrinks substantially, consumption is unlikely to decline. The only other factor that could reduce gas demand and reduce future imports is significant domestic price increases, which are not envisaged.

Summary and Conclusions

This chapter examined the gas sectors of Bahrain and Kuwait. Bahrain's economy and power sector are nearly 90 percent dependent on gas, while in Kuwait, gas satisfies nearly half of its energy needs. With rapidly depleting reserves, Bahrain will probably start importing gas around 2015. With limited ability to increase production, Kuwait faces a potentially gaping hole in its gas balance, which it is currently filling with LNG cargoes. Bahrain is a stable gas market possibly heading for a crisis within a few years, whereas Kuwait is in a temporary crisis that will probably ease in the longer term, as long as it succeeds in developing its reserves.

Kuwait and Bahrain created domestic markets for their gas three decades ago. By 2008, they were consuming 10.7 and 12.5 Bcm respectively. The bulk of the growth has been from three sectors: petrochemicals, heavy industry and power generation. As a result, the two countries share similarities in the sectoral composition of their gas demand: electricity now accounts for 33 percent of gas demand in Bahrain, and 37 percent of gas demand in Kuwait. But whereas Bahraini industry accounts for 35 percent of gas consumption, Kuwaiti petrochemicals' share has weakened to 17 percent. The oil sector in Bahrain only uses 18 percent of domestic gas, whereas in Kuwait, it is the largest consumer at 45 percent. Bahrain's aluminium industry accounts for 9 percent of GDP, whereas Kuwaiti oil-based industries account for 40 percent of manufacturing value-added and 14 percent of non-oil GDP. Hence, gas is not just a fuel, but a key pillar of domestic economic development.

Between 2002 and 2007, power generation fuelled phenomenal rises in energy consumption of 75 percent and 41 percent in Kuwait and Bahrain respectively. In Bahrain, 2008 levels of total and power sector gas demand were respectively 34 percent and 43 percent higher than in 2002, but were surpassed by production levels. For the same years, Kuwaiti gas consumption and electricity gas consumption rose by 52 percent and 92 percent each. In contrast, Kuwaiti production only rose by 35 percent over the period 2002–2008.

Supply costs in both countries have been escalating, reflecting the maturity of fields and/or dwindling reserves. Bahrain has invested substantially to increase production sufficiently to meet demand, but needs major new finds to avoid depletion in the medium term. Until the new non-associated gas discoveries in 2006, Kuwait's associated gas production fluctuated with crude production. It will take many years and multi-billion dollar investments to significantly increase supplies. In the short term, LNG imports will become increasingly important to meet peak demand in the summer. New fields could add 10–15 Bcm/year of production, but not before 2015–2016.

Both countries have responded to tightening supplies by intensifying their upstream efforts and prioritising gas projects. Foreign companies have a vital role in providing technical expertise for dealing with maturing fields and difficult reserves, and their capital would help meet development and production costs. Bahrain has modified its PSA accordingly, accepting a minority share in exchange for the financial and technical muscle of IOCs. In Kuwait, IOCs have been involved marginally in an embattled upstream context which has hampered development and contributed to the need to import. Legislative break-throughs in approving oil and gas projects in 2010 may well mark a turning point. But unless and until success is secured in the upstream, both countries will be paying market prices for imports reflecting, in the Kuwaiti case, the contradiction of a country apparently unable to commercialise its substantial reserves. Neither country has been able to secure long-term contracts or favourable prices from its neighbours. This reveals an apparent contradiction in the cooperation between Gulf states, as well as the dichotomy found in many Middle Eastern gas producers of having ample reserves but small production levels.

In both countries, high levels of demand have been stimulated by the underpricing of gas and electricity. At $1.5–$2/MMBtu, domestic prices are a half to one quarter of international levels; and in the context of the need for substantial investments, they are at least below the short-run marginal cost. Studies have shown that gas and energy demand can be reduced by increasing prices. In Bahrain, where electricity is priced at around cost recovery, price increases are currently blocked politically. In Kuwait, there is widespread agreement about the need for substantial increases in electricity prices, but no decision has yet been made in this regard. LNG imports may have opened the door for gas price rises, but again no decision has been made.

Thus, central government budgets will continue to meet explicit and implicit domestic gas and power subsidies. The fiscal consequences will increase in the medium term as domestic supply shortages evolve. The current recession may deliver a reprieve in the form of slower gas demand and stable prices. Nonetheless, Bahrain will become a gas importer by 2015, importing anything between 8–48 percent of its domestic consumption, and creating a major shock for government finances. Kuwait could meet its gas needs in the longer term, but until new domestic supplies are added it will import 2–6 Bcm, representing 15–30 percent of consumption in 2015. The speed at which both countries move towards imports depends on three factors: the extent of any recession or price led reduction in energy consumption; the rate of natural decline in gas production; and the ability of new discoveries to meet demand levels.

Notes

1 Klimstra, J., 'Optimising Fuel Efficiency', *Power Engineering – Middle East Energy*, September 2008; Razavi, H. 'Natural Gas Pricing in Countries of the Middle East and North Africa', *The Energy Journal*, 2009, vol. 30, pp.1–22.

2 Van Beurden, B., 'The Energy Challenge: Implications for the Middle East and the Global Chemical Industry', 3rd Annual Gulf Petrochemicals and Chemicals Association Forum, Dubai, December 2008.

3 In most of the region, air-conditioning and cooling account for over half of electricity consumption, which is why the residential sector has a dominant share in the latter.

4 Dargin, J. 'Prospects for Energy Integration in the GCC', Research Seminar, Dubai School of Government, 3 March 2009.

5 Dargin, J. 2009, Ibid.

6 See BP's *Annual Statistical Review 2009*.

7 Bahrain Petroleum Company, *Annual Review 2006 and 2008*.

8 See OAPEC, *Annual Statistical Bulletin 2008*, Table 60, p.78.

9 See http://www.banagas.com/b_processmain.htm

10 See Press release, Ministry of Finance, 28 August 2008.

11 Rigzone, 'Oxy, Mubadala finalise development deal for Bahrain field', 27 April 2009; *Gulf Oil and Gas*, 'Production Sharing Agreement for the Bahrain Field' 27 April 2009; *MEES*, 'Occidental, Mubadala and NOGA finalize Awali joint venture', 16 November 2009.

12 NOGA, *Annual Report 2007*.

13 Ministry of Finance, 2009; OAPEC, *Annual Statistical Bulletin 2008*. There are two updated 2009 in the list of references.

14 *Economist Intelligence Unit*, 'Bahrain: Manufacturing', 6 February 2008.

15 ALBA, *Annual Review 2008*.

16 Economist Intelligence Unit 2008, Ibid.

17 See EIA's briefing on Bahrain (March 2008).

18 *Arab News*, 27 July 2009.

19 Tabors, R.D, 'Interconnection in the GCC Grid', 42nd Hawaii International Conference on System Sciences, 2009; *Wind Energy Business News*, 'Bahrain Aims to Develop Renewable Energy in Three Years', 3 August 2009.

20 Using data from ESCWA's ESIS database.

21 OAPEC 2008, Ibid.

22 NOGA, Minister's Speech 7 February 2008,

23 Using a current exchange rate of $1 for BD0.376.

24 OAPEC, *8th Arab Energy Conference 2006*.

25 *Business 24/7 Emirates*, 28 May 2008.

26 See *Gulf Daily News*, 8 December 2008 and *Arabian Business*, 29 June 2009.

27 ESCWA, *Status of Energy Statistics and Indicators in the ESCWA Region*, March 2009.

28 Economist Intelligence Unit, 'Bahrain',2008.

29 See for example, *Arab News*, 'GCC warns Iran against making hostile re-marks', 23 February 2009.
30 MEES, 14 November 2005.
   There was also Saudi opposition to pipelines transiting through its territories. A pipeline deal negotiated in the late 1990s never happened because Saudi Arabia would not give the pipeline rights of way – Dargin, J. *The Dolphin Project*, OIES Working Paper January 2008.
31 EIA, *Kuwait*, Country Analysis Briefs, April 2009.
32 Reserves could also increase with the resolution of the ongoing dispute with Iran over the Dorra offshore natural gas field. Also shared by Saudi Arabia, it is said to hold 308 Bcm of gas.
33 ESCWA 2009, Ibid.
34 Hajiah, A., 'Energy Conservation Program in Kuwait', Orlando, 24–26 July 2006.
35 EIA, *Kuwait*, Country Analysis Briefs,
36 Excelerate Energy, 'Mina Ahmadi Gasport, 2009.
37 *The Asian Waterborne LNG Report*, Waterborne Energy, 27 February 2010, p.145.
38 OAPEC, *Annual Statistical Bulletin*, 2008.
39 Petrofrac, 'Petrofrac awarded US$543 million lump-sum contract with Kuwait Oil Company', 2008.
40 AMEINFO, 'Kuwait Oil tenders gas booster station', 10 August 2009.
41 Razavi, 2009, Ibid.
42 *Kuwait Times*, 'Kuwait signs 5-year deal with Shell', 18 February 2010.
43 Gulf Oil & Gas, 'Shell to develop gas fields in Kuwait', 17 February 2010.
44 KOC, Press release, 9 November 2008
45 *Al Qabas*, 'Khutat al Kuwait al naftiyah Tastadem bi naqs al-tiquaniyat al-haditha', 17 July 2009.
46 *MEES*, 'Kuwait oil sector struggles to arrest slide to "square zero"', 12 October 2009.
47 See AMEINFO 'Kuwait's biggest field starts to run out of oil', 12 November 2005.
48 See *MEED*: 11 September 2007, 16 January 2009. Also *MEES* 14 January 2008 and *al-Qabas* on 5 May 2009.
49 See *MEED*: 11 September 2007, 24 October 2008, 16 January 2009.
50 *MEES*, 'Kuwait looks to non-associated gas debut', 14 January 2008.
51 *MEES*, 12 October 2009, Ibid.
52 *MEES*, 'Kuwait's National Assembly Approves $107 bn Development Plan, 8 February, 2010.
53 These are al-Ahmadi, Shuaiba and Abd ullah.
54 Ministry of Oil, 'Local Energy 2008', 2009.
55 Ministry of Oil, 2009, Ibid; OAPEC, *Annual Statistical Bulletin 2008*.
56 See www.pic.com.kw/Equate.asp
57 Given shipping costs, it is better either to export naphtha and produce ethylene overseas, or go for a full ethylene-based production. Kuwait is going for both options, exporting light naphtha as of December 2009.

58 Eltony, M.N., 'Estimating energy price elasticities for non-oil manufacturing industries in Kuwait', 2008.
59 Ibid.
60 Ibid., p.193.
61 Tabors, R.D., 'Interconnection in the GCC Grid: The Economics of Change,' 2009.
62 AUPTDE, *Statistical Bulletin 2009*.
63 Darwish, M.A. et al, 'On better utilization of gas turbines in Kuwait', 2008.
64 Ministry of Oil, 'Local Energy 2008', 2009.
65 Tabors, R.D., Ibid.
66 *Arab News*, 27 July 2009.
67 See *MEED*, 18 September 2009.
68 *MEED*, 'Making the Grade', 9 November 2007.
69 See Zawya, 'Kuwait: economists stress on need to privatise water and electricity'; *Power Engineering*, 'High and Low: Kuwait's Power Problem', 2008; Al-Sayegh, O.A. 'Restructuring Kuwait electric power system: mandatory or optional', 2008; Razavi , H. 'Natural Gas Pricing in Countries of the Middle East and North Africa', 2009 and Tabors, R.D. Ibid., 2009.
70 Zawya, Ibid.; Al-Sayegh, Ibid.
71 OAPEC, 'Kuwait Country Paper', 8th Arab Energy Conference, Amman, 2006.
72 Dollar figures are obtained using average exchange rate data from the Kuwaiti Central Bank, and after converting cubic feet measures into MMBtu. The average exchange rates for 2003 and 2004 were 0.298 KD and 0.294 KD per dollar.
73 OAPEC, *Annual Statistical Bulletin, 2008*.
74 Razavi, H., Ibid., 2009.
75 Eltony, M.N., Ibid. 2008.
76 Razavi, H., Ibid., 2009.
77 Eltony, M.N., 'Industrial Energy Policy: a case study of demand in Kuwait', 2006.
78 Eltony, M.N. and Al-Awadhi. M.A., 'Residential energy demand: a case study of Kuwait', 2007.
79 Eltony, M.N., Ibid., 2008.
80 Business 24/7, Emirates, 17 June 2009
81 IMF, 'Kuwait: Statistical Appendix', 2008.
82 *Kuwait Times*, 'The ministry is spending about KD 1.6 billion on producing electricity', 15 April 2009.
83 Using an average exchange rate of KD0.289 per $1.
84 *Petroleum Economist*, 'Mideast states look for new gas sources as Qatar clams up', 2 February 2009.

CHAPTER 14

NATURAL GAS – A LIFELINE FOR YEMEN

*Franz Gerner and Silvana Tordo**

Introduction

Yemen is the poorest country in the Middle East and depends almost exclusively on crude oil exports to finance its fiscal budget. However, oil resources are depleting fast and production has been declining steadily over the last decade. If that trend continues the country could virtually run out of oil within a decade.

Natural gas production provides for a source of income that could partially offset the country's high oil dependency. Yemen Liquefied Natural Gas Company (YLNG) began exporting LNG to Korea and the United States in late 2009. The government is also aiming to develop the domestic gas-to-power market to meet future demand and to increasingly replace oil with natural gas for power generation, industrial enterprises and the commercial sector.

Developing the domestic gas market and encouraging future exploration and production (E&P) activities is absolutely indispensable for restoring fiscal sustainability and the future economic development of Yemen. While revenues from natural gas exports in the form of LNG can meet some of the fiscal needs, they are unlikely to substitute for the loss from the depleting hydrocarbon resources. Using natural gas for power generation and substituting subsidised oil-based generating capacity would yield additional fiscal savings and enhance energy efficiency.

However, this requires the development of a domestic gas infrastructure and gas-fired power plants for which the country has neither the financial nor the technological resources. Political risk and an unattractive investment environment have so far deterred investors in the upstream and downstream gas sector who will be of key importance to unlock Yemen's full hydrocarbon potential.

* The authors would like to thank Pierre Audinet, Senior Energy Economist, World Bank and Wilfried Engelke, Senior Country Economist for Yemen, World Bank for their review and valuable inputs.

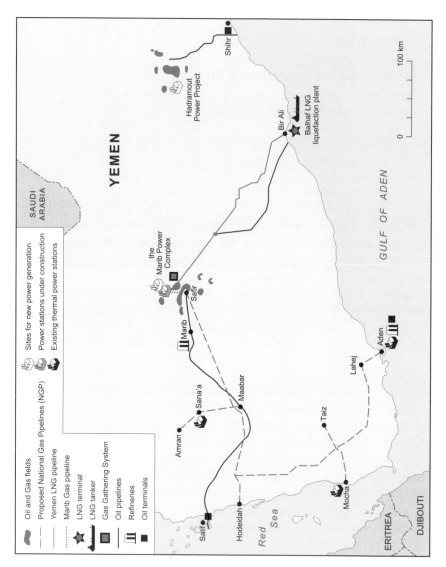

Map 14.1: Yemen's Energy Infrastructure

Yemen's Macroeconomic Challenges

Yemen's fiscal sustainability and balance of payments currently depends largely on oil revenues, while oil production is declining at an annual rate of about 6 to 8 percent. Nonetheless, nearly 60 percent of central government fiscal revenues and 85 percent of export receipts depended in 2009 on revenues derived from the oil sector (or about 15 percent of GDP). In the absence of major new oil discoveries, the long-term outlook looks challenging, as mature fields head toward the end of their economic life cycle.

Based on current knowledge, Yemen's oil reserves are unlikely to be sufficient to provide for the required financing for development spending. Public capital expenditure has been around 6 to 8 percent in recent years and without significant reforms in the way public resources are spent – right now about 31 percent of GDP are spent on various forms of energy subsidies and transfers – the reduction in oil revenues will further limit resources available for public investment and therefore development.

Several areas of the economy have been identified as potential alternative sources of growth, including agriculture and tourism. Non-hydrocarbon revenues are expected to increase from about 12 percent of GDP in 2009 to 20 percent in 2025. However, even with substantial increases in these sectors, they do not have the same potential as the hydrocarbon sector to contribute to fiscal revenues and the balance of payments, certainly not in the short term.

Yemen's Natural Gas Potential

Yemen's oil and gas reserves are located in the Marib basin in the remote eastern part of the country. There are 430 Bcm of proven gas reserves in Yemen, of which 288 Bcm are independently certified and allocated for YLNG. YLNG can use 259 Bcm for meeting its export obligations and 29 Bcm are allocated for development of the domestic market.

The remaining proven gas reserves of 142 Bcm have yet to be certified and some of those reserves are not easily produced and immediately available for power generation. Most of the gas is associated and production of some of these reserves will depend on increased oil production. The government has recently indicated that it plans to certify an additional 91 Bcm of associated gas reserves, although the timing of certification remains uncertain.

The near-term gas supply that could be mobilised is 54 Bcm. Most of this is yet to be certified. Other than these near-term reserves, there are no clear gas supply options that exist without an aggressive exploration and production programme being advanced.

Yemen's current gas reserves are relatively small but large parts of the country have not yet been explored for hydrocarbon resources. Data are in short supply on the potential size of probable and possible reserves, and on the likely cost of development. The available data would seem to indicate a relatively low chance of finding large oil and gas fields, and a relatively high chance that development costs could be higher than the regional average. This does not mean that gas reserves would not be found in Yemen, or that it would not be economic to develop them. On the other hand it does suggest that measures may need to be taken to encourage their development.

Several blocks where associated gas is available have not started oil production and substantial amounts of gas are being re-injected and flared because of the lack of gas gathering systems.

The government is in the process of reviewing and improving the fiscal incentives under the existing Production Sharing Agreements (PSA) but due to the political situation in the country and the fact that many unexplored areas lie in remote regions in the central and eastern parts of the country (Rib Al Jawf, Shabwha and Masila Basins) where political conflict prevails, it is unlikely that major E&P activities will be carried out in the near future by international oil companies. Smaller operators continue to produce from existing blocks with limited new E&P activities being carried out. Unless there are some unexpected large finds, the country will need to plan with a limited amount of incremental gas resources for the next five to ten years.

Current Barriers to the Development of Gas Exploration and Production Activities

In Yemen, an ambiguous regulatory and institutional environment is combined with relatively low prospectivity, high costs of exploration and development, and security threats – all of which are potential barriers to investment. Some of these factors are short-term in nature, and can be addressed via initiatives that have a short-term or temporary focus. Some require regulatory interventions and carry long-term effects. Others could be mitigated or addressed by companies through tailored approaches to doing business in the country.

In Yemen the contractor does not currently have the right to explore for and produce gas, whether associated or non-associated with oil, unless a gas development agreement ('GDA'), or a gas project agreement ('GPA') as the case may be, is entered into with the state. As a result, contractors do not actively explore for gas, and associated gas is re-injected – after stripping it from liquids if viable.[1] The requirement to enter into negotiations every time gas is found in potentially economic quantities may be justified by the government's need to ensure that fiscal and non-fiscal objectives are adequately taken into consideration. At the same time, the prospect of potentially long negotiations and the uncertainty of their outcome are likely to discourage investors. One possible solution could be to grant gas exploration and production rights to investors under the relevant PSA and provide for flexible, progressive fiscal terms, preferably R-factor or ROR based, so as to minimise distortions to investment decisions, and to adapt to the variety of potential project conditions. Service contracts and/or amendments to existing PSAs could be considered in respect of the development and production of known gas reserves.

The History and Current Status of Yemen LNG[2]

In Autumn 2005, the shareholders[3] of Yemen LNG (YLNG) made the decision to launch and to proceed with the construction of an LNG plant at Balhaf.[4] The location of Yemen is strategically advantageous allowing accessibility to all LNG markets, both in the Asia Pacific basin and expanding markets on either side of the Atlantic.

The government signed a Gas Development Agreement with Total of France. YLNG receives the gas today for its operation under a Feedgas Supply Agreement with the state-owned company 'Safer E&P Operation Company'. The feed gas is priced at US$0.5/MMBtu and volumes are sufficient to produce and export 6.7 million metric tonnes of LNG per annum (mtpa) to its long-term customers in the North American and South Korean markets.

In 2005, YLNG also signed Sales and Purchase Agreements for a period of 20 years with Suez LNG Trading S.A (2.55 mtpa), Total Gas and Power (2 mtpa) and Korean Gas Corporation (Kogas) (2 mtpa). The first two contracts supply the US market, at a price indexed to Henry Hub (HH). The third contract supplies the Korean market, at a price indexed to the Japan Crude Cocktail (JCC).

The total investments carried out by YLNG were about US$4.5 billion covering the construction of a pipeline from the Marib field to Balhaf, processing, liquefaction, storage and loading facilities and other support facilities. The YLNG chain comprises upstream gas processing facilities including a 25 km, 20 inch transfer line linking the two gas processing units in the gas fields of block 18 in Marib; a 320 km, 38 inch new main pipeline, which connects the gas processing facilities to the new liquefaction facilities in Balhaf, and a spur line to transport domestic gas to the Ma'bar area in central Yemen.

The main pipeline, whose construction was finalised in late 2008, supplies feed gas from Marib at a rate of 1140 million standard cubic feet per day to the LNG plant at Balhaf. The pipeline has been buried over its entire length and its route passes mainly through deserts and thinly populated regions. The two-train plant YLNG was constructed with a total annual capacity of 6.7 mtpa of LNG. In addition, two 140,000 m^3 storage tanks have been constructed as well as ancillary facilities, such as power generation, desalination, waste water treatment and steam generation, to enable the project to operate on a self-supporting basis. Yemen LNG has chartered four vessels, for a period of 20 years, to deliver LNG to fulfill its contractual obligations and all four ships have been delivered to Yemen LNG in early 2009. Yemen LNG became fully operational in late 2009.

The Economics of Developing the Domestic Gas-to-Power Market

As we have discussed, Yemen has limited proven gas reserves available for the near future. It can either export those remaining reserves or develop the domestic gas market. Currently, the only export option available is through extending YLNG and adding trains and there are no viable pipeline interconnection opportunities with neighbouring countries.

To assess the overall benefits of exporting the remaining gas reserves versus supplying the domestic market one has to assess its economic value. YLNG has signed long-term gas supply agreements to deliver gas to the United States and Korea and the cost of selling gas to the domestic Yemeni market is hence the foregone export revenue. Those foregone revenues (or opportunity costs) can be calculated by netting back the international gas price in the United States (and Korea) to the wellhead in Yemen.

Table 14.1: Economic Value of Gas through LNG Exports to the United States

	US$/MMBtu
Long-term US gas price forecasts (Henry Hub)	7.3
Regasification Cost	0.4
Shipping costs to the United States	1.5
Liquefaction costs at LNG facility in Balhaf	1.4
Pipeline cost from Marib to LNG plant	0.3
Economic Netback Gas Price at Marib	**3.7**

Source: Economic Consulting Associates (ECA) and Penspen – February 2010

The reference gas price in the United States is Henry Hub and recent long-term US gas prices are estimated at US$7.3/MMBtu. Hence, the foregone revenues from not selling the remaining gas reserves at Marib to the US market are US$3.7/MMBtu once regasification costs in the USA, shipping costs and liquefaction costs in Yemen are deducted. There are also pipeline transportation costs from the LNG facility in Balhaf to the field in Marib, which are estimated at U$$0.4/MMBtu. The government will receive only a fraction of those revenues through its Government Take under the LNG contract. In addition, YLNG pays the government US$0.5/MMBtu for the feed gas. [5]

Selling gas abroad has been an attractive option for the government to date as it generates tangible, regular and secure financial flows to support its fiscal budget. However, those financial revenues have to be compared with the potential costs and benefits of selling the gas into the domestic market. There are currently no large industries in Yemen that would justify the development of gas pipeline infrastructure and the only anchor customer is the power sector, which runs on petroleum products.

To determine whether remaining gas reserves should be exported or sold domestically one has to compare the economic netback received by selling gas through YLNG with the economic value of selling the gas to the domestic power sector. The economic netback is the maximum price an existing power plant operator would be willing to pay for the gas without losing market share or without being 'worse-off' than running the plant on current fuel. The economic netback calculation is a comparative analysis of running a new HFO plant and an OCGT or CCGT plant. The calculations in Table 14.2 are based on an average long-term oil price forecast of US$30/bbl and sets out an indicative economic netback calculation for a hypothetical new 400 MW OCGT located at Ma'bar (south of Sana'a) or a new 400 MW CCGT in Hudaidah on the Red Sea coast.

Thermal efficiency of both the oil and open cycle gas-fired plant are similar but higher at the combined cycle gas plant. Per unit capital and O&M costs of OCGT tend to be lower than CCGT. An average gas transportation tariff of US$0.8/MMBtu getting the gas from the Marib associated gas fields to the plants was assumed. Consequently, the economic netback is US$5.5/MMBtu for the Mabar OCGT and US$9.4/MMBtu for the CCGT at Hudaidah. These are the maximum prices the government can charge for its gas or the highest price a power generator is willing to pay for feed gas.

Comparing economic netbacks of selling gas abroad compared to the domestic power sector provides a good indication as to how best the government can maximise its overall economic benefits from scarce

Table 14.2: Economic Netback by Switching from Existing Oil Plant to Gas-fired
          Plants

Plant Characteristics	Oil fired boiler plant	Maber OCGT	Hudaidah CCGT
Generation Capacity (MW)	400	400	400
Load Factor	75%	75%	75%
Output (GWh/y)	2,628	2,628	2,628
Heat Rate (BTU/kWh)	10,035	10,035	6,200
Thermal efficiency	34%	34%	55%
Capital cost (US$/kW)	800	700	700
Plant cost (US$ MM)	240	280	280
Life of Plant (years)	30	30	30
Fuel Price (US$/MMBtu)	**5.3**	**6.3**	**10.2**
Per unit fuel price (USc/kWh)	5.3	6.3	6.3
Other O&M Costs (USc/kWh)	0.7	0.4	0.4
Per unit capital cost (USc/kWh)	1.4	0.7	0.7
Generation cost (USc/kWh)	7.4	7.4	7.4
Pipeline Transport cost (US$/MMBTU)		0.8	0.8
Economic Netback at Gas Plant (US$/MMBtu)		**5.5**	**9.4**

Source: World Bank estimates

gas resources. It shows that the economic return of selling remaining
gas reserves domestically is very high, and much higher than selling it
as LNG in international markets.[6]

The Challenges of Developing the Gas-to-Power Market

Yemen does not have a large industrial base and the only anchor load
for a Greenfield gas infrastructure development is the power sector. The
country has a total installed power generation capacity of 774 MW and
needs to commission an additional 1500 MW in the next five years.

Yemen is short of power and is the least electrified country in the
Middle East with only about 40 percent of the population having access
to electricity. It is estimated that an additional capacity of about 300
MW would be required to meet current demand. Power outages are
frequent and industrial consumers often generate their own electricity
using highly subsidised diesel. New connections, especially of larger
electricity consumers, are problematic and place constraints on an
already overburdened electricity supply system. The government is
aiming to gradually switch the domestic power sector to natural gas.
This would reduce the financial burden on the struggling Yemeni power
sector and free up additional oil volumes for export.[7]

The Public Electricity Company (PEC), the sole producer and supplier of power in Yemen, is using old, unreliable and inefficient oil-fired steam plants burning heavy and light fuel oil and diesel. Despite the fact that PEC receives highly subsidised fuel from state-owned domestic refineries, the utility is in a precarious financial position. Current electricity tariffs do not cover its operation costs and technical and non-technical losses remain high.

Introducing natural gas as a fuel for power generation would generate substantial benefits for Yemen. It was estimated that in 2008, PEC's real cost of power generation using diesel at market prices was almost ten times higher per kWh than it would have been for natural gas.[8] However, despite the introduction of natural gas, average electricity tariffs would need to increase from the current tariff of YR12/kWh to approximately YR25/kWh (US$0.12/kWh) to allow the power company to break even.

The development of the domestic gas-to-power market faces substantial challenges, including limited proven gas reserves, a financially constrained incumbent, insufficient electricity tariffs and an uncertain legal and regulatory framework – combined with high political risk that continues to discourage private investors from participating in the power market.

However, there are two gas-to-power developments envisaged which are located close to existing associated oil and gas fields, namely (i) the Marib Power Complex Project; and (ii) the Hadramout Power Project.

The envisaged Marib Power Complex will comprise 1365 MW of OCGT and CCGT power generation units concentrated in Marib. This complex will interconnect to the main grid that serves central and western Yemen. Marib I, OCGT producing 340 MW, should have become operational in 2009 but is delayed. It has been estimated by the World Bank that these delays cost Yemen over US$1.5 million per day in extra fuel costs for small diesel generation units that the company has to rent to maintain critical supply levels. Marib II, a 440 MW OCGT is planned for 2014 and Marib III a CCGT plant with 396 MW of capacity in 2016. All of these plants are located close to the associated gas fields. The Hadramaut Project consists of 110 MW of OCGT or 165 MW of CCGT that will serve the isolated grid in the eastern Yemen. This project will use 26.8 MMSCF/day of gas currently flared in nearby fields.

The government has yet to allocate feedgas for these developments but it is understood that negotiations are ongoing for selling the gas to PEC for US$3/MMBtu.

The Viability of a National Gas Pipeline (NGP)

The construction of a National Gas Pipeline (NGP) could further create opportunities for the Yemeni economy to reduce its dependency on oil products and switch the power sector, industrial consumers (e.g. building materials) and the commercial sector to natural gas.

The NGP would evacuate gas from Safir along a 240 km pipeline and supply various power generation plants in Marib. From Marib the pipeline will run to Ma'bar, south of Sana'a (with a spur line to Sana'a and Amran) to Hudaidah on the Red Sea coast. From there the pipeline will run along the coast to the port city of Aden with spurs to Mocha and Ta'izz. Key anchor power load was planned for Ma'bar, Hodaidah and Aden and it was assumed that several larger industrial plants, especially cement factories, could also switch to natural gas.

The investment requirements for the NGP and associated gas-fired power plants are daunting. It was estimated that the NGP would cost about US$1 billion. Gas gathering systems in the Marib fields may cost another US$500 million and power plant conversion and extension an additional US$1 billion. Thus, the entire project may cost over US$2.5 billion.

Up to 1.8 GW of OCGT and CCGT gas-fired generation capacity from existing and new plants along the NGP could be converted and built to meet future demand; this would require about 85 Bcm of gas over a 30-year life period of plants. In addition, the Marib Power Complex – which is supplied from a separate dedicated pipeline (i.e. the Marib Gas Pipeline) – would require an additional 37 Bcm of gas. In total, about 127 Bcm would be required for the power sector to run on natural gas. Unfortunately, only 54 Bcm of certified and unutilised gas is available to date, which is not sufficient to construct the NGP. However, these reserves are sufficient to supply the three Marib plants for approximately 25 years.

It has been demonstrated that the construction of the NGP will be a financially, economically and technically viable project once additional gas reserves are found in Yemen to supply large anchor customers. Until then the government should focus on providing existing proven gas reserves to the Marib Complex and the Hadramout Project and develop those projects speedily.

Conclusions

Yemen's oil reserves are depleting fast which jeopardises the future economic development of the country. Natural gas offers a lifeline to the country to compensate for the loss of some of those oil revenues. The development of the domestic gas-to-power market is crucial for the future sustainable development of the country and would create the greatest overall benefits of using scarce gas reserves. However, this requires the phasing out of electricity tariff subsidies to make the public utility financially viable and create a structure that allows for private participation in the construction of new generation plants. Unless this happens, the only remaining option for utilising remaining gas reserves is to increase LNG exports, which is a second best solution until major new reserves are discovered.

The potential demand for gas in Yemen far exceeds the supply. The government needs to create a more attractive fiscal regime to incentivise future E&P activities. It needs to establish concession and other arrangements that give clear rights and responsibilities regarding ownership and production of gas from existing and new fields. Until additional gas reserves are discovered the construction of the National Gas Pipeline (NGP) should be put on hold.

In the short run the remaining gas reserves should be utilised to develop new gas-fired power plants in Marib and Hadramout. This will require substantial private investments in the power sector to build new gas-fired power plants in Marib and Hadramout. However, it will also require that the government improves internal coordination among various Ministries to accelerate implementation of the gas-to-power programme.

An important precedent has been set by the successful implementation of the YLNG project. However, what we have experienced in Yemen to date is that the private sector has been unwilling to provide capital to invest in domestic gas infrastructure and the power sector. This is mostly caused by regulatory and political risk assumptions and, most importantly, by the perception that domestic electricity tariffs will not even allow for cost recovery.

The current gas market is also dominated by the State. The government should allow for private participation in all parts of the gas and power chain. E&P activities are limited due to political risk and fiscal arrangements that do not attract major oil companies. Consequently, creating an investor friendly environment that reduces risks for domestic gas and gas-to-power infrastructure development will be of key importance for Yemen's future.

Notes

1   The 2006 Model PSA lays out some of the criteria that should inform the drafting of the GDA/GPA. In particular, if associated gas is to be developed the 2006 Model PSA defines the time frame for finalisation of the relevant GDA, and provides for a minimum percentage participation of the government – fully carried by the contractor. Similar provisions apply for non-associated gas. It is important to note that the draft 2008 PSA, currently being considered by the government is expected to address some of these issues.

2   www.yemenlng.org

3   YNLG shareholders include: Total – Project Leader (39.62%), Hunt (17.22%), Yemen Gas Company –YGC (16.73%), SK Corporation (9.55%), Korea Gas Corporation – Kogas (6%), Hyundai Corporation (5.88%), The General Authority for Social Security & Pensions – GASSP (5%)

4   Balhaf is located on the coast of Shabwah, 200 km South-West of Mukalla and around 400 km East of Aden.

5   In 2007, the World Bank estimated the economic netback at US$2.6/MMBtu. US$5.5 at Henry Hub in the USA less regasification (US$0.3/MMBtu), shipping (US$1.2/MMBtu), liquefaction (US$1.1/MMBtu) and pipeline to Balhaf (US$0.3).

6   More detailed discussions on pricing principles for natural gas and implications for Yemen can be found in World Bank Report No. 4099-YE, Republic of Yemen, 'A Natural Gas Incentive Framework', June 2007.

7   It was estimated that over a 30-year period, about 800 million bbls of crude oil could be saved for exports by the power sector switching all units to gas.

8   This is based on a market price for diesel of YR160/litre (US$0.8/litre) and diesel consumption of 0.25 litres per kWh giving a fuel cost of US$0.2 per kWh. When gas is priced at US$3.2/MMBtu, the fuel cost is around US$0.022/kWh.

CHAPTER 15

CONCLUSION

Bassam Fattouh and Jonathan Stern

Our goal in this concluding chapter is not to repeat or summarise the conclusions of the country chapters, but rather to draw out what seem to us to be the most important themes running through the book and illustrate these themes by bringing together and interpreting the material provided by our authors. Three themes stand out above all others. The first is the challenge of rising domestic demand, which has raised concerns about gas shortages in many MENA countries, and a critical assessment of strategies that have been adopted to counter this challenge. The second theme is the problem of gas pricing in the region and its implications for the development of local, regional and international gas markets. The third theme, an important rationale for the book, is a critical examination of the prevailing assumption in much of the general gas and energy literature, that Middle East and North African countries will become an ever-larger source of internationally traded gas.

The Gas Demand Challenge

One theme that stands out throughout the book is the rising concern about critical gas shortages in many MENA countries due to rapid growth of domestic consumption of natural gas and a muted and delayed gas supply response. Between 1998 and 2008, the compound average annual growth (CAGR) of domestic natural gas consumption in the GCC has been buoyant ranging from as high as 10 percent in Dubai to over 3 percent in Qatar (see Figure 15.1). Similarly, in North Africa, domestic gas consumption grew at a fast rate, especially in Egypt, Tunisia and Morocco though in the latter country, it grew from a very low base. In the Mashreq region, natural gas has made serious inroads during the period 1998–2008 where countries such as Israel and Jordan have witnessed spectacular growth rates, though starting from a very low base. This rapid growth in gas consumption has resulted in the rising importance of natural gas in the total primary

531

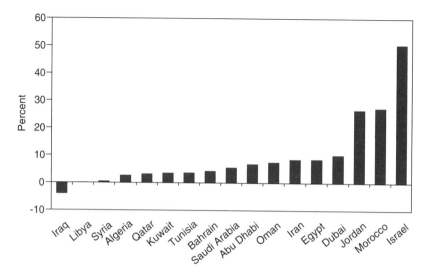

Figure 15.1: Compound Annual Growth Rate (CAGR) in Domestic Gas
Consumption in Selected MENA Countries, 1998–2008, in percent

Source: Authors' own calculations based on Cedigaz, *Natural Gas in the World*, 2009
Edition, November, Table 60.

energy supply (See Table 15.1). Natural gas is the dominant source of
energy in Algeria, Bahrain, Iran, Oman, UAE, and Qatar. Interestingly,
as seen in Table 15.1, countries such as Egypt, Tunisia, Iran, Israel,
Jordan, Oman, UAE, and Syria have witnessed a rapid rise in the share
of natural gas in the energy mix between 1980 and 2007. In contrast,
in Yemen, Morocco, Lebanon and Iraq, natural gas still plays no or a
very limited role in total primary energy supply.

While it is difficult to disentangle the importance of the various
factors in explaining the rapid growth in regional gas demand, three
factors stand out in most chapters: the rapid increase in electricity
demand; the diversion of gas into energy-intensive industries, mainly
petrochemicals; and the policy of maintaining low gas prices.

As can be seen from Figure 15.2, between 2003 and 2008, growth
in electricity demand has been phenomenal with the average annual
increase in electricity demand exceeding 10 percent in countries such
as UAE, Qatar, Libya, and Yemen. This high growth can be attributed
to a large number of factors such as rapid population growth, high
urbanisation rate, a relatively strong economic performance, and above
all low electricity prices which distort the incentive for efficient and
rational use of electricity. As Figure 15.3 shows, while electricity prices
in some MENA countries such as Palestine and Morocco are higher

Table 15.1: Share of Natural Gas in Total Primary Energy Supply in Selected MENA Countries (1980, 1990, 2000, and 2007), percent

Country	1980	1990	2000	2007
Algeria	52.01	54.82	62.30	60.55
Egypt	10.49	21.14	39.38	48.10
Libya	35.99	35.75	25.05	29.69
Morocco	1.23	0.58	0.39	3.76
Tunisia	10.70	24.85	37.35	41.29
Bahrain	86.48	81.61	84.81	83.01
Iran	9.53	25.58	44.30	51.97
Iraq	9.97	8.96	10.13	3.60
Israel	1.66	0.26	0.05	8.47
Jordan		3.07	4.26	33.47
Kuwait	37.94	64.71	38.14	37.42
Oman	35.63	57.41	65.17	67.89
Qatar	81.61	80.70	82.64	74.81
Saudi Arabia	28.96	36.53	32.61	36.65
Syria	0.78	12.04	28.34	25.56
UAE	57.62	71.28	81.51	80.93
Lebanon	0.00	0.00	0.00	0.00
Yemen	0.00	0.00	0.00	0.00

Source: IEA, *Energy Balances of Non-OECD Countries*, 2009 Edition; For Lebanon and Yemen, OAPEC, *Istihlak Al-Taqa fi al-Dowal Al-Arabiyah: Al-Hader wa Al-Mustaqbal*, (Energy Consumption in Arab Countries: Present and Future) (2010)

than those in the USA (used for comparison basis), all countries in the GCC, Libya and Egypt in North Africa, Syria and Lebanon in the Mashreq and Iraq set prices at very low levels. These prices don't often cover the cost of production, imposing a serious fiscal cost on government budgets. The difficulties facing the power generation sector in keeping pace with demographic pressures and the mounting cost of electricity subsidies, which prevented new investments from taking place in the power generation sector in some countries, have resulted in recurring power shortages in a number of countries such as Egypt, Iraq, Yemen, Kuwait, Syria, and Lebanon causing demonstrations and stirring wide public unrest.[1]

Looking ahead, the rising gas demand pressures from power generation are likely to accelerate as electricity demand is expected to grow rapidly with average annual rates between 4.2 percent (Saudi Arabia) and 18 percent (Iraq) (see Figure 15.4) during the period 2009–2020 compared to a world average of 2.4 percent.[2] Furthermore, the share of natural gas in the fuel mix for power generation has been rising in

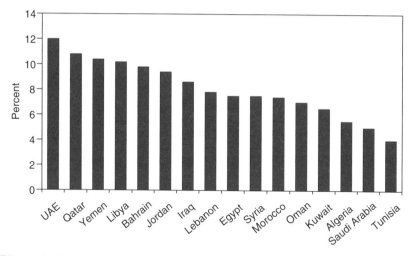

Figure 15.2: Average Annual Growth Rate of Electricity Consumption (GWH) in Selected MENA Countries, 2003–2008, in percent

Source: F. Kharbat, Istihlak Al-Taqa Fi Kitaa' Al-kahrabaa' fi al-Dowal Al-Arabiyah, (Electricity Consumption in Arab Countries) (2010), Table 4.

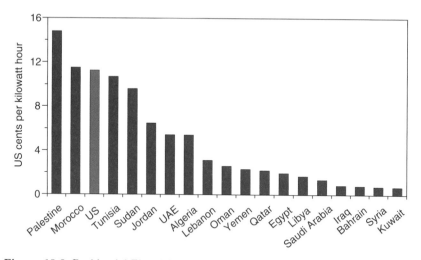

Figure 15.3: Residential Electricity Prices in Selected Arab Countries and in the USA, 2008, US Cents per kilowatthour

Source: Arab Union of Producers, Transporters and Distributors of Electricity, 'Al-Taa'rifaat al Kah'roubaeyya fil Watan Al-Arabi', (Electricity Tariffs in Arab countries), Occasional Report, November. For Kuwait, the data were obtained from Eltony, M.N. and Al-Awadi, M.A., 'Residential Energy Demand: A Case Study of Kuwait, 2007. The US data refer to the residential average (source: EIA, website).

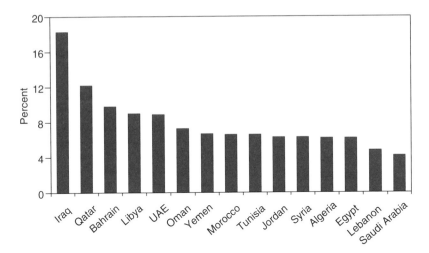

Figure 15.4: Projected Average Annual Growth Rate of Electricity Consumption in Selected MENA Countries (GWH) between 2009 and 2020, in percent

Source: F. Kharbat, *Istihlak Al-Taqa Fi Kitaa' Al-kahrabaa' fi al-Dowal Al-Arabiyah*, (Electricity Consumption in Arab Countries), Paper presented at the 9th Arab Energy Conference, Doha, Qatar, 9–12 May 2010 (in Arabic), Appendix A.

most MENA countries as the switch from oil to gas for power generation consolidated in the past three decades (see Table 15.2). However, there are some notable exceptions such as Kuwait and Saudi Arabia where these two countries have met the increase in electricity demand by burning liquid fuels in power generation reflecting a context of limited gas availability. In the absence of large finds of natural gas reserves, these countries are likely to continue to divert liquid fuels to power generation, resulting in further declines in the share of gas in power generation. In the Mashreq countries, further reduction of liquids in power generation will be dependent on availability of imported gas (Jordan, Lebanon and Syria) and the capability to develop gas reserves in Israel.

In addition to power generation, the natural gas sector lies at the heart of diversification efforts in many energy-resource rich economies, where natural gas has become the fuel of choice for industrialisation through the development of energy-intensive industries such as petrochemicals, cement and aluminium.

On the one hand, this diversification strategy has achieved some success. During the last decade or so, the MENA petrochemical industry has witnessed rapid expansion transforming the region into an important global player. This is perhaps most evident in the case of

Table 15.2: Electricity Generation from Gas, Percent of Total

	1980	1990	2000	2007
Algeria	84.1	93.7	96.7	97.3
Egypt	20.5	39.6	71.0	68.4
Libya			21.9	44.9
Morocco				13.6
Tunisia	34.7	63.7	87.6	83.1
Bahrain	100.0	100.0	100.0	96.9
Iran	24.8	52.5	76.6	78.6
Israel			0.0	19.7
Jordan		11.9	10.1	76.4
Kuwait	69.9	45.7	29.4	27.7
Oman	78.5	81.6	82.8	82.0
Qatar	97.3	100.0	100.0	100.0
Saudi Arabia	65.3	48.1	43.5	44.8
Syria	3.4	20.5	37.1	31.2
UAE	96.3	96.3	96.9	98.1

Source: IEA, *Energy Balances of Non-OECD Countries*, 2009 Edition.

ethylene where production capacity reached more than 18.5 million tonnes per annum at the beginning of 2009 compared to 12 mtpa at the beginning of 2008, with the growth mainly in Iran and Saudi Arabia (see Table 15.3). In countries such as Iran and Israel, the feedstock is more varied with naphtha playing an important role. By contrast, in the GCC countries such as Kuwait, Saudi Arabia, Qatar, and the UAE, the petrochemical industry is mainly ethane based derived from associated and non-associated natural gas. In these countries, the low cost of ethane constitutes the main source of comparative advantage and is the chief factor behind the rapid growth in the region's petrochemical industry. Many countries, including members of the European Union, consider that such low prices and the dual pricing system grant an unfair advantage to these producers and in 2009 the European Union, China and India imposed anti-dumping measures on some Gulf petrochemical imports. These measures are a constant reminder that despite the fact that countries such as Saudi Arabia have been able to join the WTO without reforming their pricing systems, the issue of gas pricing has not died away and threats of WTO actions will continue as petrochemical companies continue to put pressure on their respective governments to present their cases for WTO resolution.[3]

On the other hand, the drive towards diversification through developing petrochemicals and other energy-intensive industries raises a series of challenges in many countries analysed in this book. Given

Table 15.3: Ethylene Capacity in Middle East and North Africa, Tonnes per annum

Country	2008	2009	*Typical Feedstock Mixture*
Algeria	133,000	133,000	NA
Egypt	330,000	330,000	NA
Iran	1,214,000	4,734,000	Ethane, Propane, Butane, Naphtha
Israel	200,000	200,000	NA
Kuwait	800,000	1,650,000	Ethane
Libya	350,000	350,000	NA
Qatar	1,030,000	1,030,000	Ethane, Propane
Saudi Arabia	6,800,000	9,400,000	Predominately Ethane, Propane, but also Naphtha
UAE	600,000	600,000	Ethane

Source: *Oil and Gas Journal*, 'Ethylene Report', 2009

the increasing scarcity of natural gas and in the absence of clear price signals due to artificially low prices, the issue is whether the existing allocation of gas among the various sectors such as petrochemicals versus power generation, or exports versus domestic use, is efficient and maximises the value of a scarce resource. From a broader perspective, it raises the issue as to whether industrialisation through energy-intensive industries has been successful in achieving certain goals such as diversification and employment creation. Increasing scarcity of natural gas and more costly gas supplies also raise the issue of whether current policies and/or plans of promoting energy-intensive industries are sustainable in the long term. Due to data limitations and the scope of the analysis, the chapters in this volume do not provide adequate answers to such questions and these issues are still open for further research.

Gas Pricing Policy

Over the past 30 years in which Middle East and North African production has achieved substantial levels another extremely unwelcome trend has become evident: the era of low cost gas production – specifically gas associated with oil production and easily accessible non-associated gas which could either be considered 'free' or available at less than $1/MMBtu – has ended; for the majority of countries it probably finished at least a decade ago. The cost of new gas production can be estimated in the range of $3.50–6.00/MMBtu for countries such as UAE, Kuwait, and Saudi Arabia due to greater depth of resource discoveries, complexity of reservoirs ('tight gas') and the presence of impurities ('sour gas').

Despite the fact that the era of low cost gas finished some time ago, the vast majority of countries in the region remain in an era of *low price gas* in terms of what they charge industry, power generators, commercial and residential customers. While it is an open question whether the prices in Table 15.4 should be considered 'subsidies' in countries with no export infrastructure, these prices are a fraction of the cost of new supplies – domestic or imported – that all countries will need to develop to meet their future domestic requirements.[4]

Table 15.4: Gas Prices for Different Customer Classes in Middle East and North African Countries, $/MMBtu

	2006	
Algeria	0.85	2008: 0.5
Libya	0.90	2008: 0.12–0.20
Egypt	1.19	2008: 0.47 residential/commercial, 1.25 industry, 3.00 energy intensive industry
Saudi Arabia	0.75	2010: 0.75
Iran	0.35	2008: residential 0.33, commercial 0.74, power 0.15, industry including petrochemicals 0.47
Iraq		2008: power and industry 1.15
Qatar	0.85	2008: petrochemicals 0.75–1.00
Oman		2009: power stations 1.5, industry 1.5, methanol/fertiliser 1.00
UAE	1.05	2010: 1.00
Bahrain		2007: existing customers 1.1 rising to 1.5 in 2011; 2007 new users 1.5
Kuwait	0.60	2008: 0.6–0.9 indexed to crude oil prices which increasing prices to $2.2/MMBtu at oil prices of $121–140/bbl; petrochemical users pay $2.5

Sources: 2006 prices from Razavi, Hossein, 'Natural Gas Pricing in Countries of the Middle East and North Africa', 2009, Table 6; other data from chapters

Economic analysis by Razavi,[5] based on data from 2006, demonstrated a wide range of economic netback values for MENA gas depending on country, end-use and assumptions about oil prices and discount rates. He found values ranging from $11–12/MMBtu for oilfield reinjection and the residential sector in Iran, to $3.7 for fertiliser plants; for the power sector he estimated values in the range of $6–7/

MMBtu. It is very unlikely that any of these figures would be lower in 2010. Therefore whether we take domestic gas development costs and import prices at $3.50–7.00/MMBtu, or average netback values of $6–7/MMBtu, the task facing the majority of MENA governments with 2008–2010 prices in the region of $0.5–1.50/MMBtu is immense. As a comparison, a study of the countries of the former Soviet Union – which had similar price levels when the Union broke up in 1991 – found that by the late 2000s prices in many countries, at least to industrial customers, were in the $3–4/MMBtu range.[6]

The current pricing policy has many adverse allocation and distributional consequences. It encourages domestic gas demand above the levels warranted by their true opportunity costs. Furthermore, the optimisation of resource allocation becomes nonfeasible at subsidised prices, which often result in the misallocation of investments towards energy-intensive industries that would otherwise have not been profitable. There have been changes in some countries such as Oman where the decision as to which fuel to use is made on the basis of full economic cost and not the subsidised price.

For gas exporters, subsidies can give rise to a bias in favour of investments in export infrastructure as producers have no incentive to sell their gas on the domestic market when they can secure much higher prices from export markets. Subsidies are also regressive in nature as the bulk of the benefits accrue to households in high-income groups which consume more gas, and a greater proportion of which are connected to the natural gas network, than household in low-income groups. Perhaps this is most illustrated in the case of Iran. Data from Iran indicate that the three top income groups capture more than 40 percent of the gas subsidies compared to less than 20 percent for the three lowest income groups (see Table 15.5).

How sustainable therefore is the current policy of providing cheap gas? Here it is important to take a wider view of a group of countries with young and rapidly growing populations. In resource rich countries, low energy prices can be seen as one of the various methods for distributing rents to the local population. Furthermore, in the majority of MENA countries, low gas prices are part of a larger picture of low power prices and low charges for water use. Low price gas allows petrochemicals to be produced at low cost and therefore to compete in world markets. It also allows the generation of low price power, which allows low cost production of aluminium and water desalination. In turn this allows water to be provided at low cost (or free). Substantial increases in gas prices – our calculations above suggest the need for a six to twelve-fold increase in the majority of countries – would massively

Table 15.5: Iran – Shares in Total Subsidy in 2007, in percent

Income Groups	Natural gas	Electricity	Gasoline
1	4.10	4.19	2.43
2	5.92	5.70	3.32
3	7.62	6.75	4.17
4	8.31	7.78	5.55
5	9.11	8.53	5.93
6	10.20	9.40	7.92
7	11.70	11.02	9.64
8	12.02	11.74	13.50
9	13.73	13.68	17.76
10	17.28	21.20	29.77

Source: Salehi-Isfahani, D. (2010), 'Will Iran's Poor Lose from Subsidy Reform?'

impact those sections of the population on low incomes and hence is socially and politically undesirable. Thus, abolishing subsidies must be accompanied by measures to protect poor households from any decline in real income. This could be facilitated through graduated pricing, with preference given to low income sectors, and high income residential customers could be progressively moved to market prices. However, possible domestic opposition and potential WTO violation may preclude some governments from taking this route. Furthermore, high gas prices would impact the industrialisation and diversification strategy in many countries as it reduces the competitiveness of energy-intensive industries.

Some countries have the financial capacity to continue with their current pricing policy – whether or not this would be the most efficient strategy for maximising the utilisation of their gas reserves. Qatar's abundant low cost domestic gas means that a domestic price of $0.75–1.00/MMBtu, while it certainly does not maximise value, probably covers costs. Saudi Arabia's crude oil endowment allows it to utilise greater quantities of fuel oil for power generation while prioritising gas use for the petrochemical industry. However, such a policy is not without its costs.

In other countries, the current policy of subsidising gas prices is highly unsustainable. For instance, in the case of Egypt, Khattab estimates that Egypt had spent around 6.4 percent of its GDP on energy subsidies in 2006/2007, with the expenditure on energy subsidies accounting for around 14.6 percent of total expenditures.[7] To put this figure in perspective, expenditure on energy subsidies exceeds the expenditure on education, is twice the expenditure on defence, and four times the expenditure on health.

Thus, for the majority of MENA countries, the answer to the question of how to reform prices, given the political and economic circumstances of many of these countries, raises crucial questions of macroeconomic management and political legitimacy of governments, and ultimately how some of these countries need to develop towards a 'post-Hydrocarbon era'. The pace of reform is likely to be uneven across the region. In some countries, the government's ability to manage domestic opposition and social unrest will be the main driver of reform. In other countries a more relevant factor would be the potential impact of higher gas prices on the international competitiveness of their energy-intensive industries and the overall impact on the country's development strategy. While we are not very optimistic about *radical* price increases before 2015 in most MENA countries, it is important to note that the issue of gas pricing has been given a high priority in many MENA countries such as Egypt, Saudi Arabia, and Iran where there is recognition among policymakers of the extent of the problems caused by the low gas pricing policy. We believe that policymakers need to conclude – and will conclude – that by 2015, domestic gas prices will need to at least reflect cost recovery, even if this will not (yet) be close to international price levels.

Common Problem and Varied Responses

Rising gas demand has caused serious concerns in many countries over the security of gas supplies. Despite its dominant position in reserves, the region is no longer immune to gas security concerns. Issues such as securing long-term gas supplies at an 'acceptable' price, diversification of supplies to reduce dependency on a dominant exporter, and problems of trans-border pipelines have now become central to the energy policy agenda. In many countries, it is no longer accurate to distinguish between an 'oil policy' and a 'gas policy' and instead the two policies – combined with their contribution to the power sector – should be analysed within an all-encompassing 'energy policy'. Furthermore, developments in the gas sector have become closely interlinked with economic policy given that the gas sector is at the heart of many countries' diversification efforts.

The responses to potential gas shortages have not been uniform across MENA countries. In resource rich countries such as Saudi Arabia, the strategy has been to increase domestic gas production through an intensive exploration and development programme and by diverting natural gas to the petrochemical sector while burning liquid fuels in power generation at high opportunity cost. The current policy of no export/no import remains the dominant strategy in the Kingdom. Kuwait and UAE also burn liquid fuels in power generation, but the rise in demand has forced these GCC countries to secure natural gas supplies through imports, while intensifying efforts to secure more domestic gas supplies through intensive exploration and development programmes. In the UAE, long-term solutions beyond natural gas, such as investing in nuclear power and renewable energy technology are currently being implemented, but these will play a limited role in alleviating the gas shortage over the next decade. In countries such as Oman, Algeria, Libya and Egypt, the rise in domestic demand is already presenting these countries with hard choices regarding the allocation of natural gas between domestic uses and exports. Even in Qatar, there is reprioritisation of its natural gas monetisation strategy towards meeting domestic needs and diversifying its economy through the development of energy-intensive industries. In Yemen, on the other hand, while the analysis in Chapter 14 suggests that diverting gas for domestic use in power generation may yield a higher value for the use of the natural resource, the government has adopted the export option to secure additional revenues.

While strategies to meet the rising demand challenge vary considerably across countries, a regional default model seems to be emerging based on increasing natural gas supplies through exploration and development of associated and non-associated gas reserves. This even applies to countries with limited gas reserves such as Tunisia, Syria, and Israel. Oil-rich countries can afford to leverage on their massive oil reserves against the failure of this strategy though at a high opportunity cost. Gas exporters, such as Egypt and Oman, can switch their gas exports to domestic consumption at the expense of revenue losses. On the other hand, resource-poor countries such as Bahrain have little room to manoeuvre and must invest in infrastructure such as pipelines and a regasification policy to enable them to import their needs, otherwise they will face a gas deficit in the near future.

The default model of increasing domestic gas supplies is premised on heavily investing in the gas sector. Historically, in most MENA countries, the development of the gas sector has lagged behind the oil sector. In fact, for countries whose gas reserves are mostly in associated form, gas production was simply a by-product of crude oil production. However, rapidly expanding demand combined with fears of gas shortages and substitution between oil and gas in sectors such as power generation, water desalination and petrochemicals, mean that the issue of investment in the gas sector is currently receiving much more weight in the formulation of long-term energy policy. Since the mid 2000s, there has been a change in strategy towards the gas sector with significant increases in investment both in non-associated gas fields and gas gathering infrastructure in most MENA economies.

Interestingly, foreign investment is playing an important role in this new drive. For example, Saudi Arabia which has traditionally precluded foreign investment in its exploration activities has allowed foreign companies to explore for non-associated gas in the Empty Quarter though with limited success so far. In gas-exporting countries such as Qatar, Yemen, Oman and Egypt, foreign companies constitute the backbone of the gas industry and have been responsible for developing these countries' export capability. On the other hand, sanctions combined with unattractive upstream fiscal terms have affected Iran's ability to attract foreign companies which, at least to some extent, accounts for the fact that the country has so far failed to become an important gas exporter despite its enormous reserves. The same applies to Libya, which even after the lifting of international sanctions in 2003/4 and the return of foreign investors to the country's upstream gas industry has seen little achieved in the way of expanding proven reserves and ramping up production. Though the need for the introduction of dedicated gas upstream investment terms is recognised by some within the Libyan gas industry, institutional informality and lack of political predictability continue to preclude the realisation of Libya's elusive gas potential. In Iraq, the obstacles facing a successful gas development are paramount including the lack of a clear legal framework, security issues, and a fragile political system.

But sanctions are not the only impediment to investment. As discussed above, a common feature in most countries is that little progress has been made on the issue of adjusting gas prices to reflect opportunity cost or the long-term marginal cost of gas production. The policy of low gas prices has intensified the gas supply challenge by providing little incentive for domestic and foreign companies to invest in exploration and production of gas in some countries. Gas pricing policy has also affected the incentive to invest in local gas infrastructure. For instance, by incurring large losses by selling gas and LPG to the domestic market at below cost prices, the Egyptian state gas company (EGAS) has been unable to meet the financing requirements of connecting the residential sector to natural gas.[8]

Until very recently, few governments have been willing to raise domestic prices for natural gas. However, recognising the grave challenges ahead, there has been a slight change in attitude and some countries have already adjusted or started to consider adjusting domestic gas prices upward. For instance, in 2008, the Government of Egypt announced that it would remove subsidies on gas and electricity provided to energy-intensive industries over a three-year period, and in 2009 Iran passed legislation to remove natural gas subsidies. However, such steps remain modest compared to the investment challenge ahead. Without a structural reform of gas pricing policy, the gas supply response is likely to remain muted. Yet it is clear that many governments, especially in countries with large populations on low incomes, fear the political consequences of rapid and radical gas price increases.

Inter-Arab Gas Trade

While the region is well endowed with massive gas reserves, the distribution of these reserves is highly uneven with some countries facing potential deficits while others have turned to gas exports to secure a major source of revenue. Such imbalances should in principle give rise to an active regional gas pipeline trade and provide a regional solution to the gas challenge. Despite its great potential, regional gas trade is still very limited with very few pipelines having been built. The most well known is the Dolphin Project linking Qatar, UAE and Oman. There is also the Arab Gas Pipeline from Egypt to Jordan, Syria, and Lebanon; and the Egypt–Israel pipeline. While many other projects have been discussed (such as pipelines from Qatar to Bahrain and Kuwait, and from Iran to UAE, Oman and Syria), and in some cases contracts were signed, all of these and other regional projects face political and commercial obstacles and are unlikely to be realised in the near future.

There are many obstacles that prevent the further expansion of regional pipelines. The region has entrenched and longstanding political problems and border disputes have affected the development of the gas sector and the dynamics of gas trade. For instance, sanctions and/or threats of sanctions have constrained the growth of the gas sector in countries such as Libya, Iraq, and Iran. International and regional geo-politics and border disputes played an important role in delaying and limiting the geographical reach of the Dolphin pipeline. Suspicions and fears about Iran's hegemony in the region make many GCC countries reluctant to rely on its gas supplies. In North Africa, regional rivalry between Morocco and Algeria militated against the development of pipeline export infrastructure to Spain until the late 1980s and early 1990s. Besides gas trade, regional disputes in the Maghreb have defined the trajectory of gas market development in countries like Morocco, whose continued aversion to contracted gas imports from Algeria remains the main stumbling block to a more meaningful penetration of natural gas in its energy mix. The problems of political relations between Mashreq countries and Israel, in relation to pipeline trade, are discussed below.

Apart from political factors, expectations of inexpensive gas prices seem to be an important limiting factor in the implementation of regional agreements. Regional LNG exporters have direct experience of the price they receive from international markets which, during 2006–09 has been $7–13/MMBtu in the Pacific Basin and although somewhat lower in the Atlantic Basin (especially the USA in 2009) still above $5/MMBtu.[9] With the exception of Dolphin customers, all regional importers are already paying these prices. Since the development of its gas industry, Qatar has given priority to supplying high paying customers in Europe, the United States and Asia, rather than its neighbouring countries. Qatar has made it abundantly clear that there will be no additional exports to the region priced at $1.50/MMBtu, which is what UAE pays for Dolphin Phase 1 gas. All Iranian plans to supply regional countries have foundered (at least partly) on the issue of price. Thus, it is becoming clearer to all players that securing regional gas supplies at prices below international levels is no longer a viable option and that for regional gas trade to take off on a large scale, gas prices must eventually increase towards those levels.

Another obstacle concerns gas transit issues, which are often governed by (WTO) rules but where the Energy Charter Treaty and its transit protocol is the only specific multilateral instrument backed by binding dispute resolution procedures. The fact that a significant number of MENA countries have become observers to the Energy Charter Conference and have signed the Charter, shows a growing recognition of the relevance of this issue in the region.[10] For countries that allow gas transit through their territories there is also the issue of access to the domestic market. While the Transit Protocol of the Energy Charter Treaty makes a specific distinction between transit and third party access, this is still a hotly debated legal/regulatory issue. As in Russia and the western CIS region, many countries in MENA are still reluctant to allow regional neighbours access to their highly regulated domestic markets.[11]

Marketed Gas Production and End-User Consumption to 2015

Table 15.6 shows that marketed production and end user consumption are projected to grow strongly in almost every country in the region up

Table 15.6: Natural Gas Production and Demand in the Middle East and North Africa, 2008–2015, Bcm

| | Marketed Production* | | End-User Consumption** | |
	2008	2015 proj	2008	2015 proj
NORTH AFRICA				
Algeria	85.3	116.3	26.6	41.7
Libya	15.9	23.6	5.5	9.8
Egypt	58.9	80	40.9	60.5
Total	**160.1**	**219.9**	**73**	**112**
Syria	5.5	12	6	16
Lebanon	0	0	0	1-5
Jordan	0.2	0.3	2.9	4-5
Israel	0.8-1.0	6-8	2.5-2.7	6-8
Total	**6.5–6.7**	**18.3–20.3**	**11.4–11.6**	**27–34**
GULF				
Saudi Arabia	79.0	113	79.0	113
Iraq	1.8–5.2	10	1.8–5.2	10
Iran	116.3	191	124.3	193
Qatar	77	171.3	20.2	35
Oman	22.8	29.8	9.0	16.2
UAE	50.2	64.6	58.1	88.5
Bahrain	13.4	11–12	12.5	13–16
Kuwait	12.8	13–14	10.8	14–18
Yemen	0	10	0	1
Total	**373–377**	**614–616**	**316–320**	**484–491**

*   Marketed production = gross production minus gas flared, reinjected and used at oil and gas fields.
** End-user consumption = marketed production minus exports plus imports

Sources: compiled from data provided by the chapter authors and own estimates

to 2015. The projected increase in production relies on far more than the reserve figures in Table 1 of the Introduction. It is a judgement based on current and anticipated investment activity and plans for specific field developments in each country. By far the largest anticipated increases in production during this period are in Iran (75 Bcm) and Qatar (94 Bcm); production increases in Saudi Arabia, Algeria and Egypt are all in the range of 20–35 Bcm.

In North Africa, production is projected to grow at just under 5 percent per annum while demand will exceed 6 percent per annum over the same period. In the Gulf, production will grow at just over 7 percent per annum with annual demand growth exceeding 6 percent. This means that for the first part of the 2010s, demand growth rates are projected to be similar to the 2000s – 7 percent per annum for the Gulf and 6 percent for North Africa (see Introduction Table 2) – but with growing unease in a number of countries as to whether production will be able to keep pace with rising domestic requirements and export commitments.

Gas Export and Import Developments to 2015

Table 15.7 shows imports and exports of gas for 2008 and 2015 divided into pipeline gas and LNG. In *North Africa*, gas exports will increase modestly by 21.5 Bcm during this period, although it is difficult to be clear on the exact split between pipeline gas and LNG, which will depend on the relative profitability of costs and prices associated with different markets. The majority of the increase will come from Algeria, with Libyan and Egyptian gas exports increasing by a total of only 6 Bcm over this period. Egyptian export facilities are projected to operate at less than 60 percent capacity, reflecting a judgement that in the context of limited gas availability, priority will be given to the domestic market. In the *Mashreq, Israel and the Palestinian Territories* the overall change is not substantial with the grouping slightly increasing its imports but only by 1–2.5 Bcm over the period.

It is in the *Gulf* that we see the most dramatic changes: pipeline gas imports increase by more than 50 percent and for the first time countries in the region begin to import LNG, Kuwait having received its first cargoes in 2009. Exports of LNG nearly double, almost entirely due to Qatari exports, with Yemen having joined the ranks of LNG exporters in 2009. Pipeline gas exports increase around 50 percent due to the anticipated expansion of Iranian exports over which question marks remain for both internal economic and external and internal political reasons.

Overall, if we compare the anticipated expansion of exports in the period up to 2015 in Table 15.7 with the actual increase for 2000–09 (Introduction Table 3) we see very similar numbers for North Africa, but Gulf gas exports will increase by 66 Bcm up to 2015 compared with 45 Bcm in the 2000s. MENA gas export expansion up to 2015 will be heavily dependent on four countries: Algeria, Qatar, Yemen and Iran; but with increasing imports from Turkmenistan, net Iranian gas exports could decline slightly. Therefore, if any of these states experience domestic economic or energy problems leading to a need for greater domestic utilisation of gas then exports could be commensurately reduced; current expectations would suggest Algeria and Iran

Table 15.7: Middle East and North Africa Gas Imports and Exports, 2008–2015, Bcm

	Imports 2008		Imports 2015 proj		Exports 2008		Exports 2015 proj		Increase 2008–15	
	Lng	Png	Lng	Png	Lng	Png	Lng	Png	Imports	Exports
NORTH AFRICA	-	-								
Algeria	-	-			22	37.5	75			15.5
Libya	-	-			0.54	9.87	2.5	13		3.4
Egypt	-	-			14.06	2.86	19.5			2.6
Total					**36.6**	**50.23**	**108.3**			**21.5**
Syria	0.5	-		2.2			-	-	1.7	
Lebanon		-		0.5–2.0			-	-	0.5–2.0	
Jordan	2.7	-		3.2			-	-	0.5	
Israel	1.7	-		0			-	-	-1.7	
Total	**4.9**		**5.9–7.4**						**1–2.5**	
GULF										
Iraq	-	-					0	0		
Iran	7		14		4.25		0	12	7	8.0
Qatar	-	-			57.9	17.4	105	18.7		48.3
Oman	0.2			2.1	11.2		11.5	-	1.9–3.1	0.3
UAE	15.4		0.88	18.6	7.5		7.7	-	4.1	0.2
Bahrain			2–4	-			-	-	2–4	
Kuwait			1–4	-			-	-	1–4	
Yemen	-		-				9	-		9
Total	**22.6**	**3.9–8.9**	**34.7**		**76.6**	**21.7**	**133.2**	**30.7**	**16–22.2**	**65.7**

Lng = liquefied natural gas; Png = pipeline gas
For 2008 a blank space denotes no trade. For 2015 – denotes no plans to import or export, 0 denotes a judgement that, despite plans, there will be no exports by that date.

Source: compiled from data provided by the chapter authors and own estimates

might be most susceptible to this type of problem. Likewise internal political problems, given the opposition in Iran to gas exports, and the fragility of the political situation in Yemen could act as destabilising factors. With Qatar accounting for nearly three-quarters of total net incremental exports, any regional political difficulties between Iran and Qatar over the vexed question of demarcation of resources in the South Pars/North Field, would create anxiety about global LNG supplies and additional difficulties for Iran's relationship with the international community.

The continuity in the export picture for the first half of the 2010s is in sharp contrast to the import picture. At the beginning of the 2000s, the only significant importers in the region were Iran (from

Turkmenistan), internal transfers of UAE gas between Sharjah and Dubai, and Tunisia receiving gas from Algeria as payment for transit and
contracted imports. Indeed, aside from the Algerian pipelines to Europe
which brought additional gas to Tunisia, and the first (very small) gas
deliveries to Morocco, few of the many regional gas pipeline proposals
had succeeded. During the 2000s, two major regional pipelines were
established: the Arab Gas pipeline taking Egyptian gas to the Mashreq;
and the Dolphin pipeline taking gas from Qatar to UAE and Oman. In
addition, flows through the Egypt–Israel pipeline commenced in 2008.
Table 15.8 shows that by 2008, five regional countries had become net
importers compared with one (Iran) in 2000. With Lebanon joining the
ranks of pipeline gas importers in 2009, all the Mashreq countries will
become steadily more import-dependent, but Israel is likely to become
increasingly self-sufficient as its new gas finds are developed. Table 15.8

Table 15.8: Middle East and North Africa Net Gas Trade 2008–2015, Bcm

	----- 2008 -----			------- 2015 proj -------			
	Lng	*Png*	*Total*	*Lng*	*Png*	*Total*	*Percent Export Capacity**
NORTH AFRICA							
Algeria	22.0	37.5	59.5			75.0	83
Libya	0.54	9.87	10.41	2.5	13	15.5	
Egypt	14.1	2.9	17.0			19.5	57
Total	**36.6**	**50.3**	**86.9**			**108.3**	
Syria		-0.5	-0.5		-2.2	-2.2	
Lebanon					-0.5–2	-0.5–2	
Jordan		-2.7	-2.7		-3.2	-3.2	
Israel		-1.7	-1.7		0	0	
Total		**-4.9**	**-4.9**		**-5.9–7.4**	**-5.9–7.4**	
GULF							
Iran		-2.75	-2.75		-2	-2	27**
Qatar	40.5	17.4	57.9	105	17.4	122.4	
Oman	10.7	-0.2	10.5	11.5	-2.1	9.4	73
UAE	7.5	-15.4	-7.9	6.8	-15.4	-8.6	
Bahrain				-2–4		-2–4	
Kuwait				-1–4		-1–4	
Yemen				9		9	
Total	**58.7**	**-0.95**	**57.5**	**124.3–129.3**	**-2.1**	**122.2–127.2**	

Lng = liquefied natural gas; Png = pipeline gas; - denotes net import
* likely percent utilisation of export capacity
** contracted export commitments

Source: compiled from data provided by the chapter authors and own estimates

also shows that the regional trend towards imports will strengthen by 2015, not just in terms of pipeline gas but also LNG. Kuwait became an importer of LNG in 2009 and in 2010 will be joined by Dubai and possibly in the following few years by Bahrain. UAE became a net gas importer in 2008 as pipeline imports from Qatar exceeded its LNG exports and while Oman will not become a net importer, maintaining its LNG exports at current levels will require swift development of additional supplies.

2015 and Beyond

Looking beyond 2015, the gas export picture becomes increasingly uncertain. In *North Africa* the prospects for immediate additional exports from Algeria and Egypt are poor. Without a significant acceleration of upstream development both countries may struggle to maintain projected export levels and possibly face difficulties in meeting their contractual commitments in the late 2010s. Hopes remain high that Libya will be able to increase production and exports very substantially, but these have been dampened somewhat by slow progress towards the creation of legal and fiscal frameworks combined with somewhat disappointing exploration results under the EPSA IV framework. If and when new gas reserves are discovered the expansion of exports will be constrained by domestic demand – though a lot will depend on the size of eventual discoveries, the rate of utilisation and the commercial terms offered for foreign investors.

In the *Mashreq* the picture is one of slowly increasing imports which has already led to repressed demand due to either inability to pay higher import prices, or inability to access additional imports, or both. Israel is the only country in this region that could move from being an importer to an exporter if the size of the gas discoveries that have been announced proves to be correct. However Israel's gas trade situation will be complex both commercially and politically. If the country's production means that it has no need for the gas it has contracted from Egypt, then arrangements could be made such that the gas remains in Egypt or is exported through that country's (underutilised) LNG facilities (see Table 15.7); or alternatively through the Arab Gas Pipeline to Mashreq countries. Despite a compelling commercial incentive on both sides, Israel's political relations with its Mashreq neighbours are such that direct gas exports currently seem impossible. In the absence of pipeline markets, unless Israel can develop an LNG export capability, any gas surplus that may be discovered will remain undeveloped.

In *the Gulf*, the key countries that could increase gas exports post-2015 are Qatar, Iraq and Iran. The Qatari case is in many ways the most straightforward: the moratorium or 'gas pause' is not due to be lifted until 2015, after which a relatively rapid export increase could only be achieved by debottlenecking the existing trains, which would provide nearly 19 Bcm/year of additional exports. Assuming a decision to increase production further in 2015, any new project would require a minimum 4–5 year lead time to develop which would mean very little chance of additional exports prior to 2020. Additional production could as easily be channelled towards domestic industrial development or regional gas exports (assuming a willingness to pay international prices) as to additional LNG exports. Existing LNG trains plus debottlenecking would bring capacity close to 140 Bcm and it seems unlikely that a nation with a population of around 250,000 will want to increase exports substantially beyond that level.

The other two countries are substantially more problematic. As far as Iran is concerned, many pipeline projects have been discussed over the past four decades, and in some cases contracts have been signed. Some have come to fruition (Turkey, Armenia, Azerbaijan/Nakhichevan), others are said to be under construction (Pakistan), still others appear to be stalled or cancelled (Sharjah, Oman, Bahrain, Syria and new pipelines to Europe via Turkey). In addition, despite the cancellation of two of its projects in 2010, Iran still has five LNG projects at various stages of development. The judgement that has been made in Tables 15.7 and 15.8 is that less than half of the 27 Bcm of apparently contracted pipeline exports will actually be delivered by 2015; and none of the LNG export projects will be on stream by then. Iranian internal political problems in respect of gas exports, which tend to manifest themselves in terms of endless reopening of the price terms agreed in long-term contracts, combined with the difficulty of establishing reliable exports from a country that appears chronically short of gas for domestic consumption, have been major obstacles to export projects. We see these same problems continuing, compounded by Iranian difficulties with the international community which, at mid 2010, resulted in the imposition of additional sanctions placing yet further limitations on Iran's ability to raise finance for projects. We have serious doubts as to whether the pipeline project to Pakistan will yield any significant exports prior to 2020, and have little expectation that LNG exports will begin by the end of the 2010s unless Chinese investment can be combined with liquefaction technology which can be acquired despite international sanctions. The only development that might change this outlook would be a dramatic improvement in Iranian relations with the international community, and especially the United States (which seems unlikely at the time of writing). Without such a development, a continuation of its current position as a marginal net importer of gas seems the most likely outcome for the remainder of the 2010s.

In 2010, there was considerable optimism from international companies that Iraq could become a major exporter of gas prior to 2020, with volumes up to 15 Bcm available for the Nabucco pipeline to Europe via Turkey. This optimism is not reflected in Chapter 8 and we also do not share it (which accounts for the relatively low production and absence of Iraqi exports in Tables 15.7 and 15.8). It seems to us that resolution of the institutional problems between Baghdad and the regions – in particular the administration in Kurdistan – combined with the need to devote substantial volumes of gas to domestic reconstruction and reindustrialisation, will take most of the 2010s to resolve. We would be surprised if export volumes as large as 15 Bcm/year could be arranged prior to 2020 and should they do so, confidence in the security of these supplies would require a dramatic and lasting improvement in the security situation in the country. Assuming that gas exports were to start from the north of the country, we think it as likely that a significant share of such deliveries could be directed towards the Mashreq, given that Egypt will not be able to satisfy the needs of those countries.

With a shortage of gas in Saudi Arabia requiring increased consumption of domestic liquid fuel for power generation and a wider recognition of the high costs involved in such a strategy, there is a big possibility that Saudi Arabia itself would become a net importer of gas in the second half of the 2010s.

Thus, the outlook for incremental Middle East and North African gas exports in the second half of the 2010s is relatively bleak; the only possible bright spots being an additional 19 Bcm of export capacity from Qatari LNG debottlenecking and future (but as yet unclear) Libyan developments. However, we see no significant increase in exports from Algeria, Egypt or Iran, no substantial exports from Iraq, and other countries either struggling to maintain exports or striving to increase imports. Something fundamental needs to happen to radically change this picture and the main element of this will be to raise the near-universal level of very low gas prices coupled with increasing domestic gas/power demand throughout the region. Having said that prices need to achieve cost recovery levels by the middle of the decade, we believe that it will be necessary for governments to continue to increase them towards international levels in the second half of the 2010s. It is clear that such measures will cause a great deal of economic and political pain in many countries, and create serious challenges for their industrial and development strategies. But our view is that, even for resource rich countries (with the possible exception of Qatar), failure to implement such price increases will result in a future of increasing domestic demand for liquid fuels (with corresponding reductions in oil export availability), rationing of increasingly scarce gas between essential users (with additional negative impacts on oil production in countries using gas for enhanced recovery), and increasing power shortages.

Notes

1 In the long term, the GCC Interconnection Project (GCCIP) could help alleviate some electricity shortages by transporting power within the GCC, without necessarily importing natural gas. This is not nearly as contentious as importing natural gas as evidenced by the total cooperation of all stakeholders. Currently, however, only Qatar has spare capacity and pricing issues are likely to become important in the future. However, the GCCIP is of enormous consequence as it shows a level of cooperation beyond the relatively narrow confines of the Dolphin project and could further push the GCC states to cooperate in other power generation and sharing issues.

2 Kharbat, F., *Istihlak Al-Taqa Fi Kitaa' Al-kahrabaa' fi al-Dowal Al-Arabiyah*, (Electricity Consumption in Arab Countries), Paper presented at the 9th Arab Energy Conference, Doha, Qatar, 9–12 May 2010 (in Arabic).

3 See Chapter 7; Dargin, Justin, 'The Gulf Natural Gas Dual Pricing Regime: WTO Rules and Economic Growth in the Gulf', Dubai Initiative Working Paper, August 2010.

4 For an extensive discussion of the subsidy issue see IEA et al. World Bank Joint Report, 'Analysis of the Scope of Energy Subsidies and Suggestions for the G20 Initiative', prepared for submission to the G-20 Summit Meeting, Toronto, 26–27 June 2010 and the Introduction in this book.

5 Razavi, Hossein, 'Natural Gas Pricing in Countries of the Middle East and North Africa', *The Energy Journal*, 2009, Vol 30, No. 3, pp. 1–22

6 Pirani, Simon (ed.) *Russian and CIS Gas Markets and their Impact on Europe*, OUP/OIES, 2009.

7 Khattab, A. K. (2007), 'The Impact of Reducing Energy Subsidies on Energy Intensive Industries in Egypt', ECES Working Paper No. 124, May

8 Gerner, F. and Sinclair, S., 'Connecting Residential Households to Natural Gas', World Bank Global Partnership on Output Based Aid, 2006.

9 Prices for spot cargoes were considerably higher during 2005–2008, in some cases exceeding $20/MMBtu.

10 Algeria, Bahrain, Egypt, Iran, Jordan, Kuwait, Morocco, Oman, Palestinian National Authority, Qatar, Saudi Arabia, Syria, Tunisia and UAE all have observer status to the Charter Conference. Syria and Jordan have signed the Charter while Egypt's signature is pending. http://www.encharter.org/index.

11 For an extensive discussion of the Energy Charter Treaty's transit protocol and its application to natural gas issues, see Yafimava, K. *The Transit Dimension of EU Energy Security: Russian gas transit across Ukraine, Belarus and Moldova,* OUP/OIES, forthcoming 2011, Chapter 9.

BIBLIOGRAPHY

Introduction

BP, 2010, *BP Statistical Review of World Energy 2010*.

Cedigaz, 1999, *Natural Gas in the World 1999*, Cedigaz: Rueil Malmaison.

Cedigaz, 2001, *2001 Natural Gas Year in Review*, Cedigaz' first estimates, Cedigaz: Rueil Malmaison.

Cedigaz, 2009, Armelle Lecarpentier, *Natural Gas in the World 2009*, Cedigaz: Rueil Malmaison.

Cedigaz 2010: *2009 Natural Gas Year in Review*, Cedigaz' first estimates, Cedigaz: Rueil Malmaison.

Clements, B., Hugouneng, R. and Schwartz, G.,1995, 'Government Subsidies: Concepts, International Trends, and Reform Options', IMF Working Paper, September 95/91. Washington DC: International Monetary Fund.

Dargin, J., 2010, 'The Gulf Natural Gas Dual Pricing Regime: WTO Rules and Economic Growth in the Gulf', Dubai Initiative Working Paper, August.

De Moor, A. and Calamai, P., 1997, *Subsidizing Unsustainable Development*. Earth Council and the Institute for Research on Public Expenditure.

Farrel, D., Remes, J. and Charles D., 2008 'Fuelling Sustainable Development: The Energy Productivity Solution', McKinsey Global Institute, October.

International Energy Agency (IEA), 2009, *World Energy Outlook*, OECD: Paris.

World Bank (2008), 'World Bank's GGFR: Middle East Should Join Global Efforts in Reducing Greenhouse Gas Emissions from Gas Flaring' World Bank Website.

Chapter 1: Algeria

African Energy, 22 January 2010.

Aïssaoui, A., 'The Challenges of Diversifying Petroleum-Dependent Economies: Algeria in the Context of the Middle East and North Africa', APICORP Research Economic Commentary, 4 (6), June 2009.

Aïssaoui, A., *Algeria: The Political Economy of Oil and Gas*, (Oxford: Oxford University Press, 2001).

Aïssaoui, A., 'Algerian Gas: Sonatrach's Policies and the Options Ahead', in: R. Mabro and I. Wybrew-Bond (eds) *Gas to Europe: The Strategies of Four Major Suppliers*, (Oxford: Oxford University Press, 1999).

APS Review Gas Market Trends, various issues.

Arab Oil and Gas Directory (AOGD), various issues.

BP Statistical Review of World Energy, various issues.

CREG, 'Programme indicatif d'Approvisionnement du Marché national en

Gaz, 2009–2018', Algiers, 2009.

CREG, 'Programme indicatif des Besoins en Moyen de Production d'Électricité', Algiers, 2008.

Darbouche, H., 'Algeria's Chequered Democracy Experiment', in: M. Emerson and R. Youngs (eds) *Struggling Transitions and Proliferating Dynasties: Democratisation's Trials in the European Neighbourhood*, (Centre for European Policy Studies, Brussels, 2009).

Dillman, B. L., *State and Private Sector in Algeria: The Politics of Rent-Seeking and Failed Development*, (Oxford: Westview Press, 2000).

EC Press Release, No. IP/07/1074, 11 July 2007.

El Kadi, I., 'Le gaz algérien en passe de changer de religion', IFRI Notes, April 2009.

Entelis, J.P., 'Sonatrach: The Political Economy of an Algerian State Institution', *The Middle East Journal*, 53 (1) 1999, pp. 9–27.

Gas Matters, various issues.

Hayes, M.H., 'The Transmed and Maghreb Projects: Gas to Europe from North Africa', in: D.G. Victor et al. (eds) *Natural Gas and Geopolitics: From 1970 to 2040*, (Cambridge: Cambridge University Press, 2006).

International Energy Agency (IEA), (2008) 'World Energy Outlook', OECD/IEA, Paris.

IEA (2009a) 'Natural Gas Market Review 2009', OECD/IEA, Paris.

IEA (2009b) 'World Energy Outlook', OECD/IEA, Paris.

IEA (2009c) 'Energy Balances of Non-Energy Countries', OECD/IEA, Paris.

LNG Focus, 14 October 2007.

Middle East Economic Survey (MEES), various issues.

Observatoire méditerranéen de l'Energie (OME), *Mediterranean Energy Perspectives 2008*, OME, France, 2008.

Oil & Gas Journal, various issues.

Petroleum Economist, various issues.

Razavi, H., 'Natural Gas Pricing in Countries of the Middle East and North Africa', *The Energy Journal*, 30 (3) 2009, pp. 1–22.

World Gas Intelligence (WGI), various issues.

Chapter 2: Libya

Anon, 2005, Reformers Dash for Gas, *Petroleum Economist*, October, 2005 London.

Bencini, R., 2003. 'New Infrastructural Projects to Increase Middle East-North Africa-Europe Energy Trading', Middle East and North Africa Oil and Gas Conference, London.

BP *Statistical Review of World Energy*, 2009.

Hallett, D., *Petroleum Geology Of Libya*, Elsevier Science & Technology, 2002.

IMF Country Report No. 08/301, The Socialist People's Libyan Arab Jamahiriya, September, 2008.

IMF, The Socialist People's Libyan Arab Jamahiriya —2009 Article IV Consultation Preliminary Conclusions of the IMF Mission, 1 June 2009.Kemp.

G. A., and Otman, W, The Petroleum Development Investment Risks and Return in Libya: a Monte Carlo Study of the Current Contractual Terms (EPSA IV), North Sea Occasional Paper, Aberdeen Scotland, April 2004.

Libyan National Oil Corporation (LNOC), Gas Projects Administration, *Annual Reports* 1982, 1983, 1984 and 1985.

Libyan National Oil Corporation (LNOC), Model Exploration and Production Agreement (EPSA-III), 1989.

Libyan National Oil Corporation (LNOC), General Administration of Planning and Information: Management of Cooperation and Foreign Relations Report to the World Bank Regarding the Libyan Petroleum Industry, October 2004.

Libyan National Oil Corporation (LNOC), Model Exploration and Production Agreement (EPSA-IV), 2004.

Libyan National Oil Corporation (LNOC), Libyan Gas Plan Report, February 2005.

Libyan National Oil Corporation (LNOC), Libya: Results of the 4th Exploration Bid Round, EPSA-IV, December 2007.

Libyan National Oil Corporation (LNOC), Oil and Gas Projects Targeted by Five Years Development Plan 2009 to 2013, Libyan National Oil Corporation (LNOC), Department for Exploration, Discovery Report, April 2009.

Libyan National Oil Corporation (LNOC), General Dept. for Exploration and Production, Gas Production Report, May 2009.

Libyan National Oil Corporation (LNOC), General Dept. for Exploration and Production, Apprising Onshore Gas Discoveries located West of Libya region, July 2009.

Malecek, S.J., A Legal Framework for Gas Development: How can Host Governments Strike a Balance between Investment and Competition? OGEL, January 2002.

OAPEC, Organization of Arab Petroleum Exporting Countries, 2001 and 2009 *Statistical Reports*.

OPEC, Organization of Petroleum Exporting Countries, *Annual Statistical Bulletin* 2008, 2009.

Otman, W.A., Legal and Economic Considerations of the Re-entry of US Oil Companies to their Assets in Libya, Transnational Dispute Management (TDM), Volume 2, issue No. 05, November 2005.

Otman W.A., *Libya Oil and Gas Resources, Dar Al Rwad, Tripoli, Libya* (Book in English version), March 2008.

Otman, W.A., and Bunter, M.A., *The Libyan Petroleum Industry in the Twenty First Century: the Upstream, Midstream and Downstream Handbook*.

OGEL/Maris, 2005.

Otman, W.A., and Bin-Dehaish, H., Unrealised Potential in the Saudi Gas Industry: Fiscal and Economic Considerations. OGEL, lJune 2006. *Petroleum Economist*, October, 2005.

Townsend, D., 'The Trillions Keep Coming', *The Petroleum Economist*, March, 2003.

Van Meurs, P., *World Fiscal Systems for Gas*, Van Meurs & Associates Limited for Barrows, New York, 1997.

World Travel & Tourism Council (WTTC), 2009. Libya Travel and Tourism. Available from: http://www.wttc.org/bin/pdf/original_pdf_file/libya.pdf Accesssed 5th December 2009.

Chapter 3: North African Transit Countries

Achy, L. Fiscal Adjustment in Non-oil Producing MENA Countries: Painful but Healthy! Carnegie Endowment for International Peace. Available from: http://www.carnegieendowment.org/publications/index.cfm?fa=view&id=23976. Accessed 10th May, 2010.

Aïssaoui, A. (1999) 'Morocco to Introduce Natural Gas in its Energy Market by 2002', *Middle East Economic Survey*, 42 (37), 13 September.

Aïssaoui, A., *Algeria: The Political Economy of Oil and Gas*, Oxford: Oxford University Press, 2001.

Arab Oil and Gas Directory (AOGD), 2008.

Arab Oil and Gas Directory (AOGD), 2009.

Bank Al-Maghrib (2009), Rapport annuel, exercice 2008, Rabat.

Ben Hassine, J., 2009, Evolution de l'Activité Production et Principaux Développements, Conference of the Petroleum and Gas Sector in Tunisia; 20th Anniversary of the Tunisian Association of Petrol and Gas (ATPG) June 24, 2009.

Bergaoui, F., 2009, Tunisia: Evolution de l'Offre et de la Demande du Gaz Naturel en Tunisie, Conference of the Petroleum and Gas Sector in Tunisia; 20th Anniversary of the Tunisian Association of Petrol and Gas (ATPG) June 24.

BG Group, 2009. Available from: http://www.bg-group.com/OurBusiness/WhereWeOperate/Pages/pgTunisia.aspx#miskar. Accessed 5th September, 2009.

British Petroleum, 2009. *Statistical Review of World Energy*. Available from: http://www.bp.com/productlanding.do?categoryId=6929&contentId=7044622. Accessed 5th September, 2009.

Elfetouaki, O., 2003, 'Le Gazoduc Maghreb-Europe: Une Aubaine pour le Maroc', *L'Economiste*, 14 January.

Entreprise Tunisienne d'Activités Pétrolières (ETAP), 2009, ETAP web page, www.etap.com.tn/

Hayes, M.H., 'The Transmed and Maghreb Projects: Gas to Europe from North Africa', in D.G. Victor et al. (eds) *Natural Gas and Geopolitics: From 1970 to 2040*, Cambridge: Cambridge University Press, 2006.

IMF, 2009, Tunisia: 2009 Article IV Consultation—Staff Report; and Public Information Notice.

Mard, R., 2009, Evolution de l'Exploration petrolière en Tunisie et principales Découvertes. Conference of the Petroleum and Gas Sector in Tunisia; 20th Anniversary of the Tunisian Association of Petrol and Gas (ATPG) June 24.

MEED, 2003. Tunisia: Impact of the 1999 Hydrocarbon Law, Vol. XLVI No 2 13 January.

Middle East Economic Survey (MEES), 1977, 27 June and 31 October.

Moroccan Ministry of Energy and Mines (2008), Secteur de l'Energie et des Mines, principales Réalisations (1999–2008): Défis et Perspectives, Rabat.

Moroccan Ministry of Energy and Mines (2009), Energie et Mines: Des Chantiers en Marche, Rabat.

Petroleum Intelligence Weekly (PIW), 1977, 31 October.

Société Tunisienne de l'Electricité et du Gaz (STEG), 2007, Natural Gas Statistics, Gas Production and Transport Department, Tunis.

Tunisia, National Agency for Renewable Energy, Centre of information on sustainable energy and the environment (CIEDE), Tunis, 2004.

Tunisia, National Statistics Institute, 2007. Ministry of Development and International Cooperation.

Tunisia, 2006. National Summary of Energy in Tunisia.

Tunisia, Ministry of Industry, 2005. Tunisian Review of Energy.

UNDP/World Bank (2003) 'Cross-border oil and gas pipelines: Problems and prospects', Washington.

Wood Mackenzie (2009), *Morocco Country Overview*, December.

World Economic Forum, 2009. The Global Competitiveness Report, 2009–2010. Available from: http://www.weforum.org/en/initiatives/gcp/Global percent-20Competitiveness percent20Report/index.htm. Accessed 14th September, 2009.

Zoubir, Y.H. (2000) 'Algerian-Moroccan Relations and their Impact on Maghribi Integration', *The Journal of North African Studies*, 5 (3), pp. 43–47.

Chapter 4: Egypt

African Energy, various issues.

Alami, R. (2006) 'Egypt's Domestic Natural Gas Industry', Working Paper No. NG12, Oxford Institute for Energy Studies, Oxford.

Arab Oil & Gas Directory (AOGD), 1998, 2005, 2009 issues.

Arab Republic of Egypt, 2006. *The Country Paper for the Arab Republic of Egypt.* 8th Arab Energy Conference, Amman, Jordan May 14–17 (in Arabic).

BP Statistical Review of World Energy, various issues.

Eberhard, A. and Gratwick, K. (2005) 'The Egyptian IPP Experience', Working Paper No. 50, Center for Environmental Science and Policy, Stanford University.

EGAS Annual Report 2007–08, available at: http://www.egas.com.eg/docs/pdf/EN_mid.pdf (accessed 3/05/10).

EEHC Annual Report 2008-09, available at: http://www.moee.gov.eg/Arabic/fr-main.htm (accessed 3/05/10).

Egypt Ministry of Finance (2010) 'Financial Statement on the State's Draft General Budget for the Fiscal Year 2010–11, Cairo.

Gerner, Franz and Scott Sinclair. *Arab Republic of Egypt: Connecting Residential Households to Natural Gas. An Economic and Financial Analysis.* OBA working paper No 7, World Bank, Washington DC.

International Gas Report (IGR), various issues

Mabro, R. (1998) 'The Pricing of Natural Gas: A Discussion of Pricing Policy in Egypt', ECES working paper No 26, Cairo.

Middle East Economic Survey (MEES), various issues.

The Oil & Gas Journal, various issues.

Wood Mackenzie (2009), *Egypt Country Overview*, December, Edinburgh.

World Bank (2009) 'Project Appraisal Document on a Proposed Loan in the Amount of $600 million to the Arab Republic of Egypt for an Ain Sokhna Power Project', Washington DC.

World Gas Intelligence (WGI), various issues.

Chapter 5: The Mashreq, Israel and the Palestian Territories

Aji, Albert, 'Syrian Oil minister: Egypt will begin exporting natural gas to Syria next month', Associated Press, 23 February 2008.

Alali, Jamal, 'Jordan oil shale, availability, distribution, and investment opportunity', presented to the International Conference on Oil Shale, 'Recent Trends in Oil Shale', 7–9 November 2006, available online at http://www.sdnp.jo/International_Oil_Conference/rtos-A117.pdf, accessed 19 August 2009.

al Khayat, Faleh, 'Syria seen as future corridor for Arab gas; Looks to be link to European market', *Platts Oilgram News*, 24 June 2008.

Alexander's Gas & Oil Connections, 'Company News, Middle East: Noble Energy starts natural gas production offshore Israel', vol. 9 no. 1, 15 January 2004

APS Review Downstream Trends, 'Syria – The Syrian Decision Makers – Ahmad Al-Mu'alla', Vol. 70 No. 13, 24 March 2008.

APS Review Gas Market Trends, 'Syria – The Gas Sector', 3 March 2008.

APS Review Gas Market Trends, 'Syria – The gas development background', Vol. 70 No. 11, 10 March 2008.

APS Review Gas Market Trends, 'Syria – The Offshore Prospects', 8 March 2010.

APS Review Oil Market Trends, 'Syria – SPC Fields', vol. 70 no. 11, 10 March 2008.

APS Review Oil Market Trends 'Lebanon to have floating LNG plant', 6 November 2006.

Associated Press, 'Egypt begins pumping natural gas into Syria as part of giant pipeline project', 10 July 2008.

Bahgat, G., 'Energy Partnership: Israel and the Persian Gulf', *Energy Policy*, vol. 33 (2005), p. 676.

Baron, Lior, 'IEC to pay 40% more under new gas deal', globes-online.com, 9 November 2009.

BBC News Online, 'Hamas takes full control of Gaza', 15 June 2007, available online at http://news.bbc.co.uk/2/hi/middle_east/6755299.stm, accessed 31 July 2009.

BBC Monitoring Middle East, 'Report on Syria's efforts to increase oil, gas production', [Report by Waad al-Jarf: 'Syria's location ideal for export of gas and oil products to Europe', Syria Times website], 6 May 2008.

BMI Industry Insights – Oil & Gas, Middle East & Africa, 'Contract News

– Stroytransgaz Strikes Another Syria Deal', 15 October 2008.

BG Group, 'Gas discovery offshore Israel', Press Release, 1 November 2009, available online at http://www.bg-group.com/MediaCentre/PressArchive/1999/Pages/pr-087.aspx, accessed 25 August 2009.

BG Group, 'Israel and areas of Palestinian Authority', available online at http://www.bg-group.com/OurBusiness/WhereWeOperate/Pages/pgIsraelandAreasofPalestinianAuthority.aspx, accessed 26 August 2009.

BP *Statistical Review of World Energy* 2009.

BP Group, 'The Gaza Marine Project' (no longer publicly available), October 2007.

Carlisle, Tamsin, 'Jordan signs oil shale agreements', *The National*, 17 May 2009.

Cedigaz, *Natural Gas in the World 2009*.

CIA World Factbook – Syria. Available online at https://www.cia.gov/library/publications/the-world-factbook/geos/SY.html. Accessed 20 July 2009.

CIA World Factbook, Lebanon, available online at https://www.cia.gov/library/publications/the-world-factbook/geos/le.html, accessed 17 August 2009.

CIA World Factbook – Israel, available online at https://www.cia.gov/library/publications/the-world-factbook/geos/is.html, accessed 1 March 2010.

CIA World Factbook – Jordan, available online at https://www.cia.gov/library/publications/the-world-factbook/geos/jo.html, accessed 1 March 2010.

China View, 'Natural gas reserve in north Israel proven larger', 11 August 2009, available online at http://news.xinhuanet.com/english/2009-08/11/content_11865506.htm, accessed 17 August 2009.

Daily Star (Lebanon), 'Siniora: Lebanon needs more power plants to meet demand; State-owned utility lost whopping $1.2 billion in 2007', Staff Writer, 6 February 2008.

Daily Star, 'Lebanon receives Egypt gas to run Deir Ammar (Beddawi) plant', 20 October 2009.

DualEx Energy International Inc., 'Operations', available online at http://www.dualexen.com/operations/overview.html, accessed 12 August 2009.

Economist Intelligence Unit – ViewsWire, 'Egypt: Energy provision', 3 October 2008.

Economist Intelligence Unit (EIU), 'Palestinian Territories: Country Profile – Main report' 1 December 2008.

EIU, Jordan Country Brief, March 2009.

EIU, Syria Country Report, April 2009.

Egyptian Natural Gas Holding Company (EGAS), 'Achieved Projects – Arab Gas Pipeline', available online at http://www.egas.com.eg/Business_Opportunities/Arab_Gas.aspx, accessed 14 August 2009.

Energy Economist, 'Arab Gas Pipeline link proposed for Europe', issue 324, 1 October 2008.

Energy Information Administration (EIA), 'Country Brief – Syria', available online at www.eia.doe.gov, accessed 17 July 2008.

EIA Country Report, Jordan, available online at www.eia.doe.gov, accessed 3 March 2009.

EIA Country Analysis Brief – Syria, June 2009, available online at http://

www.eia.doe.gov/cabs/Syria/Background.html, accessed 25 August 2009.

EIA Energy Profile – Lebanon, available online at http://www.eia.doe.gov/country/country_energy_data.cfm?fips=LE, accessed 3 March 2009.

EIA, Country Reports – Israel, available online at www.eia.doe.gov

EIA, Natural Gas Weekly Update, 5 August 2009, available online at http://tonto.eia.doe.gov/oog/info/ngw/ngupdate.asp, accessed 12 August 2009.

EU Energy, 'EU energy chief sees 7 Bcm/year gas imports from Iraq, Egypt', Vol. 3 No. 183, 16 May 2008.

England, Andrew, 'Syria frets over drought's harsh harvest', *Financial Times*, 4 February 2010.

Ferzinger, Jonathan, 'BG Gaza gas deal may take months, Israel says', *Jerusalem Post*, 21 July 2007.

Ford, Neil, 'Damascus seeks to turn the tide of dwindling oil revenues', *The Middle East*, 1 March 2008.

Gavin, James, 'Syria comes out of the shadows', *Petroleum Economist*, August 2009, p. 40.

Globes-McClatchy-Tribune Information Services, 'Canada's Bontan announces two more huge Israeli gas fields: Gas at the Mira and Sarah offshore prospects, adjacent to the Tamar field, could be worth up to $7.54 billion', 2 February 2010.

Globes-McClatchy-Tribune Information Service via COMTEX, 'Gov't wants more gas from Tamar: Natural Gas Authority: We are interested in the Tamar prospect supplying added-value to the Israeli economy.' 24 November 2009.

Gulf Oil and Gas, 'Arab Gas Pipeline Agreement', 26 January 2004, available online at http://www.gulfoilandgas.com/webpro1/MAIN/Mainnews.asp?id=357.

Gulf Oil and Gas, 'Noble Energy Inc. announces startup of natural gas production from Mari-B field offshore Israel', 24 December 2003, available online at http://www.gulfoilandgas.com/webpro1/MAIN/Mainnews.asp?id=249, accessed 25 August 2009.

Gulfnews.com, 'Greek-Italian venture wins Syria deal', 8 September 2008, available online at http://www.gulfnews.com/business/Oil_and_Gas/10243579.html, accessed 26 August 2009.

Habib, Osama, 'Lebanon again plagued by power rationing amid tourist influx', *Daily Star*, 3 July 2009.

Halawi, Dana, 'Diversity key to managing fuel price swings', *Daily Star*, 26 March 2009.

Hamarneh, Yousef, 'Oil Shale Resources Development in Jordan', Natural Resources Authority of Jordan, 1998, updated November 2006, available online at http://www.nra.gov.jo/images/stories/pdf_files/Updated_Report_2006.pdf, accessed 19 August 2009.

Harif, Tal Barak and Susan Lerner, 'Israel sees energy independence in natural gas offshore fields', Bloomberg.com, 5 March 2009, accessed 5 March 2009.

Hunter, Catherine, 'Petro-Canada Prioritises Syria's Ebla Gas Project; Abu Rabah Gas Onstream', *Global Insight Daily Analysis*, 7 January 2009.

INA, Annual Report 2008, available online at http://www.ina.hr/default. aspx?id=275, accessed 12 August 2009.

International Gas Report, 'Total signs Syrian oil, gas deals', 8 September 2008.

International Oil Daily, 'Stroitransgas Plans Syria Gas Output Boost', 6 February 2009.

Jaber, J.O., A. Al-Sarkhi, B.A. Akash and M.S. Mohsen, 'Medium-range planning economics of future electrical-power generational options', *Energy Policy*, vol. 32 (2004), pp. 357–66.

KUFPEC, 'Syria', available online at http://www.kufpec.com/KUFPEC/en-US/Operations/MiddleEast/Syria/, accessed 12 August 2009.

McGeough, Paul, *Kill Khalid*, The New Press: London, 2009, p. 424.

Middle East Economic Digest, 'Al-Furat Petroleum Company: Arresting the decline', 25 August 2006, available online at http://www.meed.com/news/2006/08/alfurat_petroleum_company_arresting_the_decline.html, accessed 11 August 2009.

Middle East Economic Survey, 'Egypt raises gas supplies to Israel after reaching new price agreement', vol. LII no. 25, 22 June 2009.

Middle East North Africa Financial Network (MENAFN), 'Syria begins importing Egyptian gas', 12 July 2008.

Naff, Andrew, 'Turkey, Israel agree to move ahead with Med pipeline; Gazprom near supply deal with Israel', Global Insight Daily Analysis, 18 July 2008.

New York Times, 'Egypt and Israel sign 15-year natural gas deal', 1 July 2005.

Noble Energy, http://www.nobleenergyinc.com/fw/main/Israel-128.html, accessed 31 July 2009.

Noble Energy, 'Operations: Israel', available online at http://www.nobleenergyinc.com/fw/main/Israel-128.html, accessed 25 August 2009.

Official Journal of the European Union, 'Council Common Position 2009/7/CFSP', 27 January 2009, available online at http://eur-lex.europa.eu/LexUriServ/LexUriServ.do?uri=OJ:L:2009:023:0037:0042:EN:PDF, accessed 31 July 2009.

The Oil Daily, 'Jordan views oil shale as key to greater energy self-sufficiency', 23 March 2009.

Petroleum Economist 'Israel tenders to bring LNG to east Mediterranean', August 2009.

PRNewswire, 'Noble Energy executes letter of intent for natural gas from Tamar', 15 December 2009, available online at http://investors.nobleenergyinc.com/releasedetail.cfm?ReleaseID=430192, accessed 15 February 2010.

Raphaeli, N. and Gersten, B., 'The Iran-Syria Alliance: The Economic Dimension', *The Middle East Review of International Affairs*, vol. 12 no. 2, June 2008.

Reuters, 'S. Korea takes lead for Jordan nuclear plant deal – report', 11 March 2009, available online at http://www.reuters.com/article/idUS-SEO29770720090311, accessed 1 March 2010.

Reuters, 'CORRECTED – Iraq receives one bid for Akkas gas field', 30 June 2009, available online at www.reuters.com, accessed 14 August 2009.

Reuters, 'Iraq PM challenges Syria to explain militant aid', 30 September 2009, available online at http://uk.reuters.com/article/idUKANS349705, accessed 14 February 2010.

Sovich, Nina, 'Syria's drying wells have key role in oiling reforms', *Alexander's Oil and Gas Connections*, vol. 10 no. 20, 26 October 2005.

Stratic Energy Corporation, 'Operations – Syria', available online at http://www.straticenergy.com/operations/syria.html, accessed 12 August 2009.

Stroytransgaz, 'Arab Gas Pipeline, Phase 1', available online at http://www.stroytransgaz.com/projects/syria/arab-gas-pipeline, accessed 11 August 2009.

Stroytransgaz, 'North and South Middle Area Gas Exploitation Project', http://www.stroytransgaz.com/projects/syria/gas-processing-plant-2, 11 September 2009, accessed 17 May 2010.

Suncor Energy, 'International and Offshore', http://www.suncor.com/en/about/919.aspx, accessed 5 February 2010.

Syria Report, 'Syrian government restructures oil sector', 2 March 2009.

Total, 'Syria: Start-up of the Deir Ez Zor gas project', available online at http://www.total.com/en/finance/fi_press_releases/fpr_2002/030128_Syria_Deir_Ez_Zor_gas_project_1265.htm, accessed 12 August 2009.

United States Department of State,'Chapter 6. Terrorist Organizations', 30 April 2009, available online at http://www.state.gov/s/ct/rls/crt/2008/122449.htm, accessed 31 July 2009.

United States Geological Service, 'Assessment of Undiscovered Oil and Gas Resources of the Levant Basin Province, Eastern Mediterranean', March 2010.

United Kingdom Home Office, 'Proscribed terrorist groups', available online at http://security.homeoffice.gov.uk/legislation/current-legislation/terrorism-act-2000/proscribed-groups, accessed 31 July 2009.

Watkins, Eric, 'Egypt struggles to meet demand growth for natural gas', Oil and Gas Journal, 4 October 2008.

Watkins, Eric, 'Noble Energy to sell gas to Israel Electric', *Oil and Gas Journal*, 29 December 2009.

World Gas Intelligence, 'Egyptian, Iraqi gas maneuvers', 24 September 2008.

World Gas Intelligence, 'Syria eyeing its gas hub potential', 13 January 2010.

Xinhua, 'Jordan may build its first nuclear power plant at Aqaba', available online at http://news.xinhuanet.com/english/2008-12/22/content_10542636.htm, accessed 19 August 2009.

Chapter 6: Saudi Arabia

Aghdam, R.F., 'Why Invest in the Eastern Province', *ASharqia Chamber, 2008*.

Aïssaoui, A., 'The Likely Impact of Saudi Arabia's Accession to the WTO on the Saudi Petrochemical Industry', APICORP memo, 2004/05.

Alawaji, S.H., 'Evaluation of solar energy research and its applications in Saudi Arabia — 20 years of experience', *Renewable and Sustainable Energy Reviews* 5 (2001) 59–77.

Al-Falih, K.A., 'Saudi Arabia's Gas Sector: its role and growth opportunities',

Oil & Gas Journal, 21 June 2004.

Al-Falih, K., 'Saudi Aramco's Role in Industrial Development', *Middle East Economic Survey*, 52:16, 20 April. 2009.

Al Hayat, Interview with Khaled Al-Falih, 28 July 2009 (in Arabic).

Al-Qaradawi, I., 'Setting up Nuclear Programmes in the Arabic Peninsula', Presentation at the World Nuclear University, Summer Institute, 2009.

Al-Sa'doun, A. 'Saudi Arabia to become major Petrochemicals hub by 2010', *Oil and Gas Journal*, 2 January 2006.

Al-Salamah, M., 'On the Natural Gas Production, Transportation and Consumption in Saudi Arabia: A 2000 Perspective', King Fahd University of Petroleum and Minerals, 2003.

Arab Petroleum Research Center, *Arab Oil & Gas Directory 2009* (Paris: APRC, 2009).

BP *Statistical Review of World Energy*, June 2010.

CBS News, 'Saudi Arabia positioned to become solar power', 29 August 2008.

England, A., 'Middle East: Oil Rich Region Faces Gas Shortfall', *Financial Times*, 26 May 2009.

EIA, Saudi Arabia. *Country Analysis Briefs*, August 2008, retrieved online at http://www.eia.doe.gov/emeu/cabs/Saudi_Arabia/NaturalGas.html (October 2009).

Gas Matters, 'Is it Crunch Time for Saudi Arabia's Gas Development Programme?' April 2009.

Hart, W., R.Gist, K. Otto, 'Global LPG Market Begin Recovery from Recession', *Oil & Gas Journal*, 7 June 2010.

Hotelling, H., 'The Economics of Exhaustible Resources', *The Journal of Political Economy*, Vol. 39, 1931.

Husain, A.M., Tazhibayeva, K., and Ter-Martirosyan, A., 'Fiscal Policy and Economic Cycles in Oil-Exporting Countries', *IMF Working Paper* WP/08/253, 2008.

Husain, S., 'Saudi Arabia may go it alone on nuclear energy', *Maktoub*, 7 November 2009.

IEA, *World Energy Outlook. Middle East and North Africa Insight*, 2005.

IHS Global Insight, 'Associated Gas Demand No Longer Obstacle to Lower Crude Production—Saudi Oil Minister', 20 March 2009.

Luciani, G, 'Domestic Pricing of Energy and Industrial Competitiveness', Al Jisr Research Paper, October 2009.

Mabro, R., 'Saudi Arabia's Natural Gas: A Glimpse at Complex Issues', *Oxford Energy Comment*, October 2002.

Middle East Economic Survey (MEES), 'SKAK's Kidan-6 Well Fails To Find Gas At Khuff Target', 52:16, 20 April 2009.

MEES, 'Saudi Aramco Looks to Gulf Offshore for Gas Boost', 9 March 2009.

Mukhtar, A., 'Saudi Arabia: Water & Waste Water in Saudi Arabia', US Commercial Service, United States of America, Department of Commerce, 2007.

O&G Next Generation, 'A New Chapter', Issue 4, retrieved online at http://www. ngoilgasmena.com/article/A-new-chapter/ (October 2009).

OAPEC, The Sixth Arab Energy Conference. Country Papers, Part 1. Cairo,

Arab Republic of Egypt, 11–14 May 2002 (in Arabic).

OAPEC, The Seventh Arab Energy Conference. Energy Basics in the Kingdom of Saudi Arabia. Amman, Kingdom of Jordan, 14–17 May 2006 (in Arabic).

Ramady, M.A., 'Saudi Petrochemical Industry: The Heart of Investment', *Arab News*, 16 July 2007.

Reuters, 'Saudi Arabia Scraps Wheat Growing to Save Water', 8 January 2008.

Reuters, 'Saudi Burns more Crude for Power, Halts Fuel Oil Import", 27 July 2009.

Reuters, 'Saudi King says keeping some oil finds for future', 13 April 2008.

Salamah, M., 'Sulfur Utilization Prospects in Saudi Arabia', Paper presented at the 2004 IFA Production and International Conference, 3–5 October 2004, Dubai UAE.

Samba, 'Saudi Petrochemicals Sector: Current Situation and Future Prospects,' August 2009.

Saudi Aramco, *Annual Report* 2007.

Saudi Aramco, *Annual Review* 2009.

Saudi Arabian Monetary Agency (SAMA), *45th Annual Report*, 2009.

Saudi Arabia, Kingdom of, *Eighth Development Plan* 2005–2009, Ministry of Economy and Planning.

Seznec, Jean-François, 'Saudi Arabia's Accession to the WTO: Is a "Revolution" Brewing?' *Middle East Policy Council Capitol Hill Conference Series on US Middle East Policy*, Washington D.C., 13 January 2006.

Simmons, M., *Twilight in the Desert: The Coming Saudi Oil Shock and the World Economy* (Hoboken, New Jersey: John Wiley & Sons, 2005).

World Bank, 'A Water Sector Assessment Report on the Countries of the Corporation Council of Arab States of the Gulf' Water, Environment, Social and Rural Development Department Middle East and North Africa Region, Washington, 2005.

WTO Press Release, 'WTO Secretariat reports increase in new anti-dumping investigations', 7 May 2009.

Zawya.com, 'Saudi Arabia's Diversification Plans Take Shape as Ma'aden Receives Financing', 17 June 2009.

Chapter 7: Iraq

Al-Amir, F., 'Mulahazat hawl "Al-ittifakiya al-ulya" bayna Wizarat al-naft wa sharika Shell li-mashrua' ghaz al-janub.' *Al Ghad*, 23 Dec. 2008, available at: http://www.al-ghad.org/2008/12/23/notes-on-the-draft-agreement-between-shell-and-the-iraqi-oil-ministry/ accessed 15 July 2009.

Al-Khatib, L.J., 'Securing Iraq Gas Investment for Power and Industries', paper presented at the *Symposium for Reviewing Iraq Oil Policy* 28/2/2009, available at http://www.iraqenergy.org, accessed on 4 June 2009.

Al-Shalchi, W., *Development of Akkas Gas Field in Iraq*, Amman, available at http://www.scribd.com/doc/6435129/Development-of-Akkas-Gas-Field-in-Iraq, accessed on 25 June 2009.

Al-Shalchi, W., *Development of Mansuriya Gas Field in Iraq*, Amman, available at http://www.scribd.com/doc/8257649/Development-of-Mansuriya-Gas-Field-Iraq, accessed on 20 June 2009.

Associated Press, 'Full Text of Iraqi Constitution', *The Washington Post*, 12 October 2005, available at http://www.washingtonpost.com/wp-dyn/content/article/2005/10/12/AR2005101201450.html, accessed on 29 June 2009.

Bindemann, K., *Production Sharing Agreements: an Economic Analysis*, Working Paper WPM25, (Oxford: Oxford Institute for Energy Studies, 1999).

Business Monitor International (BMI) *Iraq Oil & Gas Report* Q1 2009.

CEDIGAZ (various years), 'Trends and Figures', *Natural Year in Review*, Paris.

Cocks, T., 'Iraq lawmaker says Shell deal lacks transparency'. *Reuters*, 8 Nov. 2008, available at: http://uk.reuters.com/article/idUKL855878520081108 accessed 12 July 2009.

Crescent Petroleum, 'Crescent in Iraq', 2009, available at http://www.crescent.ae/html/crescent_iraq.html accessed on 3 August 2009.

Energy Information Administration (EIA), *Iraq, Country Brief*, 2009, U.S. Dept. of Energy, available at http://www.eia.doe.gov/cabs/Iraq/NaturalGas.html and http://www.eia.doe.gov/cabs/Iraq/Profile.html , accessed on 13 May 2009.

Flower, A., 'Natural Gas from the Middle East', in Jonathan Stern (ed.) *Natural Gas in Asia. The Challenges of Growth in China, India, Japan and Korea*, 2nd Edition, (Oxford, Oxford University Press, 2008).

Gerner, F., Svensson, B. & Djumena, S., 'Gas Flaring and Venting', *Public Policy for the Private Sector*, World Bank, No. 279, October 2004.

Ghadhban, T. & Al-Fathi, S., 'The gas dimension of the Iraq oil industry', *OPEC Review*, March 2001.

Gulfoilandgas.com, 'MOL and OMV join Dana Gas and Crescent in Iraq', Gulf Oil and Gas, 17 May 2009, available at http://www.gulfoilandgas.com/webpro1/MAIN/Mainnews.asp?id=7938, accessed on 8 June 2009.

International Energy Agency (IEA), Statistics by Country/Region, 2009 available at http://www.iea.org/Textbase/stats/index.asp, accessed on 25 June 2009.

Iraq Oil Commission, T. Ghadhban (Chairman), 'Iraq Oil Industry. Present Status and Future Outlook', Paper presented at *Iraq Oil, Gas and Petrochemical and Electricity Summit*, Dubai, 2nd to 4th September, 2007.

Iraq Oil Report (IOR), Samuel Ciszuk, 'Iraq gas for Nabucco a tough deal', 19 May 2009, available at http://www.iraqoilreport.com/the-biz/iraq-gas-for-nabucco-a-tough-deal, accessed on 4 June 2009.

Jiyad, A.M., Preliminary assessment of the GSDPC, June 2009, available at http://www.iraq-enterprise.com/rep/jiyad62009.htm accessed on 25 July 2009.

Jiyad, A.M., Iraq-Shell Gas Deal: Who occupies the driver's seat?, April 2009, available at http://www.iraqog.com/arabresults3.cfm?keywords=ahmed%20Jiyad accessed on 25 June 2009.

Johnston, D., *International Petroleum Fiscal Regimes and Production Sharing Contracts*, (Tulsa: Penwell Books, 1994).

Kurdistan Regional Government (KRG), Statement from Minister of Natural

Resources, Kurdistan Regional Government – Iraq, 27 April 2007, available at www.krg.org/pdf/MNR_Statement_20070427.pdf , accessed on 25 June 2009.

Kurdistan Regional Government (KRG), Presidency of the Region, Oil and Gas Law of the Kurdistan Region – Iraq, Law no.22. 2007, available at http://www.krg.org/articles/detail.asp?rnr=107&lngnr=12&smap=04030000&anr accessed on 25 June 2009.

Middle East Economic Survey, (MEES) 'Nabucco partners turn to Kurdistan region for gas supply; Baghdad says no', Vol.52, No.21, May 2009.

Iraq Ministry of Oil (MOO), Wizarat al-naft al-'Iraqi (Iraq Ministry of Oil), *Waqi' wa mustaqbal istighlal al-ghaz al-tabi'i janub wa shamal al-'Iraq li al-agrad al-sina'iyyya*, Paper presented at *Iraq Oil, Gas and Petrochemical and Electricity Summit*, Dubai, 2nd to 4th September 2007.

MOO,, Heads of Agreement, 2008, available at http://www.al-ghad.org/2008/11/22/shell-iraq-oil-agreement/ accessed on 25 June 2009.

MOO, Dr Husayn Shahristani, *Ittifaq mabda'i hawl istighlal al-ghaz fi mintaqa al-busara*, 4 Sepember 2008, available at http://www.al-ghad.org/2008/11/22/shell-iraq-oil-agreement/ accessed on 25 June 2009.

MOU Iraq–EU, *Memorandum of Understanding between the Government of Iraq and the European Union on Strategic Partnership in Energy*, 2010, signed by Andris Piebalgs, European Commissioner for Energy and Hussain Ibrahim Saleh al-Shahristani, Minister of Oil, January.

North Oil Company 2009, available at http://www.noc.gov.iq/english_ver/homepage_en.htm accessed on 25 June 2009.

Oil and Gas Journal (OGJ), 'Oil reconstruction in Iraq: progress and challenges', 19 December 2009.

Oil and Gas Journal (OGJ), 'Worldwide gas processing', 22 June 2009.

Organization of Petroleum Exporting Countries (OPEC), *Annual Statistical Bulletin*, (2007 and earlier editions) available at http://www.opec.org/library/ accessed on 8 May 2009.

Peebles, M.W.H., *Natural Gas Fundamentals*, (London: Shell International Gas Ltd, 1992).

Petroleum Economist, 'Iraq seeks investment to develop its untapped gas potential', Energy Report, 12 May 2009.

Rasavi, H., 'Natural Gas Pricing in Countries of the Middle East & North Africa', *Energy Journal*, Vol.30, No.3, 2009.

Rutledge, I., *Addicted to Oil: America's Relentless Drive for Energy Security*, (London: I.B. Tauris, 2005).

SERIS, *Natural Gas Companies Worldwide Vol.6*, (Sheffield: Sheffield Energy & Resources Information Services, 2001).

South Oil Company 2007, available at http://www.socbasrah-iq.com/index.htm accessed on 25 June 2009.

Strauss, Delphine and Crooks, Ed, 'Iraq offers to supply half of Nabucco's gas'. *Financial Times*, 14 July 2009.

Van Meurs, P., 'Comparative analysis of Ministry of Oil and Kurdistan fiscal terms as applied to the Kurdistan Region', *Oil Gas and Energy Law (OGEL)*

No.3, 2008, University of Dundee.

Williams, P., 'Shell seeks to fast-track gas exports from Iraq'. *MEED* 16 Nov. 2008, available at: http://www.meed.com/news/2008/11/shell_seeks_to_ fasttrack_gas_exports_from_iraq.html accessed 15 July 2009.

Zainy, M.A., Istighlal al-ghaz al-'Iraqi mahaliya ajda min tasdirho, *Dar Babel*, 2 Nov. 2008, available at: http://www.darbabl.net/show_derasat.php?id=25 accessed 14 July 2009.

Zawya, 'Shahristani on Shell's Iraqi Gas Deal', 2009, available at: http://www. zawya.com/Story.cfm/sidv52n14-1TS01/Shahristani%20On%20Shell%20 s%20Iraqi%20Gas%20Deal/ accessed 15 July 2009.

Chapter 8: Iran

Argus Global LNG, various issues.

BBC Monitoring Middle East, 12 July 2009.

Bowden, J., 'Azerbaijan: from gas importer to exporter', in Simon Pirani, (ed.) *Russian and CIS Gas Markets and Their Impact on Europe*, OUP, 2009.

BP *Statistical Review of World Energy*, 2010.

Cedigaz News Report, 7 January 2005.

Dizaji, B.E. 'Exploration of New Oil and Gas Fields in Iran, University of Tehran, 2008.

Dow Jones International News, 4 January 2008.

Energy Economist, 1 January 2008.

EU Energy, 22 February 2008.

Fars News Agency, 23 March 2008.

Financial Times, 20 July 2010.

Global Insight Daily Analysis, various issues.

International Gas Report various issues.

Iran's Hydrocarbon Balance 2008, Institute for International Studies, Iran, 2009.

Kinnander, E., *The Turkish–Iranian Gas Relationship: politically successful, commercially problematic*, OIES, January 2010.

OPEC, *Annual Statistical Bulletin*, 2004–2008.

OPECNA Bulletin, 20 April 2001.

Oil and Gas Journal, various issues.

Pars Oil and Gas Company (POGC) website.

Petroleum Intelligence Weekly, various issues.

Petroleum Review, 29 January 2010.

Platts Oilgram News, various issues.

Reuters, various dates.

Shana News Iran website.

Stern, J., *The Future of Russian Gas and Gazprom*, OUP, 2005.

Tehran Times, 16 September 2008.

Washington Times, 6 July 2009.

World Gas Intelligence various issues.

Yeghiazaryan, A., 'Natural Gas Markets in Armenia', in Simon Pirani, (ed.)

Russian and CIS Gas Markets and Their Impact on Europe, OUP, 2009.

Chapter 9: Qatar

Alexander's Gas and Oil Connections, 'Mobil Partner in Dolphin Gas Venture,' Vol. 4, No. 15 (9 Aug.1999).

Alexander's Gas and Oil Connection, 'Qatar's Gas Sector Doubles in Size', Vol. 14, issue #10 (Aug. 7. 2009).

al-Kaabi, Saad, Presentation at the 2009 International Petroleum Technology Conference, 'World Energy Challenges Endurance and Commitment' (Dec. 7, 2009).

Al Sabah (English), 'Emir Sheikh Al-Thani: We Want a Pipeline From Qatar to Turkey', (August 18, 2009).

Al-Serkal, Mariam, 'Thousands Suffer in Three-Day Blackout', *Gulf News* (August 20, 2009).

AME Info, 'Prices Rocket for Qatar's GTL Projects', (Mar. 15, 2007).

AME Info, 'Qatar: Diversification Efforts Real, But Hidden', (Mar. 22, 2006).

American Chemical Society, 'The Shrinking World of Petrochemicals', (Feb 15, 2008).

APS Review Gas Market Trends, 'Qatar-North Field Development-Phase-1', (Aug. 14,1995).

APS Review Gas Market Trends, 'Betting On Qatar Link Up With Nabucco Pipeline Via Kuwait', (June 15, 2009).

Arabian Business, 'ExxonMobil Starts Second Phase of Al-Khaleej Project', (Nov. 30, 2006).

Arabian Business, 'Pulling Power', (Aug. 16, 2008).

Attwood, Edward, 'Qatar Utility Eyes GCC Power and Water Projects', *Utilities-ME* (May 4. 2010).

Barnett, Neil, 'Dolphin Project Surges Ahead', *The Middle East* (Feb. 2000).

Bauerova, Ladka, et al, 'Qatar Leaders Confirm Interest in Acquiring Stake in Areva', *Bloomberg* (Mar. 25, 2010).

Bloomberg News, 'Qatar has No Plans for Further Natural Gas Plants', (Dec.7, 2009).

BP *Statistical Review of World Energy*, *British Petroleum* (June 2010) Available at < http://www.bp.com/liveassets/bp_internet/globalbp/globalbp_uk_english/reports_and_publications/statistical_energy_review_2008/STAGING/local_assets/2010_downloads/statistical_review_of_world_energy_full_report_2010.pdf

Business Wire, 'Qatar Petroleum and ExxonMobil Launch Al-Khaleej Gas Phase-2 (AKG-2)', (July 10, 2006).

Business Wire, 'Qatar Petroleum and Exxon-Mobil to Launch Barzan Gas Project', (Feb. 20, 2007).

Butt, Gerald, 'Qatar to Break New Ground as Regional Gas Supplier and New Technology Developer', *Middle East Economic Survey* Vol. XLIV No.12 (Mar. 19, 2001).

Canty, Daniel, 'Qatar Matures, New North Field Projects Unlikely', *Arabian Oil and Gas* (Dec. 9, 2009).

Carlisle, Tamsin, 'UAE Dolphin Energy in Talks to Acquire Qatar Natural Gas', *The National* (June 23, 2009).

CIA World Factbook: Qatar, The Central Intelligence Agency Website. Available at https://www.cia.gov/library/publications/the-world-factbook/geos/qa.html

Cordesman, Anthony H., *The changing dynamics of energy in the Middle East, Volume 1* (Greenwood Publishing Group, 2006).

Crystal, Jill, *Oil and Politics in the Gulf: Rulers and Merchants in Kuwait and Qatar* (Cambridge University Press, 1995) p.158.

Dargin, Justin, *The Dolphin Project: The Development of a Gulf Gas Initiative*, (Oxford Institute of Energy Studies) (2008).

Dargin, Justin, 'Trouble in Paradise – The Widening Gulf Gas Deficit', Middle East Economic Survey, (Sept. 29, 2008).

Datamonitor, 'Wintershall Awarded New Exploration License in Qatar', (Oct. 29, 2007).

Dolphin Energy Website 'Initial Dolphin Gas Supplies Received in Al Ain Through Oman Pipelines', (Jan. 25 2004). Available at http://www.dolphinenergy.com/press_news_releases.html

Dow Jones News Wires, 'Qatar May End North Field Moratorium in 2014', (May 15, 2009).

El Gamal, Rania, 'Shell to Supply Kuwait LNG Starting this Summer', LNGpedia (June 23, 2009).

El Mallakh, Ragaei, *Qatar: Development of an Oil Economy* (Taylor & Francis, 1979).

El Mallakh, Ragaei, *Qatar: Energy and Development* (Routledge, 1985).

Energy Information Administration, *Kuwait, Natural Gas*.

Energy Information Administration (EIA), *Saudi Arabia: Natural Gas*, Available at http://www.eia.doe.gov/emeu/cabs/Saudi_Arabia/NaturalGas.html

Evans, Damon, 'Pearl GTL Set for Big Payback', *Upstream Online* Mar. 11, 2008).

Evans-Pritchard, Ambrose, 'Qatar Fashions Financial Oasis to go toe-to-toe with East and West', *Daily Telegraph* (May 22, 2009).

Farey, Ben, et al, 'Gas OPEC Sends Prices Lower for Worst Commodity', *Bloomberg Businessweek* (April 19, 2010).

Farey, Ben, 'Qatar LNG Outlook May Rise After Debottlenecking', *Bloomberg* (Mar. 1, 2010).

Gavin, James, 'Moving Beyond the North Field', *Middle East Economic Digest* (March 20, 2009).

Global Gas Flaring Reduction Partnership, 'Qatar: First Gulf Country Joins World Bank-led Effort to Reduce Greenhouse Gas Emissions from Gas Flaring', Home Page (Jan. 25, 2009) Available at < http://web.worldbank.org/WBSITE/EXTERNAL/NEWS/0,,contentMDK:22044056~menuPK:34463~pagePK:34370~piPK:34424~theSitePK:4607,00.html>.

Greer, Scott et al, 'Middle East Constructing: Contracting in a Roller Coaster Market', *Oil and Gas Financial Journal* (Jan. 1, 2009).

Gulfnews, 'Gulf States Face Power Shortages amid Lack of Gas', June 13, 2007.

Gulf Times, 'Dolphin to Refinance $3bn of Debt Early Next Year', (June 28,

2007).

Halstead, Kevin, 'Oryx GTL-A Case Study', *Petrochemicals* (July 2006).

Harvey, David, et al, 'The Prebisch-Singer Hypothesis: Four Centuries of Evidence', *The Review of Economics and Statistics*, Vol. 92, No. 2, (May 2010).

Hindley,Angus, 'Impact Assessment', *Middle East Economic Digest* (November 2006).

IHS Global Insight, 'Qatar Eases Off the Gas: ConocoPhillips, Marathon GTL Projects Held Back', (Apr. 27, 2005).

Iran Daily, 'Mideast Seeks to Satisfy Domestic Gas Demand', (Apr.9, 2007).

Irish, John, 'Qatar Looks to Finance $30bn Utility Expansion', *Arabian Business* (Jan. 23, 2008).

Irish, John, 'Qatar's Population Doubles Since '04', *Arabian Business* (May 15, 2008).

Joshi, Mohit, 'Turkey and Qatar Discuss Energy Cooperation and Possible Pipeline', *TopNews.in* (August 18, 2009).

Kawach, Nadim, 'Qatar's Gas Sector Share of GDP More Than Oil Now', *Emirates Business 24/7* (Sept. 15, 2009).

Kawach, Nadim, 'Strong Economy Boosts Qatari Population', *Dubai Business News* (Dec. 7, 2008).

Khaleghhu, Shahla, *Iran and Qatar: Bilateral Cooperation to Utilize Gas Market Opportunities*, Brazilian Institute of Petroleum (undated).

Lesdesma, David, 'Cost Increases for LNG projects', in Jonathan Stern, ed, *Natural Gas in Asia: the challenges of growth in China, India, Japan and Korea*, 2nd Edition, OIES/OUP, 2008.

Malik, Talal, 'Gulf Eyes Use for Gas Flares', *Arabian Business* (March 11, 2008).

MENAFN, 'Qatari Petrochemical Production All Set for Expansion', (May 5, 2010).

Mercier, Claude, *Petrochemical Industry and the Possibilities of Its Establishment in the Developing Countries*, TECHNIP (1996).

The Middle East and North Africa 2004, (Routledge, 2004).

Middle East Business and Financial News, 'Dolphin Energy Project Defines New Era for Gas', (Jan. 2006).

Middle East Economic Digest, 'North Field Inaugurated as Second Phase Progresses', (Sept. 6, 1991).

Middle East Economic Survey (MEES), 'Dolphin Makes Headway But Economic Currents May Rock Further GCC Integration', Vol.XLVIII No. 23 (June 6, 2005).

Middle East Economic Survey, 'Dolphin and Qatar in Talks About Additional Gas', Vol. LII No. 26 (Jun. 29, 2009).

Middle East Economic Survey, 'Doha Rules out New Gas Export Projects Post-Moratorium', (Dec. 14, 2009).

Middle East Electricity, 'Kuwait Seeks to Export Gas', (Mar. 17, 2008).

MidEast.Ru, 'UAE to Sign US$10bn Gas Deal', (Apr.30, 2008).

Morrow, Adam, *et al*, 'Egypt: Govt Forced to Bend on Israel Gas Deal', *Inter-Press Service* (June 18, 2008).

Nightingale, Alaric, et al, 'Qatar Idles LNG Ships as Year-End Gas 18per cent

More', *Bloomberg Businessweek* (June 3, 2010).

Klaus, Oliver, 'Germany's Wimtershall Signs a 25-yr Qatar Gas Exploration Deal', *Dow Jones Newswire* (Nov. 18. 2008).

Offshore Technology, 'South Pars, Qatar North Field, Iran,, Available at http://www.offshore-technology.com/projects/southpars/

O'Rear, Dennis, *Concepts for Reduction in CO2 Emissions in GTL Facilities*, Elsevier (2007).

The Peninsula, 'Qatar: Rising Domestic Demand Poses Big Challenge to Gas Industry', (Mar.7, 2007).

The Peninsula, 'Qatar-Power Generation to Take a Giant Leap', (Feb. 27, 2010).

Perrodon, Alain, *Dynamics of Oil and Gas accumulations* (Editions TECHNIP, 1983).

Petroleum Economist, 'GTL Investment Hits the Buffers' (Oct. 2009).

Pipeline Magazine, 'Qatar Lengthens North Field Delay', (Dec. 18, 2009).

RasGas Homepage, 'The Source: Qatar's North Field', Available at < http://www.michaelpage.co.uk/mini-site/3606/2137/the_source.html>

Reuters, 'Shell Says on Schedule with Qatar Pearl GTL Plant', (Oct. 30, 2007).

Romero, Simon, 'Natural Gas Powering Qatar Economic Boom', *The New York Times* (Dec. 22, 2005).

Romero, Simon, 'Natural Gas Powering Qatar Economic Boom Growth Likened to the Saudi Oil Bonanza', *Red Orbit* (Dec. 24, 2005).

Sambidge, Andy, 'Qatar Sees Large Increase in 2009 Power Demand', *Arabian Business* (May 7, 2009).

Sambidge, Andy, 'Qatar Aims to Cut Summer Power Blackouts', *Arabian Business* (Aug. 5, 2009).

Seddiq, Ramin, *Policy Watch/Peace Watch: Border Disputes on the Arabian Peninsula*, Washington Institute for Near East Policy (15 Mar. 2001).

Shiryaevskaya, Anna, 'Gazprom Says "Abnormal" Gas-Price Gap to Undermine Investment', *Bloomberg Businessweek* (Apr. 14, 2010).

Siddiqi, Moin, 'Exceptional Energy Prospects for Qatar', *Oil Review Middle East* (June 2007).

Siddiqi, Moin, 'Exceptional Energy Prospects for Qatar', *Oil Review* (Aug. 16, 2009).

Stanton, Chris, 'Qatar Eases off on Gas-Fired Boom', *The National*, (April 10, 2010.

The Telegraph, 'Qatari Gas to Reduce Russian Dominance', (May 12, 2009).

Tuttle, Robert, 'Qatar, Russia Shutter Gas Supply', *Bloomberg Businessweek* (June 10, 2010.

United States Geological Survey *Qatar North Arch Extension-Zagros Fold Belt Province*. Available at http://energy.cr.usgs.gov/WEcont/regions/reg2/p2/tps/AU/au203021.pdf

Upstream Online, 'Sasol Set to Open Qatar Taps', (Oct. 30, 2007).

Victor, David G. et al, *Natural gas and geopolitics: from 1970 to 2040* (Cambridge University Press, 2006).

Wilkinson, J.C. *Arabia's Frontiers: The Story of Britain's Boundary Drawing in the Desert* (London: I. B. Tauris, 1991).

Williams, Perry, 'An Inheritance Worth Protecting', *Middle East Economic Digest*,

(Sept. 14, 2007).

Williams, Perry, 'Doubts Surface Over Ras Laffan', *Middle East Economic Digest* (Sept. 12, 2008).

Williams, Perry, 'Dolphin Energy Holds Talks Over Gas Imports From Qatar', *Middle East Business Intelligence* (June 23, 2009).

Williamson, Lucy, 'Qatar's Fortunes Boom With Gas', *BBC News* (Feb. 2006).

World Gas Intelligence, 'Culprits in Qatar', Vol. XVlll, No. 10 (Mar. 7, 2007).

World Gas Intelligence, 'Approaching End of its Road', (Feb. 18, 2009).

Zhaoxia, Shu, 'Financial Crisis Impacts on Petrochemical Market Cycle', *China Chemical Reporter*, (Apr. 16, 2009).

Chapter 10: Qatar

API News, 'RasGas LNG plant receives first gas from the offshore complex', 22 April 1999.

BP Statistical Review of World Energy 2009, 2007 and 2002.

Cedigaz, 'LNG trade and Infrastructures', Paris, February 2004.

Dixon, A. and Lawson, D., 'Qatar concludes deal to develop world's biggest known gas field', *Financial Times*, 28 June 1984.

Dow Jones Newswires, 'Total-Compagnie Française in Pact for Qatar Project', 29 May 1991.

Energy Alert, 'Qatar's Rasgas Secures $2.25 Bln Financing', 30 December 1996.

Energy Alert, 'Itochu, Nissho Iwai Buy Shares In Qatar Firm', 10 December 1996, Vol. 28, No. 50.

Energy Argus Gas and Power, 'Korea Gas Takes RasGas Stake', Vol. V, No. 19, 28 September 2005.

Financial Times, 'Chubu signs up Qatar LNG', 15 May 1992.

Financial Times 'Marubeni of Japan is to have a 7.5% stake in a gas project offshore the state of Qatar', 6 September 1985.

Gas Matters Today, 'ExxonMobil Cancels Qatar GTL Project but Wins Share in North Field Barzan Project', 21 February 2007.

Gas Matters Today, 'Qatar Petroleum, ConocoPhillips and Shell Sign Multi-Billion Dollar LNG Deals', 21 December 2005.

Gas Matters Today, 'Qatargas-4 Deal with Shell Takes Qatar's Planned LNG Output to 77mtpa by 2010', 29 February 2005.

Gas Matters Today, 'Total Buys 5.2mtpa from Qatargas II and Takes a 16.7% Stake', 28 February 2005.

Gas Matters Today, 'Dahej LNG Shipment Sets Sail from Qatar', 27 January 2004.

Gas Matters Today, 'Gas Natural Signs for Another 2Bcm/yr of Qatar LNG', 15 January 2004.

Gas Matters Today, 'Qatar Petroleum Sign Deal to make RasGas II Largest Exporter of LNG to USA', 16 October 2003.

Gas Matters Today, 'Construction of third Ras Laffan train now under way', 15 January 2002.

Gas Matters, 'Trading companies to take equity in Ras Laffan', December

1996, p.31.

Hashimoto, K., Elass, J. and Eller, S. part of the Geopolitics of Natural Gas, a joint project of the Program on Energy and Sustainable Development at Stanford University and the James Baker III Institute for Public Policy at Rice University, December 2004.

Heren LNG Markets, 'CNOOC and PetroChina Join the Ranks of Qatar's Asian LNG Customers', HLM 4.4.2, 11 April 2008.

Heren LNG Markets, 'EDF Trading Takes RasGas Volume and Capacity at Zeebrugge', H.L.M 3.6.4, 22 June 2007.

ICIS Heren Global LNG Markets, 'Qatargas-3 Slips Back to Q4', Vol. 6.14, 7 May 2010.

ICIS Heren Global LNG Markets, 'Qatargas Diversions Reset Supply, Demand', Issue No 5.45, 20 November 2009.

ICIS Heren Global LNG Markets, 'Qatar to Nudge 90mtpa After Debottlenecking – Al Suwaidi', Issue No 5.39, 9 October 2009.

ICIS Heren Global LNG Markets, 'Qatar Rolls Back North Field's Moratorium Decision' Issue No 5.25, 19 June 2009.

International Gas Report, 'Adriatic LNG sends gas to the grid', 28 September 2009, p.27.

International Gas Report, 'Exxon/Qatar take Italy LNG stakes', 21 November 2003, p.10.

International Gas Report, 'Technip JV to boost Qatargas', 29 October 2001, p.23.

International Gas Report, 'Qatar's RasGas seals Indian Petronet deal', 6 August 1999, p.4.

International Gas Report, 'Rasgas clinches KGC deal', 27 October 1995, p.12.

International Gas Report, 'Italian Mid-East gas projects plunge into turmoil', 21 January 1994, p.1.

International Gas Report, 'Chiyoda lands $1.4bn Qatar Contract', 11 June 1993, p.4.

Lloyd's List International, Special Report: 'Japan shares big LNG deal', 27 December 1994.

Lloyd's List International, 'Nearly 6m tonnes of liquefied natural gas is to be bought by Japanese power and gas companies from the Australian North West Shelf' project', 3 August 1985.

Lloyd's List International, 'The Qatar government has signed a memorandum with BP and Compagnie Française des Petroles' subsidiary, Total', 22 June 1983.

Middle East Daily Financial News, 'Qatar's USD2bn third LNG JV', 27 March 2001.

MEED, 'Spain signs for Qatar LNG', 18 May 2001.

MEED, 'Japan to sign up for Qatargas supplies', 12 December 1994.

MEED, 'Finance fixed for Qatargas downstream works', 20 December 1993.

MEED, 'Qatargas signs vessel chartering agreement', 25 October 1993.

MEED, 'Qatar General Petroleum Corp establishes Ras Laffan Liquefied Natural Gas Co', 16 July 1993.

MEED, 'North Field drilling proceeds as firms bid for procurement', 19 August 1988.

Oil and Gas Journal, 'Fluxys agrees LNG supply', 12 July 2004, p.9.

Oil and Gas Journal, 'Edison Gas', 2 July 2001, p.9.

Oil and Gas Journal, 'Qatar ships first LNG to Japan, signs accord', Vol. 94, No. 53, 30 December 1996, p.28.

Oil and Gas Journal, 'BP withdraws from Qatar North LNG project', 20 January 1992, p.31.

Platts LNG Daily, 'India Plans to Lift Qatari LNG Purchases to 11.5mt/year by 2013', Vol. 7, Issue 54, 22 March 2010.

Platt's LNG Daily, 'UK's South Hook Terminal Receives First Cargo', Vol. 6, no. 54, 20 March 2009.

Platt's Oilgram News, 'News Briefs: Qatar/Italy', 17 February 1994, Vol. 72, No. 34, p.6.

Ras Gas, About RasGas, Milestones pages on RasGas website: www.rasgas.com

Reuters News, 'Qatar to sign final LNG supply deal with Distrigas', 28 February 2005.

Reuters News, 'Qatar, South Korea sign deal to double gas supply', 30 June 1997.

Reuters News, 'Qatar's Rasgas raises $1.2 billion via two bonds', 12 December 1996.

Reuters News, 'Japanese reported interested in buying Qatar gas', 18 December 1989.

Reuters News, 'Mitsui buys 7.5 pct share in Qatargas', 18 May 1989.

Stern, J.P., *Natural Gas in North America and Asia*, Gower: 1985, pp. 184–5.

World Gas Intelligence, 'Qatar in China', Vol. XIX, No. 16, 16 April 2008.

World Gas Intelligence, 'Qatar Contracts Flow', Vol. XVI, No. 39, 28 September 2005.

World Gas Intelligence, 'Qatari Delays', Vol. XVI, No. 18, 4 May 2005.

World Gas Intelligence, 'QP, ExxonMobil Finalize UK Supply Venture', Vol. XV, No. 51, p.2, 22 December 2004.

World Gas Intelligence, 'Endesa Goes Shopping', 6 August 2003.

World Gas Intelligence, 'Conoco's Qatari Partnership', Vol. XIV, No. 29, 16 July 2003.

World Gas Intelligence, 'Qatar LNG's Mega Growth', Vol XII, No 42, p.1, 16 October 2002.

World Gas Report, 'CFP seeks Qatar LNG partnership', 20 July 1981.

World Gas Report, 'Japan, Australia gas deal moves much closer', 6 July 1981.

Chapter 11: Oman

Alexanders Gas & Oil Connections, 5 October 2004, vol 9, issue #19, 'Chinese Oil in Oman'.

APS Review Downstream Trends, 30 January 2006, 'Oman – The Local Market'.

Arab Oil & Gas Directory 2007, 'Oman'.

BP *Statistical Review of World Energy*, June 2010.

Authority of Electricity Regulation, Oman, *Annual Report 2008*.

Authority for Electricity Regulation, Oman. 'Study on Renewable Energy

Resources', Oman, Final Report. May 2008.

Middle East Economic Survey, various issues.

Minister of National Economy Budget Statement on 2 January 2010 and MNE statistic.

Minister of National Economy Oman, 'Monthly Statistics'. www.moneoman. gov.om

Ministry of Oil and Gas, 'National Economy Monthly Statistics', www.mone-oman.gov.om

Muscat Daily, various issues.

Petroleum Argus, 2 March 2009, 'Oman Special Report'.

PDO *Annual Report* 2008.

World Gas Intelligence, 23 April 2008, 'Oman, Iran in unique gas buyback deal'.

Chapter 12: The UAE

ADGAS History and Evolution, ADGAS website www.adgas.com/default. aspx?tabid=132

ADMA History, ADMA Website, www.adma-opco.com/AboutADMA/History/ tabid/65/Default.aspx

Al-Abed, Ibrahim et al, *United Arab Emirates Yearbook 2005* (Trident Press Ltd, 2004).

Al-Baik, Duraid, 'Sharjah Power Crisis Could Hurt Economy', *Gulfnews*, Sept. 7, 2009.

Al Baik, Duraid, 'Why is Sharjah Suffering?' *Gulf News*, Sept. 21, 2009.

Al Serkal, Mariam M., 'Residents Battle Heat while Sharjah Blackout Continues', *Gulf News*, Aug. 19, 2009.

Al Serkal, Mariam M., 'Thousands Suffer in Three Day Blackout, *The Nation*, Aug. 20, 2009.

Alexander's Gas and Oil Connections, 'ADNOC plans Investment of $50 bn into Projects', vol. 14, issue #10, August 7, 2009.

Alexander's Gas and Oil Connections, 'Crescent-Iran Negotiations Stalled Amid Corruption Allegations', vol.13, issue #20, Nov. 12, 2008.

Alexander's Gas and Oil Connections, 'Greater Supply Deficits Force Middle East to Focus on Domestic Needs', Vol. 12, Issue 9, 10 May 2007.

Alexander's Gas and Oil Connections 'UAE Needs Gas Network and Law', Vol. 11, Issue #11, June 8, 2006.

AME Info, 'Dubai Signs Shell, QP LNG Import Deal, as Yet Another Gulf Market Tries to Escape Gas Crunch', Apr. 27, 2008.

APS Review Gas Market Trends 'UAE Gas Shortage to Triple by 2025', May 26, 2008.

APS Review Gas Market Trends, 'Sharjah's Decision Makers', June 5, 2006.

Arabian Business, 'Gulf Arab States Link Up to Foil Power Crunch', July 23, 2009.

Arabian Business, 'Energise the Emirates', June 10, 2009.

Arabian Business 24/7, 'Emal and Gasco Open Gas Pipeline to Power Smelter', Aug. 24, 2009.

Arabian Business, 'Dolphin Energy Takes Gas to All Seven Emirates', May 5, 2008.

Baxter, Kevin, 'Petrofac Drops Bid for $12bn ADNOC Refinery Job', *Arabian Oil and Gas*, Oct. 25, 2009.

Bierman, Stephen, et al, 'U.A.E. Bid for Caspian Gas May Test Russian Dominance', *Bloomberg Businessweek*, May 5, 2010.

BP Statistical Review of World Energy, June 2009.

Business Monitor, 'Second Phase of Al-Khaleej Launched as Domestic Demand Grows', May 11, 2010.

Calvin, James, et al, *An Evaluation of Nitrogen Injection as a Method of Increasing Gas Cap Reserves and Accelerating Depletion-Ryckman Creek Field, Uinta County, Wyoming*, SPE Annual Technical Conference and Exhibition, 23-26 September 1979, Las Vegas, Nevada, American Institute of Mining, Metallurgical, and Petroleum Engineers, Inc. (1979).

Carlisle, Tamsin, 'Sharjah Gas Deal Shreds Red Tape', *The National*, June 6, 2010.

Carlisle, Tamsin, 'Victim of its Own Success, Emirate Seeks New Option', *The National*, Aug. 25, 2009.

Carlisle, Tamsin, 'UAE Dolphin Energy in Talks to Acquire Qatar Natural Gas', *The National*, June 23, 2009.

Carlisle, Tamsin, 'Adnoc Finds Elixir for its Oil Finds', *The National*, May 8, 2008.

Cedigaz, 'LNG Trade and Infrastructures', Paris, February 2004.

Coker, Margaret, 'Korean Team to Build U.A.E. Nuclear Plant', *The Wall Street Journal*, Dec. 28, 2009.

Crane, Agnes, et al, 'Nuclear Power at Bay', *New York Times*, May 22, 2010.

Dargin, Justin, *The Development of a Gulf Carbon Platform: Mapping Out the Gulf Cooperation Council Carbon Exchange*, Harvard Kennedy School, Working Paper No.1, May 2010.

Dargin, Justin, 'A model in preparation for a "post-oil" world', *The National*, March 20, 2009.

Dargin, Justin, 'Trouble In Paradise – The Widening Gulf Gas Deficit', Middle East Economic Survey, September 29, 2008.

DiPaola, Anthony, 'Dolphin Plans U.A.E Gas Pipeline Work in Mid-June', *Bloomberg Businessweek* May 27, 2010.

Dipaola, Anthony, 'Golar Says Dubai Floating LNG Terminal May Start in 2010', *Bloomberg*, June 1, 2009.

Dow Jones Newswire, 'Update: Dubai Floating LNG Terminal Work On Schedule-Shell', Mar. 30, 2010.

Emirates Business 24/7, 'UAE Company Signs Deal to Transport Gas from Iran', Sept. 17, 2009.

Emirates Business 24/7, 'Demand for Electricity to Increase 6%', March 2, 2009.

Emirates Business 24/7, 'Utilities Supply Crunch in the Northern Emirates, July 10, 2008.

Ghazal, Rym Tina, 'Ajman Hopes to be Next Mini Dubai', *The National*, May 17, 2008.

Gulf Daily News, 'UAE Planning to Increase Petrol Prices', Apr. 19, 2010.

Gulf News, 'Rare UAE Gas Oil Tender Highlights Demand Fall', Apr. 2, 2009.

Gulf News, 'UAE Gas Supply is 20% Below Peak Demand', Feb. 21, 2008.

Gulf News, '*RAK to Develop 2,740 MW Power Generation Capacity for New Residential Communities*', July 15, 2008.

Gulf News, 'Dubai Eyes First Power, Water Tariff Hike Since '98', Nov. 6, 2007.

Gulf Oil and Gas, 'Dana Gas Moves Ahead with Plans for Offshore Concession in Sharjah', Jan. 27, 2009.

Henni, Abdelghani, 'Gas Crunch Dominates UAE Summit', *Arabian Oil and Gas*, Mar. 15, 2010.

Iran Daily, 'Crescent Making New Gas Offer', Oct. 8, 2008.

James, Ed, 'Gas Shortfall Leaves a Sour Taste', *Middle East Economic Digest*, Aug. 31, 2007.

Kakande,Yasin et al, 'Sharjah Swelters in the Dark Again', *The National*, Aug. 28, 2009.

Karrar-Lewsley, Tahani, 'Conoco to Exit Abu Dhabi Gas Project', *Wall Street Journal*, April 28, 2010.

Kawach, Nadim, 'UAE to Grow by More Than 3% in 2011, Says Report', *Emirates Business 24/7*, April 14, 2010.

Kawach, Nadim, 'Abu-Dhabi Says Oil Project Cost Slashed 20 per cent', *Emirates Business 24/7*, Jan. 27, 2009.

Kawach, Nadim, 'UAE Gas Output Rises by 10 bcm in Five Years', *Emirates Business 24/7*, Dec. 15, 2009.

Kawach, Nadim, 'Dana Gas to Develop 'Gas Cities', *Arabian Business 24/7*, May 8, 2007.

Krane, Kelly, 'Dubai Hit by Major Power Cut', *Gulf News*, June 10, 2005.

Kumar, Himendra Mohan, 'UAE Gas Demand Rises 7% annually', *Gulf News*, May 18, 2010.

Landais, Emmanuelle, 'Energy Efficient Lighting Cuts Bills by 80%', *Gulf News*, Sept. 18, 2009.

LNG in World Markets, 'Japanese Redouble Efforts to Finalise Price Reviews', February 2010, Poten and Partners, New York.

McGinley, Shane, 'Abu Dhabi Construction Costs Down by 30%-TDIC', *Arabian Business*, Apr. 17, 2010.

Mackenzie, Kate, 'Coal Die-off, NatGgasBoom are Already Reducing US Emissions', *Financial Times*, May 6, 2010.

Maktoob, 'Adnoc to Press Ahead with 5-Year Plan', June 2, 2009.

Maree, Karen, 'Coal is Dubai's Best Option to Meet Rising Demand', *Middle East Business Intelligence*, Feb. 22, 2008.

Maree, Karen, 'Emirates Turn to Private Sector, as the Construction Boom Continues', *Middle East Economic Digest*, Dec. 14, 2007.

Middle East Economic Digest, 'OPEC Faces Up to Cost of Output Cuts', Mar. 12, 2009.

Middle East Economic Survey, 'Dolphin and Qatar in Talks about Additional Gas', Jun. 29, 2009.

Middle East Economic Survey, 'Northern Emirates Look to Neighbors for Gas Salvation', Apr. 21, 2008.

Middle East Economic Survey, 'Iran Plans to Prove Up Extension of UAE's Offshore Saleh Gas Field', Apr. 21, 2008.

Mills, Robin, *The Myth of the Oil Crisis* (Praeger, London, 2008).

Mohan, Rakesh, *Understanding the Developing Metropolis* (Oxford University Press US, 1994).

Mortished, Carl, 'BP Offers Abu Dhabi Green Solution to Chronic Gas Shortages', *The Times*, Oct. 31, 2007.

Muthiah, Shanthi, 'Generation Asset Valuation: Are We at the Nadir for Gas-Fired Power Plants?' *Electric Lights and Power*, Nov/Dec. 2004.

The National, 'Iran: Crescent Petroleum takes NIOC to International Arbitration', Jul. 16, 2009.

National Gas Shipping Company Website, www.ngsco.com/profile/index.aspx

Naylor, Hugh, 'Emirates Left in the Dark', *The National*, Aug. 26, 2009.

Naylor, Hugh, 'Off the Grid: No Power, No Business', *The National*, Aug. 26, 2009.

Oil and Energy Trends, '*Dubai and Qatar Agree to World's Shortest LNG Route*', Vol. 33 Issue 5, May 12, 2008.

Oil and Gas Journal, 'Poten: Abu Dhabi Gas Demand Could Limit Sour Gas for LNG', July 27, 2009.

Oxford Business Group, 'Country Profile: Emirates Sharjah'. Available at http://www.oxfordbusinessgroup.com/country.asp?country=59

Oxford Business Group, 'UAE Private Supply', 2008.

Oxford Business Group, 'The Report Ras Al Khaimah', 2008.

Oxford Business Group, 'The Report: Dubai 2008', 2008.

Oxford Business Group, 'The Report Sharjah 2008', 2008.

Oxford Business Group, 'Emerging Sharjah 2007', 2007.

Patel, Kamal, 'Challenges and Prospects for the UAE Power Sub-Sector', *Zawya*, Mar. 18, 2010.

The Peninsula, 'Power Demand to Dictate More N-Deals in the UAE', Jan. 9, 2009.

Pipeline Magazine, 'Oman Starts Pumping Gas for RAK', Feb. 16, 2009.

Platts LNG Daily, 'Abu Dhabi Considering Options for LNG After 2019', Vol. 6, No 101, May 28, 2009.

Rahman, Salfur, 'Dubai Enhances Energy Security', *Gulf News*, Aug. 31, 2009.

Remo-Listana, Karen, 'Alternative Energy is an Answer to Dwindling Natural Gas Supplies', *Arabian Business 24/7*, Apr. 6, 2009.

Remo-Listana, Karen, 'Gas Shortage to Double Cost of Electricity', *Emirates Business 24/7*, March 17, 2008.

Renewable Energy World, 'Abu Dhabi Sets 7 Percent Renewables Target', Jan. 19, 2009.

Reuters, 'Dana, Crescent to Build Yemen "Gas City"', Sept. 9, 2009.

Reuters, 'UAE Short of Gas in Summer Heat', June 25, 2007.

Salisbury, Peter, 'OPEC Faces Up to Cost of Output Cuts' *Middle East Economic Digest*, March 12, 2009.

Salisbury, Peter, 'Emirates Press Ahead with Expansion', *Middle East Economic Digest* March 20, 2009.

Saudi Gazette, 'Abu-Dhabi to Build World's Largest Solar Plant', June 10, 2010.

Scandinavian Oil and Gas Magazine, 'Heritage Produces First Oil from West Bukha Field', Feb. 19, 2009.

Shaikh, Abdul Hafeez, 'Privatization of Energy in the Gulf: Selected Issues and Options' in (ed.) *Privatization and Deregulation in the Gulf Energy Sector* (I.B.Tauris, 1999).

Shamseddine, Reem, 'Gulf Petrochemical Firms Seek Alternatives to Gas', *Arabian Business*, June 9, 2010.

Shana News, 'First Train of Salman Gas Field to Inaugurate in a Month', July 4, 2009.

Singh, Timon, 'Abu Dhabi Invests \$1 Tn into Infrastructure', *Mena Infrastructure*, Nov. 3, 2009.

Stanton, Chris, 'Green Subsidy for Solar Power', *The National*, June 9, 2010.

Todorova, Vesela, 'Desalination Threat to the Growing Gulf', *The National*, August 31, 2009.

Turner, Wayne C., *Energy Management Handbook* (The Fairmont Press, Inc., 2006).

UAE Interact, 'Adnoc to Lift Curb on Oil Output', Mar. 9, 2010.

UAE Interact, 'Adnoc Boosts Output by Injecting Gas', Apr. 9, 2001.

UAE White Paper Policy Document, *Policy of the United Arab Emirates on the Evaluation and Potential Development of Peaceful Nuclear Energy*, Apr. 20, 2008 Available at: http://www.carnegieendowment.org/publications/index.cfm?fa=view&id=20070

Upstream Online, 'ADNOC Eyes 50% Boost to Drilling', Mar.8, 2010.

Upstream Online, 'Shell Signs on for Dubai LNG Supply', Apr. 21, 2008.

US Energy Information Administration, Country Analysis Briefs: United Arab Emirates, Electricity Available at <http://www.eia.doe.gov/emeu/cabs/UAE/Electricity.html>

US Energy Information Administration, 'Natural Gas Weekly Update', Aug. 27, 2009.

von Moltke, Anja, et al (eds), *Energy Subsidies: lessons learned in assessing their impact and designing policy reforms*, (Greenleaf Publishing 2004).

Webb, Simon, et al, 'Russia's Rosneft Joins Crescent in UAE Gas Venture', *Reuters* June 5, 2010.

Webb, Simon, 'Update 2-Adnoc Aims to Double Domestic Gas Supplies in 2009', *Reuters*, Feb. 19, 2009.

Zawya Dow Jones, 'Qatar's Gas Supply to the UAE will be Down 25 Pct', Feb. 10, 2010.

Chapter 13: Bahrain and Kuwait

Al Qabas, 'Khutat al Kuwait al naftiyah tastadem bi naqs al- tiquaniy-at al-haditha', 5/5/2009, http://www.alqabas.com.kw/Articleprint.aspx?id=496514&mode=print

Al Qabas, 'Khutat al Kuwait al naftiyah tastadem bi naqs al- tiquaniyat al-haditha', 17/7/2009, http://www.alqabas.com.kw/Articleprint.aspx?id=518022&mode=print

Alsayegh, O.A., 'Restructuring Kuwait electric power system: mandatory or optional' Proceedings of World Academy of Science, Engineering, and Technology', vol.35, November 2008.

Aluminium Bahrain, *Annual Review 2008*, Bahrain, http://www.aluminiumbahrain.com/en/PDF/AnnualRevie2008.pdf

AMEINFO, 'Kuwait's biggest field starts to run out of oil', 12 November 2005, http://www.ameinfo.com/71519.html

AMEINFO, 'Kuwait Oil Tenders gas booster station', 10 August 2009, http://www.ameinfo.com/206077.html

APS Review of Oil Market Trends, 'Kuwait - Part 2- Profiles of the Oilfields', 8 June 2009.

Arab News, 'GCC warns Iran against making hostile remarks', 23 February 2009.

Arab Union of Producers, Transporters, and Distributors of Electricity (AUPTDE):
  Statistical Bulletin 2009, Issue 17. http://www.auptde.org/newsite/user/User_Def1.aspx?PID=2014&ID=145
  Statistical Bulletin 2007, Issue 16, http://www.auptde.org/newsite/user/User_Def1.aspx?PID=2014&ID=133

Arabian Oil & Gas, 'Arbitration finds a home in Dubai', 18 June 2009, http://www.arabianoilandgas.com/article-5706-arbitration_finds_a_home_in_dubai/1/print/

Arabian Oil & Gas, 'Kuwait LNG terminal still waiting on first cargo', 27 August /2009, http://www.arabianoilandgas.com /article-6081-kuwait_lng_terminal_still_ waiting_on_first_cargo/

Bahrain Petroleum Company (BAPCO),
  Annual Review 2006, http://www.bapco.net/media/pdf/English2006.pdf
  Annual Review 2008, http://www.bapco.com.bh/media/pdf/engannual08.pdf

Bloomberg, 'Kuwait May Receive Three LNG Cargoes at First Import Terminal '. 13 August 2009, http://www.bloomberg.com/apps/news?pid=20601072&sid=adBaaPrWV_CU

British Petroleum, *BP Statistical Review of World Energy*, June 2009.

Business 24-7 Emirates, 'Electricity Demand to Fuel Gas Shortage', 28 May 2008, http://www.business24-7.ae/Articles/2008/5/Pages/05282008

Business 24-7 Emirates, 'Low gas prices fail to help petrochemical makers', 17 June 2009, http://www.business24-7.ae/ Articles/2009/6/Pages/16062009/

Dargin, J., *The Dolphin Project: The Development of a Gulf Gas Initiative*, Oxford Institute for Energy Studies, Working Paper NG 22, January 2008.

Dargin, J., 'Prospects for Energy Integration in the GCC', Research Seminar, Dubai School of Government, Dubai, 3 March 2009.

Darwish, M.A., Abdulrahim, H.K, and A.B. Amer, 'On better utilization of gas turbines in Kuwait', *Energy*, Issue 4, vol.33, April 2008, pp.571–88.

Economist Intelligence Unit, *Bahrain: Manufacturing*, 6 February 2008, 16 July 2009.

Economist Intelligence Unit, *World Gas: EIU's Gas Outlook*, 19 March 2009, http://viewswire.eiu.com/ index.asp?layout=ib3Article&article_id=794356064

Energy Information Administration

Bahrain, Country Analysis Briefs, March 2008.

Kuwait, Country Analysis Briefs, April 2009.

'Bahrain', Table 3a, Short Term Energy Outlook, International Energy Annual, http://tonto.eia.doe.gov/country/country_time_series.cfm?fips=BA#ng, accessed July 2009.

Kuwait', Table 3a, Short Term Energy Outlook, International Energy Annual, http://tonto.eia.doe.gov/country/country_time_series.cfm?fips=KU#ng, accessed July 2009.

Eltony, M.N, 'Estimating energy price elasticities for non-oil manufacturing industries in Kuwait, *OPEC Energy Review*, June 2008, pp.184–95.

Eltony, M.N, and M.A. Al-Awhadi, 'Residential energy demand: a case study of Kuwait', *OPEC Review*, September 2007, pp.159–69.

Eltony, M.N, 'Industrial energy policy: a case study of demand in Kuwait', *OPEC Review*, XXII, no1, June 2006 pp.85–103.

ESCWA, *Status of Energy Statistics and Indicators in the ESCWA Region*, E/ESCWA/SD/2009, March 2009.

ESCWA, 'Energy Resources and Use', Electronic Statistical Information System, http://esis.escwa.org.lb/

Excelerate Energy (2009), 'Mina Ahmadi Gasport', http://www.excelerateenergy.com/kuwait.html

Gulf Oil and Gas, http://www.gulfoilandgas.com/webpro1/MAIN/Mainnews.asp?id=8982

'Production Sharing Agreement for the Bahrain Field', 27 April 2009.

'EQUATE Completes Polyethylene Expansion Project, 15 June 2009.

'EQUATE Starts The New Styrene Monomer Unit, 17 August 2009.

'Fluor Completes Olefin II Project in Kuwait', 27 August 2009.

'Shell to develop gas fields in Kuwait' 17/2/2010.

Hajiah, A., 'Energy Conservation Program In Kuwait: A Local Perspective' Proceedings of the Fifteenth Symposium on Improving Building Systems in Hot and Humid Climates, Orlando, FL, July 24–26, 2006.

ICIS news, 'Equate to resume normal output at Kuwait PE', 17 June 2008, http://www.icis.com /Article/ 2008/07/17/9140864/equate-to-resume-normal-output-at-kuwait-pe.html, accessed August 2009.

International Monetary Fund, *Kuwait: Statistical Appendix*, IMF Country Report No. 08/192, June 2008'.

Klimstra, J., 'Optimising Fuel Efficiency', *Power Engineering –Middle East Energy*, September 2008.

Kuwait Oil Company, 'Gas Field Development Symposium Concluded', Press release, 9 November 2008 http://www.kockw.com/Press%20Releases/KOC%20gas%20production-English.pdf

Kuwait Times,

'The ministry is spending about KD 1.6 billion on producing electricity', 15 April 2009.

'Kuwait signs 5-year gas deal with Shell', 18 February 2010.

Middle East Economic Digest:

'Making the grade', 11 September 2007, vol.51, Issue 45.

'Building Kuwait's electricity supply capacity and reducing demand ', 9 November 2007.

'Gas shortfall hits utilities profit', 21 March 2008, Vol.52, Issue 12.

'Contract row stalls energy plans', 24 October 2008, Vol.52, Issue 43.

'Political disputes hold back Kuwait', 16 January 2009, Vol.53, Issue 3.

'Kuwait cuts Shuaiba fertilizers on gas shortage', 5 May 2009.

'Industry struggles to secure foodstocks', 8 May 2009, Vol.53, Issue 19.

'Oil Ministry outlines energy masterplan', 12 June 2009, Vol.53, Issue 24.

'Chevron closes head office in Kuwait', 24/ July 2009, vol 53, Issue 30.

'Al-Zour puts Kuwait to the test', 28 September 2009, Vol.53, Issue 38.

'Refiner retenders Mina al-Ahmadi deal', 25 September 2009, Vol.53, Issue 39.

Middle East Economic Survey:

'Bahrain plans new upstream drive to boost gas reserves", 22 May 2006, no.21, Vol XLIX.

'Kuwait looks to non-associated gas debut', 14 January 2008, no.2, Vol.LII.

'The widening Gulf gas deficit', 29 September 2008, no.39, vol.LII.

'GE Energy signs contracts worth more than $500 mn for al-Durr IWPP', 22 June 2009, no.25, Vol.LII.

'Kuwait oil sector struggles to arrest slide to "square zero"', 12 October 2009, no.41, Vol.LII.

'Occidental, Mubadala & NOGA finalize Awali joint venture', 16 November 2009, no.46, Vol.LII.

'Kuwait eyes non-associated gas challenge', 11 January 2010, no.2, Vol.LIII.

'Kuwait's National Assembly Approves $107 bn Development Plan', 8 February 2010, no.6, Vol LIII.

Ministry of Electricity and Water (Bahrain), 'Electricity', *Annual Report 2007*, http://www.mew.gov.bh/ar/media/pdf/statistics2007/electricity.pdf

Ministry of Electricity and Water, 'Tariffs', http://www.mew.gov.bh/ default. asp? action=article&id=43 &keywords=tariff

Ministry of Electricity and Water Kuwait, 'As'ar istihlakat al kahraba wal ma' (in Arabic)', http://www.energy.gov.kw/default.aspx?pageId=391

Ministry of Finance (Bahrain) 'Project Agreements for Al Dur Independent Water and Power Project Signed', Press Release 28 August 2008, http:// www.mofne.gov.bh/ ArticleDetail.asp ?rid=1247&ctype=news, July 2009

Ministry of Finance (Bahrain), 'Gas, Production and Distribution According to User', Economic Bulletin (last updated August 2009), Table 11 http:// www.mof.gov.bh/showdatafile.asp?rid=864&ftype=file1

Ministry of Finance (Bahrain), 'Bahrain Gas Company: Production', Economic Bulletin (last updated August 2009), Table 12, http://www.mof.gov.bh/ showdatafile.asp?rid=864&ftype=file1

Ministry of Oil (Kuwait), 'Local Energy 2008', http://www.moo.gov.kw/De-fault.aspx?pageId=53, 2009 a.

Ministry of Oil (Kuwait), 'Gas (MMSCF, Petroleum Products Refinery Output, LPG, 1990-2008' (Excel Worksheet), Economic Affairs (internal publication),

2009 b.

National Oil and Gas Authority (NOGA), *Annual Report 2007*, http://www.noga. gov.bh/ EN/PDF/NOGA%20Annual%20Report%202007_en.pdf

National Oil and Gas Authority, Minister's Speech 7 February 2008, http:// www.noga.gov.bh/EN/Default.asp?pageid=Ministerspeech&ID=154

OAPEC, 'Bahrain' and 'Kuwait' country papers, 7th Arab Energy Conference, Cairo, 2002.

OAPEC, 'Kuwait' and 'Bahrain' country papers, 8th Arab Energy Conference, Amman, May 2006.

OAPEC, *Annual Statistical Bulletin 2008*, http://www.oapecorg.org/ publications/ ASR /A%20S%20R%202008.pdf

Petrochemical Industries Company (PIC), 'Equate', http://www.pic.com.kw/ equate.asp

Petrofrac, 'Petrofac awarded US$543 million lump-sum contract with Kuwait Oil Company 13 November 2008, http://www.petrofac.com/fullArticle. aspx?m=16&amid=5808

Petroleum Economist, 'Mideast states look for new gas sources as Qatar clams up', February 2009.

Power Engineering, 'High and Low: Kuwait's Power Problem', Middle East Energy, September 2008, http://pepei.pennnet.com /display_article/340914/89/ ARTCL/none/none/1 /High-and-low:-Kuwaitrsquo;s-power-problem/

Razavi, H., 'Natural Gas Pricing in Countries of the Middle East and North Africa', *The Energy Journal*, Vol.30, no.3, pp.1–22.

Rigzone, 'Oxy, Mubadala finalise development deal for Bahrain field', 27 April 2009, http://www.rigzone.com/ news/article?asp?a_id=75474

Ross, C., 'Time for Innovation in LNG', *Petroleum Economist*, June 2009, p.11.

Reuters, 'Kuwait's offload of first LNG test cargo', 6 August 2009, http://www. reuters.com/ article/companyNews/idUKN0633615420090806

Soman, B., 'New natural gas pricing structure to spur revenues', 7 February 2008 http://www.gulf-daily-news.com/newsdetails.aspx?srch=1&storyid=207974

Tabors, R.D., 'Interconnection in the GCC Grid: The Economics of Change', Proceedings of 42nd Hawaii International Conference on System Sciences, 2009.

Toorani, N., 'Electricity Ultimatum Challenged', *Gulf Daily News*, http://www. gulf-daily-news.com/ newsdetails.aspx?srch=1&storyid=237092, 8 December 2008.

Van Beurden, B., 'The Energy Challenge: Implications for the Middle East and the Global Chemical Industry', 3rd Annual Gulf Petrochemicals and Chemicals Association Forum, Dubai, December 2008.

Wind Energy Business News, 'Bahrain Aims To Develop Renewable Energy In Three Years', 3 August 2009, http://wind.energy-business-review.com/news /bahrain aims_to_ develop_ renewable_ energy_in_three_years_090803

Zawya, 'Kuwait: economists stress on need to privatise water and electricity', www.zawya.com

Chapter 14: Yemen

World Bank Report No. 4099-YE, Republic of Yemen, 'A Natural Gas Incentive Framework', June 2007.
Yemen LNG Company, www.yemenlng.org

Chapter 15: Conclusion

Dargin, J., 'The Gulf Natural Gas Dual Pricing Regime: WTO Rules and Economic Growth in the Gulf', Dubai Initiative Working Paper, August 2010.
Eltony, M.N. and Al-Awadi, M.A., 'Residential Energy Demand: A Case Study of Kuwait', *OPEC Review*, Vol. 31, No. 3, pp. 159–68, September 2007.
Gerner, F. and S. Sinclair, 'Connecting Residential Households to Natural Gas: An Economic & Financial Analysis,' World Bank Global Partnership on Output Based Aid, OBA Working Paper Series Paper No. 7, 2006, Washington, DC: World Bank.
IEA, OPEC, OECD, World Bank Joint Report, 'Analysis of the Scope of Energy Subsidies and Suggestions for the G20 Initiative', prepared for submission to the G-20 Summit Meeting, Toronto, 26–27 June 2010.
Kharbat, F., *Istihlak Al-Taqa Fi Kitaa' Al-kahrabaa' fi al-Dowal Al-Arabiyah*, (Electricity Consumption in Arab Countries), Paper presented at the 9th Arab Energy Conference, Doha, Qatar, 9–12 May 2010, (in Arabic).
Khattab, A. K., 'The Impact of Reducing Energy Subsidies on Energy Intensive Industries in Egypt', ECES Working Paper No. 124, May 2007.
OAPEC, *Istihlak Al-Taqa fi al-Dowal Al-Arabiyah: Al-Hader wa Al-Mustaqbal*, (Energy Consumption in Arab Countries: Present and Future), Paper presented at the 9th Arab Energy Conference, Doha, Qatar, 9–12 May 2010 (in Arabic).
Oil and Gas Journal, 'Ethylene Report', Vol.107, No. 28, 27 July 2009.
Pirani, Simon (ed.), *Russian and CIS Gas Markets and their Impact on Europe*, OUP/OIES, 2009.
Razavi, Hossein, 'Natural Gas Pricing in Countries of the Middle East and North Africa', *The Energy Journal*, 2009, Vol 30, No. 3, pp. 1–22.
Salehi-Isfahani, D. (2010), 'Will Iran's Poor Lose from Subsidy Reform?', *Monthly Review*, March, Downloaded from: http://mrzine.monthlyreview.org/2010/si180310.html
World Bank (2005) 'Egypt: Toward a More Effective Social Policy: Subsidies and Social Safety Net', Social and Economic Development Group, Washington DC: World Bank.
Yafimava, K. (forthcoming 2011), *The Transit Dimension of EU Energy Security: Russian gas transit across Ukraine, Belarus and Moldova*, OUP/OIES: forthcoming 2011.

INDEX